1002

17/6n

GORHAM
AND THE
BISHOP OF EXETER

GORHAM
AND THE
BISHOP OF EXETER

by

J. C. S. NIAS, B.D.

Priest of the Oratory of the
Good Shepherd
Rector of Blandford St Mary

Published for the Church Historical Society

LONDON

S · P · C · K

1951

First published in 1951 by
S.P.C.K., Northumberland Avenue,
London, W.C.2.

Printed in Great Britain by
The Camelot Press Ltd.,
Shirley Road, Southampton

CONTENTS

ILLUSTRATIONS

AUTHOR'S NOTE

I HAVE been told that I fall into the error of making Gorham the hero of this book. But when I had read the outlines of the case and decided to write this history I had no intention of doing that: certainly I do not wish to be regarded as belonging to Gorham's "party", if there is such a thing. Whether it be possible to write a completely objective history of anything or no, is not for me to say; but this book, like all other history books, has been written from a point of view. That point of view is the belief that there was something, perhaps a great deal, in what Gorham had to say. As I read and wrote I developed an affection for Gorham and a sympathy with him in the trial he had to face. The "orthodox" in their admirable orthodoxy did not see the whole of the matter.

I wish the following to know how grateful I am for their help. First, Canon Alec Vidler, O.G.S., of Windsor, formerly Warden of St Deiniol's Library, Hawarden, without whose constant encouragement I should never have begun; secondly, the Rev R. L. P. Milburn of Worcester College who helped me greatly while the manuscript was in its early stages. My father, Mr H. R. Nias, most generously offered the time of his typists and Mr Hugh Buss gave invaluable help with proof reading and compilation of the index. Canon Charles Smyth of Westminster told me of some important material in the University Library at Cambridge. Finally, I thank the authorities of the S.P.C.K. for their kindness.

J. C. S. N.

BLANDFORD ST MARY.
All Souls' Day, 1950.

INTRODUCTION

It was in the summer of 1846 that the Reverend George Cornelius Gorham, then Vicar of St Just-in-Penwith in Cornwall, advertised for a curate "free from Tractarian error", and thus brought down upon himself the disfavour of Dr Henry Phillpotts the Bishop of Exeter. This was the beginning of the argument between a mid-Victorian Bishop and one of his clergy which led to the ecclesiastical convulsions which are recorded in the following pages.

When eventually Gorham had found a curate and nominated him to the Bishop, the latter indicated that he regarded with disfavour the acceptance of a curacy from Gorham. Perhaps the Bishop had heard that Gorham, seeking ordination in 1811, soon after his appointment to a Fellowship at Queens' College, Cambridge, had been involved in a dispute with Dr Dampier, the Bishop of Ely, on the doctrine of baptismal regeneration. At all events Dr Phillpotts summoned Gorham's prospective curate for an examination "especially on Baptism the foundation of all Christian doctrine". Hereupon Gorham remonstrated against the Bishop's insisting upon a private test of orthodoxy in addition to subscription to the Thirty-nine Articles. This protest annoyed the Bishop, and when in August 1847 the Lord Chancellor presented Gorham to the Vicarage of Brampford Speke near Exeter, Dr Phillpotts refused to institute him until he too had submitted to an examination on the soundness of his doctrine. Gorham expressed his willingness to enter upon the interrogation at once—subsequent events were to show that he was not unprepared to argue in support of his convictions—but the Bishop kept him waiting until December 17th before the proceedings began. On this day the examination lasted from 10.30 a.m. to 6.30 p.m., with short intervals for meals; it continued likewise on December 18th (noon to 11.30 p.m.), the 20th (10.30 a.m. to 6 p.m.), the 21st (1.30 p.m. to 6 p.m.) and the 22nd (11.30 a.m. to 5.30 p.m.).

At the close of the questions on December 22nd, protesting against the exacting nature and the prolonged duration of the examination, Gorham suspended his attendance at the Bishop's house indicating that he intended to seek legal redress. Even then he took away some questions from the Bishop which it was agreed that he should answer by letter. On legal advice Gorham expressed his willingness to submit to further examination, but the test was not resumed until March 8th 1848. A further fourteen hours altogether were given to it on that and the two subsequent days. On March 11th the Bishop announced that he had found Gorham's doctrine of Baptism unsound, and that therefore he declined to institute him to the living to which he had been presented by the Lord Chancellor.

Hereupon Gorham instituted a monition out of the registry of the Court of Arches calling upon the Bishop to show cause why he should not institute him. The judgment of Sir Herbert Jenner Fust in that court on August 2nd 1849 was in favour of the Bishop. Gorham then appealed to the Judicial Committee of the Privy Council, and on March 8th 1850 the judgment of the Court of Arches was reversed. The Bishop of Exeter still refused to institute Gorham; he appealed without avail to the Court of Queen's Bench, the Court of Common Pleas and the Court of Exchequer to prevent the decision of the Judicial Committee from being put into effect. In spite of the failure of these appeals, Dr Phillpotts still refused to permit Gorham to occupy his new cure; he was finally instituted on August 6th 1850 under *fiat* of the Archbishop of Canterbury. Gorham himself died in 1857, no doubt thoroughly exhausted by the nation-wide dispute of which he had become the storm-centre. This singular episode in English church history had effects deep and widespread throughout the Anglican communion: intense interest and concern were aroused among statesmen and lawyers as well as ecclesiastics. Pamphlets were written by profound and sincere thinkers as well as by professional controversialists. The Judgment of the Privy Council was an important event in the life of the nation: by some it was regarded as a blow to traditional orthodoxy, by others as a vindication of the very principles for which the Church of England stands.

The Gorham Judgment brought to a head the conflict on the doctrine of Baptism which had been taking place in the first half of the century. Mant's Bampton Lectures appeared in 1816, and in the same year Laurence published his *Doctrine of the Church of England upon the Efficacy of Baptism*. These were followed in 1821 by Bethell's *General View of the Doctrine of Regeneration in Baptism*. In 1835 Pusey wrote his three tracts on *Scriptural Views of Holy Baptism*. In 1837 G. S. Faber's *Primitive Doctrine of Justification*, bearing on the subject, was published.

Goode's *Effects of Infant Baptism* and R. I. Wilberforce's answer
to it, *The Doctrine of Holy Baptism*, both came in 1849. All this
was followed by the vast output of literature at the time of the
Gorham case itself. The controversy may be said to have been
wound up by Mozley's *Baptismal Controversy*, which was published
in 1862.

The Tractarians, with their revival of emphasis upon sacramental grace, had made the minds of nineteenth-century churchmen pulsate with the question of right disposition. But it was
historical accident rather than inevitable development that
caused this violent clash of the parties over Baptism. As a study
of the pamphlets shows, there were very few in the English
Church who opposed the practice of infant baptism, and with
agreement on practice there was widespread toleration of latitude
in doctrine. Bishop Phillpotts never identified himself with the
Anglo-catholic party and Gorham was not a typical evangelical.
The acerbity of this controversy was due to the fortuitous
encounter between the two original opponents rather than because
it was the climax of a long-standing party dispute. Phillpotts
was an irascible personality—a biographer says of him that
"His pugnacity gave him his chief reputation"[1]—and Gorham,
although no mean scholar, was a fanatic about his views of
Baptism.

When once battle was joined the controversy developed on
party lines, but it cannot be regarded as one of the disputes
brought to a head by the Tractarian movement. Whereas dispute
on the doctrine of the Eucharist flared up anew almost immediately upon the advent of the tracts and remained a heated issue
for many years, the baptismal question had been alive in the
early part of the century; it remained a mere smouldering fire
until this fierce outburst in the Gorham case, and thereafter it
soon became a secondary issue once again. The old-fashioned
high churchmen had argued with the evangelicals about the
doctrine of baptismal regeneration, but they did not raise many
of the questions which the Tractarians later brought into prominence. In 1816 a member of the S.P.C.K. had written a pamphlet[2]
declaring that the Society in publishing Dr Mant's tract on
Regeneration had overthrown its traditional evangelical doctrine

[1] J. A. Hamilton in *Dictionary of National Biography*, Vol. XLV.

[2] *A Respectful Address to the Most Rev. the Archbishops &c., and other members of the
S.P.C.K. on certain inconsistencies and contradictions which have appeared of late in some of
the books and tracts of that Society*. By a Member of the Society. London: J. Hatchard,
1816.

on the matter. But Baptism was not one of the main issues upon
which the Tractarians took their stand: several of the tracts
brought the catholic and protestant elements in the Church of
England into conflict to a greater extent than Pusey's tract on
Baptism did. Also Pusey the Tractarian was much more lenient
towards the evangelicals on the matter of Baptism than was
Phillpotts, who might be described as a bridge between the
old-fashioned high churchmen and the Tractarians, and who to
the end remained a figure upon whom no party could really
rely for support.

The language of the disputants in this case is fogged with
ambiguity and uncertainty; Phillpotts himself hardly speaks
until the appearance of his *Letter to the Archbishop of Canterbury*
which was published after the final judgment of the Judicial
Committee, and Gorham's statements abound in examples of
words being used in different senses. The last chapter of this
book is an attempt first to resolve some of the ambiguities with
which the arguments are beset, and secondly to assess some of
the ideas which each of the antagonists was striving to defend.
A survey of the whole case does seem to reveal that the theologies
of both Gorham and Phillpotts were inadequate. The thought of
F. D. Maurice, a contemporary Anglican theologian, is introduced to serve as a screen against which the limitations of both
the high church and evangelical party doctrines may be seen
more clearly. Maurice does not give a final solution of the problem: indeed his doctrine plunges us into very deep waters. But
the three points of view each have much to contribute and
together they demonstrate what an unsearchable mystery is
enshrined in this sacrament.

It is curious that in the present century, when the practice
of Baptism has been called in question much more repeatedly
than in the last, there has been such a sharp reduction in the
output of literature on the doctrine of this sacrament. With the
approach of the centenary of the Gorham case there is even
more need for the Church of England to clarify her doctrine of
Baptism than there was when this ecclesiastical *cause célèbre* was
at its height.

CHAPTER I

THE EXAMINATION BY THE BISHOP OF EXETER

On Friday, December 17th 1847, the Bishop of Exeter, Dr Henry Phillpotts, began his examination of Mr G. C. Gorham as to his doctrine of the efficacy of the sacrament of Holy Baptism. This whole examination lasted for fifty-two hours, with only short intervals for meals, spread out over eight days—the first five being in December 1847 and the last three in March 1848.[1] One wonders how many parish priests nowadays would be able to stand up to such an extended and searching doctrinal test: nay, how many bishops would have the interest and ability to maintain so prolonged an enquiry. But Mr Gorham made his defence and argued his case throughout that long period with remarkable clarity and theological exactness, and seems hardly to have made a slip. He has published the substance of all that passed between him and the Bishop on those days of examination at Exeter, together with the correspondence relating to the whole matter.[2]

His Lordship opened the first day's examination by asking Gorham to prove from Scripture that Baptism was necessary to salvation. This looked like an attempt to trap Gorham by leading him into making quotations from Scripture and then forcing him into interpretations which they will not bear when taken alongside other passages. But Gorham was ready for this, and his first answer was such as to show the Bishop of Exeter the quality of the defence he was going to make. Since this first answer contains a cardinal point in Gorham's whole position, it merits being quoted in full:

In our Lord's discourse with Nicodemus it is said: "Except a man be born of water and of the Spirit, he cannot enter into the kingdom of God" (John iii. 5). If the allusion be to Baptism[3] (which, however,

---

[1] Introduction to *The Efficacy of Baptism*, by G. C. Gorham.

[2] *Op. cit.* This is an authoritative record—"Each question and Answer was recorded by the Bishop's Chaplain, the Rev. W. Maskell and by myself, as the examination proceeded", p. 62. "All matter which is not strictly documentary, is included in brackets", *ibid.*

[3] Gorham was perhaps not aware that this passage is always referred to Holy Baptism, without exception in Christian writers who allude to it, until Calvin (so Darwell Stone, *Holy Baptism*, p. 25).

had not then been instituted), it undoubtedly affirms the necessity of complying with that solemn Institution, where no unavoidable impediment intervenes. Having been ordained of Christ, it cannot be slighted without the awful consequences of disobedience to his express command. But it does not appear to me that the being "born of water", and the being "born of the Spirit", are so indissolubly tied together by this declaration, that each is *equally and in the same sense* necessary to salvation. This view is confirmed by the fact that the expression, "born again", is used in this discourse in verses 3, 6, 7, 8, without any reference to being "born of water", but twice with express mention of being "born of the Spirit" as the great essential requisite. It is confirmed also by verses 16, 17, where "everlasting life" and salvation are *positively* connected with "belief" in the Son of God without reference to Baptism; as if for the very purpose of showing that faith is an *indispensable and essential condition*, but that Baptism is only *generally necessary*, a condition to be dutifully performed.

Precisely the same conclusion must be drawn from the terms used by our Lord, in his express institution of Baptism: "He that believeth and is baptized shall be saved" (Mark xvi. 16). The *general* connexion between the *sign* which he has ordained for admission into his Church, and the *faith* which that sign certifies, is here distinctly affirmed. But our Lord adds, "He that believeth not shall be damned." Here exclusion from everlasting salvation is grounded, not on the omission of *Baptism*, but on the withholding belief in the Son of God.

In this answer Gorham is asserting, in substance, the doctrine of Justification by Faith. If this is not presupposed the whole sacramental system of the Church is out of place. It was for precisely this tenet of biblical Christianity that Gorham conceived himself to be fighting against the so-called "high" doctrine of Baptism held by the Bishop of Exeter.

At the same time as this appeal to Scripture on the necessity of Baptism the Bishop questioned Gorham on the general necessity of the Supper of the Lord. The Bishop then went on to try to prove the absolute necessity of Baptism from the Homily of Common Prayer and the Sacraments. He quoted from this:

According to the exact signification of a Sacrament, Baptism, and the Supper of the Lord, are visible signs, expressly commanded in the New Testament, whereunto is annexed the promise of free forgiveness of our sins, and of our holiness and joining in Christ;

and then asked whether this was to be held as godly and wholesome doctrine.

Gorham replied that his subscription to the XXXVth Article

involved his assent to this passage when it was fairly construed.[1] The passage, he claimed, needs explaining in order to demonstrate the true meaning of the compiler. Without going into the question in detail at this point, Gorham said simply: "I fully assent to the wholesome truth contained in this quotation, when fairly brought into connexion with the Articles of our Church, on the nature and efficacy of the Sacraments."

The Bishop then went on to the central point upon which this whole controversy turned—whether all infants lawfully baptized were regenerated. The Bishop does not use the adverb "lawfully" in his question, but he clearly understands valid Baptism to be "by a lawful minister, with water, in the name of the Father and of the Son and of the Holy Ghost". The Bishop seems to imply that no other conditions are necessary for regeneration— and this is certainly the view which he is defending in the later parts of the examination. "Does our Church hold, and do you hold, that all infants, so baptized, are born again of water and of the Holy Ghost?" was the Bishop's question.[2]

In reply to this question,[3] Gorham enunciates what he regards as an extremely important principle in interpreting passages from the Prayer Book. He admits that passages can be quoted from the Catechism and the rites of Baptism in the Prayer Book which "in their naked verbality" appear to assert that all persons baptized with water by a lawful minister in the threefold Name are *ipso facto* regenerated without any other conditions. But Gorham finds himself in no way forced into this interpretation. He quotes with great force from the Preface to the Book of Common Prayer that the precise words of the Ritual Services or of the Catechism must be held to "contain in them nothing contrary to the Word of God, or to sound doctrine, or which a godly man may not with a good conscience use and submit unto, or which is not *fairly defensible, . . . if it shall be allowed such just and favourable construction as in common equity ought to be allowed to all Human Writings, especially such as are set forth by authority*" (italics Gorham's).

Gorham asserts that the "just and favourable construction" of passages such as those to which the Bishop refers is to be sought

---

[1] Such was not the case, in Gorham's mind, in the Bishop of Exeter's Charge, 1842, p. 21. (See *op. cit.*, p. 66, note.)

[2] Gorham, *op. cit.*, p. 67.

[3] In fact there were three questions from the Bishop, but as they are all on the same point it is convenient to treat them as one.

by reference to three standards—first the XXXIX Articles, the Church's explicit standard of doctrine; secondly, passages in her Formularies must not be abstracted in isolation, but must be brought into juxtaposition and compared with other passages; the third standard is the general view of those by whom the services were reformed and the Articles sanctioned. He insisted also that in an enquiry as to the efficacy of sacraments it is not permissible to isolate the case of infant baptism; adult baptism and the Lord's Supper must also be subject to the same three standards of interpretation.

In a lengthy reply Gorham proceeded to examine the three sources to which he had referred as standards for interpretation of passages in the Prayer Book. First the Articles: Article XXV distinctly declares that Sacraments only "have a wholesome effect or operation" upon such as "worthily receive the same". Passages from the four following articles demonstrate beyond doubt that this is the meaning intended. Article XXVI says that "the grace of God's gifts" is conferred on such as "by faith and rightly do receive the Sacraments". Article XXVII says equally clearly that "they that receive Baptism rightly are grafted into the Church etc. . . . etc. . . ." Article XXVIII maintains the same principle in relation to the Communion: "to such as rightly, worthily, and with faith, receive the same, the Bread which we break is a partaking of the Body of Christ". The same is asserted in Article XXIX: "The wicked, and such as be void of lively faith, although they do carnally and visibly press with their teeth (as St Augustine saith) the sacrament of the Body and Blood of Christ, yet in no sense are they partakers of Christ". Gorham regards himself as justified in maintaining that the view of the Articles in relation to sacraments is— "Where there is no worthy reception, there is no bestowment of grace".[1]

Gorham then deals with the second standard to which he appeals. Passages in the Formularies of the Church must be examined in juxtaposition with other passages in the same documents. He makes the comparison and contends that the Formularies as a whole, when fairly construed, teach the same doctrine as the Articles, though sometimes in a form less definite.

First he quotes the Catechism where the "inward and spiritual grace" of sacraments is clearly distinguished from the "outward and visible sign". The former accompanies the latter when the

[1] *Op. cit.*, p. 69.

latter is rightly received. This is not explicitly stated in the Catechism, but it is clearly implied by the condition of "repentance and faith" being required of all those who are to be baptized, even of infants who enter into these stipulations by their representatives. The statements in the Baptismal Services to the effect that by the rite of Baptism, just performed, the persons are in fact regenerated amount, Gorham asserts, to no more than charitable hypothesis—the hypothesis that the condition of faith is satisfied. It is true that in the Prayer Book offices of Holy Baptism[1] there are two sentences which appear to be unconditional assertions of regeneration. In the exhortation which follows the reading from St Mark's Gospel it is said, "Doubt ye not therefore, but earnestly believe . . . that he will give unto him the blessing of eternal life, and make him partaker of his everlasting kingdom". Also in the second prayer after baptism it is said, "We yield thee hearty thanks, most merciful Father, that it hath pleased thee to regenerate this infant with the Holy Spirit". Nevertheless in the concluding phrases of this same prayer the Church makes that which had, apparently, been the subject of positive declaration, to be again the matter of humble petition—"And humbly beseech thee . . . that finally, with the residue of thy Holy Church he may be an inheritor[2] of thine everlasting kingdom". This is enough to establish the principle that some apparently unhesitating assertions in the Formularies can only be "justly construed" as conditional and hypothetical. But it is important to observe here that while Gorham is insisting on the "hypothetical principle" in this passage he uses language which indicates that where the conditions are fulfilled regeneration does take place actually *in* Baptism. These are Gorham's words at this point—". . . it being impossible that such dispositions and fruits should exist, except when the Holy Ghost has imparted a new nature; which he may do *before* Baptism, *in* Baptism, or *after* Baptism 'as He listeth' ".[3]

Gorham reinforced the principle he had enunciated by quoting from the Burial of the Dead. Here there is the absolute statement, "It hath pleased thee to deliver this our brother out of the

---

[1] It is not clear why Gorham quotes from "Private Baptism"—the passages occur in "Publick Baptism" also.

[2] It might be questioned whether Gorham really makes his point here. The most we can become now is "heirs". To be an "inheritor", i.e. to enter upon possession of that to which we are heirs, must necessitate actual entry into Heaven.

[3] *Ibid.*, p. 71.

miseries of this sinful world",[1] and yet subsequently there is the prayer that "we may rest in him, as our *hope* is this our brother doth". He also quotes from the collects of the Prayer Book as showing that all the baptized who use those collects cannot be assumed to be regenerate simply from the fact of their baptism.

Gorham asserts that not only in the Prayer Book, but also in the interpretation of Holy Scripture, the principle must be allowed that "the most absolute terms must be construed sometimes in a symbolical, sometimes in a conditional sense".[2] Otherwise the Lord's words at the institution of the Eucharist commit the Church to belief in Transubstantiation, and the opening phrases of the Epistle to the Romans indicate the sanctified state of every individual member of the Church addressed.

Gorham closes his treatment of the Anglican Formularies with a short review of the whole teaching of the Prayer Book, the Articles and the Homilies, on Sacraments. Throughout these there is, Gorham maintains, a clear distinction between the Sacrament or Sign, and the grace or thing signified; and although in common speech the name of the sign is often used to describe the thing signified, the whole point of the distinction which the Formularies make is to avoid the idea of *ex opere operato* efficacy of the sacraments.

Gorham then moves on to the third criterion which he says must be applied in interpreting these passages which the Bishop quotes—that is the writings of the Anglican Reformers by whom the services were reformed and the Articles sanctioned. In the verbal examination he cited Coverdale, Latimer, Ridley, Cranmer and Hooper as marking in unmistakable language the distinction between the Sacrament or Sign and the Grace or Thing signified. He also quoted Jewel on Baptism: "in Baptism, as the one part of that holy mystery is Christ's blood, so is the other part the material water: neither are these two parts joined together in place, but in mystery; and therefore they be oftentimes severed, and the one is received without the other".[3] In the published account of the examination[4] Gorham added as

---

[1] Gorham might have quoted the even more definite passage, "Forasmuch as it hath pleased Almighty God of his great mercy to take unto himself the soul of our dear brother".

[2] *Op. cit.*, p. 74.

[3] Jewel's Reply to Harding, *On Private Mass &c.*, p. 285, edit. London, 1609, folio; *Works*, edit. Parker Society, Vol. I, p. 519.

[4] *Op. cit.*, pp. 76–9.

footnotes quotations from Coverdale,[1] Latimer,[2] Ridley,[3] Cranmer,[4] and Hooper,[5] also others from Jewel, to the same effect.

The second day's examination (December 18th 1847) was devoted mainly to the question of the necessity and meaning of the stipulations into which infants enter by their representatives at their baptism.

The Bishop began by running over some of the ground covered in the previous day's examination. First he attempted to make Gorham express explicit doubt that John iii. 5 referred to Baptism. Gorham, however, said no more than "The Church's quotation of this passage as referring to Baptism, I consider as 'not contrary to Holy Scripture'". The Bishop then fastened on to one passage of Gorham's answer of the previous day on the verses in John iii, and this led at once to the main subject of this day's examination. Gorham had said, "It is confirmed also by John iii. 16, 17; where 'everlasting life and salvation' are *positively* connected with 'belief' in the Son of God, without reference to Baptism; as if for the very purpose of shewing that Faith is an *indispensable* and *essential condition*, but that Baptism is only *generally necessary*".[6] The Bishop now questioned him, "Do you mean that Faith is an indispensable and essential condition to salvation in all persons?" Gorham replied, "Yes; I mean that". The Bishop then asked Gorham if he held that it was necessary for infants to have faith at the time of their being baptized in order that their Baptism might be effectual to salvation. To this Gorham replied that Articles XXV–XXIX[7] stated that *all* persons, without respect of age, must be *worthy recipients* of the Sacrament to benefit by it; and that worthy reception was there defined to be by "*Faith*".

The Bishop then moved on to the question of the stipulations entered into by the infant's representatives at Baptism. He asked, "Is the entering of infants into these stipulations, by their representatives, necessary to their receiving the spiritual grace of Baptism?" Gorham does not give a direct answer to this question, and he claims that no such answer can reasonably be expected. He quotes from His Majesty's Declaration prefixed to the Articles enjoining that "further curious search" into such an abstract point should be laid aside, and that such disputes should be "shut

---

[1] *Works*, edit. Parker Society, p. 411.   [2] *Ibid.*, p. 202.   [3] *Ibid.*, p. 240.

[4] E.g. *On the Sacraments*, edit. Parker Society, p. 221.

[5] *Works*, edit. Parker Society, pp. 74, 75.   [6] See p. 12, *supra*.

[7] Quoted on p. 14, *supra*.

B

up in God's promises as they be generally set forth to us in the Holy Scriptures". But he does give a partial answer to the question, and he claims that what he says is as much as can be deduced from the Formularies, and is the limit to which the Church has declared her mind on the point. Gorham's statements on this point are important in the controversy, so they will be quoted in full:

The Church requires these stipulations before administering the rite of Baptism to infants; but the spiritual grace may have been given, if it pleased God, before the stipulations were made.

He also says:

Our Church holds, and I hold, that no spiritual grace is conveyed in Baptism, except to *worthy recipients*; and as infants are by nature *un*worthy recipients, "being born in sin, and the children of wrath", they cannot receive any benefit from Baptism, except there shall have been a prevenient act of grace to make them worthy. Baptism is the sign or seal, either of the grace already given, or of repentance and faith, which are stipulated, and must be hereafter exercised.

The Bishop then asked whether the Church had not declared her mind that infants duly baptized do receive the spiritual grace of Baptism even though they have not entered into the stipulations by their representatives. This was presumably an indirect reference to the office of Private Baptism, which, without any mention of stipulations by representatives, says in its rubrics that "the child so baptized is lawfully and sufficiently baptized, and ought not to be baptized again". The only condition appears to be the existence of sufficient emergency. Against any less doughty opponent such a question might well have been a master-stroke; but Gorham appears to have been quite ready for it, and in his answer displays remarkable lucidity of thought. Gorham gives his opinion that in this case of emergency, the stipulations, though not formally made by the sponsors, are made by implication through those who earnestly desire the Baptism, and by the person who administers it. If the child lives, these implied stipulations are directed to be formally adopted in Church.

But the Bishop was not satisfied with this answer and put the question once again in a different form, asking whether the Church holds that infants baptized in an emergency were regenerated independently of any stipulations. Gorham then declared the Church to hold that infants baptized in an emergency dying before they commit "actual sin" are "undoubtedly saved" (rubric at the end of the office of Publick Baptism) and he added "therefore they must have been regenerated by an act of grace prevenient to their Baptism, in order to make them worthy recipients of that Sacrament". But he said that if the infant lives to a period in which it can commit "actual sin", then the declaration of regeneration must be construed according to the hypothetical principle which he had enunciated earlier.[1]

The Bishop did not pursue this point any further here, but reverted to Gorham's comment the day before on the passage in Mark xvi, "He that believeth and is baptized shall be saved". Gorham had said "the general connection between the sign which he [Our Lord] has ordained for admission to his Church, and the Faith which that Sign certifies, is here distinctly affirmed". The Bishop asked what he meant by "the Faith which that Sign signifies". Gorham replied, "I mean: that Baptism is a certification, pledge, and public manifestation, by the individual who is baptized, that he believes, with 'all his heart', in the Divine nature, mission, and atonement of the Son of God". Gorham said that Baptism was a Sign that the person baptized had professed that belief. Hereupon the Bishop asked whether, according to the doctrine of the Church, Baptism was a sign of anything else. To this Gorham replied:

It *may* be, and very often *is*, a Sign of *nothing more*. But, if it is received "rightly, worthily, and by faith", it is an "*effectual* Sign" of God's "grace" bestowed, which implanted a new nature and produced the faith both professed and possessed; and it is also a Sign of "God's good-will towards us", by which he "strengthens" and confirms our "faith" in him.

Gorham then asserted, in answer to the Bishop's question, that "Grace" and not "Sign" was the antecedent to "which" in the above answer; thus indicating that he held that the action of God's grace in implanting a new nature and the saving faith preceded the bestowal of the Sign by which God strengthens and confirms that faith.[2]

The Bishop then brought the Latin text of the Articles into play against Gorham. Pointing out that the Latin Articles of 1571 are of the same authority and binding force as the English, to which proposition Gorham assented, he quoted from Article

[1] See pp. 15 f., *supra*.

[2] Article XXVII—"Faith is confirmed, and Grace increased by virtue of prayer unto God".

XXVII—"Baptismus . . . est *Signum* Regenerationis, per *quod*, tanquam per instrumentum, recte Baptismum suscipientes Ecclesiae inseruntur, promissiones de remissione peccatorum atque adoptione nostra in filios Dei per Spiritum Sanctum visibiliter obsignantur. . . .". Here the antecedent to "quod" can be nothing but "Signum", and the Bishop suggested that this fact might induce Gorham to withdraw his previous answer, and attribute to the "Sign" what he had affirmed of the "Grace". But Gorham was not moved by this attack, and answered that the Latin Article did not postulate anything more of the "Signum" than he had allowed. All that the "Signum" is here said to do is to graft into the Church, and to seal the promises of God, as by an "instrument"—by which Gorham understands a legal deed.[1] Gorham affirms that the Latin Article cannot be interpreted as in any way indicating that *a new nature* is implanted by the sign. The Bishop did not press his point further.

The Bishop asked whether the Article said whose "Instrument" the Sign was, or who was said to be the efficient cause of the grafting into the Church and sealing the promises of God, of which Baptism was said to be the instrumental cause. Gorham replied that the Article stated nothing about causation; that if the Article had intended to direct those who subscribe it to that subject, it would have propounded the doctrine of the Church on the point by direct assertion, and would not have left the meaning to be gathered by implication. Such a question as the Bishop had now asked, Gorham remarked, seemed to him to depart from the principle of subscription to the Articles in their "literal and grammatical sense", and to introduce private "sense or comment".[2]

The Bishop next attempted to separate the two parts of Article XXV. He sought to obtain Gorham's assent to the clause "Sacraments ordained of Christ be . . . effectual signs of grace, and God's good will towards us, by the which he doth work 'invisibly in us' ", without the qualifying clause, "And in such only as worthily receive the same they have a wholesome effect or operation". The Bishop said, "Considered by themselves, and without reference to the qualifications of the recipients of them, are Sacraments, ordained by Christ, 'effectual signs of grace &c., &c.'?" Gorham replied emphatically, "Sacraments are

[1] "Signed, sealed and delivered" in legal language—the signing or sealing of a deed frequently does nothing more than give legal recognition to a state of affairs already existing.

[2] Quotations from the Royal Declaration, prefixed to the Articles.

NOT effectual signs of grace by themselves and without reference to the qualifications of the recipients". The Bishop repeated the question three times in different forms, but Gorham simply reaffirmed that he regarded the two parts of the Article as indissolubly connected.

The Bishop then asked Gorham to state what, if any, special grace "God doth work invisibly" in those who receive Baptism worthily. Gorham's answer to this is important, and will be quoted in full:

By this Sign and visible Symbol of his grace, he sets his seal to his "promises of forgiveness of sins, and of our adoption to be his sons", he "confirms" the "Faith" which he had previously implanted in us, and by which he made us "rightly" to receive this Sacrament; and he "increases" the "Grace" which he had previously given us: he does all this "by virtue of prayer" for which he has bestowed the disposition.

Gorham added the following as a footnote, indicating that it was his own account of the words of the Bishop, with his own comments, and not part of the written account of the examination agreed upon by himself and the Bishop:

The Bishop justly remarked, that the virtue of prayer is *not affirmed* with regard to any other blessing than the "confirming grace", as is clear from the Latin Articles—"et, vi Divinae invocationis, gratia, augetur". It is equally clear, however, that the virtue of prayer is not intended to be *restricted* to the last blessing named, though mentioned parenthetically in connection with it; on the contrary, "the Divine invocation" is beautifully suggested in the closing sentence of the Article, as *that* without which *no* blessing can be expected.

The Bishop then asked, "Does he 'work invisibly in us' the grace of our adoption to be his sons?", to which Gorham answered:

The grace of adoption he visibly *seals* by the Sign which he has ordained to be its *token*, but he "works", also, "invisibly in us", by this external pledge, *an assurance* that he *has* adopted us. In other words, he "invisibly" sends his Spirit ("the Spirit of adoption") into our hearts, by which we acknowledge our filial condition, and "cry, Abba, Father!".

The Bishop's next question was, "Does he give to us, or 'work invisibly in us' by baptism, the filial condition of which you here speak?" Gorham's reply was as follows:

That filial condition was given us by the qualification of "faith", essential to the right reception of Baptism; and, therefore, was given *before* Baptism if we were worthy recipients of that Sacrament; for he gives "power to become the *sons of God* to as many as *believe* on his name".

Gorham was next asked, "Is the faith, required of persons who are baptized, belief of any special truths stated by the Church?". This was his answer:

The faith required is stated with different degrees of distinctness, in different parts of the Formularies and Articles.

In the Catechism it is stated, generally, to be a "steadfast belief of the promises of God made in that Sacrament".

In Article XXVII those promises are more specially said to be "forgiveness of sins, and our adoption to be the sons of God by the Holy Ghost".

In the Baptismal Ritual a belief is exacted, from the recipient, of all the articles of the Christian faith embodied in the Creed.

I conclude, therefore, that the "faith" required in Baptism means faith, in the usual acceptation of that word in theology, and not belief in any *special* truth stated by the Church in any *one* part of her Services.

The third day of the examination was December 20th 1847. On this occasion the questioning lasted from 10.30 a.m. to 6 p.m. After some preliminary protestation from Gorham as to the length of the examination, and discussion between him and the Bishop to which this led, the Bishop questioned Gorham on his answer concerning infants baptized in an emergency without formal representatives.

Gorham had given his opinion that the meaning of the Church to be deduced from the general teaching of the Catechism was that in this case the stipulations were implied though not formally given. The Bishop now asked Gorham if he considered this to be the teaching of the Church. Gorham replied that in giving his view of what the Church holds on nice questions such as this, when her mind is only to be gathered from implication, he preferred to use the word "meaning". He added that the Church "teaches", using that word in the strict and definite sense, in her standard of doctrine, the Thirty-nine Articles.

The Bishop then asked what he said of the Catechism (on the implied meaning of which the foregoing discussion was based). Did he not regard it as part of the Church's dogmatical teaching, and a standard of its doctrine? Gorham replied that he had no

hesitation in allowing that the Catechism was, as its title declared
it to be, "an Instruction"; he admitted that the doctrines of the
Church, in so far as they are expressly stated therein, are to be
learnt from it, when this "Instruction" was fairly brought into
connexion with the Thirty-nine Articles. These he repeated that
he held to be, in the stricter sense of the term, the standard of
the doctrines of the Church.[1] He added that he held there was
a clear distinction between the Book of Common Prayer (including, of course, the Catechism) and the XXXIX Articles, as
regards critical and theological discussion of the tenets of the
Church contained in them. This distinction, he maintained, is
observed by Canon XXXVI, which says that every clergyman
is to declare his belief that "the Book of Common Prayer con-
taineth in it *nothing contrary* to the Word of God"; but he is to
allow "the Book of Articles to be *agreeable to* the Word of God".
The same language appears in the King's Declaration prefixed
to the Articles. Gorham said that the mind of the Church was
to be gathered, doubtless, from both; but that we must have
ultimate recourse to the Articles, when diversities of opinion
arise on the less precise language of the Formularies in the
Book of Common Prayer.

The Bishop next drew Gorham's attention to his quotation
from the Preface to the Book of Common Prayer. Gorham had
referred[2] to its plea for "such just and favourable construction
as in common equity ought to be allowed to all human writings,
especially such as are set forth by authority". The Bishop pointed
out to Gorham that the passage which he quoted was applied
by the writers of it, not to the Book of Common Prayer as it
now stands, but to the Book as it stood before the Review which

[1] Gorham added as a footnote what occurred to him afterwards and was not part
of the dialogue with the Bishop. At the Hampton Court Conference in 1604, when
this very part of the Catechism, on the Sacraments, was added to the shorter form,
King James I expressed the opinion that a Catechism should be "in the fewest and
plaintest affirmative terms that may be", and stated his wish that "old, curious,
deep and intricate questions might be avoided in the fundamental instruction of a
people" (Cardwell's *Conferences*, p. 187).

Gorham also draws attention, in the same footnote, to the views of the Nonconforming Divines at the later Savoy Conference in 1661. They asked whether "it
were not convenient to add (what seemed to be wanting) something particular
concerning the nature of faith, of repentance, the two covenants, of justification,
sanctification, adoption and regeneration". The twelve Episcopal Commissioners
gave this answer: "The Catechism is not intended as a whole body of divinity, but
as a comprehension of the articles of faith, and other doctrines most necessary to
salvation; and, being short, is fittest for children and common people" (Cardwell's
Conferences, pp. 327, 358). Gorham does not suggest that this opinion of the twelve
Bishops is in any way authoritative, but that it shows how far they were from
regarding the Catechism as a "dogmatical standard of doctrine".

[2] See p. 13, *supra*.

resulted in establishing the present Book.[1] Gorham said that he
was aware that this was the case, but that the meaning of the
writers was that this "just and favourable construction" must
be given to the present Book as much as to the former one.
They say that such "ought to be allowed to *all* human writings,
especially to such as are set forth by authority". Gorham added
that for the writers of this Preface to say, as the Bishop seemed
to be implying that they did say, that this "just and favourable
construction" was not needed for their own Book, would be to
claim that their alterations of the former Book were infallibly
the best that could be chosen, and that their own writing was a
super-human composition.

The Bishop dropped the point, and rather pursued the
doctrinal matter which Gorham had in mind in insisting upon
the "just and favourable construction" of passages in the Book
of Common Prayer. Gorham had spoken of "passages . . . which,
taken in their naked verbality, might appear to contradict the
clearest statements of Scripture". The Bishop asked what passages
of Scripture, in Gorham's opinion, would be contradicted by
the naked verbality of passages in the Prayer Book which indicated that children lawfully baptized were *ipso facto* made members
of Christ, the children of God and inheritors of the kingdom of
heaven. Gorham replied as follows:

Scripture declares that, as "the wind bloweth *where it listeth* and
thou hearest the sound thereof, but canst not tell whence it cometh,
and whither it goeth; so is every one that is born of the Spirit" (John
iii. 8). Now if the effects and blessings set forth in "naked verbality",
by the passage cited in question V[2] were absolutely, unconditionally
wrought in, and conferred on, "EVERY infant", the Spirit would, of
necessity, effect his operation, in EVERY infant, *at the moment when*
man thinks fit to direct He *shall* effect it; which is a conclusion directly
opposed to the declaration of the lip of truth in *this* Scripture.

Again: it is declared in Scripture (John i. 12, 13) that those who
are "the sons of God", "were born NOT *of blood* NOR *of the will of the
flesh*, NOR *of the will of man*, but of God"; and that they become his sons

---

[1] The passage to which the Bishop here refers, which Gorham did not quote, is:
"For we are fully persuaded in our judgements . . . that the Book, as it stood before,
established by Law, doth not contain in it anything contrary to the Word of God
&c. . . . &c. . . .".

[2] In Question V the Bishop asked, "Does our Church hold, and do you hold, that
every infant baptized by a lawful minister, with water, in the name of the Father,
and of the Son, and of the Holy Ghost, is made by God, in such Baptism, *a member
of Christ, the child of God and an inheritor of the kingdom of heaven*?". The words in italics
are an exact quotation from the Catechism.

BISHOP PHILLPOTTS

GEORGE CORNELIUS GORHAM

by "*belief* on the name" of Jesus Christ. But, if the *nakedly verbal declaration* of the spiritual filiation of "EVERY infant" were unconditionally true, then there would be no place left for its regeneration, or its being brought into the relation of a "child of God" by the means of *faith*, as here stated in the Divine Record; and the spiritual birth of "EVERY infant" would be, by "*the will of man*", and at the *precise moment when* man exercises his "will" that such new nature shall be imparted.

The same line of argument (—I mean of apparent contradiction between the supposed unconditional assertion made by "*the naked verbality*" of the passage in Question V, and the affirmation of Scripture—) might be shown from Gal. iii. 26, "Ye are all the children of God by *faith* in Christ Jesus".

And again, from James i. 18,—"Of his own will begat he us, by *the Word of truth*".

And, once more, (—to omit numerous other passages, and not to insist largely on the whole tenor of the Sacred Oracles—) the proposition which I am maintaining might be established from 1 Peter i. 3 and 23, "The God and Father of our Lord Jesus Christ . . . hath begotten us again . . . by the *resurrection* of Jesus Christ from the dead". "Being born again, not of corruptible seed, but of incorruptible, by the *Word of God*, which liveth and abideth for ever". From which passage, Bishop Latimer[1] justly insists on the truth, "Thus cometh in our New Birth;" after having directly negatived the dogma of "those firebrands" (—he clearly means the Papists—) who maintained that the New Birth was effected absolutely, unconditionally, necessarily, instantaneously, indubitably, "ex opere operato", by Baptism.

I refer your Lordship, generally, to numerous other passages (—of the class, "As many as are led by the Spirit of God, they are the sons of God," Rom. viii. 14, &c., &c.—) which speak of the disposition, character, and effects, wrought in the heart, and manifested in the life, as evidences that the Regeneration has actually taken place. All such passages would be flatly contradicted by maintaining that Regeneration, or being "made the child of God" absolutely unconditionally, peremptorily, takes place in "EVERY infant baptized by a lawful minister with water, in the name of the Father, and of the Son, and of the Holy Ghost".—FACT overthrows the supposition.

But the Bishop evidently required a further statement of belief from Gorham, so he asked again whether the passage in the Catechism on Baptism did not ascribe the blessings there mentioned to the gift of God in Baptism. Gorham once again said that faith and the filial relationship precede Baptism. He sought to prove this from Our Lord's Baptism. The actual form of his reply was:

[1] Sermon before Edward VI, *Works*, edit. Parker Society, p. 202.

. . . The Church holds, and I hold, that the worthy reception . . . implies "Faith" (see Article XXVII, and see the requirements from the sponsors in the Baptismal Service): but as the stipulation of *"Faith"* goes *before* Baptism, and as the condition of being *"the child of God"* is a blessing conferred by "Faith" (John i. 12, 13; Gal. iii. 26),—hence the blessing of "adoption", also, *precedes* Baptism, in its essence; but it is declared, attested, and *manifested by* that Sacrament, as (ordained to be) a Seal or Sign of the gift—which I maintain to be a very different proposition from this other, namely—that the blessing of regeneration, or adoption to be a member of the family of God, is to be *ascribed* TO *Baptism.*

I will illustrate what I mean, by adducing the Baptism of the Divine Founder of that Sacrament. Our Lord was the Son of God, in *fact*, in the *essential character* and *nature* of that relation to him, *before* Baptism; but when he submitted to that Sign, he was manifested, attested, Divinely proclaimed to be his "Beloved Son"; "MADE" (in *such* a sense,) the Son of God, by the affusion of water. In plain words, His Sonship must not be *ascribed* to that Sign, but it was "in and by" that sign solemnly *attested.* And this I conceive to be a fair (though I do not say it is a perfect) illustration of the way in which each of His disciples is "MADE" the child of God (—worthy reception being all along taken for granted—) "in and by Baptism".

The Bishop said that Gorham's reply seemed to be in answer to the question whether the blessings were to be ascribed "to Baptism" rather than whether they were to be ascribed "to God in Baptism". Gorham said there had not been any doubt as to the Author or Efficient Cause of the blessings—the question related to the time when, and the act by which, the blessings are conferred.

The blessing is, [he said,] "Adoption to be the sons of God;" that blessing is undoubtedly to be "ascribed TO GOD". For "*Faith* is not of ourselves, it is the gift OF GOD"; and to such as possess *Faith*, "to them giveth HE" (Jesus Christ) "power to become the sons of God". But that "faith", and that filial state, though clearly to be "ascribed TO GOD", was given to the worthy recipient (—for we are here all along assuming this worthiness—) *before* Baptism, and not "*in* Baptism".

Tuesday, December 21st 1847, was the fourth day of the Bishop's questions. On this day the examination lasted from 1.30 p.m. to 6.30 p.m. Gorham began by protesting against the length of the examination; but the Bishop said that he must continue his questions if there was any likelihood that Gorham would publish what had passed in the examination. (Gorham had not up to this time either hinted at, or denied, any such intention.) The Bishop said there were still some more considerations he ought to lay before him.

The Bishop began by referring to Gorham's quotation of Gal. iii. 26, "For ye are all the children of God by faith in Jesus Christ".[1] The Bishop asked Gorham to quote the verse immediately following this. Gorham quoted, "For as many of you as have been baptized into Christ have put on Christ". Gorham asserted that this passage was not, as the Bishop seemed to him to be implying, in the least degree at variance with his statement that faith was a pre-requisite to beneficial Baptism. On the contrary, he claimed, the passage illustrated that doctrine; St Paul says here, "As many of you as have been baptized into Christ"—that is not all who make profession by the outward and visible sign—"have put on Christ". Only those who have believed with all their hearts, and have thus come to Baptism with a lively "faith in Him" have "put on Christ". Gorham says, "You have been invested with his righteousness imputed to you for your justification, and you have been clothed with that personal righteousness (Rom. xiii. 14), which shows that you are sanctified by his Spirit".

The Bishop then turned to the King's Declaration prefixed to the XXXIX Articles, to which Gorham had referred in claiming that some of the Bishop's questions were such as could not reasonably be asked in this, or any, Examination.[2] The Bishop asked Gorham if he was aware that this Declaration had not the authority of Convocation nor of Parliament. Gorham replied that he understood it was not known at what time the Declaration was made, although it was believed to have been made in the reign of Charles I.[3] In this case he supposed the contemporary authority of Convocation for it had not been found. In any case, even if the Declaration did not receive the authority of Convocation or of Parliament, Gorham held that the "Supreme Governor of the Church of England" acted wisely in issuing this injunction "to maintain the Church in unity of true religion, and in the bond of peace, and not to suffer unnecessary Disputations, Altercations or Questions to be raised, which may nourish factions, both in the Church and Commonwealth".[4]

[1] P. 26, *supra*.   [2] Pp. 17, 20, *supra*.

[3] Gorham added, in a footnote, that the earliest copy of the Articles to which the Royal Declaration is attached is one printed in 1628 (Bishop Hacket's copy in the University Library, Cambridge). He quotes Prynne as saying that the text of the Declaration was compiled by Laud. Gorham, *op. cit.*, p. 115.

[4] Quotation from His Majesty's Declaration prefixed to the Articles.

The Bishop then asked whether Gorham held that a clergyman was not liable to ecclesiastical judgment for setting forth doctrines which were contrary to those set forth in the Prayer Book, including the Catechism, provided those doctrines were not also contrary to the teaching of the Thirty-nine Articles. Gorham replied that the hypothesis was not to be entertained that a doctrine can be set forth which is contrary to the Prayer Book and yet not also contrary to the Articles. The hypothesis would make the Church contradict herself, by doctrinal statements in her Formularies differing from those set forth in her more formal Standard of Truth.

The Bishop then asked whether Gorham held that every doctrine which is really included in the Book of Common Prayer must, as such, be in accordance with the truth as set forth in the Thirty-nine Articles. Gorham said that this must be so on the supposition, which he adopted, that the Framers of the Book of Common Prayer and the Compilers of the Thirty-nine Articles, or the persons who gave authority to them both, were consistent with themselves. He reminded the Bishop of the "just and favourable construction" which the Church claimed for her Formularies, on which he had given his views earlier.[1] He reiterated that paramount authority was to be ascribed to the Articles—the Church's more accurate standard.

The Bishop then asked again in what passages in the Articles Gorham found expressions to justify his argument on "worthy recipients" and "unworthy recipients" of the Sacraments. Gorham quoted again the passages from Articles XXV–XXIX to which he had previously referred.[2] He added in a footnote[3] that in King Edward's Articles (1552) the phrase restricting the benefit of sacraments to worthy recipients occurs at the beginning of the Article. He asserted that the phrase would have remained in this prominent place in Elizabeth's Articles if the reformers had contemplated the modern argument for essential and unconditional grace in the Sacraments. Gorham also quoted phrases to the same effect from the Exhortations in the Communion Service, and also from the Prayer of Thanksgiving—"Thou dost vouchsafe to feed us who have duly received these Holy Mysteries".

The Bishop next raised the question of the meaning of the

[1] Pp. 13, 14 and 23, 24, *supra*.   [2] P. 14, *supra*.

[3] *Op. cit.*, p. 119. This was added by Gorham subsequently, and was not part of his answer to the Bishop.

word "worthy", saying, "Do you mean that any man is 'worthy' to receive the grace of God, given in the holy Sacraments?". Gorham said that any such idea was abhorrent to his mind; the Bishop was, he asserted, using the word in very different senses, and suggesting a statement very different from that which he had, in fact, made. The same word can be applied to different ideas, and the fallacy really lies in the imperfection of human language. Gorham quoted from Canon XXXIX of 1603, where the Bishop is directed to enquire whether a Clerk presented is "worthy of his ministry"; he claimed that Canon XCV made it clear that this means, not necessarily highly meritorious, but simply duly qualified; for this latter canon adopts the term "sufficiency" and "qualities" as equivalents to the expression "worthy" in Canon XXXIX.

The Bishop reverted once more to the Declaration in the Office of Private Baptism saying that "our Lord Jesus Christ does not deny his grace and mercy to such infants", the antecedent to "such" being "born in original sin and in the wrath of God". He asked which of the XXXIX Articles affirmed that they cannot receive any benefit from Baptism, except there shall have been a prevenient act of grace to make them worthy recipients of that sacrament. Gorham answered that the "just and favourable construction" of the passage is such that the relative "such infants" cannot be so indissolubly tied to the antecedent clause, "This child, who being born in original sin &c.", as to amount to an unconditional affirmation that beneficial Baptism is applied to "a child of wrath", so that it cannot possibly have experienced an intermediate and prevenient act of grace. Secondly, he said that Article XXV is so dogmatic in its declaration that sacraments only have a wholesome effect in those who receive them worthily, that it shuts us up in the conclusion that a "child of wrath" must have been made worthy by a prevenient act of grace, in order for its Baptism to have been effective. Article XXVII limits the benefits of Baptism to such "as receive it rightly". Gorham says that he has demonstrated that by "rightly" the Church means "by Faith", "or by the gracious disposition which leads to faith, 'juxta modum recipientis' ".[1] He therefore says that this Article teaches that there must have been a prevenient act of grace to render such infants worthy.

The fifth day of the examination opened at 11.30 a.m. on Wednesday, December 22nd 1847, and lasted till 5.30 p.m.

[1] *Op. cit.*, p. 125.

After some introductory exchanges on the protracted length of the examination, the Bishop questioned Gorham again as to whether the XXXIX Articles taught the necessity for a pre-venient act of grace in order that infants baptized according to the Office of Private Baptism might receive the benefits of their Baptism. Gorham replied that he would prefer not to alter the language of his previous answer to this question.

The Bishop then drew attention to some differences between the Baptismal Offices in King Edward VI's second Prayer Book (1552) and those in the Prayer Book of 1662. Gorham said he had studied Archbishop Laurence's book published in 1816, "on the Efficacy of Baptism", and had satisfied himself that no inferential argument on the matters in hand was to be derived from the differences, in the face of the direct arguments drawn from the Articles. The Thanksgiving[1] immediately after the Baptism in the Office for Public Baptism in the 1552 book, seemed to him to have been introduced to the Office for Private Baptism in the 1662 book simply with a view to making the Public and Private Offices in that book correspond as nearly as the difference of circumstances would allow—not, as the Bishop suggested, to signify assurance of grace given to the Infant privately baptized previously to the Stipulations.[2] The Bishop also referred to the Exhortation after the Gospel: in the 1552 book, it is said, ". . . he HATH GIVEN to him the blessing of eternal life, and made him partaker of his everlasting kingdom". But in the 1662 book it reads, "And (as he hath promised in his holy Word) WILL GIVE unto him the blessing of eternal life, and make him partaker of his everlasting kingdom". The Bishop does not indicate what inference he draws from this, but Gorham said that the change of phrasing was adopted only for the purpose of stating more simply the evident futurity of the blessing of eternal life. The third alteration to which the Bishop drew attention was the position of the prayer which follows the Lord's Prayer in the 1662 book. The prayer reads, "Almighty and everlasting God &c., give thy Holy Spirit to this Infant: that he being born again and made an heir of everlasting salvation", ("as had been *certified* by the Minister before", interjected the Bishop) "may continue thy servant and attain &c., &c." The

---

[1] "We yield thee hearty thanks, most merciful Father, that it *hath* pleased thee to regenerate this infant &c. &c.".

[2] Only "previously to the stipulations" on the Bishop's hypothesis—for Gorham claims that the "Stipulations" in the Office of Private Baptism are no more than a ratification of stipulations already tacitly made before Baptism. See p. 18.

Bishop pointed out that in the 1552 book this prayer followed the Stipulations, but in the 1662 revision it precedes them. He suggested that this also was evidence of care to show that grace was given to infants privately baptized prior to the stipulations being made. Gorham replied that this change of position did not contradict what he had said previously[1] with regard to the Stipulations in the case of infants baptized privately, *viz.* that tacit Stipulations must be considered as having been given before the administration of Baptism in a private house: the Office of Private Baptism provides for these tacit and implied Stipulations, which were entered into privately, to be given formally and recognized in the face of the Church. Gorham said that these new considerations which the Bishop had brought forward could not dislodge him from the position of Article XXV, which he had so often quoted, which insists on the necessity for due reception of the Sacraments.

The Bishop said that the Godfathers and Godmothers who make the formal Stipulations in the Office of Private Baptism, are commonly not the same persons as those who, Gorham says, give the tacit Stipulations before the administration of Baptism in a private house. Therefore, the Bishop said, on Gorham's supposition, the Stipulations must be made twice, and by different parties. Gorham replied that the Stipulations are the same in substance, so he did not allow that they were made twice, although he admitted that generally speaking they would be made by different parties.

The Bishop then suggested to Gorham that he was drawing an argument, in favour of the infant's faith necessarily preceding Baptism, from the fact of the Stipulations preceding Baptism in the Office of Public Baptism. Gorham disliked the Bishop's use of the word "argument", and claimed that he had adduced the "fact" that the Church will not permit the infant to be baptized until faith has been stipulated. With regard to the capability of infants to have faith, he said further:

With regard to infants, the difficulty of their not being able to perform the condition of "*faith*", is stated in the Catechism, and is resolved by the *Stipulation* for its performance. There the difficulty is wisely left by the Church. The capability of infants to have "*faith*" (juxta modum recipientis,) or rather the new disposition which, if the Child live to years of discretion, will hereafter issue in "faith", is one of those deep Questions which I leave where the Scriptures

[1] P. 18, *supra.*

and the Church leave it. "The promise is to us and to our children":—with that gracious assurance all curious enquiry must be closed.

The Bishop then drew attention to the fact that in the office of Private Baptism, in which he claimed that the Stipulations were made after Baptism, the exhortation "Dearly beloved &c. . . ." to the godparents is omitted. The Bishop said:

Do you observe that . . . the Exhortation . . . is founded on their having just before,—"Prayed that our Lord Jesus Christ would vouchsafe to receive him, to release him of his sins, to sanctify him with the Holy Ghost, to give him the kingdom of heaven and ever-lasting life": and that it is upon this ground that the Minister addresses his demand to the Godfathers and Godmothers?. I demand *therefore*; Dost thou in the name of this child &c., &c.?

Gorham understood the Bishop to be implying that the Stipulations are not an assurance of qualifications demanded by the Church but simply a dutiful return for the promises of Christ made to us in the Sacrament.[1]

Gorham vigorously repudiated the idea that in any case the stipulations were made after Baptism. A part of his answer, which makes further use of the legal analogy[2] is as follows:

They are, indeed *subsequent* to Baptism in their absolutely chrono-logical occurrence; but they are still *prevenient* to Baptism in their theological and spiritual import. Tacit and implied Stipulations preceded, or at the least accompanied, the Private Baptism: and, when the child is brought for public Admission, those Stipulations are only orally and openly declared; they are virtually a *continuation of one and the same act*, at first tacitly commenced, and now verbally completed in the face of the Church, as required by her law if circum-stances permit. The seal was affixed *in*formally, by reason of the existing "exigence", to a valid deed; the party now *formally* (though being an Infant, by his Sponsors as his trustees), places his hand, as it were, on that seal, and more deliberately accepts his title: but who shall say that this latter act was a second sealing, *after* the conveyance of the estate?

He adds that the exhortation to which the Bishop refers is omitted

---

[1] The Bishop's point seems to be that the stipulations are made, not *on behalf of* the child, as a necessary condition of its receiving the benefit of the sacrament, but as a pious profession which the godparents make in order to call down the blessings of God on the child. In the case of Private Baptism, where the blessings have already been imparted, on the Bishop's supposition, this exhortation, which connects prayer for the blessings with the stipulations, is omitted—thus, the Bishop thinks, indicating that the giving of the blessings is not conditional upon the making of the stipulations.

[2] See p. 20, *supra*.

in the service for the admission of infants who had already been baptized in private, because its language is unsuited to such a case. The opening sentence of the exhortation presupposes that Baptism is being asked for, not that a Baptism already effected is being publicly attested and confirmed. No ground of the Minister's demand of stipulations can, he says, be inferred from this omission.

The Bishop next, once again, questioned Gorham on the basis of an apparently unconditional statement in the Prayer Book. The Bishop said that in the Office of Private Baptism, when a child is brought into Church, and it is found that he was baptized with the right matter and the proper words, "the Minister . . . thus certifies—'I certify you, that in this case all is well done, and according to due order concerning the Baptism of this child,—who, *being born in original sin* and in the *wrath of God*, is now, by the laver of *regeneration in Baptism*, received into the number of the children of God, and heirs of everlasting life', &c."

Gorham once again invokes the principle of "just and favourable construction".[1] He also added some comments on this "Certification" by the Minister. First he said the Bishop had no authority for his parenthetical remark,[2] " 'This infant . . . being born again, and made an heir of everlasting salvation' (as had been *certified* by the Minister before):" nor for the affirmation quoted above, "The Minister . . . *thus certifies*, '*I certify* you that, &c., this child, being born in original sin &c., is now, by the laver of regeneration, &c.' ". In both these instances the Bishop is, Gorham asserts, claiming more for the Certificate than it actually contains. The rubric requires that the congregation shall "be certified of the true form of Baptism having been used", and of nothing more than this. If the Minister himself has privately baptized the child, this certificate takes one form; if some other lawful Minister has baptized him, it takes another form. In either case there follow the words, "who, being born in original sin &c.", which are no part of the Certification, but, Gorham says, "are a simple *declaration of faith, hope, and charity*— the spirit which breathe through the whole of these services— beautifully harmonizing with the more SEVERELY PRECISE TEACHING OF ARTICLE XXV., but expressed with less caution (perhaps with less theological exactness) in the glowing anticipations of devotional prayer and fervid praise".

---

[1] Pp. 13, 14, 16, 24, 25, 29, *supra*.   [2] See p. 30, *supra*.

At this point Gorham protested once more against the protraction of the Examination. He seems to have been quite exhausted by the whole proceeding. He suspended for a time his attendance at the Bishop's house, on account of ill-health, and also, as he said to the Bishop, lest he should "compromise, by a dangerous precedent, the privileges of other clergymen who may hereafter be presented to Benefices"—by submitting without protest to so lengthy an interrogation. He said he thought the answers he had so far given were more than sufficient to enable the Bishop to arrive at a decision as to whether he was "worthy" of his ministry, and sound enough in doctrine to be instituted to the Benefice to which he had been presented by the Crown. Gorham also said that he must seek legal advice as to whether further attendance for examination was compulsory.

The Bishop transmitted a number of questions to Gorham which he permitted him to answer at his own house. Seven of these Gorham declined to answer;[1] they were concerned with the exceptions by the twelve Nonconforming Divines, at the Conference of the Savoy in 1662, to certain passages in the Services of Baptism and the Catechism, and the answers of the twelve Bishops who were commissioned to review the Book of Common Prayer. Gorham said that to answer these questions of the Bishop's in detail would be to introduce further almost endless conversations on the lines of so much that had gone before, and at the end of it his theological position could not be clearer than it had been made already by the answers he had given. Also he maintained that it was outside the powers of the Bishop to question him on literature so remote from the Church's formal documents.

But while Gorham declined to give formal answers to these seven questions, he made some general comments upon them which he transmitted to the Bishop. The Nonconforming Divines at the Savoy Conference said they could not agree to the Baptismal Offices and the Catechism unless certain alterations were made. The fact that the twelve Bishops did not make these alterations does not in the least mean, Gorham asserts, that the Church of England is committed to the doctrine of unconditional Sacramental efficacy which the Nonconforming Divines were objecting to. The Warrant (20 March, 13 Charles II) for the Savoy Conference expressly prohibited the Bishops from making "unnecessary alterations"; the Bishops were not, Gorham

---

[1] These seven questions do not occur in the published account of the examination.

claimed, authorized expounders of the Church's doctrine, but simply Commissioners to suggest to Convocation, for the consideration of Parliament, "reasonable and necessary alterations, corrections and amendments, for the giving satisfaction to tender consciences, and the restoring and the continuance of peace and unity". Gorham pointed out that the XXXIX Articles were not submitted to the Commissioners' judgment; therefore, whatever alterations in the Book of Common Prayer were, or were not, recommended by them, that Book, even as revised, remained, he said, under the Articles as its umpire.

Gorham also remarked that Cardwell's *Conferences* (p. 308) reveals that the Nonconforming Divines seem to have had a stronger impression that the language of the Services favoured the notion of unconditional Sacramental Efficacy than was entertained by the Prelates themselves. The following is a passage from the exceptions of the Nonconforming Divines:

Throughout the several Offices, the phrase is such as presumes all persons within the Communion of the Church to be *regenerated, converted*, and *in an actual state of grace* which cannot be rationally admitted in the utmost latitude of charity.[1]

And this was the answer made by the Bishops:

The Church in her prayers useth no more offensive phrase than St Paul uses, when he writes to the Corinthians, Galatians, and others, calling them in general the Churches of God, sanctified in Christ Jesus, by vocation Saints; amongst whom, notwithstanding, there were many who, by their known sins, were not properly such,— yet he gives the denomination to the whole from the greater part, *to whom in charity it was due*, and puts the rest in mind what *they have by their* BAPTISM *undertaken to be*; and our prayers, and the phrase of them, surely supposed no more than that they are Saints by calling, sanctified in Christ Jesus, *by their* BAPTISM *admitted into Christ's congregation*, and so to be *reckoned* members of that society, &c.[2]

Gorham added that the whole attitude and behaviour of the twelve Prelates at the Savoy Conference were such that he could not accept their opinions, as inducing him to qualify any statements he had made. He said that it was exceeding the canonical requirements governing this Examination to introduce a discussion on their theological views.

A sharp exchange of letters between the Bishop and Gorham followed. Finally it was agreed that the Examination should be

---

[1] Cardwell, *Conferences*, p. 308.   [2] *Ibid.*, pp. 342, 343.

resumed on Wednesday, March 8th 1848. On this day the Bishop and Gorham were together from 2 p.m. to 5.30 p.m.[1]

Gorham had quoted Gal. iii. 26[2] as indicating that adoption precedes Baptism in its essence. The Bishop now said, "Say whether you did not here cite verse 26, to prove that faith conferred the state of being sons of God before Baptism; which, when it supervenes, only declares, attests and manifests it, as a Sign and Seal of the gift of sonship of God already conferred". Gorham said that he would leave his answer precisely as it stood, and that he was content that his doctrine should be judged without entering into any further discussion. Gorham saw the danger of assenting to the Bishop's form of words, including as it did the word "only", which did not occur in his original answer. Gorham reiterated that in Gal. iii. 27 the Apostle does not say, "For as many of you as have been *baptized* have put on Christ," but "For as many of you as have been baptized *into Christ* have put on Christ"; by which he meant that it was by Faith, not by Baptism, that they were made the children of God—Baptism being the public attestation of this. He added, "The expression, to 'put on Christ', is applied here to the act of justifying *faith*; in Rom. xiii. 14, it is applied to the work of *sanctification*; but in neither passage to BAPTISM".

The Bishop then said "Are not all, who are in the body of Christ, sons of God?". Gorham replied, "Undoubtedly; if that expression be limited to the invisible Church; but—if it be taken, as it often *is* by theologians, as referring to the visible and merely professing Church,—I could not assent to this proposition". Gorham said that he was reminded of the remark of Bishop Nicolson, who, commenting on the answer in the Catechism, "Wherein I was made a member of Christ &c.", said that a member might be such "equivocally" as, for instance, a glass eye or a wooden leg might be said to be a member of the body.[3]

The Bishop then questioned Gorham as to whether Baptism was the instrument by which we are made members of this body. Gorham declined to add further to his previous answers in which he had set out his belief as to the sense in which he believed

[1] Gorham, *op. cit.*, p. 166, has "Two, a.m.", but this seems hardly likely and must be a misprint for "p.m.".

[2] See p. 26, *supra.*

[3] *A plain but full Exposition of the Catechism of the Church of England . . . collected out of the best Chatechists*, by the Right Reverend Father in God, William Lord Bishop of Glocester, p. 15, edit. 1678.

Baptism to be the instrument of grafting into the Church.[1]
The Bishop then referred to John i. 12, which Gorham had
quoted;[2] he observed that it was not said here, simply, that they
"that believe on his name" become, by believing, sons of God;
but that, "to them hath he given power"—ἐξουσίαν, "right
or privilege")—"to become the sons of God". The following is
the exact text of Gorham's answer to this challenge:

It appears to me, that to have the "right or privilege" to become
the sons of God, in consequence of "BELIEVING on the name" of Christ,
is the same thing in effect, though not in precise phraseology, as to
become his sons "by BELIEVING".

I should not have hesitated to adopt this view from this text alone;
but when this passage is compared with Gal. iii. 26, where we are
said to become "the children of God *by* FAITH", this conclusion seems
inevitable.

"FAITH" is the "sine qua non"; and, when IT exists, ADOPTION
commences.

The Bishop then asked whether the "right or privilege" of
becoming sons of God, stated in John i. 12, would not be satisfied
by Christ's giving them "right or privilege" to have recourse
to an Ordinance, instituted by Him, as a means or instrument,
in or by which the state of sons of God shall be given "to them
that believe". Gorham replied emphatically that the privilege
would not be satisfied in this way. First, because if adoption
were not co-existent with, or instantly consequent on, faith,
but were relegated to the period of Baptism, then the believer
would be "born of the will of the flesh", and "of the will of
man", since man can will to select the time. Secondly, he said,
Gal. iii. 26 expressly ties adoption to faith, and makes no mention
of the supposed postponement of this (ἐξουσία) "privilege" till
and opportunity for Baptism may be found.

The Bishop next drew Gorham's attention to the Greek of
John i. 13—οἳ οὐκ ἐξ αἱμάτων, οὐδὲ ἐκ θελήματος σαρκός, οὐδὲ ἐκ
θελήματος ἀνδρός, ἀλλ'ἐκ Θεοῦ ἐγεννήθησαν. The Bishop said,
"Does it not necessarily follow,—from the word ἀνδρός being used,
not ἀνθρωπού, that the inspired writer is speaking, not of man as
the general human subject, but, of the male parent; and thus ἐκ
θελήματος σαρκός and ἐκ θελήματος ἀνδρός must refer to carnal
procreation; just as in ch. iii. 6 of this Gospel τὸ γεγεννημένον ἐκ
τῆς σαρκὸς σάρξ ἐστι, has similar reference?". The Bishop's
point is that John i. 13 is saying that the becoming Sons of

[1] Pp. 25, 26, *supra*.   [2] Pp. 24, 25, *supra*.

God is due to a process quite different from that which produces
natural birth—the passage is, in the Bishop's mind, indicating
the dissimilarity between Baptism and carnal procreation. Gorham
replies that the figurative allusion is as the Bishop suggests—i.e.
that becoming sons of God is brought about by an action entirely
different from natural birth. But he cannot agree that this
passage affirms that being born into the family of God as "his
sons" is directly connected with Baptism. To say this, Gorham
asserts, is a mere Αὐτὸς ἔφη, a taking for granted the great point
discussed in this Examination.

Gorham concludes this day's proceedings with a quotation
from Cranmer: "Livery and seisin" (of that inheritance which
belongs only to "the sons of God") "is given when we first
BELIEVE, whether in Baptism, or AT ANY OTHER TIME".[1]

Thursday, March 9th 1848 was the seventh day of the Examination, which on this occasion lasted from 10.30 a.m. to 5 p.m.
The Bishop began by requiring Gorham to quote more fully the
passage of Cranmer to which he had referred. Gorham did so,
but the Bishop did not draw any new inferences from the extended
quotation. As fully quoted, the passage leaves some doubt as
to whether it will bear the meaning which Gorham ascribed
to it. But Gorham explained in a footnote[2] that it is necessary
to understand the extremely complicated discussion which was
taking place between Cranmer and Gardiner in order to interpret
this passage aright. In his footnote he sets out the arguments,
and asserts that he is right in quoting the passage in support of
his doctrine.

In his next question, the Bishop quotes from a few pages
further on in the same work of Cranmer—"For you conclude
your book with blasphemous words against both the Sacrament
of Baptism and the Lord's Supper; niggardly pinching God's gifts,
and diminishing his liberal promises made to us in them. For
where Christ hath promised to us in both the Sacraments to be
assistant with us, whole, both in Body and Spirit (in the one
to be our spiritual regeneration and apparel, and in the other
to be our spiritual meat and drink), you clip his liberal benefits. . . ."[3] The Bishop asks Gorham what he makes of Cranmer's

[1] Cranmer's *Answer to Gardiner*, Book I, p. 35, edit. Parker Society, 1844.

[2] Gorham, *op. cit.*, p. 175. As the Bishop does not make further use of this passage,
and the argument is involved, it is sufficient to refer to Gorham's footnote, and not
to set out the matter in full. As Gorham says, the effect of examining this dispute
between Cranmer and Gardiner is "to raise dust about the subject".

[3] Cranmer's *Answer to Gardiner*, Book I, *Works*, Vol. I, p. 45, edit. Parker Society.

reference to Baptism as "our spiritual regeneration and apparel"—
apparel, he supposes, being a reference to Gal. iii. 27.

Gorham said that he would not enter into any discussion of
this passage. But he recommended great caution in quoting
Cranmer in an Examination of this sort; for, he asserted, Cranmer's
opinions varied materially "in the period from the first dawning
of Protestant light into his mind, to the close of his life", and
sometimes even in the same treatise he expresses sentiments
which are not fully consistent with each other. He added that if
Cranmer's remarks on "apparel"[1] had any weight on the side
of the Bishop's conception of the Sacraments of Baptism, that
weight was more than counterbalanced by the opinion of Bishop
Jewel who, after the Articles had been framed, observed in
connection with this passage of scripture (Gal. iii. 27) that "faith"
is implied.[2] Gorham added in a lengthy footnote[3] some general
remarks on the use of the word "Sacrament" in our early reformers.
The word is used, he said, in two ways—either to denote the
outward and visible *sign* of grace; or for the inward and spiritual
grace itself. In the latter sense, always understanding the necessity
for *due* reception. He remarks that it is deeply to be regretted
that the first, and most simple, use of the word, has not been
invariably adhered to; because the introduction of the second
sense has led to so much controversy. But in fact, when the
doctrine of the reformers is carefully studied, there is seen to be
no real theological confusion.

The Bishop next referred Gorham to the chapter on Baptism
in the *Institution of a Christian Man* (1537), as expressing the
sentiments of Cranmer.[4] The *Institution* declares the absolute
necessity and unconditional efficacy of Baptism,[5] and Gorham said
he considered the work as "containing many Popish doctrinal

[1] Gorham added subsequently in a footnote that although Cranmer does not
explicitly connect his use of the word "apparel" with Gal. iii. 27, there is no objection
to this reference if it is construed with Cranmer's own caveats which he expresses
elsewhere. Gorham observes that the mode of speaking of Baptism as "apparel"
gave rise to the ceremony of the Romish ritual of investing the baptized person with
a white robe; a ceremony abolished under the influence of Cranmer in 1552.

[2] Jewel's *Answer to Harding, Works*, Vol. I, p. 473, edit. Parker Society.

[3] *Op. cit.*, pp. 176-9.

[4] This book was composed under the superintendence of Cranmer, but to what
extent he was the actual author is a matter of conjecture. See Lloyd (*Formularies
of Faith put forth by authority during the reign of Henry VIII*, ed. by Charles Lloyd, Oxford
1825, introd. p. v).

[5] E.g. "By the sacrament of Baptism they do also obtain remission of their sins
&c., &c., insomuch as infants and children dying in their infancy, shall undoubtedly
be saved thereby, and else not".

errors, as yet unhappily retained by Cranmer. . . ." The Bishop
then sought to introduce the question of whether authoritative
statements of doctrine by the Church remained in force unless
withdrawn. Gorham would not be drawn into a discussion of
this matter which, he said, was outside the limits of that "due
examination" of a beneficed clerk which is prescribed by Canon
XXXIX of 1603.

The Bishop then quoted at length from the *Necessary Doctrine*
(1543) a passage declaring the doctrine of the absolute necessity
and unconditional efficacy of Baptism.[1] He sought to connect
the doctrine of Baptism set out therein with the doctrine of
Justification in Article XI, through the mention of Cranmer's
Homily of Salvation in that Article. (There is no "Homily of
Justification" such as the Article mentions, and it is generally
agreed that the "Homily of Salvation" is meant.) Gorham said
that the reference to Cranmer's Homily was only such as to
declare that it "more largely" expresses the "wholesomeness"
and "comfort" of the doctrines of Justification contained in the
Article; not such as to contradict the very statement of the
Article on the pre-eminence of "Faith". The Article reserves
to itself the prerogative of being the dogmatical standard of
that doctrine. The Bishop referred *in extenso* to passages from
Cranmer's Homily. In particular he cited a passage on infants
baptized dying in their infancy: "Insomuch that Infants being
baptized, and dying in their infancy, are by this sacrifice[2] washed
from their sins, brought into God's favour, and made his children,
and inheritors of his kingdom of heaven". The Bishop asked
whether in this passage "being baptized" was not stated as a
condition of infants being washed from their sins by the sacrifice
of the blood of Christ.

Gorham insisted that the Homily stated no such rigid condition.
It simply declared that infants so circumstanced shall be saved,
observing a merciful and charitable silence as to infants dying
without Baptism. Gorham pointed out that in the passage relating
to this question in *The Institution* the words "or else not" occur
after the statement that baptized infants dying in infancy are
saved by baptism; words which were omitted in *The Necessary
Doctrine*. Also there is the declaration at the end of the Office
of Public Baptism which observes the same silence. (Gorham

[1] In the Article of Justification therein, there occur these words: "For as for infants,
it is to be believed that their justification is wrought by the secret operation of the
Holy Ghost in their baptism, they being offered in the faith of the Church".

[2] The sacrifice of Christ on the cross.

might also have alluded to the similar rubric before the Confirmation Service in the 1549 Book.)

At this the Bishop turned to another passage in the same Homily—"Now you shall hear the office and duty of a Christian man unto God, what we ought on our part to render unto God again for his great mercy and goodness. Our office is, not to pass the time of this present life unfruitfully and idly, after that we are baptized or justified, not caring how few good works we do. . . ." He asked whether the phrase "baptized or justified" did not imply that the words "baptized" and "justified" were equivalent. Hereupon Gorham was forced to reiterate the points which he had made so many times. That these words could not be regarded as equivalents: first, because Article XI would be contradicted, which declares that "we are justified by Faith only". Faith must precede beneficial Baptism, therefore Justification must precede beneficial Baptism and cannot be equivalent to it. Secondly, he said that if, in the passage quoted, "baptized" and "justified" were taken as equivalents, it would mean that the Homily itself were contradicted; for in the first part quoted by the Bishop it is said, "And they, which in act or deed, do sin *after* their Baptism, when they turn again to God unfeignedly, they are likewise washed by this sacrifice from their sins, in such sort, that there remaineth not any spot of sin, that shall be imputed to their damnation. This is that justification or righteousness, which St Paul speaketh of. . . ." This passage admits that Justification may *succeed* formal Baptism: it cannot therefore be equivalent to Baptism. Gorham closes his reply once again: "The conclusion seems to me inevitable; that Justification, like Faith, and Adoption, (three graces which always are co-existent, or at least immediately consequent to each other) in so far from being equivalent to Baptism, that it may take place *before, in* or *after* that Sacrament".

The Bishop next asked whether there was any passage in the Articles denying the language he had quoted from the Catechism. Gorham replied that he had never advanced any such proposition: the Formularies are not to govern the construction of the Articles, but the Articles must decide the construction of the Formularies. He was unwilling to expand the answers he had already given on the passages in the Catechism. Gorham added subsequently in a footnote that in the Catechism the exact definition of a Sacrament, and the analytical description of it which follows, are inconsistent with each other. In the first case the strictly limited sense of the word is given—"An outward and visible sign *of* an inward and spiritual grace"; in the latter case the word is given in its full sense—as covering the outward sign and the spiritual grace. This apparent confusion has already been observed as existing in the early reformers:[1] but there is no real confusion when the Catechism is interpreted alongside Article XXV.

The eighth and last day of this lengthy and exhaustive Examination began at 11 a.m. on Friday, March 10th 1848, and lasted until 3 p.m. The Bishop began by referring once again to the Catechism, saying, "Is it not specially necessary, and the peculiar duty of those who draw up a Catechism for the instruction of children, and the common people, to take care to say therein nothing which is not true according to the obvious and ordinary meaning of the words used?". Gorham declined to add anything to what he had already said on the Catechism and the necessity of interpreting it in the light of the XXXIX Articles. He defended his use of the phrase "umpire accredited"[2] in relation to the Articles by quoting from the title with which they were accepted by Convocation in 1562, and confirmed by Parliament in 1571—by which title they were stated to have been framed "for the avoiding diversities of opinions, and for establishing of consent touching true religion"; also, Gorham said that his phrase was justified by the Royal Declaration prefixed to the Articles in or about 1628.

The Bishop raised once more the points he had made so frequently before on the language of the Catechism, and Gorham was still unwilling to make further statements. The Bishop then asked Gorham to read Article XVI, asking whether the phrase "After we have received the Holy Ghost we may depart from grace given . . ." did not imply that the baptized is placed in a state of grace and receives the Holy Ghost in Baptism. Gorham once again declined to add to what he had already said on the teaching of the Articles. The Bishop then drew attention to the Latin text of Article XVI, pointing out that the phrase "such as fall into sin after Baptism" is there rendered "Lapsis a Baptismo" —he added, "Does not this confirm the statement, that in and by means of Baptism we are placed in a state of grace?" Gorham in his reply said that he had admitted earlier that the Latin

---

[1] See p. 39, *supra.*

[2] See Gorham, *op. cit.*, p. 128, where he uses the word "Umpire", though not "accredited".

Articles have the same authority as the English;[1] but he said now that on further consideration he wished to suspend his opinion on that point. He said that he found that this authority was not universally conceded to the Latin Articles in the reign of Elizabeth, and that Bishop Bilson in 1599 expressly denied it.[2] But apart from this possible objection, Gorham said he did not consider that the Latin Article confirmed the statement in the Bishop's question. He said he considered the implied sense to be "lapsis a professione in Baptismo": a view which is confirmed by the Exhortation in the Visitation of the Sick, where the patient is reminded of "*the profession* which he made to God in his Baptism".

The Bishop's next attempt to make his point was a reference to the last sentence of Article XV—". . . But all we the rest (although baptized and born again in Christ) yet offend in many things and if we say we have no sin, we deceive ourselves, and the truth is not in us". Gorham declined to make any further statement in reply to this.

The Bishop thereupon turned to Article IX, especially the phrases, "This infection of nature doth remain, yea, in them that are *regenerated* . . . and although there is no condemnation for them that believe and are *baptized*, yet . . ." He pointed out that in the Latin Article, the word "regenerated" is rendered "renatis", and also "baptized" is rendered by the same Latin word. "Does not this prove", he said, "that '*regenerated*' and '*baptized*' are in this Article used as equivalent terms?" Gorham replied by pointing out that in the Latin of this Article there was a remarkable difference from a strictly literal correspondence, not only in the choice of terms, but also in the inversion of them— e.g. the phrase "believe and are baptized" being in the Latin "renatis et credentibus". It was not, therefore, in his mind, absolutely certain that "renatis" was intended to correspond with "baptized". But even if this were admitted, his answer would not be changed—either as to the force of the Latin text, or as regards the general argument.

The Bishop's final questions drew attention to the change of wording in the English of this Article in 1571 from those of 1552 and 1562 not being accompanied by a corresponding change in the Latin. The Latin of 1552, 1562 and 1571 runs: "Manet

---

[1] See p. 19, *supra*.

[2] Gorham added subsequently in a footnote a quotation from Bilson to this effect (Bilson, *Full Redemption*, 4to, London, 1599, p. 420). See Gorham, *op. cit.*, p. 213, note.

etiam in *renatis* haec naturae depravatio"; the English of 1552 and 1562 has "in them that are *baptized*", but that of 1571 has "in them that are *regenerated*". The Bishop concludes from this that the two English words are used as equivalent. Gorham declined to enter into discussion on the point.[1]

After remarking that the Articles of 1552 were stated to have been chiefly compiled by Cranmer, the Bishop said that the Examination might be considered as terminated.

At the conclusion of this stage of the controversy, Gorham received notice from the Bishop of Exeter that he refused to admit him to the Vicarage to which he had been presented by the Crown: "To the Reverend George Cornelius Gorham, Clerk, Bachelor in Divinity . . . we have upon the said Examination found you unfit to fill the said Vicarage, by reason of your holding doctrines contrary to the true Christian faith, and the doctrines contained in the Articles and Formularies of the United Church of England and Ireland, and especially in the Book of Common Prayer and Administration of the Sacraments, and other Rites and Ceremonies of the Church, according to the use of the United Church of England and Ireland. . . . Given under our hand, this twenty-first day of March, in the year of our Lord, One thousand eight hundred and forty eight. H. EXETER".

---

[1] But Gorham said in a footnote: "I conclude that the alteration was made, from a conviction in the mind of the selector, that the former word was too indefinite to express, dogmatically and with precision, the doctrine of this Article. That doctrine is—that the infection of Adam's nature remains even in those who are partakers of the grace of God. . . . This correction was important in another view: this (as it stood till 1571, was the *insulated* passage in the Thirty-nine Articles, where the word '*baptized*' had been incautiously used, alone and without qualification, as apparently implying the necessary bestowment of spiritual grace, and THE UNCONDITIONAL EFFICACY OF THE SACRAMENT". *Op. cit.*, p. 217.

CHAPTER II

GORHAM'S CASE BEFORE THE COURT OF ARCHES

GORHAM was unwilling to accept the verdict of the Bishop of Exeter against him, and in June 1848 a monition was extracted from the registry of the Arches Court of Canterbury on behalf of Gorham, in which it was stated that he had been presented to the living of Brampford Speke by the Lord Chancellor, that he was prepared to make all the declarations and Oaths required by law, but that the Bishop of Exeter delayed to institute him to the benefice. The effect of this monition was to call upon the Bishop to institute Gorham within a time specified, or else to show cause why he should not be instituted. The *onus probandi* in the case was laid upon the Bishop. His counsel raised and developed all the points he was trying to drive home in the course of the original examination of Gorham, and eventually he won this round of the contest. The proceedings before the Court of Arches were lengthy; Gorham's advocate was an eminent ecclesiastical lawyer, Dr Bayford. His pleadings have been published,[1] and must now be examined in order to get a complete view of the case as it developed.

Bayford began his speech with a full account of the circumstances which had brought this case before the Court of Arches; he argued the unreasonableness of the Bishop's action, and the undue length of the Examination. He sought to show that the Bishop had tried to push Gorham into a corner, by pressing him to assent to Infant Regeneration unconditionally, whereas Gorham had indicated his unwillingness to treat of this matter apart from the doctrine of Baptism generally. Bayford said the Bishop was pressing, during a large part of the Examination, for an answer on an extreme question—that of infants baptized in an emergency. This was not the best way of discovering what a Clerk really held on the subject of Baptismal Regeneration. More than this, the Bishop seemed to expect Gorham to give an answer to a question into which the Prayer Book never enters— that is the effect of Baptism upon children excluding any possible previous qualifications.

---

[1] *The Argument of Dr Bayford on behalf of the Rev. G. C. Gorham, in the Arches Court of Canterbury, March 1849.*

Very soon, however, Bayford moved away from complaints of the nature of the Examination to a denial of the charges brought against Gorham by the Bishop of Exeter. It will be remembered that it was alleged on behalf of the Bishop that Gorham "held, and persisted in holding, that spiritual regeneration is not given or conferred in that Holy Sacrament, in particular, that infants are not made therein members of Christ and the children of God". It is an anticipation to draw attention to it at this stage, but it is to be observed that Sir H. Jenner Fust went further than this, and held that Gorham did not admit that grace was conferred by Baptism or through Baptism. It is an anticipation to speak of this now, because Jenner Fust's judgment was delivered after Bayford's defence; but the fact that this decision occurred in the judgment is an indication of the way in which the arguments were going against Gorham in the course of the hearing. Anyway Bayford was quick to deny both of these allegations. "He did not say, he never has said, that no grace is given in Baptism", said Bayford. Gorham had said of Regeneration, not merely of spiritual grace, that it "may be *in* Baptism, *before* Baptism, or *after* Baptism".[1] As regards the grace which is given by Baptism to those who receive it worthily, Bayford pointed out that Gorham was hardly given a chance in the Examination to set forth his doctrine on this point clearly: but in one instance Gorham did give a clear, explicit and unhesitating answer on this matter. The Bishop had asked, "In the case of those who receive Baptism worthily, is there any, and if any what special grace which 'God doth work invisibly in us' by Baptism, as the 'effectual sign' thereof?" To this Gorham answers, "There is. By this sign and visible symbol of his grace, he sets his seal to his 'promises of forgiveness of sins, and of our adoption to be his sons:' he 'confirms' the 'faith' which he had previously implanted in us, and by which he makes us 'rightly' to receive this Sacrament: and he 'increases' the 'grace' which he had previously given us: he does all this by 'virtue of prayer', for which he has bestowed the disposition." Bayford succinctly asks, "Is this denying the grace of God in Baptism, either to infant or adult?"

The next stage of Bayford's defence is worth quoting: "And, to say of Mr Gorham, after reading these answers, that he holds

---

[1] The difficulty is that Gorham means something different by "regeneration" from the meaning which his adversaries attach to the word. It is not reasonable to dub him heretical on this account because there is no scriptural or other authoritative definition of the term.

no grace to be conferred by Baptism, is impossible. The difference between the Bishop and Mr Gorham is in regard to 'worthy recipients'. Mr Gorham says, that to be a partaker of the grace of Baptism, it is necessary to be a worthy receiver of that Sacrament. The Bishop then tries to bring him to the position that every infant is necessarily a worthy recipient. We have it attempted over and over again; but Mr Gorham declines to follow so far, and why? Because the Article is silent on the subject. He does not deny that where it can be predicated of an infant, the blessing follows: he only declines to apply the proposition necessarily and universally".[1] So far it is easy to follow Bayford's argument, but he seems to say more than is warranted when, a few lines further on he declares "He would predicate through Baptism all the blessings that can be claimed by the Bishop of Exeter, or any other man: the only question is, to whom?" It really does seem that in this sentence Bayford is placing too much weight on the point of worthy reception; for even to worthy recipients Gorham will not allow Regeneration *by* Baptism—in his view regeneration must precede the reception of the grace given by the Sacrament;[2] or if regeneration has not taken place by the time of reception of baptism, then the effect of the sacrament is suspended until such time as it occurs.

Bayford points out that the Articles declare the necessity of worthy reception in order to receive the benefit of sacraments; this, he says, affords a clue to the correct interpretation of the services—which must be open to a greater latitude of interpretation than the precise dogmatical statements of the Articles. The Articles have no clear statement as to how the "worthiness" of children can be established. Nor has the New Testament any direct guidance on the matter of children, since at the time of the New Testament writings the greater number of those baptized must necessarily have been adults. From both Scripture and the documents of the Church of England, then, Gorham was com-

---

[1] *Op. cit.*, p. 33.

[2] A contemporary commentator wrote: "With him, the word 'regeneration' is used not in any inferior sense. . . . He cannot regard Baptism as conferring this, ex opere operato; but neither does he regard it as conferring it instrumentally, even when all the requisite qualifications concur and meet in the subject, the administrator, and the Church; for though it *may* take place at the time, it *may*, also, '*before*' or '*after*',—it is the sovereign and gracious act of God; baptism, therefore, is a rite which is not to be applied *for the purpose* of regeneration; the child that is properly baptized, is baptized because he is regenerate, or because he *will* be regenerate, but not that he *may* be. If anyone *happen* to be regenerate in the act of baptism, it is merely a coincidence; it is neither the effect of the rite itself, nor the result of an invariable spiritual law" (*The Great Gorham Case; a History in Five Books*, by a Looker-On, p. 95).

pelled to answer inferentially. Bayford will not allow the contention, apparently made by the counsel for the Bishop of Exeter,
that without tradition we should lose three-fourths of our religion.
The Church of England, as she expresses herself in the VIth
Article, takes her stand upon Holy Scripture, and will not,
like the Church of Rome, set up a higher authority or dogmatize
where scripture is silent.

Bayford then took up a new point, or at least approached
an old point from a new angle. Instead of trying to prove that
certain infants were unworthy, and therefore, did not receive
the grace of the sacraments, he questioned the statement of
Dr Addams, the leading counsel for the Bishop, that it was
the doctrine of the Church of England that all infants are worthy
recipients. "I desire to know", he said, "how it is established,
for no light has been given us upon it. All the public Services
for Infant Baptism, together with the Catechism, are directly
opposed to it; we have nothing but bare assertion in its
support". He then went on to quote from the services, for
instance the opening of the Office of Public Baptism—
"Dearly beloved, forasmuch as all men are conceived and born
in sin".

The advocate then draws attention to the prayer for the
blessing of the water. In this prayer there occur the words
"mystical washing away of sin". "Why", Bayford asks, "is the
word 'mystical' inserted? Why should it not have been 'Didst
sanctify the element of water, to the washing away of sin'?"
He argues that the word "mystical" is present manifestly to
show that the subject was to be considered sacramentally, that
more was to be taken into account than the idea, simple and
unqualified, of washing away sin. The conditions governing the
operation of sacraments are, he holds, brought into play by
the use of this word. Then Bayford drew the special attention
of the Court to the address to the Sponsors. The effect of this
address, he argues, is "Ye have prayed: have listened to the
promises of the Gospel: but that is not enough; for the infant
must now promise by you, his sureties, that he *will* renounce
the devil, that he will constantly believe God's Holy Word, and
that he will obediently keep his commandments". He adds,
"So far, then, as the Church, in her ordinary Services, could
provide for the case of Infant Baptism, she puts it precisely on
the same principle as that of adults; so far as it is possible, the
infant is placed in the position which the adult occupies, and the

service is the same".[1] Bayford refers to the view of the reformers that children are brought to Baptism inasmuch as being the offspring of believing parents they in some sense already belong to the people of God.[2] He asks a question which is very pertinent in twentieth-century England, "Supposing that all present, from first to last, fail in their parts, . . . suppose that all present should be mere automatons; suppose that they are all no better than Infidels, or are actually Infidels; how far does or does not such a circumstance affect the spiritual blessings which are conveyed by the Sacrament of Baptism? I repeat that it is a difficulty of which there has been no resolution, or attempted resolution, to my knowledge".[3]

Bayford next turns to the Office of Private Baptism, but on this he says little that Gorham did not adduce in the Examination. He says very forcibly that the principle should be to argue from the normal case to the exceptional, not vice versa as the Bishop has done.

In dealing with the service for Adults, Bayford says that the Bishop admits the point which it is his, Bayford's, principal object to drive home: that the receiving of the grace of baptism by adults is conditional upon the existence of faith and repentance in the parties baptized. In his Charge, the Bishop laid particular stress on the rubric requiring that due care should be taken in the examination of adults to be baptized, whether they be sufficiently instructed in the principles of the Christian religion. If the infants were old enough to profit by it, he says, they too, naturally, would be instructed. Bayford says that he can see that in this respect there is a difference between the two services; but the difference is in the situation of the parties to be baptized, and it does not involve the doctrine. There is no difference in the wording of the services, and he cannot see that there is any difference in the way the language should be interpreted. In the service for adult baptism, the priest says, "Seeing now, dearly

---

[1] *Op. cit.*, p. 39.

[2] Bayford later quotes Thomas Beacon (*Catechism*, Parker Society, p. 214): "What sayest thou of the infants of the heathen and unbelieving? Forasmuch as they belong not unto the household of faith, neither are contained in this covenant, 'I will be thy God and the God of thy seed' . . . therefore, I leave them to the judgment of God, to whom they either stand or fall. With the children of the faithful God hath made a sure and an everlasting covenant, that he will be their God and Saviour, yea their most loving Father, and take them for his sons and heirs, as St Peter saith: 'The promise was made to you and to your children'." Bayford's point, presumably, is that the baptism of infants is justified when it can be assumed that later they will be taught, and accept, the faith.

[3] *Op. cit.*, p. 41.

D

beloved brethren, that these persons are regenerate and grafted
into the body of Christ's Church". The Bishop admits that these
words are conditional, hypothetical, based upon a charitable
hope; Bayford fails to see why he will not allow the same of the
corresponding words in the infant service. Bayford aptly remarks,
"We have heard much of the plain, literal, grammatical meaning
of words which no honest man can mistake. But a mode of
interpretation is nevertheless advanced, which is totally inconsistent with any such boast; for the Bishop's counsel are driven to
maintain the necessity of construing, and the right of compelling
another to construe, the very same words in different senses. . . ."[1]
Bayford also somewhere says that he cannot imagine a Church
Service being drawn up otherwise than on the supposition that
the parties taking part in it are sincere.[2] He is not aware that
any such thing has ever been attempted.

In all these points, Bayford does not really say anything new,
but he gives new force to arguments which have been already
brought forward by Gorham. For instance he quotes the passage
from the Catechism, several times quoted already in the case,
"Why are infants baptized, when by reason of their tender age
they are not able to perform them (the promises)? Because they
promise them both by their sureties. . . ." "Not because", Bayford says, "being infants, no qualification is required, and no
condition imposed; but that must be done on their behalf by
others, which is done by adults in their own persons, and the
spiritual effect must be held liable to fail in the one case, since
it is admitted that it may do so in the other".[3] Bayford goes
farther than Gorham was willing to go in the Examination
when he says, "A present declaration of faith, and a promise of
future obedience, are therefore indispensable pre-requisites to
the Baptism of infants".

Bayford then ran through Gorham's arguments on hypothetical
language in other parts of the Prayer Book, especially in the
Burial Service; he also reviewed his contentions based on the
Articles on Sacraments and on Baptism. In all this he added
little to the propositions already set forth. But it is remarkable
to observe some of the pleading he had to meet in the course
of the hearing. Article XXV concludes with the following
sentence—"And in such only as worthily receive the same, they
have a wholesome effect or operation; but they that receive
them unworthily purchase to themselves damnation, as St Paul

---

[1] *Op. cit.*, p. 47.   [2] *Ibid.*, p. 51.   [3] *Ibid.*, p. 49.

saith". It appears that Dr Addams argued that the limitation of benefit to worthy receivers did not apply to Baptism inasmuch as this quotation from St Paul's First Epistle to the Corinthians came from a passage in which he was speaking of the Lord's Supper only. Dr Bayford was compelled to point out that in both the Latin and the English of the Article Sacraments were referred to in the plural; therefore this passage which St Paul wrote with reference to the Lord's Supper only was applied by the framers of the Articles to both Sacraments. Bayford then brings an *argumentum ad hominem*, for he says that the insistence of his opponents that infants present no obstacle to the right reception of the Sacrament is really an admission on their part that "worthy" reception is necessary even in their case. The Bishop's counsel even seems to have sought to repudiate the passage in the Catechism on Infants' promises being made by sureties.

Bayford hinted at the direction in which he thought that his opponents were leading by drawing attention to the sixth Canon of the Council of Trent passed at its seventh session—"Si quis dixerit, Sacramenta novae legis non continere gratiam, quam significant, aut gratiam ipsam non ponentibus obicem non conferre . . . anathema sit". The arguments of the Bishop's counsel came very near to saying that grace was conferred in Baptism in all cases where an obstacle was not put up to bar it. The XXVIth Article of 1552, upon which our XXVth Article is based, was drawn up expressly to refute that doctrine.[1] Bishop Burnet in his work on the Articles held that the Article of 1563 excluded the doctrine of *opus operatum* as formally as that of 1552.

Bayford held that as the Church of England in Article XVII had purposely steered a middle-course between Calvinism and Arminianism in her express doctrine on Predestination, so in her teaching on Baptism she would not drive out the Calvinist by holding every infant baptized to be elect, any more than she would exclude the Arminian by declaring some infants only to receive the grace of Baptism by virtue of special and electing grace.

[1] The XXVIth Article of 1552 contained an express condemnation of the doctrine of sacramental grace ex opere operato; but this was withdrawn in 1563, in an attempt to present a balanced view as against the inadequate sacramental theology of Anabaptists, Zwinglians and others. The Latin of the XXVIth Article of 1552 begins as follows: "Sacramenta non instituta sunt a Christo ut spectarentur aut circumferrentur, sed ut rite illis uteremur; et in his duntaxat *qui digne percipiunt* salutarem habent affectum—idque *non ex opere* (ut quidam loquuntur) *operato*, quae vox ut peregrina est in sacris literis ignota, sic parit sensum minime pium sed admodum superstitiosum."

It had apparently been argued that the Church for 1500 years had always held the same doctrine of the grace of Baptism until Gorham arose and disturbed the peace. Bayford quoted from Gregory's "Decretals" (1250) to refute this claim.[1] The Council of Trent was trying to close a question which had been much in dispute before. In the Constitution of Clement in the Council of Vienne (1312) it was said: "Quibusdam ex ipsis dicentibus, per virtutem Baptismi parvulis quidem culpam remitti, sed gratiam non conferri. . . ."[2]

Bayford next went on to examine some of the authors who were quoted in support of the Bishop. He said that on closer scrutiny it was found that these authors were not altogether agreed on the opinions they gave on the subject of Baptism. It was necessary, he held, in an enquiry of this kind, not merely to rely upon views stated in general terms, but to enquire further into the principle on which these views were maintained. Many of the authorities quoted in favour of the Bishop of Exeter were inconsistent with themselves, and speak against his theory as well as for it. Dr Waterland, for instance, Bayford admitted, did maintain to a certain extent the doctrine stated on the other side. But his evidence looks different when it is discovered how he explained it. Bayford quoted a passage from Waterland in which the distinction is made between renovation and regeneration,[3] and where the writer says that in adults there must be a certain measure of renovation ("a renewal . . . of the inward frame or disposition of the man") before regeneration ("itself a kind of renewal; but then it is of the spiritual state considered at large") can take place. Then Bayford points out that immediately after this Waterland goes on to say:

Preventing grace must go before, to work in the man faith and repentance, which are qualifications previous to Baptism, and necessary to render it salutary. Those first addresses or influential visits of the Holy Spirit, turning and preparing the heart of man, are the preparative renewings, the first and lowest degrees of renovation.

Then there is Dr Jackson whom Bayford admits to make statements in support of the other side, and yet who in another place enunciates a sort of modified election, into which persons

---

[1] Book III, tit. xlii, chap. iii—"Illud vero quod opponentes inducunt fidem aut charitatem, aliasque virtutes parvulis utpote non consentientibus non infundi, a plerisque non conceditur absolute".

[2] First Title, chap. 2, § 33.

[3] *Works*, ed. Van Mildert, Oxford, 1823, Vol. VI, pp. 349 ff. See also p. 70, *infra*.

are brought by Baptism; and, if they continue and progress in that state till they come to riper years, they arrive at a state of grace and absolute election.[1] Also Bayford cites Mant who is an authority for Baptism conferring regeneration in *all* cases, even exceeding what the Bishop of Exeter himself has predicated of it.[2] Bayford mentions these writers in order to demonstrate that although they have been quoted on the other side, as authorities in support of that case, each one presents distinct and different views on the subject.

Bayford expressed himself as extremely surprised that Bishop Jewel should have been quoted as an authority by his opponents, also that the Bishop of Exeter should have referred to him in his recent Charge. One of the several quotations which Bayford makes from Jewel should be sufficient to show the cause of this surprise:

This marvellous conjunction and incorporation, is first begun and wrought by faith; afterwards the same incorporation is assured to us, and increased, in our Baptism. The holy mysteries do not begin, but rather continue and confirm this incorporation.[3]

Again, Bishop Taylor was quoted by the other side, but Bayford points out that the following also are his words:

The Church gives the Sacraments, God gives the grace of the Sacrament. But because he does not always give it at the instant in which the Church gives the Sacrament . . . it follows that the Church may administer rightly, even before God gives the real grace of the Sacrament. . . .[4]

Bayford also quotes passages from Dr Nicholls on the Book of Common Prayer which he thinks should have made the Bishop's counsel hesitate before giving him as an authority.

Bayford next quoted the title to the XXXIX Articles and the Preface of the Book of Common Prayer, as Gorham himself had done, as indicating the different standard of interpretation which should be applied to these two documents. The Act of Uniformity (14 Car. II cap. 4) requires that every minister should give his assent "to the use of the Prayer Book". Bayford held that this meant assent simply to the "use" of the book, not

---

[1] *Works*, Vol. IX, pp. 321 ff.

[2] Mant, *Two Tracts intended to convey correct notions of regeneration and conversion etc.*, London, 1817.

[3] *Treatise on Private Mass*, Parker Society, pp. 140–1.

[4] *Works*, ed. Bishop Heber, Vol. II, p. 266.

to any doctrines which a Bishop might think to be inferred by it. In the reign of Queen Elizabeth there was passed "An Act for the Ministers of the Church to be of sound Religion" (13 Eliz. cap. 12); in this many provisions are made for dealing with irregular ministrations of the clergy, and in every case the Articles, not the Prayer Book, are held up as the criterion. The same holds good of the Act of Uniformity and the later Articles. The Canons of Convocation of 1571, 1585 and 1597 appoint the same thing. When, in 1695, there was an outbreak of unsound teaching on the Holy Trinity, the Crown sent directions to the Bishops and Archbishops to call for and enforce subscription to the Thirty-nine Articles. Bayford cites similar directions at later dates.

Bayford quotes Rogers, Chaplain to Archbishop Bancroft, on the Thirty-nine Articles.[1] He also says that Burnet "has been treated as unfairly as some of the other authors"; for at the same time as saying what he does about the Prayer Book, he prefaces his work on the Thirty-nine Articles by the statement, "They are the sum of our doctrine, and the confession of our faith".[2] Bayford then introduces a lengthy catena of quotations to the same effect; from Bishop Hall,[3] Archbishop Whitgift,[4] Bishop Prideaux[5] and Stillingfleet.[6]

Having then, as he supposes, established the supremacy of the Articles over the language of the Prayer Book, Bayford looks for explicit authority for applying the conditions which the Articles lay down in the case of Infant Baptism. This, he maintains, is to be found in Burnet:

When a person of age desires Baptism, . . . as to the effect of Baptism on the soul of him that is baptized; without doubt that depends upon the sincerity of the professions and vows made by him. The wills of infants are, by the law of nature and nations, in their parents, and are transferred by them to their sureties; the sponsions that are made on their behalf are considered as made by themselves.[7]

[1] See p. 63, note, 1.

[2] This argument of Bayford about Burnet seems rather lame, for the language quoted on p. 63 is too strong to be overthrown by this quotation, or the other which he adduces (Bayford, *op. cit.*, pp. 84, 85).

[3] *Old Religion* (*Works*, Vol. IX, p. 308. Oxford, D. A. Talboys, 1837).

[4] *Defence of the Answer to the Admonition*, Parker Society, p. 3.

[5] Dedication to *Fasciculus Controversiarum Theologicarum*.

[6] *Unreasonableness of Separation*, Second Edition, London 1681, p. 95.

[7] Burnet, *On the Twenty-fifth Article*, Oxford Edition, p. 334.

After this Bayford went to great lengths to refute the contention of the Bishop's counsel that Cranmer never changed his views on Baptism. It is indeed very surprising that this opinion should ever have been put forward, and the judge admitted that Gorham's counsel had made a successful refutation of it. It is sufficiently well known that Cranmer moved from the extremes of unreformed doctrine in the Bishop's Book to the position of the Articles in 1552, so it is not necessary to follow the whole course of Bayford's lengthy proof. In the Articles of 1536, drawn up by Cranmer, we read: "By the Sacrament of Baptism they (infants, innocents and children) do *obtain* remission of their sins, the grace and favour of God, and be made thereby the very sons and children of God".[1] In the Articles of 1552 there is the phrase "In such only as worthily receive the same they have an wholesome effect and operation"—also from Cranmer's pen. These two quotations are enough to show the strength of Bayford's point; but to make assurance doubly sure, he added many more quotations from Cranmer showing how repeatedly his later writings reverse the earlier. Constantly the word "obtain" gives place to the word "seal" in his statements on Baptism. Cranmer himself said at a later date, "I grant that then I believed otherwise than I do now".[2]

An interesting point which Bayford makes *en passant* is that in the Liturgy of Edward VI, there is the rubric: "Then shall the Priest demand of the child . . . these questions following", and each successive answer is set forth as coming from the child. This, he argues, demonstrates that the profession of faith is considered as being made by the child itself. Bayford also points out the confusion in Cranmer's language caused by his sometimes using the word "Sacrament" to denote the inward spiritual grace, to which Gorham had already drawn attention.[3]

Bayford adds that Gorham would not object to the use of any of the language about Baptism quoted by the Bishop's counsel, provided it were understood to apply only to those cases in which the conditions for receiving the blessings of the Sacrament were fulfilled. He then goes on to say, "The acknowledgement of the blessings is common to both sides; but this leaves unresolved the real question between us, viz., whether these blessings are or are not received in *all* cases". But it seems that in making this assertion Bayford is going beyond the evidence provided by the

---

[1] Translation from *Formularies of Faith*, ed. Charles Lloyd, Oxford, 1825.

[2] Cranmer's *Remains*, Parker Society, p. 218.   [3] See p. 39, *supra*.

Examination. It is questionable whether in the whole of his speech Bayford faces the fact, as does appear to be the case, that Gorham regards regeneration in Baptism as nothing more than a coincidence if it occurs.[1] It is for regeneration in and by Baptism that the Bishop of Exeter is contending, whereas Gorham will only allow a visible signing and sealing of this regeneration together with the confirming of faith and the increasing of grace as the effect of the sacrament when rightly received. This query is very much to the point when we read in Bayford's speech, "it must also be admitted that when Mr Gorham affirms, in respect of infants, that such expressions do not, necessarily, and in every case, apply to them, he is not thereby detracting from the grace belonging to the Sacrament of Baptism". But, on the Bishop's theory, he is "detracting from the grace belonging to the Sacrament". It always embarrasses an argument when one party suddenly throws in the remark, "I think we're really both saying the same thing".

Then follows a catena of quotations from Peter Martyr[2] and Martin Bucer, in which there are statements made which seem to support the Bishop's case, but Bayford is careful to point out that this extreme language is always balanced by other passages, and the result is much the same view as that of the Anglican documents. And he particularly points out that Martin Bucer, for instance, says "This only we deny, as we have clearly expressed it, that Sacraments and sacred words are such instruments and channels of grace as that they bring salvation with whatever mind or faith you partake of them",[3] and yet at the same time he voices no objection to the language of the English Prayer Book.

Bayford next turned to the Homilies. He quoted them at much greater length than Gorham, but added nothing to his arguments. He remarked that the nature and effect of Baptism had not been made the immediate subject of a single Homily. Next Bayford quoted from the Zurich Letters to show that the English Reformers, Jewel included, held the same opinions as the Continental Reformers. He then referred to an Order of Convocation in 1586 that all "inferior ministers" were to read Bullinger's *Decades*, and quoted: "Many receive the visible Sacraments, and yet are not partakers of the invisible grace

[1] Gorham's language does seem to be ambiguous. For a possible explanation, see Chap. x.

[2] E.g. from his lectures on Corinthians delivered in the University of Oxford.

[3] *Commentary on the Four Gospels*, Second Edition, pp. 18 ff.

which by faith only is received".[1] Also: "We, therefore, baptizing infants for these causes, do abundantly testify that there is not first given unto them in Baptism; but that there is sealed and confirmed that which they had before".[2] "What", asks Bayford, "is this but the doctrine of prevenient grace, taught and enjoined by all the Bishops of the Church of England then, though condemned as heresy by one of the Bishops of the Church of England now?" Nowell's Catechism and Calvin's *Institutes* were authorised for students in the University of Oxford in 1596, and Bayford proceeded to extended quotations from them.

Bayford pointed out that the Bishop's counsel had not given a single authority between Jewel and Hooker; but he quoted several authors in that period in support of Gorham. For instance Latimer,[3] Ridley,[4] Hooper,[5] Beacon,[6] Coverdale,[7] Philpot,[8] Calfhill;[9] and he gives a host of quotations from Dean Turner, Archbishop Grindal, Archbishop Sandys, Archbishop Whitgift, Rogers, Davenant, Prideaux, Robert Abbott, Whitaker, Benefield. Among these he observes many who in places use the strongest language in relation to Baptism, such as would delight the Bishop of Exeter, and yet all the while explain that faith is an essential pre-requisite.

Bayford continues his catalogue of authorities with quotations from Barlow,[10] Carleton,[11] Babington,[12] Beveridge,[13] Archbishop Usher,[14] Archbishop Sharp,[15] Nicholson,[16] Pearson,[17] Bradford,[18] Downame,[19] Andrews,[20] Hopkins,[21] Cooper,[22] Geste,[23] Bridges,[24] Fulke,[25] Mayer.[26]

[1] Parker Society, Bullinger's *Decades*, V, p. 273. [2] *Ibid.*, p. 313.
[3] *Sermons*, Parker Society, p. 202. [4] *Works*, Parker Society, p. 56.
[5] *Ibid.*, pp. 74, 75. [6] *Prayers*, Parker Society, p. 173.
[7] *Truthful Lessons*, Parker Society, p. 80. [8] *Early Writings*, Parker Society, p. 275.
[9] *Answer to Martial*, Parker Society, p. 215.
[10] *A Defence of the Articles of the Protestant Religion.*
[11] *An Examination of Montague's Appeal*, p. 193.
[12] *Comfortable Notes on Genesis*, p. 53.
[13] Beveridge's *Works*, Vol. I, p. 345, Library of Anglo-Catholic Theology.
[14] *Sum and Substance of the Christian Religion*, pp. 407 ff.
[15] Thirteenth Sermon on "Regeneration".
[16] *A Plain and Full Exposition of the Catechism of the Church of England* (Library of Anglo-Catholic Theology, p. 13).
[17] *On the Creed*, commenting on the clause, "Communion of Saints".
[18] A Sermon published by S.P.C.K. [19] *On Perseverance.*
[20] Library of Anglo-Catholic Theology, Vol. III. Eighth Sermon, "Of the Sending of the Holy Ghost", pp. 248, 249.
[21] *The Doctrine of the Two Sacraments*, in *Works*, ed. Josiah Pratt, 1809, Vol. II, pp. 417 ff.
[22] Second Sermon. [23] Appendix to his *Life and Character*, by Dugdale, p. 116.
[24] *Defence of the Government established in the Church of England*, p. 482.
[25] *Defence of the English Translation of the Bible*, Parker Society, p. 450. [26] *Catechism.*

All these quotations are set out in full in the published account of Bayford's speech. No new points are raised in them, so there is no need to transcribe the passages—it is sufficient to observe the formidable array of authors who were called into the witness-box in support of Gorham. It is interesting, however, to look more closely into Bayford's treatment of Hooker. He speaks of the change of Hooker's opinions, saying, "it is . . . grievous that the change in his views was nothing less than a departure from the avowed principles of the Reformers, and of all the divines who followed in their steps up to the time (1597), in which Hooker published the Fifth Book of his Polity, in which this partial retrogression towards the Romish doctrine of the Sacraments first appears".[1] Bayford allowed that there was a departure from the doctrine of the earlier writers, but he claimed that it was only a partial abandonment of their position. The Bishop's counsel had apparently quoted from his later writings, and Bayford now proceeds to show the earlier doctrine from which he departed. Bayford quoted from the third book of the *Ecclesiastical Polity*.

But our naming the name of Christ is not enough to prove us Christians, unless we also embrace the faith which Christ published throughout the world. Now although we know the Christian faith and allow of it; yet, in this respect, we are but entering, entered we are not, into the visible Church before our admittance by the door of Baptism.[2]

Bayford asserts that Hooker never departed from this so far as to say that every child lawfully baptized thereby receives the grace of the sacrament. The Bishop's counsel sought to prove this by his quotations which were apparently all from Book V. But Bayford quoted: ". . . the door of our actual entrance into God's House; the first apparent beginning of life; a seal, perhaps, to the grace of election before received . . .",[3] also "Grace is not absolutely tied unto Sacraments".[4]

After some general remarks about Jewel, and a sermon by Archbishop Laurence, Bayford touched upon the Savoy Conference. On this last he added little to what Gorham had said in his comments which he had transmitted to the Bishop in the course of the Examination.[5]

Bayford brought his lengthy defence to an end with some remarks on the Examination, which, it will be remembered,

---

[1] Bayford, *op. cit.*, p. 193. [2] *Eccl. Polit.*, Bk. III, ch. i, 5 and 6.
[3] *Ibid.*, Bk. V, ch. ix, 3. [4] *Ibid.*, Bk. V, ch. lx, 6. [5] See p. 26, *supra*.

was the only documentary evidence before the Court. First, it had, apparently, been asserted in the course of the proceedings that Gorham had denied that the passage in John iii related to Baptism. The text of Gorham's answer should have been enough to refute this,[1] and Bayford said, "the declaration of Our Lord could only refer to Baptism, as a *Christian* ordinance, illustratively, or by accommodation—by anticipation, at the very utmost,—because it had not been then instituted as such". But even if Gorham *had* gone so far as to deny it, he would have been in good company, for Dr Whittaker in his *Praelectiones* does so, and his statement had never been called into question as heresy. Dr Bayford had some critical things to say about the spirit in which the Examination had been conducted, but he does not dwell upon this; in asking for a decision in favour of Gorham, he says: "I have not heard it even suggested in argument, that any opinion advanced by Gorham, on his Examination, is opposed to either of the Articles. The charge against him is, I think, that of too rigid adherence to them".

Bayford's last words are an appeal that the Church of England may be found with arms wide enough to embrace both parties, and that the Court may do nothing to limit the space, or assist either to exclude the other from her bosom.

[1] See p. 11, *supra*.

CHAPTER III

THE JUDGMENT OF JENNER FUST

But in spite of this powerful defence, the Court of Arches decided against Gorham. At this stage of the controversy the position was reached that Gorham's theory was not a permissible interpretation of the Articles and Formularies of the Church of England. The Church Court proclaimed the necessity of belief in the doctrine of unconditional baptismal regeneration of infants, and it was held that the Bishop of Exeter had rightly refused to institute Gorham, who denied this doctrine, to the living to which he had been presented. It is necessary now to examine the judgment of the Court of Arches in detail.

Judgment was given by Sir Herbert Jenner Fust on August 2nd 1849, in favour of the Bishop, against Gorham. This court decided that Gorham held doctrines which were contrary to the Formularies and Articles of the United Church of England and Ireland. The judgment began with remarks on the Bishop's right to examine, the propriety of his action in appending comments of his own before transmitting Gorham's testimonials to the Lord Chancellor, and several like topics. This study is not concerned with these matters—but solely with the grounds upon which the Court decided that Gorham's views on Holy Baptism were at variance with the doctrines of the Church of England as expressed in the Prayer Book and the Articles. The judge remarked that the evidence in the case was scanty. It is important to observe at the outset that the only documentary evidence upon which the decision was reached was the book published by Gorham himself,[1] "The evidence . . . consists merely of one short affidavit by Mr Gorham, no affidavit on the part of the Bishop at all, but a book is annexed to his act on petition, containing upwards of 250 pages of introduction correspondence, and 149 questions addressed to Mr Gorham, with his answers to those questions: upon this so-called evidence the whole case turns. . . ."[2] The duty of the court was to ascertain what is the doctrine of the Church of England upon the

[1] *The Efficacy of Baptism.*
[2] *The Judgments on Baptismal Regeneration*, edited by William J. Irons, B.D.

efficacy of the Sacrament of Holy Baptism; what were the points
on which Gorham was stated to have expressed opinions contrary
to that doctrine; and whether in fact Gorham's opinions were
inconsistent with the Church's teaching.

It was alleged, on behalf of the Bishop, "that it appeared to
him, in the course of the examination, that Gorham was of
unsound doctrine respecting that great and fundamental point,
the efficacy of the Sacrament of Baptism, inasmuch as he held,
and persisted in holding, that spiritual regeneration is not given
or conferred in that Holy Sacrament, in particular, that infants
are not made therein members of Christ and the children of
God".[1] The Court proceeded to travel through Gorham's book,
which contained the record of the original questions asked by
the Bishop and Gorham's answers—the record agreed upon by
both parties. It was on the basis of these questions and answers,
which have been summarized in the first chapter of this book,
that the Court of Arches pronounced its judgment.

The judgment states that Gorham asserted, in answer to the
Bishop's charge, that he did not hold or persist in holding that
infants are not made, in Baptism, members of Christ and the
children of God;[2] nor did he maintain any views whatever
contrary to the true doctrine of the Church of England. It was,
he said, his desire and endeavour throughout the examination
to explain the language both of the articles and of the liturgy
by such just and favourable construction as would secure an
entire agreement, not only of each with the others, but of all
alike, with the plain tenor of Holy Scripture, declared by the
said articles to be of paramount and absolute authority.

The judge commented that a large portion of the proceedings
before the court had been occupied with arguments based on the
opinion of ecclesiastical authors. He said that although the
arguments were most able, and supported by a vast body of
learning, still they tended to "increase the difficulties with which
it is the lot of the Court to contend". He next said that the
doctrines of infant and adult baptism are so mixed up together
in Gorham's volume that it had become a matter of extreme
difficulty for the Court to separate the one from the other.
"I proceed", he said, "to consider the question I am called upon

[1] *Ibid.*, p. 14.

[2] Gorham may be assumed to have made this reply, either meaning that he
assented to the use of this language, provided it was given its proper construction,
or else on the basis of his answer that being made a member of Christ depends upon
an act of grace which may occur before, *in*, or after baptism.

to decide: the question is allowed to be, what is the efficacy of baptism in the case of infants only?"[1]

The judge prefaced that part of the judgment which contained his real decisions by remarking that whereas Gorham appeared to take his stand upon the Articles, the Bishop took his upon the Articles and Formularies of the Church conjointly. He then went on to refer to the opening questions in the Bishop's examination, and Gorham's answers to them. First there was the Bishop's question as to whether Holy Scripture declared Baptism to be necessary to salvation, and Gorham's answer that Baptism was not so declared to be indispensably necessary, although it was to be understood from Scripture that it was generally necessary as a duty to be observed. Then there was Gorham's admission that John iii. 5—"Except a man be born of water and of the Spirit he cannot enter into the kingdom of God"—showed "the great necessity of the Sacrament of Baptism where it may be had". There followed the Bishop's reference to the Homily of Common Prayer and the Sacraments, which says that Baptism and the Supper of the Lord are "visible signs expressly commanded in the New Testament, whereunto is annexed the promise of free forgiveness of our sins, and of our holiness and joining in Christ". Gorham had answered to this that he fully assented to this passage "when fairly brought into connexion with the Articles of our Church on the nature and efficacy of the Sacraments". The judge remarked that in all this Gorham was making the Articles the principal standard by which he wished to be judged.

The judge next reviewed Gorham's answers to the Bishop's questions on the passages in the Formularies which apparently stated that all infants duly baptized were thereby regenerated. Gorham's answer had been that such passages contained nothing contrary to the Word of God when they were given such just and favourable construction as they deserved. The judge observed that Gorham did not give a precise answer to the question proposed to him by the Bishop, but in reply adopted, in part only, certain words to be found in the preface to the Book of

---

[1] The judge's complaint of the amount of extraneous matter introduced into the proceedings would seem to indicate a desire on his part to treat of nothing but Gorham's opinions on the one side and the doctrines of the official documents of the Church on the other. But this is not the plan which is followed; the judge very soon undertakes to pronounce on a question the existence of which Gorham's arguments does not allow. Early in the Examination Gorham had said that it was not permissible to isolate the case of infant baptism. They were talking, he said, of general principles relating to Sacraments.

Common Prayer. Gorham had gone on to say that the just and favourable construction of the passages to which the Bishop referred was to be sought by reference to three standards of judgment; the Thirty-nine Articles; other passages in the Formularies; and the views of those by whom the services were reformed and the Articles sanctioned. The judge said that he had no intention of pursuing the evidence given in this last direction; he was going to limit himself to what the Church's official documents said about the baptism of infants.

In the opinion of the judge Gorham's counsel had been right in saying that in order to ascertain the doctrine of the Church on any subject the Thirty-nine Articles are, in the first place, to be consulted. The judge quoted Rogers,[1] chaplain to Archbishop Bancroft to this effect, also Archbishop Whitgift[2] and Bishop Stillingfleet[3] and he cited Bishops Hall and Prideaux. He admitted, then, that the Thirty-nine Articles are the standard of doctrine, but he said, "if they fall short, if they are silent on any particular point, to what then are we to resort?" He says that in this case what is to be done is not to resort to the supposed opinions of those by whom the Articles were framed and the Formularies of the Church compiled, but to refer to the language of the Formularies themselves. He quotes Bishop Burnet (*Pastoral Care* at the commencement of Chap VI.):

The truest indication of the sense of a Church is to be taken from her language in her public offices; this is that which she speaks the most frequently and the most publicly. Even the articles of doctrine are not so much read or so often heard of as her Liturgies are. And as this way of reasoning has been of late made use of, with great advantage, against the Church of Rome, to make her accountable for all her public offices in their plain and literal meaning; so I will make use of it on this occasion. It is the stronger in our case, whose offices being in a tongue understood by the people, the argument from them does more evidently conclude her.

Also Dr Waterland, who says:

The Church's public acts are open and common, and he is the best Church of England man that best understands the principles there

[1] In his Preface to his work on the Articles, Rogers says: "The purpose of our Church is best known by the doctrine which she doth profess; the doctrine by the Thirty-nine Articles established by Act of Parliament; the Articles, by the words whereby they are expressed, and other purpose than the public doctrine doth minister, and other doctrine than in the said Articles is contained, our Church neither hath nor holdeth. . . ."

[2] Preface to *Defence of the Answer to the Admonition*, Parker Society, p. 3.

[3] *Unreasonableness of Separation*, Pt. II, Sec. 1, p. 95, London, 1681.

laid down, and argues closest from them; the rest are but assertions, fancies, or practices of private men, and are not binding on us.[1]

And Bishop Conybeare[2] says the same.

The judge then proceeded to examine whether what the Articles have to say about infant baptism is conclusive, or whether recourse must be had to the declarations of the Church as manifested in her services and offices. He refers to Article XXV and observes that it is there said that to be worthy is necessary for the beneficial receiving of baptism. But, he remarks, the Article leaves it doubtful what worthy reception is. Gorham had said, "Faith and repentance are necessary—are pre-requisites to the Sacrament of Baptism, as well as to that of the Lord's Supper", but these conditions are not to be found in this Article. The judge also points out that another question which is left unanswered by the Articles is that of what Regeneration is in infants. Article XXVII says, ". . . the promises of forgiveness of sin, and of our adoption to be the sons of God by the Holy Ghost, are visibly signed and sealed; faith is confirmed and grace increased by virtue of prayer unto God", and also "The baptism of young children is in any wise to be retained in the Church, as most agreeable to the institution of Christ". The judge's comment on all this is as follows: "Now the first question which suggests itself to one's mind is,—if faith is to be confirmed, and grace increased by virtue of prayer unto God,—how is it that young children are to be baptized? They can have neither faith nor repentance. They cannot have faith, because they know not the promises; they cannot have repentance because they have not committed actual sin. They may have faith and repentance in after life, but in infancy they can have neither the one nor the other; the one they cannot have for want of understanding; the other they cannot have, and are not required to have, since they have not been guilty of actual sin".

The position reached so far in the judge's argument is that Article XXV declares that worthy reception is necessary; infants by reason of their tender age seem to be incapable of faith or repentance; and yet Article XXVII says that the baptism of infants is to be continued. What can this "worthy" reception be, of which infants must be presumed to be capable since the

[1] *Works*, Oxford, 1823, Vol. 10, p. 186. Quoted by Jenner Fust in his judgment without reference.

[2] *Treatise on the case of Subscription to Articles of Religion considered* in *Enchiridion Theologicum, or a Manual for the use of Students in Divinity*, by John Randolph, Bishop of London, Vol. III, Oxford Edition, 1792, pp. 262, 263, and 267.

XXVIIth Article advocates their continued reception of baptism?

Gorham had said that children "being born in sin" were by this original sin hindered from being worthy recipients of baptism. "Our Church holds, and I hold, that no spiritual grace is conferred in baptism, except to worthy recipients, and as infants are by nature unworthy recipients, 'being born in sin and the children of wrath', they cannot receive any benefit from baptism, except there shall have been a prevenient act of grace to make them worthy".[1] Gorham had said then, "Baptism is the sign or seal, either of the grace already given, or of the repentance and faith which are stipulated, and must be hereafter exercised". The judge's comment on this is: "According to this Mr Gorham does not admit that it is by baptism or through baptism that grace is conferred. . . ."[2]

As regards the stipulations made at Baptism, Gorham had said that the Church requires them; but he had not committed himself to the view that they were a pre-requisite to beneficial reception of the sacrament. The Bishop had suggested that the Office of Private Baptism, which provided for the baptism of infants in emergency in private houses, without any mention of stipulations, was an indication that infants could receive the spiritual grace of baptism independently of the stipulations of representatives. Gorham's reply to this had been that in this case the Church tacitly understood the stipulations to be implied —they were required to be absolutely entered into afterwards, though not formally given at the time. Gorham had said that infants baptized in emergency without formal stipulations, dying before they committed actual sin were undoubtedly saved— according to the declaration at the end of the office of Public Baptism. In this case, infants so baptized must have been regenerated by an act of grace prevenient to their baptism.

On all this the judge remarks: "There may be grace imparted at the reception of Baptism, at the very identical moment the rite is administered; or there may be no grace imparted at that time. . . . Whether there may be a 'prevenient act', or whether

[1] See p. 18, *supra*.
[2] The judge does not seem to have understood the whole of what Gorham held to be effected by Baptism. He held that if the prevenient act of grace had been given, then grace was given *in* the Sacrament—". . . it is also a Sign of 'God's good-will towards us', by which he 'strengthens' and confirms our 'faith' in him". See p. 19, *supra*.
The passage quoted here by the judge might, in isolation, be taken as meaning that Gorham denied that grace was given by or through the sacrament; but Gorham is here speaking of what Baptism does as a sign or a seal, not of what it does as an instrument.

E

there may be an act concurrent with the rite, or whether there may be an act subsequent to the rite, are points upon which the Court is not called upon to express an opinion.[1] It is sufficient for it to observe that Gorham's position is, that it is not by baptism, or through baptism, that grace is conferred."

Having now dealt with such Articles as bear on the case, and Gorham's interpretation of the Articles, the judge proceeds to examine the Formularies of the Church—which, he says, must be his guide and authority in ascertaining the doctrines of the Church in the absence of clear direction from the Articles. He first looks at the Office of Public Baptism of infants. Gorham had said that its language was to be considered as hypothetical, conditional upon the fulfilment of certain promises which were made for the children by their godfathers and godmothers; it is language which requires a "just and favourable construction"; it is a "charitable hope" on the part of the Church. The judge, however, held that the construction of the service indicates a meaning different from Gorham's interpretation. The prayers and exhortations before the actual baptism anticipate the reception of spiritual benefits—adoption, regeneration and the like. The parts of the service after the baptismal act assume that the child has been regenerated, washed from its sins, etc. The structure of the service cannot allow of the language being no more than a charitable hope—it all assumes that a turning point has been reached in the act of baptism.

According to Gorham's interpretation, the Church admits an infant to Baptism in the form prescribed on the assumption that he will do all that is promised for him by his sponsors. But the judge held that this interpretation could not stand. "I confine myself to the case of infants; for the case of adults is totally different", he said.[2] In the latter case, he held, it is allowed without question that the declarations of the Church are made on the hypothesis that the recipients (adults) are sincere in their profession of faith and repentance. But he added "in the case of infants, the declaration in the service of public baptism, of which we are now speaking, is positive, precise, and distinct, that the child 'is regenerate', and that thanks are returned to

---

[1] As the late Editor of the *Christian Observer* (W. Goode) points out (*Review of the Judgment of Sir H. J. Fust*, p. 20), it is difficult to reconcile this sentence with the decision of the judge.

[2] It must be remarked here that to say this is to beg a large question. It is part of Gorham's thesis that the two cases cannot be separated. The judge summarily dismissed this point.

God for that benefit". As regards the Office of Private Baptism, it had been maintained in support of Gorham that since that office only provided for cases of great necessity therefore nothing with respect to the efficacy of baptism without stipulations could be fairly drawn from that formulary. The judge differed from that view. He asserted that the provision that "so many of the collects appointed to be said before in the form of public baptism as the time and present exigence will suffer" were to be made use of, was an indication that the Church intended to declare that the child so baptized is entitled to all the benefits of an infant publicly baptized. The administration of the Baptism is complete when the infant has been baptized with water in the threefold Name. The counsel for the Bishop had said that if this were not so the child ought to be brought into Church on recovery and baptized again. The judge remarked, "I must say I think there was something in that observation. But, according to the Church that, which is directed to be done afterwards, is not a repetition of the baptism, as we shall presently see".

The judge next proceeded to deal with the certification which is made by the minister when the child baptized privately is brought into the Church. Whereas Gorham had held that the "certification" ended with the statement that the true form of baptism had been used, the judge regarded as included in the "certification" the words "who, being born in original sin, and in the wrath of God, is now, by the laver of regeneration in baptism, received into the number of the children of God, and heirs of everlasting life". Gorham had held that these words were "a simple declaration of faith, hope, and charity". The judge now says that this form of private baptism is conclusive proof that godparents are not essential to baptism, therefore there is no ground for saying that either of the offices of public or private baptism of infants is merely conditional or founded upon an hypothesis. The judge adds that if the child lives it may commit actual sin and fall away from the benefits given in baptism; then faith and repentance would be requisite, not to regenerate him, for that has been already done, but to renovate him and place him back in that state in which he was placed by baptism.

The judge closes his treatment of the infant baptismal offices by one more reference to the declaration at the end of the office of public baptism. Here, he says, we have a positive declaration on the part of the Church, not a mere hypothetical or charitable hope. "It is certain by God's Word, that children which are baptized, dying before they commit actual sin, are undoubtedly saved"—the statements in the baptismal offices are equally positive, and the judge cannot understand how Gorham's qualification can be engrafted on the words.

The next matter to which attention is given in the judgment is the service for adult baptism. The judge's argument is not immediately apparent, but it seems that he is accepting the necessity for worthy reception of the sacrament in order for its benefits to be received. He appears to regard "worthiness" as constituting freedom from actual sin, and makes the distinction between adult and infant baptism on the ground that adult baptism is conditional upon true repentance, whereas in the case of infants there is no actual sin, and therefore "worthy" reception can be assumed in all cases.[1] These are the judge's words: "There is then, I say, this marked distinction—that the Church knows in the case of an infant that it cannot have committed 'actual sin' before baptism; whereas, in the case of an adult, it can only rely upon his outward profession of faith and repentance".[2] No argument can be drawn, he says, from the application of the one case to the other; in the case of adult baptism the Church can only act on the charitable supposition that the party is sincere. There is no such hypothesis necessary in the baptism of infants.

Next the judgment deals *in extenso* with the Catechism. It is pointed out that the language of the Catechism is in strict conformity with that of the baptismal offices. "I heartily thank our heavenly Father that he hath called me to this state of salvation. . . . And I pray unto God to give me His grace that I may continue in the same unto my life's end". "Continue", observes the judge—"there is no doubt, no hypothesis, here expressed as to the state in which he was placed by baptism". He cannot understand how any doubt can be raised upon these words. Baptized children, when they arrive at years of discretion, are bound to take upon themselves the performance of the vows which are made by their sureties in baptism—but it is not this, nor prevenient grace, but baptism, the judge argues, which, according to the Prayer Book, places the children in the

---

[1] No space is given in the judgment for a discussion of Gorham's definition of "worthy"; nor does sufficient attention seem to be given here to the statements of the Prayer Book that children are conceived and born in sin, and are by nature the children of wrath.

[2] This section of the judgment ignores the question of faith in infants.

state of salvation. " 'Prevenient grace' is not the mode", says the judge—"the Church says nothing about prevenient grace".

The judge quoted at length Dean Nowell's *Catechism*,[1] maintaining that the doctrine which he alleged to be found in the Prayer Book was also taught there. "Nam sicuti Deus peccatorem condonationem et vitae novitatem nobis vere in baptismo offert, ita a nobis certo recipiuntur. Absit enim ut Deum vanis nos imaginibus ludere atque frustrari putemus." He quotes a great deal more, including a passage on infants which, he holds, shows that Nowell is in line with his interpretation of the Church Catechism: "Ut fides et poenitentia baptismo praecedant, tantum in adultis, qui per aetatem sunt utriusque capaces, exigitur; infantibus vero promissio Ecclesiae facta per Christum, in cujus fide baptizantur, in praesens satis erit, deinde postquam adoleverint, baptismi sui veritatem ipsos agnoscere, ejusque vim in animis eorum vigere, atque ipsorum vita, et moribus repraesentari omnino oportet."

Next the judge turned to the Confirmation service in the Prayer Book. In the prayer for the Holy Spirit there is the assumption that the children now to be confirmed have been regenerated in baptism. The judge interprets this as a positive declaration, and with this further piece of evidence he gives his opinion that the doctrine of regeneration in the baptism of infants is established.

After this the judge adverted to the question of the precise meaning of the word "regeneration",—whether it implies an absolute change of nature, character, and feelings, or whether it implies only a change of state and of relation; that is, a change from being a "child of wrath" to being a "child of grace". He gave his view that the term did not mean such a total change of character as precluded the possibility of the person regenerated ever falling again; but that it meant a change of station, a placing under grace instead of under wrath, the becoming a member of Christ and an inheritor of the kingdom of heaven. He quoted Dr Bethell,[2] Bishop of Bangor at the time: "No reasonable doubt can be entertained that it [the word "regeneration"] was appropriated to that grace, whatever may be its nature, which is bestowed on us in the Sacrament of Baptism (including perhaps occasionally, by a common figure of speech,

---

[1] *Enchiridion Theologicum*, Oxford Edition, 1792, Vol. II, pp. 212–16; also Nowell's *Catechism*, Parker Society, p. 86.

[2] *General View of the Doctrine of Regeneration in Baptism*, pp. 6–8, Third Edition.

its proper and legitimate effects, considered in conjunction with it). . . ." Also Dr Bethell gives a summary of the view of Dr Waterland:[1]

Regeneration is distinguished from renovation.—Regeneration is a change of the whole spiritual state; renovation a change of inward frame or disposition; which in adults is rather a qualification or capacity for regeneration, than regeneration itself. That in infants regeneration necessarily takes place without renovation, but in adults renovation exists (or at least ought to exist) before, in, and after baptism. . . .

Regeneration comes only once—in or through baptism. Renovation exists before, in, and after baptism, and may be often repeated. Regeneration, being a single act, can have no parts, and is incapable of increase. Renovation is in its own nature progressive. Regeneration, though suspended as to its effects and benefits, cannot be totally lost in this present life. Renovation may be often repeated and totally lost. . . .

Grown persons coming to baptism properly qualified, receive at once the grace of regeneration; but, however well prepared, they are not regenerate without baptism. Afterwards, renovation grows more and more within them by the indwelling of the Holy Spirit. As to infants, their innocence and incapacity are to them instead of repentance, which they do not want, and of actual faith, which they cannot have: and they are capable of being born again, and adopted by God, because they bring no obstacle. They stipulate, and the Holy Spirit translates them out of a state of nature into a state of grace, favour and acceptance. In their case, regeneration precedes, and renovation follows after, and they are a temple of the Spirit, till they defile themselves with sin.[2]

And the judge quotes Bishop Van Mildert[3] to the same effect.

Without saying any more the judge had decided against Gorham that infants were regenerated absolutely in baptism, not conditionally upon the performance of faith and repentance. The rest of the judgment was taken up with arguments in support

---

[1] *General View of the Doctrine of Regeneration in Baptism*, Ch. 2, pp. 14, 15.

[2] In all this the judge seems to have been supposing that Gorham was confusing regeneration with renovation. He seems to miss the point which is Gorham's main contention, that the act of faith is necessary before regeneration can take place. The judge seems to be imagining that Gorham's view is that infants cannot be regenerated because they cannot be renovated—that "renovated" is the meaning of worthy. Once again (see p. 68, note 1) he does not take cognizance of Gorham's definition of "worthy" (see pp. 18 and 29, *supra*). Gorham is arguing for the necessity of actual faith in all cases, not merely for the absence of need for repentance, much less for actual goodness.

[3] *Bampton Lectures*, 1814, pp. 195, 196, 2nd Edition (*Inquiry into the General Principles of Scripture Interpretation*).

of the decision which had been reached, and in refutation of some more of the points which Gorham had adduced for his view.

First, he makes clear that his saying that infants are changed in their relation to God does not involve a doctrine of indefectible grace. If such infants fall away, commit sin and die without faith and repentance, they forfeit their title. But the title is given in Baptism, and that is why the Church can declare her belief that infants baptized and dying before they commit actual sin are undoubtedly saved.

Then he considers Gorham's assertion that the burial service contains statements which cannot be regarded as other than a charitable hope, and that therefore it is legitimate to treat passages in the baptismal offices in the same manner. The judge declares that this is no argument in support of Gorham's contention. Nothing more is expressed in the burial service than "hope" that the deceased will partake of the resurrection; the body is committed to the ground "in sure and certain hope of the resurrection to eternal life". The Church must necessarily assume that God has taken the deceased "unto Himself": that in whatever state he was, God has taken him from this world into a world where there is no possibility of committing sin. We pray that we may rest in Christ "as our hope is this our brother doth". The judge does not admit that in the burial service there is any positive declaration on which Gorham can base his argument.

Then there was Gorham's claim that the Articles were not to be construed by the Formularies but vice versa. It was argued that when a clergyman is required to declare his assent to the Articles and to the Book of Common Prayer it was not in the same terms in each case. Whereas he was required to declare the Articles to be "agreeable to the Word of God", in the case of the Prayer Book he declares "his unfeigned assent and consent to the *use*" only of that book, as containing "nothing contrary to the Word of God".[1] The judge decided that this difference of wording cannot indicate that a different standard of truth is applied to the Prayer Book from that which is applied to the Articles.

The judge next gave his attention to another point which was

---

[1] Gorham does not draw attention to the word "use" in his original answer to the Bishop of Exeter. This point must then, presumably, have been brought up for the first time before the Court of Arches (see Bayford, p. 78).

not raised by Gorham in the original Examination, and which was raised by his counsel before this court presumably for the first time. The contention was that the English reformers were Calvinists, and therefore could not have held the doctrine of baptismal regeneration. This point was made, it seems, after a successful refutation, as the judge admitted, of a plea by the Bishop's counsel that Cranmer had never changed his opinions with respect to baptism. The Bishop's counsel had presumably argued that Cranmer's earlier views on Baptism were what they ever were. At all events the judge allowed that the principles of Calvin did make considerable advances in England; but he seriously questioned whether the doctrine of predestination was held so firmly by those who framed the Articles and Service Books in the reign of Edward VI as to exclude baptismal regeneration from their minds. Gorham's counsel had apparently given the opinion that the XVIIth Article determined the question. The judge, however, decided that by this article the Church decided nothing with respect to predestination and election; it is said that it is "full of sweet, pleasant, and unspeakable comfort to godly persons", but with respect to "carnal persons", for them "to have continually before their eyes the sentence of God's predestination is a most grievous downfall, whereby the devil doth thrust them either into desperation or into wretchlessness of most unclean living, no less perilous than desperation". It appears that Gorham's counsel allowed that this particular question was left open in this article by the reformers, but asserted that it was left open for the purpose of inducing as many people as possible to sign the Articles. The judge said he could not adopt this opinion—if the reformers had entertained the doctrines of absolute predestination and election they could not but have expressed themselves in the plainest language.

The judge then quoted from the 6th and 7th articles of the Synod of Dort on predestination, and said that Cranmer and Ridley could not have held this doctrine at the same time as having a share in the preparation of the Baptismal Offices and the Confirmation service in the Prayer Book of Edward VI. Even if the reformers expressed different views privately, the judge insisted that it was his duty to be guided by the public declarations in the Offices of the Church. It is true, the judge allowed, that there was a considerable influx of Calvinistic thought into this country with the return of the clergy from Germany after the death of Queen Mary; but even so, such thought can only be held to be that of private individuals—not in any way committing the Church as a whole.

Peter Martyr and Martin Bucer may, the judge observed, have gone so far as to say that faith and repentance are necessary in all cases to receive the benefit of Baptism; but Cranmer cannot be held responsible for everything they taught and said, although he did consult them in reference to the first service book of Edward VI. The judge questioned whether even the German reformers adhered to the doctrine of predestination for any length of time, quoting from Burnet's *History of the Reformation*:

The Germans soon saw the ill effects of this doctrine; Luther changed his mind about it, and Melancthon openly writ against it. And since that time, the whole stream of Lutheran churches has run the other way. Both Calvin and Bucer were still for maintaining the doctrine of these decrees; only they warned the people not to think much of them, since they were secrets which men could not penetrate into; but they did not so clearly show how those consequences did not flow from such opinions. Hooper and many other good writers did often dehort the people from entering into these curiosities; and a caveat to that same purpose was put afterwards into the article of the Church about predestination.[1]

Speaking generally of Gorham's quotations from writers of the period of the Reformation,[2] the judge said that it must be admitted that many of them were men of great learning; but in spite of that fact, there were writers equally eminent who expressed contrary opinions. If the Articles are silent on any point, he must look to the Services which were confirmed by Act of Parliament and adopted by convocation, rather than to opinions expressed by private individuals.

The judgment ends with the opinion that the points referred to are sufficient for a decision against Gorham; the doctrine of the Church of England is that children baptized are regenerated at Baptism. Gorham maintains opinions opposed to the doctrines of that Church of which he professes himself a member and a minister. The Bishop therefore has shown sufficient cause why he should not institute Gorham to the vicarage of Brampford Speke, and is entitled to be "dismissed with costs".

[1] Vol. II, p. 234 (Oxford Edition, 1829).

[2] In the original Examination before the Bishop of Exeter; in the footnotes of *The Efficacy of Baptism*; and also, presumably, in his defence before this Court.

CHAPTER IV

THE BISHOP'S CASE BEFORE
THE JUDICIAL COMMITTEE

EVEN after the decision of the Court of Arches, Gorham remained convinced that his doctrine of Baptism was tenable within the Church of England, and so he appealed to the final court of appeal in ecclesiastical matters, the Judicial Committee of the Privy Council. In order to see how Gorham's views ultimately became legally and officially declared to be in keeping with the doctrines of the Church of England, we must now examine the proceedings before this court. Just as when the Court of Arches decided against Gorham, Bayford's speech in support of him was published, so as to present a balanced view to the public at each stage, so now when the Privy Council vindicated him, there emerged from the press the speech of Mr. Edward Badeley, Barrister, on behalf of the Respondent, the Bishop of Exeter. Mr Badeley's speech was delivered before the Judicial Committee of the Privy Council on Monday and Tuesday, December 17th and 18th 1849, and it was published with an introduction by Mr Badeley himself in 1850.[1]

Mr Badeley began by drawing attention to the extreme importance of the decision which the present court was called upon to reach. It involved, he said, that adherence of the Church to primitive doctrine and to Catholic truth, which must be, beyond aught else, the "Articulus stantis vel cadentis ecclesiae". He said he believed the decision of the Court of Arches to be right, both as to the principles upon which it was founded and their application to Gorham's case. He pleaded the learning, ability, care and experience of the judge in the court below, lest his judgment should easily be set aside. "We have no right and no power," he said, "to put any interpretation of our own upon any doctrine which the Church has declared: the Clergy generally as well as the lay members of the Church of England,

---

[1] *Substance of a speech delivered before the Judicial Committee of the Privy Council,* by Edward Badeley. Badeley was a distinguished ecclesiastical lawyer who had espoused the tractarian cause. He was associated with the leaders of the high church party who drew up resolutions to the effect that the Judgment should be disowned by the Church of England. When no such action was taken he, with Manning and others, seceded to the Church of Rome.

are estopped from denying that anything is the doctrine of Scripture, if the Church of England has so declared it".[1] He goes on to insist that the Articles and the Prayer Book are to be looked at concurrently—"if either be not sufficiently clear, or need any explanation, the explanation must be sought from the other". It is erroneous, he maintains, to assert that Liturgies and authorized Forms of Prayer are not to be taken as indications of the belief of a Church. He quotes the doctrinal language of the proper preface for Trinity Sunday in the Office of Holy Communion. Badeley cites other instances of doctrinal expressions in the services of the Church, and then quotes Jeremy Taylor:

Public forms of Prayer are great advantages to convey an article of faith into the most secret retirements of the spirit, and to establish it with a most firm persuasion and to endear it to us with the greatest affection. . . .[2]

At this point Sir James Knight-Bruce, one of the judges present, interjected a question—"Does Taylor use the maxim, 'Lex orandi est lex credendi'?" Apparently Dr Addams, the Bishop's advocate in the court below, had cited this maxim in his argument. Badeley replied that he did not know Taylor used it, but he quoted from some "Capitula" or "Decreta" which he said were "of a very early date, not later than the fourth or fifth century"—"obsecrationum quoque sacerdotalium sacramenta respiciamus, quae, ab Apostolis tradita, in toto mundo et in omni Ecclesia Catholica uniformiter celebrantur, *ut legem credendi lex statuat supplicandi*".[3] He gives his opinion that it is from this source that the maxim has been derived, and adds, "Thus . . . we have the testimony of the early church to the connection of doctrine with devotion". To the same effect he quoted Selden— "To know what was generally believed in all ages, the way is to consult the Liturgies, not any private man's writing".[4] Of course, he wanted the question at issue to be settled by appeal to liturgies and he points out that whereas his opponents emphasized Canon XXXVI of 1603, which declares the necessity of assent to the "use" of the Book of Common Prayer, the Act of Uniformity of Charles II insists upon "unfeigned assent and consent to all and everything contained and prescribed in and by the book. . . ."

[1] *Ibid.*, pp. 5, 6.   [2] *Works*, ed. Bishop Heber, Vol. VII, p. 375.

[3] Harduin's *Councils*, Vol. I, p. 1,257.

[4] *Table Talk*—but was Selden talking simply of Liturgies as opposed to individual opinions? It is doubtful if Badeley is justified in quoting this in support of Liturgies as opposed to Articles, which is what in effect he is doing, although not explicitly.

He also referred to the first Act of Uniformity, that of Edward VI, which enforced the 1549 Prayer Book. While admitting that the book of 1662 had many important differences from that of 1549, he asserted that with respect to Baptism there was no substantial variation in any edition of the book; and he drew attention to an expression in the first section of the Act of Edward VI:

. . . one convenient and meet order, rite, and fashion of Common and Open Prayer and Administration of the Sacraments to be had and used in his Majesty's realm of England and Wales. The which at this time, by the aid of the Holy Ghost, with one uniform agreement, is of them concluded, set forth, and delivered to his Highness, to his great comfort and quietness of mind, in a book entituled "The Book of Common Prayer and Administration of the Sacraments and other Rites and Ceremonies of the Church, after the use of the Church of England".

Here was a belief, Badeley affirmed, that those who drew up the Prayer Book did so by the aid of the Holy Ghost, who, they trusted, had led them to formulate the book in a manner consistent with true religion and with the usage of the primitive Church. He quoted the statute of the 5th and 6th, Edward VI, Chapter I, to the same effect. This spoke of the Prayer Book as ". . . agreeable to the Word of God and the Primitive Church, very comfortable to all good people desiring to live in Christian conversation, and most profitable to the estate of this realm. . . ."[1] Similarly, Elizabeth's Act of Uniformity spoke of the suspension of the book in the reign of Mary as "to the great decay of the due honour of God, and discomfort to the professors of the truth of Christ's religion". Charles II's Act of Uniformity speaks of the Prayer Book in the same manner as "agreeable to the Word of God and usage of the primitive Church". All this, Badeley argues, means authorization of the Prayer Book by the Legislature not merely as a form of devotion, but as a doctrinal document. He maintained that any clergyman preaching doctrine contrary to anything contained in the Prayer Book would be open to prosecution according to the Laws Ecclesiastical of the realm, without referring at all to any one of the Thirty Nine Articles. The two, in his mind, stand on equal footing. "The Church and the State

---

[1] When Lord Campbell, another of the judges, interjected that the Prayer Book of Edward VI underwent very important alteration later, Badeley did not deny this, although he said that there was no alteration of the doctrine of Baptism. But these sonorous phrases of the statutes apply to the whole book, not merely to the passages on Baptism: they presumably apply to passages which it was thought necessary to alter later.

have alike promulgated both, and given them equal sanction".[1]

But Badeley went further even than this, and claimed for the Prayer Book authority superior to that of the Articles, since it was the later confirmed by the Legislature. He appealed to the rule of law for the construction of statutes, that if two are in conflict the later in time must prevail and override the former. He then quoted from the 51st Canon of 1603, which censures anyone who "shall publish any Doctrine either strange or disagreeing from the Word of God, or from any of the Articles of Religion agreed upon in the Convocation House, Anno 1562, or from the Book of Common Prayer. . . ." Again, he quotes from Canon 57 with special reference to the doctrine of Baptism: "forasmuch as the Doctrine both of Baptism and the Lord's Supper is so sufficiently set down in the Book of Common Prayer to be used at the administration of the said Sacraments, as nothing can be added unto it that is material and necessary, we do require and charge &c. . . ." He quotes in support of the Prayer Book generally from Canon 73, and from Canon 59 with respect to the Catechism. As regards the Catechism, too, he draws attention to Bishop Burnet's remark that "the Catechism is the most solemn declaration of the Doctrines of the Church of England".[2]

Badeley next proceeded to an attack on the Articles of a kind that we have not hitherto met is this controversy. He admits the force of Gorham's phrases such as "severely rigid standard of doctrine" in relation to the Articles so long as the Articles do "clearly and explicitly and completely" enunciate the doctrine on any particular point of theology. But there are many of the Articles, he says, which have not the severe precision which Gorham ascribes to them. He quotes from the XXVth Article: "Those five, commonly called Sacraments, that is to say, Confirmation, Penance &c., are not to be counted for Sacraments of the Gospel, being such as have grown partly of the corrupt following of the Apostles, partly are states of life allowed in the Scriptures". Of Confirmation Badeley says there can be no dispute that it is a most solemn rite binding on the Church following the example of the Apostles, to which the Church is committed by the Act of Uniformity, the Rubric, the Canons and the general law of the Church. Yet if the doctrine of Confirmation were made to rest on the Articles it would only be concluded that it was a result of "the corrupt following of

[1] *Op. cit.*, p. 21.　　[1] *Pastoral Care*, quoted by Badeley, *op. cit.*, p. 24.

the Apostles", for it is clearly not a "state of life". At this point
Baron Parke, another of the judges, interjected, "It does not
state that the two parts include the whole. It only says they are
partly one and partly the other; not that the two parts embrace
the whole". In his reply to this observation of Baron Parke,
Badeley makes his point more precisely:

> But the Article makes no exceptions; it embraces all the five
> ordinances under the two descriptions; and I submit that, according
> to the ordinary rules of interpretation Confirmation would have to
> range itself either under one or under both of these: at all events, it
> seems to be a very strange and very loose mode of dealing with a
> solemn Apostolic rite, which is undoubtedly binding upon all the
> members of the Church, but yet may be thought to be condemned.
> This, at least, has been contended to be the case with respect to
> Extreme Unction, and the Article does not distinguish between them.

And he goes on to point out what he thinks are other instances
of lack of care and precision in the framing of the Articles. In
the same Article (XXV) there is the declaration, "The Sacraments were not ordained of Christ to be gazed upon, or to be
carried about, but that we should duly use them". These words
can, he says, only properly be applied to the Lord's Supper.
Who ever thought of "carrying about" the water of Baptism?
And as to "gazing upon" the Sacrament of Baptism, this seems
to be the very thing which is encouraged in the rubric before the
Office of Public Baptism—"Baptism should not be administered
but upon Sundays and other Holidays, when the most number
of people come together. . . ." Next he goes on to the XIth
Article, which says, "wherefore that we are justified by faith
only is a most wholesome doctrine, and very full of comfort. . . ."
Badeley says on this, "this expression of 'being justified by faith
only' occurs only once in the whole of the New Testament,
and there it is used to contradict it". The passage is "Ye see
then, how that by works a man is justified, and not by faith
only" (James ii. 24).[1] The Article incorporates the Homily of
Justification (which, however, is wrongly entitled)[2] which
expresses more fully the very doctrine which is only mentioned
in Scripture to be condemned. Badeley then expresses the opinion
that the Articles were framed rather to meet the controversies
of the day than to form part of a complete code of doctrine;

[1] Perhaps this particular point is of more importance in Badeley's whole argument
than he indicated at the time.
[2] See p. 40, *supra*.

they are explicit and clear in their expression of subjects which were then being controverted with the Roman Church, but doctrines which then excited little or no attention were left largely unnoticed and unexplained. There are many important doctrines, (he mentions those of the office of the Holy Ghost and the existence of the Devil) which, if a clergyman were to deny, it would be impossible to proceed against him on the basis of the Articles alone; these doctrines could be substantiated from the Prayer Book but not from the Articles. Apart from the preaching of the ministers the Prayer Book is the chief source of doctrine for the people; with some few exceptions the Laity generally have nothing to do with the Articles.

Having then, as he supposes, triumphantly proved the equal status of the Prayer Book and the Articles as evidence of doctrine—although he has once claimed a higher authority for the former—Badeley proceeds with his argument that the official documents of the Church of England declare the unconditional spiritual regeneration of infants in and by the Sacrament of Baptism. He begins with the Articles, saying that even in these there is more than sufficient to prove that what he is contending for is the doctrine of the Church of England.

He quotes from the Latin of Article XXV—"Sacramenta . . . certa quaedam testimonia, et efficacia signa gratiae, atque bonae in nos voluntatis Dei, per quae invisibiliter Ipse in nos operatur, nostramque fidem in se non solum excitat, verum etiam confirmat". He points out the difference in the language of the Fathers between the words "signum" and "signaculum", saying that in their usage "signum" has a stronger meaning than our word "sign"; "signaculum" is used for a mere outward ordinance, for example circumcision, but "signum" has the sense of the effective operation of direct spiritual agents. He quotes from St Zeno, the fourth-century Bishop of Verona who, speaking of Baptism, says ". . . hoc Spiritus Sancti non signaculo, sed signo censemur".[1] Our XXVth Article says that Sacraments are "efficacia signa gratiae"; and if anyone asks of what Baptism is the "efficax signum" he has only to turn to Article XXVII where he is told that it is "signum regenerationis". Not a word is said about prevenient grace, but by the use of the word "signum" it is expressly declared that regeneration is conferred by this Sacrament. Upon those who rightly receive it, the benefit of this sacrament is conferred immediately on reception; neither

[1] Lib. I, Tract XIII, xi.

here nor in the case of the Lord's Supper is there any question of the grace being subsequent or prior.

Then in connexion with the Baptism of infants, Badeley goes on to say that in the terms of the Article there are two classes of persons only—those who receive "worthily" and those who receive "unworthily": there is no third class of receivers. Inasmuch as the Article advocates the continuance of the Baptism of infants, it must be understood that they were considered as belonging to the former class. Therefore, infants receive at once the full benefit of the Sacrament—spiritual regeneration. The infant cannot possibly be an unworthy receiver, if his Baptism "cum Christi institutione optime congruat". Badeley shows that he regards "worthy" as meaning the absence of obstacle, for he says "there is therefore in his case no hindrance or drawback at all; and if there is not, then the benefits are conveyed immediately".[1] From this he goes on to say that he knows of no regeneration in the Articles except by Baptism, so "baptized" and "regenerated" are convertible terms; in the Latin "regenerati", "renati" and "baptizati" are equivalents.[2] He reinforces his argument by quoting from the 16th Article, but in this he adds little to what he has said before.

It will be seen that Badeley never directly faces the challenge of Gorham's arguments against the identification of "regeneration" and "Baptism" in the Articles, nor does he even allude to the points which Gorham makes. But upon these pleadings he claims to have demonstrated that the Articles alone do teach Baptismal regeneration unconditionally. He then turns to the Prayer Book, saying that even if it were not admitted that the Articles settled the matter beyond doubt, there—in the Prayer Book—the doctrine is clear and indisputable.

There is no need to set out Badeley's arguments from the Prayer Book. The Bishop of Exeter and Sir Herbert Jenner Fust have used them all before him. He adds little to the previous presentations of this case. Of the exhortations after the gospel in the office of Public Baptism he says that it considers infants as at once, from their mere infancy, from their innocence and helplessness, the proper subjects of Baptism. The Office of Private Baptism demonstrates, he argues, that sponsors are not of the essence of Baptism—nor is the signing with the sign of the cross. All that is essential is the element of water and the use of the proper words. Badeley, however, is the first in this controversy

[1] Op. cit., p. 44.   [2] Cf. Gorham's arguments, p. 43, supra.

to say explicitly not merely that infants are equally qualified with "worthy" adults, but that in their case a different standard of qualifications is accepted. He says, "The Church . . . justifies the bringing of infant children to be baptized, considering that their mere helplessness and freedom from actual sin authorizes them to be admitted to the Christian covenant, and that no further qualification is requisite. This differs entirely from the case of adults; they being required to have 'faith and repentance'; graces which infants cannot have".[1] But he does not completely close the door to conditions for infant baptism, for he allows the Augustinian theory that infants are received "on the faith of the Church",[2] or "on the faith of those that bring them" as Badeley puts it.[3] As regards adult Baptism, Badeley allows that in this case the receiving of the grace is conditional upon the existence of faith and repentance in the party; but he insists again that the grace is spiritual regeneration, nothing less.

When he came to the Catechism, Badeley brought up a new point. There had apparently been some argument in the course of the hearing about the punctuation of the answer on Sacraments. Some editions of the Prayer Book had "An outward and visible sign of an inward and spiritual grace, given unto us, ordained by Christ", while others omitted the comma between "grace" and "given"—thus, it was held, indicating a different meaning. But Badeley quoted from the Latin Prayer Books of 1733 and 1768, also from a Greek version of 1666, also from a French version (1616) and a Spanish translation (1715), all showing clearly that "given unto us" agreed with "grace" and not with "sign". Throughout he is arguing from the point of view that infancy is a qualification for reception of baptismal grace, inasmuch as it presents no "obex" to its operation.

He quotes from the Homily of Common Prayer and Sacraments:

For although absolution hath the promise of forgiveness of sin, yet by the express word of the New Testament it hath not this promise annexed and tied to a visible sign, which is imposition of hands. For this visible sign (I mean laying on of hands) is not expressly commanded in the New Testament to be used in absolution, as the visible signs of Baptism and the Lord's Supper are; and therefore absolution is no such sacrament as Baptism and the Communion are.

---

[1] *Op. cit.*, p. 57.   [2] Augustine, Ep. 98, 5.

[3] This seems to go rather ill with his statement above that sponsors are not of the essence of Baptism.

F

He uses this passage as an argument that whereas sacramental absolution has not of necessity a visible sign, the graces of Baptism and Communion are inseparable from their outward signs.

Then in answer to a question of Lord Campbell as to "prevenient grace", Badeley gave a spirited repudiation of Gorham's doctrine on this point. He said " 'prevenient grace' is not mentioned in the Articles, in the Formularies, or in the Catechism; we know nothing about it; . . . the doctrine on the subject in Mr Gorham's book does not appear to me to be Roman, or Anglican, or Catholic, or Protestant, or anything else".[1]

Lord Campbell interrupted Badeley's speech at this point to ask him what was the difference between his argument and the "opus operatum" of the Roman Catholic Church. His answer was that he conceived that the term "opus operatum" was one that had been very much misunderstood. He held that at the Reformation many writers used the term with different meanings. By some it was understood as though the outward act conferred grace independently of the Divine Agency, by others as meaning that the Sacraments conferred grace through the act of the minister rather than through the operation of the Holy Spirit. He alleged that Bishop Barlow and most of our divines regarded the doctrine of "opus operatum" as meaning that the Sacraments conferred grace on those who were capable of faith and good dispositions, but still did not possess them—"sine bono motu utentis". But of course this question could not have any reference to the case of infants who were not capable of faith and good dispositions. The doctrine of the Baptismal regeneration of all infants was not derived from the Schoolmen, and, he held, formed no ingredient in the controversy respecting grace "ex opere operato". The Article of 1552 on Sacraments excluded the doctrine of "opus operatum"—pointing only to the case of adults, the only case to which it could have any application, so Badeley held. He submitted that the omission of any mention of the doctrine in the corresponding article of 1562 indicated that the Church of England finally declined to condemn the doctrine even in relation to adults.

Lord Campbell observed that as far as he could see in Badeley's view there was no difference between the doctrine of the Church of England and that of the Church of Rome on Infant Baptism. Badeley assented—at least so far as concerned the aspects of the

[1] *Op. cit.*, p. 66.

doctrine under discussion. When asked by Dr Lushington what he understood by "due performance" of the rite, Badeley mentioned the necessity of water and the threefold formula, but would not enter into a discussion on intention; he pointed out that the Prayer Book (Private Baptism of Infants) only enquired into matter and words. He left the matter where the Prayer Book left it. He held that the word "recte" in the phrase "recte baptismum suscipientes" in the Latin of Article XXVII had the primary meaning of the proper outward performance of the rite. The word "digne" might have meant something else; but that word was not used.

The next question to be raised was that of baptized infants dying before they commit actual sin. Badeley held that Gorham qualified the doctrine of the Church on this point a good deal. Gorham's meaning he took to be that infants so dying were regenerated, not by their Baptism, but by an act of prevenient grace received prior to their baptism;[1] their death was evidence of their having received this prevenient grace, and having died in a regenerated state. The doctrine of the Church, on the other hand, Badeley held, is that these children are saved by reason of their Baptism.

Lord Campbell then said, "It would appear that both sides agree, that all children that are baptized are in a state of grace . . .[2] the issue seems to be, whether *that* is produced simply by the act of Baptism, or whether it is produced by the grace of God being communicated *at* the time of Baptism, or *before* Baptism". Badeley of course claimed that from the earliest times the Church had taught that the grace was tied to the Sacrament. If the child is a "worthy" recipient it must receive the grace immediately, otherwise there was no telling when it received it[3] and no assurance that it would ever receive it. If the child was an "unworthy" recipient then it receives the Sacrament to its damnation (Article XXV)—and this was an idea too horrible to conceive.

Badeley's chief objection to the theory that the grace of the Sacrament of Baptism remains inoperative until faith exists in the subject is on the grounds that it seems to him to imply some

---

[1] See Gorham's opinion set out on p. 18, *supra*.

[2] It is surely a big assumption to say that Gorham would assent to this. See p. 18, *supra*.

[3] But it can be assumed on Gorham's system that as soon as faith and repentance are manifested there may be assurance that the grace of the sacrament has followed. Gorham does not postulate any other condition remaining to be fulfilled.

goodness in the child which could operate upon the Sacrament and so render it effective, rather than that the Sacrament operates upon him or conveys to him the seeds of grace. But any such idea of goodness existing in the subject in the first place is emphatically excluded by Gorham.[1] Badeley presses his point by asking questions about the foreknowledge of God. "If the foreknowledge of God is to apply in the one case, why not in the other? If the Baptism of the infant is to confer grace and regeneration, only because the Almighty foresees that he will, at some distant date, acquire a right frame of mind, why is that of the adult, who is ultimately to fall away, to put him into a state of grace?" All this seems to be bringing in questions on which the Church does not declare her mind, and which Gorham would have been prepared to say that he was ready to leave unanswered.[2] Badeley claims that the only way to avoid getting into such mazes of doubt and difficulty is to construe the language of the formularies in its plain and literal sense. What, he asks, is to be the reaction of a congregation, which sees plain language in the services, and yet receives an interpretation so different from the clergyman?

Badeley allows the existence of conditions in the Marriage Service, and in Adult Baptism, and he allows that the words of the Burial Service are based on hope—because in each case the conditions are explicit in the service. But in the case of Infant Baptism no trace of mere "hope" or any doubt whatever is expressed.

He makes a great point out of the clause in Article XXV which says that those who receive the Sacraments unworthily receive them to their damnation. If Gorham's theory of prevenient grace be correct, how is a parent to know beforehand whether a child has prevenient grace or not—that is whether when it is brought to the font it will there receive grace or damnation? Will parents bring their children to be baptized on the chance of receiving grace when they know that the alternative is so disastrous? And yet the Church encourages parents to bring

---

[1] See p. 29, *supra*, and p. 21, where he says "he 'confirms' the 'Faith' which he had previously implanted in us". Also p. 26—" 'Faith' is not of ourselves, it is the gift of God".

[2] It also assumes that Gorham thinks grace *is* given at the time of the administration of the sacrament, but remains inoperative until the conditions are fulfilled. It is more likely that Gorham would have said that grace was not received until the conditions were fulfilled, but he nowhere clearly pronounces on this. That is, he nowhere gives an answer to this specific question, though he says "no spiritual grace is conveyed in Baptism, except to worthy recipients", p. 18, *supra*.

their children![1] If they are not baptized, they may not even receive Christian burial, according to the rubric in the office for the Burial of the Dead. Badeley takes care to safeguard himself against implying that because he believes that the grace of regeneration is given in Baptism therefore he believes that the grace of final perseverance is also given.

Badeley next declares his intention of appealing to antiquity to prove that Baptismal Regeneration of Infants is a doctrine of the Church of England. He conceives himself to be justified in making this appeal, rather than referring to the writings of the reformers themselves, inasmuch as this was the method of those who took part in the Reformation and finally settled our Articles and Formularies. "They were fully conscious, that if they attempted to alter the Church any otherwise than according to its ancient model, it would crumble to pieces altogether, and probably bury them in its ruins".[2] He quotes from Jewel's Apology—". . . Inde enim putavimus instaurationem petendam esse, unde prima religionis initia ducta essent. . . ."[3] In the Preface to the Prayer Book, in the Articles and in the Homilies, there are frequent references to the Fathers and the Primitive Church. There was no intention at the time of the Reformation to depart from the doctrine of the early Church; the early Fathers, therefore, will give us certainty, he maintains, where the writings of the Reformation period leave any doubt.

But before Badeley was able to begin his appeal to the Primitive Church he was asked by Dr Lushington whether when he said that "Regeneration" and "Baptism" were convertible terms he meant that there could be no such thing as Regeneration independent of Baptism. He replied that the words were frequently used as convertible terms by the early fathers. Dr Lushington then asked whether in the case of an adult, if he was baptized not having faith and repentance, and yet afterwards came to have faith and repentance, his Baptism conferred regeneration at the time of its administration. Badeley said that in this case he would hold that regeneration took place at the time of the administration of the sacrament. When pressed by Dr Lushington as to whether this would not be contrary to the doctrine of the

---

[1] At first sight these arguments seem very cogent, but Gorham's answer, no doubt, would be that receiving Baptism unworthily would not add to the damnation to which a person is already destined unless he comes to faith.

[2] *Op. cit.*, p. 97.

[3] *Apologia Ecclesiae Anglicanae*, Parker Society, p. 42.

Church of England which demanded the conditions, he made what seems to be a purely arbitrary distinction—"The adult would not receive the full benefit of the Sacrament; he would not receive remission of sin: but regeneration, as I understand the doctrine of the Church, he would receive".[1]

Badeley referred to the canons of 1571[2] and to direction by the Lords of the Council to the Bishops in 1582[3] as supporting his appeal to the early fathers. He cites two writers of the English Church who have examined the works of the early fathers in respect of Infant Baptism: Wall (*On Infant Baptism*, 1705), and Bingham (*The Antiquities of the Christian Church*, 1708). Wall adduces passages from the Fathers to show that infant baptism was a practice of the primitive church; but Badeley asserts that his extracts go further than this and show that the fathers believed that the effect of the sacrament on infants was such as he himself had stated. He begins with a quotation from Hermas which he conceives to demonstrate that the writer held Regeneration to be the immediate result of the Sacrament:

Necesse est, inquit, ut per aquam habeant ascendere, ut requiescant. . . . Antequam enim accipiat homo nomen Filii Dei, morti destinatus est: at ubi accipit illud sigillum, liberatur a morte, et traditur vitae. . . .[4]

Also from Justin Martyr:

. . . Then we bring them to some place where there is water; and they are regenerated by the same way of regeneration by which we were regenerated: for they are washed with water in the name of God, the Father and Lord of all things, and of our Saviour Jesus Christ, and of the Holy Spirit.[5]

He makes similar quotations from Irenaeus,[6] Clement of Alexandria,[7] Origen,[8] Cyprian,[9] Gregory Nazianzen,[10] Zeno,[11]

[1] *Op. cit.*, p. 99.

[2] "Imprimis vero videbunt, ne quid unquam doceant pro concione, quod a populo religiose teneri et credi velint nisi quod consentaneum sit doctrinae Veteris aut Novi Testamenti, quodque ex illa ipsa doctrina Catholici Patres et veteres episcopi collegerint". Liber Quorundam Canonum 1571, De Concionatoribus, Cardwell, *Synodalia*, p. 126.

[3] "You shall call for the interpretation of the old Doctors, such as were before Gregory I, for that in his time began the first claim of the supremacy of the Patriarch of Constantinople, and shortly afterwards was usurped by the Bishop of Rome". Brett *On Tradition*, ch. 1.

[4] Hermas, Lib. 3, Similitud 9, c. 16.   [5] Apol. i, 61, trans. Wall, Vol. I, ch. 2.
[6] *Contra Haeres*, lib. 2, c. 22, s. 4.   [7] *Paedag*, i, 6.
[8] 14th Homily on the Gospel of St Luke.   [9] Ep. lxxii, 10.
[10] Oration XL, on Holy Baptism.   [11] 43rd Sermon.

the Council of Carthage 253[1] and the Council of Milevis 416,[2] and particularly Augustine.[3] He quotes from Prosper of Aquitaine as refuting the idea that the doctrine of Baptismal Regeneration is incompatible with the doctrine of Predestination.[4]

Badeley next refers to the ancient liturgies. He quotes from the Apostolic Constitutions,[5] and the Sacramentary of Gelasius.[6] The earliest office expressly for infants from which he quotes is the "Ordo Baptismi Parvulorum" of the Church of Milan,[7] roughly contemporary with the Gelasian Sacramentary. He also cites Syrian and other eastern rites.[8] After this he quotes from the ancient rites of Confirmation, indicating that the prayers in them assume regeneration to have been given in Baptism.[9]

After these quotations from the Fathers and the early liturgies he comes to some passages from Anglo-Saxon writers. He quotes Bede,[10] Archbishop Aelfric[11] and a canon of Archbishop Egbert.[12] Badeley sees the same doctrine in all these places, as also in the Constitutions of Richard, Bishop of Sarum in 1217;[13] similarly the Constitutions of Richard, Bishop of Durham 1220,[14] and he gives several other quotations from the same period: from a Synod of Exeter 1287, a canon of 1306, the "Pupilla Oculi" of 1385, and some others. He also cites Lyndwood.[15] And before coming to the documents of the Reformation he cites the mediaeval English Service Books.

He begins his treatment of the Reformation with a quotation from the "Articles about Religion" of 1536:

. . . it is offered unto all men, as well infants as such as have the use of reason, that by Baptism they shall have remission of sins &c., &c. . . . and be made thereby the very sons and children of God, insomuch as infants dying in their infancy shall undoubtedly be saved thereby, and else not.[16]

---

[1] Harduin's *Councils*, Vol. I, p. 147.   [2] Harduin, *op. cit.*, p. 1,217.

[3] *De Peccat. Mer. et Remiss.* I, 10—Benedictine ed., 1733, Vol. X, p. 7; and also in his Anti-Pelagian treatises, *ibid.*, Vol. X, p. 466.

[4] *Pro. Aug. Responsiones*, II (Aug. Benedict, ed. Vol. X, Appendix, p. 198). Prosper was a disciple of Augustine in the doctrine of predestination.

[5] Book vii, 39.

[6] Quoting from Assemani *Codex liturgicus*, Vol. II. The passage quoted is from the Benedictio Fontis in the Gelasian Sacramentary.

[7] Assemani, Vol. II, p. 43.   [8] *Ibid.*, Vol. II, p. 75.

[9] *Ibid.*, Vol. III, esp. Gelasian Sacramentary.   [10] Comm. on Mark xvi.

[11] See Maskell, *Holy Baptism*, p. 351.   [12] Spelman's *Concilia*, Vol. I, p. 263.

[13] Spelman, Vol. II, p. 141.   [14] Spelman, Vol. II, p. 66.

[15] *Provinciale*, lib. iii, tit. 24.   [16] Lloyd, *Formularies of Faith*, p. 7.

After this quotation, Badeley remarks, "The only alteration which our Church has made since is this; it has not chosen to pronounce that infants cannot be saved without Baptism. . . ."[1] He also quotes passages from *The Institution of a Christian Man* (1537) and *The Necessary Doctrine and Erudition for any Christian Man* (1543) such as we have seen before.[2] This brings him to the question of Cranmer's views, upon which he makes the following observation: ". . . his belief was unsettled upon almost every other question, but upon Baptism he seems to have remained unshaken. I have looked carefully into his works for the purpose of ascertaining this point, and I do not find any evidence of his having departed from the Catholic faith on this Sacrament. . . ."[3] He quoted from "A Sermon on Baptism" in Cranmer's Catechism (1548):

... And so by Baptism we enter into the Kingdom of God. . . . By Baptism the whole righteousness of Christ is given unto us. . . .[4]

Badeley dismisses summarily the possibility that Peter Martyr influenced the opinions of Cranmer, on the ground that he was a Zwinglian and consequently could have found nothing in common with Cranmer on the subject of Baptism. Bucer, however, he quotes in support of a high doctrine of Baptism:

Electum genus Dei, id est, per generationem Baptismi filios Dei factos.[5]

He did not believe that Melanchthon differed from Bucer on Baptism; he denied that these continental theologians who were in touch with Cranmer were Calvinists, but claimed that even if they could be proved to have been so, this was not incompatible with Belief in Baptismal Regeneration: Augustine's position was an example of this, also that of Peter Lombard, Aquinas and Anselm.

If the English reformers had been full Calvinists, Badeley argued, they would surely have expressed their beliefs in the Anglican documents. In the XVIIth Article, for instance, there is nothing inconsistent with the rest; and if the reformers had held their views to be incompatible with the doctrine of baptismal regeneration they would not have allowed the language of the

[1] *Op. cit.*, p. 146.   [2] See pp. 39–40, *supra*.

[3] *Op. cit.*, p. 151. This at least implies that Cranmer, who was responsible for so much of the finally agreed Anglican Formularies &c. *did* depart from the Catholic faith on some matters; whereas elsewhere Badeley has asserted that at the Reformation the Church of England did not so depart. See p. 85, *supra*.

[4] Cranmer's *Catechism*, Oxford, 1829, p. 182.

[5] *Epitome of the Christian's Doctrine and Religion.*

formularies to remain as it is. If they let the Prayer Book stand as it is and really believed in high Calvinism, they were guilty of the grossest hypocrisy. Badeley pointed out that Calvin's first work on predestination—*De Aeterna Dei Predestinatione*—did not appear until 1552, whereas the greater part of our 1552 Articles were prepared in 1551. The Prayer Book of 1549 must, he said, be interpreted in the light of Cranmer's Catechism which appeared in 1548. Cranmer approved the Articles of 1536; those of 1552 and 1562 do not materially differ from them on the subject, so the three sets of Articles may be taken as maintaining the doctrine of Baptismal Regeneration concurrently with the succeeding Prayer Books. Any opinions expressed privately cannot be taken as impairing the consistent statements of the Church's Articles and Offices.

Badeley then quotes from the Baptismal Offices of 1549, saying that not a word is mentioned of "Prevenient Grace"; the child is declared to be, without any qualifications, the proper recipient of the sacrament, and to obtain the whole benefit, Regeneration, Remission of Sin, Sanctification and Adoption, "in" and "by" Baptism, as the Article of 1552 says—"Tanquam per instrumentum". He then gave parallel quotations from the Second Prayer Book (1552). He points out that in this book, in the Office of Private Baptism, the Minister's certification[1] has the additional words "in Baptism" inserted—"is now, by the laver of regeneration *in Baptism*, received. . . ." This, he said, was added with the intention of making even clearer and more positive the faith of the Church on the subject.

Badeley then drew attention to a paper of Cranmer's which has survived,[2] showing that it was due to him that the Articles of 1552 have a fuller exposition of the doctrine of Sacraments than that given in the Augsburg Confession upon which they are largely based. In the former, sacraments are spoke of as "Efficacia signa gratiae per quae Deus invisibiliter operatur in nobis" rather than as merely "Ad excitandam et confirmandam fidem" as in the Augsburg Confession. He also pointed out that the 1552 Article on Baptism is much more definite than the corresponding passage in the Augsburg Confession.

So, he argued, the doctrine remained until the 1562 Articles, in which no change was made on the matter in question. The

[1] It will be remembered that Gorham only allowed the word "certification" or "certificate" to apply to the statement of the form and matter of the Baptism. See p. 33.

[2] Cranmer's *Works*, ed. Jenkyns, Vol. IV, p. 273.

Hampton Court Conference made no change, but after that Conference the passage in the Catechism explaining the effect of the Sacrament of Baptism was added. He then quotes some answers to Nonconformist objections at the Hampton Court Conference. For instance, in dealing with the thanksgiving prayer after Baptism, the Nonconformists objected: "We cannot in faith say, that every child that is baptized is regenerated by God's Holy Spirit; at least it is a disputable point, and therefore we desire it may be otherwise expressed". To this the Commissioners replied:

Seeing that God's Sacraments have their effects, where the receiver does not 'ponere obicem', put any bar against them (which children cannot do); we may say in faith of every child that is baptized, that it is regenerated by God's Holy Spirit; and the denial of it tends to anabaptism, and the contempt of the holy sacrament, as nothing worthy, nor material whether it be administered to children or no.[1]

He gives other such quotations.

Then with reference to the latest revision of the Prayer Book, Badeley brings a new piece of evidence which he considers establishes the supremacy of the Formularies over the Articles as expositions of the Church's doctrine. It is a minute or order of Council dated May 31st 1661:

It was ordered by his Majesty in Council that Mr Attorney-General should forthwith prepare a Commission to authorize the Convocation to consult of matters relating to the settlement of the Church, and not to insert therein the clause or proviso in the words following, nor any other clause or proviso to the like effect: 'Provided always that the said Canons, orders, ordinances, constitutions, matters, and things or any of them, so to be considered, consulted, and agreed upon as aforesaid, be not contrary or repugnant to the Liturgy established, or the Rubric in it, or the nine-and-thirty Articles, or any doctrine, order, or ceremonies of the Church of England already established.[2]

Badeley's comment on this is: "The Articles, therefore, were to be no hindrance to any alterations which might be thought advisable, and we may consequently, with greater reason, regard the Formularies as the true exposition of the Church's doctrine, and the proper commentary upon the Articles; for, while the Articles were left unaltered, the Prayer Book was revised and settled with great care. . . ."

[1] Cardwell, *Conferences*, p. 356.

[2] Bishop Kennett's *Register*, p. 455; also cited by Wilberforce, *The Doctrine of Baptism*, p. 251.

As against the argument that many of those who lived after the Hampton Court Conference entertained high Calvinistic notions, and therefore could not have subscribed to the doctrine of Baptismal Regeneration, Badeley reiterated what he had said earlier about St Augustine, and also quoted Bradford[1] as holding equally Predestination and Baptismal Regeneration. Badeley then made use of the argument which Dr Bayford had used in his turn, that many of the writers of the Reformation period appear to be inconsistent with themselves. For instance, Peter Martyr at the same time as expressing a low doctrine of Baptism also in another place seems to hold the high view.[2]

Of Bullinger's *Decades* which were ordered by Convocation to be read by the clergy,[3] Badeley said that passages in this work were so heretical that even Mr Turner, Gorham's advocate before the present court, did not like to read them. He asserted that Bullinger's *Decades* were never officially authorized by the Church, and suggested that they were simply recommended as notes for preachers who had not had the benefit of a university education—there being a number of such at the time, and very little literature adapted to the use of these persons. He pointed out that at about the same time the dignitaries of the Church were recommended to possess copies of Fox's *Book of Martyrs*,[4] a work which was now generally agreed to abound in falsehoods and inaccuracies.

Badeley drew the attention of the court to the fact that it is stated that at the time of the final revision of the Prayer Book in 1662 about two thousand ministers resigned their benefices on this very point—because the Formularies expressed the doctrine of Baptismal Regeneration so plainly. They did not, he said, seek to twist the language of the Prayer Book to fit their own meaning, but found it clearly contrary to their views.

Badeley then made some quotations from Gorham's book, and claimed that his position was incompatible with the uninterrupted tradition of the Church as he had traced it above. The Bishop of London then questioned Badeley as to whether he denied that there was a promise implied in the very fact of a child receiving Baptism. In reply to this, Badeley said that he admitted that Baptism was "in one point of view a Covenant", but he denied that the promises, ordinarily made by the Sponsors,

---

[1] *Works*, ed. Parker Society, p. 311 and pp. 217–18.

[2] Cf. Bayford's quotations, pp. 52, 53, *supra*.   [3] See p. 56, *supra*.

[4] Liber Quorundam Canonum, 1571, De Episcopis. Cardwell, *Synodalia*, p. 115.

were "ex necessitate". Once again it appears that those of the
Bishop of Exeter's side of this controversy regard absence of
"obex" as sufficient qualification for reception of the grace of
sacraments, and they do not look upon the qualifications as
being positive demands. Badeley says that whereas Gorham
declares the operation of the grace of Baptism to be suspended
until faith and repentance are present, or to be non-existent if
they never supervene, he believes the grace to be conferred in
all cases and to operate unless and until the child eventually
falls away by its own act. Gorham asserts that a disposition must
have been conferred by the Holy Ghost in order for the grace
of Baptism to operate. Badeley says that this is a most presump-
tuous defining of the powers of the Almighty: who is to limit the
use He can make of the Sacrament? Nowhere in the tradition
of the Church is there a word about the necessity of prevenient
grace for due reception of the benefits of Baptism; by his doctrine
Gorham makes the sacrament a mere sign or seal. Arguing on
Gorham's hypothesis is not the child just as unworthy to receive
the prevenient grace as he is to receive Baptism?

Badeley then goes on to a lengthy criticism of Gorham's
answers in the original examination. In most of this there are
no points which we have not already seen before. But it is
interesting to observe that, because Gorham denies regeneration
in Baptism, Badeley, like Jenner Fust,[1] refuses to allow that
Gorham believes in any spiritual grace being conferred by the
sacrament at all. He quotes a question and answer from Gorham's
Efficacy of Baptism.[2] The Bishop had asked what grace was
conferred by Baptism, and Gorham replied ". . . By this sign . . .
He confirms the faith which He had previously implanted in us,
and by which He made us rightly to receive the Sacrament, and
He increases the grace which He had previously given us. . . ."
On this Badeley comments, "But all this represents Baptism as a
mere seal or confirmation of something already given; not as
an active agent, itself the means of grace and remission of sin".
It is unfortunate that Badeley over-simplified Gorham's doctrine
in this way.

It is an illustration of the difficulty felt by the disputing parties
in grasping the points in the controversy, that at this point
Dr Lushington interjected: "Mr Gorham agrees with you,
according to his answer here, as to the effect of infant Baptism
when they die Infants". Gorham would certainly agree that

[1] See p. 65, *supra*.   [2] P. 93; see also p. 21, *supra*.

such infants are "undoubtedly saved", but he would not agree that their salvation was due to Baptism—he would presumably say that their Baptism was a sign of the grace of regeneration already given, and a confirming and increasing of that grace.

Badeley said that Gorham's doctrine of prevenient grace was destructive of the nature of the sacrament and entirely contrary to the whole stream of the Church's doctrine and tradition. He then added that Gorham's doctrine was not merely contradictory of the Church's Articles and Formularies, but also annulled an article of the Nicene Creed—that which professed acknowledgement of "one Baptism for the remission of sins". He quotes Bishop Bull's *Judicium Ecclesiae Catholicae*[1] describing how the writers of the early Church, Irenaeus especially, were concerned to denounce those heretics who denied the doctrine of regeneration and remission of sin in Baptism. Pearson in his work on the Apostles' Creed gave the same view under the article "the forgiveness of sins"—that Baptism was the medium through which forgiveness was obtained.

With this, and a final reference to some cases in which ministers of the Church had been refused admission to benefices solely on the grounds of denial of doctrines in the Prayer Book independently of the Articles, Badeley brought his speech to an end. He commended the question to the decision of the judges, adding his fears that if they reversed the decision of the court below, thousands of the clergy and laity of the Church of England would regard the decision as a sentence of the highest tribunal in the land that the Church had betrayed her trust.

[1] *Works*, Oxford, 1827, Vol. VI, p. 147.

CHAPTER V

SUBSIDIARY SPEECHES BEFORE
THE JUDICIAL COMMITTEE

THE speeches of Dr Bayford before the Court of Arches and of Mr Badeley before the Privy Council are the only pleadings in this case which have been published separately. But as well as these there were presumably subsidiary speeches before both courts. I have been unable to trace any reports of such subsidiary speeches before the Court of Arches; but in view of the length of Sir Herbert Jenner Fust's judgment and Dr Bayford's argument, it is unlikely that such speeches would have contained any points which were not included in them. As regards the case as heard by the Privy Council, there were speeches on behalf of Mr Gorham by Mr Turner and Dr Bayford, and for the Bishop of Exeter by Dr Addams as well as the great speech of Mr Badeley. These speeches have been published at length in *The Case of the Rev G. C. Gorham against the Bishop of Exeter* by E. F. Moore (1852), and in briefer form in *Gorham v. the Bishop of Exeter: a Full Report* (1850). Those defending Gorham said little that had not been already said by Dr Bayford or that was not soon to be said in the Judgment; and Dr Addams added little to what is recorded in Sir H. Jenner Fust's judgment and Badeley's speech. Such points as are made in these subsidiary speeches and do not occur elsewhere are summarized in this short chapter.

Turner said that he was unable to collect from the judgment of the court below what was the opinion of the judge himself as to spiritual regeneration. In one place, he alleges, he speaks of it as a "change of nature", in another as a "change of condition", and in a third place as amounting "almost to justification". He avers that Gorham holds regeneration to be a change of nature and not of condition only.

Turner quotes at length the various statutes enforcing the successive Prayer Books, endeavouring to demonstrate that their object was to establish uniformity in public worship, and not to determine doctrine. He also pointed out that while the VIIIth Article of 1562 declared that the three creeds contained in the Prayer Book are to be received by all, the article purposely avoided reference to the Prayer Book itself. He also gives a long

catena of quotations from Anglican Divines, but adds little to
that of Bayford given in the court below; he gives much the
same arguments as to the statements in the services of the Church
being based upon charitable presumption. He complained that
the judge in the court below was acting on entirely wrong
principles in distinguishing between the doctrine involved in
adult Baptism and that in the case of infants.

Turner resented the attempt to dub Gorham a Calvinist. All
he said was being maintained on behalf of Gorham was that the
framers of the Articles and Formularies would not have done
their work in a way which precluded a Calvinistic interpretation.

Bayford in his short speech before the Privy Council said that
the decision of the court below was against the policy which
the Church of England had consistently adopted since the
Reformation. Heylin says that the liturgy was framed with a
view to admitting of Papists continuing to attend Church.[1]
He did not claim that Gorham's opinion was the only possible
one,[2] and he quoted Heylin in support of the view that the
Articles were drawn up to allow latitude of opinion so far as
this was consistent with peace and charity.[3] Adult Baptism, he
argued, was scarcely known at the time of the framing of the
Articles; the service of Adult Baptism was not drawn up until
1661—a point which seems to have been lost sight of both by
the Bishop and the judge in the court below.

Dr Addams, in his speech on behalf of the Bishop of Exeter,
says little which is not either in the Dean of Arches' judgment
or in Badeley's long speech. He asserts that the passages in
Gregory's Decretals and the Constitutions of Clement quoted
by Bayford[4] do not allow latitude of opinion as to whether
grace was or was not conferred in Baptism, but only as to the
amount or degree of grace given. He gives an interesting opinion
on the question of adults who receive Baptism unworthily,
saying, "no doubt it is by implication the teaching of the Church
that the grace of the sacrament is 'suspended' ".[5]

Addams declares that it cannot be said that it would have
been impossible to draw up baptismal offices which avoided

[1] *History of the Reformation*, Vol. I, p. 153. See also *op. cit.*, Vol. II, p. 285, for similar
comment on the second revision of the Prayer Book.

[2] It is important to observe the change in the Gorhamite claims as they are made
before the Privy Council. Originally it was "Our Church holds, and I hold . . .",
but now it is only claimed that Gorham's view is a tenable one, which may exist
alongside others.

[3] *Op. cit.*, Vol. I, p. 228.   [4] See Bayford, p. 52, *supra*.

[5] Moore, *op. cit.*, p. 285. Contrast Badeley's view on this, pp. 85-6, *supra*.

saying one thing and meaning another. Zwingli, Calvin and John Knox all evolved forms in which not a single sentence implied that spiritual grace was given in Baptism.

After Badeley's speech Turner made a short reply. He denied that Gorham said that regeneration can never be given in Baptism—"He nowhere denies that grace may be conferred in Baptism worthily received, nor that regeneration, by which he understands to mean a new nature, may take place in Baptism".[1]

Turner also added some patristic evidence on Gorham's side which had been rather passed over previously. The most apt of the quotations which he makes is the following from St Basil:

> But faith and Baptism, two means of salvation, are closely connected with each other and inseparable. For faith is perfected by Baptism, and Baptism has its foundation in faith, and both are fulfilled through the same names. For as we believe in the Father, Son, and Holy Spirit, so also we are baptized into the name of the Father, and of the Son, and of the Holy Spirit. And the confession that leads to salvation precedes, but Baptism that puts the seal upon our engagement follows.[2]

[1] Moore, *op. cit.*, p. 445. Cf. my observations on Gorham's language, pp. 173-4, *infra*.
[2] *De Spiritu Sancto*, ch. 12.

CHAPTER VI

THE JUDGMENT OF THE JUDICIAL
COMMITTEE OF THE PRIVY COUNCIL

THE Judicial Committee of the Privy Council met on Friday,
March 8th 1850, and the judgment was given by Lord Langdale.[1]
The Archbishops of Canterbury (Sumner) and York (Musgrave)
and the Bishop of London (Blomfield) attended the hearing of the
appeal; the two Archbishops expressed their approbation of the
judgment, but the Bishop of London did not concur. Sir James
Knight-Bruce also expressed dissent.

Lord Langdale began by giving a brief outline of the circumstances which had led up to the present judgment. He made
the complaint that the court had not been called upon to decide
upon specific propositions distinctly stated, but upon a charge
of unsoundness of doctrine based upon a long series of questions
and answers: questions sometimes abstruse and perplexing, and
answers often not given plainly and directly. The court did not
have before it any precise statement of what the Bishop of
Exeter alleged to be the doctrine of the Church of England
upon the matters in question, nor was there any specific declaration of the doctrine held by or imputed to Gorham and alleged
to be unsound. As before, the only evidence was the original
examination of Gorham by the Bishop embodied in Gorham's
book, *The Efficacy of Baptism*. The counsel on both sides had done
much to assist the court, but they had not been able entirely to
remove the difficulties. Lord Langdale said that in considering
the evidence it was necessary to have regard to the general scope,
object and character of the whole examination rather than only
to the particular question to which each answer is subjoined.
He said he found it difficult to reconcile some of the answers
with each other, but justice required that an endeavour should
be made to reconcile them in such a manner as to obtain the
result which seemed most consistent with the general intention
of Gorham in the exposition of his doctrine and opinions.

The judge said that, adopting this course, the doctrine held by
Gorham appeared to be this:

[1] *Gorham v. Bishop of Exeter. The Judgment of the Judicial Committee of Privy Council,
delivered March 8 1850, reversing the decision of Sir H. J. Fust.*

G

That Baptism is a Sacrament generally necessary to salvation, but that the grace of regeneration does not so necessarily accompany the act of Baptism that regeneration invariably takes place in Baptism; that the grace may be granted before, in, or after Baptism; that Baptism is an effectual sign of grace, by which God works invisibly in us, but only in such as worthily receive it,—in them alone it has a wholesome effect; and that without reference to the qualifications of the recipient, it is not in itself an effectual sign of grace. That infants baptized, and dying before actual sin, are certainly saved; but that in no case is regeneration in Baptism unconditional.

The judge then observed, what it is very important to notice, that the question which the court was called upon to decide was not whether these opinions were theologically sound or unsound, nor whether they were the only opinions upon this matter tenable within the Church of England; but, whether these opinions were contrary or repugnant to the doctrines of the Church of England as expressed in its Articles, Formularies and Rubrics and required to be held by its ministers, and whether upon the ground of these opinions the appellant could lawfully be excluded from the benefice to which he had been presented.

The question, the judge said, must be decided from the Articles and Liturgy. As to the interpretation of these documents, he said, the rules that must be applied were those which by law were applicable to the construction of all written instruments; and he added, "We must endeavour to attain for ourselves the true meaning of the language employed, assisted only by the consideration of such external or historical facts as we may find necessary to enable us to understand the subject-matter to which the instruments relate, and the meaning of the words employed".

The judge observed that there were different doctrines and opinions prevailing and under discussion at the time when the Articles and the Liturgy were framed. But in the interpretation of the Church's documents it is not permissible to be influenced by the particular opinions of the eminent men who had a share in formulating them, nor by the authorities by whom the ideas of the framers were supposed to have been moulded; nor, he added, "by any supposed tendency to give preponderance to Calvinistic or Arminian doctrines". The Articles and the Liturgy must be considered as the final result of the discussions which took place at the time. The judge presumably meant by this that the Articles and the Liturgy must be taken to be the mind of the Church of England on the various doctrinal issues which were being debated—they must not be allowed an interpretation made from the standpoint of one of the parties involved in the general conflict of ideas out of which the Anglican settlement arose.

From the first dawn of the Reformation to the time when the Articles and Formularies of the Church of England were settled, the Church was harassed with a great variety of opinions respecting Baptism. In the Articles the Church aimed at avoiding diversities of opinion and establishing consent touching true religion—to this end it made decisions on points of doctrine upon which it was thought practicable and proper to reach a conclusion. But the Articles were never intended to be an authoritative statement of all Christian doctrine—"other points and other questions were left for future decision by competent authority, and in the meantime to the private judgment of pious and conscientious persons". This being the case, the judge continued, it must be allowed that the framers of the Articles intended such latitude of interpretation as would not imperil any doctrine necessary to salvation—always, of course, assuming that such interpretation was not contradictory of something which the Church has elsewhere allowed or required.

Lord Langdale said that the first and great question which arises in a case such as the present is whether the disputed point is or was meant to be settled at all, or whether it is left open for each member of the Church to decide according to his own conscientious opinion. If there is a doctrine upon which the Articles are silent or ambiguously expressed, it must be supposed that it was intended to be left to private judgment unless the Formularies clearly decide it. But if the Rubrics and Formularies are ambiguous, it cannot be held that the Church intended to declare a point of doctrine indirectly there, which it had failed to declare directly in the Articles.

The judge then pointed out that very different opinions as to the Sacrament of Baptism were held by different promoters of the Reformation, and that great alterations were made in the Articles on the subject. He began with the Articles about Religion of 1536 with their extreme high doctrine that all infants baptized receive remission of sin, and the promise of grace and everlasting life; that unbaptized infants dying in infancy are not saved. Then he went on to the King's Book of 1543 (*A Necessary Doctrine for any Christian Man*) in which the phrase "duly received" begins to appear, and which also speaks of the necessity of infants

being offered "in the faith of the Church". Then he referred
to the Articles of 1552 and 1562 which adopt very different
language from those of 1536 as to the qualification of worthy
and right reception, having special regard to the necessity of
these qualifications. The XXVth Article of 1562 distinctly
states that in such only as worthily receive them do the Sacraments have a wholesome effect or operation. The Article on
Baptism, in describing the benefits conferred by that sacrament,
speaks only of those who receive it rightly; and in the place of
the clear statement of the Article of 1536 that the salvation of
infants depends upon Baptism, the XXVIIth Article of 1562
has no more than its vague and general commendation of the
practice of infant baptism, without any declaration as to the
state of infants, whether baptized or not.

The judge declared that the Articles did not determine what
is signified by right reception, although Gorham said the expression always means or implies a fit state to receive—in the case
of adults "with faith and repentance", and in the case of infants
"with God's grace and favour". Another point which he said
was left undecided by the Articles was the distinct meaning and
effect of the grace of regeneration—whether it is a change of
nature, a change of condition, or a change of the relation between
sinful man and his Creator. That differences on these points
which were left open were thought consistent with subscription
to the Articles is shown, his Lordship added, by the Royal
Declaration added to the Articles in the reign of Charles I,
which said, "even in those curious points in which the present
differences lie, men of all sorts take the Articles of the Church
of England to be for them; which is an argument, again, that
none of them intend any desertion of the Articles established".

From this the judge went on to say that if members of the
Church were left at liberty to draw different inferences in matters
of faith not expressly stated in the Articles, which were drawn
up to be the code of faith, we may reasonably expect such
differences of opinion to be allowable in the interpretation of the
devotional services, which were drawn up not for the purpose
of determining points of faith but of establishing a uniform order
of common prayer. The judge then made a distinction between
different parts of the Prayer Book. There are, he said, parts of
the book which are instructional and parts which are devotional.
The former are to be regarded as dogmatical, declaring what is
to be believed and not doubted, but the latter which are framed

for the purpose of stirring Christian people to the due honouring of God need some further consideration. The judge then pronounced upon a point around which there had been much argument in the course of the controversy. He declared that the formularies cannot be held to be evidence of faith or doctrine without reference to the distinct statements of doctrine in the Articles. This is a final pronouncement that the Formularies are to be interpreted by the Articles and not vice versa. The example which he gave, and said that he regarded as conclusive, was that of the Service for the Burial of the Dead. Of this he said, "So far as our knowledge or powers of conception extend, there are, and must be, at least some persons not excommunicated from the Church, who, having lived lives of sin, die impenitent—nay, some who perish and die in the actual commission of flagrant crimes; yet, in every case in the Burial Service, as the earth is cast upon the dead body, the priest is directed to say, and doth say, 'Forasmuch as it hath pleased Almighty God, of his great mercy, to take unto himself the soul of our dear brother here departed, we therefore commit his body to the ground, earth to earth, ashes to ashes, dust to dust, in sure and certain hope of the resurrection to eternal life'": And then he commented, "In this service, therefore, there are absolute expressions implying positive assertions; yet it is admitted that they cannot be literally true in all cases, but must be construed in a qualified or charitable sense. . . ." In this case, and in other passages in the services, he added, there were devotional expressions involving assertions which cannot be taken to bear an absolute and unconditional sense.

Lord Langdale then proceeded to set out the passages in the Office for Infant Baptism which fell, in his judgment, within the same category. Before the Baptism is actually performed the sponsors are questioned and make their answers, and then comes the prayer that the infant to be baptized may receive the grace of the sacrament—"so firm is the belief expressed that God will favourably receive the infant—so confident is the negation of all doubt but that God favourably alloweth the charitable work of bringing the infant to Baptism". And after the act of Baptism there is the same "undoubting confidence of a favourable reception and allowance". All this, the judge holds, must be construed in a charitable and qualified sense, and cannot with any appearance of reason be taken as proof of doctrine. The conditions entered upon by the sponsors in the case of infants, and by the party himself in the case of an adult, must be considered as the rule of the Church. The emergency allowed for in the Office of Private Baptism cannot be regarded as anything but exceptional. "Any other conclusion would be an argument to prove that none but the imperfect and incomplete ceremony allowed in the exceptional *case would be necessary in any case*".[1]

The conditions of faith and repentance are the rule of the Church—and this view is confirmed by the Catechism. When the question is asked as to why children are baptized when they cannot perform the conditions, the answer given is not that infants qualify by their innocence or cannot present any hindrance to the grace of regeneration, but that sureties make the promises for them. "The answer has direct reference to the condition on which the benefit is to depend".

The allowance of the necessity of the fulfilment of the conditions is a large step in the direction of permitting Gorham's opinions on Baptism. But the judge goes on to allow the theory of the suspended operation of grace: ". . . those who are strongly impressed with the earnest prayers which are offered for the Divine blessing, and the grace of God, may not unreasonably suppose that the grace is not necessarily tied to the rite; but that it ought to be earnestly and devoutly prayed for, in order that it may then, or when God pleases, be present to make the rite beneficial".

The judge then deals with the rubric at the end of the office of Public Baptism to the effect that infants baptized and dying before they commit actual sin are undoubtedly saved. He comments that this rubric does not, like the Article of 1536, say that such children are saved by Baptism. The Article of 1536 says that children dying unbaptized are not saved; the rubric makes no statement on this point. He then goes on to say that there are other points of doctrine respecting the Sacrament of Baptism which are capable of being honestly understood in different senses—points which are left undetermined by the Articles are not decided by the Rubrics and Formularies. Upon such points ministers of the Church, having duly made the subscriptions required by law and taking the Holy Scripture for their guide, are at liberty to exercise their private judgment without offence or censure.

The judge once again emphasized that it was the work of this court to decide whether Gorham's opinions were contrary

[1] For a trenchant criticism of this opinion see p. 150.

or repugnant to the doctrine of the Church of England, upon the true and legal construction of her Articles and Formularies. It was not the function of the court to decide what the doctrine of the Church of England ought to be, and if any Article is really a subject of dubious interpretation it would be highly improper for the court to fix on one meaning or to condemn contrary opinions.

While refusing to rely upon the doctrinal opinions of Anglican writers, however eminent, in the examination of the case, the judge remarked that men of the learning, ability and piety of Jewel, Hooker, Ussher, Jeremy Taylor, Whitgift, Pearson, Carlton, Prideaux,[1] and many others, had been allowed to maintain opinions which cannot in any important particular be distinguished from those of Gorham. The judge then makes four quotations to substantiate this statement:

Jewel says:

This marvellous conjunction and incorporation with God, is first begun and wrought by faith; afterwards the same incorporation is assured to us, and increased by Baptism.[2]

Hooker says:

We justly hold Baptism to be the door of an actual entrance into God's house—the first apparent beginning of life—a seal, perhaps, of the grace of election before received; but to our sanctification, a step which has not any other before it.[3]

Ussher, when asked whether in the baptism of infants the grace of the Sacrament always accompanies the outward sign replies:

Surely, no; the Sacrament of Baptism is effectual only to those, and to all those who belong to the election of grace.[4]

Jeremy Taylor writes:

Baptism and its effect may be separated, and do not always go in conjunction. The effect may be before, and therefore, much rather may it be after its susception: the Sacrament operating in the virtue of Christ, even as the Spirit shall move.[5]

He also drew attention to a circular issued by Whitgift in 1588 enforcing an order made in 1587 whereby every minister under the degree of Master of Arts was required to study

---

[1] See Bayford's evidence, pp. 53, 54 and 57–8, *supra*.
[2] *Treatise on Private Mass*, Parker Society, pp. 140–1.   [3] *Eccl. Polit.*, Bk. V, lx, 3.
[4] *Sum and Substance of the Christian Religion*, p. 415.
[5] *Works*, ed. Bishop Heber,. Vol II, p. 259.

Bullinger's *Decades*. In these it is declared, "The first beginning of our uniting in fellowship with Christ is not wrought by the Sacraments". And it is also said in this work that Baptism seals and confirms to infants what they had before.

In support of his declaration that the statements in the Baptismal Offices about children are suppositions, he quotes Hooker again: "The Church speaks of infants, as the rule of charity alloweth both to speak and to think".[1] And he quotes Pearson, who says: "When the means are used, without something appearing to the contrary, we ought to presume of the good effect".[2] Also he quotes from Carleton who writes: "All that receive Baptism are called the children of God, regenerate, justified; for to us they must be taken for such in charity, until they show themselves other".[3] And Prideaux says: "Baptism only pledges an external and sacramental regeneration, while the Church in charity pronounces that the Holy Spirit renders an inward regeneration".[4]

He adds that the court expresses no opinion on the theological accuracy of these writers; many writers of equal eminence have expressed contrary views, and the authors he has quoted are not always consistent with themselves. Nevertheless he holds that the mere fact that these opinions have been held by men of such eminence is sufficient to show that the opinions come within the liberty allowed by the Articles and Formularies.

Once more pointing out that the Court refrained from expressing any theological opinions of its own, Lord Langdale concluded his judgment by saying that with the exception of Knight-Bruce the Court was unanimous[5] in holding that Gorham's doctrine was not contrary or repugnant to the declared doctrine of the Church of England, and that therefore the judgment of Sir H. Jenner Fust in the Arches Court of Canterbury ought to be reversed.

[1] *Eccl. Polit.* Bk. V, lxiv. In fact this is a slight misquotation: Hooker's phrase is "the rule of piety".

[2] *On the Creed*, commenting on the clause, "the Communion of Saints".

[3] *An Examination of Montague's Appeal*, p. 193.

[4] *Fasciculus Controversiarium Theologicarium*, p. 240.

[5] The Bishops, although present, were not members of the Court.

CHAPTER VII

DR PHILLPOTTS' LETTER TO THE
ARCHBISHOP OF CANTERBURY

THE Judgment was pronounced on March 8th 1850. The Bishop
of Exeter had for some time been preparing for the eventuality
of an adverse decision, and he was expecting that if such a
decision were reached a strong wave of pro-Roman feeling would
be one of the results. Pusey had been supplying him with material[1]
for a letter to the Archbishop of Canterbury which he could
publish if the necessity arose. On March 25th this letter appeared.[2]
Liddon says "Few documents of the kind, since Law's letters
to Hoadley, can rank in importance with this famous Protest.
Deep conviction and common sense, trenchant logic and indignant irony are in their turn brought to bear with triumphant
effect on the judgment of the Judicial Committee". This letter
is of particular importance, since it is the first public statement
which the Bishop of Exeter himself makes in the course of the
controversy as to his own doctrine of Baptism.

Dr Phillpotts begins, "My Lord Archbishop, I address your
Grace under circumstances the most unusual, and with feelings
the most painful. In the whole history of the Church of England
I am not aware that anything of a similar kind has ever before
occurred: that the Primate of all England has ever before thrown
himself upon the judgment of the world as the writer of a
controversial book: if he have, the statements contained in it
must have been so manifestly accordant with the doctrines of
the Church, that they carried with them the universal assent of
Churchmen. Your Grace has been pleased to descend from the
exalted position in which your predecessors were wisely, I think,
content to stand". The Bishop's opening criticism is directed
against the Archbishop's republication of his book, *Apostolical
Preaching*. Dr Sumner's book first came out in 1815; it had run
through several editions, and he published a ninth edition with
a new preface in 1850. The alterations to the book itself, to which
the Bishop of Exeter draws attention, were first made in an
edition of 1817, not in 1850. The Bishop later admitted this and

---

[1] Liddon, *Life of E. B. Pusey*, Vol. III, p. 229.
[2] *A Letter to the Archbishop of Canterbury*, by the Bishop of Exeter.

acknowledged his error. His charges on this score, therefore, are false; but it is interesting to see the accusations which the Bishop of Exeter did in fact make, thinking that the Archbishop of Canterbury had altered his position to justify the part he played in the Gorham case.

Dr Phillpotts observes that the Archbishop says in his new preface that the book as republished is substantially the same as when it first came from his pen. But in Chapter IV—"on Grace"— he points out changes which dilute "what was originally a strong and uniform expression of Catholic Truth". The Bishop then gives a quotation, a passage which he says he rejoices to see remaining in the 1850 edition:

It is indeed sufficient confutation of the doctrine of special grace, that it [absolutely nullifies the Sacrament of Baptism] (These last words are omitted in 1850—still we continue to read "the Bishop says", and rejoice to read—"what follows".) . . . After His Baptism, the descent of the Holy Spirit in visible form was surely intended to confirm His followers in a belief, that their Baptism would confer upon them a similar gift: and, besides the washing away of their sins, and the remission of the penalty entailed upon the posterity of Adam, would bestow upon them power enabling them to fulfil the covenant laws of their religion.[1]

And he proceeds to give more quotations designed to show that a high doctrine of Baptism was not entirely expunged from the Archbishop's 1850 edition. Among them the following (p. 160):

On the authority of this example (that of St Paul, Rom. vi. 3, viii. 15; Gal. iii. 26) and of the undeniable practice of the first ages of Christianity, our Church considers Baptism as conveying Regeneration, instructing us to pray, before Baptism, that the infant "may be born again, and made an heir of everlasting salvation"; and to return thanks, after Baptism, that it hath pleased God to regenerate this infant with his Holy Spirit, and receive him for his own child by adoption.

But he goes on to say that he regrets that passages such as these, although they remain, can hardly continue to express the Archbishop's views on Baptism. The sense of these passages becomes much obscured by some of the new matter which is introduced. For instance, the following (p. 166):

I do not deny, that there may be a danger in addressing a congregation collectively, as regenerate, since the term has neither been

_____
[1] Pp. 176–7. In the 1850 edition Sumner substitutes the words, "reduces Baptism to an empty rite. . . ."

accurately defined in Scripture, nor restricted to one sense in the common language of divines.

The Bishop of Exeter says that in this passage there is startling intimation of His Grace's altered view. Scripture does not fully describe regeneration, but it defines it clearly as a spiritual change. And whereas at one time the Archbishop had said, "the baptized person has his nature amended, and is regenerate by the Spirit"; now he neutralizes the force of such phrases and talks about those who have been "pronounced" regenerate, saying, "Many who have once been pronounced regenerate, have revolted from their baptismal vows. . . ."

Next the Bishop points out some new matter inserted at p. 171:

How many more of them might be saved, if parents and sponsors universally made the baptism of infants a spiritual service, and accompanied it with that prayer of faith. . . .

He says that he would gladly try to interpret this to mean that grace is merely increased by the parents' prayers. But he is unable to do so when he places it alongside the following passage from the Archbishop's *Exposition of the Gospel of St John*:

And so there is reason to believe that he will hear and favour the prayers of all parents who concur in like simplicity of heart and faith. . . . Would to God, my brethren, that this truth were better understood, and this primitive, this Scriptural, this reasonable baptism more generally practised. Then we should not find so many who, though born of water, as far as concerns the baptismal rite, are evidently not made new creatures by the Spirit, who renews and sanctifies the soul.[1]

On this the Bishop comments, "My Lord, I have already said that to require as necessary to the efficacy of the Baptism of Infants that there be faith on the part of those who present them, is little short, if indeed short, of heresy".

The Bishop uses his best polemical style in condemning this view of the Archbishop, for he turns the tables on him and accuses him of Popery for introducing the necessity of other mediators with God besides Christ. The Council of Trent only calls having recourse to such other mediators as "pious and useful", but "your Grace makes it to be necessary to salvation". Bishop Phillpotts declares, "It is rank Popery—and worse than Popery. . . . My Lord, I stand aghast when I hear such teaching

[1] *Exposition of the Gospel of St John*, p. 83, commenting on John iii. 5. This commentary was published in 1835.

from such a place". He deplores the idea that the first motion
of grace in Baptism depends upon man rather than God.

Then in connexion with the Archbishop's mention of primitive
Baptism, Phillpotts refers to a canon of the Fourth Council of
Carthage as being "received generally", and as having had "the
authority of the whole Catholic Church".[1] In giving rules for
the examination of one elected to be a Bishop the canon directs:
"Quaerendum etiam ab eo si credat . . . si in Baptismo omnia
peccata, id est tam illud originale contractum, quam illa quae
voluntarie admissa sunt, dimittantur". Dr Phillpotts says he
hopes the Archbishop held this doctrine when he was made a
Bishop in 1828; because he had abandoned it by 1841 when in
the appendix to his Charge of that year he said, "in my judgment
a clergyman would be departing from the sense of the Articles . . .
if he were to speak of justification by faith, as if baptism and
newness of heart concur towards our justification". The Bishop
says, "My Lord, I know not how to understand this sentence. . . .
For 'newness of heart', as well as justification, is a fruit of
Baptism. . . ."

In his *Exposition of the Gospel of St John*, the Archbishop had
spoken of our Lord's "approving of the zeal of those parents"
who brought their children to Him as if this were the moving
cause of his blessing them. Phillpotts challenges him to produce a
passage of Scripture to justify this idea. "The text, which you have
produced in the passage I am considering, has been, I grieve to be
obliged to say, perverted by you, and 'added to' most awfully".

Phillpotts goes on to lament "the miserable uncertainty
respecting the efficacy of his Baptism" which, according to the
Archbishop's scheme he thinks everyone baptized in infancy
must have; and the dreadful cruelty of the idea that our one
opportunity of being born again depends upon the qualities of
others at the time of our baptism. He also criticizes severely the
Archbishop's quotation (p. 166) from the twentieth chapter of
Gibbon's *Decline and Fall of the Roman Empire*. The Archbishop
had argued from the abuse of Baptism—the postponing of it
until deathbed and meanwhile revelling in a life of sin—that this
was the result of regarding its efficacy independently of the
disposition of the recipient. This abuse, Dr Phillpotts maintained,
was a sure sign that the early Church did believe that full remission of sins was conferred by Baptism. It was absurd to argue

---

[1] See Goode's criticism of this statement, p. 135, *infra*, and Pusey's defence of
Phillpotts on the point, pp. 127–8.

from a corruption of a belief against that belief itself: what the Archbishop had said against deathbed Baptism might equally well be said against deathbed repentance. Dr Phillpotts averred that in all his pastoral ministry he had not come across one instance of "fallacious security" in the regeneration of Baptism such as the Archbishop was condemning.

But the passage which Phillpotts seemed to deplore above all is from pp. vii, ix and x of the new Preface:

Unquestionably there is much difficulty, much mystery in the case, as regards the Baptism of infants . . . a difficulty which has more or less perplexed the Church in every age, since the Baptism of infants has been the general practice, and which many divines have solved by supposing that the spiritual benefit of Baptism, 'a death unto sin and a new birth unto righteousness', is only received where there has been an antecedent act of grace on the part of God. . . .

. . . Without concurring in these opinions, I cannot doubt that a minister of our Church may justly maintain them, sanctioned as they have been by some of her worthiest members, and relating to a subject upon which, confessedly, Scripture does not speak definitively.

He cannot understand how the Archbishop can say this and at the same time retain the passage from the earlier edition at p. 160—"On the authority of the example of St Paul our Church considers Baptism as conveying Regeneration". It seems to him that the Archbishop can find no objection to the Church having ministers who deny its official doctrine. Phillpotts points out other instances of what he considers contradictions in the Archbishop's book. On p. xi of his 1850 preface the Archbishop says that Scripture does not determine the actual effect of infant baptism, and yet he assents to the rubric, "It is certain *by God's word* that children which are baptized, dying before they commit actual sin, are undoubtedly saved".

Dr Phillpotts says that by concurring in the decision of the Privy Council the Archbishop has done all he can to cut off the Church, in which he holds the highest place, from the Holy Catholic and Apostolic Church of all ages. He has mis-led the court, mis-stated the doctrine and mis-quoted the authors whom he has cited.

At p. iv of his Preface, the Archbishop, in speaking of the recent "distressing controversy" implies that Gorham says: " 'A death unto sin and a new birth unto righteousness' is the spiritual benefit of Baptism, but it is only received in Baptism where there has been an antecedent act of grace on the part of

God" (p. ix). But this is inaccurate, Phillpotts argues, for Gorham says: "That filial state . . . was given to the worthy recipient . . . *before* Baptism, and not *in* Baptism."[1]

Phillpotts charges the Archbishop with falsification of the evidence from Hooker. Hooker says that Baptism is a "seal, perhaps, of the Grace of Election before received"[2] but the Archbishop is not justified in implying that Hooker regards Baptism as a mere seal. Hooker in this passage is refuting Cartwright who held that view. But while Hooker allows that Baptism has the aspect of a seal of election, that election or predestination is not enough in itself; for a few sentences earlier, in a passage not included in the Archbishop's quotation, Hooker says, "Predestination bringeth not to life without the Grace of external vocation, wherein our Baptism is implied".

Phillpotts next flatly denies that the passage quoted by the Privy Council as from Archbishop Ussher belongs to that divine at all. The passage in question is, "The Sacrament of Baptism in infants is effectual to all those, and to those only, who belong to the Election of Grace", from *The Sum and Substance of the Christian Religion* (p. 415). The evidence against the authenticity of this passage which Phillpotts brings is from Elrington's *Life of the Most Rev James Usher*.[3] Elrington says that the book was published under the Archbishop's name by a Mr Downham, and he quotes a letter of Ussher written on May 13th 1645 disowning the work, though not by name. As against this allegedly false quotation, Dr Phillpotts quotes from a sermon of Ussher:

And God hath appointed his Sacrament of the Lord's Supper to strengthen and continue that life which we received in Baptism, as by spiritual nourishment. In Baptism our stock of life is given us, by the Sacrament it is confirmed and continued.[4]

As regards Jeremy Taylor, Phillpotts says, "Your Grace will be glad to hear that he really wrote what you cite from his *Treatise on Infant Baptism*". The passage in question, quoted in the Judgment and in the Archbishop's Preface was:

Baptism, and its effects, may be separated, and do not always go in conjunction. The effect may be before, and therefore much rather it may be after its susception. . . .[5]

[1] Gorham, *Efficacy of Baptism*, p. 113; and see p. 26, *supra*.
[2] *Eccl. Polit.*, v. 60.   [3] Pp. 248–50.
[4] *Eighteen Sermons, preached in Oxford, 1640, by the Right Rev James Usher, late Bishop of Armagh, in Ireland*, London, 1660, Thirteenth Sermon, p. 448.
[5] *Works*, ed. Bishop Heber, Vol. II, p. 259.

But the Bishop adds "You have been seduced by an unhappy confidence in some most untrustworthy informant", because Taylor only says this in speaking of Cornelius (Acts x) whom he is treating as an exception in that he received the Spirit before being baptized. The general rule Taylor gives at the beginning of the very same paragraph as that from which the Archbishop has quoted:

Baptism is the first ordinary current in which the Spirit moves and descends upon us. . . .

Phillpotts next attacks the Archbishop's use of Bullinger, and in so doing he uses a complicated argument. Bullinger, he says, makes contradictory statements—and he gives instances. He then says that our divines of the sixteenth century commended many writers who opposed Popish errors so long as they had in their writings statements in agreement with the doctrine of the Church of England; they overlooked the fact that some of them also said things which contradicted that doctrine, or perhaps it would be more accurate to say that our divines in their charity gave them an unduly favourable interpretation. It was so with Bullinger—in commending his *Decades* it must not be supposed that our divines endorsed everything that Bullinger said there. Apart from this, Phillpotts argues that the Archbishop is quite wrong in saying that the *Decades* were "authoritatively taught" in our Church. In the minutes of the 13th session of Convocation in 1586[1] it is said that the Archbishop of Canterbury introduced an order about the *Decades*, but there is no mention in the Acts of Convocation of any canon recording that this motion was passed.

The quotation which the Archbishop gives from Pearson— "When the means are used, without something appearing to the contrary, we presume the good effect"[2]—Phillpotts says is referring in its context to the case of adults only. He also detects an inaccuracy in the Archbishop's quotation from Hooker. Whereas the Archbishop quotes him as saying, "We speak of infants as the rule of *charity* alloweth"[3] in every edition of Hooker which Dr Phillpotts can find there is "piety" not "charity". Anyway, he says, Hooker is engaged here in an *argumentum ad hominem* against Cartwright. He gives what he considers as other instances of Hooker's use of this kind of argument, and also statements

[1] Wilkin's *Concilia*, iv, 321.
[2] *On the Creed*, commenting on "the Communion of Saints".
[3] *Eccl. Polit.*, v. 64. Quoted in Sumner's 1850 Preface, p. xii.

from him as to the Church's *absolute*, not *charitable* belief about baptized infants.

The Bishop goes on to assert that the quotation from Carleton[1] is similarly wrenched out of its context and distorted. Even the "charitable presumption" which the Bishops at the Savoy Conference speak of is referring to adults, not infants.

The Bishop of Exeter then leaves Dr Sumner's book and proceeds to attack the Privy Council's Judgment itself. He begins by setting out what he regards as the two chief heresies of Gorham—(a) Remission of sins, which depends upon an act of prevenient grace, must precede Baptism, if the sacrament is to be received worthily, (b) Regeneration and Adoption must likewise precede Baptism if it is to be received worthily.

These heresies, the Bishop avers, are glossed over and almost unnoticed in the Judgment. The Judgment speaks of Gorham believing "that in no case is regeneration in Baptism unconditional", but the Bishop alleges that in his answers Gorham denies regeneration *in* Baptism altogether. Then the Judgment says that Gorham means by right reception "in the case of adults 'with faith and repentance', and in the case of infants 'with God's grace and favour' ". "God's grace and favour" the Bishop says he will readily allow; what sacrament could be healthfully administered without these? But this is to say something very different from the "prevenient grace" on which Gorham insists. "What would any of those judges have thought", Phillpotts remarks, "if . . . a man were charged with wilful murder, and the Judge were, in summing up, to omit noticing any evidence, beyond such as established manslaughter?"[2]

Bishop Phillpotts complains that the Judgment does not take into account what Gorham really says. The Judgment refers to Gorham as holding "That grace may be granted before, in, or after, Baptism". The Bishop says that if this means the grace of regeneration, first it is a heretical statement to say that it may be received before Baptism, and secondly it is inaccurate since Gorham does not allow that regeneration may take place *in* Baptism at all. It is interesting to see what the Bishop says at this point about "Justification", for he grudgingly allows that in exceptional cases this may take place before Baptism. If the word "grace" in the above sentence means "Justification", "it might, as an abstract statement of what in the nature of things

[1] *An examination of Montague's Appeal*, p. 193.
[2] This all sounds very convincing, but see my comments on p. 117.

is possible, have a sound sense". The Bishop continues: "Justification, if understood of God's first acceptance of one unbaptized, who turns to God in true faith with the desire of Baptism, would in an adult be uniformly *before* Baptism: if understood of that act whereby God washes away his sins, it would be *in* Baptism". He complains that the Judgment never quotes a sentence of Gorham when he is saying that "regeneration" and "adoption" precede beneficial Baptism. Also the Judgment does not take into account that Gorham holds that Baptism works all those things which infants cannot have—confirming of faith (which they cannot begin to have), increase of grace (which the Bishop holds they lack before Baptism, being "children of wrath"); and none of those graces of which, by God's mercy, infants are capable —remission of sins, regeneration, sanctification, adoption, &c.

The Bishop concludes his comments on what he considers as the oversights of the Judgment with the following magnificent paragraph:

So much suppression of the truth converts a formal absolution of Gorham into a virtual condemnation of his doctrine. Grave charges thus glossed over are tacitly acknowledged, while the individual is acquitted. My Lord, truth does not usually thus shun the light.

Next Dr Phillpotts goes on from condemning the court for glossing over Gorham's words to charging the judges with a violation of their duty in using what he regards as unsound argument for approving what they did approve. The judges should not, he maintains, have said that uncertainties in the Articles should not be clarified by reference to the Prayer Book, since this was precisely the procedure recommended in Canon LVII of 1603—"The doctrine of Baptism is sufficiently set down in the Book of Common Prayer. . . ." The Court compared the 1562 Articles with those of 1536 and 1552 and professed to observe a progressive abandonment of Catholic doctrine as to Baptism. This was a false method—especially as the 1536 Articles were of a popular nature, drawn up for a purpose quite different from that for which the 1562 Articles were intended. The proper method, the Bishop insists, would have been to compare the Articles with the confessions of faith of other reformed communions—for instance the Confession of Augsburg; it would then have been seen how tenaciously the Church of England adhered to the traditional Catholic faith.

The Bishop says that it is "a most amazing specimen of, I

H

cannot call it, reasoning", to say, as the Judgment does, that the
rubric at the end of the office of Public Baptism does not say
that infants baptized, dying before they commit actual sin, are
saved by Baptism. Coming where it does, the Bishop argues,
the rubric can mean nothing else. What if he, the Bishop, were
to apply the court's principle of charitable hypothesis to that
rubric? The whole argument of charitable hypothesis cannot
be proved from the burial service, since there "hope" is explicitly
mentioned, whereas no such uncertainty is even hinted at in
the language of the baptismal offices.

The Bishop next charges the court with encouraging breaches
of the Act of Uniformity. That statute was passed for the express
purpose of exacting from ministers "unfeigned assent and consent
to all and everything contained and prescribed in and by the
book . . ." as against mere consent to the use of the book. If
there had been any doubt as to the meaning of the legislature
as to the authoritative exposition of any words in the Book of
Common Prayer, it is removed by the Acts of the Savoy Conference. The Bishop gave a number of quotations, designed to
show that the episcopal commissioners at the Savoy Conference
endorsed the plain meaning of the language of the Prayer Book;[1]
for instance, the Nonconformists objected to the phrase "May
receive remission of sins by spiritual regeneration" in the second
prayer before Baptism.[2] The Bishops answered to this, " 'Receive
remission of sins by spiritual regeneration'. Most proper; for
Baptism is our spiritual regeneration (St John iii, 'Unless a man
be born again of water and of the Spirit &c.'); and by this is
received remission of sins, Acts ii, 'Repent and be baptised every
one for the remission of sins'. So the Creed, 'One Baptism for
the remission of sins' ".[3]

Dr Phillpotts suggests that the Archbishop was moved by a
desire to temporize. He would not, he thinks, have given his
support to such a judgment had he not been afraid that a large
number of clergymen would otherwise have resigned their
offices or left the Church. Dr Phillpotts did not believe that this
would have followed if the judgment of the Archbishop's Court
had been affirmed, for Gorham's was a clear case of heresy, no
mere matter of perplexity arising out of the misuse of words.[4]

---

[1] But see also Gorham's treatment of the Savoy Conference, pp. 34–5.

[2] Cardwell's *Conferences*, p. 324.   [3] *Ibid.*, p. 356.

[4] But Goode said (*Letter to the Bishop of Exeter*, p. 21): "Prepared they were, and that
in no inconsiderable numbers, to quit a Church that should make your Lordship's
doctrine on the subject of Baptism its own".

If the judgment of the Privy Council is accepted there is no certain teaching on Baptism—the flocks committed to the pastors' charges cannot be told anything definite; the Articles are left to individual ministers to affirm or contradict. But happily, the Bishop says, this is not so. The Judgment declared contrary to faith, and it must therefore be set aside. The Church of England retains Catholic truth. This means rebellion against the authority of the Archbishop, which is to be deplored; but even that is not so bad as the dislocation of the faith itself which is threatened otherwise.

The Bishop contrasted the state of affairs which would follow if the Judgment be accepted, with the Day of Pentecost—"Then the multitude wondered when 'they heard, in divers tongues, the wonderful works of God' one and the same truth. Now the same words of prayer are to cover, not different truths (for different truths there cannot be), but conflicting *opinions*". He demands of the Archbishop to seek the mind of the Church. "Call together your com-provincial Bishops", he says, "invite them to declare what is the faith of the Church on the Articles impugned in this Judgment".

The Bishop's two concluding paragraphs merit being quoted in full:

Meanwhile I have one most painful duty to perform. I have to protest not only against the Judgment pronounced in the recent cause, but also against the regular consequences of that Judgment. I have to protest against your Grace's doing what you will be speedily called to do, either in person, or by some other exercising your authority. I have to protest, and I do hereby solemnly protest, before the Church of England, before the Holy Catholic Church, before Him who is its Divine Head, against your giving mission to exercise cure of souls within my diocese, to a clergyman who proclaims himself to hold the heresies which Mr Gorham holds. I protest that anyone who gives mission to him till he retract, is a favourer and supporter of those heresies. I protest, in conclusion, that I cannot, without sin— and, by God's grace, I will not—hold communion with him, be he who he may, who shall so abuse the high commission which he bears.

I am, my Lord Archbishop, with that "due reverence and obedience" which I have pledged to you, and with earnest prayer that such reverence and obedience to you may never be forbidden by my duty to our common Master, your Grace's affectionate friend for nearly thirty years, and your now afflicted servant, H. EXETER.

CHAPTER VIII

SOME REVERBERATIONS OF THE JUDGMENT

EVEN after the decision of the Privy Council, Bishop Phillpotts did not consider himself beaten: he tried to obtain a ruling that Gorham's case should never have gone before the Privy Council at all. He applied to the Court of Queen's Bench for a Rule to prohibit the institution of Gorham on the ground that an appeal from the Court of Arches lay properly to the Upper House of Convocation and not to the Privy Council. This was refused on April 25th, but a month later the Bishop made the same application to the Court of Common Pleas and this was no more successful. His next attempt was with the Court of Exchequer, but once again he obtained no satisfaction, and then it became clear that he could obtain no remedy in the Civil Courts. The Bishop of London, too, who had not concurred in the judgment, was active in support of the Bishop of Exeter. On June 3rd he introduced a Bill in the House of Lords for the Royal Supremacy in causes spiritual to be exercised by judges of the spirituality. Although this Bill had the support in principle of twenty-five bishops, it was rejected.

The next step was that the Court of Arches issued a monition calling upon the Bishop to bring Gorham's Presentation into Court. This the Bishop did, but he accompanied his action by a further solemn protest in which he pointed out what he regarded as differences between the statement of Gorham's teaching upon which the Judicial Committee based its decision and those statements of Gorham himself which had made him refuse to institute him to the living of Brampford Speke. It is important to observe what those alleged differences were, for it might be held that they show the limits of what the Judicial Committee declared to be tenable within the Church of England. The Bishop affirmed that Gorham had stated that without any exceptions, remission of sins, adoption into the family of God, and regeneration, must take place in the case of infants, not in, or by means of, but before Baptism, in order for the sacrament to have any effect at the time of its administration.[1] Regeneration when it took place, according to his teaching, so the Bishop

---

[1] See pp. 18 ff., *supra*.

understood, took place quite independently of the sacrament. This was something different from what the Judicial Committee allowed, Dr Phillpotts argued. In the Judgment[1] Gorham's doctrine had been defined as follows: ". . . the grace of regeneration does not so necessarily accompany the act of Baptism that regeneration invariably takes place in Baptism; that grace may be granted before, in, or after Baptism . . . in no case is regeneration in Baptism unconditional". The Bishop's point in making his protest seems to be that Gorham denies that regeneration ever takes place in and by the sacrament; but this cannot be said absolutely, for throughout the controversy the term "regeneration" is used somewhat loosely, and it can be shown that in one sense of the word Gorham does allow it to be applicable to the grace of Baptism.[2] On the ground of this isolated quotation from the Privy Council Judgment it might be held that it had failed to take into account Gorham's real position; but other passages and the general tenor of the judgment seem to indicate allowance of everything he said in the original examination. Nevertheless this verbal disagreement made the Bishop feel that he had refused institution to Gorham on grounds which had not been taken into consideration by the body which ultimately decreed that he should be instituted.

On these grounds the Bishop made the following trenchant repudiation of the Privy Council's judgment:

Now we, the said Henry, Bishop of Exeter . . . do, by virtue of the authority given to us by God, as a Bishop in the Church of Christ, and in the apostolic branch of it planted by God's providence within this land, and established therein by the laws and constitutions of this realm, hereby solemnly repudiate the said judgment, and declare it to be null and utterly without effect *in foro conscientiae*, and do appeal therefrom in all that concerns the Catholic faith to "the sacred Synod of this nation when it shall be in the name of Christ assembled as the true Church of England by representation".

And further, we do solemnly protest and declare, that whereas the said George Cornelius Gorham did manifestly and notoriously hold the aforesaid doctrines, and hath not since retracted and disclaimed the same, any Archbishop or Bishop, or any official of any Archbishop or Bishop, who shall institute the said George Cornelius Gorham to the cure and government of the souls of the parishioners of the said parish of Brampford Speke, within our diocese aforesaid, will thereby

[1] See p. 98, *supra*.

[2] See pp. 15, 21, *supra*, and Gorham's counsel before the Privy Council argued this, see p. 96.

incur the sin of supporting and favouring the said heretical doctrines, and we do hereby renounce and repudiate all communion with anyone, be he whom he may, who shall so institute the said George Cornelius Gorham as aforesaid. . . .

But this protest was unavailing. The Bishop persisted in his refusal to institute Gorham, but he was finally instituted on August 6th 1850, under *fiat* of the Archbishop of Canterbury, by Sir Herbert Jenner Fust, Dean of Arches, the person who, at an earlier stage of the case, had formally judged Gorham's condemnation to be right. This meant, as Warre Cornish says, that "A Bishop excommunicated an Archbishop";[1] and Dr Phillpotts wrote to Archdeacon Manning about this time, "I can no longer attend Convocation for the Archbishop of Canterbury has, by his act of inducting Mr Gorham, denied an article of the Creed and forfeited his right to spiritual authority".[2]

On August 15th 1850 the Bishop of Exeter wrote an open letter to the Churchwardens of Brampford Speke, the parish to which ten days before Gorham had been instituted under *fiat* of the Archbishop of Canterbury.

He began:

BELOVED IN CHRIST,—I feel it my imperative duty to address you, and through you the parishioners of Brampford Speke generally, on an occasion which has excited the liveliest interest, not only throughout the Church of England, and of Ireland, and of Scotland, but also in every portion of the Western Church.

I say not this lightly. I have now on my table an address from the ministers of more than twenty congregations of Protestants in Germany, expressing their warm sympathy with a Bishop in the Church of Christ, placed under the special difficulties with which it has pleased God that my faithfulness to my Consecration Vows should be tried, and under which He hath (most humbly do I thank him for it), by His merciful goodness, hitherto sustained me.

He goes on to declare that the Book of Common Prayer teaches in unmistakeable terms that every baptized infant receives the full benefit of the sacrament. Gorham denies this, and although he, the Bishop, had decided that on these grounds Gorham was not a fit person to be Vicar of Brampford Speke, the Judicial Committee of the Privy Council—a court incompetent to decide such an issue—had ruled that Gorham ought to be instituted. He had in fact been instituted on the authority of the

[1] A *History of the English Church in the Nineteenth Century*, Pt. I, p. 327.
[2] Purcell, *Life of Cardinal Manning*, Vol. I, p. 594.

Archbishop of Canterbury over the Bishop of Exeter's head.

Dr Phillpotts says that the question arises as to what duty he should indicate to the parishioners of Brampford Speke in this very painful case. It had been suggested that he should license some other minister to reside amongst them and preach the pure word of God. But since it is the Archbishop, and not merely the State, who has authorized the institution of Gorham, to do so would be to offend against the law of the Church. Similarly, since Gorham had already been officially and authoritatively installed to the living it would be an act of schism to suggest that the people should seek the pure doctrine in another Church.

The Bishop gets out of the difficulty by saying that although in his examination of Gorham he has found him to be of unsound doctrine as to Baptism, he has no evidence that he has ever preached his heresies. If this should ever happen it would be their duties as Churchwardens to bring the matter to the notice of the Bishop or the Archdeacon. But as regards the teaching of the Catechism, the Bishop says he can see no human remedy: "those who have superseded me in the discharge of my duty, have overlooked, or disregarded, this great practical consideration, strongly as it was urged upon them. But although there is no human remedy, let us hope, and earnestly pray, that it may please God to give more largely of His own Heavenly aid to the young among you, and enable them to learn from the words of the Church that Faith which their Minister may be disqualified by misbelief from inculcating".

The Bishop says the people of Brampford Speke may console themselves in concentrating more upon the worship of the Church than on that which is spoken from the pulpit. The sacraments of the Church are what the Prayer Book declares them to be in spite of the opinions of one heretical minister. He says he will transmit to every house in the parish a copy of Archdeacon Bartholomew's sermon on "The Holiness of Baptized Infants". At the end of this letter there is printed the Protest which the Bishop of Exeter made on bringing Gorham's Presentation into the Registry of the Court of Arches.

When the judgment was pronounced it produced many ramifications throughout the country. This "great ecclesiastical drama", as Purcell, Manning's biographer, calls it, had shaken the religious world to its depths for nearly three years. And the religious world then did not consist merely of bishops and other clergy, but included well-known statesmen and lawyers and men of letters. Manning, who was then Archdeacon of Chichester, Robert Wilberforce (Archdeacon of the East Riding), W. H. Mill (Regius Professor of Hebrew at Cambridge), Pusey (Regius Professor of Hebrew at Oxford), John Keble, Bennett of St Paul's Knightsbridge, and other well-known parish clergy such as Henry Wilberforce and Dodsworth had met together with lawyers such as James Hope and Edward Badeley and statesmen such as Gladstone and Sidney Herbert in March 1850 to await the outcome of the case and take counsel together. Gladstone's interest in the case is shown by his collection of the documents and his notes and marginalia in the volumes on the case which are preserved at St Deiniol's library at Hawarden.

Gladstone wrote to Manning on December 30th 1849, "Were we together I should wish to converse with you from sunrise to sunset on the Gorham case. It is a stupendous issue. . . ."[1] Morley remarks, "The religious world in both of its two standing camps was convulsed, for if Gorham had lost the day it would or might have meant the expulsion from the establishment of calvinists and evangelicals bag and baggage".

The comments of the secular Press were such as to indicate that the matter was regarded as one of national importance. The following is an extract from a leading article in *The Times* of March 9th 1850:

The Church of England has from the dawn of the Reformation, and still more under the great Protestant reign of Elizabeth combined the spiritual element of Catholic tradition with some of the great principles of the continental reformers. Seeking rather to include the several shades of opinion which might arise from the exercise of the right of private judgment, than to exclude all variations from the standard of rigorous orthodoxy, she laid no claim to universal despotic power over conscience, because she owed no claim to infallibility. The decision of the Privy Council has altered nothing in the policy of the church or in her teaching. It is an undoubted fact that for the last three centuries one portion of the clergy and the laity has inclined more to the views of the Calvinistic school, and another to the secular traditions of Catholic theology. Even the Church of Rome, in the great Jansenist controversies of the 17th century, was not free from similar divergencies. But such differences having an acknowledged existence, it remained to be decided in our time that a condemnation of one class of opinions by the authority of the other, so as to exclude the holder of such opinions from a benefice, and even to exercise a *veto* upon the patronage of the Crown, on the express ground of a

[1] Morley, *Life of Gladstone*, Vol. I, p. 378.

diversity of interpretation of the received formularies, would not be sanctioned by the law. Such a case may serve for a lesson in toleration and justice. We render homage to the principle, without any undue consideration for the individual, who perhaps sought to provoke this painful investigation by his own refractory and disputatious character. But the Lords of the Council have wisely shown no disposition to narrow the sacred precincts of the Church of England, or to decide this important question upon a mere point of personal fitness or conduct.

This decision has in all probability saved the Church and the country from a great calamity. As the matter stands, the orthodox doctrine of the Bishop of Exeter will be professed by the majority of English Churchmen, without suffering any disparagement from the fact that a minority in the Church continue, as they have done for centuries, to lay peculiar stress on a clause in the Articles, admitting the same efficacy in the sacrament of baptism but by different means of operation. A change and a novelty would have been introduced if such a variation had on a sudden been condemned as heresy, subjecting the holder of it to a penalty of forfeiture. Had Mr Gorham been excluded from the vicarage of Brampford Speke, he ought, by a parity of reasoning, to be ejected from his former living of St Just in the same diocese; and it can hardly be doubted from the temper of a portion of the clergy on this subject, and from the recent example in the church of Scotland, that a considerable schism and secession of conscientious or irritable men, not perhaps all of them sharing Mr Gorham's own opinions, would have ensued. That most fatal consequence of the Bishop of Exeter's proceedings against Mr Gorham, and of Mr Gorham's contentious conduct towards his diocesan, has now, we trust, been averted.

The same issue of *The Times* records the excited scenes near the Privy Council chamber before the proceedings opened. There seems to have been almost a riot, and "the court room of the Privy Council never, perhaps, on any former occasion, presented a more crowded and animated appearance. . . . It was some time before, amidst the scramble for places and the general confusion, the proceedings could be opened with becoming decorum".

The whole matter had a profound effect upon the mind of Archdeacon Manning. Writing on the influence of the Judgment on the position of Manning, Purcell in his *Life of Cardinal Manning* says: "The Gorham Judgment, pronounced by the highest court in the land, inflicted on the High Church party and the Church to which they belonged a twofold blow. It struck out an article of the Creed; and asserted afresh, as an inherent right,

the Royal Supremacy in matters of faith."[1] And James Hope-
Scott[2] the eminent barrister, friend of Newman and Gladstone,
writing to Manning on January 29th 1850—before the decision
of the Privy Council—said: "But if a false judgment be pronounced
in Gorham's case, and that judgment be acquiesced in by the
Church of England, then indeed a new feature will arise for
which I find no place; whatever be the mouthpiece which utters
the judgment, if the Church does not repudiate it, there is an
article of the Creed struck out, and then indeed there will be a
weight thrown into the scales against my allegiance, which it
would seem ought to prevail".[3] Hope-Scott eventually seceded
to Rome as well as Manning, and so did Edward Badeley, the
Bishop of Exeter's advocate before the Privy Council. The
Judgment also led to the secession of Robert Wilberforce, the
author of *The Doctrine of Holy Baptism* which was published in
1849. But, so far as it is possible to separate the two, it seems to
have been the question of the Royal Supremacy rather than the
doctrine of Baptism which finally settled his mind.

Cardinal Manning at the end of his life recalled some of the
meetings and negotiations between this group about the judgment.
Manning said that it was he who informed Gladstone about the
decision. Gladstone was in bed with influenza in Carlton Terrace
at the time, and when Manning told him he started up and
threw out his arms exclaiming, "The Church of England is
gone unless it releases itself by some authoritative act".[4] It was
then agreed that a Declaration should be drawn up and signed
by the group. At a meeting at which Pusey and Keble were not
present a statement was agreed upon that by the Gorham
Judgment the Church of England had forfeited its authority as
a divine teacher. Later, however, when Pusey and Keble were
present they would not agree to this, and it was changed to:
"If the Church of England shall accept this Judgment it would
forfeit its authority as a divine teacher". Manning observed that
this change was made because it did not say whether the Church
of England had or had not *de facto* accepted the Judgment. At
one point Hope said, "I suppose we are all agreed that if the
Church of England does not undo this we must join the Church
of Rome". Manning says that this led to an outcry. Gladstone,

---

[1] *Op. cit.*, Vol. I, p. 524.

[2] James Hope assumed the name of Hope-Scott in 1853 on succeeding to the estate
of Abbotsford.

[3] *Ibid.*, p. 526.   [4] *Ibid.*, p. 528.

it seems, was all for delay and preferred the idea of an address to the Bishops rather than the Declaration. In the end he did not sign the Declaration. Pusey and Keble, too, were for moderation, and uttered warnings against alarm. Keble said that some were in a mood to see in all these events a sign from heaven that they should no longer stay in the Church of England. In a public letter on March 19th, he warned his friends against "amusing themselves, as if nothing sacred were in jeopardy", but also deprecating "losing patience and rushing fretfully on, as though it were our duty to make the worst of everything".

The final form of the Declaration drawn up by the group and later known as the "Nine Resolutions" was as follows:

1. That whatever at the present time be the force of the sentence delivered on appeal in the case of Gorham *v* the Bishop of Exeter, the Church of England will eventually be bound by the said sentence, unless it shall openly and expressly reject the erroneous doctrine sanctioned thereby.

2. That the remission of original sin to all infants in and by the grace of Baptism is an essential part of the article "One Baptism for the remission of sins".

3. That—to omit other questions raised by the said sentence—such sentence, while it does not deny the liberty of holding that article in the sense heretofore received, does equally sanction the assertion that original sin is a bar to the right reception of baptism, and is not remitted, except when God bestows regeneration beforehand by an act of prevenient grace (whereof Holy Scripture and the Church are wholly silent), thereby rendering the benefits of Holy Baptism altogether uncertain and precarious.

4. That to admit the lawfulness of holding an exposition of an article of the Creed contradictory of the essential meaning of that article is, in truth and in fact, to abandon that article.

5. That, inasmuch as the faith is one and rests upon one principle of authority, the conscious, deliberate, and wilful abandonment of the essential meaning of an article of the Creed destroys the divine foundations upon which alone the entire faith is propounded by the Church.

6. That any portion of the Church which does so abandon the essential meaning of an article, forfeits, not only the Catholic doctrine in that article, but also the office and authority to witness and teach as a member of the universal Church.

7. That by such conscious, wilful, and deliberate act such portion of the Church becomes formally separated from the Catholic body, and can no longer assure to its members the grace of the sacraments and the remission of sins.

8. That all measures consistent with the present legal position of

the Church ought to be taken without delay, to obtain an authoritative declaration by the Church of the doctrine of Holy Baptism, impugned by the recent sentence; as, for instance, by praying licence for the Church in Convocation to give legal effect to the decisions of the collective episcopate on this and all other matters purely spiritual.

9. That, failing such measures, all efforts must be made to obtain from the said Episcopate, acting only in its spiritual character, a re-affirmation of the doctrine of Holy Baptism, impugned by the said sentence.

It was signed by H. E. Manning (Archdeacon of Chichester), Robert I. Wilberforce (Archdeacon of the East Riding), Thomas Thorp (Archdeacon of Bristol), W. H. Mill (Regius Professor of Hebrew at Cambridge), E. B. Pusey (Regius Professor of Hebrew at Oxford), John Keble (Vicar of Hursley), W. Dodsworth (Perpetual Curate of Christ Church, St. Pancras), W. J. E. Bennett (Perpetual Curate of St Paul's, Knightsbridge), Henry W. Wilberforce (Vicar of East Farleigh), John G. Talbot (Barrister), Richard Cavendish, Edward Badeley (Barrister), James R. Hope-Scott (Barrister) and George Anthony Denison (Vicar of East Brent).

This alone is enough to show that the Gorham Judgment was causing considerable misgivings and searching of hearts in the Church of England. It was driving Manning onward towards his decision to secede to the Church of Rome. Manning himself records that on March 19th 1850 he "convened the clergy of the Archdeaconry of Chichester in the Cathedral library, and we unanimously voted (8 only excepted out of 100) a protest against the Gorham Judgment and the interference of civil authority in questions of doctrine".[1] Of course a great deal of the opposition to the judgment was on the ground of State interferences in ecclesiastical matters, and it must not be supposed that this vote of the clergy of the Archdeaconry of Chichester was representative of the views of the Anglican clergy as a whole on the doctrine of Baptism which was at issue. The Chichester clergy did indeed agree in sending an address to the Bishop of Chichester in which they declared their belief that all infants baptized with water in the Threefold Name were regenerate by the Holy Spirit, but the whole proceedings at this meeting were dominated by Manning's scheme for a purely ecclesiastical court to deal with matters of faith in the place of the Judicial Committee of the Privy Council.

[1] Purcell, *op. cit.*, p. 533.

Many protest meetings were arranged all over the country and addresses and declarations drawn up in the months following the Judgment, but since the two matters were so closely intertwined it is difficult to say whether the real issue which provoked these protests was the doctrinal issue or the question of the independence of the Church. It is certain, of course, that Manning and his associates were violently opposed to the official toleration of Gorham's views on Baptism in the Church of England, but a large part of their protestations and deliberations was taken up with the matter of the intervention of the State in questions of faith. Cardinal Manning wrote in his journal in 1887, "The violation of the doctrine of Baptism was of less gravity to me than the violation of the divine office of the Church by the supremacy of the Crown in council". Nevertheless this interference of the State which gave rise to such protests was on the doctrine of Baptism, and in May 1850 Manning thus wrote to Robert Wilberforce:[1]

Is not this the true statement of baptism?
1. That it unites the baptized to the Holy Trinity, to the Father by adoption, to the Son by remission, to the Holy Ghost by indwelling.
2. That the agent is the Holy Ghost.
3. That the infusion of grace is the *one* principle which brings also Adoption and Redemption.
4. That Regeneration comprehends *the whole threefold idea.*

As well as differing from Pusey as to the situation created by the intervention of the State, he seems to have had some doctrinal difference with him, for he adds after giving the above definition, "If so, what does our dear friend Pusey mean by taking the second effect, and the Second Person?"[2] He was presumably criticizing, on second thoughts, the inadequacy of resolution No. 2 of the Nine Resolutions, which Pusey did, however, later admit.[3]

In the hope of keeping Manning in the Church of England, Gladstone tried to induce Bishop Wilberforce to obtain from a majority of Bishops a statement that they adhered to the high doctrine of Baptism in spite of the Gorham Judgment. This attempt, however, proved abortive; but Gladstone believed that

[1] Purcell, Vol. I, p. 556.

[2] By "second effect" Manning means the second effect in 1, above: "to the Son by remission", upon which he thought that Pusey laid undue and exclusive emphasis.

[3] Letter to *Guardian*, June 19th 1850. See also Dodsworth's similar objection, pp. 131-2 and 145. But it is curious that Manning signed the Nine Resolutions, apparently without any objection.

if such a statement could have been obtained Manning would not have left the English Church.[1]

If their alarm was due equally to State interference as to heresy, the Tractarian party should logically have been almost as indignant if the Privy Council had reached a decision in keeping with what they regarded as orthodoxy. But it is unlikely that they would have been so, and obviously the doctrinal issue was at the back of their minds the whole time. H. W. Wilberforce, preaching at St Barnabas Pimlico in 1850, exhorted the Bishops to "defend the sacrament of baptism against attack, and to preserve the unity of the faith". Dr Mill declared that with the Gorham Judgment "the last vestiges of Catholicism are gone, or are at least rapidly passing away from sight".

Dr Pusey naturally followed the controversy carefully throughout. The tracts on Baptism which he had written earlier were an indication that he would be interested in any discussion of the doctrine of this Sacrament. In 1835 he had written a tract entitled *Scriptural Views of Holy Baptism* (Tract 67) in which he said:

The Christian Church uniformly, for fifteen centuries, interpreted these His words (John iii. 5) of Baptism; that on the ground of this text alone, they urged the necessity of Baptism; that upon it, mainly, they identified regeneration with Baptism. If, then, this be an error, would our Saviour have used words which (since water was already used in the Jews' and John's Baptism) must inevitably, and did lead His Church into error?

But it is important to observe that he also says in the same tract:

But it is one thing to hold Baptismal Regeneration, and another to hold merely that there is no regeneration subsequent to Baptism. . . . In like manner individuals who oppose the same doctrine, are wont to refer to the time when they suppose they held it, as a period of religious apathy, during which they lulled their consciences with the notion that, having by Baptism been made children of God, they had nothing further to do.

At the same time as insisting on Baptismal Regeneration he is careful not to say that the grace of Baptism includes final perseverance.

Pusey made great efforts to get the tract reprinted in time for the trial, but he did not succeed in this.

But in spite of his decided views on the doctrine of Baptism

[1] Purcell, *op. cit.*, p. 567.

stated above, Pusey contemplated a decision of the Privy Council against the Bishop without despair. He regretted that the Bishop of Exeter had ever brought matters to a head, because he thought that agreement could have been reached on this question if matters had not been rushed. Writing to Archdeacon Harrison of Maidstone after Gorham's appeal from the Arches Court had been announced, Pusey said, "A judicial decision on a doctrinal question, reversing an ecclesiastical judgment and deciding against the Creeds, would be a miserable thing, though one must, if God avert it not, make the best of it, and sit down by the waters of Babylon, toiling on under bondage".[1] All along he held that the shortcomings or misfortunes of the Church of England did not prove the claims of the Church of Rome, so throughout the controversy he was in different case from Manning.

During the Privy Council stage of the case Pusey was of great assistance both to the Bishop of Exeter and to Badeley his counsel. What Badeley said in his speech about the *opus operatum* seems to have come straight from Pusey's mind. Pusey also carried on a lengthy correspondence with Manning, but this was mainly on the supremacy of the Crown. Pusey undoubtedly held Gorham to be a heretic, but he felt that the best policy would have been to leave him alone, and he would then probably have modified his views. He never regarded the case as putting the whole position of the Church of England in the balance in the same way as Manning and some of the others did, and he was not willing to subscribe to some of the exaggerated resolutions which Church societies drew up at the time. Nevertheless, from the correspondence which has survived, it seems that Pusey supported the Bishop of Exeter in his uncompromising attitude when once the issue was joined, and he passed on to the Bishop Keble's suggestion of a Diocesan Synod to make a protest and demand a Provincial Council to settle the doctrine. And when Goode[2] pointed out a historical error in the Bishop's *Letter to the Archbishop of Canterbury*, Pusey came to the Bishop's defence.[3] Dr Phillpotts had referred to the Canons of the Fourth Council of Carthage as having been received by the whole Church, and Mr Goode, the champion of the evangelical party, in denouncing this misstatement said that "when proceeding from a Bishop" it was

---

[1] Liddon, *Life of E. B. Pusey*, Vol. III, p. 204.
[2] *A Letter to the Bishop of Exeter*, see p. 135.
[3] *Guardian*, May 1st 1850, p. 307.

"a discredit to us all". The Bishop undoubtedly had made a mistake, but Pusey pointed out that at a late date, though before the Reformation, the canon quoted by the Bishop was accepted by the Eastern and Western Church. He was also able to cite the authority of Baronius, Schelstrate and Tillemont in favour of these Canons.

Pusey also engaged about this time in a correspondence in the press about "prevenient grace". Badeley had said[1] "The offices of the Church are to be used for each Infant so brought, . . . there can be no distinction between them—no question whether one has 'prevenient grace' or another: no such doctrine is once heard of;—'prevenient grace' is not mentioned in the Articles, in the Formularies, or in the Catechism; we know nothing about it . . . the doctrine on the subject in Mr Gorham's book does not appear to me to be Roman, or Anglican or Catholic, or Protestant, or anything else". This statement had been hotly disputed in the columns of the *Morning Chronicle*, and Pusey wrote a letter to the public Press[2] in December 1849 in which he said that Badeley was not dealing with "prevenient grace" in general, but only as the doctrine was applied by Gorham to infants. He said that the traditional doctrine of prevenient grace, and the statement of it in the Xth Article—"the grace of God preventing us, that we may have a good will"—is plainly inapplicable to unconscious infants, who are incapable of any good will at all. Gorham holds that infants, being born in original sin, are thereby unworthy recipients of Baptism unless there be an act of "prevenient grace" to make them worthy; that this act of "prevenient grace" confers regeneration, justification, adoption. "In a word", Pusey says, "he substitutes this act of 'prevenient grace' for Baptism, so that Baptism becomes the outward seal of a grace already given, and he says that it 'confirms faith', which our Church in the Catechism asserts that infants cannot have". It is in this sense, Pusey says, that Badeley declares that the phrase "prevenient grace" is unknown to the primitive Catholic Church or the Roman Church.

In the same letter Pusey points out that the article "One Baptism for the Remission of Sins" existed in the Baptismal Creed, as attested by St Cyprian, before the Council of Nicaea. In the Pelagian controversy, on both sides, it was allowed that children were baptized "for the remission of sins". The Council

---

[1] See p. 82, *supra*, and Badeley, *op. cit.*, p. 66.
[2] Text preserved in Liddon, *op. cit.*, p. 235.

of Carthage (A.D. 418) declared the same. So far from a prevenient act of grace being necessary for the remission of sins,
Pusey declares, the remission of sins in and by Baptism itself is
implied by the very practice of infant baptism alone. He allows
Goode's assertion[1] that an adult is not necessarily in a state of
grace simply because he was baptized in infancy, but he will
not allow that it follows from this that original sin is not remitted
in Baptism. Pusey concludes his letter: ". . . God does, in St
Augustine's words, 'gratiam latenter infundit et parvulis'.
'Prevenient grace', by its very nature, they cannot have: since
this is grace 'disposing us that we may have a good will', and
when received is followed by co-operating grace, 'working with
us when we have a good will', whereas infants plainly can neither
have a good will, nor act upon it".

On April 29th 1850, largely owing to Pusey's influence, a
Protest was drawn up at Oxford and signed by forty-five dons,
which showed that the matter was regarded with considerable
concern in the University. The main points of this protest were
as follows—Whereas (a) All tutors are required by the University
Statutes to instruct their pupils in the XXXIX Articles, and
(b) the eighth of those articles declares belief in the Nicene
Creed which has the clause "I acknowledge one Baptism for
the remission of sins", and (c) the Formularies of the Church
of England declare the doctrine of Baptismal Regeneration;
and whereas, in spite of all this, principles of interpretation have
been applied to the formularies which make it possible for
ministers of the Church to hold entirely conflicting views on the
efficacy of the sacrament of Baptism "thereby endangering the
One Faith of Christ"; those who sign the Protest "teach and
maintain, and, by the help of God, will continue to teach and
maintain, the remission of sins to all infants, in and by the
grace of Holy Baptism, and also the regeneration of the same
universally by that Blessed Sacrament, not only as a tolerated
opinion, but as an essential doctrine of the Church of England
in common with the Universal Church of Christ".

As well as this Protest, which was intended for the parents of
undergraduates, two other declarations were drawn up to the
same effect at Oxford, and circulated among members of the
University and also addressed to the Queen and the Archbishop
of Canterbury. Those to the Queen and the Archbishop as well
as dealing with the theological question, referred also to the

---

[1] *Effects of Infant Baptism*, p. 275.

unsatisfactory character of the final court of appeal in ecclesiastical matters.

The London Church Union held a large and mixed gathering on July 23rd 1850 at which Pusey, Keble, R. I. Wilberforce and Manning spoke. The Bishop of Bath and Wells (Dr Bagot) and Mr J. G. Hubbard (afterwards Lord Addington), and many other eminent laymen were present. Various petitions to the Queen and the Bishops were drawn up on the subject of the final court in ecclesiastical matters; and also a Protest was adopted on the doctrinal issue. The main points in this Protest were as follows:

Gorham holds:

(i) A prevenient act of grace is necessary to make infants worthy recipients of Baptism, otherwise no spiritual grace is conveyed by the sacrament. "Declaring Original Sin (the remission of which is a promised effect of Baptism), to be a bar to the due reception of Baptism".

(ii) Infants baptized dying before they commit actual sin are undoubtedly saved, but these must have been regenerated by an act of grace prevenient to their Baptism.

(iii) Regeneration, Adoption, Remission of Sins and Justification are given before Baptism.

But the belief of the Church of England in the doctrine of Baptismal Regeneration is declared as follows:

(i) In the Nicene Creed.
(ii) In her two forms of Public and Private Baptism.
(iii) In the Order of Confirmation.
(iv) In the Catechism.
(v) In the XXVth Article.

Those who signed the protest therefore denied that the deliberate and unambiguous expressions in the Baptismal Formularies were to be taken in a qualified or uncertain sense, and hold "that original sin is remitted to all infants by spiritual regeneration, through the application of the merits of Our Lord and Saviour Jesus Christ in and by the Sacrament of Baptism". The Protest also declares that there is a difference between the statement of Gorham's beliefs in the Privy Council Judgment and Gorham's own words.[1]

All these protests and memorials and speeches show a unity of the High Church Party in opposition to the Gorham Judgment;

[1] See the Bishop of Exeter's protest on the same point, p. 112, *supra*.

but at the same time there were signs of cleavage in the ranks. On the one hand there were those like Pusey and Keble who were opposed to the Judgment, but who were not in despair as to the doctrine of the Church of England as a result of it; and on the other hand there were those like Manning, Hope and Dodsworth who took a more extreme line. Keble wrote, in the course of a letter in the *Guardian* of March 20th 1850 over the initials "J.K.":

. . . A chance we have of a certain degree of success could we be brought just now to concur in the earnest yet temperate move for a specific purpose, viz. the obtaining of a synodical declaration, that in the Church of England hereafter no person shall maintain that infant baptism does not in all cases convey remission of original sin. This is the one point on which for the present I would fain concentrate all the Catholic feeling of the country. It is *the* point raised.

Also I have a good hope, by taking this particular stand, we shall do something more towards the peace of the Church. For surely there are many, who while through misapprehension they shrink from what are called high views of baptismal grace, would yet be glad to disavow the extreme view which has just been sanctioned. They are afraid of making broad statements of regeneration because they think it disparages conversion, but they would not willingly be thought to deny God's grace and mercy given to those infants. . . .

On this Dodsworth comments: "So according to this advice we are to seek 'the continuance' of those who it is admitted shrink from declaring what we believe to be *vital* and *fundamental* truth, in order to get this little modicum of success."[1] Manning and Dodsworth not only thought that the whole Catholic position of the Church of England was threatened by this latest assertion of the Royal Supremacy, but also regarded Pusey's and Keble's doctrine of baptismal grace as showing signs of being incomplete. Manning, in writing of his belief in the tri-personal activity of God in the sacrament said, "What does our dear friend Pusey mean by taking the second effect, and the Second Person?"[2] and Dodsworth who also signed the Nine Resolutions also seems to have thought Pusey's Statement of the doctrine of Baptismal grace to be inadequate. In a pamphlet entitled *The Gorham case briefly considered*, Dodsworth criticised Pusey's views—Pusey had presumably been largely responsible for drawing up the form of the Nine Resolutions. Pusey thought that Gorham's view would be adequately challenged by stating that "the remission of

---

[1] *The Gorham Case briefly considered*, p. 13, note.   [2] See p. 125, *supra*.

original sin to all infants in and by the grace of Baptism is an essential part of the article, "One Baptism for the remission of sins' ". Dodsworth complained in his pamphlet that the doctrine of baptismal grace meant much more than the remission of original sin; that its great and positive effect was the gift of membership in Christ as the Church Catechism teaches.[1] Pusey in reply admitted that in asserting the remission of original sin he had not said everything about baptismal grace, but he conceived this to be enough for the time to meet the truth impugned by Gorham.[2]

But this was not the only point of difference. Dodsworth—and it is probably true to say that Maskell[3] and Allies[4] were with him in this—were suspicious of Pusey's attitude towards some of the Low Churchmen who supported the Judgment. In a postscript to his book on the Royal Supremacy, Pusey defended those Low Churchmen who were afraid that the doctrine of Baptismal Regeneration meant that no further change was needed to conform the soul to the mind of God. He wrote:

Many, not the least devout and earnest of the so-called Low Church, are not opposing the truth of Baptismal Regeneration but an untrue imagination of it. . . . The question which they suppose to be at issue is not, I am persuaded, as to the real grace of the Sacrament, but as to the *actual* change in the infant's soul, and the need of any further change, by which the grace imparted in Baptism may actually take up all the powers of the man, and being continually enlarged and renewed, may conform the whole soul to the mind of God.[5]

Dodsworth regarded this as a dangerous compromise, and he wanted to force the issue for the Low Churchmen. He says in a public letter that Pusey's words leave "a loophole for another doctrine, namely, that sufficient grace indeed is given in baptism to save infants, if they die; but if they live, their salvation flows not from that source, to be perfected in succeeding sacraments; but from a gift perfectly distinct which they can only receive through active faith, and their own intellectual apprehension. And what is this but Pelagianism under a more subtle form?

[1] Liddon, *Life of E. B. Pusey*, Vol. III, p. 262.

[2] Letter to *Guardian*, June 19th 1850.

[3] The Rev W. Maskell was a scholar in the front rank of ecclesiastical antiquaries. He published *Holy Baptism: a dissertation* in 1848 in which while domestic Chaplain to the Bishop of Exeter he defended the high doctrine of Baptism. He seceded to Rome in 1850.

[4] The Rev T. W. Allies was a distinguished historian. He seceded to Rome in 1850 and became Professor of History at the Roman Catholic University at Dublin.

[5] *Royal Supremacy*, pp. 220, 221.

What is it in effect, and to all practical purposes, but to bring back the doctrine of Mr Gorham and Mr Goode?"[1] This certainly seems to be an approximation to the doctrine that the grace of Baptism includes the grace of final perseverance. At the end of his letter to Dr Pusey he shows how acute the difference was. After saying how valiant a champion of the Catholic cause in the Church of England Pusey had been he continues,

And yet now, when, by God's mercy to us, a great opportunity has occurred, of asserting and enforcing the very keystone of this system, and apart from which the whole must crumble away—forgive me for speaking so plainly—you seem to shrink from the front rank. You seem ready to hide yourself under soft assertions of truth, "which", it is said, "not six men in the Church of England will be found to deny", and behind ambiguous statements which can be subscribed in different senses.[2]

Pusey's position which he adopted in opposition to Dodsworth is a very interesting one, and may point towards a statement of the doctrine of Baptism which takes into account the points maintained by both sides in this controversy. In a speech in Freemasons' Hall Pusey referred to Dodsworth's cricitisms and said:

The low Churchmen . . . were anxious to secure three points— 1st. That adults who receive the Sacraments unworthily do not then receive the grace of the Sacraments. 2ndly. That it does not avail to a man's salvation to *have* received the Sacraments, if he is no longer living as a child of God. 3rdly. That one so living must by the grace of God be turned back to God, by a true and thorough conversion. And therefore I believe that peace will be best secured by laying down truly, and in all its depth and fullness, and in its connexion with the Incarnation and death and merits of Christ, the truth of Baptismal Regeneration, but also by laying down the other truth, that those who have been made in Baptism the children of God, must by God's grace, live as the children of God, and those who have fallen from that grace must be restored by a thorough conversion to God.[3]

The question of the Royal Supremacy led to still further differences between them: Pusey allowed the state rights in connexion with the Government of the Church so long as there was no inter-ference in matters of doctrine. The extremists, however, held that any control even over discipline was indefensible.

The ecclesiastical press gave up a large amount of space to

---

[1] *A Letter to the Rev E. B. Pusey,* pp. 13, 14.
[2] *Ibid.,* pp. 16, 17.   [3] Liddon, *op. cit.,* p. 264.

the controversy. *The Guardian* bitterly opposed the Judgment and its correspondence columns were filled with the matter for months afterwards, but it must not be supposed that all the agitations and protestations in the Church at this time were directed against the Judgment. Gorham was not without his staunch supporters. The low Church papers were as glad of the decision as *The Guardian* was opposed to it. For instance, *The Record* had published these words in a leading article on August 6th 1849:

We are members of the Church of England, because we have believed, and do believe, that in all material points she is a true expounder of Holy Scripture, and, therefore, a fellow-worker with God, and a partaker of his favour and blessing. But, if she herself declares, by her recognized judicatories, that in an important point she, in common with Rome, and in opposition to all the Reformed Churches, teaches what all these Churches pronounce to be important error, her foundations are changed, and her living members will speedily change also.

On April 18th 1850 the Rev William Goode, Rector of Allhallows the Great, wrote an open letter to the Bishop of Exeter[1] criticizing the latter's *Letter to the Archbishop of Canterbury*. Mr Goode had been for some years editor of the *Christian Observer* and was the recognized champion of the evangelical party in the English Church. He was the author of a large number of tracts and pamphlets directed against the tractarian movement, and had also written *The Doctrine of the Church of England as to the Effects of Baptism in the case of Infants* which was first published in 1849, and which appeared in a second edition in 1850.

Goode begins by saying that the attack which the Bishop of Exeter makes in his letter upon "our common ecclesiastical Ruler and Primate" alone was enough to "justify any of the faithful sons of the Church in placing before the public a calm review of your statements". When the Bishop says that it has never happened before in the history of the Church of England for an Archbishop to take sides in a controversy, Goode reminds him of Archbishop Cranmer's *Answer to Bishop Gardiner*. Goode denies that Archbishop Sumner in republishing his book *Apostolical Preaching* with its new preface was showing partiality in a controversy in which he was called upon to exercise a judicial function. Quite the reverse. The book appeared first in 1815. The opponents of Gorham had culled passages from it and separated them from

[1] *A Letter to the Bishop of Exeter*, from William Goode.

their contexts; they had ignored the Archbishop's public utterances on the matter in the meantime, and thus made it appear
that His Grace's sentiments in the cause *sub judice* were quite
other than they were. It was this that moved the Archbishop to
write his new preface to the book and republish it. He did so
not before the Judgment, but after it—to show to the public
that the passages that had been quoted were misused, and that
in fact the book was in accordance with the Judgment to which
he had just given his sanction.

Bishop Phillpotts had attacked the Archbishop of Canterbury
for changing his views on a fundamental article of the creed,
but Goode denies that it is a contradiction of a fundamental
article of the creed to admit that the effects which at one time
were supposed to attend the administration of infant baptism
do not invariably and necessarily attend it. Anyway, Goode
declares, the passages which Dr Phillpotts implies have been
inserted into the latest edition for the purpose, he thinks, of
meeting the Gorham case, are all to be found in the second
edition of 1817.

So much for the Bishop's charge of change of view. The next
point to which Goode gives his attention is the Bishop's accusation
of popery and heresy. The Archbishop's statements in his commentary on St John as to the duty and efficacy of earnest prayers
to bring down the baptismal blessing on the child is a very
different thing from a declaration of the indispensability of such
prayers which Dr Phillpotts ascribes to him. Goode remarks
that it is curious to hear a charge of popery from one whose
doctrine of Baptism is identical with that of the Church of Rome.
Goode says that he is amazed that the Bishop of Exeter should
speak of the Archbishop's observations on the value of interces-
sory prayer as making the first motion of grace in Baptism
dependent upon human agency, when his, the Bishop's, doctrine
of Baptism is such that the grace of regeneration is entirely at
man's disposal—whenever he shall decide to administer the
sacrament.

Goode proceeds: "In kindness to His Grace, however, and to
facilitate his answer to your enquiry, you present him with a
specimen of your Lordship's researches into the Councils of the
Church. . . ." He then points out that the Bishop's statement
that the first canon of the Fourth Council of Carthage, declaring
the necessity for Bishops to hold the remission of original sin in
Baptism, had the authority of the whole Catholic Church is

false.[1] Harduin[2] says that all the collectors of canons, both Greek and Latin, are silent on this Council.

Goode criticizes the Bishop's statements that there is nothing in the New Testament to show that our Lord approved the zeal of those who brought children to Him. But the Lord blamed those that kept them away, and this is surely the equivalent of commending those who brought them. It was the Bishop's interpretation of the Archbishop, not the Archbishop himself, which made the grace of Baptism dependent upon the feelings of the parents. Dr Phillpotts' condemnation of the effects of such a "scheme" of Baptism he must keep to himself and not level it at the Archbishop, who never entertained such an idea.

In spite of the Bishop's remarks on Gibbon's account of those in the early church who delayed their Baptism until their death bed, hoping thereby to receive full remission of sins, Goode holds that this kind of thing is a natural consequence of the Bishop's theory of the automatic operation of grace in the sacraments.

Goode seems certain that the doctrine of regeneration, as held by the High Church party, means complete sanctification, for he says, "there are few, *comparatively* very few ungodly persons who really *believe* what I must be permitted to call the false doctrine of those who would fain teach them, that they are spiritually regenerate persons. Their conscience, their common sense, tells them that they are not". He then enters upon a long argument to show that the new matter in the Archbishop's latest preface is not out of keeping with the doctrine in the original edition of the book.

Goode severely strictures the Bishop of Exeter for the language he uses about the Archbishop mis-leading the Privy Council, and the judges violating their duty. "My Lord", he says, "it may be that such language will be permitted to pass without legal notice. But it will only be on one ground—that its character, and the quarter from which it proceeds, render it harmless." He regards Dr Phillpotts as a merciless tyrant, and he is thankful that someone has arisen to challenge his actions. He informs the Bishop that large numbers of the evangelical party were prepared to leave the Church if his doctrine of Baptism had been made authoritative.

Next follows an interesting passage on adults receiving Baptism

---

[1] See Pusey on this, p. 128, *supra*.
[2] *Councils*, ii, 975.

unworthily. Goode rejects the Bishop's resting of his doctrine
on the article in the creed, "one Baptism for the remission of
sins". The Bishop allows that the efficacy of Baptism in the
case of adults is conditional; it is therefore impossible for him
to rest his doctrine of unconditional efficacy in infants on these
words in the creed alone. If the words themselves, taken alone,
mean unconditional remission of sin in infants, then they must
mean the same for adults; this point, Goode asserts, Mr Badeley
saw, and he boldly laid down this doctrine.[1] Archdeacon
Wilberforce holds the same.[2]

This view, stated by Badeley and largely adopted by Archdeacon Wilberforce but not fully accepted by the Bishop of
Exeter, Goode puts on one side. On the other side there is the
view that the privilege of sonship is given independently of
Baptism, and that only when the privilege has been given does
the rite have efficacy. Those who hold the latter view are divided
into two parties according to the effect they believe Baptism to
have upon the children of Christian parents. The view of one
party is that the children of Christian parents are within the
bond of the covenant, so that the mere fact of their having
such parents means that the guilt of original sin will not be
imputed to them; consequently this party holds that the remission
of original sin is formally handed over to such infants in Baptism.
The other party however, which includes Gorham, and which
is equally opposed to the Bishop of Exeter, holds that there must
be an act of prevenient grace conferring remission of original
sin for even the Baptism of the infants of Christian parents to
be efficacious.[3]

Goode makes much of this "formally made over" doctrine.[4]

[1] See p. 86, *supra*; and see what Dr Addams said on the point, p. 95, *supra*.

[2] Goode says that this doctrine can be seen "without any timid reservations and
scruples" in Wilberforce. But Wilberforce does not express himself very plainly on
adults. He does, however, say, "But the Church finally ruled the matter as it is
expressed by St Augustine, that Baptism is valid where those things that are required
on the part of God are truly administered, but that its benefit does not come out till
fitness on the part of the receiver co-operates with the validity of the rite" (*The
Doctrine of Holy Baptism*, p. 48). See, however, p. 27, where he says: "What is
regeneration? It is the effect of that gift of grace . . . received by those happy members
of the family of man to whom the Gospel comes, and by whom it is not rejected through
unbelief or impenitence." But this sentence is at most ambiguous, and Goode seems
to have misconstrued Wilberforce's meaning.

[3] In other words, the former party holds that being born of Christian parents
takes the place of that act of prevenient grace which otherwise is regarded as necessary
to confer remission of original sin.

[4] Goode's "formally made over" doctrine also appears in a pamphlet of his entitled
A Letter to Sir W. P. Wood, Q.C., M.P., published in 1852.

He declares that, as opposed to the Bishop's view that Gorham holds Baptism to be a mere sign, in fact he holds that in suitable cases regeneration and adoption are "formally made over, and in that sense given, in and by Baptism". Goode claims that Gorham's denials were only directed against the Bishop's *opus operatum* doctrine.[1] Hence when the Privy Council declared that Gorham held regeneration in Baptism to be possible they were not glossing over his statements, but using the word in a limited sense—but a sense which Gorham did allow, for it is clear that he did on occasion apply the word "regeneration" to the grace which he believed to be given by the sacrament.

Goode proceeds to give an extremely able exposition of Gorham's doctrine, and in so doing is as conciliatory towards the Bishop of Exeter's views as is possible without sacrifice of the principles for which Gorham is standing. One paragraph quoted in full will show the lines upon which he is working:

The object for which I bring this illustration, is to show that it may be held, that spiritual regeneration has been given before Baptism, and yet that in that same case the party baptized is made the son of God in and by Baptism; because the former words refer to God's original act, corresponding to the act of the Sovereign in the case of which we have been speaking; and the latter to the act of the Church which, as God's minister, publicly and formally makes over to the party that which God has given.

Goode gives a piece of patristic evidence which is worth mentioning, since quotations from the Fathers are somewhat scarce on Gorham's side. It is from Cyril of Jerusalem, referring to Cornelius. Cyril says that Peter directed Cornelius to be baptized "in order that, his soul having been regenerated through faith, his body also might, through Baptism, receive grace".[2] He adds, after some other references, "So the use of the word 'regeneration' by the Fathers in connection with Baptism, can be of no avail to show that they did not hold that a rightful claim to sonship might be possessed before Baptism".

Goode goes on to deal with the passages from Anglican Divines in the Archbishop's preface which Phillpotts had alleged to be

[1] Goode adds in a footnote (p. 26): "Hence the apparent contradiction in the statements that adoption &c. may be given before or in or after Baptism [Gorham, p. 71; see p. 15, *supra*], and that adoption is *not* given *in* Baptism [Gorham, p. 113; see p. 26, *supra*] is only apparent and not real. The former relates to the *Divine grant*, the latter to the mere *opus operatum* of the Baptismal act."

[2] Catech., 3, § 2.

either misquoted or *nihil ad rem*. First he claims that Hooker in speaking of "a seal, perhaps, of the grace of election before received" was adopting and admitting the truth of these words of Cartwright.[1] Next he disputed Elrington's opinion that the work attributed to Ussher was entirely spurious. He adduced evidence that if not actually his work it received his approbation as conveying his own mind on the subjects discussed.[2] He quotes other passages from Ussher, saying that his objective language is to be interpreted in the sense which he, Goode, gives above—that Ussher means "formally making over", and in that sense giving. The evidence from Jeremy Taylor he treats in the same way, saying that the Bishop of Exeter has passed over much in his writings which supports Gorham's views. He runs through several other writers claiming that they speak in favour of the position he is maintaining. He disputed at length what the Bishop had said as to the authority of Bullinger's *Decades*, and he employed biting sarcasm against the Bishop's allegation that certain passages in Hooker are a mere *argumentum ad hominem*. He claimed that the Bishops at the Savoy Conference laid down a principle for interpreting certain passages from the Prayer Book. They were forced to apply this principle to a number of passages, but we are not bound to apply the principle precisely as they did. Goode presumably means by this that the Bishops could not allow a liberal interpretation of all the passages to which the Nonconformists objected for fear of diluting all the dogmas of the Church; but that we are not bound in the same way since at the moment we are not engaged in defending the faith from attacks from without.

Goode claims that the Bishop's allowance of "God's grace and favour" as being necessary for the administration of the sacrament is a tearing up of his doctrine by the roots—for what is God's grace and favour but an act of God's prevenient grace? But the Bishop contradicts himself, for elsewhere he says that infants are "children of wrath" until they have been baptized.

Having pointed out the sense in which he understands Gorham to accept the doctrine of Baptismal Regeneration, Goode goes on to deny the Bishop's assertion that the Judgment failed to take into account Gorham's real views.

Goode will not allow the Bishop's point that the Articles of 1562 should not have been compared with those of 1536 because the latter were drawn up for a purpose different from the former.

---

[1] See p. 110, *supra*.   [2] See p. 40, *supra*.

The 1536 Articles, he asserts, were expressly drawn up as a guide to the clergy in their teaching of the people as well as for the people themselves. He points out that language such as "certa efficacia signa gratiae" is used by the highest Calvinists, and therefore cannot be held to prove the doctrine which the Bishop maintains—such language need never mean more that Gorham believes.

Goode claims that canon LVII to which the Bishop referred does not bind the Church to a literal interpretation of the language of the Prayer Book. He maintains that in saying that the doctrine of Baptism is sufficiently contained in the Prayer Book it was refuting the idea of some of the Puritans that sacraments were invalid unless accompanied by preaching—a refutation set out at length in the canon entitled "The Sacraments not to be refused at the hands of unpreaching ministers". Many other objections which the Bishop raised to the Judgment were met by Goode on lines which have been seen before. The Declaration in the Act of Uniformity was added only because it was required as a public acknowledgement, not because some more comprehensive subscription to the Prayer Book was required, he maintained. He quotes authorities as to the binding nature of the subscription prescribed in the canon. It was absurd, he said, to distinguish between assent to the use of the Prayer Book and subscription to the doctrine contained in it.

Goode makes a vigorous refutation of the Bishop's theory that the Savoy Conference expresses the sense in which the legislature accepted the Prayer Book. Contrary to the Bishop's statement, the Savoy Conference presented no "resolutions and determinations" to the King: the whole of its time was spent in useless altercations between the parties, and no results were achieved. He referred to his account of the Savoy Conference proceedings in his *Effects of Infant Baptism*.[1]

Goode brings his letter to an end with a severe stricture on the ecclesiastical and civil disobedience which is contemplated in the closing paragraphs of the Bishop of Exeter's letter. He draws an amusing parallel between the Bishop's position and the Devonshire Rebellion of 1549:—"If you mean . . . that you will place yourself in a state of open rebellion against the laws of your country; then, my Lord, I leave you, without fear, to reap the due reward of broken vows and violated oaths; feeling well assured, that the majesty of the law will obtain as easy a triumph

[1] Pp. 480, 481.

over Devonshire and Cornish rebels *now* as it did three centuries ago".

He then gives some extracts from William Maskell's *Second Letter on the Present Position of the High Church Party in the Church of England* written after his decision to leave the English Church. In this letter Maskell recognizes the Judgment as giving a true and just statement of the doctrine of the Church of England; he feels it to be un-Catholic and therefore he leaves the Church. Goode recommends this attitude to the Bishop as being the only honest one in the circumstances.

Goode's last point is a contrast between the Bishop's friendly attitude towards Independent and Wesleyan Dissenters in his Primary Visitation Charge of 1833 and his intolerant spirit of 1850. At the end of his letter Goode adds a postscript in which he acknowledges that in a postscript to a postscript to his letter the Bishop of Exeter apologizes for his false charge against the Archbishop about the "new matter" in the last edition of *Apostolical Preaching*. The Bishop explains that he only had before him the 1815 edition and that of 1850. If he had had that of 1817 he would have seen that much of the matter which he had taken to be new in 1850 had appeared in that.

CHAPTER IX

PAMPHLETS ON THE GORHAM CASE

THE leading performers in this ecclesiastical drama may be grouped roughly in four classes. First there were those who held an extreme high doctrine of Baptism; who believed in the unconditional regeneration of all infants in and by Baptism, and who regarded the Gorham judgment as an intolerable challenge to sound doctrine and an indication that the Church of England had betrayed her trust. First among these was, of course, Dr Henry Phillpotts, the Bishop of Exeter. He only grudgingly allows that a man is ever accounted righteous in the sight of God before his Baptism; he regards justification, the redeemed status, as well as the beginning of actual holiness, as part of the grace always imparted in the baptism of infants. He says " 'newness of heart', as well as justification, is a fruit of Baptism,"[1] expressly refuting Archbishop Sumner who had denied that Baptism and newness of heart "concur towards our justification". All that Phillpotts will say about the doctrine that justification precedes Baptism is "it might, as an abstract statement of what in the nature of things is possible, have a sound sense".[2] William Maskell, the Bishop's chaplain, also falls into this class. He says: "herein then also are we justified or both accounted and made righteous, since we were made members of Him Who is alone Righteous".[3] He, with Manning, Badeley and Dodsworth regarded the Judgment as undermining the Catholic foundations of the Church of England, and seceded to Rome. Dodsworth approximated to the belief that final perseverance and assurance of ultimate salvation were included in the Grace of Baptism.[4]

The second class includes Pusey and Keble and those who with them regarded the Judgment as wrong, but did not consider that it irreparably compromised the English Church. They thought that it was not impossible for agreement to be reached between those who at the time were divided on the doctrine of Baptism. They thought that there was a great deal of misunderstanding of the high position by the evangelicals: the latter

---

[1] See p. 108, *supra*.   [2] See p. 112, *supra*.

[3] W. Maskell, *Holy Baptism: a Dissertation*, p. 354.   [4] See pp. 132–3, *supra*.

seemed to think that belief in complete sanctification and final perseverance was involved, and hence went further than they would naturally have done in qualifying baptismal grace. Those in this second class saw some positive value in the Judgment inasmuch as it refuted these ideas of Baptism which the low-church party abhorred and they themselves regarded as false.[1]

The third class is headed by Goode who supported Gorham against the Bishop of Exeter but did not accept an extreme interpretation of his doctrine. For instance he is prepared to say that "regeneration" is given in Baptism in suitable cases, and to interpret Gorham as meaning this;[2] and also he does not refute the doctrine that the children of believing parents have remission of sins formally made over to them in Baptism. Goode, in short, allows the doctrine of Baptismal Regeneration but insists upon certain qualifications as being necessary for the reception of that grace.

It is widely held that Gorham himself heads the fourth class which denies the doctrine of Baptismal Regeneration altogether.[3] There is indeed much language in Gorham's book strongly suggesting that regeneration, adoption &c., must invariably precede Baptism in order for it to have any spiritual effect at all, or else that its effectiveness is suspended until these graces have been given, quite independently of the sacrament. At all events there was a party in the Church which held this view, and there were some who even regarded Baptism as a mere sign and nothing more.

But as well as the protestations of the leading ecclesiastics of the day there were considerable agitations among the rank and file of the clergy. A pamphlet entitled *The Exeter Synod* by Gorham himself reveals that two protests were drawn up and signed by the clergy of the diocese of Exeter against a synod which the Bishop convened for June 1851 to affirm the doctrine of Baptismal Regeneration "virtually denied" by the Judicial Committee of the Privy Council. The first protest was signed by 45 clergy of the diocese and the second by 79. Someone was so moved by the dispute that he wrote a play entitled *A Vision, or the Romish Interpretation of "Be ye converted"*. The following is a sample of this singular dramatic work. The characters are:

[1] See, e.g., Pusey's attitude on p. 132, *supra*, and Keble's letter, p. 131. See also Archbishop Whately's charge, p. 169, *infra*.

[2] See *supra*, p. 138, and p. 138, note 1.

[3] As to whether Gorham really belongs to this extreme category see the reconsideration of Gorham's position on pp. 173-4, *infra*.

> Henry, Bishop of Exeter
> Paul, an Apostle
> Peter, an Apostle
> Pio Nono
> George Cornelius Gorham, Vicar of St Just
> Cardinals Innocent, Urban, Wiseman etc.
> Servants

The following is Henry's final speech, waking up at midnight after a dream in which he saw himself having fallen into the popish trap:

> Where have I been? where am I? What, alone—
> Is this a Roman dungeon? do mine eyes
> Give me a true report, or taunt me only,
> With sight of freedom, while in slavery?
> Is this my couch, my room, these walls my home?
> Sing those sweet birds their matins to console,
> Or as rejoicing in my liberty?
> Yes, I am here, safely within the sound
> Of the deep peal in yonder Norman tower.
> What melody! the clank of chains, the laugh
> Of fiends have filled mine ears; now breathes the morn,
> Laden'd with music as of Seraphim.
> Forms! Ceremonies! Rites! avaunt! ye snares.

But to come to the more serious pamphlets published in connexion with the controversy. Just as the leading figures in the dispute fell roughly into four groups, so the large number of pamphlets on the matter which were showered on the public in the years 1849-50 can be grouped in the same four classes. In addition we shall observe a fifth group of pamphlets, made up of some which express opinions in particular points not hitherto seen in the course of the controversy and which do not fall conveniently into any of the categories set out above. The purpose of this chapter is to examine a few of the pamphlets representative of the four positions. A complete list of the pamphlets collected by Mr Gladstone, now in St Deiniol's Library at Hawarden, together with those in the Bodleian Library at Oxford and in the University Library at Cambridge, is given at the end of this volume.

A. Pamphlets Expressing an Extreme High Doctrine of Baptism

The first publication which must be mentioned is Dr Phillpotts' *Letter to the Archbishop of Canterbury* which was published in the form of a pamphlet, and which has been examined in full above.

Also mention must be made of Dodsworth's two pamphlets: he seems to regard the effect of Baptism as including something approaching final perseverance. In his *Letter to the Rev E. B. Pusey* he condemns the doctrine that "sufficient grace indeed is given in baptism to save infants, if they die; but if they live, their salvation flows not from that source, to be perfected in succeeding sacraments; but from a gift perfectly distinct which they can only receive through active faith and their own intellectual apprehension".[1] And in his *The Gorham Case briefly considered* he certainly seems to say that the grace of the sacrament is more than merely the beginning of sanctification—"the grace of Holy Baptism, instead of being taught as a substitute for personal holiness, is urged as the very source and foundation of it".[2] This is at the most ambiguous, but in a pamphlet entitled *The Outward Means of Grace*, published in 1848, he had put his doctrine even more clearly: ". . . Baptism: in which, by the infinite mercy of the Father, by the infinite merit of the Son, by the infinite grace and sanctification of the Spirit, we were placed once for all, 'in the right way'. . . ."

In *A Letter to the Archbishop of Canterbury*, by W. B. Barter, the writer says much the same, declaring that sufficient grace for salvation is given to all in Baptism. And the same kind of doctrine is to be seen in *The Gorham Controversy Briefly Noticed* by Eneas Macdonnell. The writer of this pamphlet brings Bede's *History of the English Church*, Book I, Ch. 27 to bear on the subject. The passage to which he refers is St Gregory's answer, about 598, to Augustine's question whether a pregnant woman ought to be baptized. Macdonnell claims that in Gregory's answer there is nothing about prevenient grace or supplemental grace or any suggestion "of the insufficiency of baptismal grace". On the contrary, he points out, we meet the explicit doctrine of "Sacri baptismatis gratia", "donum gratiae" and "sancti mysterii gratia"; and the same doctrine is implied in the words "redemptionis mysterium" and in the phrase "illo mysterio in quo omnis culpa funditus extinguitur". And, he adds, there is not a word about a sign or seal, or anything of that sort. Macdonnell then goes on to point out that in 1565 a translation of Bede's *History* by the Rev Thomas Stapleton was published. This was three years after the final form of the English Articles was drawn up, and two years after the Council of Trent closed its sittings. In the volume containing this translation of Bede's *History* there is

[1] Pp. 13, 14.   [2] P. 18.

K

a statement entitled "Differences between the primitive faith of England continued about these thousand years, and the late pretended faith of Protestants; gathered out of the History of the Church of England, compiled by Venerable Bede, an Englishman, about 800 years past". Stapleton was an eminent Catholic controversialist, strictly opposed to the Protestant Reformation, and under the head of "Differences in Doctrine" he enumerates eighteen differences, but he does not include the doctrine of baptismal regeneration, or infant baptism, or any doctrine concerning this sacrament.

Another pamphlet written from a completely different standpoint, but having the same doctrinal force, was William Maskell's *Second Letter on the Present Position of the High Church Party in the Church of England*. The writer claims an extreme doctrine of Baptism as the true one, although he says that the Anglican reformers do not maintain it. This pamphlet, in which Maskell argues for the unconditional efficacy of infant baptism and regards the Gorham Judgment as completely heretical, was written after he had decided to resign his benefice, but before joining the Church of Rome. These are his words:

I have learnt, that perhaps with two exceptions, all the divines, bishops and archbishops, doctors and professors, of the Elizabethan age—the age, be it remembered, of the present common prayer book and its chief particulars, and of the book of homilies, and of the 39 articles—held and taught doctrines inconsistent (I write advisedly) with the true doctrine of baptism. . . .

It is one thing for a religious community to allow its ministers to hold and to teach a particular doctrine; it is quite another that they should be enjoined to teach it, as being certainly and exclusively true. There are some books of the Elizabethan writers, which are examples of the first of these positions, namely, the permission: but I do not remember any example of the second: on the contrary, numberless proofs that it could scarcely have been intended.

"A Scottish Presbyter" wrote in *A Letter to the Right Reverend the Bishop of Glasgow and Galloway* that the Judgment was so harmful to true religion that the Episcopal Church of Scotland should break away from the English Church.

B. Pamphlets Opposed to Gorham yet Expressing a Moderate Doctrine of Baptism

Pusey and Keble were perhaps unconsciously the leaders of this school of thought.[1] They saw that there was some value

[1] See pp. 131–2, *supra*.

in the Judgment if it disabused the evangelical party of the idea that the doctrine of baptismal regeneration precluded the need for any subsequent growth in holiness; nevertheless they were adamant in insisting that the grace of the sacrament was inseparably united to its administration. There was a large number of pamphlets published which argued along these lines, but did not regard the Judgment as irreparably compromising the doctrine of the English Church.

Archdeacon Hare of Lewes wrote *A Letter to the Hon. Richard Cavendish* in which he declared Baptismal Regeneration to be the doctrine of the Church of England, but condemned any action which would drive out the evangelicals while there was still time for agreement to be reached. He remarks, "the hypothetical view of Baptismal Regeneration is still very common among the so-called evangelical clergy". He is particularly afraid of a doctrine of Baptism which leaves no room for subsequent sanctification by the Spirit. He averred that although the Privy Council decided that Gorham's views were not such as to give legal ground for refusing him institution, there was no question of giving equal sanction to two views of Baptism. In his attempt to conciliate he even goes so far as to say that forgiveness of sins cannot be said to be always exactly contemporaneous with Baptism.[1] Baptism forgives future sins as well as past ones, and he quotes Jeremy Taylor: "Baptism does not only pardon our sins, but puts us into a state of pardon for the time to come".[2]

Lord Redesdale wrote a pamphlet entitled *Observations on the Judgment in the Gorham Case: and the way to unity*. In this he complains particularly of one phrase in the Judgment—"it is not particularly declared in them (the Articles) what is the distinct meaning and effect of the Grace of Regeneration; whether it is a change of nature, a change of condition, or a change of relation subsisting between sinful man and his Creator". Article XXVII, Lord Redesdale claims, declares the grace of Baptism to be all three. The writer has no objection to the manner in which Gorham holds that infants may become worthy recipients, but it cannot be imagined that God wishes the damnation of any (Art. XXV), therefore Article XXVII must mean that all infants are worthy recipients. He says "In these two points of doctrine all the others, raised in the questions, answers and

[1] Hare's words were (p. 8): "Now the Article in the Creed in no way defines the various modes in which this mighty power manifests itself . . . it does not declare that the sins of all persons who are baptized are straightway forgiven. . . ."

[2] *Discourse of Baptism*, s. 18.

arguments are resolved. . . ." The Bishop, he maintains, could have proceeded against Gorham on the ground of Article XXVII for denying that all infants are worthy. Lord Redesdale is in general opposed to Gorham, but in another pamphlet entitled *Reflections on the Doctrine of Regeneration and its connexion with both sacraments* he seems to make a concession to him in saying, "the presence of the Spirit properly precedes the administration of the sacrament; that water as well as the Spirit, even in its most miraculous form, is necessary to perfect Christian baptism; and that without the Spirit, it is the baptism of John only".

In a pamphlet called *An Apology for the Plain sense of the Doctrine of the Prayer Book on Holy Baptism*, the Rev Alexander Watson, then curate of St John's, Cheltenham, began with a bold defence of the idea of baptismal grace being at the disposal of man:

> Every lawful minister of God *has* "power and authority given him by God to make over" "remission of sins and spiritual regeneration" "by performing the rite of Baptism". But it is not "at his pleasure"— it is not as the "author" of grace—it is not with "an absolute power", nor because he regards Baptism as the "source" (!!) of grace that he then acts—No, the Sacraments "be effectual because of Christ's institution and promise". It is He who worketh, not man. And although man is entrusted with the perilous endowment of acting contrary to God's commands, there is no authority given to man to compensate for this disobedience by constructing a theory founded on this exceptional anomaly.[1]

The writer is answering Goode's *Letter to the Bishop of Exeter*, and he attacks Goode's treatment of the evidence from Reformation divines. But at the same time as opposing the evangelical position, Watson is careful to refute the idea that the doctrine of baptismal regeneration precludes the necessity for subsequent sanctification: "Birth", he says, "is not a continuous state, but an act referable to a particular period". "They in whom the law of life works towards everlasting salvation, not only were new-born, but are living the new life; they are not only spiritually regenerate, but they are day by day sanctified by the Spirit of Truth". He then proceeds to a long jeremiad on the effects of an hypothetical construction of the passages in the Prayer Book which speak of baptismal regeneration.

In a pamphlet entitled *The Present Position of the Church*, *Letter III: Effect of the late Judgment on the Church*, the Rev W. H. Hoare pleads for a literal interpretation of the statements on Baptism

[1] Pp. 23, 24.

in the creeds and the Catechism. But he adds, "That the grant is free and unconditional—though in after life the continuance of the grace must depend on the use made of it—might be further insisted on. But these and such other points might be regarded as deductions from the main truth, more than as essential parts of it". All the time this writer is assuming a close union between Church and State, and that the State recognizes its duty to teach religion and morality through the medium of the National Church. In *Letter II* Hoare points out the obscurity of this controversy owing to misunderstandings as to the meaning of the term "regeneration".

In *The Baptismal Controversy* by the Rev R. Montgomery there is a violent condemnation of Bishop Hopkins' idea that "regeneration" means simply visible admission to ecclesiastical privileges. "It really appears almost like a solemn mockery", the writer says, "to render solemn thanks unto God the Spirit, for a sacramental appearance, which man alone is quite competent, *ad extra*, to achieve".

In *A Pastoral Letter to the Clergy of the Diocese of Ripon* Dr Longley, the Bishop, took a severe view of Gorham's doctrine, but did not maintain an extreme position himself. He said that Gorham's views "seem to leave Baptism an empty rite, conveying no real benefit, nor advancing the receiver one step in the way of salvation; they seem to overthrow the nature of a Sacrament, robbing Baptism of all its inward and spiritual grace". He himself seems to concentrate upon remission of sins as though that were the particular grace of Baptism, saying "Remission of sins is the grace of Baptism", and "the peculiar grace of Baptism; namely the remission of sins". In this he is in company with Pusey and Keble. But he does say that remission of sins begins a new life, and seems to suggest that Baptism is a part of sanctification as opposed to justification. "It will be perceived how clear a course the Church of England holds between the Romanizing extreme on the one hand . . . and the other extreme . . . as if there were not the same relation between our natural birth and our natural growth, as there is between regeneration and progressive sanctification. It will be felt also, I believe, that the preaching of Baptismal regeneration in the sense which avoids each of these extremes, is entirely consistent with the fullest and freest recognition of that blessed truth, so full of all comfort to the believer, that we are justified by faith only for the merit of our Lord and Saviour Jesus Christ".[1]

[1] P. 21.

In *A Letter to the Most Rev John Bird, Lord Archbishop of Canterbury
and the Most Rev Thomas, Lord Archbishop of York* written anonymously by "A Rural Dean", the view is expressed that Archbishop Sumner's *Apostolical Preaching* is sound on Baptism, but
that the Judgment is inconsistent with this. The writer accuses
Gorham of spurious Calvinism:

Your Grace has declared that *Apostolical Preaching* was aimed against
the Calvinistic doctrine of particular election, but Mr Gorham's
heresy is spurious Calvinism. Calvin never taught that *regeneration
was separated from Baptism.* He upheld the dignity of the sacrament,
though he set limits to the mercy of God; he confounded regeneration,
which is the act of a moment, with repentance, which is a continuous
habit; he preached regeneration as progressive, but *always commencing
in Baptism.* This gift of God he limited to his fancied *elect*—to Mr
Gorham's recipients "*with God's grace and favour*", but he never separated
the grace of regeneration from Baptism.

*A Letter on the Recent Judgment in the case Gorham v the Bishop
of Exeter,* also published anonymously, is severely critical of the
Judgment while maintaining a moderate high doctrine. The
writer is scathing in his denunciation of the statement in the
Judgment on the necessity for sureties at infant baptism. The
Judgment said:

The adult person is not pronounced regenerate until he has first
declared his faith and repentance; and before the act of Infant Baptism,
the child is pledged by its sureties to the same condition of faith and
repentance. And these requirements of the Church, in her complete
and public services, ought, upon a just construction of all the services,
to be considered as the rule of the Church, and taken as proof that
the same promise though not expressed, is implied in the exceptional
case, when the rite is administered in expectation of immediate death,
and the exigency of the case does not admit of sureties. Any other
conclusion would be an argument to prove, that none but the imperfect
and incomplete ceremony, allowed in the exceptional case, would be
necessary in any case.

The writer says that this contradicts the rubrics of the service
of private baptism, which clearly declares that in such a case
the child "is lawfully and sufficiently baptized". Secondly, he
says, "Consider the *extreme folly* of the statement. According to
it—if the Baptized Child live, then Baptism is not complete—
if the Baptized Child die, then the Baptism is complete.—For
'*it is certain by God's word, that children, which are Baptized, dying
before they commit actual sin, are undoubtedly saved*'. Therefore (as

it has been remarked) according to the judgment of the Court— DEATH MAKES THE SACRAMENT VALID!!!" Nevertheless, in a note at the end of this pamphlet, entitled "A plain statement of the doctrine of Holy Baptism", the writer allows the doctrine of the suspended operation of grace in the case of adults, saying, "If Faith and Repentance be professed by Adults in hypocrisy or be not real, then the adult baptized *is* baptized, and cannot be baptized again; but his sins are not remitted but increased, nor is the wrath of God removed but confirmed. Nevertheless, the Sacrament, unworthily received, may upon *future repentance*, operate, by virtue of Christ's institution, to a wholesome effect". But he holds that infants are qualified for reception of the sacrament simply through absence of *obex*. Baptism is a change of nature, not merely of condition—"God assumed man's nature; man, through Baptism, the channel of grace, is made partaker of the Divine Nature".

Another pamphlet is this class is *Baptism misunderstood, the great trouble of the Church* by the Rev Alfred Gatty. The writer declares his belief in regeneration *in* Baptism, and points out that the faithful adult is not called regenerate until he is baptized. Infants are regenerate in Baptism, but his view is that regeneration is conditional in this case also, not merely on the faith of the sponsors, but on the faith of the whole congregation—which, however, he says, can always be assumed. He is careful to distinguish between regeneration and final perseverance.

In *The Gorham Case, and the doctrine which it contains considered*, James Collins, Dean of Killala, declares that the Judgment does not bind the Church to Gorham's view. Among his remarks are the following: ". . . Regeneration, namely the depositing of the sacred seed . . ." and ". . . to be sanctified 'wholly' (1 Thess. v. 23); but this is a remote and progressive blessing—it is Sanctification and not Regeneration".

The Subjective and Objective Theories of Regeneration explained and examined by "A Clergyman of the Diocese of Exeter" concentrates primarily on remission of sins as the grace of Baptism: "regeneration", the writer says, means this, and is clearly to be distinguished from Repentance, Conversion and Renewal.

C. Pamphlets Supporting the Judgment but taking a Moderate Low View of Baptism

The leading pamphleteer in this class is the Rev William Goode whose *Letter to the Bishop of Exeter* has been examined in full above. Goode was for some years editor of the *Christian Observer* and was the recognized champion of the evangelical party at the time; he was also the author of *The Effects of Infant Baptism* published in 1849. The characteristic of this group of pamphlets is to allow the doctrine of Baptismal Regeneration, but to insist upon the conditions of faith and repentance, albeit not always denying that infants may receive the grace of the sacrament.

As well as his other writings, Goode published in 1850, under the name of "the late editor of the *Christian Observer*", a pamphlet entitled *Review of the Judgment of Sir H. J. Fust*. This contains criticisms of the judgment in the Arches Court largely on lines which we have observed before. When the judge commented on Gorham's doctrine of prevenient grace, he said, "That there may be 'prevenient grace' is not for me to deny. There may be grace imparted at the reception of Baptism, at the very identical moment the rite is administered; or there may be no grace imparted at that time, but it may be accorded hereafter. Both these are suppositions to which Mr Gorham resorts, and which the Court is not bound in any manner to deny". The writer observes that these remarks are difficult to reconcile with the final decision of the court. He quotes Pusey *on Baptism*, apparently admitting that Hooker allowed an hypothetical construction of the services.[1] An interesting passage in this pamphlet of Goode's is the following: "It does not follow that nothing is given by Baptism to infants supposing that there is no present bestowal of grace. . . . The sacrament becomes effectual as soon as the moral condition of the party becomes such as to call into operation and give life to the sacramental act".[2] The writer says that the child may be said to be possessed of the blessing of the covenant in the same way as a child inheriting an estate upon some condition is in some way possessed of it even before the condition is fulfilled.

In the same sort of position is Lord Lindsey's pamphlet, *A Brief Analysis of the Doctrine and Argument in the case of Gorham v the Bishop of Exeter*. The only section of the pamphlet which is of interest to the present enquiry is that which discusses the present position of the Church of England. The writer's theory is that the Church of England embraces both the objectivity of Catholicism and the Subjectivity of Protestantism. It is very advantageous to have these two elements within the one field—

[1] Pp. 146, 7.   [2] P. 27.

"every struggle has left the Church on a higher vantage-ground than before, and nearer the recognition of Universal Truth". The high-church party, represented by the Bishop of Exeter, dwells upon the objective grace given in the sacrament of Baptism; the low-church upon the subjective condition of the recipient. Gorham dwells upon the subjective qualifications of the recipient to such an extent as to diverge into heresy—he differs from the majority of the low-church party. The writer holds that the judgment allows the general low-church view, but does not sanction Gorham's doctrine inasmuch as it does not really take it into account at all. The Church of England ought not to be troubled about the Judgment—it merely sanctions one of the views which make up its unique comprehensiveness, and does not in any way threaten orthodoxy.

A Letter to the Bishop of Exeter, by "A Layman", asserts that the rule laid down in the Judgment is not wrong: the mistake comes in deciding that Gorham's case comes within it—so it is not a vindication of Gorham's views. The decision is an error of fact, not of rule.[1]

Another pamphlet in this class is *A Remonstrance to the Bishop of Exeter on his recent letter to the Archbishop of Canterbury* by the Rev L. Vernon Harcourt. The writer of this pamphlet was the author of a work on baptismal regeneration entitled *The Doctrine of the Deluge*. In the *Remonstrance* he takes up a position midway between Gorham and Dr Phillpotts, saying:

> Moreover, though I am a great stickler for baptismal regeneration, I cannot shut my eyes to the fact, that the language of the Liturgy, even in that most earnest persuasion to which you allude, is most plainly conditional, and based upon charitable presumption; for it exhorts us earnestly to believe, not only that the child will be received with favour and mercy, but that Christ will give unto him the blessing of eternal life, and make him partaker of his everlasting kingdom. Can we really believe this of every infant that is baptized, except upon the charitable presumption, that he also will perform his part of the covenant, and keep the promises made in his behalf?

And yet he will not go the whole way with Gorham, for he says a little later:

> This strange fancy, that worthiness is a predisposition indispensable to a participation in the graces of a sacrament, is neither warranted by Scripture, nor acknowledged by our Church: . . . But if the

[1] The author of this pamphlet was Sir Edward Hall Alderson (Baron Alderson), a distinguished judge of the Court of Exchequer.

unworthiness attributed to infants disqualifies them for the reception
of sacramental grace, who can hope to be qualified for the other
Sacrament?

And he adds:

If, on the one hand, nothing is said about the state of unbaptized
infants, and therefore there can be no assurance that they are
undoubtedly saved, and on the other hand, it is averred as a most
certain truth, that baptized infants are undoubtedly saved; to deny
that baptism is the means by which they are saved, merely because
they are not said *totidem verbis*, to be saved by Baptism, is a specimen
of that hard sophistry which has hitherto been considered the peculiar
property of the Jesuits.

But he also puts forward a suggestion which would reduce the
whole controversy to a matter of hair-splitting, and which would
hardly be acceptable to Gorham. He says, "If Mr Gorham will
allow that his prevenient grace accompanies the affusion of the
water, all parties may rest contented; for his theory is then
satisfied, and he does not deny the article of the creed, and
does not separate entirely the inward and spiritual grace from
the sacrament". But if the writer holds this view, and regards
the first motions of grace towards the soul as being contemporaneous with the affusion of the water, it somewhat cuts across
his assertion that justification is not one of the fruits of Baptism,
which he appears to make in another place.

In *Notices of the late Judgment of Sir Herbert Jenner Fust in the
Court of Arches* by the Rev John King, the writer complains that
Sir Herbert's "own preconceived notions may, unconsciously,
have led him to overlook important arguments which deserved
consideration. . . ." The judge had rejected as a false principle
reference to the sentiments of the Reformers. King says that this
was a mistake, since to suggest a discrepancy between the views
of the Reformers and the doctrines of the Church would be to
say that the Reformers who drew up the services, were lacking
in integrity, that the Prayer Book was full of self-contradictions
and absurdities, and that the Church of England had adopted
formularies dishonestly framed.

The Reformers, he declared, held Calvin's views on Election,
Predestination and Final Perseverance, so they could not have
believed the doctrine of the universal regeneration of baptized
infants: it could not, therefore, have been their intention to
leave this doctrine in the services. The writer criticizes the
judge's comments on Article XVII. He had said it "determines

nothing as to Predestination and Election: and it appeared that those questions were left open. . . ." King remarks, "It is styled 'An Article on Predestination', but there is no Predestination in it!" Perhaps the intention was to leave the door open to Arminianism, but certainly not to nullify the Article altogether. The continental Calvinists worked upon the hypothetical principle in interpreting baptismal formularies: the English Reformers may be presumed to have done the same.

In addition to the above, there were a number of less important pamphlets, for instance, *A Letter to the Right Rev the Lord Bishop of Ripon on Baptismal Regeneration*, by Joseph Wolff, which affirmed Gorham's doctrine of prevenient grace as well as declaring regeneration in Baptism: this writer believed that the children of believing parents qualified for reception of the grace of the sacrament. Also there was *The Judgment of Charity*, by Thomas Vores, which, like Goode, allowed baptismal regeneration in suitable cases.

D. Pamphlets denying Baptismal Regeneration and taking an Extreme Low View of the Sacrament

The question as to whether Gorham himself really belongs to this class is one which cannot hastily be answered. There is much in his book which suggests this; yet there are other passages which suggest that in the heat of the argument he may have been driven into a position which he was not really willing to hold. However that may be, there were a few pamphlets published at the time which gave an extreme interpretation of Gorham's language, some of them regarding the grace of the sacrament as being simply an increase of something already given or having the power to enlarge something which was to be given in the future, and there were some which even regarded Baptism as no more than an outward sign.

The Rev J. Jordan, Vicar of Enstone, wrote *An Appeal to the Evangelical Clergy against the Doublesense Use of the Baptismal and Confirmation Services and the Catechism of the Church of England*. He holds Gorham's view that Regeneration, Adoption etc. are given apart from Baptism. He declares Baptism to be an "effective sign", but the sense in which he uses that term is shown by the following: "As by being thus reminded of its Baptism, and itself calling to mind the privileges into which it has been outwardly admitted, the sign is made effectual, that it works in and impresses upon the mind of the child the truth which it signifies. . . ." He gives his opinion that in this dispute one party has given a literal interpretation of the Prayer Book, and thus arrived at an unscriptural doctrine, while the other party has sought to evade the meaning of the Prayer Book language. The Church should be allowed to hold its own synods and draw up a baptismal formula which expressed the conditional efficacy of the sacrament.

An anonymous pamphlet entitled *The Sacrament of Baptism considered in reference to an examination of the Rev G. C. Gorham by the Bishop of Exeter and the Judgment of Sir Herbert Jenner Fust* boldly declared Baptism to be no more than a sign: ". . . the Sacrament of Baptism, which on our part is a sign of our solemn renunciation of our past sins, and of our faith in God through Christ, and of our obedience to him; and which on God's part is a sign to us, that he has washed away and cleansed us from all our sins, and will fulfil all his promises made to us, and to our children". In another place, however, he says, "God works invisibly in them who worthily receive the sign, that is, he quickens or excites, strengthens and confirms *their pre-existent faith*". This, however, is ambiguous, and must be taken in the light of his insistence elsewhere that the Baptism of infants is a mere sign of God's good-will towards them, which they may reject.

In *The True Idea of Baptism*, by Lord Congleton, the writer declared himself opposed to the practice of infant baptism altogether, and he says: "Baptism is not the means whereby a man is born again of the Holy Spirit, but the outward and visible act whereby penitent and believing sinners do outwardly and visibly obtain the remission of their sins". An even more clearly extreme view is taken in a pamphlet entitled *Baptismal Regeneration Refuted: A Letter to the Lord Archbishop of Canterbury*, by W. E. Pope. He says: ". . . even in adults, baptism is but an external, yet a solemn rite—an outward mark of allegiance. . . ."

E. Pamphlets Expressing Views on Particular Points, which do not fall conveniently into Any of the Above Categories

One passage in the Rev L. Vernon Harcourt's pamphlet, *A Remonstrance to the Bishop of Exeter*, is interesting because it is written by someone who believes in baptismal regeneration, and who is trying to make some logical definition of the terms "Regeneration", "Justification" and "Sanctification" in their relation to Baptism. His language is not completely clear, but he seems to be groping in the direction of a definition of baptismal grace which confines the operation of the sacrament to the process of sanctification, and excludes it from justification.

These are his words:[1]

It might seem, at first, as if sanctification and justification must be the same thing; for what is the difference between being made holy, and being made just or righteous? But justification is a forensic term, signifying acquittal from guilt in the sight of God, so that he can treat the justified as if they were really just. When a man is baptized, faith enables him to lay hold of that privilege, and his sins being washed away through the water and the blood, he is reputed holy; and if he dies without forfeiting it again, he is saved. When an infant is baptized, the faith of the parent, or of the sponsors, or of the minister, or of the congregation, is accepted vicariously, and he is justified by that faith, inasmuch as he is acquitted from the guilt of his sinful nature; original sin is then forgiven. In this sense, it is true, that "justification and newness of heart are contemporaneously given in Baptism"; but it is an unwise and dangerous language to employ. For what is the dogmatic teaching of our Church? Does it tell us that we are justified by Baptism or by faith?

And this seems to be much what is in his mind later when he says (p. 36), "Mr Gorham . . . divides the grace of regeneration into two parts, of which one must of necessity precede the other, but without assigning any specific interval between them". This is also the general tenor of a pamphlet entitled *Baptism accompanied by conditional and unconditional grace*, by C. R. Cameron. The writer believes Regeneration to be the equivalent of Justification, and holds that the grace of Baptism is a seal of this and also "such a measure of the Spirit as may enable us to attain that holiness without which we cannot enter into the kingdom of heaven".[2]

In *A Review of the Gorham Case in its aspects moral and legal*, J. D. Chambers, Recorder of New Sarum, expresses a lawyer's opinion on the chaotic results that would follow from an application to all legal documents of the principles which the Privy Council had applied to the Prayer Book. It is contrary to the purpose of the Articles, which were drawn up to avoid diversity and to establish consent as to true religion, to allow contradictory doctrines to exist side by side. The decision, he holds, violates the rules of law, grammar, reason and equity, and ought not therefore to affect the conscience of a single member of the Church of England.

[1] P. 8.   [2] See also the charge of Bishop McIlvaine of Ohio, p. 170.

A View of Baptism which supersedes Exeter v Gorham, written anonymously, claims to be an appeal, after the example of Article XX to Holy Scripture as the sole standard. As there is no record of infant baptism in the New Testament, and the conditions which surround Baptism there—repentance (Luke iii. 3); teaching (Matt. xxviii. 19) belief (Mark xvi. 16)—are all such as can apply to adults only, it is wrong for the Church to baptize infants. Article XXVII is wrong about infant baptism: it is not "agreeable with the institution of Christ", but resting solely on the counsels of men, has "neither strength nor authority" (Art. XXI). The writer commends Gale's answer to Wall in the eighteenth century. Up to the time of Justin Martyr, he says, every mention of Baptism is incompatible with Infant Baptism. Tertullian denounced it; all sorts of corruption follow its introduction. A new Reformation is needed in the Church, on this matter. If the Church abandoned infant baptism anyhow one ground of contention between Gorham and the Bishop of Exeter would be removed—it would be agreed by both sides that faith and repentance must precede the administration of the sacrament. As to the exact effect of Baptism, we cannot say. "All that we know from God—all that we can gather from the sure warrant of Holy Scripture, is this—namely, that when, but not until we have sincerely repented of our past sins, and have a hearty faith in Christ, we are to be baptized. What is the precise virtue of Baptism we neither know, nor are concerned to know. Suffice it however for us, that God commands it. . . . One thing is quite clear: the more virtue and importance we attach to the rite of Baptism, the more essential it is that it should be received by rational beings, and not by senseless babies".

A pamphlet entitled *The Sacrament of Baptism with remarks on the ambiguity of the modern use of the word Regeneration* by the Rev R. W. Bosanquet declares that "regeneration" means a change of state and not a change of heart or disposition. The grace of Baptism, then, the writer holds, is Justification, and he concentrates particularly on the remission of sin. In infants this grace is worked prior to any preparatory conversion; in adults it is suspended until "repentance and faith had their effectual work in the heart". Baptism "increases grace" in those who have experienced conversion before receiving the sacrament.

The Rev Henry James Hastings, in a pamphlet called *Reasons for not signing the proposed Address to the Lord Bishop of Worcester*, says that a grace is conferred in infant baptism, but that it is not the full regeneration which accompanies adult baptism in faith and repentance. He quotes approvingly a passage from Dean Milner to this effect. In 1816 Milner prepared materials for publishing a work on Baptism which, however, never came out; but passages are preserved in his *Life*—for instance, the following:

To trace the manner and the circumstances by which baptism of adults led to the baptism of infants has ever been considered a very intricate and difficult enquiry in the history of the Church of Christ. . . . This, however, I think, is sufficiently clear, that the term regeneration, which had constantly been applied to adult converts, continued to be still applied to infants, though it was impossible that faith and repentance could exist in the young subjects. . . . This subject is very important in a practical sense. Thus if the terms regeneration—born of God—Sons of God—New creature—Conversion of heart, and such like, are all allowed to have in Scripture the same meaning (which no student of Scripture can deny,)—then, as it is impossible to predicate these same things of baptized infants, whatever be the meaning of regeneration when applied to them in our Church service, it will be a most dangerous inference for them, when they shall have become adults, to make, that because they were baptized in infancy they possess of course a regeneration of the same nature and efficacy as that arising from the baptism of adults. . . .

The kind of thing that is implied by this is that infant baptism confers justification alone, but that adult baptism gives justification and as well a certain measure of sanctification; for a few paragraphs later the writer of this pamphlet says, "We must, in fact, make a distinction between a spiritual change of state and a spiritual change of heart". He quotes Augustine in support of his view:

Ita et in baptizatis infantibus praecedit regenerationis sacramentum et (si Christianum tenuerint pietatem) sequitur in corde conversio. . . . Et baptismus quidem potest inesse ubi conversio cordis defuerit conversio autem cordis potest quidem inesse non percepto baptismo, sed contempto baptismo non potest.[1]

As well as these there were a few pamphlets which dealt with the cosmic aspect of justification as opposed to the individual. So much thought in this controversy had been concentrated upon the salvation of the individual that it is a great relief to find some writers dealing with the solidarity of the whole Christian family and the redemption of the race in Christ. Hastings' pamphlet *Reasons for not signing the proposed address*, quoted above,

[1] *Contra Donat*, Lib. iv, c. xxiv, § 31, and c. xxv, § 32.

has some allusion to this. The writer does not agree with Gorham's theory that some special grace must necessarily be infused into the heart of an unconscious babe before it can be fit to receive the benefits of baptism. The grace of Calvary must go before; but to say more, Hastings holds, is to go beyond human ken. The whole Christian family is redeemed by the cross, the grace of which is sealed in Baptism. This is how he puts it:

The great transaction at Calvary, the one full, perfect, and sufficient sacrifice, oblation, and satisfaction made on the cross for the sins of the whole world, is a grace bestowed on infants to which the children of Christian parents are mercifully admitted. *This* grace goes before baptism—in baptism it is sealed. Infants are allowed to enter into covenant with God under the Christian as well as under the Jewish dispensation. To me it seems that we are intruding into those things which we have not seen, and which we cannot know, in determining that, in any other sense than has been stated, a prevenient act of grace is required for infants to be right recipients of baptism.

This doctrine is treated extensively in a pamphlet entitled *The Gorham Case. Which are we to believe?* by "A Country Rector". The writer says that if the decision of the Privy Council is right, Baptism "cannot be a sign of grace . . . it is therefore a sign of nothing, but a snare and a delusion". He repeatedly stresses that the whole race is redeemed, and that Baptism is admission to the commonwealth of Israel. Baptism does not work salvation, it admits into a state of salvation which already exists. The following are some quotations showing how the writer expresses his point of view:

The question is . . . whether . . . in giving this plain and simple ordinance to all nations, Christ did not intend to bestow a visible rite for the admission of His professing households to the fold of that Apostolic Church in all those nations to which His providence should assign the high prerogative of possessing the Gospel as their proper light and religion? And if He did intend to give that visible admission to His Church, and we have that Church amongst us, which has grown out of that ordination, there is no human reason that can draw a plainer or more self-evident induction from the charge given by our Lord with that institution, than that Baptism in the name of the Holy Trinity is the true and sole means of admission to that Church, and to whatever share in the grace of God, that Church can ever attain, as a national Church in the commonwealth of Israel.[1]

[1] P. 90.

And the following occurs among his comments on infant Baptism:

Infant Baptism then appears to be the natural state, if we may use such an expression of the Christian dispensation. In no other state can that imputed worthiness be so properly attributed, as to that of childhood in its innocence; and that too for a cause which is not of themselves who are baptized, but of an inheritable favour, out of regard to the faith of their progenitors.[1]

He believes in baptismal regeneration, but confines that grace in the case of infants to those who are born of believing parents. Whereas Goode thinks of this from the point of view of the individual this writer has in mind the whole time the doctrine of the redemption of the race; and uses such phrases as "the national church", "the commonwealth of Israel", etc.

Whatever then may be the real opinions of Mr Gorham on the questions of personal election and its consequents, his answers, so far as they are shown in Dr Fust's Judgment, are judicially satisfied by a reference of them to the inherited grace in those children, which are born of Christian parents. And his position, that children are by nature unworthy recipients, being born in sin and children of wrath, is satisfied by the difference the Church recognizes between the children born in the households of faith, and those which are born in unreclaimed families.[2]

But he will not have Gorham's "secret grace of regeneration" necessary to make Baptism effective.

This same position is taken up in *The Church of England not high, not low but broad as the Commandment of God*, by Dr T. W. Peile, Headmaster of Repton. He assumes England to be the proper Church-State—"In what we well pray for as the 'most religious and gracious' Person of our Sovereign, I see (under the God-Man Jesus Christ our Lord) the one anointed head of one Anglo-Catholic Church-and-Kingdom". He sees Baptism as admission to membership of this redeemed Church and Realm:

But now, if as Christians we must have submitted ourselves to the Civil Power, viewed simply as an "ordinance of man"—and this both "to the King, as supreme," and "to governors, as being sent by him"—what shall we say, when this same Power claims our obedience and homage as the Lord's own anointed head of a body whose every member also has received its unction from THE HOLY ONE? the same *Lord over all* being rich in mercy unto *all* who come to His holy Baptism, and wash away their birth-sin by calling, in the midst of His Congregation, upon the saving Name of the Lord. On the one hand, what in

[1] P. 46.   [2] P. 61.

the course of this world had been simply Cæsar's—our obedience as
citizens, our loyalty, our devotedness of heart and hand to the cause
of our Queen and Country—all these have become consecrated, and
are seen now to be *rendered unto* GOD, in one whom we *doubly* reverence
as "GOD's minister to us for good". On the other hand, what in His
Congregation is purely GOD's—His engrafted Word and Sacraments,
and with these the power of an Apostolically descended ministry to
build up, and not (at a man's own peril) pull down or profane His
spiritual Temple—these too are seen to be not the less *administered
for* GOD, because from one Head and Fountain of honour, in one
never-to-be-divided "Church and Kingdom", we trace the visible
presence among us of those "Two Anointed Ones"—*Ecclesiastical
Order*, namely, and *Civil Government*—"that stand before the Lord of
the whole earth".

Dr Peile enlarges on the theme in another pamphlet, *The Christian
Temple and its Representative Priesthood.*

F. A Dissenting Commentary on the Controversy

Protestant, just as much as Romanist, Dissenters were quick
to make capital out of the discomfiture of the Church of England
which was caused by the Gorham controversy. A book, published
in 1850, entitled *The Great Gorham Case; A history in five books*,
was a reprint of a series of articles which had appeared in the
Christian Times—"an unsectarian religious journal", as it called
itself—at intervals during the course of the whole case from its
commencement in the Court of Arches in April 1849 to its
conclusion in March 1850. The writer imagines himself to be
installed in what he calls the "Crow's Nest", a viewpoint at the
top of St Paul's Cathedral. He tells his story as though looking
down from that lofty eminence upon London and observing the
proceedings in Doctor's Commons—where the Court of Arches
met—and in the Privy Council chamber in Downing Street;
and noticing the effect of the decisions upon Londoners at large.
The book is written from the point of view of Nonconformity,
and therefore what it says on doctrine is not of great importance
to those who are seeking the faith of the Church of England.
Some of the questions which the writer raises, however, are a
challenge to Anglicans, but for the rest it may be regarded as a
brief interlude in the midst of the arid technicalities of the
controversy.

The following extract from the Preface gives some indication
of the impression which the Gorham case made on Dissenters
at large:

I have never been reluctant to express my high estimation of many things in the established Church. I like parts of her ecclesiastical system; I admire the Collects, the Liturgy, and the general tone of her Services and worship. Often have I cordially attended that worship, and so experienced the power of some of the formularies, as to have been melted into tears—to have had my heart broken and healed at once—and to have felt that I could dispense with the sermon altogether. To me—to my feelings, judgment and taste—the Church has many and strong attractions. I can not only understand how powerful may be the inducements to devout minds to turn away from theological objections, that would disturb their repose or diminish their enjoyment, but I can also appreciate the nature of the struggle with which minds of deeper insight may endeavour to bring themselves to accept or tolerate the terms of subscription. *With all this, however,* the more I have attempted distinctly to understand the Church Offices, and fairly and honestly to estimate all that they legitimately involved, on whatever theory of interpretation explained, the more have I been confirmed in the soundness and sufficiency of those objections which the Fathers of Nonconformity urged against them. The late decision in the Gorham case may minister relief to some minds, and mitigate or remove the difficulties of others, since it legalizes a somewhat broader interpretation of what is supposed to be *the mind of the imposer* at the time of subscription, than we Nonconformists could ever make out from our unaided, personal study of the book. That book, however, still remains just as it was; it is still a matter of individual obligation "to be fully persuaded in one's own mind", as to what its sense actually is to *us*; the advocates of the opposite, though alike and equally authenticated, readings, are all earnest in denouncing each other; in spite of the authority of the Committee of the Privy Council, a conscientious man may, without presumption, question the correctness of their reasoning and judgment; or he may feel dissatisfied to be guided in what he has to utter to God by the cold technicalities of legal interpretation; or, if not, he may certainly hesitate about the claims of a Church, in which two directly opposite opinions, on what each party designates *"vital"* truth, are authoritatively endorsed,—the respective opinions being to their advocates the truth itself, and being regarded, of course, as *so* "vital" as to warrant their mutually anathematising each other![1]

It is interesting to observe these comments of an outsider on the width of interpretation which the final decision allowed. After this passage the writer gives his opinion that both sides in the controversy are wrong since, he holds, both theories of Baptism "spring from an original seminal falsehood—a first

[1] Pp. ix–xi.

and fatal fundamental lie common to them both". This "first and fatal fundamental lie" he declares to be:

They alike assume the universal liability of all infants, *as* such, to GOD'S EVERLASTING WRATH AND DAMNATION;—that every babe is born into the world fitted for HELL;—fitted for, that is, or righteously exposed to, intense, inconceivable, immitigable, and conscious eternal anguish!

His doctrine need not detain us, but what he says about the principle of interpretation which the Judgment allows is worth noticing:

At the same time, it would have been proper to have adverted to what cannot be denied,—the fearful price, namely, at which latitude of opinion and diversity of interpretation are secured in a national Established Church, with such dogmatic standards as ours;—on the one hand, by nothing less than by open infidelity to solemn subscriptions, or, on the other, by applying principles of interpretation to the language of formularies, which, if applied by gentlemen to their intercourse with each other, or by merchants and tradesmen in the transaction of business, would sap and destroy the foundations of society, by destroying that good faith which alone renders society possible. If a class of men were to construct forms of speech for their communications with the world, such as some others use in their speaking to God and their utterances in the Church,—and if they were to attempt to do working-day business after such a fashion,— they would throw matters into such mystery and uncertainty, that they would be hooted from the ordinary walks of life as simpletons or cheats, that the sensible and honest might conduct their affairs through an intelligible language.[1]

The following is the comment on the judgment of the Court of Arches:

It is impossible to estimate the results that may flow from the present decision of this celebrated case. With clergymen on the one hand turning papists, and on the other infidels;—oratories opened by the first, and scoffing books written by the second;—and with the doctrine of the Church so interpreted, as virtually to expel from it evangelical religion, as the Fathers of Nonconformity were once expelled,—we cannot but feel that we live in times of no ordinary interest, and that great events must be on the wing. May the God of love and truth be glorified by his servants in the battle that is before them!

We are constrained to add, that we deem Sir H. J. Fust's judgment

[1] Pp. xv, xvi.

perfectly correct, sound, and, in equity, inevitable; and that we are glad he attempted no miserable compromise that, while it might have saved both parties, would and could have satisfied no honest, clear-headed, and truth-loving man.[1]

The writer also has some challenging remarks to make about the idea of aiming at comprehension in this matter. After remarking that both parties to the dispute regard the other as preaching "another Gospel", he says:

Has it come to this, that they will be satisfied to stand side by side, and on the same level, with the men who preach "another Gospel",— these men being equally authorized and sanctioned by the Church as themselves? There is something cutting in Dr Addam's remark, which Mr Gorham and his friends will do well to ponder,—"Mr Gorham described the doctrines of the Bishop as unscriptural and soul-destroying doctrines". If the doctrine held by Mr Gorham were the true doctrine, then that laid down in the Prayer-book was not the true doctrine; and that might be a very good reason for altering the Prayer-book, but not for instituting Mr Gorham.[2]

Perhaps the most amusing passage in this book, which is full of sardonic humour, occurs when the writer describes what he sees through his imaginary telescope at the top of St Paul's Cathedral when the Judicial Committee of the Privy Council begins its work:

Just at ten o'clock, the fog unfortunately gathered on the glass, so that we lost the sight of any formalities that might have attended the opening of the Court. When we looked again the business had begun. Mr Turner was addressing the Committee, and the members were beginning to take notes of his argument. He stood close to the end of the table at which the Judges (if we may so call them) sat, and had a sort of desk, on which his notes lay, and from which he appeared to read carefully. No one sat at the higher end of the table, as if *presiding* over the Committee of Council, by occupying a seat between, and at the head of, the two rows of members on each side. The members present were arranged in these two rows, and sat in something like the following order:—On the right side of the table, the Marquis of Lansdowne, Lord Langdale, Baron Parke, Vice-chancellor Knight-Bruce, Mr Pemberton Leigh; on the left, the Archbishop of Canterbury, the Archbishop of York, the Bishop of London, Lord Campbell, and Dr Lushington. The two Archbishops, and the Bishop of London, it will be remembered, are *not* actual members of the Committee. They were not present as judges. They have no vote, and will not sign the report that the Committee may submit to the Queen. It is well and decent that they attend; though we must confess to something almost amounting to shame and mortification, with a spice of burning and indignant displeasure, when we saw our condescending and venerable friend, his Grace of Canterbury, occupying the mean position which he did, instead of sitting, as he ought, in the chair and throne of ecclesiastical supremacy whenever questions are to be formally entertained and officially determined, respecting the doctrines of the English Church.

It was excessively humiliating to us, occupying, as we do, this roost in the Cathedral, to have to look on a parcel of lawyers and laymen, listening to abstruse theological arguments on a subject of experimental or doctrinal divinity—a subject which none of them, perhaps, understood, and which some of them are supposed, in *all* senses, utterly to repudiate,—to see such men clothed with the *judicial* function, and empowered to decide on the teaching of the Church, while the true ecclesiastical head of the Church sat by their side, destitute of authority, only to be spoken to if necessary, and only to speak if asked!—The sight was so mortifying and melancholy, and suggested so much against the present constitution of things,—the royal supremacy in causes ecclesiastical, and the nature and results of the union of Church and State,—that we were obliged to turn away from the glass that revealed it, lest the glow that we felt crimsoning our countenance, and the sparks of indignation that were darting from our eye, might, by possibility, have so acted through the lenses of the telescope, as to have burnt the whole spectacle to ashes,— lawyers and advocates, judges and doctors—Canterbury, York, London, and all![1]

The writer clearly enjoyed making fun of the curious predicament in which the established church found itself.

G. *Opinions of Some Bishops*

The pamphlets noticed above show that there were wide divergencies of view among the English clergy. The bishops as a whole seem to have made it their policy to avoid making public pronouncements during the controversy—presumably so as not to cause increased confusion which would have followed from episcopal trumpets giving uncertain notes.

Nevertheless, there is sufficient evidence to show that there were considerable variations of opinion about Baptism even among the bishops. The Archbishop of Canterbury maintained a careful silence, but his concurrence in the Judgment, and his re-publication of his *Apostolic Preaching* in 1850 showed the

[1] Pp. 113–15.

breadth of his views—he allowed the evangelical doctrine, though not in its extreme form.

The Archbishop of York (Musgrave), on the other hand, had been much more outspoken in his Charge of 1849.[1] In commending Goode's *Effects of Infant Baptism*, he said that it had been proved that the sixteenth-century English reformers were Calvinists, "Hence they taught that spiritual regeneration in baptism could only result in the case of those who had been from all eternity elected to everlasting life by the free and sovereign grace of God. . . . With the knowledge of this *historical fact* before us, we cannot insist on it as a *ruled doctrine* of our Church that all baptized children are, as such, spiritually regenerate". He says that those who interpret the baptismal services in the hypothetical sense approach nearest to the minds of the Reformers. In short, the Archbishop of York believed in regeneration in Baptism being conditional: he belongs to class C above.

The Bishop of London (Blomfield), however, did not concur in the Judgment. In his Charge of 1842 he had said: "The opinion which denies Baptismal Regeneration might possibly, though not without great difficulty, be reconciled with the language of the Twenty-seventh Article; but by no stretch of ingenuity, or latitude of explanation, can it be brought to agree with the plain unqualified language of the Offices for Baptism and Confirmation."[2] But his dissent from the decision seems to have been due to his opinion that the judges did not interpret accurately what Gorham's true position was rather than because he regarded the doctrine which they allowed as wrong. He held that Gorham categorically denied baptismal regeneration, not merely declared it to be conditional. As to saying that regeneration was not necessarily, nor unconditionally, the accompaniment of Baptism, he declared in his Charge of 1850: "Had this been a full and accurate account of Mr Gorham's opinions on the subject of Baptism, as set forth by himself, and had the reasoning, by which the judgment of the Judicial Committee is supported, been omitted, in part at least, I might have felt less difficulty in assenting to the judgment".

The Bishop of St David's (Thirlwall), in his Charge of 1851, held that Gorham was right in denying baptismal regeneration,

---

[1] A Charge delivered to the Clergy of the Diocese of York, June 1849.

[2] These quotations from the Bishop's charges are taken from *Memoir of Bishop Blomfield*, by Alfred Blomfield, Vol. II, pp. 118–19.

since he, Gorham, held regeneration to be a change of condition and nature, and not merely of status. He, the Bishop, regards Baptism as conferring justification and not sanctification:

It is an incorporation into the body of Christ, adoption into the family of God, a title to the inheritance of the kingdom of heaven,—that is, a present, but defeasible title, to a future contingent possession. It is a state of salvation: the state of those who should be saved, who may be saved, who will be saved, if they fulfil the conditions on which their salvation depends. The chief, if not the only doubt on this point relates to that gift of the Holy Spirit, for which prayer is made on behalf of the child before Baptism, and which, unless we adopt the so-called charitable hypothesis, must be held to have been conferred in Baptism. But it appears to me that we may very well believe this gift to be really received, and yet need not adopt the theory of an *infused virtue*, or *a mysterious earnest of the Holy Spirit*, or of an *initial and seminal grace*. This theory seems to proceed on the arbitrary assumption, that the gift cannot be really bestowed unless it takes immediate effect. . . .[1]

And he continues:

. . . It is plain that one whose idea of regeneration implies a moral change, if he denies that such a regeneration invariably accompanies Baptism, even when rightly administered, does not contradict those who, maintaining the unconditional and universal efficacy of Baptism, describe it as consisting in a change of state or relation.

But he will not allow Gorham's view that the death of a baptized infant is a sure sign that it possessed graces which other infants did not enjoy.

The Bishop of St David's is prepared throughout to give Gorham considerable latitude of interpretation:

I am aware that in the course of that Examination expressions were used by the respondent, which, taken by themselves, would seem to convey an opinion, that there may be cases in which the Baptism of infants, regularly administered, is not only attended with no subsequent benefit to the recipients, for this it is admitted on all hands may often happen, but confers no present and immediate benefit of any kind or degree, and is a mere empty inoperative form. But these expressions ought in common candour to be construed in connexion with the general subject of the inquiry: and then I think it will appear, that they really relate to that benefit which depends on the fulfilment of the conditions stipulated in the baptismal contract. At all events this point was not so distinctly brought forward, or so

[1] *A Charge delivered to the Clergy of the Diocese of St David's.*

fully discussed, as to make it clear that the proposition was meant to be understood in a strictly literal and absolutely unqualified sense. No one who reads that Examination can fail to observe, that Mr Gorham was led, and almost compelled, to fix his attention almost exclusively on the negative side of the subject, that he was more concerned to state what Baptism does not give, than what it gives. His one main object throughout was to guard himself against any admission implying a belief, that the sacrament, *ex opere operato*, imparts a gift involving not merely the possibility, but the absolute certainty of future spiritual benefits, reaching perhaps, in his view, even to the attainment of everlasting life.

The Bishop of Lincoln (Kaye) expressed the following opinion in *A Charge to the Clergy of the Diocese of Lincoln* in 1852:

The decision of the Privy Council is regarded by many as having sanctioned an innovation in the doctrine of the Church respecting the efficacy of Infant Baptism. I cannot concur in that view of the effect of the decision: the question of Baptismal Regeneration, in my opinion, remains precisely on the same footing as before . . . from the time of the Reformation to the present, persons maintaining opinions similar to those maintained by Mr Gorham had held the highest dignities in the Church and had held them unquestioned.

He goes on, however, to express his own opinion that infants are regenerated in Baptism.

The Archbishop of Dublin (Whately) also entered the arena with *Infant Baptism considered in a Charge* (1850). The following extract epitomizes his view:

As for "remission of sins" at Baptism . . . it seems to denote that those duly baptized are considered as no longer children of the condemned and disinherited Adam . . . have thrown open to them, as it were, the treasury of divine grace, through which, if they duly avail themselves of it—though not otherwise—they will attain final salvation. . . . But no one can suppose that they (the reformers) regarded the sowing of seed as the same thing with the full maturity of the corn for harvest, or as necessarily implying it.

The voice of the Bishop of Llandaff (Copleston) was also heard. In a charge to the clergy of his diocese in 1848 he had favoured latitude:

There is a latitude or comprehensiveness of meaning in words that denote abstract truths and religious mysteries, which cannot be reduced to an exact definition excluding all possible variation. . . . I might specify *absolution, inspiration, justification, regeneration* as examples of this kind . . . to fix *one sense* in which they must always be understood, whatever be the context, and to make these niceties the object of legal adjudication, after forensic pleading in which the temporal interests of the accused are involved, would, I think, introduce more discord into the Church, and give occasion for more extensive evils, than the permission of some latitude of opinion as to the precise significance of the terms through which religious doctrines can alone be conveyed.

As well as these, two episcopal utterances from the United States of America were heard in this country. The Bishop of Ohio (McIlvaine) delivered a charge in 1852 entitled *Spiritual Regeneration*. The following three extracts give an idea of the position which he adopted:

We have no doubt that infants are sometimes spiritually regenerated in the receiving of baptism, and we have no doubt that great spiritual blessings would be much more frequently bestowed in that sacrament, were children brought thereto with more effort of prayer, and a more devout preparation of mind altogether on the part of those who bring them. . . .
. . . Unquestionably, the two great doctrines of the Gospel . . . are those which treat of our *justification* before God, and our *sanctification* by His Spirit. To be delivered from condemnation, so that sin is not imputed unto us, and to be delivered from the unholiness of our fallen nature, so that sin hath no dominion over us. . . .
. . . But sanctification has no beginning except in regeneration. . . .

The Bishop of Vermont (Hopkins) added, in 1849, a contribution to the appeals for freedom of interpretation. In *An Address to the Clergy of the Diocese of Vermont* he said:

We cannot safely assume, and we ought not to desire, any enlargement of the episcopal prerogative, in requiring our clergy to subscribe to the theological opinions of their diocesan, where the uniform course of all our predecessors, justified by the primitive practice, has left them free.

For the most part the charges of archdeacons which dealt with the dispute were not distinguished for originality of thought or expression. One, however, should be mentioned, since it drew a reply from the Bishop of Exeter. This was *Church Difficulties of 1851: a Charge to the Clergy of the Archdeaconry of Middlesex*, by John Sinclair. Archdeacon Sinclair expresses the view that a baptized infant is regenerate; but he denies that Gorham contravenes the creed of the Council of Constantinople, since that council, he alleges, was not dealing with the efficacy of infant baptism but with the impropriety of repeating the initiatory ordinance. This, the writer said, made him read the Nine Resolutions of Manning and the others with surprise and alarm. Sinclair went on to point out the apparent contradictions in Augustine between assertions of the necessity of faith and of Baptism. Dr Phillpotts replied in a *Letter to the Clergy of the Diocese of Exeter* (1851) in which he works out a long argument that the Archdeacon of Middlesex is wrong in saying that the council of Constantinople is only dealing with re-baptism in laying down "One baptism for the remission of sins".[1]

[1] The Bishop calls this a reply to the prefatory epistle to the second edition of Archdeacon Sinclair's charge.

CHAPTER X

THE CONTROVERSY RECONSIDERED

ALTHOUGH it has for long been almost forgotten, and regarded by many as little more than a curious episode in English church history, this controversy raised by Mr Gorham and the Bishop of Exeter in the middle of the nineteenth century is the only instance of a large-scale doctrinal clash on the subject of Baptism in the annals of the Church of England. It is therefore worthy of notice, and the issues it raises are of greater import to the Church of a hundred years later than is generally supposed. The conditions with which the Church is surrounded in the mid-twentieth century make it even more necessary to clarify the doctrine of Baptism than it was in Gorham's day. A hundred years ago it could much more reasonably be assumed that a child brought to the font would be brought up in the nurture and admonition of the Lord than it can to-day. It has been pointed out more than once in recent years that the twentieth is a post-Christian century in England; having once been a Church-State the nation now remains nominally Christian while in fact a majority of its institutions and its individual members are indifferent to the Gospel. As regards baptismal theory and practice this means that the situation in England is neither that of the mission field, where the Gospel is being brought to a people for the first time, and where therefore it becomes clear who are the real members of the Church and who are not; nor is it that of the mediaeval and later polity where the relations between Church and State were such that Christian dogma was accepted as the body of statements about God and Man assumed to be true in all the corporate acts of the nation, and not merely tolerated along with other conflicting ideas. The life of the nation—politics, education, industry, civic life and the rest— has become so alienated from Christian dogma and practice that it may be that in many cases it is little more than lingering custom or superstition which prompts a family to present its new-born infants at the font of a parish church of one of our great cities. It can hardly be denied that this indiscriminate administration of Baptism year after year, this distribution of

the rights of membership of the Church without a corresponding recognition of obligations, is exposing the sacrament to
disastrous dishonour. The question is, Do either of the main
parties in the Gorham dispute offer a theory of Baptism which
will solve the problems with which the present practice is
beset?

There is an immediate inclination to regard the principle at
issue between Gorham and Phillpotts as being the old prophet-
priest controversy in another dress, or as simply the age-long
problem of objective grace and subjective disposition in relation
to sacraments. This view of the dispute is tenable if Gorham is
held to deny that either regeneration or any other spiritual grace
is ever conferred in and by the sacrament of Baptism. At the
time the heat of the controversy was such that many writers,
unable to appreciate fine distinctions of thought, regarded this
as being Gorham's true view. But close examination of Gorham's
own words and the pleadings of his advocates suggests that there
is much truth in Bishop Thirlwall's remark that Gorham "was
led, and almost compelled, to fix his attention almost exclusively
on the negative side of the subject; that he was more concerned
to state what Baptism does not give, than what it gives".[1]
Although there is much in his book limiting the operation of the
sacrament, there are also several passages which indicate that
he could not have denied completely that spiritual grace was,
under proper conditions, conveyed through it.

For instance, he says:

I refer your Lordship, generally, to numerous other passages . . .
which speak of the disposition, character, and effects, wrought in
the heart, and manifested in the life, as evidences that Regeneration
has actually taken place. All such passages would be flatly contradicted
by maintaining that Regeneration, or being "made the child of
God", absolutely unconditionally, peremptorily, takes place in
"EVERY infant baptized. . . ."[2]

Here he must be taken to be allowing the possibility of regeneration taking place in *some* infants baptized. And he says:

. . . it being impossible that such dispositions and fruits should exist,
except when the Holy Ghost has imparted a new nature, which He
may do *before* Baptism, *in* Baptism, or *after* Baptism, "as He listeth".[3]

[1] See p. 169, *supra*.   [2] See p. 25, *supra*.   [3] See p. 15, *supra*.

He also affirms that Baptism rightly received "confirms" faith and "increases" grace.[1]

But as well as these passages, we have to take into account statements like the following which undoubtedly preponderate in his book:

> ... The blessing of "adoption", also *precedes* Baptism, in its essence ... which I maintain to be a very different proposition from this other, namely—That the blessing of regeneration, or adoption to be a member of the family of God, is to be *ascribed* TO *Baptism*.[2]

But Gorham presumably assented to the pleadings of Turner, one of his advocates before the Privy Council, who said, "He nowhere denies that grace may be conferred in Baptism worthily received, nor that regeneration, by which he understands to mean a new nature, may take place in Baptism".[3] Also the judges of the Privy Council must have given the matter the careful consideration of their trained logical minds before they allowed the doctrine of conditional *regeneration* in Baptism, believing that to be Gorham's view. And there is no evidence that Gorham himself questioned the relevance of the judgment or opposed it as not expressing his opinion.

Throughout the controversy, as more than one commentator pointed out, there was confusion and misunderstanding as to the meaning of the term "regeneration", and even Gorham himself does not confine his use of it to one sense. Sometimes it means a change of status before God or being reckoned righteous —what in one usage of the word is indicated by "justification"; sometimes it means a change of nature and condition or actually becoming righteous, not merely reckoned so—what is sometimes indicated by "sanctification". Sometimes in this controversy the word "regeneration" is used to mean a combination of

---

[1] See p. 21, *supra*. Gorham's widow presented his collection of pamphlets on the case to the University Library at Cambridge. Bound up with them there is a MS. note of Gorham's (inserted in the middle of his copy of the Bishop of London's Charge of 1850) which bears on this point: "Sacramental grace. Fallacy. Is it initial g; or additional g? G conf*erred* or g conf*irmed*? G inherent in the sac., one of its inseparable parts, or gr. sealed by the sac. only to those who have been made worthy by prevenient gr.?" Gorham also makes an interesting marginal note in his copy of the Bishop of Ripon's pastoral letter. Beside the Bishop's comment "thus maintaining that the remission of original sin, adoption into the family of God, and Regeneration, must take place, in the case of infants, not in Baptism, nor by means of Baptism but before Baptism", Gorham pencils "Who receive benefit *at the time* (underlined) of Baptism", and he underlines "infants" in the Bishop's sentence. This is ambiguous, but it indicates that he is prepared at times to profess a closer connexion between the outward sign and the grace than many of his critics imagine.

[2] See p. 26, *supra*.   [3] Quoted on p. 96, *supra*.

justification and sanctification in these senses. Gorham certainly does not make his use of "regeneration" either clear or consistent. In the light of the general tenor of his argument the most reasonable interpretation is that in the first passage quoted above from his book he uses the word to mean sanctification, and that in the last, where he denies baptismal regeneration, he uses it in the sense of justification.

These are not the only meanings of the terms "justification" and "sanctification" in the history of Christian doctrine; but the antithesis between being reckoned righteous and the actual process of becoming righteous through the progressive operation of the Holy Spirit in the life of the Church is one which has a firm place in dogmatic tradition. For the purpose of convenience these are the senses in which I will use these two terms in this chapter.

Not only do the ideas of justification and sanctification which I have outlined above occur from time to time in the history of Christian doctrine, but they are more than once found to be existing contemporaneously, side by side in the same theological system. In St Paul's epistles there are double lines of teaching as to man's salvation: he says that we are "justified by faith"—he seems to mean by this that at any given moment the believer stands before God acquitted by virtue of his faith in the atoning work of Christ, which faith is the gift of God. On the other hand St Paul has also the notion of sanctification: justification having occurred, union with Christ and actual holiness are being gradually and progressively built up in the believer through the operation of the Holy Ghost in the Church.

Generally speaking the Fathers and Schoolmen did not distinguish clearly between justification and sanctification; they for the most part regarded "justified" as meaning "made righteous". At the Reformation there came the cleavage in the West between Catholicism and Protestantism; where the conflict was acute the former, broadly speaking, stressed the doctrine of sanctification at the expense of that of justification, the latter exalted justification to the disparagement of sanctification. But it was part of the genius of Anglicanism to blend these two apparently incompatible notions in one system—to be in a sense both Catholic and Protestant at the same time, and so perhaps more than any other Christian communion to return to the position of the Pauline epistles. The XXXIX Articles dwell predominantly on the note of justification, the Prayer Book mainly on sanctification; the Articles speak largely of Justification and the worthlessness of man's works before justification; the Prayer Book preserves the Catholic sacramental system and speaks of the incorporation of the believer into Christ by the operation of the Holy Spirit. Although in the centuries following that in which the Articles and the Prayer Book were drawn up this balance may have been from time to time obscured, it was nevertheless preserved in essence by the mere existence of the Articles and Formularies alongside each other.

Tyndale and Cranmer referred to the first and second justifications to indicate what I have defined respectively as justification and sanctification above.[1] Hooker says:

For in the Sixth to the Romans he [St Paul] writeth, "Being freed from sin, and made servants to God, ye have your fruit in holiness, and the end everlasting life". "Ye are made free from sin, and made servants unto God": this is the righteousness of Justification: "Ye have your fruit in holiness"; this is the righteousness of Sanctification.[2]

Also he says in connexion with Baptism:

Baptism . . . we justly hold it to be the door of our actual entrance into God's House, the first apparent beginning of life, a seed perhaps to the grace of election before received: but to our sanctification here, a step that hath not any before it.[3]

Archbishop Leighton in part of a charming discourse on Isa. lx. i, has the same idea:

Now every faithful soul is espoused to Christ, and therefore such may well shine, seeing the Sun himself is their husband. He adorns them with a double beauty of *justification* and *sanctification*: by *that*, they shine more especially to GOD, by *this* to men. And may not these two be signified by the double character given to the spouse in Cant. vi. 10? *She is fair as the moon, and clear as the sun.* The lesser light is that of sanctification, *fair as the moon*; that of justification, the greater, by which *she is as clear as the sun*. The sun is perfectly luminous, but the moon is but half enlightened; so, the believer is perfectly justified, but sanctified only in part: his one half, his flesh, is dark; and as her *partial* illumination is the reason of so many changes in the moon, to which changes the sun is not subject at all, so all the imperfections of a Christian's holiness is the cause of so many waxings and wanings, and of the great inequality of his performances, whereas in the meanwhile his justification remains constantly like itself. *This* is imputed

---

[1] See A. H. Rees, *The Doctrine of Justification in the Anglican Reformers*, p. 18.
[2] *A Discourse on Justification, etc.*, §. 6.　　　　[3] *Eccl. Polit.*, V, 60.

righteousness, *that* inherent. The light of sanctification must begin in the understanding, and from thence be transfused into the affections, the inferior parts of the soul, and from thence break forth and shine into action. This is, then, the nature of the duties, *Arise and shine*.[1]

Waterland expresses the same distinction, using, however, the terms "regeneration" and "renovation".[2]

But lest it be thought that the antithetical ideas to which I have attached the names "justification" and "sanctification" are only to be found in post-Reformation interpreters of St Paul, it is well to consider the thought of St Augustine, whose name at once raises the mind from the confines of any provincial theological controversy. At one time St Augustine seems to think of faith as being the vital factor in the salvation of man; at another he lays all the emphasis on Baptism. In short, in Augustine's writings there is to be found what is positive both in Gorham's and Phillpotts' positions.

In places in his anti-Pelagian treatises, Augustine's emphasis is pre-eminently on faith. For instance:[3]

By faith, therefore, in Jesus Christ we obtain salvation,—both in so far as it is begun with us in reality, and in so far as its perfection is waited for in hope; "for whosoever shall call upon the name of the Lord shall be saved".

And the same occurs in his sermons, for example:[4]

The beginning of the good life, to which eternal life is due, is right faith. Moreover faith is to believe in what thou dost not yet see.

And, of course, "The merit of faith is itself also the gift of God".[5]

But in other passages Augustine equally clearly lays down the indispensability of Baptism. In his *opus imperfectum contra Iulianum* he declares:[6]

Behold there lie two infants: one of them expires having been baptized, the other unbaptized: upon which of them dost thou say that God showed mercy? . . . one is taken and the other left, because the grace of God is great and the justice of God is true . . . the judgments of God are past searching out.

And again, in his *de peccatorum meritis et remissione:*[7]

[1] Sermon II, *Sermons and Charges*, ed. William West, 1869, p. 22.
[2] *Works*, ed. Van Mildert, 1823, Vol. VI, pp. 349 ff.
[3] *De Spiritu et Littera*, 51.   [4] *Serm.* XLIII, c. 1.   [5] *Retract.*, XXIII, 3.
[6] *Op. imperfect. c. Iul.*, i, 39.   [7] *De peccat. merit. et remiss.* I, 21.

M

It may therefore be correctly affirmed, that such infants as quit the body without being baptized will be involved in the mildest condemnation of all. That person, therefore, greatly deceives both himself and others, who teaches that they will not be involved in condemnation.

Then to take a modern writer, Dr O. C. Quick in his last book *The Gospel of the New World* is following a Catholic master in saying that the conceptions of justification and sanctification exist together in St Paul's thought:

In St Paul's theological use of the expression, to "justify" a man means neither to acquit him by a sort of legal fiction, nor yet to make him actually just or righteous whereas he had before been a sinner; rather it means to set him in that right relation to God which he would have enjoyed if he had been actually righteous.[1]

and a little later he continues:

Although the transformation wrought by the new creation affects man's whole being and has already begun in Christians, it is still incomplete, and must remain incomplete as long as this world lasts and the Christian continues to exist in it.

St Paul explains this incompleteness by teaching that the Christian, although spiritually and in respect of his spirit he has already risen with Christ into newness of life, nevertheless still awaits the redemption of the body together with the transformation of the whole material universe.[2]

It is possible to interpret Gorham as holding that the grace of Baptism is a part of sanctification and not a part of justification; that justification must precede Baptism in order for the sacrament to be effective. He firmly believes in justification by faith and not by Baptism. Whether he was right in sometimes withholding the name "regeneration" from the grace which he believes Baptism to confer, it is not necessary to decide. The New Testament uses the notion of new birth to indicate the beginning of the Christian life generally, without making any nice definitions. The Bishop of Exeter, however, seems to regard Baptism as conferring both justification and the beginning of sanctification.[3] And this is really the issue between them—that Gorham believes in justification by faith and that Baptism, provided justification

---

[1] *Op. cit.*, p. 54.   [2] *Ibid.*, p. 61.

[3] See especially p. 108, *supra*. And this seems to be the underlying assumption in all the questions embodied in Gorham's book; that Baptism is invariably the means by which God takes the first step towards raising the individual soul.

has preceded it, confers a measure of sanctification;[1] the Bishop of Exeter on the other hand believes in justification and sanctification by Baptism.

And there does seem to be a very great deal to be said for the doctrine that Baptism is the beginning of sanctification, and no part of justification. This view seems to follow properly both from the true Catholic and the true Protestant views of redemption. The Catholic conception is that the whole Church, or the whole race or nation, is redeemed in Christ or justified; the Protestant view is that the individual enters the realm of justification through his individual faith, and that it is not until that has happened that sacraments are of any avail. The paramount importance of justification as the beginning of the Christian life in Protestant theology hardly needs to be demonstrated. It also has its place in the Catholic tradition, for example in Augustine who says (*Ep.* 23) that children are brought "on the faith of the Church". On either the Catholic or the Protestant hypothesis therefore justification ideally precedes Baptism.[2] It was interesting to observe one isolated instance of this idea among the pamphlets—the doctrine was adumbrated by L. V. Harcourt in *A Remonstrance to the Bishop of Exeter*.[3]

But although Gorham recognizes this principle, his view of the place of Baptism in the scheme of salvation is inadequate. He suffers from the Protestant preoccupation with the idea of the redemption of the individual from the sinful mass—affirming that the *individual* must either believe or receive prevenient grace before he can receive the grace of Baptism. He is absorbed with the psychological idea of justification and ignores its cosmic aspect. Similarly Phillpotts' high churchmanship is inadequate: he, with his adviser Dr Pusey, thinks of the salvation of individuals too, and he differs from Gorham really only in substituting individual reception of Baptism for "prevenient grace", while equally ignoring the cosmic aspect of justification.

Both Phillpotts and Gorham were standing for great truths: the former insisting that a receptionist view of Baptism does violence to the nature of the sacrament, the latter refuting the idea that God is tied by his sacraments. But in each case it was

---

[1] A reflection of Gorham on the doctrine of sanctification is to be observed on p. 27, *supra*.

[2] "The promise is to you and to your children" (Acts ii. 39); and see Augustine's statements on the primacy of faith (p. 177, *supra*), and he says that children are brought to the font on the faith of the Church (*Ep.* 98, 5).

[3] See pp. 156–7, *supra*. See also the charge of Bishop McIlvaine of Ohio, p. 170, *supra*.

a defensive action that was being fought; neither had a really full or properly catholic doctrine of Baptism. A theologian of the time who saw deeper than either of the conflicting parties was F. D. Maurice. He has a full understanding of the cosmic significance of justification, the solidarity of the Christian family and the redemption of the race. In *The Kingdom of Christ* he complains of the inadequacies of the Puseyite doctrine of Baptism:

I would earnestly intreat Dr Pusey and his friends, to consider whether by this phrase ["Change of Nature"] they are not getting rid of a *mystery* for the sake of introducing a *mystification*;— . . . For, *first*, no persons are more anxious to assert the dignity and glory of the church than they,—to upset the notion that it is composed of a number of individual atoms, instead of being a Divine constitution into which men, from age to age, are brought; and yet, by representing Baptism as that which confers a portion of grace on each particular child, and not as that which brings him out of his selfish and individual condition, into the holy and perfect body, they do very much, as I think, to destroy the idea of the church, and to introduce a Genevan, individualizing notion in the place of it . . . for they, looking at Baptism as an act done in an instant, and accomplishing its purpose in an instant, and not rather as to witness of an eternal truth, the sacrament of constant union, the assurance of a continual living presence, are driven to this conclusion,—that the moment after it has been performed is a period of ideal purity and excellence, from which the future life even of a saint is a deflection, and which those who have wandered far into sin cannot hope to recover;—these must be content, by much prayer and fasting, to seek for God's mercy, which may perhaps, though there is no certain promise to uphold the flattering expectation, once again redeem them out of sin and hell.[1]

But he does not lose sight of the doctrine of justification by faith:

. . . The notion of building up a church upon the assertion of a fact, expressly concerning the distinct life of each man, is an absurdity and a contradiction which, in the first place, tends to destroy the meaning of that doctrine itself; in the second place, leads to interminable strife and separation. I say, that the life of a church is based upon a deeper foundation than this, even upon that foundation upon which the doctrine of justification itself is based,—the ATONEMENT made for *mankind*, in the person, and by the incarnation and death of Jesus Christ.

[1] Vol. I, pp. 95–7. The kind of passage to which Maurice was objecting was as follows: "The child of the regenerated or Christian parent brings into the world with it nothing but the corruption of our fallen nature, and God's promise to restore it by Baptism. . . ." Pusey, *Scriptural Views of Holy Baptism*, p. 162.

In this assertion, as far as it is opposed to the doctrine of particular redemption, i.e. a redemption made for those who believe in the redemption, I am supported by your early Friends.[1]

His point here is that we are not justified *by* our faith any more than we are justified by any other excellences which we display. Our justification is in a context of faith which itself is a gift of God, and he presupposes membership of a society in which the Christian faith is accepted as true.

In all he says about Baptism Maurice supposes the context of a Christian State; we may say that his doctrine of Baptism is based upon the assumption of a justified nation. This comes out, for instance, in the following passage on education in England:

... And then, after this, we ascertained that our nation was provided with an education—that this education did proceed upon the principle of delivering man from the chains of his animal nature—that it had addressed itself to something which is common to all men, and yet had done reverence to all the particular faculties which men are endowed with for the sake of helping their brethren—that it had not limited itself to the mere work of teaching, but had incorporated itself with the forms of society, and brought every influence which man acknowledges as helpful to bear upon him—that it had not violated the sacredness of family life—that it had actually given life to the state—lastly, that it was founded upon that principle which men, by their own researches, had ascertained to be the only support of education the recognition of a Divine Being, who announces himself as the Deliverer of Man, and formally enters into relations with him, for the purpose of effecting and completing the deliverance.[2]

This is the outlook which we observe in the pamphlet *The Gorham Case. Which are we to believe?* written anonymously by "A Country Rector".[3]

We have then before us three main views of Baptism. First, that of Dr Phillpotts who believes that Baptism confers justification and sanctification; secondly that of Gorham, who believes Baptism to convey a measure of sanctifying grace only after individual justification; and thirdly that of Maurice who, with his views of the corporate and permanent effects of baptismal sanctification, also assumes that it follows the justification of the race or nation.[4]

[1] *Ibid.*, pp. 38–9.   [2] *The Kingdom of Christ*, Vol. III, p. 170.   [3] See pp. 160–1, *supra*.

[4] It is sometimes maintained that Maurice takes a merely obsignatory view of Baptism, but this can hardly be the case. See the quotation on p. 180—where he refers to Baptism as "that which brings him (the child) out of his selfish and individual condition".

Does any one of these views speak to our present condition? The Church evidently does not accept Phillpotts' doctrine, for mass baptismal campaigns—not necessary in his day when the majority of English infants were baptized as a matter of course— are not advocated. Gorham's doctrine receives no general support: if it did it would not permit the present indiscriminate administration of the sacrament. Thirdly, England cannot be regarded any longer as being a Church-State in which faith over-arches the life of the nation and corporate justification can be assumed. The present baptismal practice cannot be defended on any of these three theories. Maurice's is the richest doctrine of Baptism, but we can scarcely follow him in thinking of England as a justified nation. The furthest we can go with Maurice is in baptizing those infants which are born within the environment of justifying faith.

The difficulty for the parish priest in post-Christian England lies in deciding which infants are within that environment. The problem of determining the proper regulation of the administration of Baptism to-day is precisely the problem of discovering the extent to which the nation is still Christian, and how far the Church of England in truth remains the National Church.

LIST OF PAMPHLETS

A. Pamphlets bearing on the Doctrine of Baptism

ARNOLD, T. K. *An Examination of some portions of the Rev W. Goode's "Letter to the Bishop of Exeter"*, London: F. & J. Rivington, 1850 (pp. 68).

BARNE, HENRY. *A New Year's Address to his flock on the subject of Baptism.* The *Gazette* Office, Devizes, 1850 (pp. 16).

BARTER, W. B. *A Letter to the Archbishop of Canterbury.* London: F. & J. Rivington, 1850 (pp. 16).

—— *The Opponents of Baptismal Regeneration solemnly warned.* London: F. & J. Rivington, 1849 (pp. 49).

BINNEY, THOMAS. *Conscientious Clerical Nonconformity.* London: Jackson and Walford, 1848 (pp. 16).

BLACKBURNE, J. *"Why are they then baptized for the dead?"* Cambridge: J. Deighton, 1850 (pp. 116).

BONNIN, S. T. *A Letter to the Churchmen of Hull.* London: Seeleys, 1850 (pp. 8).

BOSANQUET, R. W. *The Sacrament of Baptism with remarks on the ambiguity in the modern use of the word Regeneration.* London: Simpkins, Marshall & Co., 1850 (pp. 52).

BRICKNELL, W. SIMCOX. *The Charitable Hypothesis Defended: A Letter to the Right Rev Henry Lord Bishop of Exeter.* London: W. E. Painter, 1850 (pp. 48).

CAMERON, C. R. *Baptism accompanied by conditional and unconditional grace.* London: Wertheim & Macintosh, 1849 (pp. 23).

CAVENDISH, RICHARD. *A Letter to Archdeacon Hare on the Judgment in the Gorham Case.* London: John Ollivier, 1850 (pp. 36).

CHAMBERS, J. D. *A Review of the Gorham Case in its aspects moral and legal, with a critical examination of the Judgment: A Letter to the Lord Bishop of Salisbury.* London: William Benning, 1850 (pp. 72).

CLAUGHTON, T. L. *Our present duties in regard of Holy Baptism.* A sermon. London: F. & J. Rivington, 1850 (pp. 14).

COLLES, W. M. *The Doctrines, Dangers and Duties of Churchmen at the Present Crisis.* London: Hamilton Adams, 1850 (pp. 24).

COLLINS, JAMES, Dean of Killala. *The Gorham Case, and the doctrine which it concerns considered.* Dublin: Hodges & Smith, 1850 (pp. 40).

CONGLETON, LORD. *The True Idea of Baptism.* London: James Ridgway, 1850 (pp. 24).

COPLESTON, EDWARD, Bishop of Llandaff. *A Charge delivered to the Clergy of the Diocese of Llandaff.* London: F. & J. Rivington, 1848 (pp. 34).

DAVISON, JOHN. *Remarks on Baptismal Regeneration.* Oxford: J. H. Parke, 1847 (pp. 71).

DODSWORTH, W. *A Letter to the Rev. E. B. Pusey, D.D., on the position which he has taken in the present crisis.* London: William Pickering, 1850 (pp. 20).

—— *The Gorham Case Briefly considered.* London: William Pickering, 1850 (pp. 40).

FARLEY, W. M. *A Voice from the Font: Regeneration not necessarily connected with Baptism.* London: Wertheim & Macintosh, 1850 (pp. 16).

FORESTER, O. W. W. *One Baptism.* London: Seeleys, 1850 (pp. 34).

GARSIDE, CHARLES. *The Impiety of Bartering Faith for Opinion.* London: William Pickering, 1850 (pp. 30).

GATTY, ALFRED. *Baptism misunderstood, the great trouble of the Church.* London: George Bell, 1849 (pp. 30).

GOODE, WILLIAM. *Review of the Judgment of Sir H. J. Fust, Kt, in the case of Gorham v. The Bishop of Exeter.* By the late editor of the *Christian Observer.* London: Hatchards, 1850 (pp. 52).

—— *A Letter to the Bishop of Exeter.* London: Hatchards, 1850 (pp. 107).

—— *A Vindication of the Defence of the XXXIX Articles.* London: Hatchards, 1848 (pp. 83).

—— *A Letter to Sir W. P. Wood, Q.C., M.P.* London: Hatchards, 1852 (pp. 32).

GORHAM, G. C. *Extracts from the writings of Martyr and Bullinger on the effects of Baptism.* London: Hatchards, 1850 (pp. 42).

—— *The Exeter Synod. A Letter to the Bishop of Exeter on the Diocesan Synod convened by his Lordship in the Chapter House of Exeter, June 25, 1851.* London: Hatchards, 1851 (pp. 27).

GRUEBER, C. S. *A Letter on the Recent Judgment in the case of Gorham v. the Bishop of Exeter, with an appendix on Baptism.* By "G". London: F. & J. Rivington and J. Masters, 1850 (pp. 17).

—— *A Complete Statement of the Church's Doctrine on Holy Baptism.* London: Joseph Masters, 1850 (pp. 58).

HARCOURT, L. VERNON. *A Remonstrance to the Bishop of Exeter on his recent letter to the Archbishop of Canterbury.* London: F. & J. Rivington, 1850 (pp. 45).

HARE, J. C. *A Letter to the Hon. Richard Cavendish on the recent judgment of the Court of Appeal, as affecting the doctrine of the Church.* London: J. W. Parker, 1850 (pp. 44).

—— *The True Remedy for the Evils of the Age: A Charge to the clergy of the Archdeaconry of Lewes.* London: J. W. Parker, 1850 (pp. 126).

HASTINGS, HENRY JAMES. *Reasons for not signing the proposed Address to the Lord Bishop of Worcester, and remarks on the late decision in the appeal Gorham v. Bishop of Exeter.* London: Hatchards, 1850 (pp. 44).

HOARE, E. H. *Baptism according to Scripture.* London: Seeleys, 1850 (pp. 91).

HOARE, E. H. *The Present Position of the Church. The Baptismal and Educational Questions, Three Letters to the Right Hon. Sir George Gray, H.M. Secretary of State for the Home Department.* London: F. & J. Rivington, 1850 (pp. 47 + 36).

HOOK, W. F. *A Letter to Sir Walter Farquar, Bart.* London: John Murray, 1850 (pp. 21).

HOPKINS, J. H., Bishop of Vermont. *Address to the Clergy of the Diocese of Vermont.* Burlington, U.S.A.: E. Smith, 1849 (pp. 40).

JORDAN, J. *An Appeal to the Evangelical Clergy against their concurrence in the Doublesense Use of the Baptismal and Confirmation Services and the Catechism of the Church of England.* London: James Nisbett, 1850 (pp. 39).

KAYE, JOHN, Bishop of Lincoln. *A Charge to the Clergy of the Diocese of Lincoln.* London: F. & J. Rivington, 1852 (pp. 47).

KING, JOHN. *Notices of the Late Judgment of Sir Herbert Jenner Fust in the Court of Arches: in the case of Gorham versus the Bishop of Exeter.* London: Seeleys, 1849 (pp. 28).

KNIGHT, JAMES. *Remarks on Baptismal Regeneration.* Sheffield: *Times* Office, 1850 (pp. 12).

LINDSAY, LORD. *A Brief Analysis of the Doctrine and Argument in the case of Gorham v. The Bishop of Exeter; and observations on the present position of the Church of England with reference to the recent decision.* London: John Murray, 1850 (pp. 56).

LONGLEY, CHARLES THOMAS, Bishop of Ripon. *A Pastoral Letter to the Clergy of the Diocese of Ripon.* London: F. & J. Rivington, 1850 (pp. 31).

MACDONNELL, ENEAS. *The Gorham Controversy Briefly Noticed.* London: Sears, 1850 (pp. 8).

MCILVAINE, C. P. *Spiritual Regeneration.* A Charge delivered to the clergy of Ohio, by the Bishop. London: Sampson Low, 1852 (pp. 53).

MCNEILE, HUGH. *"Baptism doth save": A Letter to the Right Rev. the Lord Bishop of Exeter.* London: T. Hatchard, 1851 (pp. 28).

MASKELL, WILLIAM. *A Second Letter on the Present Position of the High Church Party in the Church of England (The Want of Dogmatic Teaching).* London: William Pickering, 1850 (pp. 90).

—— *A Letter to the Rev. William Goode.* London: William Pickering, 1848 (pp. 20).

—— *The Outward Means of Grace.* A sermon. London: William Pickering, 1848 (pp. 37).

MASSINGBERD, F. C. *A Letter to the Rev. William Goode.* London: J. W. Parker, 1850 (pp. 41).

MAYOW, M. W. *A Second Letter to the Rev. William Maskell.* London: William Pickering, 1850 (pp. 154).

MONTGOMERY, R. *The Baptismal Controversy,* being an extract from the third edition of *The Gospel in advance of the Age* (pp. 12).

N

MUSGRAVE, T. *A Charge delivered to the Clergy of the Diocese of York. June, 1849.* By Thomas, Archbishop of York. London: J. W. Parker, 1849.

MUSHETT, WILLIAM. *The Popular Delusion.* London: B. L. Green, 1850 (pp. 24).

NEALE, J. M. *A Letter to Archdeacon Hare.* London: Joseph Masters, 1850 (pp. 24).

PEILE, T. W. *The Church of England not high, not low, but broad as the Commandment of God.* London: J. W. Parker, 1850 (pp. 35).

—— *The Christian Temple and its Representative Priesthood.* London: J. W. Parker, 1850 (pp. 60).

PHILLPOTTS, HENRY, Bishop of Exeter. *A Letter to the Archbishop of Canterbury.* London: John Murray, 1850 (pp. 91).

—— *A Letter to the Churchwardens of The Parish of Brampford Speke.* London: John Murray, 1850 (pp. 24).

—— *A Pastoral Letter to the Clergy of the Diocese of Exeter.* London: John Murray, 1851 (pp. 126).

—— *A Letter to the Clergy of the Diocese of Exeter.* London: John Murray, 1851 (pp. 45).

—— *A Pastoral Letter to the Clergy of his Diocese.* London: John Murray, 1854 (pp. 84).

POPE, W. E. *Baptismal Regeneration Refuted: A Letter to the Lord Archbishop of Canterbury.* London: Henry Pope, 1849 (pp. 22).

REDESDALE, LORD. *Reflections on the Doctrine of Regeneration and its connexion with both sacraments.* London: F. & J. Rivington, 1849 (pp. 26).

—— *Observations on the Judgment in the Gorham Case, and the way to unity.* London: F. & J. Rivington, 1850 (pp. 28).

RICHARDSON, JOHN. *A Letter to the Rev. William Goode.* London: John Ollivier, 1850 (pp. 49).

ROBERTSON, J. C. *The Bearings of the Gorham Case: A Letter to a friend.* London: F. & J. Rivington, 1850 (pp. 31).

SCHOLEFIELD, JAMES. *Baptismal Regeneration as maintained by the Church of England.* A sermon. Cambridge: University Press, 1849 (pp. 24).

SIMPSON, MICHAEL F. *The Sacrament of Responsibility.* 2nd edit., 1851.

SINCLAIR, JOHN. *Church Difficulties of 1851: a Charge to the Clergy of the Archdeaconry of Middlesex.* London: F. & J. Rivington, 1851 (pp. 46).

—— *Church Difficulties of 1851: Second Letter to the Clergy of the Archdeaconry of Middlesex.* London: F. & J. Rivington, 1851 (pp. 32).

THIRLWALL, CONNOP. *A Charge delivered to the Clergy of the Diocese of St David's.* London: Rivingtons, 1851.

TOWNSEND, GEORGE. *Baptismal Regeneration:* A reprint of a note on St John iii, 3–6, from the arrangement of the New Testament by the Rev George Townsend, D.D. London: F. & J. Rivington, 1850 (pp. 35).

TROWER, W. J., Bishop of Glasgow and Galloway. *A Pastoral Letter to the Clergy of the Diocese of Glasgow & Galloway, in reference to questions connected with the recent decision of the Judicial Committee of the Privy Council.* Glasgow: Maurice Ogle & Son, 1850 (pp. 44).

VORES, THOMAS. *The Judgment of Charity. A Plea for the hypothetical interpretation of the baptismal services of the Church of England.* London: Hatchards, 1849 (pp. 46).

WARD, W. P. *The Union of the Spiritual and Temporal Authorities in one and the same Ecclesiastical Court: a letter to the Right Hon. William Gladstone.* London: Joseph Masters, 1850 (pp. 24 + xxiii). (The appendix contains a doctrinal criticism of the judgment.)

WATSON, ALEXANDER. *A Letter to all members of the Church of England . . . on "One Baptism for the Remission of Sins".* London: Joseph Masters, 1850 (pp. 35).

—— *An Apology for the Plain Sense of the Doctrine of the Prayer Book on Holy Baptism in answer to the Rev. W. Goode's letter to the Bishop of Exeter.* London: Joseph Masters, 1850 (pp. 197).

—— *Judgment in Re Gorham v. Bishop of Exeter* (pp. 3).

WHATELY, RICHARD, Archbishop of Dublin. *Infant Baptism considered in a Charge.* London: J. W. Parker, 1850 (pp. 70).

WILBERFORCE, R. I. *A Charge to the Clergy of the East Riding.* London: John Murray, 1850 (pp. 36).

WOLFF, JOSEPH. *A Letter to the Right Rev. The Lord Bishop of Ripon on Baptismal Regeneration.* London: Hatchards, 1850 (pp. 20).

B. Anonymous Pamphlets on the Doctrine

Appeal in the cause "Gorham versus the Bishop of Exeter" to the Judicial Committee of the Privy Council against the judgment of the Court of Arches. Answer to a pamphlet by the Rev. T. Vores entitled "The judgment of charity". By "Amicus Curix" (Henry Winckworth Simpson). London: F. & J. Rivington, 1849 (pp. 28).

The Sacrament of Baptism considered in reference to an examination of the Rev. G. C. Gorham by the Bishop of Exeter & the judgment of Sir Herbert Jenner Fust. London: James Nisbet, 1849 (pp. 148).

A View of Baptism which supersedes Exeter v. Gorham. By "A Churchman". London: Houlston & Stoneman, 1850 (pp. 15).

Is a decision of the privy council a reason for secession, or for retiring into lay communion? A Letter to a clergyman of the evangelical school by another clergyman. London: George Bell, 1849 (pp. 24).

The Letters of "A Diocesan Practicioner" on Baptismal Regeneration which appeared in "The Western Times" Newspaper. Exeter: Balle, 1849 (pp. 65.)

A Brief vindication of Jewel, Hooker, Ussher, Taylor and Pearson from misrepresentations in the recent baptismal judgment. By "A Fellow of a College". Cambridge: J. Deighton, 1850.

A Letter to the Bishop of Exeter. By "Layman" (pp. 14). *A Second Letter to the Bishop of Exeter.* By "A Layman" (Sir Edward Hall Alderson) (pp. 18). London: Joseph Masters, 1850.

Letters to the primate upon the Gorham Case, and the dangers to which the laity are exposed in consequence of the recent judgment of the judicial committee. By "A Layman". Part I. Signed "M. J. R." London: F. & J. Rivington, 1850 (pp. 43).

Reasons for not supporting the Baptist Missionary Society. By "A Paedo-Baptist". Norwich: Charles Muskett, 1850 (pp. 23).

Two Notable Errors of the Bishop of Exeter. By "An Old Presbyter". London: James Nisbet, 1850 (pp. 47).

A Voice from the North: An appeal to the people of England on behalf of their Church. By "An English Priest" (Samuel Brown Harper). No. 1: *State of Dogmatic Teaching of the English Church.* London: Joseph Masters, 1850 (pp. 32).

The Gorham Case. Which are we to believe? By "A Country Rector". Oxford: J. H. Parker, 1851 (pp. 91).

Report on the proceedings of the general meeting of clergy and laity (on the Gorham Case) at St. Martin's Hall, July 23, 1850. London: 1850.

A Letter to the Most Rev. John Bird, Lord Archbishop of Canterbury, and the Most Rev. Thomas, Lord Archbishop of York: in reference to the late Judgment of the Judicial Committee of Privy Council, in the case of Gorham v. the Bishop of Exeter. By "A Rural Dean". London: George Bell, 1850 (pp. 78).

Remarks on the Judgment of the Judicial Committee of the Privy Council in the case of Gorham v the Lord Bishop of Exeter. By "A Solicitor". Oxford: J. H. Parker, 1850 (pp. 32).

The Church as it is: with special reference to the judgment of the final court of appeal in the cases of Gorham v. The Bishop of Exeter etc. By "A Worcestershire Vicar". Worcester, 1865.

A Vision, or The Romish Interpretation of "Be ye converted": a dramatic poem representing a dream of the Bishop of Exeter on the Gorham case. London: Seeleys, 1851 (pp. 30).

The Subjective and Objective Theories of Regeneration explained and examined. By "A Clergyman of the Diocese of Exeter". London: Simpkin Marshall & Co., 1850 (pp. 64).

Neither Exeter nor Gorham. By "Clericus Oxoniensis". London: W. E. Painter, 1850.

Remarks on some portions of the Recent Pastoral Letter of the Bishop of Exeter. By a Clergyman of the Diocese. London: Seeleys, 1851 (pp. 31).

C. *Some Pamphlets on the Subject of the Royal Supremacy in Matters Ecclesiastical which were Published in Connexion with the Controversy*

ANDERSON, J. S. M. *The Trials of the Church a quickening of her zeal and love.* Two sermons. London: F. & J. Rivington, 1850 (pp. 47).

BENNETT, W. J. E. *The Church, The Crown, and the State, their junction or their separation.* Two sermons. London: W. J. Cleaver, 1850 (pp. 41).

BLUNT, W. *A Few Words of Expostulation on the present excitement addressed to my clerical brethren.* London: J. Masters, 1850 (pp. 8).

DENISON, G. A. *An Appeal to the Clergy and Laity of the Church of England to combine for the defence of the Church and for the recovery of her rights and liberties.* London: F. & J. Rivington, 1850 (pp. 39).

—— *The Warning of the Church of England.* A sermon. London: F. & J. Rivington, 1850 (pp. 32).

DODSWORTH, W. *A House Divided against Itself.* A sermon. London: Joseph Masters, 1850 (pp. 24).

—— *The Things of Cesar, and the Things of God.* London: Joseph Masters, 1850 (pp. 22).

EDMONSTONE, ARCHIBALD. *A Letter to the Lord Bishop of Glasgow and Galloway on the present aspect of Church matters.* London: Joseph Masters, 1850 (pp. 24).

FORTESCUE, R. H. *The Tudor Supremacy in Jurisdiction Unlimited.* A sermon. London: Joseph Masters, 1850 (pp. 37).

GLADSTONE, W. E. *Remarks on the Royal Supremacy as it is defined by Reason, History and the Constitution: A Letter to the Lord Bishop of London.* London: John Murray, 1850 (pp. 88).

IRONS, W. J. *The Present Crisis in the Church of England, illustrated by a brief enquiry as to the Royal Supremacy.* London: Joseph Masters, 1850 (pp. 62).

KEBLE, J. *Church Matters in 1850.* I. *Trial of Doctrine* (pp. 32). II. *A Call to Speak Out* (pp. 32).

MANNING, H. E. *The Appellate Jurisdiction of the Crown in matters spiritual: a letter to the Right Rev. Ashurst Turner, Lord Bishop of Chichester.* Chichester: W. H. Mason, 1850 (pp. 48).

MASKELL, W. *A First Letter on the Present Position of the High Church Party in the Church of England.* London: William Pickering, 1850 (pp. 68).

MAYOW, W. *A Letter to the Rev. William Maskell.* London: William Pickering, 1850 (pp. 22).

MILL, W. H. *Human Policy and Divine Truth.* A sermon. Cambridge: J. Deighton, 1850 (pp. 26).

MONRO, EDWARD. *A Few Words on the spirit in which men are meeting the present crisis in the Church.* London: J. H. Parker, 1850 (pp. 44).

RANDALL, JAMES. *A Letter to the Ven. Edward Berens, on the constitution of the Ultimate Court of Appeal in causes ecclesiastical.* Oxford: J. H. Parker, 1850 (pp. 16).

ROBINS, SANDERSON. *Some Reasons against the Revival of Convocation.* London: William Pickering, 1850 (pp. 36).

SEWELL, WILLIAM. *Suggestions to minds perplexed by the Gorham Case.* Oxford: J. H. Parker, 1850 (pp. 30).

WARD, W. P. *The Union of the Spiritual and Temporal Authorities in one and the same Ecclesiastical Court: a letter to the Right Hon. William Gladstone.* London: Joseph Masters, 1850 (pp. 24 + xxiii).

D. Anonymous Pamphlets on the Royal Supremacy, etc.

Opinion of the Judges on the Jurisdiction of the Convocation in matter of Heresy: given in the year 1711. Oxford: J. H. Parker, 1850.

Church and State. Reprinted from the *Christian Remembrancer*, April, 1850. London: J. & C. Mozley, 1850 (pp. 48).

The Anglo-Catholic Theory. Reprinted from the *Christian Remembrancer*, 1851 (?) (pp. 527–58).

A Letter to the Right Reverend the Bishop of Glasgow and Galloway. By "A Scottish Presbyter". Edinburgh: R. Grant & Son, 1850 (pp. 46).

A Provincial Convocation. Reprint of two letters to the Editor of the *English Churchman* by "Laicus" (pp. 4).

Circular with memorial to the Most Holy Patriarchal Synod of the Russian Church.

On Pleas alleged for separation from the Church. A sermon (pp. 19–42).

Considerations preliminary to the summoning of Convocations for debate and the revival of Church legislation. By "S. T. P." (pp. 12).

E. Pamphlets on the Roman Catholic Question called forth by the Controversy

ANDERSON, JAMES. *Bishop Berkeley on the Roman Catholic Controversy.* London: F. & J. Rivington, 1850 (pp. 30).

MONRO, EDWARD. *Reasons for feeling secure in the Church of England.* London: J. H. Parker, 1850 (pp. 27).

WARD, W. G. *Heresy and Immorality considered in their respective bearing on the Notes of the Church.* London: Burns & Lambert, 1851 (pp. 102).

WISEMAN, N. *The Final Appeal in Matters of Faith.* A sermon. London: Thomas Richardson, 1850 (pp. 39).

—— *The Papal and Royal Supremacies contrasted.* A Lecture. London: Thomas Richardson, 1850 (pp. 48).

F. Party Tracts of a General Kind called forth by the Controversy.

NEALE, J. M. *A Few Words of hope on the Present Crisis of the English Church.* London: Joseph Masters, 1850 (pp. 24).

SCOTT, WILLIAM. *A Letter to the Rev. Daniel Wilson occasioned by his recent "Appeal to the Evangelical Members of the Church of England".* London: J. & C. Mozley, 1850 (pp. 40).

WILSON, DANIEL. *Our Protestant Faith in Danger: An Appeal to the evangelical members of the Church of England in reference to the Present Crisis.* London: Hatchards, 1850 (pp. 45).

Tracts of an Anti-Tractarian. No. 11. By "A Barrister". London: C. Gilpin, 1850 (pp. 163–76).

The Morality of Tractarianism: A Letter from one of the people to one of the clergy. London: William Pickering, 1850 (pp. 34).

BIBLIOGRAPHY

Gorham v. Bishop of Exeter: The Judgment of the Judicial Committee of Privy Council, delivered March 8, 1850, reversing the decision of Sir H. J. Fust. London: Seeleys, 1850.

Gorham v. The Bishop of Exeter: A Full Report of the Arguments of Counsel in this important case, before the Judicial Committee of the Privy Council. London: W. E. Painter, 1850.

ANONYMOUS. *The Great Gorham Case: A History in Five Books, including expositions of the rival baptismal theories.* By "A Looker-on". London: Partridge & Oakey, 1850.

BADELEY, E. *Substance of a speech delivered before the Judicial Committee of the Privy Council, upon an Appeal in a cause of Duplex Querela, between the Rev. George Cornelius Gorham, Clerk, Appellant, and the Right Rev. Henry, Lord Bishop of Exeter, Respondent.* With an Introduction. London: John Murray, 1850.

BALLEINE, G. R. *A History of the Evangelical Party in the Church of England.* London: Longmans, 1908.

BAYFORD. *The Argument of Dr Bayford on behalf of the Rev. G. C. Gorham, in the Arches Court of Canterbury, March 1849.* London: Seeleys, 1849.

BETHELL. *General View of the Doctrine of Regeneration in Baptism.* 4th edn. revised 1845. London: F. and J. Rivington.

BLOMFIELD, A. *Memoir of Bishop Blomfield.* Vol. II. London: John Murray, 1863.

CARDWELL, E. *A History of Conferences.* Oxford University Press, 1840.
—— *Synodalia.* Oxford University Press, 1852.

CORNISH, F. WARRE. *A History of the English Church in the Nineteenth Century.* Part I. London: Macmillan, 1896.

FABER, G. S. *The Primitive Doctrine of Justification.* London: Seeleys, 1837.

GOODE, W. *Effects of Infant Baptism.* London: Hatchards, 1850.

GORHAM, G. C. *The Efficacy of Baptism: Examination before Admission to a Benefice by the Bishop of Exeter.* London: Hatchards, 1848.

HARDWICK, C. *A History of the Articles of Religion.* London: Rivingtons, 1851.

IRONS, W. J. *The Judgments on Baptismal Regeneration.* London: John Masters, 1850.

LAURENCE, R. *The Doctrine of the Church of England upon the Efficacy of Baptism.* Oxford University Press, 1816.

LIDDON, H. P. *Life of E. B. Pusey.* Vol. III. London: Longmans, 1894.

LLOYD, C. *Formularies of Faith.* Oxford: Clarendon Press, 1825.

MANT, R. *An Appeal to the Gospel.* (Bampton Lectures, 1812.) London: Rivingtons, 1816.

MASKELL, W. *Holy Baptism:* A Dissertation. London: Pickering, 1848.

MAURICE, F. D. *The Kingdom of Christ.* Vols. I and III. London: Darton & Clark, 1838.

MOORE, E. F. *The Case of the Rev. G. C. Gorham against the Bishop of Exeter.* London: Stevens & Norton, 1852.

MORLEY, J. *Life of Gladstone.* Vol. I. London: Macmillan, 1903.

MOZLEY, J. B. *The Baptismal Controversy.* London: Longmans, 1862.

ORNSBY, R. *Memoir of James Hope-Scott.* Vol. II. London: John Murray, 1884.

PURCELL, E. S. *Life of Cardinal Manning.* Vol. I. London: Macmillan, 1896.

PUSEY, E. B. *Scriptural Views of Holy Baptism.* (Tracts for the Times, Nos. 67, 68 and 69.) London: Rivingtons, 1836.

—— *Royal Supremacy.* Oxford: J. H. Parker, 1850.

QUICK, O. C. *The Gospel of the New World.* London: Nisbet, 1944.

REES, A. H. *The Doctrine of Justification in the Anglican Reformers.* London: S.P.C.K., 1939.

STONE, DARWELL. *Holy Baptism.* London: Longmans, 1899.

SUMNER, J. B. *Exposition of the Gospel of St. John.* London: Hatchards, 1835.

—— *Apostolical Preaching.* Ninth edition. London: Hatchards, 1850.

WICKHAM, J. A. *A Synopsis of the Doctrine of Baptism.* London: George Bell, 1850 (pp. 589).

WILBERFORCE, R. I. *The Doctrine of Holy Baptism.* London: John Murray, 1849.

INDEX

Unconscionable Crimes

Unconscionable Crimes

How Norms Explain and Constrain Mass Atrocities

Paul Morrow

The MIT Press
Cambridge, Massachusetts
London, England

Testimonies, and the United States Holocaust Memorial Museum provided access to the primary and secondary sources I employed in this study. Ron Coleman, Rebecca Erbelding, Vincent Slatt, and Megan Lewis of the United States Holocaust Memorial Museum's Library and Archives gave particularly valuable guidance during an early phase of this project and continued their support long after my residence in Washington came to an end.

Other members of the staff at the Mandel Center for Advanced Holocaust Studies furnished material and intellectual assistance. Conversations with Jo-Ellyn Decker, Emil Kerenji, Jürgen Matthäus, and Suzanne Brown-Fleming substantially aided my work. Among my fellow visiting scholars, Mark Celinscak and Istvan Pal Adam have proved deeply inspiring friends. Special thanks go to Steve Feldman, whose patience watching this book develop was matched only by his confidence that it would one day be complete.

Teachers and colleagues at three universities have helped shape this project in its various phases. At Vanderbilt University, Lucius Outlaw, Marilyn Friedman, Jeffrey Tlumak, and José Medina taught me how to think like a philosopher, while Mona Frederick and Edward Friedman encouraged my tendency toward interdisciplinarity. Rob Talisse challenged me at a crucial stage to say what exactly I meant by the word *explanation*; his question has critically informed the text that follows. Larry May proved the ideal dissertation supervisor and offered unstinting support during the completion of this book.

At the University of Virginia, Colin Bird, George Klosko, Jennifer Rubenstein, and Murad Idris supplied helpful comments on various chapters while I was writing them. Jim Childress kindly allowed me to sit in on his Just War Theory seminar, and Gaby Finder, Jennifer Geddes, and Asher Biemann welcomed me into their Jewish studies reading group. My fellow postdocs Brookes Brown, Shruta Swarup, and Chris Berk offered trenchant readings of individual chapters, while Liya Yu delivered inimitable criticism of the project as a whole.

After an unplanned (and unfunded) career detour to the Netherlands, I had the good fortune to be included in the Ethics Institute Seminar Series hosted by the Department of Philosophy and Religious Studies at Utrecht University. Ingrid Robeyns graciously devoted time and energy to ensuring that I could continue my research, while Colin Hickey and Uğur Üngör helped me feel included in Utrecht's scholarly community. Well-timed visits from Shannon Fyfe and Neal Palmer brightened the gray North Sea winter. Friends and colleagues at Utrecht in Dialoog facilitated lively conversations about many topics entirely unrelated to atrocity.

Some academic debts are all the more substantial because the institutional ties that normally underpin them are absent. In my case, I owe Colleen Murphy particular thanks; she has kindly read and commented on multiple chapters in this book while sharing her own expert perspective on the theory and practice of transitional justice. Berel Lang and Noah Shenker also provided valuable feedback despite their own busy careers. Sven-Erik Rose first fostered these concerns more than a dozen years ago and has maintained an interest in my work for all that time.

Along with these individuals, I thank audiences at the University of Virginia, Utrecht University, the University of Glasgow, Collegio Ghislieri in Pavia, Tilburg University, the University of Minnesota, Western Galilee College, the University of Dayton, and the University of Southern California for listening to portions of this book while it was in preparation.

No academic work wholly escapes the personal. In my case, family support has been crucial. My parents, Lee and Becky, kept faith in this project even when it carried me across the Atlantic. My brothers, Ed and Brian, and my sister-in-law, Theresa, provided hospitality during successive research trips to Washington DC, while my brother-in-law, Matt, joined me on a memorable visit to Berlin. Ann Smith and Beryl Parrington gave me uncommon support, fully welcoming me into their Scotch-Coloradan family. Finally, my partner, Megan, has made this book all it is and showed me what it could be.

Part of the material in chapter 1 appeared previously in *Genocide Studies and Prevention* under the title "The Thesis of Norm Transformation in the Theory of Mass Atrocity" (vol. 9, no. 1, 2015). I thank the editors of the journal for their permission to reprint this material.

Introduction

This book presents the first general theory of the influence of norms on genocide and mass atrocity. It does so by combining conceptual and empirical arguments. At the conceptual level, the book offers a clear account of norms and norm transformation, one that is rooted in recent work in moral and political philosophy, but intended for readers approaching these topics from a broad range of backgrounds. At the empirical level, the book examines numerous historical cases of large-scale crimes, employing documentary and testimonial sources in order to illustrate the various roles norms perform before, during, and after such crimes. Ultimately the book argues that norms—moral, legal, and social—are integral to both the explanation and the prevention of mass atrocities.

Research on genocide and other kinds of large-scale crimes has long been the province of empirical social scientists. Historians and psychologists, sociologists and political scientists have all tested their respective disciplinary methods on the hard problems of mass killing, mass rape, forced removal, and other forms of mass atrocity.[1] More recently, anthropologists, economists, and scholars of language have added their observations to the expanding literature on such crimes.[2] Through this interdisciplinary research program, it has become possible to regard even the most grievous harms as phenomena with a long history, a typical etiology, and an internal rationality.

For all the insights offered by contemporary social science, it would be wrong to conclude that mass atrocities must be viewed merely as empirical facts. This is because genocide and other large-scale crimes are also matters of profound normative concern. In studying such crimes, we not only seek to discover the conditions that make them possible or the causes that make them actual. We are equally concerned with the wrongs these acts embody, the punishments they merit, and the interventions they license.

Philosophy has an important part to play in uniting these empirical and conceptual strands of inquiry. As a discipline, philosophy has long assessed the structure and coherence of explanatory theories. It has equally appraised the soundness of normative claims. By bringing the analytical tools of philosophy to bear on findings advanced by historians, psychologists, and other social scientists, this book demonstrates the central place of norms in efforts to explain and constrain mass atrocities.[3]

I.1   The Notion of Norms

Norms are practical prescriptions, permissions, or prohibitions, accepted by individuals belonging to particular groups, organizations, or societies, and capable of guiding the actions of those individuals. Accepting norms entails adopting various practical commitments and normative attitudes. These include a commitment to obey the requirements embodied in specific norms, as well as a disposition to disapprove of, and perhaps punish, fellow group members who fall short of those requirements.

Philosophers frequently distinguish between empirical and normative notions of norms—between the prescriptions, permissions, and prohibitions that are in fact accepted by individuals, on the one hand, and the prescriptions, permissions, and prohibitions that individuals *ought* to accept, on the other.[4] This study focuses on norms in the former, empirical sense. I am concerned chiefly with explaining the power of accepted norms to guide individuals' decisions and actions in times of severe social and political upheaval. Studying the influence of norms under such straitened conditions serves several aims. It will aid efforts by historians and other scholars to account for widespread participation by "ordinary" individuals in atrocities. It will assist policymakers seeking to use norms to prevent recurrences of large-scale crimes. And it will amend recent philosophical work on the social and political significance of norms, in which norms feature chiefly as sources of stability rather than as vectors for violence.

The urgency of these undertakings stems from the conviction that genocide and mass atrocity are manifestly, even supremely, wrong. Activists and institutions whose missions start from this conviction regard it as an expression of basic normative truths: such actions *are* wrong, they *deserve* opprobrium, they *must be* prevented. I share these views. But it is not my aim in this study to convince readers of the unconscionability of mass atrocities.[5] Instead, I advance the less obvious claim that such crimes depend on the persistence of norms within the groups that perpetrate them and those that suffer them. Mass atrocities, in other words, typically reflect the presence, not the absence, of norms.

Vindicating this claim requires that I defend the baseline definition of norms I just offered. It requires that I draw distinctions among various kinds of norms—notably, moral, legal, and social norms—and contrast these with other forms of social ordering, such as taboos or conventions. Finally, it requires that I show how norms can become legitimate objects of historical and social scientific inquiry. All of these issues will be addressed in the course of this study. For now, however, another problem demands attention: the problem of defining mass atrocity.

I.2   The Concept of Mass Atrocity

Raphael Lemkin, the Polish lawyer who coined the term *genocide*, saw it as a specific kind of crime, conspicuous for the intention among its perpetrators to destroy not just large numbers of individuals but whole groups.[6] The definition embedded in the 1948 UN Convention on the Prevention and Punishment of the Crime of Genocide narrows this category of criminality still further, singling out a small set of groups as legally recognizable targets of genocide.[7] Such definitional restrictions have fueled heated debates among scholars, jurists, and activists about the essential features of genocide. They also raise questions about the extent to which genocide exemplifies mass atrocity.

It might be possible to conduct a study of norms focusing solely on the crime of genocide. Such a project would face two major hurdles. First, as has often been noted, genocide presents researchers with a "small-N" problem: the number (N) of recognized cases is too small to support robust statistical analyses of the causes and conditions of this crime.[8] This problem reflects, in part, the definitional disputes I mentioned. But it also reflects the fact that under any plausible definition, genocide seems to occur less frequently than mass killing, mass rape, and other forms of mass atrocity.

The second challenge for a study focusing solely on genocide is not statistical but conceptual. Starting with Lemkin, numerous authors have argued that genocide need not involve any bodily harm, but may at times proceed bloodlessly, through the destruction of shared group identities. Such identities are rooted in part in shared norms. Hence, it is conceivable that coercively imposed changes to group norms could sometimes *constitute* genocide. The difficulties this line of thinking raises are substantial, and although they should be addressed, I do not seek to do so here.[9] Instead, my focus falls on what Lemkin called "physical genocide," along with non-genocidal acts of mass killing, mass rape, and forced removal.[10]

Over the past few decades, various terms have been adopted to refer to such acts. Two of the most common terms, which I employ throughout this study, are *mass atrocity* and *large-scale crimes*. In order to head off potential confusions arising from this usage, I must address two issues.

First, both *mass atrocity* and *large-scale crime* imply a particular magnitude of harm. There are two rival approaches to specifying this magnitude. One approach is quantitative and focuses on the precise number of victims of such crimes. So in recent years, academics and activists have proposed the bright-line number of 1,000 civilian deaths occurring over a discrete period of time as a minimum threshold for mass killings.[11] The other approach is qualitative and focuses on the extent of perpetration as well as on the scale of suffering. According to this approach, mass atrocities are defined as temporally extended assaults *by* large numbers of individuals *on* large numbers of individuals, where the latter are often further qualified as people particularly vulnerable to harm.[12]

In this study, I adopt the qualitative approach to the scope of mass atrocity. In my view, the numerical threshold that quantitative scholars now propose is too low to support an inquiry into the influence of norms on mass atrocities. The killing or maiming of a thousand civilians, though morally disastrous, may result from the chance detonation of a single explosive or the misdirected fire of a single infantry unit. It is unreasonable to suppose that laws, social norms, or moral permissions must be implicated in explanations of such tragedies. It is equally unreasonable to hope that changes in norms might suffice to prevent them. The qualitative definition, while still referencing the scope of harm, does not propose an implausibly low numerical threshold. At the same time, it highlights the widespread nature of perpetration—something that scholars of mass atrocity have long sought to understand. Ultimately, this definition provides better access to the acts I am concerned with, and a better index of the questions I address.[13]

Turning to a second potential point of confusion, both *mass atrocity* and *large-scale crime* cast the acts and policies they name as criminal. This is obvious in the case of large-scale crime. It may be less so in the case of mass atrocity. The term *atrocity*, as Mark Osiel has observed, descends from Roman military law, where it denoted actions deemed unlawful even when ordered by a duly authorized commander.[14] Elsewhere, I have argued that the set of actions that can be plausibly called atrocities is subject to substantial semantic variation, swelling or shrinking in order to fit political needs.[15] I do not wish to downplay the difficulty of identifying legitimate referents of mass atrocity. But I do reject the claim, sometimes advanced by social scientists, that it is in principle inappropriate to define genocide, mass killing, mass rape, and other mass atrocities as crimes.[16] To be sure, such actions have not always been, and are not always now, criminalized. Nor do legal definitions of such actions align perfectly with popular or scholarly conceptions—as indicated by the term *genocide* or by proposed alternatives, such as *atrocity crimes*.[17] Nevertheless, it is both etymologically accurate and analytically appropriate to refer to mass atrocities as large-scale crimes.[18]

I.3   The Enigma of Explanation

In his 2017 study, *Why? Explaining the Holocaust*, historian Peter Hayes observes that the adjectives most often employed in public discussions of the Shoah are *unfathomable*, *incomprehensible*, and *inexplicable*.[19] Against such suggestions of unintelligibility, Hayes arrays the tools developed by historians, political scientists, and other social scientists for explaining temporally and geographically extended events. "The Holocaust," he concludes, "is no less historically explicable than any other human experience, though the job is not easy."[20]

Philosophers and other readers encountering this claim may wish to know precisely what types of explanations are on offer. Whereas the explanations of physical events and processes supplied by natural scientists tend to be nomological—that is, grounded in appeals to general causal laws—social scientific explanations of large-scale crimes display a different structure. Historians and other scholars of mass atrocity do not typically seek to show that particular mass killings, forced removals, or other crimes had to occur precisely when they did, where they did, and how they did. Rather, they aim to identify social and political factors that allow attacks to proceed against certain populations and to distinguish psychological factors underlying individual participation in atrocities. The most common way of framing such explanations is to speak of factors that promote the occurrence of mass atrocities, on the one hand, and factors that constrain atrocities, on the other.[21]

One problem with this approach is that it can be difficult to determine which particular factors are most relevant in any given case. Consider the following list of factors scholars have cited in order to explain the fact that men, rather than women, predominate among perpetrators of mass atrocities:

1. The different susceptibility of men and women to peer pressure[22]
2. "Entrenched gender norms and expectations" that frequently restrict women's "opportunities to perpetrate harm"[23]
3. Colonial-era policies of forced labor (*corvée*) applied solely to male subjects[24]
4. Traditional associations between masculinity and military service[25]
5. The preponderance of "bored young men" in refugee camps[26]

In some cases of large-scale crimes, we can exclude one or more of these factors as inapplicable. But in most cases multiple factors retain at least a prima facie claim to relevance.

I do not hope to dissolve this general concern about the structure of social scientific explanations of mass atrocity. Instead, my aim is to eliminate some particular confusions arising from inadequate conceptual approaches to norms within existing explanatory theories. Historians and social scientists regularly refer to moral and social norms in their accounts of perpetration, victimization, and resistance, but they rarely state clearly how they understand those different types of norms or display a firm grasp of the distinctions between them. Legal scholars have strenuously debated the abstract question of whether legality is compatible with mass atrocity, but they have largely ignored the more mundane ways in which legal norms can help explain large-scale crimes. Finally, scholars of genocide often issue sweeping claims about the absence or inversion of norms during historical episodes of this crime, without recognizing that in many places, their own sources refute those claims. Exposing these problems and proposing alternative ways of integrating moral, legal, and social norms into explanatory accounts of mass atrocity is one major goal of this book.

I.4   The Problem of Prevention

Since the end of the Cold War, international institutions and individual nations have devoted considerable resources to the prevention of mass atrocities. Over the same period, scholars of large-scale crimes have clarified the notion of prevention itself. They have distinguished "proximate" and "structural" approaches to preventing mass atrocities.[27] They have contrasted "early-warning systems" with "risk-assessment" initiatives.[28] At the most basic level, researchers have shown that the forward-looking task of preventing mass atrocities differs substantially from the backward-looking task of explaining them.[29]

Not all strategies for preventing large-scale crimes implicate norms directly. Military approaches to atrocity prevention emphasize the power of armed soldiers to forcibly counter specific episodes of mass killing, mass rape, or forced removal.[30] Proposals focusing on education or economic opportunities tend to treat norms simply as vehicles for distributing social goods.[31] Finally, some scholars suggest that the causes of mass atrocities are so various, and the motives of perpetrators so diverse, that no effort at prevention that centers on specific moral, legal, or social norms can succeed.[32]

In arguing that norms are integral to the prevention, as well as the explanation, of large-scale crimes, I do not take myself to be denying the complexity of such crimes; rather, I am affirming it. When humanitarian aid workers question the traditional rules that prescribe neutrality during ongoing conflicts, they are asking whether fundamental moral norms require them to make a more explicit stand against atrocities. When lawyers at domestic or international tribunals prioritize prosecutions for high-level officials, their decisions reflect beliefs about how the enforcement of legal norms can help deter large-scale crimes. Finally, when schools adopt curricula that teach students to be "upstanders" (that is, to intervene against harms directed at third parties), they embrace the idea that social norms structure both everyday acts of bullying and extraordinary outbreaks of violence.

We must look to empirical research to determine what evidence supports the preventive effects claimed in each of these cases. In some areas, such as the study of bystanding, empirical inquiries are well established, but conclusions concerning preventive power remain equivocal. In other areas, such as investigations of the deterrent power of international criminal trials, only preliminary assessments are possible. One aim of this book is to establish a shared conceptual framework for scholars interested in the preventive power of moral, legal, and social norms. Another aim is to distinguish short-term, medium-term, and long-term contributions that norms can make to this end.

I.5   The Argument of This Book

Three main claims make up my argument in this book. The first is that genocide and other kinds of mass atrocity are social processes, reflecting larger social structures. The second claim is that historical cases of mass atrocity typically reflect the presence, rather than the absence, of norms. The third claim is that norms are crucial to both the explanation and the prevention of large-scale crimes.

Each of these claims cuts against common views of the causes and characteristics of mass atrocities. Studies of genocide often hypothesize the collapse of morality or the failure of legality as preconditions for violent group destruction. Some of the weightiest literary reflections on the Holocaust go further, suggesting that the very possibility of linking causes to effects broke down within the confines of Nazi concentration camps.[33]

Besides the belief that genocide entails the absence or progressive disappearance of norms, there is another view of large-scale crimes that my argument contests. This is the view that such crimes generally proceed from decisions taken by state leaders in response to the requirements of instrumental rationality. This explanation of mass atrocity takes different forms in different contexts. In contexts of war, especially international armed conflicts, the decisions that military commanders or state leaders take to bomb, starve, or displace civilians may be said to reflect *Kriegsraison*, or hard-headed calculations of military necessity.[34] In contexts of domestic upheaval, the decision to torture or abduct citizens en masse may be said to reflect a dominant strategy of "draining the sea."[35] Implicit in such accounts is the idea that norms, or at least norms that go beyond the bare requirements of instrumental rationality, have no place in explanations of mass atrocities.

I believe both of these approaches to explaining large-scale crimes fail, and for the same reason: both proceed from a desire for simplicity in explaining events that appear to defy comprehension. To those who fear that large-scale crimes are unintelligible, the theorist of norm collapse responds that such attacks are just what we should expect when all accustomed limits on human conduct vanish. To those who claim that mass atrocities are incomprehensible, the instrumentalist responds that these crimes reflect the same calculations that spur the dredging of harbors or the enforcement of quarantines. It is commendable to offer an explanation where none appears forthcoming. But not all explanations fit the features, including the normative features, of the events in question. The view of mass atrocity defended in this study surpasses accounts based on norm collapse or instrumental calculation. To show why, I must unpack my main claims.

First, I claim that mass atrocities are social processes, reflecting larger social structures. To be a social process means to draw on the sorts of institutions, resources, and relationships that make any substantial human undertaking possible.[36] To reflect larger social structures means to use those institutions, resources, and relationships in ways that do not radically break with, but instead extend, prior social arrangements. When soldiers or police kidnap civilians or torture dissidents, their actions reflect capacities that also make possible the legitimate functions of armies and police forces. When the men in a community join together to kill or displace their neighbors while their wives plunder those neighbors' homes, a preexisting gendered division of labor directs the progress of violence. While I do not go so far as to say that mass atrocities are normal outgrowths of modern social arrangements, I do think that all existing societies have features that make such crimes possible and affect their course when they occur.[37]

Second, I claim that historical cases of mass atrocity typically reflect the presence, rather than the absence, of norms. Identifying the existence of norms "in the wild" presents serious methodological challenges.[38] Undertaking this task for historical cases of mass atrocity compounds the difficulty. Nevertheless, basic assumptions about the nature of human agency, combined with the testimony of those who have lived through, suffered from, or perpetrated large-scale crimes, give us reason to investigate the influence of norms on such crimes. By reviewing a wide range of historical cases and focusing on salient distinctions among moral, legal, and social norms, I hope to show how norms help guide the actions of perpetrators, targets, and resisters of mass atrocities.

Third, I claim that norms are crucial to both the explanation and the prevention of large-scale crimes. I have already observed that the tasks of explanation and prevention differ in important ways. Much of the discussion in the chapters that follow is devoted to drawing out those differences. Here it may suffice to say that I believe explanations of genocide and mass atrocity must consider the conduct of individual agents, highly organized institutions, and loosely unorganized collectives—and that efforts to prevent large-scale crimes must also address each of these different levels of social reality.

I.6   Sources and Methods

Philosophers have long consulted historical cases in order to test key conceptual and normative claims. This is especially true of those philosophical subfields that focus on issues of war and peace. My strategy in this study goes beyond established philosophical uses of history insofar as I give sustained attention to primary, as well as secondary, sources. In light of this, I shall briefly describe these sources, their value, and their limits.

Letters and diaries, reports and memoranda are the main primary sources I use in this book. Such materials have the advantage of being contemporaneous with the crimes they describe. In addition to these documentary sources, my argument draws on oral testimony offered in courtrooms, classrooms, and recording studios by survivors, witnesses, and perpetrators of atrocities. Though not contemporary with events, such testimony conveys key details about the kinds of harm involved in large-scale crimes and about the normative beliefs and attitudes of their subjects. As will become clear in the chapters that follow, I am especially interested in using these sources to spotlight moments in which historical actors reflect on relevant norms; embrace particular legal, moral, or social norms as guides to action; or else reject their authority.[39]

The use of primary sources poses challenges well known to historians but less familiar to philosophers. Questions of authenticity cloud some documents; barriers to access at relevant archives prevent researchers from consulting others. Many primary sources that scholars of mass atrocity employ derive from documents compiled or testimonies recorded during specific legal proceedings, such as the International Criminal Tribunal for Rwanda or the International Military Tribunal at Nuremberg. The standards of evidence used in these proceedings were not identical, and they often differed substantially from the standards that historians and other scholars accept.[40] Finally, in the case of oral histories in particular, problems of memory, motivation, and context must be considered when assessing the credibility of each individual witness to atrocity.[41]

While primary sources are invaluable for exhibiting the historical operation of norms, this study draws more heavily on the large body of secondary scholarship on genocide and other kinds of mass atrocities. Beginning in the immediate post-Holocaust period, when scholars like Raphael Lemkin and Raul Hilberg drafted the first major studies, the crime of genocide has been analyzed from an enormous range of perspectives. Important work has also been done on the related crimes of mass killing, mass rape, and forced removal.[42] This literature conveys essential details about the historical examples discussed in this study, ranging from the concentration camps erected in South Africa at the start of the twentieth century, through the mid-century horrors of fascism and communism, up to the atrocities observed in postcolonial societies in recent decades. At the same time, this secondary literature provides a crucial starting point for the theoretical interventions I undertake.

Specifically, I argue that the action-guiding power of norms, though assumed in most studies of genocide and mass atrocity, is rarely analyzed explicitly, and never with sufficient clarity. Few scholars draw clear distinctions among moral, legal, and social norms or recognize the different ways in which these several kinds of norms influence action before, during, and after large-scale crimes. Many scholars assert that mass atrocities proceed from inversions of moral norms, or breakdowns in legal norms, without providing proof of these dynamics. Across the various chapters of this study, I develop a more principled framework for integrating norms into the study of mass atrocity.

The account of norms I defend is grounded in the scholarship of numerous philosophers and political theorists. Comprehensive studies of norms by Robert Goodin, Geoffrey Brennan, Nicholas Southwood, and Lina Eriksson, as well as work done specifically on social norms by Cristina Bicchieri, form the backbone of my discussion. In addition, investigations of legality rooted in the mid-century work of H. L. A. Hart and Lon Fuller have informed my account of legal norms, and philosophical studies of failures of professional ethics during historical mass atrocities by Berel Lang and Jonathan Glover have aided my discussion of moral norms. Turning to a different disciplinary tradition, the work of constructivists in the field of international relations, including such leading theorists as Martha Finnemore, Kathryn Sikkink, and Alex Bellamy, has enriched my understanding of how norms function in international politics. Studies of specific norms by Tuba Inal, Phil Orchard, Richard Price, and Karisa Cloward underpin my arguments about the constraining power of legal norms. Finally, the work of philosophers and legal scholars such as Ruti Teitel, Colleen Murphy, and Larry May on transitional justice has been critical to my understanding of the aftermath of large-scale crimes. Strengthening the connections among these various branches of scholarship is an important secondary aim of this study, as will be seen in my chapter summaries.

I.7 Chapter Summaries

Chapter 1 sets out the basic theory of norms employed in this study and addresses some fundamental questions about the power of norms to explain and constrain large-scale crimes. I first distinguish my conception of norms from mere statistical regularities or behavioral patterns, focusing instead on agents' practical commitments and normative attitudes. Next, I describe my strategy for differentiating moral, legal, and social norms on the basis of salient distinctions in the ways such norms appear within the practical point of view. Briefly, I argue that (1) moral norms are *not* grounded in real or perceived social practices and are *not* subject to standing procedural rules governing their creation, modification, or elimination, whereas (2) legal norms *are* grounded in real or perceived social practices and *are* subject to standing procedural rules governing their creation, modification, or elimination, while (3) social norms *are* grounded in real or perceived social practices but are *not* subject to standing procedural rules governing their creation, modification, or elimination. These distinctions, discussed in more depth below, are schematically represented in table I.1.

Turning to the substantive aims of this study, the second half of chapter 1 defends three assumptions underlying any effort to exhibit the influence of norms on large-scale crimes. The first is that it is possible reliably to identify differences in the norms accepted by individuals across two or more places or moments in time. The second is that norms have a nonreducible power to guide the actions of individuals and pattern the conduct of groups. The third is that it is possible to pinpoint specific mechanisms by which changes in norms have been, or might be, achieved.

Chapter 2 shows how moral norms help explain genocide and mass atrocity. Moral norms, I argue, are distinguished from legal and social norms

Table I.1
Salient Distinctions among Moral, Legal, and Social Norms

	Practice Grounded	Governed by Standing Procedural Rules
Moral norms	No	No
Legal norms	Yes	Yes
Social norms	Yes	No

by their independence from real or perceived social practices, combined with the absence of standing procedural rules governing their emergence, modification, or elimination. The chapter first examines the widespread scholarly view that mass atrocities proceed from an inversion of preexisting moral norms among perpetrators. Against this thesis, I argue that processes of norm evasion and norm erosion are more useful for explaining most cases of individual participation in large-scale crimes. I illustrate my account of the erosion of moral norms by discussing historical cases of demoralization and brutalization before and during mass atrocity. I illustrate my account of the evasion of moral norms by considering how techniques of euphemism and dehumanization obscure the immorality of such crimes. In the final section of the chapter, I consider whether professional complicity in mass atrocities provides conclusive evidence of inversions in moral norms.

Chapter 3 assesses how moral norms assist in preventing large-scale crimes. I begin by describing a special class of moral norms against deliberation, or norms that morally prohibit even thinking about performing certain actions or calculating the costs of doing so. I next consider the significance of moral norms against deliberation for individuals specially trained to perform violent acts: soldiers serving in regular armies or irregular armed groups. After describing traditional just war principles that aim to shape the deliberative agenda for soldiers and commanders considering various courses of conduct in war, I introduce alternative principles proposed by so-called revisionist just war theorists and show that these proposals stem largely from a concern to prevent mass atrocities. In the second part of the chapter, I turn to another set of agents active on the front lines of large-scale crimes: humanitarian aid workers. Reviewing recent debates about the adequacy of the traditional humanitarian principles of impartiality and neutrality, I show that these debates equally reflect a concern for atrocity prevention. The chapter concludes by critically evaluating philosopher

Jonathan Glover's account of the moral resources that might empower ordinary citizens to take an active part in preventing mass atrocities.

Chapter 4 examines the power of legal norms to help explain large-scale crimes. Legal norms are distinguished from moral and social norms by their grounding in real or perceived social practices, combined with the existence of standing procedural rules governing their emergence, modification, or elimination. One long-running debate within Anglo-American jurisprudence concerns the question of whether the rule of law can be upheld even during mass atrocities. While such debates usually focus on the validity of legal norms in contexts where mass atrocities occur, I argue that we should consider the broader range of roles that legal norms play in the etiology of large-scale crimes. Legal norms contribute to the creation of invidious social categories; the progressive marginalization and persecution of persons placed in those categories; the restriction of information concerning such marginalization and persecution; and the closure of escape routes that might otherwise provide a final refuge from mass atrocity. In light of their contributions to such social transformations, I conclude that legal norms play a crucial role in creating conditions for large-scale crimes. At the same time, these norms provide a privileged source of evidence for scholars of mass atrocities.

Chapter 5 addresses the value of legal norms as constraints on mass atrocities. I first briefly survey the many laws and legal institutions developed during the twentieth century in response to large-scale crimes. Here I distinguish efforts aimed at preventing such crimes from occurring in the first place from efforts designed to save victims or deter perpetrators once those crimes are underway. Next, I consider the argument that legalization, that is, the development of legal norms that are highly precise, obligatory, and delegated, is necessary for law to effectively constrain mass atrocities. While this argument is plausible for societies that are not currently threatened by large-scale crimes, it fails to capture the needs of societies undergoing transitions in the wake of such crimes. Building on Colleen Murphy's recent study of such societies, and particularly her analysis of the circumstances of transitional justice, I show that these circumstances commonly require departures from the precision, obligation, and delegation of relevant laws. Rather than reflecting an unwillingness to use law to prevent mass atrocities, such departures may be defended precisely in these terms.

Chapter 6 introduces the third major category of norms considered in this study, namely, social norms. Social norms are distinguished from legal and moral norms by their grounding in real or perceived social practices, combined with the absence of standing procedural rules governing their emergence, modification, or elimination. Such norms, I argue, contribute to large-scale crimes in two fundamentally different ways. On the one hand, preexisting social norms within particular groups or societies often influence atrocities from the moment they begin. On the other hand, novel social norms may arise once atrocities are underway, structuring subsequent patterns of perpetration, victimization, and resistance. My discussion in this chapter focuses on the first of these pathways. I am particularly concerned with exploring the role of preexisting social norms in creating and sustaining gender-based patterns of violence during large-scale crimes. Preexisting gender norms do much to explain the profiles of perpetrators during large-scale crimes, as I argue. They also help determine the specific types of harms that targeted individuals and groups suffer and the strategies for escape that they pursue.

Chapter 7 explores the power of social norms to help prevent mass atrocities. The chapter begins by rebutting a common misconception about rescuers during atrocities, according to which such individuals are comparatively insensitive to social norms. While social norms in fact play an important part in guiding rescuers' decisions and actions, I argue that rescue is of limited significance for thinking about atrocity prevention. Next, I examine how the elimination of existing social norms within particular populations can help constrain large-scale crimes. Focusing on three kinds of social norms prescribing silence about past or ongoing atrocities, I distinguish three means by which these "bad" norms can be disrupted. Finally, I turn to consider how the intentional creation of new social norms can help prevent mass atrocities. My discussion centers on the example of social norms prohibiting incitement to atrocities. These norms avoid many of the objections that legal prohibitions on this form of expression commonly encounter. At the same time, a social norm against incitement might spread more rapidly within particular societies through the influence of norm leaders. The chapter concludes by considering the future prospects of social norms as tools for atrocity prevention and by restating the need to unite moral, legal, and social norms in this cause.

1 Norms in the World: Agents, Action Guidance, and Historical Inquiry

On September 11, 1940, Dr. Leonardo Conti of the Reich Interior Ministry addressed a letter to his former medical school teacher, Professor Gottfried Ewald. Conti's letter came in response to a memo Ewald had composed condemning the secret Nazi euthanasia program known as *Aktion T4*. Conti wrote his erstwhile instructor as follows:

Dear Professor Ewald,

With the deepest gratitude I acknowledge the receipt of your letter of August 21. I still remember with great pleasure your lectures in Erlangen. Your analysis contains much that is right, I am sure. Nevertheless, I take a different view, although I cannot and will not set it down in writing at this time. I would only like to say, that I am fully convinced that the views of the entire German people [*Volk*] concerning these things are undergoing a transformation, and I can very easily imagine that things which in one period are considered objectionable [*verwerflich*] can in the next period come to be regarded as the only right choice. This is something we have experienced countless times in the course of history. As the most recent example, I would note the sterilization law: here, the process of a transformation in thought [*Umformung des Denkens*] is today already quite far advanced.[1]

Conti's letter has previously been cited in studies of professional complicity in the Holocaust.[2] His words are of interest here because of the glimpse they provide into the views of one high-ranking German official during an early phase of industrialized killing. Aktion T4, as historian Henry Friedlander has shown, contained the "origins of Nazi genocide."[3] It was in hospitals and sanatoriums like Hartheim, Sonnenstein, and Hadamar that Nazi officials first tested the method of mass murder using poison gas.[4] It was in reference to mentally and physically disabled persons that German academics coined the term "life unworthy of life."[5] Whether this term aimed more at euphemism or at dehumanization when it was introduced is hard to say.

But both euphemism and dehumanization were integral to the "transformation in thought" that preceded, and made possible, the Holocaust.

Conti was just one member of an extensive network of doctors, nurses, and administrators charged with implementing Aktion T4. I begin this chapter with his letter not because of the significance of his contributions but because of the suggestiveness of his claims. Conti's account of attitudes toward euthanasia in Germany in this period gives us reason to reflect on the nature of such views. At the same time, his letter raises several serious historiographical questions: about the sincerity of his arguments and the accuracy of his claims; about the methods available for testing his conclusions and the reasons why their truth or falsity might resist definitive proof.

In this chapter, I address these issues. The answers I offer take the form of a particular theory of norms. In case it is not already clear, I believe the disagreement between Conti and Ewald about Aktion T4 was in fact a disagreement about norms. I also believe the philosophical and historiographical questions that Conti's letter raises are largely questions about norms. My goal in this chapter is to develop and defend a baseline theory of norms and show how that theory can aid ongoing efforts to explain and constrain mass atrocities. While subsequent sections of this study focus on specific kinds of norms—moral, legal, and social—the arguments I present all begin from the general account of norms developed here.

The chapter proceeds as follows. In section 1.1, I explain my core definition of norms, showing how it is informed by recent work in moral and political philosophy and unpacking key component concepts. In section 1.2, I introduce a distinction between norm acceptance and norm guidance. Section 1.3 explicates the various terms used in this study to trace changes in norms, including *norm emergence, norm transformation,* and *norm elimination.* Section 1.4 turns from conceptual to historiographical issues, isolating three assumptions underlying efforts to discern norms in historical contexts. Section 1.5 addresses two challenges to these assumptions, one rooted in concerns about the circularity of normative explanations and the other in claims about the reducibility of such explanations to more fundamental cognitive processes.

1.1 Norms

In everyday life, we encounter norms in various contexts and discuss them in various ways. We say there is a norm requiring students to be vaccinated before starting kindergarten. We read that polar ice coverage has shrunk below historic norms. We find that faculty meetings start five minutes late as a norm. We praise our favorite artists or musicians for defying industry norms.

Not all of these expressions pick out the notion of norms under consideration in this book. Some refer simply to human behavioral regularities.[6] Others emphasize changing features of the natural world. The kinds of statements about norms that form the core of this study are those that seek to capture specifically normative views—views about what ought to be done, or ought not to be done, by some set of agents. I define norms, understood in this sense, as follows:

> *Norms* are practical prescriptions, permissions, or prohibitions, accepted by individuals belonging to particular groups, organizations, or societies, and capable of guiding the actions of those individuals.

On this definition, the mere fact that a particular behavior occurs widely within a specific group, organization, or society does not establish the existence of a norm prescribing that behavior. Nor does the absence of a given mode of conduct imply a norm prohibiting such action. Rather, it is the practical commitments and normative attitudes held by members of specific populations that establish the norms prevailing within those populations.[7] Among those practical commitments, two of the most important are a commitment to comply with the prescriptions, prohibitions, or permissions embodied in specific norms and a commitment to sanction fellow group members who fail to meet those requirements. Among those normative attitudes, one of the most significant is the feeling that a particular prescription, permission, or prohibition ought to be followed for its own sake rather than merely conformed with for instrumental reasons.[8]

Over the past two decades, philosophers have devoted significant efforts to explaining the sources and dynamics of norms, understood in the sense I have identified. Some have applied the findings of evolutionary biology to the analysis of norms, modeling possible pathways for the emergence of normative attitudes within humanity's ancestral past, and using evidence from child psychology and primatology to gauge the plausibility of those models.[9] Others have adopted the methods of behavioral economics, designing experiments intended to demonstrate empirically the existence of norms concerning fairness, trustworthiness, and reciprocity within specific populations.[10] A third strand of research focuses on the structures of shared intention required for groups to maintain particular norms over time.[11] Finally, a few philosophers have published comprehensive accounts of norms and norm cognition.[12]

Each of these lines of inquiry informs the theory of norms presented in this study. Each helps to establish distinctions between norms and other forms of social ordering, such as customs, conventions, and taboos. For example, conventions lack any intrinsic connection to agents' normative attitudes and are capable of guiding and coordinating action merely by engaging agents' self-interest.[13] Taboos, for their part, are distinguished from norms on the basis of their brute resistance to rational reflection.[14] In my discussion of norm guidance and norm transformation later in this chapter, I draw substantially on the work of Geoffrey Brennan, Cristina Bicchieri, and other philosophical theorists of norms. Before turning to those topics, however, I want to augment my baseline definition of norms by explaining my views of action, practical deliberation, and social identities.

In the first place, I believe that norms belong chiefly to the practical domain—the part of human experience that concerns action and deliberation about action.[15] "Action" should be understood broadly, denoting not just physical exertions but also the design of experiments, the management of political campaigns, and the creation of works of art. Borderline cases can be found in the rules governing the production and preservation of knowledge. Sometimes called "epistemic norms," these rules are practical insofar as they direct the distinctly interpersonal activities of instruction, disputation, and reason giving. They are theoretical insofar as the ends toward which they aim are truth, justification, or knowledge sought for their own sake.[16] Although epistemic norms are clearly relevant to the problems considered in this study, I do not single them out for separate treatment.

In the second place, I believe that norms are capable of guiding the actions of individuals who accept them. It is certainly possible to talk about norms in a third-personal sense, describing beliefs and attitudes underlying the words or actions of individuals and groups. This is precisely the way Dr. Conti characterized the views of the German people concerning sterilization and euthanasia circa 1940. A credible philosophical theory of norms, however, has to take up the first-person perspective and explain how norms appear from the standpoint of agents who accept and follow them. Philosophers refer to this perspective as the *practical point of view*. In subsequent sections of this study, I distinguish the different ways in which moral, legal, and social norms are apprehended from this point of view.

In the third place, I believe that norms circulate within particular groups, organizations, or societies. Some scholars use the term *reference group* to describe the collectives in which given norms circulate.[17] I will use the term *population* for this purpose. This notion of population is not equivalent to the raw aggregate of persons occupying a given locale at a given time, since different groups, guided by quite different norms, may inhabit the same cities, streets, and buildings. Not all members of the particular populations within which norms circulate need accept those norms, and not all who do accept them will comply with them in all cases. Though complex, these qualifications reflect the intricate nature of human groups, organizations, and societies—whose members are exposed to the hazards of birth and death, entry and expulsion; whose charters are subject to peaceful revision or forcible retraction; and whose identities, as understood by both members and nonmembers, are often in flux.[18]

This last relationship, between norms and identities, has been the subject of extensive research over the previous half-century. Philosophers, psychologists, political scientists, and sociologists have all analyzed the ways in which norms inform social identities—those sets of characteristics by which individuals and groups are distinguished in social life.[19] One reason for this robust research agenda is that social identities are perennial sources of political and ideological conflict.[20] In subsequent sections of this study, I consider whether moral norms, in their connection with individual and group social identities, sometimes serve to constrain individual participation in atrocities. I also show how changes in legal norms can foster changes in social identities, thereby easing perpetration of large-scale crimes. For now, it is enough to note that norms always circulate within particular populations and that although the boundaries of those populations are usually fluid, they can suddenly become quite fixed in circumstances of mass atrocity.

1.2 Norm Guidance

Norms inform agents' decisions and actions in a variety of ways. Some norms serve as default constraints on the paths of practical reasoning, rarely rising to the level of conscious awareness, but nevertheless influencing a wide array of decisions and actions.[21] So norms of rationality enjoin agents to avoid adopting incompatible ends, to pursue all the means that are necessary to their ends, and to update both means and ends in response to new information.[22] Other norms become salient only in the most extreme circumstances, such as moral norms prohibiting killing or legal norms banning torture.[23] While this study focuses on decisions and actions taken in contexts of genocide and mass atrocity, it gives equal consideration to norms at each end of this spectrum.[24]

In analyzing the influence that norms exert over action, philosophers commonly distinguish between norm compliance, on the one hand, and norm guidance, on the other. Agents can be guided by norms even when they refuse to comply with the specific prescriptions, prohibitions, or permissions set out by those norms. Sometimes agents intentionally violate norms they consider immoral; where those norms enjoy the backing of official institutions, such violations may be styled acts of civil disobedience. In other cases, agents who support specific norms but find prevailing interpretations or modes of enforcement inadequate may deliberately infringe those norms in order to force changes. Less principled, but more typical, are violations of norms driven by self-interest, self-importance, or scofflawery. Even in such cases, offending agents often show themselves to be guided by norms insofar as they take steps to conceal or cover up their actions.[25]

A second philosophical distinction concerns the difference between norm guidance, on the one hand, and norm acceptance, on the other. I have suggested that agents who accept specific norms tend to feel that those norms ought to be followed for their own sake rather than merely conformed to for instrumental reasons.[26] We may now consider this same normative attitude from within the practical point of view. Seen from this perspective, accepting a norm involves (1) recognizing its claim to serve as a guide to conduct and (2) acknowledging this claim to be legitimate. The bases for such acknowledgments, and hence the conditions for norm acceptance, differ across different kinds of norms. The specific accounts of moral, legal, and social norms developed later in this study draw out those differences. For now, however, I want to complete my baseline account of norms by describing some major forms of norm transformation.

1.3 Norm Transformation

By "norm transformation," I refer to changes in the norms prevailing within particular populations. Such transformations are rooted in changes in the practical commitments and normative attitudes that individual agents hold.[27] They may nevertheless first manifest themselves at the level of larger groups, organizations, or societies. Three types of transformations are especially significant for this study: the emergence, modification, and elimination of norms.

Norm Emergence

By "norm emergence," I mean the various processes by which new norms take hold within specific populations. Current social scientific accounts of norms focus on a small number of factors facilitating the emergence of norms. These include the presence of strong shared identities among members of particular groups; the intrusion of external events or crises that demand rapid responses by members of such groups; and the conscious efforts of "trendsetters" or "norm entrepreneurs," who use their social capital to urge the adoption of specific prescriptions, prohibitions, or permissions.[28]

Social identities comprise the characteristics by which individuals and groups are distinguished in social life. Norms or, rather, patterns of acceptance of particular norms often figure prominently among those characteristics. Clear examples of such core norms are norms of honor or professionalism within military organizations, norms of masculinity within political or corporate environments, and norms of maternal care or nurturing within traditional families. What is crucial about social identities is that they offer the individuals and groups who share them common resources for determining what norms should govern the conduct of group members in both routine situations and novel circumstances.[29]

Changes in circumstances can often be accommodated by norms already prevailing within particular populations. In cases of more extreme transformations, however, explicit calls for new norms may arise. Such scenarios represent "norm shocks" or "norm crises." Examples of specific crises that have prompted the adoption of new norms include the development and deployment of poison gases during World War I and the massive accumulation of displaced persons in Europe following World War II.[30] What is crucial about such shocks is that they expose the failure of existing prescriptions, prohibitions, or permissions to resolve problems affecting the interests of individuals within particular groups, organizations, and societies.[31]

Even when catalyzed by crises, new norms frequently benefit from promotion and translation by agents who enjoy specialized knowledge of the problems those norms aim to resolve, or unusual freedom to advocate for changes. These agents are referred to as "trendsetters" or "norm entrepreneurs."[32] A great deal has been written in recent years about specific instances of norm entrepreneurship, with historical examples including Francis Lieber (International Humanitarian Law), Raphael Lemkin (the Convention on Genocide), and Princess Diana (the UN Land Mine Protocol). What is crucial about norm entrepreneurs is that they not only seek to model new practical commitments and normative attitudes within specific populations, but that they also take pains to monitor other agents' acceptance of, and compliance with, emerging norms. Ultimately, as political scientist Lisbeth Zimmerman observes, "a norm is something that has to be brought to life in its new context by a process of discursive interaction, negotiation and contestation."[33]

Norm Modification

By "norm modification," I refer to the various changes that specific norms may undergo without thereby ceasing to exist. Just as norms reflect the complexity of social and political life, so too do the modifications to which they are subject. Accordingly, I will not attempt to enumerate all possible forms of changes in norms here, but instead discuss only the modifications most relevant for this study. These include changes in scope, changes in normative character, and changes in modality.

First, norms may undergo changes in scope, expanding or contracting to apply within a wider or narrower range of circumstances and to guide a greater or smaller set of actors. In some cases, these changes reflect newly discovered analogies between various situations in which specific norms might apply. In other cases, such changes in scope are driven by the interests of particular individuals seeking to extend existing norms to new contexts. Philosopher Margaret Gilbert refers to "tendentious" invocations of norms within situations where those norms were not previously held to apply.[34] In the legal domain, such changes in scope supply ready material for lawsuits, with judges asked to adjudicate competing claims about the applicability or inapplicability of particular legal norms.[35] Where moral and social norms are concerned, however, formal venues for resolving disputes about the scope of norms rarely exist.

Second, norms may undergo changes in the specific type of normativity they exhibit. Such changes are grounded in the practical commitments and normative attitudes held by the individuals who accept those norms, though other factors are also relevant. So what was once accepted as a social norm within a particular group, organization, or society may later become a moral norm, and what once was a moral norm may later become a legal norm.[36] While many aspects of agents' practical commitments and normative attitudes are implicated in such changes, my account focuses on just two salient distinctions: the dependence or independence of those commitments and attitudes on real or perceived social practices and the presence or absence of standing procedural rules which agents consider to govern changes in specific norms.[37]

Third, norms may undergo changes in modality, by which I mean changes in their status as prescribing, prohibiting, or permitting particular actions. Within certain areas of social life, all of the leading norms tend to exhibit a single modality. In laissez-faire economies, the leading norms tend to be permissive. In the laws of armed conflict, by contrast, key norms tend to be prohibitive. We can imagine that in the future, certain actions permitted under the norms of a given economy may come to be prescribed, or certain actions prohibited under current laws of war may come to be permitted. It would then be appropriate to speak of changes in the modality of existing norms rather than of one norm replacing another.[38]

What about cases in which an action prohibited under current norms comes to be prescribed, or vice versa? The question is apposite, since this is precisely the sort of transformation that Dr. Leonardo Conti predicted in his letter to Professor Ewald. In Conti's words, "Things which in one period are considered objectionable can in the next period come to be regarded as the only right choice." The last part of this claim indicates that Conti had in mind not just the erosion of a prohibition, but the shift from a prohibitive norm to a prescriptive norm. It is also evident from Conti's letter that he expected this change in norms to occur not only within a subset of the German population, but throughout "the entire German *Volk*."

I think inversions in norms of the kind Conti predicted should be understood not in terms of the modification of a single norm, but rather in terms of the elimination of an old prescriptive or prohibitive norm, combined with the emergence of a new norm bearing the opposite modality.[39] In such cases, the only constants will be a certain population and a certain area of human activity; the relevant attitudes, commitments, and patterns of enforcement are all, by hypothesis, reversed.[40] In order to understand this specific dynamic, we must turn from the modification of norms to their elimination.

Norm Elimination

Norms that have lost their utility, shed their intelligibility, or otherwise ceased to serve valued ends may finally disappear from the populations in which they once prevailed. To speak of "eliminating norms" suggests a conscious effort to dispose of disvalued practical prescriptions, prohibitions, or permissions. Such deliberate acts of norm elimination do sometimes occur. Statutes may be superseded by new acts of legislation; agency rules may be invalidated by judicial decision. Nevertheless, it often happens that norms lose their place in social life through less formal processes. In such cases, we may refer to the erosion, or breakdown, of norms.

It is not entirely clear from Conti's letter to Ewald whether Conti thought that ordinary German social and moral beliefs concerning euthanasia would be eliminated through overt means or if they would be discreetly undermined. The fact that Aktion T4 had its legal basis in an executive order long kept secret, coupled with the fact that the program was continued covertly after several German clergy spoke out about the assault on "life unworthy of life," suggests that the latter path toward norm elimination predominated.[41] For all the success of National Socialism in creating new norms concerning health, masculinity, and fertility during the 1930s and 1940s, however, there is little evidence that practical commitments and normative attitudes in favor of killing disabled persons ever became widespread.

We should pause here to acknowledge the reality of conflicts between norms. Such conflicts often occasion campaigns for norm elimination. In cases of conflicts between legal and moral norms, we have an established vocabulary for discussing agents' decisions to prioritize their moral commitments and engage in civil disobedience. The opposite dynamic, where legal norms are leveraged by state officials to undercut moral norms, has no widely recognized name.[42] Nor are there ready turns of phrase for describing clashes between social norms and legal norms or between social norms and moral norms. Conflicts of each sort will nevertheless receive consideration in the course of this study, as will cases where two norms of the same kind conflict with each other.

It is important not to overgeneralize when describing the dynamics of norm elimination. Some paths to norm elimination are limited to legal norms; others apply only to social norms; still others are restricted to moral norms. For this reason, it is difficult to give a summary account of "norm breakdown" or, as it has sometimes been called, "norm death."[43] In light of this, and with my baseline account of norms now in place, I want to turn to the historiographical task of this chapter and argue that we can in fact detect the influence of norms in historical cases of mass atrocity.

1.4   Norms in the World

On June 12, 1944, a young Hungarian woman named Olga Kovacs was deported from her hometown of Salgótarján to Auschwitz. Olga was eighteen years old at the time; her mother and aunt were deported, and survived, with her. Reflecting on this period in postwar audiovisual testimony, Olga described a significant subterfuge she and her family adopted upon entering the camp:

> Somehow, I don't know what made us think, from then on I never called her mother, only called her Sari. They did not know, except the people from our town, that we are relatives. Because it was not good to have a relative in Auschwitz. I don't know who told us. But we saw at the, on arrival that families are torn apart. Probably that's what gave us the idea.[44]

Like the letter from Leonardo Conti cited at the start of this chapter, Olga Kovacs's testimony raises significant interpretive and normative questions. Is Olga making a claim about the presence of a norm against acknowledging relatives in Auschwitz or merely recalling perceived strategic reasons for such concealment? Can we say that Olga, her mother, and her aunt, a group of just three people, created and followed such a norm, even if none had previously existed? What sanctions, if any, were used to maintain this norm within the family circle or within the camp more broadly? And how, if at all, does this informal practice of refusing to acknowledge relatives connect to the legal prohibitions against various kinds of relationships promulgated by the perpetrators of the Holocaust?

The conceptual distinctions established in the first half of this chapter can refine the ways in which we ask these questions. They do not suffice to answer them. For these are not questions about norms in the abstract, but questions about norms in the world: in the *univers concentrationnaire* that Hitler and his executioners created and in the many other societies riven by mass atrocities during the long twentieth century.[45] Only by addressing such questions at the outset can we hope to understand how norms—moral, legal, and social—contribute to the explanation and prevention of mass atrocities.

Fortunately, these questions have not gone unnoticed by scholars. A significant literature exists in which the normative underpinnings of large-scale crimes are debated. By studying that literature, we can isolate the key assumptions underlying efforts to use norms to explain and constrain large-scale crimes. We can also gain a better sense of the main objections to those assumptions, and of how those objections might be overcome.

Explaining Atrocities through Norms

In a 2004 article on the Rwandan genocide, political scientist Lee Ann Fujii argues that norms exerted a substantial causal influence on that mass atrocity.[46] "Put simply," she writes, "genocidal leaders had to transform the normative environment such that actions that were once considered verboten (such as killing thy neighbor) could be viewed as not only legitimate but imperative."[47] Both official records and testimonial accounts provide clues to the mechanisms by which, in this case, "genocide became normalized."[48] Ultimately Fujii sketches a more general theory of why norms remain salient during mass atrocities. "Norms," she avers, "become more important when reality is confusing, contradictory, or changing. The more ambiguous the situation, the more likely people are to rely on norms as guides for behavior; and the clearer the prescription of a given norm, the more likely people will follow that norm and not others."[49]

Fujii's claims concerning the causal influence of norms on large-scale crimes rest on three principal assumptions: that it is possible to reliably identify differences in the norms accepted by individuals across two places or moments in time; that norms have a fundamental, or nonreducible, power to guide the actions of individuals and pattern the conduct of groups; and that it is possible to pinpoint specific mechanisms by which changes in norms have been, or might be, achieved. These assumptions are not restricted to Fujii's analysis of the Rwandan genocide. The exchange between Dr. Conti and Professor Ewald embodies at least the first two, and perhaps all three, of these assumptions. Historian Christopher Browning's well-known analysis of participation by "ordinary men" in mass killings on the Eastern Front during World War II also rests on these assumptions.[50] Consider the first assumption identified above. In the course of his study of the actions and decisions of members of Reserve Police Battalion 101, Browning contrasts two different norms accepted by members of this particular unit at different moments in time. Browning first posits a norm prescribing killing among participants in mass shootings in German-controlled territory in Eastern Europe. He then posits a reversion to norms prohibiting such actions during the decades of investigations and trials that followed the Holocaust. Browning writes,

> To concede that the morally inverted world of National Socialism—so at odds with the political culture and accepted norms of the 1960s—had made perfect sense to them at the time, would be to admit that they were political and moral eunuchs who simply accommodate to each successive regime. That was a truth with which few [former members of Reserve Police Battalion 101] either wanted or were able to come to grips.[51]

In order to see how the second assumption identified underlies norm-based explanations of large-scale crimes, it is helpful to consider cases of apparent norm breakdown. Argentinean legal scholar Carlos Santiago Nino supplies an example in his discussion of judges' contributions to the "Dirty War" in his country. By officially recognizing "the legitimacy of coups d'état," Nino argues, the Argentinean judiciary fostered a broader social environment of anomie, undermining support for the rule of law and impeding accountability for the thousands of disappearances and other atrocities that the military government sponsored.[52] Similar claims about breakdowns in norms encouraged by the malfeasance of legal actors have been made by scholars of legal institutions under National Socialism, apartheid-era governments in South Africa, and elsewhere.[53] In each of these cases, the assumption is that relevant legal norms should have led the persons implicated to substantially different decisions and actions.

Consider, finally, the assumption that it is possible to pinpoint specific mechanisms by which changes in norms have been, or might be, achieved. Here we should return to Fujii's analysis of the Rwandan genocide. Fujii identifies three distinct stages in the emergence of what she calls a "genocidal norm," with each stage associated with different mechanisms for provoking norm transformation. First came the stage of spreading a message of threats posed by Rwandan Tutsis to the Hutu majority. Second was the stage of producing "objective" evidence of those threats through fabricated attacks, sensationalized reporting on real crimes, and so on. Third came the stage of making an escalation in risks appear imminent so as to require immediate action.[54]

These examples illustrate the assumptions underlying efforts to identify norms, and the influence of norms, in explanatory accounts of large-scale crimes. Precisely the same assumptions underlie efforts to harness the action-guiding power of norms to prevent mass atrocities, as I shall now show.

Preventing Atrocities through Norms

In his 2009 book, *Making Sense of Mass Atrocity*, legal scholar Mark Osiel argues that modifications to existing legal norms may help prevent large-scale crimes. After asking how changes in law might "create and cultivate within modern armies the institutional characteristics enabling them to steer clear of mass atrocity," Osiel suggests that one promising strategy is to impose civil liability on officers whose subordinates take part in mass killings, mass rapes, or other large-scale crimes.[55] Expanding the scope of legal norms imposing civil liability for such crimes, Osiel contends, avoids the problems of procedural justice raised by comparable proposals to extend criminal liability and penalties. At the same time, this change in law could help weaken social norms prohibiting "snitching" on fellow members of one's military unit.[56]

Osiel's proposal for using law to counteract pernicious social norms depends on the possibility of identifying differences in the norms accepted by particularly situated individuals across two or more places or moments in time. It thus parallels the explanatory invocations of norms already discussed. What is different about this case is the forward-looking nature of the appeal to norms—the prediction that practical benefits will follow from modifications to the legal norms by which officers are held accountable. A similar prospective quality appears in arguments supporting the emerging international legal doctrine of responsibility to protect.

Unlike Osiel's proposed modification to domestic military law, the doctrine of Responsibility to Protect (R2P) aims chiefly to guide the actions of high-level state officials and institutions.[57] And unlike Osiel's proposed change in norms, R2P is supposed to be capable of guiding those actions even in the absence of statutory changes in law. Further clarification comes from distinguishing primary and secondary bearers of the responsibilities established under R2P. Primary bearers of responsibilities are individual states and their leaders. Secondary bearers are the various state and nonstate actors composing the international community, who are tasked with taking up protective responsibilities when primary bearers fail to fulfill them.[58]

Advocates of R2P generally avoid calling protective actions by secondary parties *punishments* for failures by primary parties to meet their responsibilities.[59] Furthermore, as Luke Glanville observes, there are currently no legal sanctions in place for failures by secondary bearers to act in cases of malfeasance by primary bearers of responsibility.[60] What this example shows is that while preventive applications of the thesis of norm transformation depend on the assumption that norms have the power to guide actions, both the identity of the actors guided by such norms and the forms of accountability tied to such guidance vary substantially across different normative domains.[61]

Preventive appeals to norms, and changes in norms, place particular emphasis on the mechanisms by which desired transformations in norms are to be achieved. Political scientists, as noted, offer numerous interpretations of the efforts of norm entrepreneurs to change norms in order to prevent war and mass violence.[62] In addition to highlighting the accomplishments of such individuals, these scholars suggest that catastrophic events in the domestic or international sphere may equally serve as catalysts for key changes in norms. In all of these cases, theorists assume that it is possible to pinpoint specific mechanisms that have caused, or might yet compel, changes in norms that serve to constrain mass atrocities.

1.5 Two Problems: Circularity and Reducibility

The assumptions underlying efforts to use norms to explain and constrain mass atrocities may be widely shared, but they are hardly uncontroversial. Here, I consider two objections to these assumptions. The first objection targets the assumption that it is possible reliably to identify differences in the norms accepted by individuals across two or more places or moments in time. The second objection targets the assumption that norms have a fundamental, or nonreducible, power to guide the actions of individuals, and thereby pattern the conduct of groups. Taking these objections seriously should strengthen my argument for integrating the philosophical theory of norms into scholarly accounts of genocide and mass atrocity.

The Circularity Problem

Efforts to explain atrocities through norms rest on the assumption that it is possible reliably to identify differences in the norms accepted and followed by individuals across two or more places or moments in time. It is not obvious that this assumption is justified. The circularity problem raises questions about the verifiability of claims about the existence and influence of norms within any given population. Although this objection applies to claims about norms circulating in present-day contexts, it seems still stronger when leveled at claims about norms prevailing in past epochs. Addressing this problem is, accordingly, crucial to the success of this study.

The risk of circularity arises because of the evidentiary gap between the observable conduct of actors and their unobservable cognitive and conative states. In everyday life, we routinely infer things about individuals' beliefs, attitudes, and intentions from their actions.[63] But in cases of ostensibly norm-guided conduct, such inferences may give rise to a circular pattern of reasoning, as follows. First, observed patterns of behavior are taken as evidence of the existence and influence of particular norms within specific populations. Second, these same inferred norms are used to explain, or account for, the observed patterns of behavior.[64]

Some of the most promising strategies for breaking out of this explanatory circle are not available to scholars studying norms in historical cases of mass atrocity. Philosopher Cristina Bicchieri has pioneered experimental methods for identifying, and measuring the strength of, norms regarding fairness, reciprocity, and truthfulness in present-day societies.[65] These methods depend on the experimenters' ability to control the beliefs that subjects form concerning the kinds of interactions in which they are involved. They depend equally on the experimenters' ability to change the structure of incentives subjects face for certain kinds of conduct. So in experiments designed to elicit fairness norms, subjects may be selectively fed information about the past behavior of their experimental partners, or they may be told that the experiments have been structured in such a way as to prevent partners from detecting unfair divisions of monetary rewards.[66]

Carefully controlled experiments of this kind are not possible when it comes to the study of norms in contexts of mass atrocity. Even if reliable simulations of large-scale crimes were technically feasible, they would surely violate the rules of ethical scientific inquiry. Indeed, the most famous experimental approximations of such scenarios undertaken in the late twentieth century—Stanley Milgram's experiments in New Haven and Philip Zimbardo's Stanford Prison Experiment—are today subject to serious methodological, as well as ethical, critiques.[67] Fortunately, there are other sources, besides the observed actions of historical actors themselves, that can provide independent evidence of the influence of norms on those actions.[68] The most important of these sources are documents and testimony.

Holocaust scholars have exhaustively debated the merits of documents and testimony as sources of historical knowledge about large-scale crimes. Pioneering figures like Raul Hilberg once insisted on the primacy of documents created by the planners and perpetrators of genocide themselves as sources of information concerning the Shoah.[69] Such documents often do provide substantial evidence concerning norms. One important example concerns the language rules (*Sprachregeln*) developed by various parties within the German military and political hierarchies to conceal the truth about the policies of deportation and mass killing from the targets of such policies and from third parties. The existence of letters and memos in which officials were reprimanded for failing to conform to these language rules provides clear, noncircular evidence for the existence and influence of such norms.[70]

For Hilberg, who belonged to the founding generation of Holocaust historians, the evidentiary advantage of documents over testimony was clear. More recently, testimonial sources have achieved high standing in studies of large-scale crimes. As historian Yehuda Bauer explains, privileging documents produced or preserved by the organizers of mass atrocities threatens to distort the historical record by obscuring the experiences of the targets of such crimes. Treating testimony as an independent source of historical knowledge is far from unproblematic, but it is a mistake to think historical understanding could be improved by excluding such material.[71]

Philosophers do not draw the same distinction between testimonial and documentary evidence as historians. For philosophers, the evidence that any particular agent possesses for his or her beliefs is typically termed "testimonial" if it originates in the perceptions, conceptions, or simply the words of others.[72] From this perspective, many of the Holocaust-era documents discussed by Hilberg and Bauer, as well as many of the thousands of documents presented as evidence at recent international criminal trials, count as testimonial evidence of atrocities.[73] They are testimonial in two senses: first, their evidentiary value consists chiefly in the words that certain individuals use to convey information about particular acts or policies to other individuals; second, the authenticity of these documents must be attested to by their creators, witnesses to their creation, or experts with specialized knowledge of such documents.[74]

In this study, I aim to reconcile these contrasting conceptions of testimony. That reconciliation does not, however, extend to the level of terminology. In general, when I refer to testimony, I use it in the current historiographical sense, excluding official reports, documents, and pronouncements created by perpetrators before and during atrocities, but including many different written, oral, and audiovisual texts supplied by targets, bystanders, or rescuers before, during, and after large-scale crimes. Retrospective statements by perpetrators about their reasons for participating in past large-scale crimes also count as testimonial in this sense. When I want to invoke the alternative, philosophical notion of testimony, I say so explicitly.[75]

When testimonial sources are admitted as a basis for explaining large-scale crimes, it opens a second way of overcoming the circularity challenge.[76] It is important to be clear about the nature and limits of this resource. Bauer suggests testimony is most reliable when multiple individuals provide consistent statements concerning the existence or effects of a particular policy or event.[77] This argument accords with the principles endorsed by Alvin Goldman, Tony Coady, and other philosophers concerned with testimonial knowledge.[78] In the context of inquiries into the historical influence of norms, corroboration by multiple witnesses takes on added importance, since it is always possible for individual actors to be mistaken about the norms accepted or followed by other members of specific populations. The risk of mistakes rises when opportunities for communication are constrained or the contents of communications censored, as commonly occurs during large-scale crimes.[79]

At this point, we do well to return to the postwar testimony of Olga Kovacs. We may never know whether a general norm, as opposed to a local strategy, of concealing adult family relationships existed at Auschwitz-Birkenau during the summer of 1944. The question never became relevant during the postwar investigations, disciplinary hearings, and trials at which much testimony was elicited—in contrast to concentration camp rules concerning birth and parental ties to young children, which are well attested and played a part in the postwar trials of nurses and camp guards.[80] Nevertheless, many other details from Olga's three-and-a-half-hour testimony, such as her description of the latrine as a place for exchange of news, or her use of the folk name "Kanada" for the section of the camp where confiscated goods were sorted, are confirmed in statements given by other survivors.[81] This suggests that neither her memory nor her sincerity as a giver of testimony can be used as reasons for challenging her claims.

The Reducibility Problem

"People pass away, and everything a man had in his head is lost forever." So observed one witness called by prosecutors at the 1961 trial of Adolf Eichmann.[82] Acts of testimony offer a way of avoiding this fate, establishing a public record of individuals' private impressions and attitudes. But the problem may be worse than this witness admits. Not only are the true contents of our experience rendered inaccessible by death; they may also be inaccessible in life. Statements about norms and the influence of norms are, on this skeptical view, at best linguistic approximations of more primitive, prelinguistic attitudes.[83] At worst, such statements represent post hoc justifications of essentially involuntary behaviors. Pursuing the objection to its limit, critics may contend that any effort to characterize action from within the practical point of view must fail, since such characterizations necessarily depict decisions and actions in ways that distort the fundamental cognitive and conative bases of human conduct.[84]

Kristen Renwick Monroe's 2012 study, *Ethics in an Age of Terror and Genocide*, extends one version of this cognitive model to the specific circumstances of mass atrocity.[85] Monroe aims to show how individuals' social identities, rooted in specific social relationships, constrain the range of choices available to them in contexts of moral decision making. Three concepts are crucial to Monroe's account of moral choice. First is the concept of identity. Drawing on the findings of social identity theory within social psychology, Monroe suggests that differences in identity do much to explain the different actions of perpetrators, bystanders, and rescuers during episodes of genocide and mass atrocity.[86] Second is the concept of categorization. Monroe defines this as "the process by which ideas and objects are recognized, differentiated, or distinguished from one another and then understood."[87] Third is the concept of cognitive stretching. This concept seeks to capture the fact that patterns of categorization can change over time in response to a variety of environmental or social factors. Put differently, cognitive stretching seeks to explain how situations or events that once seemed morally salient to particular individuals can subsequently cease to be categorized in this way, or vice versa.[88]

To the extent that Monroe addresses the ability of norms to guide decisions and actions, she suggests that they do so nonreflectively. Her entire account is designed to challenge moral theories that focus on deliberation and rational reflection about right and wrong. Indeed, the central framing device for her study is the idea that both bystanders and resisters of genocide tend to assert that they had "no choice" in acting or failing to act.[89] A second, and more consequential, feature of Monroe's model is the claim that the acceptance of norms often occurs unreflectively and may be difficult to elicit at the level of conscious awareness. Monroe argues that an individual's identity, or self-conception, largely determines both which facts that individual recognizes as morally salient and which choices seem available to that individual in the face of such facts.[90]

Both of these claims are, in principle, compatible with a study of mass atrocity centering on norms, though they suggest a very different picture of both the acceptance of norms and the way in which norms guide actions. There is, however, a case to be made that on Monroe's model, norms themselves are simply superfluous. Norms are not fundamental to the explanation of individual and group conduct during large-scale crimes, since cognitive processes of categorization and social processes of identity formation seem to do all the explanatory work. And norms are not fundamental to the prevention of large-scale crimes, since what really seems to matter is transforming individuals' self-conceptions and in this way altering the categories they deploy and the facts they take to be legally or morally salient.[91] In my view, this is the strongest way to frame the challenge that Monroe's model of agency poses to the theory of norms I have advanced in this chapter.

In response to this challenge, I suggest that the acceptance of norms is not just a consequence of, but also constitutive of, individual and group social identities. That is, changes in the particular profile of prescriptions, permissions, or prohibitions that individuals accept often serve as steps toward claiming, or retaining a claim on, particular social identities.[92] Two types of changes in accepted norms are worth distinguishing. First are identity-instituting norm transformations, or changes in norms that serve as conditions for the adoption of new identities. Second are identity-vindicating norm transformations, or changes in norms that serve as conditions for preserving, in the face of some significant threat, existing identities.[93]

How do identity-instituting norm transformations bear on theories of genocide and mass atrocity? Here, the history of Aktion T4 is instructive. The ideas underlying this euthanasia program existed in Germany (and indeed, outside Germany) well before the ascendancy of National Socialism.[94] In terms of changing norms, particularly legal norms, to reflect these ideas, however, it was Hitler's takeover of power that "made the implementation of the race hygiene utopia possible."[95] It is this utopian aspect of the Nazi policy toward the disabled, emphasized by historian Eric Weitz, that makes it appropriate to consider the relevant changes in laws regarding so-called life unworthy of life as a form of identity-instituting norm transformation: a change in norms coinciding with, and seen as a condition for, the development of a new *Völkisch* identity.[96]

Shifting to identity-vindicating norm transformations, it is useful to consider the Nuremberg Code of medical ethics, promulgated in the first so-called successor trial at Nuremberg. While lead prosecutor Telford Taylor considered it possible to "pass very briefly over matters of medical ethics" in his opening statement at this trial, retrospective accounts have called the Nuremberg Code "the most important document in the history of the ethics of medical research."[97] Chiefly at issue in the Nuremberg Code is the requirement that doctors obtain voluntary and informed consent from prospective research subjects. As historian Paul Weindling has pointed out, a major aim of the scientists and physicians who assisted Taylor in developing his prosecutorial strategy was to avoid "too strong a denunciation of Nazi medicine [which] might jeopardize their own position" and to articulate "conditions under which risky experimentation was ethically permissible."[98] The development of the principle of informed consent, on this reading, is an example of an identity-vindicating norm transformation. It is a norm that had not been clearly articulated or widely accepted before World War II, but that became part of the basis of the continuing legitimacy of the medical profession after that conflict. Importantly, this change in norms was not so radical as to completely destroy the existing identity of medical professionals. It allowed physicians to continue drawing on a tradition of medical experimentation designed to improve future care, even while ruling out certain previously accepted methods of research.[99]

By addressing objections based on concerns about circular reasoning and the reducibility, or nonfundamentality, of norms, I hope to have strengthened the baseline theory of norms I employ in this study. The concerns underlying these objections are not idle; they point up real risks that historians and other scholars run when trying to trace the influence of norms on historical events. Analyzing these risks has exposed limits to testimonial and documentary evidence that will remain relevant for the discussions of moral, legal, and social norms that follow. At this point, I have only indicated some strategies by which such risks might be averted. It is up to the remaining chapters of this study to vindicate these strategies and prove the power of norms to explain and constrain mass atrocities.

2 "Necessary—and Even Proper": Moral Norms and the Explanation of Mass Atrocities

On December 26, 1917, Sir Arthur Conan Doyle published a letter in the *Times* under the heading, "The Uses of Hatred." In his letter, Doyle discussed strategies for restoring enthusiasm among British soldiers and civilians for the unrelenting conflict in Europe. After reciting several stories of abuses inflicted on British officers by their German captors, Doyle asked, "Why should we recall these incidents? It is because Hate has its uses in war.... It steels the mind and sets the resolution as no other emotion can do." "Scatter the facts," Doyle continued, "put them in red hot fashion." He concluded, "We have to win, and we can only win by keeping up the spirit and resolution of our own people."[1]

The circulation of reports of shocking acts performed by enemy soldiers in war dates from antiquity. During the Republican period, Roman orators decried atrocities ascribed to the Carthaginian general Hannibal.[2] In the Middle Ages, claims of cruelties committed by Muslims against Christians helped spark the series of clashes now called the Crusades.[3] World War I extended, but did not seriously alter, this tradition. Working in various media, writers and artists in France, Germany, and Britain conveyed lurid tales of enemy outrages to credulous publics. As political scientist Harold Lasswell argued after the war's end, it was not the novelty of such stories but their adherence to long-established tropes that gave them the power to win belief and spur action.[4]

Today, scholars commonly associate propaganda with the hardware of war. One historian speaks of "munitions of the mind," another of "weapons of mass seduction."[5] Such comparisons accord with Doyle's description of the "uses of hatred." But propaganda need not be seen solely in these terms. It may also be viewed as a technique for overcoming constraints on the use of more tangible weapons against enemy soldiers, neutral civilians, and even fellow citizens. Atrocity propaganda, in particular, belongs to the stock of provocations that planners of large-scale crimes use to evade or erode moral prohibitions on mass killing, forced removal, and other types of mass atrocities.

An analysis of this kind might appear to exculpate the individuals who actually carry out atrocities. In fact, this is not so. As Christopher Browning has observed, "Explaining is not excusing; understanding is not forgiving."[6] Though I criticize some of the explanatory notions that Browning and other scholars of mass atrocity employ—notably, their claim that such crimes are best explained by reference to *inversions* in moral norms—I share their conviction that accountability for such crimes is not foreclosed by efforts to understand the beliefs and attitudes of perpetrators.

The chapter proceeds as follows. In section 2.1, I set out my basic account of moral norms, distinguishing them from legal and social norms on the basis of their independence from real or perceived social practices, combined with the absence of standing procedural rules governing their emergence, modification, or elimination. Section 2.2 introduces and critiques the explanatory thesis of moral norm inversion. This is the thesis that planners and perpetrators of mass atrocities occupy an "inverted moral universe" that makes their crimes possible. Section 2.3 begins to develop an alternative framework, analyzing two important forms of erosion of moral norms. Norm erosion occurs when previously accepted norms cease to be accepted or followed by members of particular groups, organizations, or societies. Moral norm erosion is exemplified by processes of demoralization and brutalization that commonly accompany large-scale crimes. Section 2.4 turns to consider the evasion of moral norms during genocide and mass atrocity. Norm evasion occurs when the scope of norms that individuals within such populations accept is intentionally narrowed or altered in order to legitimate some behavior. Moral norm evasion may appear in the adoption of specialized euphemisms or manifest itself in broader patterns of dehumanization. Section 2.5 returns to the thesis of moral norm inversion in order to address the special problem of professional complicity in mass atrocities. Norms of professional ethics are distinguished from other kinds of moral norms by their formal codification, together with the existence of standing procedural rules governing their modification. It is precisely these exceptional features of professional codes of ethics that make the thesis of moral norm inversion plausible in such cases.

2.1 Moral Norms

Philosophers offer numerous and conflicting accounts of the features that distinguish moral norms from legal or social norms. Some locate these features in intrinsic properties of the norms themselves, defining moral norms as objectively true or universally binding.[7] Others hold that the special character of moral norms stems from the particular ways in which those norms are apprehended by agents—for example, via intuition or rational reflection under ideal conditions.[8] Still others reject all claims of special status for moral norms, offering error theories designed to show that the alleged distinctiveness of moral norms rests on features wrongly ascribed to some norms or wrongly denied to others.[9]

I do not hope to settle these meta-ethical disagreements here. As noted in chapter 1, my focus in this study is on accepted norms, and particularly on the different ways in which specific kinds of norms influence decisions and actions within the practical point of view. Moral norms, I argue, have two features that distinguish them from legal and social norms when seen from this perspective. First, moral norms are not grounded in real or perceived social practices. Second, there are no standing procedural rules governing changes in the scope, force, or content of moral norms. Taken together, these two features establish salient distinctions between moral norms and legal or social norms.

In the first place, moral norms are not grounded in real or perceived social practices. This distinguishes them from social norms, which depend for their normative character on shared beliefs—accurate or not—about existing social practices. It may also help to distinguish moral norms from legal norms, though legal scholars differ on the question of whether laws must be widely followed to remain valid. Considered from the practical point of view, this first feature of moral norms entails that it is a mistake for individuals engaged in practical deliberation to reject the guidance of accepted moral norms simply because other agents are not following those norms.

Philosopher Nicholas Southwood captures this feature of moral norms when he writes, "Certain grounds are incompatible with being a moral judgment; and the existence of a presumed social practice is a case in point."[10] Elaborating on this claim, Southwood imagines asking a companion why he or she refrains from murder and receiving as a reply, "Murdering people is just not done around here." This reply is morally inapt, according to Southwood, because "appealing to a practice of refraining from murder as constituting any part of a defence of the requirement not to murder is ruled out by the nature of moral judgment." The conclusion Southwood draws, which I share, is that "what is 'done around here' is just the wrong kind of thing to appeal to" when describing the grounds of moral norms or defending particular practical judgments.[11]

The second distinguishing feature of moral norms that I want to highlight consists in the absence of standing procedural rules governing changes in the scope, force, or content of moral norms. This feature is particularly important for differentiating between moral norms and legal norms. While legal systems vary substantially in their structures and procedures across traditions and cultures, certain second-order principles, typically described in terms of "legality" or "the rule of law," can be found in most of these systems. Some legal scholars argue that minimal adherence to such principles, such as the principle of nonretroactivity, belongs to the very definition of a legal system.[12] Without insisting on that point here, I claim that moral norms lack any standing procedural rules governing their emergence, modification, or elimination.[13]

It might be objected that certain views of moral norms, most notably theological views, do contain procedural rules for changing the scope, force, or content of those norms. According to such views, church leaders provide binding interpretations of key texts, religious traditions supply public and prospective statements of moral rights and obligations, and religious laws govern relationships between individuals and institutions. I have no knock-down argument capable of showing that this view of moral norms is incoherent when considered from within the practical point of view. But I think a powerful argument against this understanding of moral norms can be found in the widespread acceptance of the moral value of autonomy.

The idea of autonomy can be interpreted most broadly as holding that there is value to be found in assessing for oneself the moral prescriptions, prohibitions, or permissions accepted and followed by others. The value of autonomy can be accounted for in several ways. It is valuable for resolving conflicts among the various moral norms individuals accept, for its egalitarian implications (that is, for suggesting that all human beings can be sources of valid moral judgments), and for stimulating the development of individuals' diverse moral beliefs and commitments into coherent worldviews.

As far as the significance of autonomy is accepted within commonsense morality, this helps explain the absence of standing procedural rules governing changes in moral norms. In everyday life, it is common to hear complaints about efforts to "legislate morality," sometimes voiced by social conservatives and sometimes by progressives. In both cases, they express the idea that moral norms do not emerge from formally constituted, majoritarian processes in the way that legal norms do within democratic societies.[14] No similar agreement exists concerning the procedures by which prevailing moral norms *should* be changed, if at all.

My account of moral norms in this section has proceeded largely negatively. I have argued that moral norms, seen from the practical point of view, are not grounded in real or perceived social practices in the manner of social norms or governed by standing procedural rules in the manner of legal norms. For readers wishing to know more about the sources of moral norms, I suggest that the relevant practical commitments and normative attitudes can arise in a variety of ways. They may be rooted in intuitions or ideologies.[15] They may emerge from agents' rational reflections or from their encounters with compelling moral testimony.[16] They may develop out of analogies to previously accepted principles or from direct observation of "intolerable harms."[17] This last, perceptual source is especially significant when it comes to the moral prescriptions and prohibitions bearing on mass atrocity. In the remainder of this chapter, I show how even such closely held moral norms can be evaded, eroded, or overturned.

2.2 The Thesis of Moral Norm Inversion

Mass atrocities constitute the worst things human beings can do to each other. Mass killing, genocidal rape, and state-sponsored torture "shock the conscience of mankind" and exhibit "man's inhumanity to man."[18] Given this general opprobrium, historians and social scientists face a significant challenge in explaining how and why these acts occur. In particular, theorists of large-scale crimes are hard-pressed to explain how large numbers of "ordinary" individuals come to participate in mass killings, mass rapes, and other mass atrocities, performing acts that in different contexts they might themselves condemn.

In response to this challenge, many theorists have embraced a particular explanatory thesis, which I call the *thesis of norm inversion*. According to this thesis, planners and perpetrators of genocide, mass killings, and other mass atrocities accept and follow moral norms that are the opposite of the norms accepted by people who deplore such crimes. Perpetrators of mass atrocities, it is argued, inhabit "an inverted moral universe, shaped by brutalization, in which right has become wrong; healing has become killing; and life has become death."[19] In the course of large-scale crimes, "the moral world that the law assumes" is rendered "topsy-turvy, its familiar furniture rearranged."[20] Historian Paul Bartrop puts the point most plainly when he claims that genocide occurs not in spite of morality's demands but because "some people deem it both necessary—and even proper—to eliminate" their enemies.[21]

As a framework for explaining genocide and other kinds of mass atrocity, the thesis of norm inversion has several advantages. In the first place, it represents a genuine attempt to explain large-scale crimes. It rebuts the view that such crimes are unintelligible or incomprehensible. In the second place, the thesis clearly outperforms certain alternative theories that have sometimes been advanced to explain mass atrocities. These include the idea that planners and perpetrators of such crimes are "murderous robots" or that they suffer as a group from certain shared cognitive or psychological disorders.[22] Finally, the thesis of norm inversion enjoys a certain degree of historical support, at least for cases of mass atrocity that have been studied in sufficient depth to disclose the moral commitments and attitudes of particular participants.[23]

These advantages notwithstanding, the thesis of norm inversion suffers two serious defects. First, it risks circularity. This is especially true of static, as opposed to dynamic, versions of the thesis—versions that simply posit the existence of moral norms prescribing, rather than prohibiting, acts of killing, looting, rape, and mutilation in the times and places in which large-scale crimes occur. Such static claims of norm inversion invite charges of circularity because their authors cite as evidence of inversions in morality the very acts and policies that those inversions are supposed to explain.[24]

Dynamic versions of the thesis of norm inversion seek to avoid circularity by providing an account of exactly how particular moral norms developed or disappeared over time within the societies in which such crimes have occurred. Some of the richest investigations of historical mass atrocities—such as Claudia Koonz's *The Nazi Conscience* and Eric Weitz's *A Century of Genocide*—adopt this approach.[25] What links these dynamic accounts of norm inversion is their focus on totalizing ideologies or utopic visions under which no sacrifice is held too great if it advances essential social goals.[26]

There is, however, a second reason to resist the thesis of norm inversion as a general explanation of genocide and mass atrocity. This reason is rooted in the logic of norm inversion itself. The phenomenon of norm inversion, as I argued in chapter 1, can be broken down into two parts: the erosion of a previously accepted norm coupled with the emergence of a new (and in some relevant sense contrary) norm. It seems clear, however, that not every instance of collapse in moral norms prohibiting killing, rape, mutilation, or other offenses is accompanied by the emergence of moral norms prescribing such actions. An undue emphasis on full-scale inversions in moral norms obscures the power of mere erosions in moral norms to help explain large-scale crimes.

In the remainder of this chapter, I examine processes leading to the erosion of moral norms in the context of mass atrocity, notably brutalization and demoralization. I also consider processes of evasion of moral norms, showing how dehumanization and euphemism work to encourage participation in large-scale crimes even while leaving preexisting moral norms intact. My aim is to see how far these alternative explanations can go in making sense of individual participation in mass atrocity. In both cases, I argue, the resulting analysis better fits the documented beliefs and attitudes of perpetrators of large-scale crimes than explanations in terms of norm inversion.

2.3 Eroding Moral Norms: Demoralization and Brutalization

Norm erosion occurs when previously accepted norms cease to be accepted or followed by members of particular groups, organizations, or societies. In the case of moral norms, individuals and groups do not generally acknowledge any standing procedural rules governing changes in moral norms. Accordingly, an account of moral norm erosion in contexts of genocide and mass atrocity must focus on informal processes, which may resist conscious awareness on the part of affected agents. Two of the most important processes are demoralization and brutalization.

Demoralization

The concept of demoralization has two different meanings—one specifically martial, the other embracing a broader range of contexts. In its military usage, *demoralization* refers to decreases in troops' (or their supporters') "cohesion," "efficiency," and "will to fight."[27] It is this sense of the word that Harold Lasswell employed shortly after World War I when describing the power of propaganda to "Demoraliz[e] the Enemy." As Lasswell remarked, "It is possible to employ propaganda as a weapon of direct attack against the morale of the enemy by seeking to break up or divert the hatred of the enemy from a belligerent."[28]

The second sense of demoralization is related to its military usage, insofar as it also indicates a weakening of shared standards or shared goals. John Stuart Mill used the term in this way in his 1861 *Considerations on Representative Government*, writing, "It would not be a matter personally indifferent to the rest of the country if any part of it became a nest of robbers or a focus of demoralization, owing to the maladministration of its police."[29] One hundred years later, Great Britain's Committee on Homosexual Offenses and Prostitution employed this same sense of the word in rebutting claims that decriminalizing consensual adult homosexual behavior would lead to "the demoralization and decay of society."[30]

Both the martial and nonmartial notions of demoralization occur in Raphael Lemkin's pioneering studies of genocide. The term appears in Lemkin's analysis of Axis occupation policies, his autobiographical account of his experience in Lithuania as a Polish refugee, and his unpublished case studies of historical genocides. In general, Lemkin depicts demoralization as a process through which previously accepted moral norms cease to guide the actions of members of particular groups. More specifically, he suggests demoralization involves the substitution of self-interest for other-directed concerns in agents' practical deliberations, as well as the eclipse of long-term aims by short-term advantages.

Throughout his various writings, Lemkin maintains that both the perpetrators and the targets of genocide are susceptible to demoralization. Within both groups, he suggests, breakdowns in moral norms may result from either the manipulative policies of conniving leaders or broader changes in social relationships. Reviewing German occupation policies in Poland, Lemkin claims that "the occupant attempt[ed] to create an atmosphere of moral debasement" by legally authorizing pornography, gambling, and alcohol consumption. "Important for the realization of such a plan," Lemkin remarks, was "that the desire for cheap individual pleasure be substituted for the desire for collective feelings and ideals based upon a higher morality."[31]

Lemkin spotlighted a quite different process of demoralization in his case study of genocide carried out against the native peoples of South America by Spain's conquistadors. Discussing Francisco Pizarro's sixteenth-century expedition to Peru, Lemkin notes that the conquering European forces showed "increasing rapacity and contempt for the Peruvians with increasing loot and success," so that in the years and decades following conquest, "demoralization not only persisted but became part of the conqueror's and colonist's behavior."[32] Once again, the substitution of self-interest for higher ideals is emphasized, but Lemkin here casts this as the unplanned consequence of a dramatic change in fortune. The Spaniards' "sudden transformation from bedraggled, isolated, and miserable explorers" to "owners of mountains of gold and treasures went to their heads," exploding constraints rooted in notions of honor and the obligation to spread Christianity.[33]

What lessons should we draw from Lemkin's descriptions of demoralization in societies experiencing mass atrocities? First, his account supports my claim that breakdowns in moral norms within particular groups or societies occur through informal processes, unbeholden to any standing procedural rules for norm elimination. In the Polish case, as Lemkin describes it, the erosion of moral norms was pursued indirectly, through the occupiers' creation of laws and policies encouraging activities previously seen as morally prohibited. In the Spanish colonial case, the breakdown of prohibitions on killing, torture, and other egregious harms was associated with what might appear to be unrelated changes in economic standing.[34]

Second, Lemkin's account of demoralization clarifies how explanatory appeals to the erosion of moral norms operate. His account highlights the fact that it is breakdowns in the moral prohibitions or prescriptions previously accepted by members of specific populations that are supposed to do the explanatory work. Scholars of mass atrocity need not themselves endorse sixteenth-century European views of martial honor or religious piety in order to argue that the erosion of such accepted norms might help to explain historical crimes. Nor must scholars disavow alcohol, gambling, or nonconjugal sex in order to argue that occupying powers sometimes promote hedonistic pleasures as a means of quashing resistance.

There are of course limits to what Lemkin's studies of genocide can tell us about the dynamics of moral norms during mass atrocities. Some of those limits have to do with his understanding of genocide and of the facts involved in various historical cases of this crime. Philosophers have criticized Lemkin's definition of genocide and his explanation of what makes this crime uniquely wrongful.[35] Historians, for their part, have amended many of his case studies of genocides.[36] Lemkin's account of demoralization, by contrast, has received little critical consideration. Philosophers may doubt his premise that ideals centered on group flourishing are necessarily more valuable than those focused on individual well-being.[37] But his autobiographical reflections on demoralization, particularly his memoir of life among World War II refugees, gain support from psychological research suggesting that demoralization is a useful concept for capturing the experience of individuals fleeing conflicts in Iraq, Syria, and elsewhere today.[38] All things considered, his concept of demoralization captures one important way in which breakdowns in moral norms can help to explain large-scale crimes. In order to broaden our account of moral norm erosion, we should next consider the concept of brutalization.

Brutalization

Taken literally, *brutalization* refers to the reduction of human beings to the condition of nonhuman animals. The term has not always been reserved for discussions of war and mass violence, though this is the domain in which it appears most frequently today.[39] Indeed, theorists of genocide and mass atrocity have recently adopted brutalization as a key explanatory concept.

James Waller and Christopher Browning both associate brutalization with soldiers and other direct witnesses of war who have become desensitized to violence through long exposure to human suffering. These theorists do not simply repeat traditional complaints about war reducing soldiers to the condition of wolves, sheep, or other beasts. Rather, they argue that brutalization actively erodes the moral misgivings that soldiers and other witnesses of war might otherwise feel when contemplating killing noncombatants or attacking gravely wounded enemies. Waller contends that "as our psychological system grows used to events that initially produced a strong reaction, extraordinary evil becomes habitual and routinized."[40] Brutalization, according to this view, always involves decreased sensitivity to others' suffering and sometimes culminates in "perverse enjoyment of, and sadistic pleasure in" such suffering.[41]

It is easy to find instances of brutalization in the annals of armed conflict. We can see this process at work in the prison ships, or hulks, that the British army employed during the American Revolution in which American soldiers were subjected to arbitrary beatings, insufficient rations, and undignified burial.[42] We can see it as well in International Red Cross founder Henry Dunant's description of the Battle of Solferino in 1859, during which, he writes, local Italian peasants stole eagerly from the wounded and "wrenched [boots] ruthlessly off the swollen feet of the dead."[43] And we can see it in the degrading treatment of prisoners of war by American soldiers staffing Iraq's military prison at Abu Ghraib in 2003. Not all of these examples meet the definition of mass atrocity I use in this study, but each helps illustrate the notion of moral norm erosion at work in many leading explanations of large-scale crimes.

I have mentioned Waller's suggestion that brutalization helps create an "inverted moral universe," one "in which right has become wrong; healing has become killing, and life has become death."[44] Elsewhere in the same book, Waller argues that brutalization fundamentally involves a "repression of conscience."[45] I am not certain that these two claims are compatible. If, as I have suggested, moral inversions require that the breakdown of some moral prescription or prohibition be followed by the emergence of a contrary prohibition or prescription, then we must ask whether brutalization tends to bar the second stage of this process. According to Waller's own analysis, brutalization is characterized by the eclipse of moral commitments rather than by their replacement.

I believe the concept of brutalization can make an independent contribution to the explanation of large-scale crimes. It designates a key pathway through which previously accepted moral prohibitions on the intentional infliction of pain and suffering are extinguished. This form of norm erosion is narrower than that of demoralization, since it rests on direct exposure to acts of extreme violence—something that not all individuals at risk of demoralization have experienced.[46] Nevertheless, we can see clear connections with the account of demoralization offered above, particularly with the sadistic forms of harm that Lemkin described in his discussion of Pizarro's men.[47]

It might be objected that the processes of norm erosion considered in this section run counter to the overarching claim of this study: that mass atrocities typically reflect the presence, rather than the absence, of norms. Both brutalization and demoralization, as I have portrayed them, involve the collapse of previously accepted moral commitments and attitudes. One response to this challenge is to say that only a subset of moral norms, not all norms, disappear in such contexts. Perpetrators brutalized by long experience of war often continue to accept and adhere to gender-based social norms.[48] Targets of atrocities suffering demoralization often continue to be guided by relevant legal prohibitions, even where they do not follow them.[49] A second response is to note that norm erosion is not the only, or the most significant, threat to previously accepted moral norms that arises during large-scale crimes. Processes of norm evasion, which differ from both norm inversion and norm erosion, are equally crucial for explaining mass atrocities.

2.4   Evading Moral Norms: Euphemism and Dehumanization

Norm evasion occurs when the scope of the norms that individuals belonging to particular populations accepted is intentionally altered in order to legitimate some otherwise prohibited behavior. In the case of moral norms, I have argued, the force of such prohibitions is supposed to be independent of the actual patterns of norm acceptance or norm following by other group members; this is what the independence of moral norms from real or perceived social practices entails. Nevertheless, there are well-known tactics by which planners of large-scale crimes seek to evade accepted moral prohibitions against such actions. Two such tactics are euphemism and dehumanization.

Euphemism
The Holocaust exhibit at London's Imperial War Museum contains a powerful display titled "The Final Solution." A small, glass-walled room stands empty save for a low table supporting a typewriter. Inserted in the typewriter is a single sheet of paper containing a list of code words employed by the planners of the genocide of European Jews. Included in this list are *Umsiedlung* (relocation), meaning deportation, as well as *Sonderbehandlung*

(special treatment), meaning execution. After seeing this display, museum visitors are supposed to reflect on the role euphemistic language plays in promoting mass atrocities and shielding perpetrators of such crimes from detection.[50]

The use of euphemistic language to describe acts and policies of killing, maiming, torture, rape, and other egregious harms is not unique to the Shoah. Marguerite Feitlowitz has described the "lexicon of terror" developed by officials and security forces during Argentina's "Process of National Reorganization."[51] Uğur Üngör has traced the obfuscations used by Turkey's Committee of Union and Progress (CUP) during the Armenian genocide.[52] During the decade following September 11, 2001, some of the most contentious policies in America's "War on Terror" were debated using such plainly euphemistic phrases as "extraordinary rendition" and "enhanced interrogation tactics."

One reason for the proliferation of specialized terminology in discussions of military or paramilitary violence centers on participants' desire to evade detection or criticism by outside parties. This was the reason emphasized by the judges at Adolf Eichmann's 1961 trial in Jerusalem. When introducing or discussing documents related to the expropriation, forced relocation, or murder of Jews and other targeted populations, the judges and the Israeli state prosecutor regularly described specific terms as providing "camouflage" for illegal acts. A similar purpose can be imputed to some of the terms prescribed in the Argentine army manual analyzed by Feitlowitz, according to which guerrilla operations were to be labeled "criminal actions," while the words "wearing uniform" (in descriptions of captured or killed enemies) were to be replaced by the phrase "usurping the use of insignias, emblems, [or] uniforms."[53]

There is, however, a second reason for the use of obfuscatory language in discussions of illicit acts or policies. Such language serves not only to hide the illegal or immoral character of perpetrators' actions from outside parties but may also conceal that character from perpetrators themselves. The terms are "euphemistic" in the sense that they direct agents' attention away from the true nature of the acts they perform. James Waller suggests that euphemisms "facilitate moral disengagement" among perpetrators of large-scale crimes. "As they live within their euphemistic labels, and use them with each other," he contends, "perpetrators become bound to a psychologically safe realm of dissociation, disavowal, and emotional distance."[54]

To take another example from Feitlowitz's study, the use of the Spanish verb *trasladar* (move) to refer to the removal of prisoners for execution could, according to this view, have the effect of "creat[ing] psychological distance between the doer and his act."[55]

Such scholarly descriptions support my characterization of euphemism as a technique for evading, rather than eroding, moral norms. The very introduction of euphemistic terminology signals awareness of an accepted moral norm that might ordinarily prohibit the actions masked by the euphemism.[56] According to the framework I set out in chapter 1, the introduction of euphemistic words and phrases thus represents a case of norm guidance without norm following. Over time, of course, routine exposure to the sorts of violent acts masked by euphemistic terminology may prompt a more thoroughgoing erosion of moral commitments and attitudes, following the paths of demoralization or brutalization I have described. Nevertheless, euphemism should be regarded as a qualitatively distinct technique by which ordinary moral prohibitions on individual participation in genocide or other mass atrocities can be evaded.[57]

Dehumanization

Although euphemism plays a role in the explanation of large-scale crimes, it applies only to a portion of the communications that accompany such crimes. Technical or neutral-sounding terms may be mandated in official reports on executions, expropriations, and forced relocations, but public calls for attacks on targeted groups are often couched in highly explicit words and images. Here, putative enemies of the state, race, or nation are described as rats or cockroaches, as plague germs or cancer cells. Recent studies of martial propaganda by David Welch and Michael Kearney confirm what Arthur Conan Doyle argued a century ago: hate has its uses in war, as well as in other situations of severe social and political conflict.[58] One of the chief aims of such hateful expressions is to dehumanize the targets of organized violence.

There is an ordinary notion of dehumanization that we sometimes use to describe scenarios where we feel ourselves roughly handled or rudely dealt with.[59] This is not the sense of dehumanization I have in mind. Instead, I will consider the more precise notion of dehumanization described by philosopher David Livingstone Smith in his book *Less Than Human*. Smith defines dehumanization as "the act of conceiving of people as subhuman creatures rather than as human beings."[60] This act has biological roots, it depends on our evolved cognitive capacities for cultural differentiation, and it helps make humans capable of cruelties unmatched by other animals.[61]

In my discussion of brutalization, I highlighted that term's etymological connection to the word *brute* and glossed the process of brutalization as one of reducing human beings to the condition of nonhuman animals. Superficially, this process resembles dehumanization.[62] There are, however, important differences between these two pathways for explaining individual participation in mass atrocities.

A first difference has to do with the direction of causation implied by brutalization and dehumanization, respectively. In the case of brutalization, it is the fact that certain human beings have been placed in circumstances where their animal needs and functions predominate that is supposed to explain particular actions performed by those individuals—for my purposes, the vicious acts performed by perpetrators during episodes of forced relocation, extermination, and the like. In the case of dehumanization, by contrast, it is the fact that certain human beings are regarded as nonhuman that is supposed to explain the persecution to which those individuals are subjected. The two processes can, of course, overlap. Stories of marginalized groups living in degraded conditions often serve as fodder for dehumanizing depictions of those groups and as excuses for mistreatment. Nevertheless, the two pathways remain distinct.

A second reason for regarding brutalization and dehumanization as different processes comes from the specific analysis of dehumanization Smith provides. When we dehumanize others, Smith argues, we do not merely regard them as nonhuman, but rather as beings who appear to be human but are not. That is, we operate according to the assumption that there is some indeterminate essence that all and only human beings have. Dehumanized individuals, despite their similarity to ordinary people, lack this essence, and so cannot be human.[63]

One advantage of this analysis of dehumanization is that Smith is able to explain why dehumanized individuals and groups are commonly seen as threatening by those who dehumanize them. In some cases, dehumanized persons are viewed as dangerous agents of infection; in other cases, they are regarded as fearsome predators. In both cases, Smith suggests, proposals for the destruction or expulsion of the dehumanized can take on a "hefty moralistic component" as politicians and commanders call for the purification of society or the punishment of evildoers.

This discussion of dehumanization suggests that it is possible for some perpetrators of atrocities to describe themselves as engaged in a highly moral struggle—as participants in the construction of "utopias of race and nation."[64] Nevertheless, it is misleading to describe such true believers as inhabiting an "inverted moral landscape," if that term is meant to signify a dynamic reversal of previously accepted moral norms. Instead, dehumanization denotes the drawing of a line between those individuals and groups with whom we can actually stand in relationships defined by moral rights and obligations, and those dangerous beings who threaten the existence of such relationships. Ultimately, dehumanization is a key process through which individuals or groups are placed beyond "the boundaries of the universe of obligation."[65] It should thus be understood as a mode of evading, not inverting, moral norms.

2.5 Breakdowns of Professional Ethics: Proof of Moral Norm Inversion?

The general tendency of this chapter has been to resist the thesis that inversions in moral norms provide a good general explanation of individual participation in large-scale crimes. My method has been to analyze alternative processes, particularly processes of norm erosion and norm evasion, that offer more plausible explanations of this phenomenon. At this point, it might be objected that by focusing my discussion on participation by "ordinary individuals" in such crimes, I have overlooked a significant class of actors whose contributions to mass atrocities can be explained only in terms of inversions in moral norms. This is the class of professional actors—doctors and lawyers, pharmacists and psychologists—who in specific historical contexts have played crucial roles in planning or perpetrating large-scale crimes.[66]

Studies of professional participation in atrocities typically distinguish two broad categories of professional contributions to such crimes. First are the contributions that directly inflict physical or mental harms on victims.[67] This category encompasses medical professionals, such as doctors, nurses, and psychologists, who oversee the administration of lethal or painful drugs and procedures; it also encompasses the lawyers and judges who defend manifestly unjust laws and authorize wholesale executions.[68] Second are so-called complicitous contributions made by professionals to large-scale crimes. Historian Robert Ericksen characterizes such contributions as words or actions undertaken by respected persons which, though not themselves violations of core moral norms, have "a measure of influence in shaping public attitudes and behavior" and effectively signal "permission" for individual participation in atrocities.[69]

There are difficult questions concerning the assignment of particular professional historical actors to one or both of these categories of professional contributions to large-scale crimes. Additional puzzles surround the levels of legal and moral responsibility incurred by actors falling in each of these categories. For my purposes, it is enough to note that scholars commonly explain both modes of professional participation in atrocities by reference to inversions in the norms governing the professions in question.

In order to assess such explanations, it is necessary to get a grip on the nature of professional codes. Here I focus on the account developed by philosopher Michael Davis, who argues that professional codes comprise "morally permissible standards of conduct governing members of a group simply because they are members of that group."[70] The principal aim of such codes, he contends, is to solve coordination problems faced by professionals who share particular ethical ideals in morally permissible ways.[71] The specific ideals shared by professionals vary across professions—justice in the case of legal professionals; well-being in the case of medical professionals; knowledge or truth in the case of academics. Davis concludes that the presence of some such ideal is a necessary, though not a sufficient, condition for the formal authority of professional codes, that is, their power to cause members of the profession to exclude considerations contrary to the code's teaching in their professional deliberations.

If Davis's account is correct, professional codes of ethics diverge from the picture of moral norms defended in this chapter in three ways. First, professional codes are at least partially grounded in real or perceived social practices, specifically, the practices prevailing among professionals. Second, professional codes are subject to standing procedural rules governing their emergence, modification, or elimination. Finally, professional codes owe their action-guiding power to more fundamental moral ideals.

I think the first two features of professional codes identified above account for the greater plausibility of the thesis of norm inversion when applied to professional participation in large-scale crimes. Members of professional groups are identified partially on the basis of their acceptance of particular moral norms, which are typically formally codified and publicized. Since professionals are widely identified with particular practical prohibitions or prescriptions, widespread violations of those prohibitions or prescriptions seem to require an explanation that is similarly rule based, suggesting an inversion of previously accepted moral norms. In this way, consistent explanations are preserved for sharply divergent group-level patterns of behavior.[72]

While consistency is a virtue, I think it is outweighed by consideration of what actually tends to happen to professional groups' codes of ethics in contexts of mass atrocity. Writing about German society between World Wars I and II, philosopher Berel Lang describes the "breakdown of professional ethics" within a broad range of professions. On Lang's view, this breakdown is characterized by four features: (1) the introduction of a new practice that departs substantially from prior practices, (2) common knowledge that this practice conflicts with norms governing comparable spheres of professional activity in other countries, (3) a close affiliation between the professionals spearheading the change in practice and the leaders of the dominant political movement, and (4) bans or restrictions on the kind of "open discussion" that usually characterizes proposals for changes in professional norms or practices.[73]

Historians and legal scholars offer similar accounts of professional life under National Socialism and other deeply immoral regimes. Konrad Jarausch uses the term *deprofessionalization* to describe the broader patterns of sociological change in which Lang's breakdown of professional ethics occurred.[74] David Dyzenhaus, a legal philosopher focusing on transitional justice efforts in South Africa, has devoted numerous works to pointing out just this gap between judges' and lawyers' claims of independence from state oversight during the transition in that country and the serious lack of judicial independence exhibited during apartheid.[75] What is significant about these examples is that they undercut the first two distinctive features of professional codes named above: showing how the formal procedures by which professional norms are usually formulated and applied can cease to function and revealing a significant gap between the norms that purportedly govern professional life and actual practices.

The upshot of this discussion is that the thesis of moral norm inversion does not fit all cases of professional participation in mass atrocities. First, there are significant differences in the form and ground of professional norms when compared with moral norms more generally. Second, even considering those professional norms in themselves, it is rare for a full inversion of such norms to occur publicly and via ordinary procedures. Third, it seems possible to explain the changes in practices that underlie claims about both the breakdown and the inversion of professional ethics by way of motivational factors, such as the desire for self-preservation, that stand apart from properly moral considerations. Nevertheless, as we saw in the exchange between Dr. Conti and Professor Ewald discussed in chapter 1, professionals sometimes express a belief that inversions in the norms governing their social roles are forthcoming in contexts of mass atrocity. Where evidence of this sort exists, it is easier to make the case that individuals and groups who previously accepted prohibitions on some actions later came to regard those actions as "the only right choice." It is easier, in other words, to substantiate the thesis of norm inversion.

3 Better Never to Deliberate? Moral Norms and the Prevention of Mass Atrocities

On June 15, 1917, Captain Siegfried Sassoon of the Royal Welch Fusiliers drafted a statement declaring his opposition to Britain's continued prosecution of World War I. Sassoon began as follows:

> I am making this statement as an act of willful defiance of military authority, because I believe that the War is being deliberately prolonged by those who have the power to end it. I am a soldier, convinced that I am acting on behalf of soldiers. I believe that this War, upon which I entered as a war of defense and liberation, has now become a war of aggression and conquest. I believe that the purposes for which I and my fellow-soldiers entered upon this War should have been so clearly stated as to have made it impossible for them to be changed without our knowledge, and that, had this been done, the objects which actuated us would now be obtainable by negotiation.[1]

This declaration led directly to Sassoon's referral for treatment at Scotland's Craiglockhart War Hospital. It later supplied the climax for his 1930 *Memoirs of an Infantry Officer*. Though condemned by one recent biographer as "quite startlingly naïve," Sassoon's statement raises questions that remain relevant today for students of the ethics of war and peace. It also offers a starting point for thinking about how norms—specifically, moral norms—can help constrain large-scale crimes.[2]

This chapter examines the action-guiding role of moral norms in the practical deliberations of soldiers, humanitarian aid workers, and other individuals active on the front lines of war, civil upheavals, or other intergroup conflicts. Such individuals stand in the vanguard of what James Waller has called "midstream prevention strategies": "real-time relief efforts ... to slow, limit, or stop the continuation or escalation of genocidal violence."[3] Although societies on the brink of genocide or other kinds of large-scale crimes are, as we have seen, frequently beset by the erosion or evasion of previously accepted moral norms, I believe norms of this kind also provide crucial support to individuals seeking to impede mass atrocities. Moral norms, I contend, count among the most important "moral resources" available to individuals actively working toward atrocity prevention.[4]

Assessing the preventive power of moral norms requires that we consult the same sorts of documentary and testimonial sources that ground explanations of large-scale crimes. Contemporary statements, whether publicly aired like Sassoon's or privately recorded in letters, reports, or diaries, offer clues to the kinds of moral deliberations that occur during war and humanitarian emergencies.[5] At the same time, such sources point up disagreements surrounding specific moral norms currently accepted by soldiers, aid workers, and other agents directly exposed to mass violence. Accordingly, this chapter also examines debates among philosophers and other scholars about the moral norms that ought to govern the decisions and actions of these agents. Studying these debates clarifies the ways in which moral norms come to be accepted by individuals and groups. It also further illuminates the distinguishing features of moral norms.

The central argument of this chapter is that moral norms against deliberation are of particular importance for individuals on the front lines of large-scale crimes. Norms against deliberation block specific paths of practical reasoning. They occur most commonly in groups that face recurring practical dilemmas; their justification depends on higher-order normative considerations. Moral norms against deliberation seek to secure morally valuable goods by constraining agents' deliberations in specific ways—saying, in effect, that certain courses of action are not fit even to be considered.

To date, little empirical work has been done on the power of moral norms to prevent mass atrocities. One book-length study of this issue, Alex Bellamy's *Massacres and Morality*, identifies a clear, if fragile, trend toward universal acceptance of a moral norm prescribing civilian immunity in war.[6] His account differs from mine insofar as he focuses on the ability of moral norms to guide the actions of high-ranking military leaders and politicians, whereas I am concerned with the power of moral norms to guide the actions of front-line agents before and during mass atrocities. Despite this difference, I share Bellamy's view that "there is simply no room for complacency" when it comes to understanding how moral norms can constrain large-scale crimes.[7]

The chapter proceeds as follows. In section 3.1, I provide a preliminary analysis of moral norms against deliberation. In section 3.2, I demonstrate the significance of such norms for soldiers fighting wars in accordance with the moral tenets set out in traditional and revisionist versions of just war theory. I also explain why the killing of large numbers of healthy soldiers during war, when carried out by permissible means, should not count as a case of mass atrocity. Section 3.3 turns to consider another set of actors on the front lines of atrocity prevention, namely, humanitarian aid workers. Here, the traditional humanitarian principles of impartiality and neutrality furnish further examples of moral norms against deliberation. Section 3.4 critically examines Jonathan Glover's claim that broad educational campaigns about past mass atrocities can empower ordinary citizens to help prevent large-scale crimes.

3.1 Moral Norms against Deliberation

In their 2013 book *Explaining Norms*, philosophers Geoffrey Brennan, Lina Eriksson, Robert Goodin, and Nicholas Southwood single out a special set of "norms concerning how we are supposed to *think* about—deliberate about, judge, value—certain kinds of things."[8] Although the authors do not offer a full analysis of such norms, they do discuss one telling example. Starting from standard moral prohibitions on killing, they note that most societies not only have moral norms prohibiting the act of killing itself, but "also norms about how one is supposed to *think* about killing people: one should not think about it; not at all."[9] Brennan et al. suggest that we should interpret this type of norm as removing certain courses of action from the agenda of agents engaged in practical deliberation. Although they remain neutral on the question of whether this norm complements, or is somehow entailed by, the basic moral prohibition on killing, I believe we see here a clear example of what I am calling a moral norm against deliberation.[10]

Moral norms against deliberation hold that agents are morally required to disregard certain considerations, or to avoid contemplating certain courses of action, when dealing with specific practical problems.[11] In some cases, these norms work in tandem with other legal, moral, or social norms requiring that agents explicitly examine certain facts before taking action. In other cases, they exercise an independent influence within the practical point of view. Like all other moral norms, moral norms against deliberation are distinguished from legal and social norms by their independence from real or perceived social practices, combined with the absence of standing procedural rules governing their emergence, modification, or elimination.[12]

It is easy to multiply examples of moral norms against deliberation—examples much more likely to affect the everyday lives of agents than the prohibition on thinking about killing already discussed.[13] It remains to ask under what conditions agents are justified in following such norms, despite the countervailing considerations that may arise in any given scenario. Why should norms against deliberation not be open to criticism, or subject to revision, during the very deliberations they help guide?[14] This question is especially pressing if one thinks that the moral norms that individuals accept and follow must always in principle be open to rational reflection if they are not to transform into mere taboos.[15]

One answer to this question comes from considering the temporal character of practical deliberation. Within the practical point of view, agents are centrally concerned with discovering, assessing, and embracing specific courses of action.[16] These courses of action are typically time limited. Failing to decide on and undertake some particular action in a reasonable amount of time is often just as consequential, from the practical point of view, as choosing to act would have been.[17] For this reason, agents generally accept that their practical deliberations cannot be drawn out indefinitely, as full-scale theoretical reflections on moral principles might require.

The time-limited nature of practical deliberation goes some way toward justifying agents' reliance on norms against deliberation when comparing various courses of action. Two other factors offer more substantial support for this distinctive form of norm guidance. The first concerns the position of agents who face recurring moral problems. The second concerns agents who are subject to extraordinary pressures during practical reasoning.

Within a wide range of institutions, from hospitals to prisons, colleges to accounting firms, agents confront certain recurring moral problems. These include problems of how to administer care to patients who lack knowledge of relevant medical facts, problems of how to reconcile obligations to shareholders with duties to employees, and problems of how to determine whether students' work was produced honestly. Where such problems predictably recur, norms against deliberation can serve the valuable purpose of rendering responses to those moral problems consistent across the many members of such institutions or across various phases of individual agents' careers.

Related to the role of moral norms against deliberation in resolving recurring moral problems is the role of such norms in insulating agents against extraordinary adverse pressures on practical deliberations. These pressures may arise from considerations of self-interest, group or organizational biases, or situational factors. Moral norms against deliberation insulate agents against such pressures by committing them to prescind from specific considerations or to rule out certain courses of action. The value of such norms is especially evident when we consider the lack of standing procedural rules governing changes in moral norms, which tends to amplify the pressure agents face to adjust their existing moral commitments and attitudes when confronting difficult practical dilemmas.

The several benefits of moral norms against deliberation that I have identified provide only conditional justifications for withholding those norms from scrutiny. Some individual commitments lack meaningful connections to moral ideals or values. Some organizations achieve consistency only by making wrongdoing standard policy. Given these dangers, moral norms against deliberation cannot ultimately be immune to criticism. The point is that in order to play their distinctive action-guiding roles, these norms must be held fixed during specific instances of practical deliberation, coming in for reevaluation only afterward. As we shall see, one context in which norms against deliberation are particularly valuable is the sphere of war, with its attendant risk of mass atrocity.

3.2 Soldiers and Moral Norms against Deliberation

In his 2015 essay, "Military Means of Preventing Mass Atrocities," retired US Army Colonel Dwight Raymond distinguishes two paths by which soldiers and their commanders can contribute to the prevention of large-scale crimes. One path consists of "deliberate actions" aimed at atrocity prevention, such as safeguarding vulnerable populations, gathering vital intelligence, and forcibly deterring perpetrators. The other path is summed up by the slogan "Do no harm." It requires soldiers and their commanders to abide by specific legal and moral prescriptions and prohibitions in order to protect innocent parties and prevent unnecessary suffering.[18]

While Raymond centers his discussion on the positive actions soldiers can perform, my concern in this chapter is with the "do no harm" side of his distinction. Here, I argue, we find clear evidence of the ways in which moral norms against deliberation can contribute to atrocity prevention. At the same time, we encounter substantive philosophical debates about the justifiability of widely accepted moral norms.

Two different kinds of moral questions regularly encountered by soldiers structure my analysis: questions about the morality of going to war in the first place, which often reduce to questions about the justice of one's own party in a potential conflict, and questions about the morality of actions taken in war, especially actions intended to spare civilians. Following a long tradition of philosophical thinking about just and unjust wars, I shall refer to these as *ad bellum* and *in bello* questions and divide my discussion accordingly.[19]

Ad Bellum Norms against Deliberation

Siegfried Sassoon's 1917 statement notwithstanding, ordinary soldiers and junior officers are not generally required by the laws of armed conflict to form independent judgments about the justice of the causes for which they fight. Many philosophers hold that these agents are not morally required to undertake searching investigations of this issue either. The reasons offered for this conclusion differ. Some philosophers stress the youth and limited education of most ordinary soldiers.[20] Others emphasize the general epistemic challenges that war creates, citing the prevalence of propaganda, restrictions on access to classified information, and other aspects of the "fog of war."[21] Finally, some philosophers observe that even the best informed, most experienced statesmen frequently fail to reach agreement on the justice or injustice of particular conflicts, and they infer from this that low-ranking officers and common soldiers cannot be expected to succeed where these epistemically privileged agents fail.[22]

The authors I have cited typically speak in terms of a lack of obligation to investigate the ad bellum justice of wars. I think it is more precise to refer to a permissive moral norm against deliberation. A mere assertion of nonobligation carries no implications about the practical commitments or normative attitudes of the agents in question. A permissive norm against deliberation suggests, by contrast, that ordinary soldiers generally do believe that they are morally permitted to follow the judgments of their superiors on such matters, except in cases of manifest injustice.[23] Furthermore, while soldiers who accept such a permission may believe that they are in no way prohibited from undertaking more extensive investigations, they can at the same time believe it would be wrong for other parties—say, war protesters, or opposition leaders—to criticize them for not making independent inquiries.[24] Indeed, soldiers may plausibly regard it as part of their professional duty to accept, in all but the most extreme cases, the ad bellum decisions made by their civilian or military leaders and to focus their deliberations on issues more in keeping with their distinctive professional identity.

It is not my aim to explain how the permissive norm against deliberation that I have described came to be part of what Michael Walzer calls the "war convention": "the set of articulated norms, customs, professional codes, legal precepts, religious and philosophical principles, and reciprocal arrangements that shape our judgments of military conduct."[25] A full history of the emergence of this moral norm would have to comprehend the classical and medieval antecedents of current moral theories of war, the transition from professional to democratic armies that began around the time of the French Revolution, and the substantial increases in soldiers' literacy and educational attainments achieved in the modern period. My point is that this permissive moral norm against deliberation emerged well before the experience of twentieth-century mass atrocities and that in reaction to this experience, substantial philosophical challenges have been raised against this permissive norm. Those challenges are worth considering for two reasons. First, they help us understand how moral norms against deliberation are assessed at the level of theoretical, rather than practical, reasoning. Second, they illustrate my basic claim that moral norms are not subject to standing procedural rules governing their emergence, modification, or elimination.

In his 2009 book, *Killing in War*, philosopher Jeff McMahan offers a vigorous critique of the standard permissive view of soldiers' ad bellum moral responsibilities. "That most people appear to have few scruples about setting off unquestioningly at the behest of their government to kill members of other nations," McMahan begins, "is a phenomenon that has been studied by psychologists and historians" but rarely by philosophers.[26] The aim of philosophical inquiry, on his view, is to replace unreflective and unjustified moral beliefs held by individuals with justified beliefs. Ultimately this process might result in "institutional accommodation to people's changed moral beliefs."[27] Recasting these claims slightly, McMahan contends that philosophical inquiry can eventually prompt changes in the moral norms that individuals and groups accept and follow. The urgency of such inquiry is heightened by the historical connection between unreflective participation in war and mass atrocities.

McMahan rejects the traditional view that soldiers are morally permitted to defer to the judgment of their commanders about the justice of the cause for which they fight. He rejects, in other words, the permissive moral norm against deliberation. Instead, McMahan contends that ordinary soldiers are not morally permitted, but at best morally excused, for deferring to their leaders' judgments that a particular war is just. To be clear, he does not condemn deference to leadership in all cases. He suggests that soldiers are rightly prohibited from following their own judgment and making war in cases where their leaders deem such a war unjust. Acknowledging that this account of the moral norms that ought to govern soldiers' ad bellum moral reflections is asymmetric, McMahan suggests that this asymmetry does not affect soldiers' first-order practical deliberations, but rather the ways in which they resolve conflicts between their own moral judgments and those of their superiors.[28] Ultimately, McMahan argues, soldiers do not have the right to decide unilaterally to resort to war, but they do have the right, and indeed the duty, to decide for themselves whether the wars their leaders have launched are just.[29]

What practical effects, what "institutional accommodation," might we expect to occur if McMahan's revisionist account of soldiers' ad bellum moral obligations ultimately succeeds in replacing the permissive moral norm against deliberation? One result, according to philosophers Michael Robillard and Bradley Strawser, is that the bar for states to launch just wars would rise considerably. They write:

> If revisionist just war theory is correct, the moral demands on individual soldiers are radically higher than the traditional view takes them to be, for those demands include *ad bellum* responsibility. As these demands are ratcheted up, the likelihood of just behavior occurring in the real world goes down. ... But this difficulty does not make those moral duties any less true. Even on a strong commitment to an "ought implies can" principle, just war theory reminds us that refraining from war in the first place if it cannot be waged justly is something that can (and should) be done. It is no objection to just war theory (revisionist or traditional) to argue that its high demands make fighting war justly very difficult.[30]

Let us assume that this interpretation of the institutional consequences of rejecting current permissive norms against deliberation is correct. What then are the implications for mass atrocity prevention? Quite possibly the increased difficulty of waging just wars would lead, practically, to an increased reluctance to wage war at all.[31] Then one way of answering the question is to return to Dwight Raymond's distinction and ask whether the active use of military force, or the passive avoidance of unjustifiably using force, is more effective as a means of preventing large-scale crimes.

McMahan explicitly frames his revisionist account of soldiers' ad bellum deliberative duties as a contribution to mass atrocity prevention. He remarks, "We as individuals are protected from becoming Nazis by ideas, and by the cultural and political institutions they inspire."[32] Nevertheless, the bulk of McMahan's discussion focuses not on the role of moral theory in preventing mass atrocities, at least as traditionally conceived, but rather on transforming traditional views about the morality of killing soldiers in war.[33] Furthermore, certain elements of McMahan's analysis cut against common scholarly understandings of mass atrocity, as when he argues that civilians who are not themselves armed, but contribute causally to unjust war efforts (for example, by developing new weapons or technologies) are liable to attack in war.[34] Indeed, based on the argument of *Killing in War*, it is hard to see why episodes of large-scale killing of "innocent" soldiers who are not hors de combat should not themselves be considered cases of mass atrocities.[35] These features of McMahan's account make it difficult to draw conclusions about the power of the particular moral norms he defends to constrain mass atrocities.

At this point, I want to turn from considering soldiers' ad bellum moral deliberations to discuss their in bello decisions and actions. Doing so promises to bring us closer to discovering connections between norms against deliberation and the project of atrocity prevention. It also sheds further light on the concept of mass atrocity itself.

In Bello Norms against Deliberation

Soldiers' deliberations about the justice of their nation's cause for going to war are vulnerable to propaganda, patriotic fervor, and official secrecy concerning relevant facts. Traditional just war theorists, as we have seen, respond to these adverse conditions by endorsing a permissive moral norm against deliberation; revisionist just war theorists repudiate that norm. But how do the conditions of practical deliberation change for soldiers who are already engaged in war and must make morally consequential decisions about targeting and risk taking while exposed to potentially lethal violence?

I start by citing one specific testimonial account. The philosopher J. Glenn Gray, a veteran of World War II, provides the following description of a soldier's experience "in an exposed position on the battlefield during action":

> All the time, he acts as he feels he must, swept by moods of exultation, despair, loyalty, hate, and many others. Much of the time he is out of himself, acting simply as a representative of the others, as part of a super-personal entity, on orders from elsewhere. He kills or fails to kill, fights courageously or runs away in the service of this unit and unity. Afterwards, he hears no voice calling him to account for his actions, or, if he does hear a voice, feels no need to respond.[36]

This description might seem to tell against the account of practical deliberation that I have relied on so far in this study. The picture Gray presents is not one of individual agents carefully considering the reasons, moral or otherwise, that count for or against certain actions. Instead, it parallels what social psychologists call a state of deindividuation, involving "decreased focus on personal identity, loss of contact with general social norms, and the submergence of the individual in situation-specific group norms."[37] In fact, however, Gray's description underscores the significance of norms against deliberation in war, for norms of this kind, as I have argued, are most valuable in circumstances where situational factors place extraordinary pressure on practical reasoning. We should, then, consider which particular moral norms against deliberation are most salient in these circumstances and how they affect efforts at atrocity prevention.

Current international law contains clear prohibitions on many actions soldiers and their commanders might consider strategically valuable.[38] Despite this broad coverage of legal norms concerning in bello deliberations, many important moral questions remain unaddressed. These include questions about the degree to which soldiers must actively take greater risks on themselves in order to reduce the risk of collateral harm to noncombatants during war, as well as questions about whether healthy soldiers in the field can ever be so vulnerable as to make their killing morally impermissible.[39] Far from being mere armchair quandaries, these are real problems that soldiers and junior officers face in war, which moral norms against deliberation promise to resolve.

In his 2016 book, *Sparing Civilians*, philosopher Seth Lazar provides a novel defense of a widely accepted moral principle that he believes rightly informs soldiers' responses to such practical quandaries.[40] He argues further that this principle underlies existing international legal norms that afford protection to noncombatants in war.[41] Lazar defines this principle as follows:

> *moral distinction*: In war, with rare exceptions, killing non-combatants is worse than killing combatants.[42]

Lazar's main aim in providing new defenses for the principle of moral distinction is to safeguard its acceptance among people who believe that many combatants who fight in wars are not themselves liable to be killed. Put differently, Lazar hopes to vindicate the intuition that "killing innocent civilians is worse than killing innocent soldiers."[43] It is for this reason that his arguments are relevant to our study of mass atrocity, for if it is possible to identify features that make the killing of innocent civilians morally worse than the killing of innocent combatants, then it may be possible to show that those same features justify excluding most cases of large-scale killing of combatants from the analytical category of mass atrocity. This is just the issue that our study of McMahan's revisionist account of soldiers' ad bellum moral obligations raised but did not resolve.

Of the five arguments Lazar advances for the principle of moral distinction, some are more relevant to the project of mass atrocity prevention than others. One argument Lazar considers holds that killing noncombatants is morally riskier than killing combatants due to the greater likelihood that any given noncombatant is innocent than any given combatant. This argument seems unlikely to tell us much about mass atrocities, since the wrongfulness of such large-scale, systematic acts of violence does not seem to be a function of mere recklessness or inattention to the moral risks involved.[44]

Another argument Lazar offers for *moral distinction* is more promising. This is the argument that noncombatants are generally both more vulnerable and more defenseless than combatants and that harming vulnerable and defenseless persons is morally worse than harming persons capable of defending themselves.[45] Lazar defines vulnerability in terms of the harm that an agent is likely to suffer from a given threat.[46] He defines defenselessness as the inability of an agent to reduce, for herself, her vulnerability to that threat.[47] With respect to the threats that arise in war, Lazar argues, noncombatants will generally be both more defenseless and more vulnerable than combatants. But attacking innocent parties who are comparatively more vulnerable and more defenseless is morally worse than attacking innocent parties who are less vulnerable and less defenseless. Hence, killing innocent noncombatants is morally worse than killing innocent (but armed) combatants.[48]

I think the distinctive wrongs involved in killing persons who are both substantially vulnerable and substantially defenseless give us good reason to exclude the large-scale killing of soldiers who are not *hors de combat* from the concept of mass killing within studies of mass atrocity. This exclusion does not entail that no wrong is done to soldiers in the field who are killed unnecessarily or are killed despite their nonliability. Those soldiers may be wronged, but the wrong is not of the distinctive kind involved in mass atrocities, to which the testimonial accounts cited elsewhere in this study attest.[49] This argument preserves the standard scholarly inclusion of "combatants removed from fighting" within the set of persons who may become targets of mass atrocity.[50] At the same time, it allows that soldiers who are not hors de combat may be the victims of other kinds of legally and morally prohibited attacks, such as killing or maiming via weapons that are legally forbidden due to the extraordinary suffering they cause.[51] What it rules out is the idea that the deaths of large numbers of soldiers in battle, who are killed by permissible means, should count as a case of mass atrocity.[52]

Some readers may doubt the moral or conceptual significance of the greater vulnerability and defenselessness of noncombatants. But there is, I think, another reason to ground a distinction between combatants' and noncombatant's susceptibility to mass atrocity on these qualities. Planners of genocide, mass killing, and other mass atrocities themselves tacitly admit the moral significance of these features of noncombatants when they use propaganda, euphemism, and dehumanization to try to make targeted groups seem formidable rather than vulnerable, dangerous rather than defenseless. Where these techniques of norm evasion are in play, in bello moral norms against deliberation, of the kind Lazar seeks to shore up, may provide soldiers with a last defense against pressures to participate in large-scale crimes.

Empirically minded scholars of mass atrocity prevention may be surprised by my focus in this section on ad bellum and in bello moral norms against deliberation. Compared to legal or social norms, moral norms seem to resist integration into comprehensive prevention strategies.[53] But I believe a full survey of strategies for constraining large-scale crimes must consider the norms that can, and at times do, deter agents on the front lines of armed conflict from using their specialized training in violence to engage in mass killing, forced removal, or other large-scale crimes. Parallel considerations give us reason to attend to the moral norms accepted by another set of actors regularly present on the front lines of atrocities, namely, humanitarian aid workers.

3.3 Humanitarian Aid Workers and Moral Norms against Deliberation

Humanitarian aid workers, acting in a voluntary capacity or employed full time by nongovernmental organizations, spend significant periods in war zones and sites of civil upheaval. Like soldiers, these aid workers face recurring moral challenges and have adopted a variety of norms for dealing with them. In this section, I analyze two traditional moral principles governing actors in "humanitarian space" and explain how those principles are realized in specific moral norms against deliberation. My goal is to show that these norms aim at constraining large-scale crimes while making clear that, here too, significant debates exist concerning their capacity to do so.

Humanitarian Neutrality
In an anthology published on the occasion of the fortieth anniversary of Doctors Without Borders (Médecins Sans Frontières), sociologist Marc Le Pape identifies a recurring moral dilemma faced by members of this pioneering humanitarian aid group. This is the choice between "provid[ing] medical assistance" to vulnerable populations, on the one hand, and "issu[ing] public criticism" of the conduct of domestic or occupying authorities, on the other.[54] A "tension between medical action and speaking out," Le Pape contends, "is, in fact, inherent to the organization's work and may always provoke contradictory judgments that are, to a greater or lesser degree, inflexible."[55] Rather than trying to resolve this tension by arguing for the greater value of one or the other form of action, Le Pape concludes that Doctors Without Borders, like other humanitarian groups, "must reach a compromise" between these competing goals.[56]

The moral significance Le Pape attaches to the act of speaking out against political authorities' involvement in humanitarian catastrophes cuts against a core principle in an older tradition of humanitarian thinking: the principle of neutrality. Articulated as early as Article 1 of the First Geneva Convention of 1864 and expanded to include more than doctors, nurses, stretcher bearers, and other medical personnel during the rapid growth of humanitarian activity that took place over the twentieth century, the principle of humanitarian neutrality has been endorsed by many frontline actors during historical large-scale crimes.[57] By studying this principle and the debates surrounding it, we can gain insights into the processes by which particular moral norms against deliberation are justified and by which they may subsequently be transformed.

In his 2015 book, *Humanitarian Ethics,* written "to help humanitarian workers apply their ethics more consciously and effectively on the ground," political theorist Hugo Slim characterizes neutrality as a "political principle" of humanitarian action, one that traditionally encompasses both military and ideological forbearance.[58] Neutrality, as Slim points out, is not usually seen as a virtue in everyday moral life. Instead, humanitarian neutrality paints a role-specific picture of the focus of practical deliberations for actors trying to relieve suffering during war or mass atrocities.[59]

So far, Slim's description of the traditional humanitarian principle of neutrality accords with philosophical accounts of professional codes more generally. Mike Davis, as we saw in chapter 2, defines professional codes as "morally permissible standards of conduct governing members of a group simply because they are members of that group."[60] What Davis's definition does not capture, and what much of Slim's analysis addresses, is the persistence of disagreements among members of particular professions concerning both the basic acceptability of received moral principles and the realization of those principles in specific action-guiding norms. Slim documents disagreements among contemporary humanitarians concerning both of these aspects of neutrality. Here I focus on disagreements about some specific moral norms against deliberation meant to help humanitarian actors maintain their neutrality.

Norms prescribing military neutrality on the part of humanitarian actors are less controversial than norms prescribing ideological neutrality.[61] It is not up for debate, among most humanitarian actors, whether they should share military intelligence derived from behind-the-lines relief work with the opposing side in a conflict. Nor are bona-fide humanitarians inclined to defend colleagues who supply weapons to belligerents. By contrast, many humanitarian actors and organizations do contest prevailing moral norms that prescribe ideological, or expressive, neutrality. Most significant, traditional norms of ideological neutrality bar humanitarian actors from stating publicly which side(s) they consider blameworthy for ongoing conflicts.[62]

In a study like Slim's, which focuses on the hard choices humanitarian actors are likely to face in the field, it is natural to find that most of the discussion concerns methods for deepening deliberation rather than norms against deliberation. Nevertheless, Slim's remarks on the widespread humanitarian commitment to military neutrality help fill out my picture of moral norms against deliberation. These norms differ in content from the norms accepted and followed by soldiers and junior officers, but structurally they are quite similar. Adapting the language Geoffrey Brennan and his coauthors employ to sum up this sort of moral prohibition, we may say that the principle of humanitarian neutrality is reflected not just in norms against giving weapons to fighters on any side of a conflict but also in "norms about how one is supposed to *think* about [supplying weapons]: one should not think about it; not at all."[63]

In contrast to the moral prohibitions rooted in the principle of military neutrality, considerable debate surrounds the principle of ideological neutrality and its attendant norms. The impetus to rethink restrictions on the views humanitarian actors can publicly express stems from various sources, including the growing size and resources of humanitarian organizations; the retreat of traditional state actors from providing many of the relief services required in contexts of war or natural disasters; and the controversy surrounding responses of nongovernmental organizations to particular humanitarian crises, such as the Haitian earthquake of 2010 or the Rwandan genocide of 1994.[64] This last example is especially important for my purposes, since it indicates doubts about the connection between humanitarian neutrality and the prevention, or mitigation, of large-scale crimes. While humanitarian actors have long claimed a right to denounce such crimes whenever they occur during war, the debate about neutrality is directed chiefly at the question of whether remaining neutral as to the ad bellum justice of states' participation in war fails effectively to constrain mass atrocities. Hugo Slim seems to believe that ideological neutrality is an acceptable price to pay for gaining (or retaining) the "access and trust" required for humanitarian relief in circumstances of mass atrocity.[65] But the very existence of competing opinions on this issue reveals that there is no strongly established norm against deliberation to speak of here, but at most a very weak one.[66] Humanitarian actors may still largely refrain from speaking out about the ad bellum justice of particular sides in inter- or intrastate conflicts, but speaking out is increasingly something they think about, write about, and otherwise express doubts about. Those doubts center, as I have suggested, on the preventive efficacy of this policy.

The different degrees of acceptance evident in norms surrounding military and ideological neutrality among humanitarian aid workers point up one of the distinguishing features of moral norms: the absence of standing procedural rules governing their emergence, modification, or elimination. As Slim notes, much of humanitarian ethics falls in the category of "soft law," consisting of policies drawn up voluntarily by humanitarian organizations over the past several decades and increasingly embodied in the governing principles of the largest humanitarian nongovernmental organizations.[67] Particular aid agencies may choose to reject specific norms, thereby incurring sanctions that may include exclusion from certain coalitions or denial of funding but not the more stringent penalties associated with hard law. Even these quasi-legal sanctions do not extend to norms against deliberation, however. Instead, as I have suggested, such norms have the structure of moral norms, developed in conjunction with certain deep moral principles, but subject to revision or rejection when those principles come under suspicion. As with the ad bellum deliberative responsibilities of soldiers already discussed, moral arguments may ultimately succeed in transforming the moral norms against deliberation accepted and followed by humanitarian actors. If that happens, we should expect institutional changes to follow.

Humanitarian Impartiality

Despite its verbal similarity, humanitarian impartiality differs from humanitarian neutrality in important ways. Impartiality does not prohibit humanitarian actors from ranking beneficiaries according to their respective merits or expressing the results of such comparisons. Rather, it bans the use of unfair or arbitrary criteria for making such judgments. In the actual practice of humanitarians, we can observe a further difference: whereas neutrality usually affects how humanitarian agents conduct themselves toward states or other large-scale actors, impartiality applies more commonly to decisions about how to treat individual recipients of aid or protection.

Political scientist Janice Gross Stein claims that the principle of impartiality helps aid workers operate more efficiently in contexts of war and mass atrocity. Traditionally, she observes, "impartiality was not only principled, it was functional: on the ground, it helped facilitate access to all sides in a conflict zone, and it avoided explicit discussion of difficult political choices."[68] This final phrase suggests how the principle of impartiality is expressed in the form of norms against deliberation, where the difficult choices involved may concern which wounded or diseased patients to treat first in field hospitals, which refugee populations to prioritize with deliveries of food or water, or where economic assistance for rebuilding in the wake of war or forced removal should focus. To reiterate, impartiality does not require humanitarians to disregard any comparative factors that could inform such choices, only those deemed unfair or arbitrary. So the race, ethnicity, nationality, and religion of aid recipients count among the qualities that are supposed to be excluded from humanitarian deliberations, but relative need, likelihood of success, and comparative accessibility are factors that can and should be taken into consideration.[69]

The principle of humanitarian impartiality bears on mass atrocity prevention in several ways. In the first place, it helps aid workers resist the invidious categorizations that often dominate government actors' preferred divisions of scant resources before, during, and after large-scale crimes.[70] This is valuable both in cases where humanitarian actors operate at the discretion of existing states and in cases where humanitarian agencies become the only effective governing agencies after total state collapse.[71]

At a second level, the principle of humanitarian impartiality, and the related norms that prohibit dividing aid according to political convenience, may help inhibit mass atrocities by calling attention to patterns of violence that state actors and foreign allies would prefer to ignore. It is here that the analysis of state leaders' moral commitments provided by Alex Bellamy and my own analysis of moral commitments and attitudes held by front-line actors intersect. Whereas Bellamy's account highlights the interest state leaders have in preserving "sufficient legitimacy" even in the face of persecutory policies, norms against deliberation furnish humanitarian actors with a standing defense against the ethnic, racial, or religious biases of their political sponsors.[72] It is this defense that Janice Gross Stein has in mind when she writes of the "functional" value of impartiality for humanitarian actors. By cultivating norms against deliberation, humanitarians can tell state actors who would prefer their silence or complicity that their rules forbid even considering such courses of action. This does not remove humanitarian actors from the pressures of politics—far from it—but it does provide a distinct form of leverage in the fraught political debates that accompany mass atrocities.[73]

As political theorist Jennifer Rubenstein has observed, humanitarian actors face an array of ethical predicaments, recurring across contexts and conflicts, that cannot all be settled simply by applying traditional humanitarian principles.[74] In some cases, as when aid organizations take on the responsibilities of local or national governments, this is because the guidance offered by norms rooted in those traditional principles proves contradictory.[75] In other cases, as when relief workers must decide whether to release emotionally charged images in order to raise badly needed relief funds, this is because those traditional principles are largely silent.[76]

I agree with Rubenstein that there are substantial areas where traditional humanitarian principles do not supply clear norms capable of guiding humanitarian actors' practical deliberations. In this section, I have explored how two of the longest-standing humanitarian principles provide important moral resources for front-line actors seeking to prevent or mitigate mass atrocities. Those resources take the form of moral norms against deliberation.

3.4   Mass Moral Education as a Means of Atrocity Prevention

The moral norms I have considered in the course of this chapter circulate within highly specialized populations. Those populations—common soldiers, junior officers, and humanitarian aid workers—were selected because of their firsthand experience dealing with recurrent moral dilemmas in contexts of real or threatened mass atrocities. My analysis of the various moral norms against deliberation accepted and followed by members of these groups was enhanced by attention to debates among philosophers and other theorists concerning the justifiability of those norms and their ability to help constrain large-scale crimes.

Some readers might suppose that our investigation should go further and consider the preventive potential of moral norms circulating within political societies at large. Over the past few decades, a number of philosophers have argued that this is precisely the level at which we should focus when cultivating defenses against mass atrocities. By sharing "sympathetic stories" and publicizing the deeds of "moral exemplars," these authors hope to induce changes in the moral norms accepted and followed by ordinary citizens around the globe, which will assist those citizens in resisting large-scale crimes whenever and wherever they occur.[77]

One of the more careful efforts to identify such macrolevel opportunities for atrocity prevention appears in philosopher Jonathan Glover's book *Humanity*.[78] Glover starts from the premise that in the absence of transcendent moral laws, it is necessary to show that human moral psychology can sustain absolute prohibitions on mass killing, mass rape, and other mass atrocities. Reviewing a range of twentieth-century cases of moral dilemmas encountered by individual agents in such contexts, Glover discerns two distinct "moral responses" to these dilemmas. First, there are attitudinal responses such as sympathy, shame, and respect occasioned by encounters with the suffering of others.[79] Second, there is the effort to sustain a coherent self-image, or identity, in the midst of real or threatened atrocities.[80]

How do these moral responses inform specific strategies for preventing mass atrocities? Glover sketches two preventive pathways and claims that both can help constrain large-scale crimes. The first pathway is fairly clear-cut: Glover believes that sharing stories of historical mass atrocities with broad audiences can increase democratic support for international efforts to prevent future large-scale crimes.[81] The types of international efforts he has in mind include humanitarian interventions, international administration, and monitoring by peacekeeping forces in contexts where atrocities are likely. In general, this proposal coincides with the active component of Dwight Raymond's "military means of preventing atrocities."[82]

The second preventive pathway Glover outlines is less straightforward. In several places, he suggests that by spreading "awareness of collective disasters," historians, philosophers, and other educators can help ordinary individuals avoid participation, or complicity, in large-scale crimes.[83] Beyond this general description, it is difficult to say exactly what Glover has in view, though the historical case studies at the heart of his text draw attention to many different individual actors whose responses (or nonresponsiveness) to prevailing attitudes and policy have changed the trajectory of particular mass atrocities. In many cases, it should be noted, these individuals occupied the kinds of specialized social roles I have highlighted rather than being mere private citizens.[84]

While I admire Glover's historical discussions and support his call for popular moral education concerning large-scale crimes, I am skeptical about the specific preventive pathways he defends. It is not that Glover fails to offer robust empirical evidence for his preventive claims; like my own study, he is concerned chiefly with identifying possible preventive pathways, which may later be taken up for empirical confirmation. My concern is, rather, that the particular pathways he sketches are unpromising on their own terms. Three central objections stand out. They concern (1) the fragility of individual and group moral identities, (2) the uneven distribution of mass atrocities, and (3) the inherent riskiness of military intervention.

Glover's call for cultivating more robust moral identities among ordinary citizens seems to me unlikely to increase most individuals' ability to resist participation in, or publicly oppose, large-scale crimes. At the end of his book, Glover acknowledges the malleability of moral identities, citing cases of apparent dynamic moral norm inversion among German National Socialists, Soviet party members, and other groups in order to make the point that agents' "self-images" can and sometimes do become detached from the "human responses" of sympathy and respect, and thus prove "useless or worse" for preventing mass atrocities.[85] But the fragility of moral identities, and of the practical commitments and normative attitudes that compose them, runs deeper than this. As I argued in the previous chapter, inversions of moral norms help to explain some, but by no means all, mass atrocities. The techniques for norm evasion and norm erosion that I analyzed may in many cases leave individuals' moral identities largely intact— for example, by suggesting that victims of large-scale crimes are less than human or by concealing the real import of perpetrator's actions. Beyond these explicit cases of manipulation of citizens' moral responses, government agencies and other institutions frequently use censorship, geographic remoteness, and other forms of concealment to prevent most citizens from knowing that mass atrocities are underway. In these cases, individuals may sense that something unusual is happening without knowing exactly what or even how to find out definitively.

This points to one way in which soldiers and humanitarian aid workers differ from the ordinary citizens whom Glover wants to enlist in the cause of atrocity prevention. Such front-line agents generally possess more direct knowledge of real or threatened acts of persecution than the public at large. The ability to know what actions to take in response to the persecution of others does not only depend on correct weighing of relevant moral norms; it also requires sufficient acquaintance with the facts on the ground.[86] It is one thing to ask whether ordinary citizens have a moral responsibility to pursue such information in light of their political leaders' decisions about war. It is another to ask whether atrocity prevention efforts can succeed absent such knowledge.

My second concern about Glover's proposal to advance mass atrocity prevention is related to the first.[87] It hinges once again on a distinction between the experiences of soldiers and humanitarian aid workers, on the one hand, and ordinary citizens, on the other. This objection starts from the fact that mass atrocities are unevenly distributed: for individuals living in some countries, these events are troublingly common, whereas for individuals living in more stable nations, they are exceptionally rare. Even indirect exposure to those contexts of war or civil conflict where large-scale crimes most frequently occur is unusual for many people today, especially in nations that lack compulsory military service.

I have argued throughout this chapter that the moral norms against deliberation accepted by soldiers and humanitarian aid workers gain their practical relevance from their power to resolve recurring moral problems. For individuals working in these specialized professions, the objection from the uneven distribution of atrocities does not apply. But it seems to me a defect of the preventive pathway proposed by Glover that the moral capacities he hopes to cultivate will only rarely, if ever, be confronted by the challenge of real or threatened large-scale crimes. Support for this claim comes from the fact that the kinds of stories Glover tells are most commonly used in the United States and other developed countries today to address more quotidian moral challenges that children and adults may face, including bullying, police brutality, corporate malfeasance, and whistle-blowing. If the general goal of telling compelling stories about large-scale crimes is to help individuals resist wrongdoing, then these common moral problems are more likely to show results than the extraordinary circumstances of mass atrocity.

Glover might respond that, however rare large-scale crimes are in any given nation, they are not rare in the world at large. Indeed, this points to the importance of his first, and more straightforward, preventive pathway, according to which popular education about past large-scale crimes will make ordinary citizens more likely to support their governments in

undertaking military and diplomatic action to prevent future mass atrocities. This is precisely the sort of decision that citizens of stable democracies
are likely to face repeatedly in the course of their lives. The problem, from
the perspective of mass atrocity prevention, is that it does not seem right
to counsel ordinary citizens to withhold skepticism concerning their governments' claims about the motives for military action, or the necessity of
armed intervention to prevent large-scale crimes. In part, this is because
humanitarian wars have yet to establish a successful record of atrocity prevention. In part, this is because the risks of unsuccessful military action
are so severe; indeed, humanitarian interventions sometimes occasion or
accelerate mass atrocities despite their directors' honest efforts to prevent
them. Finally, it seems to me that if it is doubtful whether soldiers should
accept a permissive moral norm against deliberating about the justice of
their nation's cause for going to war, then it is even less plausible to say
that ordinary citizens should refrain from serious reflection on this point.
For the same reason that I am skeptical about Glover's proposal, I worry
about discursive strategies that seek to use the human responses of sympathy produced by shocking descriptions or images to quell skeptical doubts
about humanitarian intervention.[88] Moral norms circulating among specialized agents, such as soldiers and humanitarian aid workers, are in my
view far more plausibly linked to atrocity prevention than efforts to engage
the moral sensibilities of mass publics for the purpose of constraining large-
scale crimes. This is why philosophical debates about the justification of such
norms, and empirical investigations of their efficacy, deserve our ongoing
attention.

4   The Etiology of Inhumanity: Legal Norms and the Explanation of Mass Atrocities

In March 1945, the German jurist Gustav Radbruch resumed writing his memoirs. Radbruch, who had served as minister of justice under successive Social Democratic governments during the Weimar Republic, was forced from his chair at Heidelberg University with the rise of National Socialism. Now, in the closing weeks of World War II, Radbruch linked the course of his life to a series of events that had transformed European society during the late nineteenth and early twentieth centuries. He started by citing various technological breakthroughs achieved in his lifetime. He then noted the promise those inventions had seemed to hold out—a promise that had, by 1945, proved false:

> The greatest technological development for myself and my contemporaries was the conquest of the air through the human spirit. I remember seeing tears fill the eyes of those who caught their first glimpse of a Zeppelin from the Neue Brücke in Heidelberg. On that day, no one could have guessed that this invention and others like it would not make men better or happier, but would instead lead towards the destruction of mankind.[1]

Today, Radbruch is remembered chiefly for his contributions to legal philosophy, particularly his critique of the doctrine known as legal positivism. "Positivistic legal thinking," he argued in a 1946 essay, had "prevailed for decades among German jurists, without real opposition."[2] Summarized by the slogan "law is law," this doctrine denied legal officials the right to seek guidance for their decisions from an ideal of justice independent of, and superior to, enacted laws.[3] Beguiled by positivism, Radbruch contended, German lawyers and judges had acceded to the wicked policies of National Socialism. They had thus enabled the acts and policies that the Nuremberg Tribunal would soon condemn as crimes against humanity.

Radbruch's critique of positivism has long fueled debates among law-yers and philosophers about the relationship between law and morality. One typical way of framing these debates is to ask whether there could be an "exterminatory legality"—a scenario in which officials carry out atroci-ties exclusively by means of duly enacted laws.[4] This might seem to be an empirical question. But the jurisprudential debates to date have focused mainly on conceptual claims about the nature of law and legal systems. Some theorists, such as the American legal scholar Lon Fuller, believe that defining features of law render an exterminatory legality impossible.[5] Other theorists, such as the English legal philosopher H. L. A. Hart, hold that no decisive protections against state-sponsored crimes can be found in the concept of law itself.[6] The best safeguard against "wicked legal systems," Hart argues, is to admit their possibility and oppose their emergence.[7]

In this chapter, I aim to show how legal norms contribute to the explana-tion of genocide and other kinds of mass atrocity. My discussion is informed by Gustav Radbruch's jurisprudential legacy; however, I depart from Rad-bruch's example in the questions I ask and the resources I use to answer them. Whereas Radbruch asked what World War II–era mass atrocities could tell us about the foundations of law, I ask what law can tell us about the foundations of mass atrocities. Whereas Hart and Fuller used "fables" and thought experiments to support their arguments, I will be concerned with tracing specific laws and legal institutions that have facilitated histori-cal large-scale crimes.

My thesis is twofold. I first argue that legal norms are integral to the eti-ology of large-scale crimes. Legal norms create social categories, legitimate discriminatory policies, and restrict the spread of knowledge about perse-cution and violence. The power of legal norms to produce these effects is rooted in the features that distinguish them from moral and social norms. I then argue that legal norms stand as crucial sources of evidence about large-scale crimes. This evidence consists not just of the laws themselves, codified in statutes or secret decrees, but also in the troves of documents produced by the institutions tasked with implementing them. Both the special place of legal norms in the etiology of large-scale crimes and their status as key sources of evidence concerning such crimes render these norms integral to the explanation of genocide and mass atrocity.

The chapter proceeds as follows. In section 4.1, I set out my basic account of legal norms and discuss two salient distinctions between legal norms and moral or social norms. In section 4.2, I consider contrasting approaches to the etiology of large-scale crimes and defend an approach adapted from the work of Deborah Mayersen. Sections 4.3 to 4.5 discuss three ways in which legal norms can escalate the risk of genocide and other forms of mass atrocity: by creating or reinforcing social out-groups through legal categorization, helping state leaders maintain external legitimacy while directing internal persecution, and providing cover for denials of large-scale crimes. Section 4.6 turns to consider a different kind of contribution that legal norms can make to the explanation of large-scale crimes, namely, the distinctive documentary evidence they furnish. Section 4.7 considers the challenge posed by an alternative explanatory pathway rooted in Christian Gerlach's notion of "extremely violent societies."

4.1   Legal Norms

In his 2014 book, *A World without Jews*, historian Alon Confino details the regulations that German officials used during the 1930s to exclude Jews from the nation's social and political life. In 1933, Jews were banned from the bar, from editorial positions at newspapers and magazines, and from the management of lotteries.[8] In 1935, they were prohibited from working as tax consultants or as army officers.[9] In 1938, they were barred from employment as auctioneers.[10] And in 1939, they were blocked from using public air raid shelters and subjected to a nightly curfew.[11]

We know that German officials and institutions progressively excluded Jews from communal life in this period because we have records of their public pronouncements and private deliberations. We know, more concretely, because we have the texts of the exclusionary laws themselves.[12] By reflecting on our ability to access and understand these laws today, we can gain insight into the distinguishing features of legal norms.[13]

In the first place, legal norms are at least partially grounded in real or perceived social practices. Such practices differ depending on the particular type of law in question: domestic or international, ecclesiastical or colonial. They also differ depending on the specific institutions and traditions found within given jurisdictions. What this claim concerning the practice-grounded feature of legal norms entails is simply that the existence or perception of certain social practices plays a part in justifying the acceptance of legal norms by individuals and groups and informs the action-guiding roles those norms perform within the practical point of view.

What sorts of social practices are relevant? At the limit, as in some cases of international law, as well as domestically in common-law jurisdictions, long-standing customs may ground legal norms. Here the relationship between law and social practices seems straightforward: were the practices different, so the laws would differ. Acts of genocide, crimes against humanity, and other kinds of large-scale crimes are today considered *jus cogens* violations in international customary law, and so this type of legal norm is relevant to individuals and groups seeking to assess accountability for such crimes. However, for an account of the place of legal norms in the explanation of large-scale crimes, customs are less relevant than the institutionalized practices of courts, legislators, and administrative agencies.[14]

Distinct from customary law is positive or statutory law: law explicitly created by an individual or institution endowed with legislative authority. Today in many countries, statutes are created by elected parliaments, legislatures, or assemblies. There is nothing in the nature of statutes that requires that they be created by such democratic bodies, however. In 1920s Russia, laws were enacted by high officials in the Communist Party; in 1920s Morocco, laws were instituted by the French governor-general. The positive laws created during earlier periods in the history of particular societies often continue to influence events in the present, largely because of their effectiveness in shaping the beliefs and guiding the actions of individuals raised under their jurisdiction. So, for example, the ethnic categories created under Belgian colonial law in Rwanda notoriously continued to influence postindependence politics in that country until the time of the 1994 genocide.[15] The activities of legislative authorities in creating laws, and of courts and agencies in interpreting and implementing them, constitute what I am calling the practice-grounded nature of legal norms.

Some philosophers of law take this point further and argue that legal norms are grounded exclusively in certain social practices. This position is known as the "social fact thesis." Put more precisely, the social fact thesis holds that what law there is within a given jurisdiction is determined exclusively by relevant social facts.[16] Proponents of the social fact thesis offer different accounts of which particular facts are relevant. Some hold that what law there is can be determined chiefly by reading statutes, constitutions, and other published law texts, treating these texts as the prime sources of law. Others argue that the content of the laws should be determined chiefly by analyzing the ways in which specific legal actors (such as judges, jurors, or administrators) are disposed to act when presented with specific legal problems. One claim that proponents of the social fact thesis overwhelmingly deny is that questions about what law there is can be answered directly by appeal to moral principles.[17] They deny, in other words, what Radbruch affirmed in his 1946 essay: that certain principles of justice stand above positively enacted laws and in some cases can render those laws invalid.[18]

It is not my intention to defend the social fact thesis against Radbruch's arguments, or vice versa. My claim is that legal norms are at least partially grounded in real or perceived social practices, and that this helps distinguish them from moral norms. One advantage that the social fact thesis offers is that it provides insight into how the relationship between legal norms and social facts gives those legal norms a special power to pattern the conduct of groups. As philosopher Joseph Raz writes, "Law ... helps to secure social co-operation not only through its sanctions providing motivation for conformity but also through designating in an accessible way the patterns of behavior required for such co-operation."[19] This special capacity of law to coordinate activity need not be beneficial to all individuals living within particular jurisdictions.[20] It is equally crucial to explaining the contributions that legal norms make to the planning and perpetration of mass atrocity.[21]

Legal norms can be distinguished from moral norms on the basis of their grounding in real or perceived social practices, but this fact does not suffice to differentiate them from social norms, which are equally practice grounded.[22] The second feature of legal norms I highlight helps distinguish them from both moral and social norms. Legal norms, unlike norms of these other kinds, are subject to standing procedural rules governing their emergence, modification, and elimination. Taken together, these rules constitute the basic requirements named by the term *legality*.

Lon Fuller offers one of the most influential inventories of these standing procedural rules.[23] In his 1964 book, *The Morality of Law*, Fuller identified "eight ways to fail to make law."[24] Prospective lawmakers fail to make law, Fuller argued, when they issue rules that are ad hoc; fail to publicize the rules they make; make laws retroactive, unintelligible, contradictory, or impossible to follow; change laws too frequently; and fail to administer laws in the correct way.[25] Fuller considered these eight failures to correspond to basic requirements of legality; he argued as well that such requirements provide safeguards against immoral laws. Subsequent authors have largely accepted Fuller's list of criteria for legality, or the rule of law, while rejecting his metanormative claim. Joseph Raz argues that only minimal adherence to Fuller's requirements is necessary in a functioning system of law and flatly denies that such adherence provides a safeguard against institutional immorality.[26] Jeremy Waldron suggests that the eight features of law Fuller identified must be supplemented by certain additional features, related to the roles of particular legal actors, in any complete account of legality.[27]

There is a clear link between the distinctive features of legal norms that Fuller set forth and the evidential value of law for explaining large-scale crimes. When laws are passed publicly, rather than in secret; when they are designed as general rules, requiring interpretation to apply to particular cases; and when they are made intelligible rather than unintelligible, these features help ensure that laws can be accessed and understood not just by those within a particular society while they are operable, but also by those outside a society, even long after they have lapsed. Legal apartheid no longer exists in South Africa, but it is still possible to access and understand apartheid-era racial segregation laws. France no longer governs Morocco as a protectorate, but it is still possible to access and understand French colonial laws and policies mandating the separation of colonizers from colonized. The evidential quality of laws that conform to the requirements of legality is so great that many regimes bent on wicked ends have departed from the use of clear, well-publicized laws in order to conceal their actions. This was the case with the secret euthanasia program Aktion T4, discussed in chapter 1. It is also one reason why Fuller defended a necessary connection between law and morality.

The two features of legal norms that I have identified—their grounding in real or perceived social practices and the existence of standing procedural rules governing their emergence, modification, and elimination—serve to distinguish them from both moral and social norms. The debates about the relationship between legal and moral norms that have long occupied philosophers of law are useful insofar as they indicate that in practice there are few contexts in which just one of these kinds of norms is implicated in the deliberations of social and political actors. More commonly, both legal and moral norms accepted by individuals will be relevant. Sometimes these norms are well aligned. In other cases they conflict, setting the stage for shows of civil disobedience or troubling acts of moral compromise.

It is not only the decisions and actions of individuals that legal norms help explain, however. Just as important, legal norms help pattern the conduct of whole populations. To be sure, the practical commitments and normative attitudes of individual agents are fundamental. This is the upshot of the methodological individualism I endorsed in chapter 1.[28] But we often find it convenient to refer to the power of legal norms to guide the decisions and actions of institutional actors, such as the League of Nations, the UN High Commissioner for Refugees (UNHCR), or specific state ministries. In what follows, I focus chiefly on the explanatory power of legal norms at this level: analyzing their place in the etiology of large-scale crimes and their status as privileged sources of evidence about such crimes.

4.2 Legal Norms and the Etiology of Large-Scale Crimes

To talk about the etiology of a phenomenon is to talk about the conditions that make it possible and intelligible.[29] The processes of moral norm erosion and moral norm evasion discussed in chapter 2 count among such conditions. Few studies of the etiology of large-scale crimes focus on the adverse moral pressures that individual agents face, however. Most focus instead on institutional factors, including, notably, transformations in legal norms. Laws stripping rights from minority groups, decrees granting extraordinary powers to police forces or militias, and administrative rules restricting the freedom of journalists and other observers to speak out about abuses all exemplify such factors. I will consider each of these examples in more detail, but, first, it will be helpful to introduce a more general model of the conditions contributing to large-scale crimes.

Not all studies of the etiology of genocide and mass atrocity share the same analytical goals. While many strive to explain large-scale crimes, others are concerned with predicting these events. Predictive projects can be further divided into those concerned with identifying long-range risk factors and those concerned with providing early warnings to national minorities and the international community. As political scientist Ernesto Verdeja points out, the project of prediction differs from that of explanation in numerous ways.[30] Most significant, predictive models seek to identify factors or conditions correlated with large-scale crimes, while explanatory models seek to identify factors or conditions that causally contribute to such crimes.[31] As a result, not all of the factors included in risk assessment models or indexes of warning signs can be incorporated directly into explanations of mass atrocity.

Compounding these differences in purpose are differences in methods. Some theorists favor quantitative methods and endeavor to build data sets extensive enough to support robust statistical generalizations.[32] Others adopt a qualitative approach and discover potential causal factors by conducting detailed case studies of particular occurrences of large-scale crimes.[33] Still others seek to identify structural features of human societies that make mass atrocities possible in the first place.[34]

A third distinction concerns the ambitiousness of studies of the etiology of large-scale crimes. Here I am concerned specifically with studies aimed at explaining mass atrocities. Some authors announce the fairly modest goal of making large-scale crimes intelligible—showing, in other words, that such crimes do not violate basic principles commonly used to make sense of the behavior of individuals and groups. The political theorist Benjamin Valentino, for example, has shown that orchestrating mass killings can be rational for political leaders, at least under certain circumstances.[35] Similarly, the sociologist Christopher Powell has argued that genocide, in particular, is not a departure from modern "civilizing processes" but rather compatible with them.[36]

Far more ambitious, as genocide scholar Deborah Mayersen observes, are studies that seek to identify necessary and sufficient conditions for large-scale crimes.[37] Such studies straddle the divide between prediction and explanation, boldly aiming at both goals. Like Mayersen, I doubt any such account can succeed in the limited case of genocide. The challenge is still greater in the more variegated terrain of mass atrocity.

I believe Mayersen's model of the etiology of genocide exhibits just the right level of ambition, focusing as it does on "escalatory" and "inhibitory" conditions along "the path to genocide."[38] Because I am concerned not just with genocide but with a broader range of large-scale crimes, I cannot adopt Mayersen's model whole cloth. Nevertheless, key elements of her model apply to mass atrocities generally, and are especially useful for identifying ways in which legal norms contribute to such crimes.

Mayersen identifies eight conditions that progressively escalate the risk of genocide. These conditions are as follows:

1. Presence of an out-group within a society
2. Significant internal strife
3. Perception of an out-group as an existential threat
4. Case-specific precipitating or constraining factors
5. Processes of retreat from or escalation of violence
6. Emergence of a genocidal ideology
7. Creation of an extensive propaganda campaign
8. Further case-specific precipitating or constraining factors[39]

A society's progress through these eight conditions need not be linear. Nor must it be unidirectional: both temporary and permanent (or indefinite) deescalations are possible.[40] Nevertheless, these conditions, in this order, do seem to help explain the occurrence of genocide in the specific cases that Mayersen details (the Rwandan genocide and the genocide of Armenians in Turkey). Analogous conditions are apparent in other twentieth-century cases of genocide.

I have said that I cannot adopt Mayersen's model without qualification, since her focus is on genocide specifically, not large-scale crimes more generally.[41] Some of the conditions she identifies also clearly precede nongenocidal forms of mass atrocity, such as mass killing, mass rape, and forced removal. The presence of an out-group within a society is one such example; so are some of the case-specific precipitating or constraining factors Mayersen discusses, such as the perceived willingness of external powers to intervene in case of attacks on national minorities. Focusing on such factors individually and explaining how they escalate the risk of large-scale crimes seems to me legitimate, even if I cannot claim that nongenocidal large-scale crimes exhibit precisely the same tendency to progress through all eight of the conditions listed.

In what follows, I first discuss the power of legal norms to create or maintain out-groups within societies, via processes of legal categorization. Next, I discuss the power of legal norms to legitimate violence as it is occurring, which I identify with the fourth stage of Mayersen's model. Finally, I consider the role of legal norms in concealing or hiding evidence of large-scale crimes from the international community—a power that counts as one of the further case-specific precipitating factors that Mayersen discusses. In each of these cases, I argue that an understanding of the two distinguishing features of legal norms enhances our understanding of the significance of legal norms within explanations of genocide and mass atrocity.

4.3   Legal Norms and the Creation of Social Out-Groups

Laws create social categories and entrench social distinctions. This is true even in societies where equal treatment under the law is a fundamental principle. The construction of legal categories frequently proceeds from benign reasons and often serves egalitarian aims.[42] But the power of legal norms to establish and enforce social categories is regularly exploited by leaders seeking to vilify, degrade, or expel members of specific groups.

The exclusionary laws that Confino listed in *A World without Jews* furnish clear examples of the use of legal norms to enforce social categories. Confino distinguishes between the work of categorization done by laws directed at German Jews and those directed at colonized subjects outside Europe, who from the time of first contact were regarded by Germans "as distinctly outside their own European civilization."[43] More recently, Peter Fritzsche has described the proliferation of racial, ethnic, and religious categories within Europe between 1933 and 1945, arguing that laws and regulations establishing such categories had clear effects on the beliefs and judgments of the individuals and groups bound by them. On the one hand, "thinking in terms of categories ... required paying attention to differences that had previously not been thoroughly scrutinized."[44] On the other hand, "once set in motion, the process of division and subdivision could go on for a long time, until only lonely individuals remained to fend for themselves."[45] The "breakdown of solidarity" that Fritzsche sees as the result of this process of categorization is quite similar to the phenomenon of demoralization I described in chapter 2.

The significance of legal categorization for large-scale crimes is not limited to the era of National Socialism. Historian Eric Weitz, in his comparative study, *A Century of Genocide*, identifies categorization as one of the key features linking large-scale crimes in such geographically and temporally distant contexts as the early Soviet Union, Nazi Germany, Cambodia under the Khmer Rouge, and late twentieth-century Bosnia-Herzegovina. In each of these cases, Weitz argues, the categories of "race" and "nation" became "categories through which states organized the most extreme violations of human rights."[46] His discussion of the importance of legal categorization prior to the commission of atrocities in the former Yugoslavia supports Mayersen's claim that the creation of out-groups constitutes one of the first escalatory conditions "on the path to genocide."[47]

Because of their central focus on group destruction, acts of genocide necessarily involve some effort at categorization. But the use of laws to categorize and render vulnerable members of particular groups is not limited to this specific type of large-scale crime. Episodes of mass killing perpetrated against colonized subjects, for example, were made possible by the fact that the laws governing these subjects typically did not afford the same protections against state violence as laws governing citizens in the metropole.[48] Likewise, legal restrictions placed on Jews in Imperial Russia, which confined them to the Pale of Settlement, increased their vulnerability to pogroms.

It is important to stress, once again, that legal norms do not always deprecate those they categorize. The Third Geneva Convention of 1949 offers a lengthy definition of the category of prisoners of war, applied to members of the regular armed forces of nation-states and irregular fighters in nonoccupied territories who respect the laws and customs of war.[49] The explicit purpose of this legal categorization, as stated in Article 3 of the Convention, is to ensure the "human[e]" and "civilized" treatment of prisoners and to protect captives against "humiliating" or "degrading" usage.[50] Other, less effective, efforts at protective legal categorization include the distinction made in international law between fortified and nonfortified towns as targets for attack.

Confronted with such contrasting evidence, we may wish to conclude that the effects of legal categories are knife-like: they may cut either way, for the good or the ill of the individuals and groups categorized.[51] But this would be premature, for we have yet to consider whether the negative effects of legal categorization are in any way constrained by the reality, or unreality, of the categories created. My own view is that social identities, or the identities attributed to individuals and groups in social life, need not be grounded in real features or characteristics of those individuals or groups, but are often grounded in merely perceived characteristics. But these perceptions are themselves deeply influenced by social practices and institutions, including laws designed to create or distinguish different categories of people.[52]

A particularly powerful example of the ability of legal norms to create enduring social categories comes from Rwanda. In that country, as

Mahmood Mamdani has shown, racial identities that were first "legally enforced and institutionally reproduced" during the period of Belgian colonial rule provided a basis for judgments about indigeneity and foreignness that long outlived colonization and proved crucial to the 1994 Rwandan genocide.[53] Even before that grim event, the legally produced racial categories helped give rise to massacres in the 1960s during Rwanda's social revolution.[54] The role of legal categorization as an escalatory factor in those nongenocidal mass killings seems as clear as in the subsequent case of genocide.

4.4 Legal Norms and the Legitimation of Persecution

Pursuing policy objectives through duly enacted laws is an important signal of political legitimacy. So too is avoiding actions that clearly violate domestic or international legal norms. A concern for legitimacy may seem unlikely to crop up in contexts where state leaders contemplate attacks on their own populations. However, historical evidence suggests that leaders and officials in such states often take steps to maintain at least the appearance of legitimate rule. The use of laws to create or preserve this appearance before and during mass atrocities thus constitutes a second important contribution of legal norms to the explanation of large-scale crimes.

In speaking of states' efforts to create or maintain the appearance of legitimacy, I have in mind the framework developed by Alex Bellamy in his 2012 book, *Massacres and Morality*. Bellamy, as noted in chapter 3, believes that state actors planning or perpetrating mass atrocities seek to avoid negative judgments by external observers about their legitimacy.[55] One way that state actors seek to maintain legitimacy is by preventing particular legal norms from becoming widely accepted at the international level.[56] At the 1899 International Peace Conference at the Hague, for example, the British delegation sought to prevent the passage of a declaration condemning the use of expanding bullets, arguing that these munitions were necessary for conflicts in their colonies.[57] Similar resistance to the development of special prohibitions on aerial warfare in international law has proved more effective, so that now states may be legally condemned for disproportionate or indiscriminate bombardment, but not simply for the act of aerial bombardment itself.[58]

Absence of law is not the only way in which legal norms can help states engaged in large-scale crimes maintain their legitimacy. Bellamy describes several other tactics that are relevant here. One is the creation of new domestic laws that challenge existing international legal norms. Although not yet rising to the level of mass atrocity, US policies on targeted killings carried out by drones, developed over the Bush and Obama administrations, appear to pursue this strategy for contesting long-standing international legal prohibitions on assassination in war.[59]

Another tactic Bellamy describes is the appeal to other norms to legitimate behavior that violates a particular norm. Here, the practice-grounded nature of legal norms is particularly significant, for it means that there is less likely to be disagreement about whether the alternative norms appealed to exist, and only about whether those legal norms actually justify or excuse the behavior engaged in. In the run-up to mass atrocities, states may pass any number of laws stigmatizing particular members of the population, suspending ordinary requirements of due process, and allowing indefinite detention. The mere existence of such laws does not morally justify the policies pursued, but it may make it more difficult for both internal and external actors to conclude that large-scale crimes are underway. This is especially true when such laws employ camouflaged language or euphemisms of the kind discussed in chapter 2.

One of the most disturbing ways in which legal norms help states maintain sufficient legitimacy is when laws are used to compel members of targeted groups to participate in their own expropriation, expulsion, or annihilation. In the case of the Holocaust, German authorities employed this tactic both before the policy of physical destruction began, with laws requiring Jewish business owners to sell their concerns to "Aryan" partners, and, more controversially, after the camps and ghettos had been created, with the use of Jewish Councils to help enforce persecutory regulations within the carceral universe. Jews implicated in this task were subjected to judgments in honor courts immediately after the war, and the topic stirred significant historiographical debate from the late 1960s to the 1990s.[60] The most recent literature has shown that significant debates did occur among Jews within various ghettos about whether their cooperation with the laws and orders of the oppressors would help ameliorate the effects of those policies, even at the cost of lending them apparent legitimacy.[61]

Having discussed various ways in which legal norms help state leaders maintain sufficient legitimacy while engaging in assaults on their own citizens, it remains to say where this function of legal norms fits in the etiology of large-scale crimes. Here we should return to the case-specific escalatory and inhibitory factors that Mayersen discusses. In particular, she describes the expectation of diplomatic sanctions or military intervention by other states as a case-specific inhibitory factor. The legitimizing role of legal norms, insofar as they decrease the chances of such diplomatic or military responses by other states, removes this inhibitory factor. For this reason, it makes sense that some of the changes in legal norms considered here occur well before large-scale crimes, while others occur while those crimes are ongoing or about to conclude.

4.5   Legal Norms and the Denial of Violence

Mass atrocities, I have argued, are sometimes carried out by means of ordinary laws and legal institutions. But many large-scale crimes are conducted extralegally, executed in secret by hired mercenaries or paramilitary forces.[62] In such cases, we may still find that legal norms play an important explanatory role insofar as they provide officials with pretexts for denying atrocities while they are ongoing and after they have occurred. In some ways, this is an extension of state efforts to maintain sufficient legitimacy despite sponsoring mass atrocities. But it seems to me different enough to call for separate treatment.

The crudest way of rejecting reports of genocide or other forms of mass atrocity is to say that they cannot be true because existing laws prohibit such actions. Sociologist Stanley Cohen terms this approach "magical legalism."[63] He illustrates this form of denial using the example of state-sponsored torture. First, Cohen explains, governments invoke domestic laws and international conventions prohibiting torture. Then they offer a "magical syllogism: torture is strictly forbidden in our country; we have ratified the Convention Against Torture; therefore what we are doing cannot be torture."[64] Such appeals to existing laws may sometimes help states engaged in large-scale crimes maintain their legitimacy, but this is a risky strategy. Frequently, international observers will be able to collect and disseminate contrary evidence. Besides, it is now common knowledge that states can pursue mass atrocities despite legal prohibitions. For this reason, we should turn to more sophisticated forms of legal denials of violence.

One form of legal denial consists of the passage of censorship laws and the criminalization of unpatriotic or slanderous forms of expression. This form of denial prevents individuals living both within and outside the bounds of particular societies from gaining accurate information about ongoing atrocities. The German-Jewish diarist Victor Klemperer provides compelling evidence of such censorship under National Socialism during World War II. In his diaries, first published in 1995, he repeatedly registers his fear that letters describing lack of medical care or the rigors of forced labor will result in charges of spreading "atrocity propaganda."[65] The fact that most countries employ censorship of some kind during armed conflicts means that states employing this strategy to conceal large-scale crimes sometimes succeed in maintaining sufficient legitimacy.

A second form of legal denial occurs after large-scale crimes have been committed, but while they remain unacknowledged by a ruling government. The best-known example of this phenomenon comes from contemporary Turkey, where citizens face sanctions under a law prohibiting "denigrating Turkishness" for referring to early twentieth-century attacks on Armenians as genocide.[66] As sociologist Fatma Göçek observes, this post hoc denial of violence has precedents in the history of Ottoman rule in Turkey, as well as in the censorship employed in the wake of previous episodes of mass killing.[67]

A third significant form of legal denial occurs after atrocities have taken place and after officials responsible for ordering or orchestrating crimes have left office. This form of denial consists of amnesty laws that offer immunity for and restrict investigations into past atrocities. Legal philosopher Carlos Santiago Nino describes in detail the so-called self-amnesty law passed by Argentinean president Reynaldo Bignone in September 1983, which not only provided amnesty for individuals who had engaged in "subversive and countersubversive acts" between 1973 and 1982 but also prohibited subpoenas and interrogations of persons likely to be covered by the amnesty.[68] Today this type of transitional settlement, which serves neither the interests of truth nor of justice, has been supplanted by transitional justice arrangements that at least encourage truth telling. Still, it provides an example of a third form of legal denial.

What links these three forms of denial is that each seeks to use laws to eliminate evidence concerning ongoing or historical crimes, thus constraining knowledge about such crimes either domestically or within the international community. At the same time, however, the public nature of the relevant legal norms frequently creates a record of the fact that something is being covered up. For this reason, legal denial appears at least partially self-undermining.

It might be objected that the strategy of legal denial has no place in the model of the etiology of large-scale crimes that I have adopted. How, after all, can laws that prevent discussion or investigation of past crimes belong to the factors that escalate the risk of such crimes? The answer is that the availability of legal means of denial may be something that planners or perpetrators of mass atrocities take into consideration when deliberating over such courses of action. When political leaders have the power to declare states of emergency and possess under such conditions legal rights to engage in censorship, along with the institutional capacity to do so, this can make the decision to engage in attacks on vulnerable populations appear less risky. When state archives have control over official documents, this may convince bureaucrats or military planners that evidence of their role in large-scale crimes is less likely to come to light. In both cases, the prospect of future deniability serves to reduce existing constraints on mass atrocity.

4.6   Legal Norms as Evidence of Mass Atrocities

Legal norms, as we have seen, play a significant role in the etiology of genocide and other kinds of mass atrocities. Their power to preserve legitimacy and impede accountability goes some way toward establishing the place of legal norms in explanatory accounts of large-scale crimes. But there is another way in which legal norms advance such explanations: their special evidential qualities.

Laws generate documents. In open societies, the texts of laws themselves are routinely published in official organs. But the paperwork produced in the codification of laws makes up only part of a much larger accretion of documents. Judicial institutions charged with interpreting laws and providing remedies in case of violations produce piles of materials yearly. So too do administrative agencies tasked with implementing laws and coordinating the enforcement of new statutes alongside existing ones. Much of this documentation continues to be produced even where the laws themselves are kept secret, or where ordinary legislative and judicial functions are taken over by military governors and courts-martial. Such documents provide a valuable stock of evidence for lawyers and historians seeking to explain the progress of large-scale crimes.

In his opening statement to the International Military Tribunal at Nuremberg, American chief prosecutor Robert Jackson assessed the different forms of evidence available for prosecuting perpetrators of Nazi-era crimes. He discounted first-personal accounts from victims of those crimes, telling the court, "We will not ask you to convict these men on the testimony of their foes."[69] Instead, Jackson favored the use of documentary evidence, declaring, "There is no count in the Indictment that cannot be proved by books and records."[70]

Jackson's reference to "books and records" does not place explicit emphasis on the documents generated by laws themselves as sources of evidence about Nazi criminality. But Uğur Üngör and Mehmet Polatel, in their study of "confiscation and destruction" during the Armenian genocide, exploit precisely this phenomenon in order to reconstruct the progress and methods of state-sponsored robbery.[71] "The expropriation of Ottoman Armenians," these authors argue, "was a functionally necessary phase linking persecution to destruction."[72] Through this process, targets of persecution were deprived "not only of their possessions, but also of possibilities for escape, refuge, or resistance."[73] In documenting this process of deprivation, the authors draw in part on the collection of official documents from the period 1915 to 1920 published in the 1980s by the office of Turkey's prime minister with the aim of justifying the wartime policy of the Committee of Union and Progress (CUP) toward the Armenians.[74] But they also rely on the contemporary publication of the early "temporary law" regarding deportation and expropriation in 1915 in the semiofficial newspaper of the CUP, the *Ottoman Gazette*.[75] The publication of laws in government documents and in more widely circulating newspapers reflects the publicity requirement of legality, exacerbated, in this case, by the need for the ruling party to be able to cite a formal basis for confiscations in their dealings with foreign governments and firms that held debt from Armenians.[76] What Üngör and Polatel characterize as the "legalization of pillage" served the short-term aims of a government engaged in forced removal and mass killing. But it also, and ironically, serves the aims of historians and other scholars seeking documentation of the etiology of such crimes.

To be sure, laws and the documents they generate cannot be the sole or complete source of evidence concerning large-scale crimes, since states that engage in such crimes often deploy extralegal tactics at particular stages and since, as I have shown, states often try to conceal or deny the legal basis for destructive policies. But while these considerations suggest that a complete explanation of genocide and mass atrocity cannot be found by focusing solely on legal norms, the argument of this chapter is in fact the reverse: that no complete explanation can deny a central place to such norms. The special evidential value of legal norms, like their distinctive power to marginalize groups, legitimate persecution, and curtail communication, helps prove this claim.

4.7 Extremely Violent Societies: An Alternative Etiology?

Publicly promulgated laws, created in accordance with standing procedural rules, help create social categories, legitimize discriminatory policies, and restrict the spread of knowledge about violent acts. State actors seeking to carry out genocide or other types of mass atrocities typically supplement legal measures with extralegal tactics and secret orders. But the desire of such actors to maintain legitimacy before, during, and after large-scale crimes creates pressure to preserve at least a veneer of legality through the continued use of legal norms. This helps support the main argument of this study, which is that mass atrocities typically reflect the presence, not the absence, of norms.

In response to these claims, some might cite specific instances of large-scale crimes that do not exhibit the legal dynamics already discussed. Others might argue that secret orders and extralegal tactics have played a far greater role than ordinary laws and regulations in most historical cases of genocide and mass atrocity. I will consider such extralegal rules in detail later in this study, when I turn my attention to social norms. For now, I consider a different, and more thoroughgoing, challenge to my account of the explanatory significance of legal norms. This challenge takes the form of an alternative etiology of mass atrocity.

In a 2010 study, historian Christian Gerlach develops a theory of what he calls "extremely violent societies."[77] His aim is to provide an alternative to the "genocide approach" to mass violence.[78] Gerlach's objections to that approach are epistemological. He believes that viewing historical cases of mass violence through the lens of genocide tends to serve political, rather than explanatory, goals. Although his critique is directed at genocide specifically, it extends to some other forms of large-scale crimes, such as ethnic cleansing. Most significant for my purposes, he takes a broadly skeptical view of the action-coordinating function of legal norms in situations of mass violence, denying in particular that the focus on institutional actors encouraged by a study of laws aids our understanding of large-scale crimes.

Drawing on detailed case studies of societal conflicts in Indonesia, Turkey, Greece, and elsewhere, Gerlach argues that four features characterize the violence experienced in those societies. First, "various population groups" are victims of the violence—variously suffering rape, torture, displacement, or murder.[79] Second, "diverse social groups participate," directly or indirectly, in these violent acts.[80] Third, the reasons and motives that individuals and groups have for participating in violence are complex and subject to change over time.[81] Fourth, the origins of violent acts and policies are not limited to high officials but implicate broader segments of society.[82]

This empirically grounded characterization of mass violence departs from the traditional framework of genocide studies in two important ways. First, the concept of genocide, from its inception in the writings of Raphael Lemkin to its current existence in international criminal law, conceives of mass violence as directed at specific social groups. It also assumes that the social identities of those groups help shape the violent intentions of perpetrators.[83] Gerlach departs from this framework by acknowledging a plurality of victim groups and recognizing the complexity of perpetrator motivations.

The second departure from standard analyses of genocide has less to do with the features tracked by this concept and more to do with the presumed reasons for its prominence in contemporary political life. Genocide, according to Gerlach, is "an action-oriented model designed for moral condemnation, prevention, intervention, or punishment."[84] The desire of genocide scholars to make their concept an effective tool for political advocacy "leads to simplification, with a focus on government policies."[85] This focus on government action is exacerbated by the fact that "state operations are better documented" than popular participation in mass violence.[86] Doubtless Gerlach would deem the analysis of legal norms offered in this chapter entirely symptomatic of this last tendency.

Several of the criticisms Gerlach lodges against the conceptual framework of genocide can be extended to other specific types of large-scale crimes. It is true that the concepts of mass killing and mass rape do not inherently make reference to specific social groups or assume unified perpetrator intentions. Nevertheless, a focus on state officials and institutions, grounded in a desire for both political efficacy and thoroughness of evidence, is manifest in much of the historical and social scientific work on such crimes. Put most strongly, Gerlach's critique holds that existing approaches to the study of large-scale crimes privilege political and legal goals over explanatory power. This is what his alternative etiology, which emphasizes cross-cutting social fissures and informal coalitions for violence, is meant to correct.

Three responses to Gerlach's argument are available. The first is to note that my approach in this study aims to accommodate precisely the plurality of actors and interests that Gerlach identifies at the core of large-scale crimes. Not only are moral, legal, and social norms distinguished by their relationship to social practices and standing procedural rules; these differences themselves create differences in the value of each kind of norm for explaining various kinds of individual and institutional actions. Gerlach's claim that much scholarship on genocide (and, by extension, other forms of mass atrocity) focuses unduly on official institutions and actions may apply to my account of legal norms in this chapter, but this is precisely why I have tried in the other chapters of this book to describe pathways for explaining large-scale crimes that are not directly tied to official laws and institutions. Each level of analysis has a part to play in explaining crimes that, by definition, implicate broad swathes of the societies in which they occur.

The second response is to double down on my claims concerning the distinctive features of legal norms that make them particularly relevant to the explanation of genocide and mass atrocity. Social categorization, legitimation of persecution, and denials of violence do sometimes proceed through the devices of unofficial institutions, whose declarations and actions lack the force of law. Julius Streicher's newspaper, *Der Stürmer*, engaged in all of these activities in 1920s Germany before Streicher rose to an official position as Gauleiter (district leader) in Nuremberg in the 1930s. Nevertheless, legal norms can create categories that are enforceable in court, they can legitimate the taking of property without hope of compensation or relief, and they can smother testimony about past or present violence with the cloak of censorship.

My third response to Gerlach is to acknowledge that there is indeed an asymmetry between the legal norms developed in international criminal law for the prosecution of large-scale crimes, on the one hand, and the motivations and identities of individuals and institutions that use domestic laws to plan and perpetrate such crimes, on the other. Not every institution that helps clear the path to genocide, mass rape, or forced relocation does so due to prevailing beliefs in the fundamental inferiority or dangerousness of particular out-groups. Nor are all individual perpetrators of large-scale crimes significantly influenced by changes in laws or institutions. Nevertheless, legal norms, with their distinctive features, are central to understanding the contributions that laws and institutions make to the etiology of mass atrocities.

5 The Limits of Legalization: Legal Norms and the Prevention of Mass Atrocities

In 1902, the English activist Emily Hobhouse published a scathing account of the conduct of British and Boer forces in the South African War.[1] Hobhouse's book, *The Brunt of the War and Where It Fell*, used photographs, eyewitness testimony, and firsthand reporting to recount hardships imposed on Boer women and children by fighters on both sides of this late Victorian conflict.[2] Two tactics struck Hobhouse as especially egregious: the burning of farms belonging to suspected guerrilla fighters and the confinement of families displaced from rural areas in concentration camps.[3]

Hobhouse opened her exposé by reciting several articles from the recent Hague Convention on the Laws and Customs of War on Land.[4] These included Article 47 (prohibiting pillage), Article 45 (prohibiting demands that occupied populations swear oaths of loyalty), and Article 50 (stating that "no general penalty ... can be inflicted on the population, on account of the acts of individuals for which it cannot be regarded as collectively responsible").[5] The implication of the hundreds of pages of documentary and testimonial evidence that followed was that these articles had been violated, not just incidentally, but systematically, during the South African conflict.

The 1899 Hague Convention, along with its 1907 sequel, forms one part of a larger body of law created with the express aim of curbing war's worst excesses. Referred to collectively as international humanitarian law (IHL), this system of customary and treaty-based legal norms grounds prohibitions on torture, maiming, indiscriminate killing, and other illicit tactics during war. During the past six decades, IHL has been supplemented by norms belonging to two other legal traditions: international human rights law (IHRL), originating in the 1948 Universal Declaration of Human Rights, and subsequently extended by various Covenants and court rulings; and international criminal law (ICL), originating in the International Military Tribunal at Nuremberg and subsequently extended by the creation of the International Criminal Court. Taken together, these three bodies of law establish extensive protections for combatants and noncombatants in contexts of war. At the same time, they set limits on the forms of coercion states may legitimately employ within their domestic spheres.

It remains to ask whether the various prescriptions, prohibitions, and permissions set out in these bodies of law succeed in protecting individuals and groups from mass atrocities. Building on the account of legal norms developed in chapter 4, I argue that the distinguishing features of legal norms underpin both their advantages and their disadvantages as instruments for preventing large-scale crimes. My account focuses, once again, on the power of legal norms to guide the decisions and actions of institutional actors. Ultimately, I argue, efforts to render legal protections against atrocities more obligatory and more precise hold promise when it comes to preventing large-scale crimes from occurring in the first place, but such efforts may prove counterproductive in transitional societies, where a key aim is to avoid recurrences of mass atrocities.

The chapter proceeds as follows. Section 5.1 briefly reviews the development of laws and legal institutions in response to twentieth-century mass atrocities. Here I consider such distinct laws and institutions as the Convention on Genocide, the pre–World War II effort to establish prohibitions on aerial bombardment, and the doctrine of individual criminal accountability for mass atrocities set out by the Nuremberg Charter and the Rome Statute of the International Criminal Court. Section 5.2 focuses in on the specific arguments by which scholars and practitioners defend the preventive power of these laws and legal institutions, distinguishing deterrent from expressive arguments. Section 5.3 takes up the idea that legal norms with certain formal features, namely, precision, obligation, and delegation, are best suited for constraining mass atrocities. Drawing on the work of Kenneth Abbott, Tuba Inal, and others, I argue that the technical concept of "legalization," defined as the refinement of existing laws so that they exhibit these three features, sharpens our understanding of the strengths and weaknesses of legal norms as resources for constraining large-scale crimes. At the same time, I suggest that the strategy of legalization runs into difficulties in societies that have recently experienced mass atrocities. Section 5.4 focuses directly on these transitional societies, discussing the special problems that dominate their politics. Because of breakdowns in obligation, precision, and delegation in law that coincide with political transitions, legalization must often be put on hold in such contexts. Nevertheless, I conclude the chapter by arguing that the international community should continue developing precise and obligatory laws, along with institutions for enforcing them, in response to the challenge of mass atrocity.

5.1 Laws, Institutions, and Liability for Atrocities

Three trends define domestic and international legal responses to twentieth-century mass atrocities. First is the proliferation of laws prescribing or prohibiting particular modes of conduct by state and nonstate actors. Second is the development of institutions tasked with codifying, interpreting, and enforcing these laws. Third is the entrenchment of the doctrine of individual criminal liability for violations of these laws. Taken together, these developments have helped generate a legal framework that places the security of persons and peoples, rather than the security of states, at the center of international affairs.[6]

The Proliferation of Laws

During the early 1900s, new technologies like the submarine, the airplane, and poisonous and asphyxiating gases became widely available for military use. The laws of land warfare proposed in the 1899 and 1907 Hague Conventions did not effectively address these developing technologies; consequently, those laws failed to limit the deployment of gas, submarines, and aerial bombers during World War I.[7] In the interwar period, fresh efforts were made to place legal constraints on these novel technologies. A treaty drawn up at the 1930 London Naval Conference required submarines to follow the customary laws of war applied to surface vessels.[8] Earlier international conferences in Washington and Geneva resulted in the Protocol for the Prohibition of the Use in War of Asphyxiating, Poisonous or Other Gases and of Bacteriological Methods of Warfare.[9] And in 1923, jurists from six nations met at the Hague to draft comprehensive Rules of Aerial Warfare, intended for acceptance by all Great Powers.[10]

Legal restrictions on the use of specific tactics or technologies in war aim to reduce harms suffered by soldiers or civilians once fighting is underway. A different legal approach to atrocity prevention consists of curtailing policies that marginalize particular populations in peacetime. This tactic is represented at the domestic level by laws passed in Rwanda following the genocide in that country, whereby racial identities rooted in colonial administration cannot legally be evoked in political discourse.[11] At the international level, many of the prescriptions laid out in the UN's 1966 Covenant on Civil and Political Rights aim to prevent the marginalization of groups within particular countries, for example, by ensuring freedom of religion and conscience for citizens.[12] Finally, in Europe, many nations prohibit public espousal of specific prejudicial views, such as views historically tied to National Socialism.[13]

When efforts to prevent states from pursuing genocide, mass killing, or forced removal fail, a final legal safeguard lies in the protections offered to individuals and groups fleeing such attacks. The major development in this area over the past century is the creation of binding legal norms meant to safeguard refugees from persecution in their countries of asylum, as well as from removal (*refoulement*) to countries where they face serious risks.[14] Even in the nineteenth century, bilateral treaties between specific states created legal protections for some asylum seekers, but in the twentieth century, multilateral agreements were negotiated, first at the League of Nations and later, after the failure of those agreements during World War II, at the United Nations.[15] These agreements universalized the rule of nonrefoulement, along with other legal norms relating to refugees.[16] Although serious controversy surrounds current treatment of asylum seekers by countries as widely dispersed as Hungary, Israel, the United States, and Australia, all of these states maintain laws requiring some form of legal process for asylum claims.

The Development of Institutions

Laws are not likely to inhibit mass atrocities unless they are coupled with institutions capable of codifying, interpreting, and enforcing them. This reflects the practice-grounded nature of legal norms. Unlike moral norms, which retain a claim to guide the actions of individuals even under conditions of widespread noncompliance, legal norms lose their claim to guide action when they are not generally followed within relevant populations.[17] Legal institutions are, accordingly, integral to what philosopher Christopher Kutz calls "the social reality of norms." Such institutions are key sources of legal norms; at the same time, they furnish forums for the "labelling, (dis)approbation, and punishment" of violations.[18]

In the 1930s, Raphael Lemkin drafted his first proposal for an international legal prohibition on efforts by states to destroy specific groups.[19] In the 1940s, living as a refugee in the United States, Lemkin published a book introducing the concept of genocide and called for the creation of an international agency capable of monitoring wartime occupation policies.[20] In the last years of that decade, Lemkin lobbied steadily in favor of the UN Convention on the Prevention and Punishment of the Crime of Genocide, which finally came into force in 1951.[21]

The history of the Genocide Convention reveals contributions by several kinds of legal institutions. Lemkin's earliest proposals for prohibitions on "barbarism" and "vandalism" were prepared for an academic symposium on the unification of penal law.[22] His call for an international monitoring agency in his 1944 book was conceived as a continuation of the laws of occupation drawn up at the Hague Conferences.[23] Since the adoption of the Genocide Convention by the UN General Assembly, three-fourths of the world's states have acceded to this treaty, and genocide has been included in the charge sheets of the International Criminal Tribunal for the former Yugoslavia (ICTY), the International Criminal Tribunal for Rwanda (ICTR), and the International Criminal Court (ICC). Finally, in 2004, the UN secretary general hired a special adviser on the prevention of genocide.

Other laws aimed at constraining mass atrocities exhibit similar institutional trajectories. During the 1920s and 1930s, the first major international organizations devoted to upholding legal protections for refugees were formed.[24] After the clear failure of these institutions before and during World War II, an international Convention on Refugees was adopted at the United Nations, and an independent agency, the United Nations High Commission for Refugees, was created with the power to monitor and respond to crises.[25] As in the case of the Genocide Convention, negotiations over the precise definition and prescribed treatment of refugees in international law remain contentious, and the application of swift and serious sanctions for violations is hardly guaranteed.

I have emphasized the development of international institutions as a major element of twentieth-century legal responses to mass atrocities. I do not wish to depict this project as a fait accompli. Genocides have occurred and refugee crises have developed even after the rise of the institutions I have discussed. International awareness of these events is partly a product of these institutions—especially those tasked with monitoring compliance with relevant legal norms. But legal institutions, like the laws they administer, provide no panacea against large-scale crimes. I consider some of the specific arguments for and against the preventive power of these laws and institutions in subsequent sections of this chapter. First, I discuss a third major legal innovation, which concerns individual accountability for large-scale crimes.

The Emergence of Individual Criminal Liability

States have long asserted the right to prosecute their own citizens and soldiers for infractions of the laws of war. In Civil War–era America, political scientist Francis Lieber included in his "Instructions for the Government of Armies of the United States in the Field" a discussion of the procedures for trying soldiers charged with violating statutes or the customary laws of war.[26] During the South African War, British military authorities used a special tribunal to try one soldier accused of unlawfully shooting a Boer civilian at the command of his superior officer.[27] And in Cold War–era West Germany, trials of Holocaust perpetrators commonly relied on ordinary German penal law, their verdicts reflecting the basic elements and assumptions of that code.[28]

International criminal trials for individual participants in mass atrocities are of more recent vintage. They reflect a claim of authority by the international community at large, rather than by any single state, to bring criminal charges against men and women implicated in mass killings, mass rapes, or other large-scale crimes. This claim of authority was first decisively advanced at the military tribunals convened in Nuremberg and Tokyo after World War II. In the former trial, American prosecutor Robert Jackson went to considerable lengths to defend the legitimacy of the prosecutions of high Nazi officials while admitting the "novel and experimental" nature of the tribunal.[29]

Two key categories of actors appear as defendants in international criminal trials. In the first category are soldiers and junior officers, paramilitary fighters and commanders, and ordinary citizens who stand on the "shooting end" of atrocities. In the second category are heads of state, government ministers, and other high-level planners of large-scale crimes. Prosecuting individuals belonging to each of these categories has required overcoming certain traditional legal defenses, as I shall explain.

International law grants two types of immunity to heads of state and other high officials. The immunity that they enjoy from prosecution in the domestic courts of other states while they remain in office is called immunity *ratione personae*. The immunity that they enjoy from prosecution once out of office for actions previously taken amid their official functions is called immunity *ratione materiae*.[30] Though differing in application, these two forms of immunity share similar rationales. Both reflect the idea of the sovereign equality of states, as well as the shared interest all states have in the orderly conduct of international relations.[31]

The traditional immunity of heads of state from prosecution for crimes committed while in office generated one of the great controversies surrounding the peace settlement that ended World War I. Article 227 of the Treaty of Versailles called for the creation of a special tribunal to try Germany's Kaiser Wilhelm II—at this time abdicated and living in the Netherlands—for "a supreme offence against international morality and the sanctity of treaties."[32] This provision, never carried out, was controversial because the offenses it listed were not included in the contents of any specific international convention.[33] It was even more controversial because it appeared to overturn the doctrine of sovereign immunity.[34]

Since Versailles, a significant shift has occurred in international jurisprudence with respect to this doctrine. Described variously as a "justice cascade" or as the "end of impunity," this shift represents both a modification of laws and a change in institutions.[35] The legal recognition of international crimes like genocide, combined with the creation of institutions like the ICC charged with investigating and prosecuting such crimes, has undermined the assumption that state leaders will not face legal justice for violating the rights of their citizens or of other groups within their control. At the same time, domestic courts and tribunals in countries afflicted by severe social upheaval have proven increasingly capable of holding past political leaders legally accountable. Though it is not yet clear how far this shift in laws and legal institutions may go, many scholars consider the real possibility of legal consequences for state leaders implicated in mass atrocities to supply an important constraint on large-scale crimes.[36]

An equally important development, and one slightly preceding the legal changes noted, is the decline of the "superior orders" defense for ordinary soldiers accused of atrocities. According to the strongest formulation of this defense, ordinary soldiers are not to be held legally responsible for committing crimes in war when ordered to do so by their commanders, save in cases where those orders are manifestly unjust. Importantly, the superior orders defense is distinct from the defense of duress, under which an individual claims a reasonable fear of injury or death consequent on refusal to follow orders.[37] At Nuremberg, superior orders was formally rejected as an acceptable defense for soldiers accused of war crimes, though a defense of duress could in principle still be made.[38] The undermining of this defense in cases of major international crimes such as crimes against humanity appears to offer a further constraint on mass atrocity.[39]

At this point, it might be objected that whereas I previously characterized legal norms as applying mainly to institutions, the rise of individual criminal responsibility for mass atrocities points in the opposite direction. This objection is misplaced. Both the end of impunity for heads of state and the decline of superior orders as a defense for ordinary soldiers represent substantial institutional changes. The laws of armed conflict circulating at the start of the twentieth century already contained provisions for the adjudication and punishment of individuals who were not members of any particular army but nevertheless took up weapons in defense of their nation or in revolt against an occupier. The shifts in laws, institutions, and forms of liability I have outlined are not aimed at such lone individuals, but at fighters embedded in armies or recognized rebel groups, in state ministries or civil service apparatuses, or at the very apex of states. Implicit in each of these changes in laws is the belief that mass atrocities are closely bound up with such institutions and not, as is sometimes argued, products of their weakness or absence.[40]

In this section, I have surveyed major changes in international laws, institutions, and forms of liability taken in response to twentieth-century mass atrocities. Although I have registered the hope prevailing among legal scholars, diplomats, and norm entrepreneurs that these changes will contribute to the prevention of mass atrocities, I have not yet stated explicitly how such preventive effects might work. The next section addresses this issue.

5.2   Legal Norms and the Prevention of Large-Scale Crimes

The laws and institutions I have surveyed are in many cases too novel to permit robust empirical investigation of their power to prevent large-scale crimes.[41] In the case of specific international crimes, particularly genocide, this problem is exacerbated by the comparative rareness of acts of attempted group destruction, along with the basic logical difficulty of proving a negative.[42] It remains important to identify the specific mechanisms by which these legal norms are supposed to constrain mass atrocities.

In a 2016 book, *Reconstructing Atrocity Prevention*, Sheri Rosenberg, Tibi Galis, Alex Zucker, and other contributors distinguish two particular pathways by which legal norms might discourage planners and perpetrators of large-scale crimes from carrying out assaults.[43] One is that the risk of investigations, trials, and prison sentences handed down by legal institutions like the ICC might serve to deter these agents before, or even during, mass atrocities. The other is that the expressive effects of international laws and institutions—that is, their power to project and alter extralegal norms, values, and ideals—might defuse tensions in divided societies and in this way make large-scale crimes less likely.

The deterrent effects of laws and legal institutions may be either specific or general. In the first case, the prospect of civil or criminal penalties is communicated to specific individuals or groups—for example, through the announcement of an investigation by the ICC or the deployment of monitoring teams from the United Nations. In the second case, publicizing those potential penalties to broad audiences and actually imposing them on a few individuals or groups may serve to discourage a wider set of actors from pursuing comparable courses of action in the future.

For either specific or general deterrence to succeed, scholars generally agree that laws and legal institutions must possess certain qualitative features. In particular, civil or criminal penalties for violations of relevant legal norms must be swift, certain, and severe.[44] These features should not be construed as sufficient conditions for successful legal deterrence, since empirical research on the deterrent effects of criminal laws remains inconclusive.[45] Even considered merely as regulative ideals, however, it is clear that current international laws and institutions fall short. Punishments for planners or perpetrators of large-scale crimes remain far from certain and far from swift, even if they are sometimes severe.

Given the difficulty of assessing the deterrent effects of current legal responses to mass atrocity, some scholars of atrocity prevention have focused instead on the expressive functions of these laws and legal institutions. Sheri Rosenberg contends that contexts of mass atrocity are characterized by social norms that prescribe, rather than prohibit, killing, maiming, or displacing members of perceived "enemy" groups.[46] In such contexts, she argues, "where social norms have been turned upside down," the main value of laws and legal institutions may be to "shif[t] social norms and meanings" over the medium term rather than deterring atrocities contemplated or underway.[47]

Rosenberg's analysis directs our attention to the relationship between the legal and social norms circulating within and across particular populations. It also highlights the idea of multiple timescales for atrocity prevention efforts. We need not accept, without further analysis, her claim that large-scale crimes are generally accompanied by inversions of social norms—a claim that implies quite particular shifts in the practical commitments and normative attitudes of perpetrators and witnesses of atrocities. But we should pause to note two different ways in which legal norms can influence social norms. In the first case, which Rosenberg emphasizes, legal norms at the international level can over time create new profiles of normative beliefs and attitudes within particular populations and may motivate practices, such as informal social sanctions, of the sort that ground social norms. In the second case, legal norms may actually cause the erosion of social norms by calling attention to relevant social relationships and thereby revealing that practices of mutual respect, fair and equal treatment, or peaceful resolution of conflicts do not actually exist.

Turning to the multiple timescales of prevention, we may distinguish between short-term, medium-term, and long-term prevention strategies. The specific deterrent effects of legal norms, so far as they exist, reflect a form of short-term prevention, as do other strategies (such as direct moral suasion, humanitarian intervention, or power-sharing negotiations) that seek to prevent particular individuals or groups from picking up their weapons and actually using them. Long-term prevention strategies, by contrast, seek to change the political and economic conditions that heighten the risk of atrocities, even where none are actually underway. Such strategies include efforts to reconcile rival religious ideologies within divided populations, as well as attempts to create diversified and thriving economies in order to stave off conflicts.[48] Like James Waller's distinction between upstream, midstream, and downstream prevention strategies, Rosenberg's distinction between short-term, medium-term, and long-term prevention strategies enhances our understanding of the general notion of atrocity prevention while also providing insights into the contributions existing legal norms aim to make to this goal.

5.3   Legalization: The Best Path to Prevention?

Whatever their deterrent, expressive, or other preventive effects, existing international laws and legal institutions clearly have not succeeded in eliminating large-scale crimes. This is evident from ongoing reports of mass killing, mass rape, and forced displacement of civilians in Syria, Iraq, Yemen, and elsewhere. Of course, we should not conclude that existing legal norms have exerted no influence on these mass atrocities. Planners and commanders of ground raids, bombing campaigns, and kidnappings often seem to be minimally guided by relevant legal norms, insofar as they disclaim responsibility for particularly well-publicized attacks or smear victims of those attacks as suspected fighters. It is even possible that laws like the Convention on Genocide and institutions like the UN Security Council have helped prevent attempts by state or nonstate actors to destroy groups in Libya, Sudan, and elsewhere. But the evidence for success in genocide prevention remains disputed, and the adequacy of existing laws and legal institutions remains in doubt.[49]

Rather than focusing on the mere existence of laws prohibiting or prescribing certain actions in armed conflict or domestic governance, an emerging scholarly literature draws attention to the formal properties of legal norms that enable them to constrain the actions of institutional actors in particular circumstances. This approach has been adopted by some scholars of legal means of atrocity prevention, who argue that the "legalization" of existing international laws and institutions represents a critical step toward making those laws and institutions effective in constraining large-scale crimes. In this section, I analyze this argument, first explaining the (rather counterintuitive) meaning of legalization and then assessing whether this process reliably enhances the power of laws to prevent large-scale crimes.

The technical term *legalization* should not be confused with the familiar notion of rendering some activity, behavior, or possession legal. The word refers instead, in this case, to the reform of existing laws or bodies of law so that they display three formal features: obligation, precision, and delegation.[50] As examples of international laws and institutions characterized by high levels of obligation, precision, and delegation, the originators of this technical term point to the European Human Rights Convention and the International Criminal Court, each of which explicitly defines various forms of prohibited conduct by state actors and involves standing bodies for interpreting relevant laws and punishing violations.[51] As examples of legal arrangements with high levels of delegation but low precision and low obligation, these scholars cite the World Bank and the International Monetary Fund.[52]

The technical notion of legalization was not originally conceived as a measure of the efficiency of domestic or international laws and legal institutions.[53] Subsequent commentators have, however, argued that initiatives aimed at increasing the precision, obligation, and delegation of relevant international laws can play an important part in reducing institutional tolerance for large-scale crimes. Political scientist Tuba Inal makes a particularly forceful case for the value of legalization in solidifying legal constraints on the specific large-scale crime of wartime rape. Inal's 2013 study, *Looting and Rape in Wartime*, traces the rise of international criminal prohibitions on this particular form of mass atrocity.[54] It thus helps to illustrate my claims about the distinguishing features of legal norms and shows how those features give legal norms a clear part to play in the prevention of large-scale crimes.

The basic question Inal addresses is why so many years elapsed between passage of the first binding legal prohibitions on wartime looting, on the one hand, and passage of comparably strict prohibitions on wartime rape, on the other. She locates the first binding international legal prohibitions on looting in the Hague Conventions of 1899 and 1907; she locates the first strict prohibition on wartime rape in the 1998 Rome Statute of the International Criminal Court.[55] Inal's explanation of this gap can be reduced to two related claims. First, she finds that the increased involvement of women in official rulemaking delegations and summits was strongly correlated with increasing precision, delegation, and obligation in domestic and international laws targeting wartime rape.[56] Second, she suggests that military commanders and civilian leaders first had to shed a longstanding belief that acts of rape in wartime were inevitable, and therefore not susceptible to constraint by legal prohibitions or any other institutional interventions.[57]

Because Inal believes these changes occurred in stages, she frames her account of legalization around a few key moments of international lawmaking. At the Hague Conferences, themselves informed by earlier diplomatic meetings, rape was not explicitly discussed, though an imprecise, nonprohibitory call for states to respect "family honors and rights" was adopted.[58]

After the shocks of World Wars I and II, the 1949 Geneva Conventions stipulated in Article 27 that "women shall be specially protected against any attacks on their honor, in particular against rape, enforced prostitution and any form of indecent assault."[59] While this norm is more precise than its Hague predecessor, Inal claims it failed to establish a legally binding obligation on the part of states to prevent rape by members of their armed forces.[60] Finally, in the 1998 Rome Statute, Inal finds that Article 8 precisely defined rape as a war crime, clearly obliged states to take responsibility for preventing acts of rape by their troops, and delegated prosecutorial authority to the ICC in cases of violations.[61]

Inal's analysis of the processes producing greater legalization of international responses to wartime rape tracks the two key features of legal norms that I have identified. First, Inal's analysis emphasizes the practice-grounded character of legal norms—that is, their dependence on real or perceived social practices. The long delay in the international adoption of strict legal prohibitions on wartime rape was driven by the received view that "rape in war was normal because it was a combination of two normal things: aggression (normal in war) and sexuality."[62] Although this perception by itself might not rule out efforts at legal regulation, Inal goes on to state that "the fact that rape was thought to be inevitable because of the biological nature of men and women made it virtually impossible, in the eyes of the states, to prevent it, especially in war."[63] This observation reinforces my claim that legal norms are practice grounded insofar as it suggests that lawmakers are not eager to pass prohibitions that they do not believe will actually influence the behaviors they wish to regulate.

Turning to the second distinguishing feature of legal norms—the presence of standing procedural rules governing their emergence, modification, or elimination—we also see the influence of this feature in Inal's account. Her historical narrative consistently calls attention to the procedures for drafting new laws, updating or replacing old laws, and seeking formal ratification from states. What is interesting is that we also discover parallel changes in the moral and social norms accepted by relevant populations participating in those legal negotiations. As Inal reports, the relationship between changes in those extralegal norms and changes in legal norms is complex, with social or moral norms surrounding rape sometimes more, sometimes less strictly prohibitive than law. Finally, while we might wish that moral strictures against rape would suffice to turn soldiers against such conduct, Inal suggests there is an independent value to precise, obligatory legal norms in preventing episodes of mass rape. She writes, "Soldiers on the ground need additional incentives to comply with the laws of war to which their governments have committed."[64] The chief additional incentive she lists is the realistic chance of facing individual criminal prosecution for acts of rape in wartime. This reflects an overall perspective in which the preventive potential of legalization is attributed chiefly to the greater deterrent effects of laws that are precise, obligatory, and delegated.

The legalization of international laws and institutions holds great potential for strengthening their power to constrain large-scale crimes. Nevertheless, serious objections have been raised against efforts at legalization in this context. I consider three such objections here. The first reflects assumptions about the ways in which states seek to erode or undermine legal norms in order to pursue their perceived interests. The second starts from claims about the changed nature of warfare in the twenty-first century. The third objection centers on observations about the fragility of law in societies recovering from mass atrocities.

Skeptics of legalization sometimes claim that legal norms, however precise, obligatory, or delegated, cannot be expected to restrain the conduct of state actors and institutions where they run counter to substantial interests—and that making laws more precise or strictly obligatory will only call attention to this fact. The classic statement of this objection is the claim, made by German Chancellor Bethmann Hollweg in the early days of World War I, that an international treaty becomes nothing more than "a scrap of paper" under the pressure of military necessity.[65] Modern states rarely express quite so explicit a contempt for the bedrock legal principle *pacta sunt servanda* (treaties are to be honored). But deliberate efforts to evade or erode legal norms are readily detected in the activity of modern states—for example, in efforts to avoid entering into binding treaties related to the use of particular tactics or technologies or in attempts to evade accepted restrictions through tortuous distinctions and tendentious arguments. These and other strategies of the sort discussed in chapter 4 are often cited as support for a realist approach to international relations—one that holds that it is not (or is not directly) legal or moral considerations, but rather leaders' assessments of their own interests, that drive international relations and domestic conflicts.[66]

Advocates of legalization often respond to such arguments by claiming that maneuvers by state actors and institutions to evade or avoid acceptance of legal norms simply confirm the action-guiding power of those norms. Otherwise, they contend, these actors would not go out of their way to reject or deflect norm-based criticisms. This may be true with respect to legal norms generally, but is it true of processes of legalization specifically? Here I think we have reason to be more circumspect due to a potential contradiction arising from the two distinguishing features of legal norms. Briefly put, these two features create the possibility for situations in which particular laws or whole legal regimes remain officially in force (having never been eliminated in the manner prescribed by relevant procedural rules), but where the perception of their grounding in relevant practices cannot be sustained due to routine breaches or blatant violations by domestic or international institutions. This reflects a failure of congruence between laws and institutional conduct, to use Lon Fuller's terminology.[67] The worry is that, especially in cases of thoroughgoing legalization, where laws are spelled out precisely and made obligatory, discrepancies between institutional action and enacted laws will be harder to overlook, and the commitments and attitudes that support legal norms will erode more rapidly.[68]

In the final section of this chapter, I argue that there are good reasons to suspend some measures of legalization in societies that are trying to rebuild fragile institutions following mass atrocities. But in the case of most domestic and international legal institutions, I think that this objection to legalization fails. After all, the record of the twentieth century shows that state leaders are likely to seek creative interpretations of law, or to avoid being bound by restrictions, even when those laws are quite vague or simply advisory. This suggests that legalization by itself does not increase leaders' incentives to evade legal norms. Furthermore, as political scientists Phil Orchard and Richard Price have argued, certain legal regimes, such as those relating to refugee protection or chemical weapons prohibitions, have proved of great value in protecting vulnerable populations despite efforts within some states to evade or avoid their strictures.[69] For these reasons, I think the "realist" challenge to legalization fails.

A second objection to legalization starts from a different direction. This objection holds that the kinds of interstate conflicts that international humanitarian law, in particular, was designed to restrain have been largely superseded by new forms of armed conflict, making many existing legal prescriptions and prohibitions obsolete. Legal scholar Sarah Sewall argues that the decreasing role of traditional state actors in armed conflicts, combined with decreased interest, among developing nations, in enforcing humanitarian norms, means that "increasing the standards of positive law may not be the most effective route toward enhancing civilian protections."[70] Instead of seeking to make international humanitarian law prescriptions and prohibitions more obligatory and more precise, Sewall suggests that atrocity prevention efforts should focus on extralegal norms, such as the informal norm of seeking to minimize civilian casualties in military operations, even where those casualties are legally permitted or excused.[71]

Sewall's argument raises two distinct questions. The first is whether, under the pressure of changing empirical realities, states and international organizations should pull back from long-standing efforts to render humanitarian legal protections more precise, more obligatory, and more completely delegated. The second question is how far informal social norms are needed to support the power of laws and legal regimes to prevent mass atrocities. I will say more about the second question in the final two chapters of this book. With respect to the first question, I believe Sewall overstates the case for refraining from legalization as a strategy for atrocity prevention. Political scientist Hyeran Jo has shown that nonstate rebel groups often express considerable interest in complying with humanitarian prescriptions and prohibitions, seeing this as a key means of achieving legitimacy on the international stage.[72] Furthermore, as I noted at the start of this chapter, a focus on international humanitarian law as the primary source of international legal efforts to prevent atrocities is too narrow, since international human rights law and international criminal law have also become substantially more precise, obligatory, and delegated in recent decades. Finally, while there was a clear shift from international armed conflicts (IACs) to noninternational armed conflicts (NIACs) over the second half of the twentieth century, state institutions and international organizations frequently do end up entangled in those conflicts—meaning that legal norms directed primarily at such institutions are far from obsolete. For these reasons, I do not think Sewall's objections to legalization are decisive.

A third objection to the strategy of legalization as a means of atrocity prevention is narrower than the first two. It does not deny the value of legalization across domestic and international affairs generally, but argues that this strategy may backfire in countries emerging from episodes of severe political turmoil. In such situations, what I have called the practice-grounded character of legal norms is weak or absent, faith in existing legal institutions is low, and the application of existing legal norms is likely to spur strong resistance. Broadly, these are the conditions highlighted by scholars of transitional justice, who are just as concerned with preventing future atrocities as are advocates of legalization but argue that a temporary suspension of the precision, obligatoriness, and delegation of specific laws may be necessary to achieve that goal.

I am inclined to accept these claims about the distinctive character of transitional societies, and the need for transitional exceptions to legalization. But I believe it is important to spell out, as clearly as possible, the conditions under which such limits to legalization apply. In the next section, I analyze those conditions and show how far the demands of transitional justice cut against the strategy of legalization pursued by promoters of mass atrocity prevention.

5.4   Transitional Justice as Suspended Legalization

Legal norms and institutions are not intrinsically hostile to mass atrocities. Legal norms may be employed, as we saw in chapter 4, to marginalize minorities, legitimate their persecution, and conceal evidence of atrocities after they have ended. Legal institutions—such as courts, prosecutors, and law enforcement agencies—may be implicated in each of these different phases of large-scale crimes. The aim of recent investigations of transitional justice is to explain what changes in laws and legal institutions best serve the needs of societies recovering from war and mass atrocities.

Two particular needs appear most urgent in such contexts. The first is the need to restore social and political stability, thereby discouraging recurrences of mass killings, assaults, or displacements. The second is the need to pursue accountability for individuals and groups implicated in such crimes. Scholars have introduced several conceptual distinctions in their efforts to assess the compatibility of these aims. They have contrasted the prospective goal of social stabilization with the retrospective focus of campaigns for accountability.[73] They have suggested that an emphasis on punishment may run contrary to efforts at reconciliation.[74] Above all, they have debated the extent to which principles of "transitional justice" overlap with principles of justice applicable in "ordinary" times.[75]

I have no wish to add a new dualism—between legalized and nonlegalized interventions in laws and legal institutions—to the transitional justice literature.[76] Rather, I want to explain why each specific aspect of legalization—obligation, precision, and delegation—may need to be suspended in transitional contexts. In order to do so, it is necessary first to give an account of the general social and political features that characterize those contexts and then review specific changes to laws or legal institutions that have been undertaken in particular societies after mass atrocities.

The Circumstances of Transitional Justice

What features define life in transitional societies? Legal scholar Mark Drumbl argues that these societies are characterized by recent experiences of widespread deviance, which strain ordinary legal mechanisms for accountability.[77] Ruti Teitel and Christine Bell suggest that such societies are marked out by the delicate negotiations and compromises required for successful peace settlements.[78] Other scholars insist that nothing distinguishes transitional societies from so-called stable or peaceful or ordinary societies—adding that no distinct principles of transitional justice exist either.[79]

In her 2017 book, *Conceptual Foundations of Transitional Justice*, philosopher Colleen Murphy provides a novel account of the core features of transitional societies, one that is more capacious than studies focused on mass deviance and more constructive than the views of transitional justice skeptics. Murphy identifies four "circumstances of transitional justice" that are "widely recognized as characteristic of paradigm transitional societies":[80]

1. Pervasive structural inequality
2. Normalized collective and political wrongdoing
3. Serious existential uncertainty
4. Fundamental uncertainty about authority

Each of these circumstances sets transitional societies apart from what Murphy calls "reasonably just, stable democracies."[81] Taken together, these four circumstances have important implications for what justice can demand, or legal institutions achieve, in societies recovering from mass atrocities.

While Murphy's focus falls on the "moral salience of these features" of transitional societies, my interest is different.[82] I consider the implications of these circumstances for movements toward, or away from, precision, obligation, and delegation in the laws and legal institutions of societies that have experienced large-scale crimes. My basic argument is that these four circumstances create substantial pressure to suspend, or even reverse, processes of legalization within the domestic legal institutions of transitional societies. At the same time, the circumstances of transitional justice provide international institutions with good reasons to pursue greater legalization at the level of international law. In the long run, such developments may reduce the inequalities and uncertainties that currently define transitional societies.

The inequalities that constitute Murphy's first circumstance of transitional societies include economic and social disadvantages, as well as formal and informal modes of exclusion. Inequalities are "pervasive," according to Murphy's view, when they exist both within particular institutions—such as courts, schools, or professions—and across all or most institutions integral to social life.[83] When such inequalities are formally enshrined in law, as in the antebellum United States or in East and West Germany on the eve of reunification, transitional justice initiatives may require rejecting the precise terms of particular laws. Thus, in the early 1990s, several former East German border guards were tried for shooting attempted border crossers, despite the fact that their conduct was permitted under relevant East German laws and that the legal terms of reunification specified that only actions criminalized in the codes of both East and West Germany would be actionable in the newly united Germany.[84]

If the inequalities characterizing transitional societies put pressure on the precision of legal norms, the obligatory character of law faces still greater pressure from the circumstance of normalized collective and political wrongdoing. In describing this second circumstance of transitional societies, Murphy makes clear that she understands "normalized" in the statistical, rather than the normative, sense; that is, she means that wrongdoing is statistically widespread, whether or not relevant beliefs and attitudes about the permissibility of killing, torture, or other atrocities have changed.[85] This statistical sense of normalized wrongdoing challenges the obligatory character of legal norms on two fronts. First, by undermining the perception of practice groundedness for laws against killing, maiming, rape, and theft, widespread violations erode the action-guiding power of these legal norms from within the practical point of view.[86] Second, widespread violations create considerable logistical difficulties for courts and tribunals charged with holding lawbreakers accountable, producing pressure to either relax legal requirements of due process or pursue extralegal forms of accountability.

The pressure directed at the obligatory character of law and legal institutions is increased if we turn to the third circumstance of transitional justice: the fact of serious existential uncertainty. This is the characteristic of transitional societies that centers most directly on the threat of recurrences of large-scale crimes, reflecting "a real risk that peace will not stick and violence will return."[87] In the face of this risk, even highly credible reformers elected to high government positions after atrocities may be forced to endorse amnesties for planners or perpetrators of large-scale crimes, despite the obligations created in law to hold such individuals and groups accountable. A parallel retreat from obligation occurs when such policies depend on discretionary judgments from elected leaders rather than on formal processes governed by independent institutions.

Finally, the fourth circumstance of transitional justice, the fundamental uncertainty about authority prevailing in such contexts, disrupts the delegation of law-making, law-enforcing, and law-interpreting functions. Murphy describes two kinds of uncertainty here: uncertainty about whether existing leaders and institutions are too compromised to carry out their legal functions, and uncertainty about which among a range of new or temporary institutions has the authority to create, modify, or eliminate legal norms.[88] Insofar as delegation implies the existence of clear hierarchies and coordination among legal institutions, transitional societies seem to be characterized by a drift away from, rather than toward, legalization.

We can perceive the threat to delegation in transitional societies most clearly if we consider the suspicions that courts and judges have historically come under for failing to apply laws and preserve the integrity of legal institutions during large-scale crimes. South African legal scholar David Dyzenhaus has eloquently described the failures of judges in that country to uphold legal protections for black South Africans during the apartheid era, and has criticized the refusal of judges to appear in the "Justice Session" of that country's Truth and Reconciliation process.[89] Hakeem Yusuf has assessed the appropriateness of truth commissions as vehicles for judicial accountability in transitional societies and condemned the exclusion of the Nigerian judiciary from the inquiries into human rights abuses conducted by that country's Oputa Panel on human rights violations in the early 2000s.[90] And Lisa Hilbink has argued that specific institutional features of the Chilean judiciary left judges in that country poorly equipped to resist antidemocratic actions and large-scale abuses carried out by the government of Augusto Pinochet.[91]

The departures from legalization demanded by the circumstances of transitional justice are paradoxical when we consider that international organizations and foreign governments typically focus their efforts on shoring up laws and strengthening legal institutions during transitional periods. International lawyers fly in to countries emerging from upheaval in order to write new constitutions that enshrine precise, obligatory protections for citizens.[92] Members of the judiciary, whether newly appointed or renewed, are invited to attend training seminars on rules of evidence and requirements of due process.[93] In a few cases, the United Nations has itself temporarily taken up the duties of administration in transitional societies (specifically, in Kosovo and East Timor in the late 1990s).[94] In the course of such efforts at "promoting the rule of law abroad," international agencies and activists committed to legalization often find that the inequalities, uncertainties, and inherent instability of transitional societies require relaxing the precision, obligation, and delegation of both preexisting and newly created legal norms.[95]

Legal Institutions and the Mitigation of Structural Inequalities

The distinctive circumstances of transitional societies, as we have seen, put pressure on the precision, obligation, and delegation of laws, leading to temporary suspensions of legalization. In light of this, it might seem that simultaneous efforts to legalize international laws and legal institutions must be misjudged. But this need not be the case, for there are forms of legalization that could, if adopted, mitigate one or more of Murphy's circumstances of transitional justice. Consider the first circumstance, that of "pervasive structural inequalities." The challenge of redressing such inequalities, and of securing both formal and informal protections for human rights and economic freedoms within transitional societies, is certainly serious in the immediate aftermath of large-scale crimes. Internal or external conflicts may have drained state coffers, while employers in the regions hit hardest by violence may have ceased operating. In many cases, wars and mass atrocities magnify existing social inequalities. Emily Hobhouse made just this point in the wake of the South African War, which overturned the agrarian economies of the two defeated Boer republics and left young Boer women, in particular, without good economic prospects. Such inequalities would likely be exacerbated, Hobhouse argued, by the failure of the British government to release sufficient funds for rebuilding the local economies—allocating 3 million pounds sterling for the purpose, where 50 million pounds sterling were required.[96]

But what if an international institution existed with the specific mission of distributing resources needed for rebuilding transitional societies? Philosopher Larry May has recently proposed such an institution, in the form of "a worldwide no-fault insurance scheme for paying the restitution and reparation costs of those who are the victims of war and mass atrocity."[97] Under this plan, all the world's nations would contribute to a fund that would be used to "rectify" the harms imposed by war or mass atrocity, without requiring contentious determinations of fault for those harms.[98] Such a pooling of responsibility for rebuilding reflects that fact that victorious nations or factions, as well as defeated ones, frequently face financial strains at the conclusion of international or noninternational armed conflicts. It also reflects that fact that in some immediate postconflict settings, local populations are more concerned with recovering the means of making a living than with ensuring that perpetrators of wrongdoing receive criminal penalties.[99]

May's focus on restitution and reparation as the guiding aims of this proposed insurance scheme is not fully in line with the need to confront preexisting structural inequalities within transitional societies. It is also not clear how obligatory the contributions to (and disbursements from) such an institution could be, how precise the language of its establishing legislation should be, and how far states would be willing to delegate authority over its operation. Nevertheless, the very creation of such an institution would represent a step toward greater legalization, as compared with the charity schemes and strategic aid payments that are currently the main source of funding for rebuilding in transitional societies. If this institution made the rectification of underlying structural inequalities a mandatory part of the use of funds, it could go beyond restoring an (unequal) status quo ex ante and, in tandem with other long-term strategies, help reduce the risk of future occurrences of large-scale crimes.

6   The Grammar of Violence: Social Norms and the Explanation of Mass Atrocities

In June 1934, Dr. Victor Klemperer logged a conversation with long-time friend Johannes Scherner in his diary. Klemperer, a German-Jewish professor employed at the Technical University of Dresden, had hosted Scherner and his wife for lunch during the couple's holiday visit to the city. Amid complaints about career setbacks and the pains of provincial life, Scherner noted the shallow character of anti-Semitism in rural Saxony:

> He told us: In Falkenstein one is not allowed to buy from the "Jew." And so the people in Falkenstein travel to the Jew in Auerbach. And the Auerbachers in turn buy from the Falkenstein Jew. However, on bigger shopping expeditions the people from the one-horse towns travel to Plauen, where there's a larger Jewish department store. If you run into someone from the same town, no one has seen anyone else. Tacit convention [*Stillschweigende Konvention*].[1]

Klemperer's diary, kept up at substantial personal risk during World War II, offers a prime source for what Saul Friedlander has called an "integrative and integrated history" of the Holocaust.[2] This form of history does not limit its focus to official acts or policies. Instead, it studies the fates of a wide range of people in order to exhibit the full scope of the Shoah. The "tacit convention" Scherner mentioned may mark just a passing feature of provincial life, but it deserves a place in such a history, attesting to the mixed success of National Socialism's early efforts to reshape German society.[3]

Is there anything else we can learn by studying such minute features of mass atrocities? Can greater attention to social norms and conventions improve our understanding of the causes of large-scale crimes or of the paths they take once underway? In this chapter, I argue that social norms are integral to the explanation of mass atrocities. Social norms, I suggest, are especially important for making sense of the experiences of unstructured collectives—"mothers," "young men," or "neighbors"—during large-scale crimes. Ultimately, I hope to convince historians and other scholars to incorporate social norms into their basic explanatory frameworks for mass atrocities.

Uncovering the influence of social norms during large-scale crimes is no easy task. Unlike legal norms, social norms are not created by judicial fiat or legislative enactment. Unlike moral norms, social norms rarely count among agents' most deeply held practical commitments. Given the relative silence of official records, we have to rely on testimonial descriptions of social norms circulating during mass atrocities. Those descriptions appear in private writings, such as Klemperer's diary, and in post-atrocity memoirs, trial depositions, and oral histories. Each of these sources presents risks of misperception or misinterpretation, rendered more complex by the fact that social norms sometimes emerge from just such misperceptions and misinterpretations.[4] Even so, I believe key features of large-scale crimes cannot be understood without due attention to social norms. The specific set of features I consider in this chapter concern gender-based patterns of violence during mass atrocities.

Explaining gender-based patterns of violence during mass atrocities does not necessarily require any appeal to new or emergent social norms. Rather, these patterns generally exhibit the continuing influence of preexisting gender-based social norms. Studying such gender-based social norms supports the basic thesis of this book: that mass atrocities typically reflect the presence, rather than the absence, of norms. It also illuminates the ways in which members of loosely organized collectives respond to large-scale crimes as targets or as perpetrators of violence.

Before I begin, I should briefly state how I understand gender and gender-based social norms. I take gender to be one of several key social identities through which individuals identify themselves and are identified by others in social life.[5] Like race, class, and other identity elements, it is possible for individuals to identify themselves in ways that differ from the gender identifications that others make; it is also possible for individuals and groups to be singled out for exceptional treatment—for good or ill—on the basis of their perceived gender identities.[6] While recent work in philosophy and political theory has focused on gender formations that stand outside traditional notions of masculinity or femininity[7] and while increasing attention is being paid to the ways individuals bearing such nonstandard identities have historically been targeted for violence, my focus in this chapter falls on the decisions and actions of individuals bearing traditional male or female social identities.[8]

I understand gender-based social norms as social norms that prescribe, prohibit, or permit specific courses of conduct to some individuals within particular societies but not to others, where the relevant distinction resides in individuals' gendered social identities. Such norms are present in many domains of social and political life. Some of the most consequential gender-based social norms concern the division of labor within families, including the division of tasks inside and outside the home, as well as the types of careers available to men and women and the opportunities for advancement on offer. While these norms are by no means fixed across time or space, they always reflect, in Cristina Bicchieri's words, a "situation where particular norms are embedded in a thick web of values, beliefs, and other norms."[9] Untangling that web, and showing how gender-based social norms help explain historical episodes of mass violence, is the aim of this chapter.[10]

The chapter proceeds as follows. In section 6.1, I lay out my basic account of social norms, arguing that they can be distinguished from legal and moral norms on the basis of (1) their dependence on real or perceived social practices, combined with (2) the absence of any standing procedural rules governing their emergence, modification, or elimination. In section 6.2, I discuss scholarly approaches to gender as an explanatory factor in large-scale crimes, focusing on two competing views of the significance of gender for the study of genocide. Section 6.3 analyzes the influence of gender-based social norms on the practical decisions and actions of targets of large-scale crimes, especially concerning escape, survival, or hiding. Section 6.4 turns to the influence of gender-based social norms on perpetrators of large-scale crimes, raising questions about theoretical distinctions between "direct" and "indirect" perpetration, and contrasting two patterns of wartime rape. Section 6.5 answers some objections.

6.1 Social Norms

Social norms are practical prescriptions, permissions, or prohibitions that are grounded in real or perceived social practices, but lack standing procedural rules governing their emergence, modification, or elimination. The grounding relationship with social practices serves to distinguish social norms from moral norms. The lack of standing procedural rules serves to distinguish social norms from legal norms. While these distinctions are important, social norms exhibit other features that cannot be conveyed contrastively. In this section, I review some of these features of social norms before turning to consider the various roles these norms play before, during, and after large-scale crimes.

Philosophical investigations of social norms and conventions began in the mid-twentieth century with the influential work of H. L. A. Hart and David Lewis.[11] A second wave of scholarship by Margaret Gilbert, Edna Ullman-Margalit, and others placed more explicit emphasis on distinctions between social norms and other forms of social ordering, such as customs or conventions.[12] Over the past two decades, a number of philosophers, drawing on the work of economists, political theorists, and psychologists, have published full-scale theories of social norms. These theories offer clear definitions of social norms; provide guidance to behavioral experiments intended to gauge the existence and influence of such norms; and integrate social norms into broader accounts of political stability, economic rationality, and just social institutions.[13] Key findings advanced by their authors include the claim that social norms depend on shared normative beliefs and attitudes among members of particular populations, as well as the claim that those beliefs and attitudes are stabilized in part by the use of sanctions against violators of social norms.[14]

Although methodological and conceptual differences distinguish these philosophical accounts of social norms, I will focus on three features accepted by proponents of each of the leading theories. These features, I suggest, suffice to establish the explanatory power of social norms within theories of mass atrocity. The three features I will consider concern the kinds of accountability social norms establish, the types of transformations social norms undergo, and the forms of evidence that individual actors rely on when weighing social norms during practical deliberations.

With respect to the kinds of accountability established by social norms, several points stand out. For one thing, judgments of compliance or non-compliance with social norms are not usually governed by the sorts of procedural safeguards associated with legal norms. Individuals can be, and often are, sanctioned for violations of social norms that have not been publicly articulated, conflict with other accepted norms, and may not have even existed at the time those "violations" occurred. The absence of rule-of-law requirements of publicity, noncontradiction, and nonretroactivity may be deemed an advantage by those who would use social norms to speed social transformations—facilitating swift responses to collective action problems or allowing for incompletely theorized agreements about the reasons for regulating people's conduct in new ways.[15]

Social norms are also characterized by widely distributed powers of enforcement within the populations in which they circulate. Everyone who accepts a given social norm is, in principle, authorized to criticize or punish those who are presumed to accept, but fail to follow, that norm.[16] Because there are costs associated with norm enforcement and because additional social, legal, or moral norms may govern which members of specific populations are permitted to carry out punitive actions, we should not expect that every individual who accepts a given social norm will take tangible steps to enforce it in cases of violations.[17] But this does not change the fact that acceptance of a social norm entails a practical commitment to seeing it enforced.[18]

The lack of standing procedural rules governing the enforcement of social norms, combined with the wide distribution of authority to sanction violators, has important implications for the types of transformations that social norms undergo. While some social norms are openly cultivated by actors eager to steer the conduct of individuals and groups, others arise in other ways. Particular social norms may emerge as a consequence of some group members observing the conduct of other members and (wrongly) taking that conduct as evidence of a social norm. Alternatively, interested agents may seek to manipulatively shift social norms—for example, by lying to new members about the prescriptions or prohibitions circulating within particular populations or offering self-serving descriptions of situations in order to make one norm rather than another seem salient.[19]

Turning from the emergence to the modification of social norms, such norms may easily migrate from one population to another or from one set of practical dilemmas to another. Developmental psychologists suggest that even young children are prone to look for and articulate norms governing behavior in specific group activities, such as unstructured game playing, and philosophers claim that this tendency persists in adults facing new environments or practical dilemmas.[20] This is not to say that all efforts to transplant or translate old social norms within new contexts succeed. Anyone who compares a typical email sent in 2018 to a typical letter sent in

1998 can see this. Yet the very fact that we often hear complaints about the informality of emails sent by students or colleagues reflects a sense that old social norms might yet be applied to this new mode of communication.[21]

Finally, much philosophical research on social norms has focused on the ways in which they break down. Intentional norm breaching is one important strategy for activists seeking to undermine unjust social norms.[22] In other cases, flagrant flouting of norms of civility, reciprocity, or truthfulness by powerful figures gives rise to concerns that larger populations will cease to accept social norms undergirding honest social relations. Philosophers working in decision theory have shown that it is in principle possible for a single prominent breach of a social norm to cause that norm to collapse via information cascades in which practical commitments and normative attitudes thought to be widespread are shown to be illusory.[23] Here again, an instructive contrast with legal norms can be drawn, for in most cases of breakdowns in social norms, there will be no authoritative text or verdict that proves a norm invalid, but only informal signals and shaky inferences about prevailing normative and empirical expectations.[24]

This leads directly to the last feature of social norms that I want to consider: the forms of evidence that individuals have within the practical point of view concerning the social norms prevailing among their peers. As with legal and moral norms, much of this evidence will be testimonial, passed on in childhood or upon entry into new groups.[25] Some may be documentary, read in guidebooks, reported in newspapers, or specified in letters of introduction. But a good deal of evidence is more ephemeral, based on inferences that are grounded in the observed conduct of other group members and that aim to connect public conduct with the practical commitments and normative attitudes held by those people. The existence of such "second-order" beliefs about the normative beliefs of others is, as Bicchieri argues, crucial for distinguishing social norms from conventions, customs, and other forms of social ordering.[26]

In discussing efforts to connect private beliefs and attitudes with public courses of action, we may seem to confront once again the problem of circular reasoning discussed in chapter 1. But there is a crucial difference. Circularity is indeed a problem from the perspective of social scientists seeking to achieve well-supported observations about the norms prevailing within particular populations or to explain observed patterns of conduct by reference to such norms. But from the point of view of agents living within those populations, circularity is not a problem, or at least not a major one. This is because the risks of wrongly imputing a norm standing behind the conduct of others are usually lower than the risks of wrongly assuming no norm exists relevant to that conduct. Individuals are regularly sanctioned for violating social norms they did not know of, but sanctions for wrongly assuming a social norm exists where it does not are rare.[27]

With this picture of social norms in place, we may consider whether the "tacit convention" described at the start of this chapter would not be better characterized as a social norm. The theoretical literature on social norms, conventions, and other forms of social ordering that underpins this study did not exist in the 1930s. There is, accordingly, no reason to place great weight on Victor Klemperer's specific form of words in his diary. As I noted in chapter 1, a key feature of conventions is that they are self-enforcing: no person who follows a convention has a reason to deviate unilaterally, owing to the negative effects that will predictably occur independent of any normative judgments or sanctioning decisions by others.[28] But the negative effects that provincial Germans might expect to incur from acknowledging the presence of their Christian neighbors in socially proscribed stores existed only because of the second-order normative belief that others think one ought not to "buy from the 'Jew'"—and that one might be blamed for doing so.[29] Hence we do better, on the strength of Scherner's evidence, to treat this as a social norm. Further obstacles to identifying social norms in historical contexts and strategies for overcoming them are discussed next.

6.2 Gender-Based Social Norms in Explanations of Large-Scale Crimes

Early reporting on mass atrocities tends to emphasize departures from the patterns familiar from ordinary social life. Emily Hobhouse ended her account of conditions in Britain's South African concentration camps by stressing the hardships faced by women seeking to uphold basic domestic standards.[30] Victor Klemperer's diary registers, in painful detail, the progressive marginalization of Jews in wartime Dresden. The French writer David Roussett, author of one of the earliest postwar memoirs of life in Hitler's *univers concentrationnaire*, describes the erosion of age-based courtesies among male prisoners at Buchenwald:

In these sordid conditions, one of the most surprising results is the destruction of all hierarchies based on age. All the conventions [*conventions*] that maintain a certain respect for the aged are annihilated. Old men are subject to common constraints. It is right for teenagers to hit and insult them, to chase the aged from their place in line and take it for themselves.[31]

Descriptions of wholesale transformations in social relations during large-scale crimes are compatible with current philosophical research on social norms, but they have not yet been subjected to close analysis. In the philosophical literature, social norms appear chiefly as instruments for harmonizing the conduct of diverse populations or for solving social dilemmas created by competing individual interests. Philosophers and political theorists who work on social norms frequently treat them as tools for reinforcing legal institutions or resolving disagreements rooted in the "burdens of judgment."[32] Although some philosophers, including Cristina Bicchieri, Geoffrey Brennan, and Robert Goodin, have noted how "bad" social norms serve to prop up practices like bribery, academic backbiting, or child marriage, their focus has not yet turned to the place of social norms in the more exigent circumstances of mass atrocity.[33]

I believe preexisting social norms can and frequently do persist during large-scale crimes and that they continue to guide the deliberations and actions of both perpetrators and targets of atrocities. Studying the survival of gender-based social norms, in particular, enriches our understanding of the decisions made by targets of atrocities and provides novel insights into the conduct of perpetrators.[34] It equally provides a corrective for current philosophical accounts of the moral and political significance of social norms. Where some philosophers consider it a "condition of social norms" that they "tend to preserve the central order and hierarchy of a given society," I will show that gender-based social norms may facilitate radical transformations in social hierarchies.[35] Where others suggest that social norms supply the "grammar of society," I will argue that social norms are equally integral to the grammar of violence.[36]

There are two contrasting lines of argument concerning the significance of gender and gender norms for explaining large-scale crimes. On the one hand, feminist historians contend that the peculiar forms of victimization and the specific obstacles to escape encountered by women and girls during genocide and mass atrocity tend to reflect preexisting conditions of patriarchy and gender inequality. In the words of Elisa von Joeden-Forgey,

"Peacetime violence against women and girls sets the stage for their violation at times of conflict."[37]On the other hand, some scholars, most prominently Adam Jones, argue that men and boys are statistically the most likely to suffer sex-selective killing or other serious forms of violence during genocide and note that this disproportionate killing of men and boys reflects "cultural codes," "humanitarian biases," and "ingrained norms" that place greater restrictions on the killing of women than on the killing of young men.[38]

Jones has been criticized for his claims about the disproportionate victimization of men and boys during genocide. Some critics have focused on the empirical basis for Jones's claims about death rates and suggest that his conclusions are too hastily drawn.[39] Others argue that a singular focus on killing unduly excludes certain forms of gender-based violence characteristic of genocide and other kinds of mass atrocity.[40] In her own work, von Joeden-Forgey uses the concept of "life-force atrocities" to explain the prevalence of both coordinated and opportunistic rape during mass atrocities. Life-force atrocities are defined as "ritualized pattern[s] of violence that targe[t] the life force of a group by destroying both the physical symbols of its life force as well as its most basic institutions of reproduction, especially the family unit."[41] Rape is the primary, though not the only, example of such an atrocity. Crucially, rape "provides a model for genocide in its perceived ability to destroy both the outer and inner dimensions of human life."[42]

I believe the patriarchal and gendercide approaches to victimization during mass atrocity are, on reflection, complementary. A closer focus on the part that gender-based social norms play during such crimes substantiates this claim. The "cultural codes" and "ingrained norms" that Jones cites as reasons for greater resistance to killing women and girls during war are historically intertwined with patriarchal features of many societies, such as the exclusion (until recently) of women from combat roles in national armies. Closer analysis of the influence of gender-based social norms on genocide and other kinds of mass atrocities enhances our understanding of these crimes in two basic ways. It helps explain differences in the courses of action adopted by targets of atrocities, and it sheds light on the conduct of perpetrators of large-scale crimes. The following two sections address each of these topics in turn.

6.3   Gender-Based Social Norms and the Targets of Atrocities

In audiovisual testimony recorded for Yale's Fortunoff Archive, Holocaust survivor Yvette L. was asked why she thought so few Jews from her home city of Thessalonika managed to escape deportation during the German occupation of Greece. In response, Yvette first cited the secrecy surrounding the policy of annihilation. She then noted the language barrier that divided the city's Ladino-speaking Jews from their Christian neighbors. She concluded by giving a more principled reason: the strength of family ties among Greek Jews of this period. Few Jews offered the opportunity to escape with their own lives, Yvette mused, would have seriously considered leaving their parents or grandparents behind.[43]

Yvette does not describe the normative bases of these familial obligations, and so it is hard to say whether she meant to refer to moral prescriptions, social prohibitions, or some combination of the two. We may be tempted to think that only a closely held moral norm could keep individuals from taking steps to flee the Nazi threat. No social sanctions, we might suppose, could be of any moment compared to this. However, Yvette's reference to the secrecy surrounding the policy of annihilation challenges this inference, making it possible that in circumstances of real but concealed danger, Greek Jews might have continued to observe familial obligations grounded in social norms.[44]

Escape is one of the first strategies that targets of atrocities pursue once the reality of existential risk sets in. We saw in chapter 4 how legal norms have in various times and places helped or hindered refugees fleeing from war and other emergencies. But social norms, and especially gender-based social norms, also affect agents' deliberations about emigration and their assessments of the dangers of remaining behind. In 1930s Germany, as historian Marion Kaplan observes, married Jewish women were typically less integrated into political and economic life than their husbands due to social norms suggesting that women should focus on their families and avoid newly opened professional careers.[45] Consequently, "women, whose identity was more family-oriented than men's, struggled to preserve what was central to them by fleeing with those they loved."[46] Rather than regarding this gender-based pattern of Jewish women plotting escapes as the result of an emergent social norm (which would entail that those women were socially required to construct plans for escape and faced sanctions if they failed to do so), Kaplan's analysis suggests we should connect this pattern to preexisting social norms that helped maintain a gendered division of labor within German society at large.[47]

Compared to Jewish emigration on the eve of the Holocaust, the 1994 Rwandan genocide did not feature a massive exodus of Rwandan Tutsis.[48] Historians have offered multiple reasons for the relative rareness of escape, citing the rapidity with which the violence unfolded, the fact that large numbers of Tutsis had already fled during prior episodes of mass killing, and the effectiveness of roadblocks set up by Hutu officials on the country's frontiers.[49] But the postconflict testimony of perpetrators suggests that local social norms also affected judgments about whether certain persons—notably, women and children—posed a threat and so ought not to be allowed to flee. Several of the perpetrators Scott Straus interviewed for his 2006 study, *The Order of Genocide*, pointed out that Paul Kagame, leader of the Rwandan Patriotic Front (RPF) forces, had been allowed to leave Rwanda as a child refugee; some derived from this the lesson that it was necessary to kill not just Tutsi men but also Tutsi children and the women who bore them.[50] The following exchange shows an interviewee invoking, however tendentiously, a permissive local social norm in order to explain such conduct:

Straus: But why kill all Tutsis?

Interviewee: That, no! Ehhh! That is the reasoning of an American. People are created like that. If you do something bad to me, will I have good intentions for your children? That is the logic of Africans.[51]

For individuals and families who do not manage to escape the environs of large-scale crimes, social norms may yet substantially affect their chances of survival. At the extreme, outliving atrocities might require individuals to make "choiceless choices," or to deliberate in a moral "gray zone."[52] But survival in contexts of ghettoization, hiding, internment, or forced marches can also depend on apparently trivial decisions, as preexisting gender-based social norms continue to influence choices about trust, hiding, and betrayal.

Beginning with Emanuel Ringelblum's sociological work on life within the Warsaw Ghetto, scholarship on the ghettoization of European Jews has emphasized the ways in which adult men and women responded differently to the constraints of ghetto life.[53] Jewish men previously employed in a profession had serious difficulties adapting to the economic realities of life in a context where their skills were rendered worthless. Jewish women consequently took up much of the role of providing for their families—in one sense, overturning prior gendered divisions of labor, but in another sense, extending those divisions, since the skills that proved economically useful in the ghettos were commonly those confined to unremunerated domestic work in earlier periods.[54]

An episode reported in Victor Klemperer's diary illustrates the continued influence of gender-based social norms from an alternative perspective. Klemperer's wife, Eva, had suffered serious health problems even before the years of Nazi persecution, leading Klemperer to take on many domestic tasks. During the war years, the Klemperers were required to move from their private home to a communal "Jews' House" closer to the city center. Multiple entries in Klemperer's diary record the chidings he received from female residents for taking over the work of cooking for himself and his wife in the house's shared kitchen.[55] Though this case is trivial, it points up the fact that during the first stages of persecution, members of targeted groups may continue to be guided by (and even inclined to enforce) social norms that seem nonsensical to persons possessing knowledge of subsequent atrocities.

Strategies for survival change qualitatively once individuals are placed under the direct control of authorities intent on their destruction. In the contexts of concentration camps, gender-based social norms could directly influence death rates across interned populations. In the infamous selections that took place among new arrivals to Auschwitz, individuals with some sort of experience in skilled or manual labor were more likely to be assigned to work duties than to be sent for immediate killing. As Peter Hayes notes, this helped contribute to the fact that "the female mortality rate upon arrival was much higher than the male."[56] By contrast, in the case of the German war of extermination against the Herero people in Southwest Africa in 1904–1905, Herero men who survived starvation in the desert and sought to turn themselves in at detention camps were typically executed immediately as suspected combatants, whereas women survivors were not killed outright but instead exposed to sexual assault or slave labor.[57]

Finally, for individuals seeking to keep themselves or their families safely hidden for the duration of large-scale crimes, gender-based social norms could contribute to the success or failure of their efforts. Closely parallel examples drawn from the Holocaust and the Rwandan genocide illustrate the significance of masculine social norms of revenge in protecting families in hiding from betrayal. In her article "Gender and the Daily Lives of Jews in Hiding in Eastern Galicia," Natalia Aleksuin notes that "while Jews in general could only appeal to the mercy of their Polish and Ukrainian caretakers while making them financially invested in sheltering the Jews, Jewish men were also feared for the possibility that they might take revenge."[58] She cites testimony from one woman living in hiding with her two sons who overheard discussions by her paid helpers about the possibility of poisoning them; as long as the woman's husband remained alive, the helpers worried he might later "come and kill" them.[59]

Genocide scholar Sara Brown shares an example from the Rwandan genocide that is strikingly similar, despite the substantial differences in national and cultural contexts. Ruth, a Rwandan Hutu, had hidden a man and two girls in her home. One day the paramilitary groups known as Interahamwe entered her home, found the man, and killed him. They threatened to kill Ruth and the one child she was still harboring, but "in the end, one of the Interahamwe stopped them, insisting that they cease on account of Ruth's husband. `If this man, the husband of this wife, finds that you've killed his wife, I'm telling you, this war will never end.'"[60]

Gender-based social norms—whether focusing on actions as innocent as housework or as bloody as revenge killings—belong among the factors that explain the strategies adopted by the targets of large-scale crimes. A full account of the influence of social norms on such decisions and actions would have to cover social norms relating to bribery, "passing," and so on. None of these social norms has received systematic investigation from scholars of mass atrocity. Because of this oversight and because analysis of gender-based social norms helps indicate how other types of social norms may play a role in large-scale crimes, it is valuable to examine their influence on the practical deliberations of targets of atrocities. It is also valuable to examine their influence on the decisions and actions of perpetrators, to which I now turn.

6.4 Gender-Based Social Norms and the Perpetrators of Atrocities

Profiles of perpetrators of mass atrocities often include references to social norms.[61] Legal scholars Mark Drumbl and Sheri Rosenberg suggest that local social norms may outweigh domestic or international legal norms during the deliberations of potential perpetrators.[62] According to Rosenberg, although trials or tribunals are frequently convened in the wake of large-scale crimes, "in this context, criminal law is not punishing deviant behavior. In fact, it is punishing conduct that, in the time and place it was committed, was in conformity with social norms."[63] Both Drumbl and Rosenberg argue that ordinary legal proceedings must be modified in response to widespread participation in mass atrocities.

Without greater precision and evidentiary support, these claims about perpetration risk succumbing to the circularity objection discussed in chapter 1. That is, the pattern of facts that social norms are supposed to explain—in this case, the fact of widespread popular participation in historical cases of mass atrocity—is also offered as the sole or most significant evidence for the existence of such a social norm. One advantage of looking at gendered patterns of perpetration of large-scale crimes, and noting the specific statements perpetrators themselves have offered concerning such patterns, is that it helps overcome such concerns about circularity by more narrowly framing explanatory claims about social norms.

Studies of the Rwandan genocide commonly point out that although the victims of murder, expulsion, and expropriation included men, women, and children, the patterns of perpetration were largely divided along gender lines. Male Hutus carried out most killings, while female Hutus engaged chiefly in looting and other forms of theft.[64] Different explanations are given for this gendered pattern of perpetration, including the colonial-era existence of a state-centered *corvée*, or forced labor, requirement for men, the prior organization of Interahamwe for Hutu boys and young men, and the mere fact that men were more likely to be out in the fields doing farmwork at the time that groups chasing fleeing Tutsis formed. All three of these explanations implicate gender-based social norms, though in different ways. The forced-labor precedent, for example, suggests that a preexisting legal norm became the pattern for an extralegal social norm requiring Hutu men to participate in killings. Scott Straus summarizes many of his interviewees' responses about their reasons for killing with the remark, "Attacking Tutsis was like a 'law'—and disobedience, claimed both those pressuring and those being pressured, would have carried a heavy price."[65] Straus's scare quotes around the term *law* mark the fact that participation in killing was not actually mandated by formally enacted laws, even though the sanctions applied for abstention could be as severe as any in the penal code.

Looting after mass killings or forced displacements in some cases may be purely opportunistic, with little explanatory space available for social norms. However, across diverse cases of large-scale crimes, gender-based social norms seem to play a decisive role in driving participation in this apparently indirect form of perpetration. In the case of Rwanda, according to one perpetrator interviewed by French journalist Jean Hatzfeld, among male Hutus, "it was the rule to kill going out and to loot coming back."[66] In cases where a man was too tired or had other business to attend to after killing, "[he] could send his wife."[67] Goods looted in this way included household wares, cattle, and sheet metal, with expropriated land parceled out in a more centralized manner. While women were permitted to stand in their husbands' places during the looting of houses, however, they were not regarded as proper substitutes during killings. As another of Hatzfeld's informants remarks, "There were even healthy men who sent their wives to replace them for a day on the expeditions [i.e., killings], but that didn't happen often because it was not legitimate."[68]

The power of gender-based social norms to explain patterns of looting during large-scale crimes has been cited by scholars of numerous other historical mass atrocities, including the Armenian genocide and anti-Jewish pogroms during the 1918–1921 Russian civil war.[69] Historian Wendy Lower has provided the most extensive account of how the gendered division of labor in German society affected patterns of Nazi genocide.[70] Like Straus and Hatzfeld, Lower highlights the place of women in looting goods expropriated from victims of killings, sometimes directly buying them at auctions or depots in the course of their domestic tasks, sometimes pressuring their boyfriends or husbands to acquire items made scarce by the war.[71] But Lower also notes that women played a more direct role in the centers of killing in the East, acting as secretaries, typists, telephone operators, and in other roles reflecting prewar career opportunities available to women in Germany.[72]

Although women might play organizational roles in mass killings and less commonly help to kill victims directly, rape as a form of mass atrocity is almost exclusively perpetrated by men.[73] The reluctance of scholars like Jones and Straus to recognize rape as a direct form of perpetration comparable to killing—not just in the harms it imposes but in the political goals it may serve—has provoked some of the sharpest disagreements with feminist scholars of large-scale crimes.[74] Scholars working in this area generally recognize the role of social norms in shaping patterns of wartime sexual violence.[75] At the same time, they commonly distinguish two types of wartime rape: opportunistic rape during war or just after war's end and coordinated or "strategic" rape, undertaken with the aim of achieving specific wartime objectives.[76] Although both of types of rape can constitute large-scale crimes, they display substantially different etiologies.

Opportunistic rape is a form of wartime sexual violence that was hinted at, however ineffectually, in the Hague Conventions, with their references to the protection of "family honor," and in the Second Geneva Convention, with its assertion that women should be protected "in particular against rape, enforced prostitution, or any form of indecent assault."[77] As Tuba Inal has shown, this form of sexual violence was long regarded as a lamentable but unpreventable consequence of the socialization of military-aged men and the license accorded to soldiers in war.[78] We saw, in chapter 5, how the progressive legalization of international criminal law with respect to wartime rape aims to curb this practice. But outside of the strengthening of legal prohibitions, political theorists and historians have argued that social norms may help to explain where opportunistic rape occurs in war and where it does not. Elisabeth Jean Wood suggests we should distinguish between the "cultural norms" that incoming military recruits have internalized concerning the permissibility of sexual violence, on the one hand, and the norms cultivated within combat units or armies regarding sexual violence, on the other.[79] In cases where those unit-level social norms are permissive with regard to sexual assault or prohibitions are not supported by practices of monitoring and enforcement, the background cultural norms that individual soldiers accept may be decisive in guiding their deliberations about opportunistic rape. It should be noted how very different this norm-guided model is from the "biological" model of male sexual desire described by Inal as operative in the late nineteenth century, where deliberation played no part in a picture of uncontrollable male sexual urges leading "naturally" to acts of opportunistic rape in war.[80] Both explanations put gender at the center, but the biological model focuses on physiology, whereas Wood's model focuses on social contexts and gender-based social norms.

Opportunistic rape, even when not officially sanctioned, can rise to the level of mass atrocity. But there is another mode of large-scale sexual violence in war that has received considerable attention in the past several decades, which seems to exhibit a very different etiology. This is what has been termed variously "systematic" or "genocidal" rape—in philosopher Claudia Card's words, "rape as a weapon of war."[81] This type of centrally organized sexual assault was widely reported during the Balkan wars of the 1990s and has been attested in conflicts ranging from Guatemala to Sudan.[82] When conducted in order to permanently destroy or change the composition of a targeted population, the name "genocidal rape" seems appropriate, and in such cases, social norms may play a role in explaining patterns of perpetration.[83] In this case, however, it is not the norms circulating among the perpetrators that do the explanatory work, but rather the norms circulating among the targets of sexual violence that are most significant. As Elisa von Joeden-Forgey argues, those who order sexual violence are, at least in some cases, well aware of the social stigma and sanctions associated with nonmarital sex or pregnancy within targeted populations.[84] She writes:

> As some perpetrators seem to know, when female victims are allowed to live, the consequences of sexual violation extend well beyond the genocide.... In many cases women rape victims are rejected by their families and communities, are unable to find work, and remain left to raise children born of war alone and in abject poverty.[85]

It is worth noting that perpetrators of genocide need not share the normative beliefs and commitments grounding such sanctions of victims of sexual assault in order to exploit them as a means of advancing group-destructive goals. In addition, it is not inevitable that peacetime social norms regarding sexual activity or pregnancy should be applied to victims of sexual assault during large-scale crimes. Given appropriate interventions and policies of material restitution and social reconciliation, such collateral harm to women who have suffered rape may be averted. However, as I have argued throughout this chapter, the distinguishing features of social norms mean that they can sometimes take hold without anyone intending them to, based on mere presumptions about the practical commitments and normative attitudes of others. This is why it is all the more important that we study the effects of gender-based social norms before, during, and after mass atrocities.

This discussion has touched on many ways in which preexisting social norms can influence the actions of targets and perpetrators of large-scale crimes. It might yet be asked why this should be the case: why, that is, societies undergoing violent turmoil, in some cases (as in Cambodia during the rule of the Khmer Rouge) accompanied by efforts at the complete transformation of society, continue to show patterns reflecting preexisting, gender-based social norms?[86] The answer, I think, is twofold. In the first place, large-scale crimes are frequently characterized by severe limits on the free flow of information because of either the breakdown of ordinary channels of communication or the imposition of state censorship, or both. In these cases, local actors will not be able to freely express views about what standards ought to apply to their conduct, whether that conduct consists in hiding and flight or direct or indirect forms of perpetration. Such euphemistic phrases as are permitted, including the common call during the Rwandan genocide for men to "go to work," may tend to reinforce preexisting gender roles and gender norms.[87]

A second reason for the considerable influence of preexisting social norms during large-scale crimes concerns the specific kinds of collectives that are implicated at this level of explanation of atrocity. Unlike hierarchical groups such as military units, university teaching staffs, or political parties, the sorts of collectives affected by gender-based social norms, including mothers and military-aged young men, lack centralized deliberative procedures for making collective decisions about matters that could affect their fates as perpetrators or as victims of violence. Furthermore, while some scholars have argued that men or women, as such, can constitute the core targets of genocide or other types of large-scale crimes, most twentieth-century mass atrocities targeted groups defined by ethnic, racial, national, religious, or ideological grounds, with the gendered composition of those groups representing a secondary level of complexity in the patterns of violence. As a result, the forms of solidarity that might arise from being singled out for persecution on the basis of a specific feature of one's social identity, whether or not one recognizes that identity, are less likely to occur for men or women as such during large-scale crimes. All this tends to the preservation of preexisting gender roles and gender norms, and to their continued influence even under the drastically changed circumstances of mass atrocity.

6.5 The Limits of Social Norms

A number of challenges can be raised against my account of the influence of social norms on mass atrocities. Here I consider three of them. The first challenge holds that I have not really shown that social norms feature among the causes of large-scale crimes. At best, I have demonstrated that social norms, whether preexisting or emergent, can influence the course that mass atrocities take once underway. While such a demonstration is of value in showing how mass atrocities occur (for example, by clarifying the distribution of perpetrators of large-scale crimes across specific populations, or revealing consequential aspects of hiding or resistance), it does not address the basic question of why they happen, and so falls short of the explanatory roles assigned in previous chapters to moral and legal norms in making sense of such crimes.

In response to this objection, I suggest that it assumes that discrete instances of decision and action can be isolated as the proximate causes of large-scale crimes. It may be that some mass atrocities begin like this. However, as the microlevel discussions of the persecution of Armenians in Turkey, Tutsi in Rwanda, and Jews in Nazi Germany considered in this chapter have shown, many of the harms that targets of mass atrocities have suffered are the work of relatively unstructured collectives, forming what Christian Gerlach describes as "coalitions for violence."[88] In such cases, it is perhaps an error to look for a single cause of all the harms perpetrated in the course of mass atrocities. Better to focus on understanding why specific patterns of perpetration and victimization developed as they did. Here, attention to social norms can make a signal contribution.[89]

A second challenge to my argument concerning the explanatory value of social norms is that I have not provided clear tools for distinguishing between social norms and other forms of social ordering, such as customs, conventions, or traditions. This objection rightly flags the fact that a posited norm, whether gender based or otherwise, cannot be called a social norm without theoretical consequences. Calling it so implies that it is based on certain normative attitudes absent from mere conventions and that it is supported by a threat of sanctions that may be absent in the case of customs or traditions. Calling it so also implies that certain counterfactual statements are true, such as that if a given practice ceased to exist, the practical commitments and normative attitudes supporting those practices would also vanish. As a counterexample, we could consider the challenge Nechama Tec describes for Jewish men passing as Christians in occupied Poland, who found it hard to mimic their peers' pattern of heavy drinking and rough talk.[90] We need not assume these behaviors are objects of normative beliefs and attitudes, but only that they form part of the empirical expectations of local populations, in order to understand the necessity of imitating them. It may also be, to borrow Cristina Bicchieri's typology, that these behaviors represented mere customs within the relevant populations—practices pursued by individuals because they met certain needs, independent of second-order assessments of the beliefs or commitments of others.[91]

A final challenge suggests that my use of examples from multiple instances of twentieth-century mass atrocities, occurring in quite disparate geographical, political, and cultural contexts, gives a misleading impression that gender identities, gender roles, and gender-based social norms are the same across these various contexts and that it is not necessary to do more careful, microhistorical analyses in order to fully demonstrate the existence and influence of particular social norms.

Nothing could be further from my view. In each case in my discussion of social norms among targets and perpetrators of large-scale crimes, I have drawn on the indispensable work of historians richly attentive to the specifics of local normative contexts. As a philosopher, I cannot reproduce the contextual richness of their discussions. My aim in this chapter has been simply to provide a more precise conceptual framework for future investigations of social norms in the context of explanations of large-scale crimes. That account can be extended through the analysis of the place of social norms in the prevention of mass atrocities, to which I now turn.

7 Arresting Incitement: Social Norms and the Prevention of Mass Atrocities

In the early 2000s, international monitors observed an increase in violence in the western Sudanese region of Darfur.[1] The pattern of attacks defied prior Western understandings of the main geopolitical fault lines in Sudan. A second aspect of the violence that puzzled outsiders concerned the overlapping ethnic and religious identities of perpetrators and victims.[2] Initial reports diverged, finally, on the question of whether the killings, rapes, and displacements in Darfur constituted war crimes, crimes against humanity, or acts of genocide.[3]

Against this backdrop, one humanitarian aid effort stood out for the simplicity of the relief it promised and the roster of support it received. This was a plan to distribute high-efficiency cook stoves to Darfuris living in refugee settlements in Sudan and neighboring Chad. Although the aims of this plan were multiple, a key goal was to reduce the vulnerability of women and girls to sexual assault during trips made outside the bounds of settlements in search of firewood.[4] Better stoves, advocates argued, would decrease the quantity of wood needed for everyday tasks, thus reducing the frequency and duration of collection trips.[5] Nongovernmental organizations working on the ground in Darfur eventually abandoned claims about the power of cook stoves to constrain wartime rape, but similar programs have been launched in subsequent conflicts.[6] Through such "technological solutions," critics of the contemporary international aid system contend, "sexual assault and abuse are depoliticized," while "the perpetration of the violence and the social norms which legitimize and cause such violence … are made invisible."[7]

My discussion in the previous chapter demonstrated the central place of social norms in explanations of mass atrocity. My aim in this chapter is to show that social norms are just as integral to efforts to prevent large-scale crimes. Compared to moral and legal norms, the preventive power of social norms has received scant scholarly attention.[8] Existing studies of "bad norms"—those that undermine substantial interests of some or all members of particular groups, organizations, or societies—concentrate on social norms within unequal but relatively stable societies.[9] Philosopher Cristina Bicchieri and political scientist Karisa Cloward have independently analyzed the social norms that support early marriage and female genital mutilation in communities where these practices are commonplace.[10] Cloward holds that "persuasion" is the principal mechanism for eliminating these social norms. Bicchieri divides the process of transforming social norms into the discrete tasks of changing individuals' empirical expectations, on the one hand, and changing their normative expectations, on the other. While these studies are instructive, it is not clear whether the specific strategies they recommend apply in the more turbid circumstances of mass atrocity.

In this chapter, I consider several ways in which attention to social norms can aid efforts to prevent large-scale crimes. I assess the value of eliminating certain existing social norms within particular populations, notably norms prescribing silence about past atrocities. And I explain how the intentional creation of new social norms, notably norms against incitement, can contribute to atrocity prevention. Along the way, I rebut one argument commonly encountered in the scholarly literature on rescue and rescuers, according to which these agents are distinguished from bystanders by the fact that they are unusually insensitive to social norms. This argument misrepresents the motives and conduct of most rescuers. More important, it overstates the significance of rescue for our understanding of atrocity prevention.

Throughout the chapter, I seek to distinguish different kinds of collectives that can be recruited for the task of constraining large-scale crimes. These collectives range from highly structured institutions like the United Nations to ephemeral coalitions of activists or citizens. Each kind of collective possesses different capacities for shared agency, but even collectives lacking expansive agential powers can sometimes help prevent mass atrocities by adopting or abandoning specific social norms.

The chapter proceeds as follows. In section 7.1, I survey how social norms typically feature in the literature on rescuer behavior during large-scale crimes and argue that rescue is of only limited significance for our understanding of atrocity prevention. Section 7.2 discusses strategies for eliminating social norms that prescribe silence about past or ongoing atrocities and explains how this can advance atrocity prevention efforts. Section 7.3 analyzes the opposite dynamic: the intentional creation of social norms designed to give loosely organized collectives greater capacities for constraining large-sale crimes. Here I propose the creation of social norms against incitement to atrocities. A brief conclusion follows in section 7.4.

7.1 Social Norms and the Limited Significance of Rescue

It is difficult to frame a definition of rescue that applies to all cases of mass atrocity. In part, this reflects the political nature of past and present campaigns to identify and honor rescuers.[11] More substantially, it reflects the complex character of rescue itself. That complexity becomes apparent when we consider a few of the distinctions scholars have drawn when discussing this broad category of action. One such distinction differentiates short-term and long-term acts of rescue.[12] Another asserts a stark moral division between rescuers and "paid helpers."[13] A third distinction challenges our tendency to associate individuals with one particular category of action, forcing us to reflect that the same person may act as a rescuer at one moment, a collaborator at another, and a bystander for the balance of any specific episode of wrongdoing.[14]

For my purposes, it is sufficient to define rescuers as agents who, acting alone or in groups, offer aid to persons targeted for atrocities despite substantial costs or personal risks of harm.[15] Social norms have been taken up in several ways by scholars seeking to explain rescuer behavior during large-scale crimes. One argument, often encountered in prosopographical studies, holds that individual rescuers hail disproportionality from groups occupying a marginal social position before or during mass atrocities. They may be foreign born, belong to a minority religion, or perform a socially stigmatized occupation such as sex work.[16] This line of analysis receives some support from the philosophical theory of social norms, according to which individuals on the margins of any given population are less likely to internalize group norms and may be better positioned to avoid sanctions for violations.[17] That said, acts of rescue are often legally, as well as socially, prohibited during mass atrocities. It is unclear whether a marginal social position tends to shield individuals and groups from legal penalties or instead renders them all the more vulnerable to punishment. Nor does this line of analysis distinguish differences in sensitivity to social sanctions, on the one hand, from differences in the perceived likelihood of actually being detected, and sanctioned, on the other.[18]

A second way that social norms inform accounts of rescue turns on the plurality of social norms. As Bicchieri and Cloward observe, there are usually multiple social norms that plausibly apply to agents' deliberations and actions in any given situation. Individuals are often able to make strategic judgments about which particular norms to follow.[19] Indeed, narratives of rescue often feature agents who find ways to call attention to, and stubbornly insist on, specific social prohibitions or prescriptions, in order to prevent the enforcement of other social or legal norms. This dynamic appears in Sara Brown's interviews with Hutu women who rescued Tutsis during the Rwandan genocide, where Brown found that some of her subjects were able to exploit local norms prohibiting male nonrelatives from entering a family's compound while the head of household was absent.[20] It also describes the case of non-Jewish concierges in Budapest ghetto buildings during the Holocaust who, as historian Istvan Pal Adam has shown, sometimes chose to treat their Jewish tenants as employers deserving deference rather than as prisoners subject to the decrees of the occupying authorities.[21]

There is a third way that social norms have been incorporated into studies of rescue, an approach developed by Samuel Oliner and Pearl Oliner in their 1988 book, *The Altruistic Personality*.[22] In that study, based on interviews with four hundred Holocaust-era rescuers, the authors identified three forms of rescuer motivation, which they call "empathic" motivation, "normocentric" motivation, and "principled" motivation.[23] The smallest proportion of rescuers in their sample described principled motivations for rescue: deeply internalized beliefs about justice or due care that compelled the agents in question to offer aid to others.[24] The second-largest proportion of rescuers described empathic reasons for helping: reasons rooted in personal concern for the well-being of specific individuals singled out for harm.[25] But the plurality of rescuers, according to the Oliners, described normocentric reasons for their acts of rescue: reasons rooted in the norms circulating within one of the specific groups to which they belonged, such as their church, profession, or family.[26] The authors conclude that the action-guiding influence of social norms need not undermine properly moral agency. Rather, "empathy and concern with social norms ... represent alternative but equally profound ways of apprehending moral claims."[27]

The Oliners' study has shaped much subsequent research on rescuer behavior during large-scale crimes. Leading scholars such as Ervin Staub, Kristen Renwick Monroe, and Jacques Semelin draw heavily on their methodology and their general conceptualization of rescue.[28] But there are three problems that should cause us to question whether any of the preceding accounts of the relationship between social norms and rescuer behavior can be applied directly to the study of mass atrocity prevention. The first problem is that none of the historical cases of rescue highlighted in these accounts actually succeeded in preventing large-scale crimes. The second problem is that coalitions formed for the purposes of rescue are usually either ephemeral or dedicated to peacetime missions far removed from atrocity prevention. The third problem concerns the hostility that individual rescuers often encounter within the fragmented communities left after atrocities end. I discuss each of these problems in turn.

In order to make the first point clear, we should distinguish between the moral significance of acts of rescue, on the one hand, and their preventive significance, on the other. Philosopher Lawrence Blum provides a perceptive account of the moral value of acts of rescue during large-scale crimes, focusing on the altruistic character of rescuers' actions and identifying additional bases of moral value in the way such acts manifest resistance to racism or resistance to evil.[29] Blum notes the paradoxical fact that when we learn about parents who have offered aid in historical cases of mass atrocity, thereby risking the lives of their own children, we are not on reflection inclined to blame them for this, but instead deem their conduct morally exemplary.[30] He argues that such assessments reflect the existence of moral ideals that go beyond, and sometimes trump, even the strongest associative duties.

Blum expressly rejects consequentialist evaluations of the moral significance of rescue. He argues that assessments of altruistic action that focus on outcomes do not illuminate altruism at all and suggests that the value of rescue as a gesture of resistance to evil or racism lies in its expressive qualities rather than its practical results.[31] Even failed acts of rescue, or short-term acts of rescue that nevertheless did not suffice to save the lives of those assisted, realize profound moral value on this view.

If we accept Blum's analysis, we should conclude that the moral value of rescue does not depend, even in part, on its preventive effects. But atrocity prevention is precisely the subject with which we are here concerned. It is true that some scholars of rescue and rescuers, including the Oliners and, more recently, Ervin Staub, suggest that we can learn from the study of rescue how to craft policies and institutional reforms aimed at atrocity prevention. These are, in large part, educational policies and reforms, exemplified by the Oliners' call for schools to become "caring institutions" that help students "acquire an extensive orientation to others."[32] Whatever the general desirability of such initiatives, however, their contributions to atrocity prevention remain unproved. They cannot stand as evidence of a correlation between successful forms of rescuer intervention and successful strategies for atrocity prevention.[33]

A second reason for doubting whether studies of rescue meaningfully inform theories of atrocity prevention does not focus on the gap between the moral and the preventive significance of rescue, but rather on the long-term aims and capacities of the individuals and groups involved. Out of the many cases of rescue on which the Oliners based their study, a substantial number involved individuals acting together to offer aid to targets of large-scale crimes. Paralleling Christian Gerlach's analysis of perpetrators, we may wish to call these "coalitions for rescue." In some cases, these coalitions reflected preexisting social relationships, such as membership in the same church, school, or office. In other cases, individuals without preexisting social ties worked together to offer aid or ease escape. In either case, there is reason to question whether such groups will continue to exist and work together for shared goals once the immediate menace of atrocity ends. Churches and professional associations are just as likely go back to being focused centrally on the spiritual lives or the vocational skills of their members rather than directing their efforts toward the prevention of large-scale crimes. The "goal-oriented collectives" that engage in rescue commonly break up after direct threats dissipate, in some cases splintering because of differences in visions for the social and political future and in other cases because of urgent practical needs.[34] Although an increasing number of permanent organizations are devoted to atrocity prevention, few of these feature in accounts of rescue. Nor does success at the relatively short-term task of rescue necessarily presage success at the longer-term challenge of mass atrocity prevention.

It might be objected that while groups or coalitions of rescuers often break up after atrocities end, individual rescuers may yet play a leading part in prevention efforts. After all, several prominent individual rescuers (as well as attempted rescuers) from specific episodes of large-scale crimes have gone on to become leading advocates of mass atrocity prevention. Roméo Dallaire, the commander of UN peacekeeping troops in Rwanda at the start of that country's genocide, is one such example. The unnamed Holocaust-era rescuer interviewed by the Oliners who founded a "House of Reconcili-ation" at Versailles immediately after World War II is another.[35] One way of viewing these cases is to say that rescuers, or attempted rescuers, enjoy the standing to serve as spokespeople for policies and institutions designed to prevent large-scale crimes. Is this not a clear connection between the work of rescue and atrocity prevention?

Against this objection, we should set the fact that across many different contexts of mass atrocity, rescuers are not welcomed as heroes or moral authorities in the immediate aftermath of conflict, but instead treated as social pariahs. This is true of the Polish rescuer Janka Polanska, interviewed by Nechama Tec, who, after the end of World War II, found "that to most Poles her protection of Jews was unacceptable," and she soon "came to feel like an outsider in the country she loved."[36] It is also true of the Rwandan rescuer whom Sara Brown interviewed, who reported that after the geno-cide, her former neighbors "took us as the same as the Tutsis. They said we are traitors."[37] Another rescuer Brown spoke with never went public with her story, saying, "I always kept quiet. I didn't want to be in the spotlight because I was afraid they would kill me."[38] The fragmented circumstances of transitional societies, so well described by Colleen Murphy, often encourage rescuers to play down their experiences after atrocities end, thus limiting the extent to which rescue can become a springboard for atrocity prevention.

Rather than transplanting findings about the influence of social norms on acts of rescue into proposals for atrocity prevention, I want to describe two independent pathways by which social norms can help constrain large-scale crimes. The first pathway focuses on the elimination of social norms that hinder atrocity prevention efforts by blocking or smothering informa-tion about past or present crimes—silencing not only rescuers, as in the case cited above, but also perpetrators, survivors, and bystanders to large-scale crimes. The second pathway focuses on creating new social norms within broader publics, focusing specifically on the advantages of a prospective social norm against incitement to atrocities.

7.2   Eliminating Social Norms as a Means of Atrocity Prevention

Not every widespread pattern of behavior observed during large-scale crimes indicates the existence or influence of social norms. When perpetrators all wield similar weapons, this may simply reflect the tools available in their communities. When displaced persons require fuel for cooking, cleaning, or other domestic tasks, they may spend hours every day searching for firewood without forming any normative attitudes toward the foraging activities of their fellow refugees. To borrow Cristina Bicchieri's language, these "action patterns" may be "created and sustained by the motivations of actors acting independently," reflecting customs, perhaps, but not social norms.[39]

That said, some facts about the pattern of firewood collection in Darfur described at the start of this chapter do seem to warrant explanation via social norms. Responsibility for obtaining cooking fuel, here and in many others places around the globe, falls largely to women and young girls, though it is not the case in Darfur (as in many other developing countries) that women are generally confined to domestic work rather than wage-paying employment.[40] At the same time, the risk of sexual assault that women and girls face during firewood collection trips appears closely tied to gender-based social norms: norms about sexual consent, norms about female "purity" or "honor," and norms about the treatment due to women who report such crimes.[41] Moving from theoretical posits to empirical proof of the power of social norms to help explain sexual violence in Darfur requires careful ethnographic research.[42] But identifying, and altering, inequitable social norms clearly deserves a place within the project of atrocity prevention.

In what follows, I consider in more detail how social norms that escalate risks of large-scale crimes can be eliminated. My focus falls on several examples of social norms prescribing silence about ongoing or recently ended atrocities. Some of these social norms center on sexual or reproductive harms; others relate to diffuse forms of perpetration and victimization. I first explain the bad effects of social norms prescribing silence about atrocities as suggested by current theories of atrocity prevention. I then describe several pathways by which those norms might be eliminated.

The simplest cases of social norms prescribing silence about atrocities appear in groups directly implicated in large-scale crimes. Members of a military unit, for example, may share a norm according to which "ratting" on fellow members who violate the laws of war is prohibited. Norms of this kind are "bad" in the sense that they serve to protect the interests of one set of individuals (those who commit or permit atrocities) against the interests of victims of those crimes.[43] Such norms are also bad from the perspective of more conscientious men and women in uniform, who have internalized the rules of engagement but may reasonably fear reprisals for reporting infractions by their peers.

Social norms circulating within the groups to which perpetrators of mass atrocities belong are not the only ones that can inhibit the disclosure of large-scale crimes. Social norms accepted and followed by victims of atrocities can also prompt silence about abuses. As I noted in the previous chapter, one explanation for the prominence of sexual violations in many twentieth-century cases of genocide and ethnic cleansing holds that perpetrators exploit preexisting social norms within target populations that subject women who have been assaulted to shame or exclusion. The same social norms, as Bina D'Costa has noted, may guide fathers or husbands whose daughters or wives have been raped to avoid disclosing those crimes due to the social sanctions they themselves might incur.[44] Such patriarchal social norms also seem to fit the model of norms that are bad for some, good for others, though in the circumstances of mass atrocity, some prior beneficiaries of these norms may find their interests harmed by them instead.[45]

Finally, we should consider how social norms that prescribe silence about personal experiences of mass atrocity can arise from misperceptions about the normative beliefs and attitudes prevailing within particular populations. Holocaust scholars writing on shifts in the prevalence of acts of testimony by survivors over the last half-century often cite survivors' early impressions of norms prescribing silence about their experiences within their countries of immigration or refuge. Annette Wieviorka, in her book *The Era of the Witness*, reports the advice one émigré survivor received from an aunt living in the United States: "If you want to have friends here in America, don't keep talking about your experiences. Nobody's interested, and if you tell them, they're going to hear it once and then the next time they'll be afraid to come and see you."[46] Lawrence Langer, in his *Holocaust*

Testimonies, provides a comparable account of survivor silence in the initial postwar era:

> The seeds of anguished memory are sown in the barren belief that the very story you try to tell drives off the audience you seek to capture.... Reluctance to speak has very little to do with the *preference* for silence.[47]

Philosophical studies of social norms suggest that these beliefs about the likely responses of hearers of testimony, even if unfounded, could in principle lead to the emergence of a social norm against sharing personal experiences of large-scale crimes. Such a norm, which would in fact be bad for everyone, could arise without anyone intending it, as the natural disposition of newcomers to err on the side of caution, "combined with an initial misestimate of the other's intentions," leads survivors to interpret the discomfort or avoidance their stories elicit from new neighbors as a sanction based on an existing social norm.[48] Following Bicchieri, we may wish to say that the "reluctance to speak" that Langer described reflects a *conditional preference* for silence on the part of survivors, capable of being activated by a misjudgment of the preferences of their interlocutors.[49]

Some readers might object that the negative responses reported by survivors of large-scale crimes, such as physical discomfort or future avoidance by interlocutors, cannot reasonably be construed as sanctions and so cannot give rise to belief in the existence of a social norm prescribing silence. Such responses might be disheartening, but they are not punitive. They hardly suggest that a standard of conduct has been violated. However, as philosopher Linda Radzik has noted, "social avoidance" is in fact a common sanction for violations of shared norms.[50] It is true that not all instances of social avoidance reflect practical commitments or normative attitudes; in some cases, social avoidance may follow from sheer physical unease on the part of the hearer.[51] But this simply opens new opportunities for misperception and creates new chances for the emergence of a social norm prescribing silence.[52]

I have suggested that social norms prescribing silence about large-scale crimes should be of interest to scholars and practitioners of atrocity prevention. But how exactly do such social norms contribute to the etiology of mass atrocities? In the case of social norms against "ratting" in military units, the causal pathway is fairly clear: soldiers who are bad actors will not be eliminated from their units, and so will have further opportunities to violate legal or moral norms. In addition, those who fail to report them may thereby become susceptible to blackmail and face pressure to participate in future abuses. But what about silence among survivors of large-scale crimes? How can this sort of silence serve as a causal factor in *future* atrocities—such that eliminating social norms prescribing silence would aid prevention efforts?

Here we can distinguish several ways in which silence among survivors or witnesses to atrocities and the resulting lack of information about past assaults contribute to the etiology of large-scale crimes. In the first place, much like the military case, silence can leave perpetrators or planners of atrocities in positions of power, with barely reduced legitimacy, and so in a position to carry out further attacks. This pathway for large-scale crimes is particularly important for scholars who stress the rationality of mass killings or forced displacements, that is, the ways in which such acts advance the aims of calculating political leaders.

A second way in which norms of silence about past crimes render future abuses more likely is by impeding understanding of ongoing conflicts, and thereby hindering effective interventions. As noted in the discussion of Darfur at the start of this chapter, international observers are not always able to tell who the responsible parties are in given conflicts or what motives stand behind attacks. Where such understanding fails and no single group can be credibly charged with responsibility for mass atrocities, the political case for intervention becomes harder to make. As Alex Bellamy observes, states "tend to be risk averse and are unlikely to adopt strong positions when faced with incomplete, inconsistent, or uncertain information."[53]

Finally, some scholars of atrocity prevention contend that intergroup dialogue is crucial to efforts to end cycles of violence in deeply divided societies. Where social norms obstruct such dialogue, they may hinder prevention. Political scientist Elazar Barkan provides a clear explanation of how lack of dialogue can hamper long-term prevention efforts. First, he argues, "Conflict between groups is often transgenerational, and the historical animosity [between those groups] remains if it is not addressed." Second, he contends, both "fear and desire for revenge often linger … and are prone to be awakened by nationalists or fundamentalists as carriers of xenophobia," thus establishing a reservoir of animus that can be tapped to recruit coalitions for violence. Historical dialogue, by contrast, "aims to defuse such hatred by engaging government and civil society in conversations about history and introducing empathy and even sympathy toward the other."[54]

Barkan acknowledges that such long-term strategies for atrocity prevention remain undertheorized. He suggests that "for historical dialogues to be meaningful, new norms will have to be evolved."[55] This accords with Kerry Whigham's observation that "ensuring free and open debate about the past is not always easy, especially when certain groups uphold a version of the past that rationalizes the violence that occurred."[56] But if the argument I have developed in this chapter is correct, it will not be enough, in confronting this challenge, to craft new norms for structuring intergroup dialogue. It will also be necessary to eliminate existing social norms prescribing silence about past atrocities.

How can these detrimental social norms be eliminated? Cristina Bicchieri provides the most detailed account of the multiple routes to social norm elimination. According to her model, the elimination of social norms requires the elimination of both shared empirical expectations that others will act in a certain way and shared normative expectations that others ought to act in a certain way.[57] In addition, on Bicchieri's account, the change in empirical expectations must generally precede the change in normative expectations when eliminating norms.[58] Let us now consider several means by which changes in such expectations might be induced.

In some cases, the adoption of other kinds of norms, such as legal norms, within specific populations may help to erode social norms prescribing silence. The proposal by Mark Osiel, discussed in chapter 1, to make military officers civilly liable for atrocities committed by troops under their command is designed to erode the social norm against reporting on one's fellow soldiers by vesting a form of legal accountability in figures responsible for shaping the culture of military units.[59] The legal lustration programs adopted as part of many transitional justice mechanisms similarly seek to erode the norm-supported practice of blackmail against officials implicated in atrocities—in this case, through the rather drastic step of making sure that they do not hold office in the first place.[60]

In the case of social norms prohibiting disclosure of sexual assault, which are supported by sanctions such as social shaming, banishment, or other harsh treatment, two distinct strategies have been pursued, one of which is more akin to norm evasion, the other to norm elimination. In the former case, activists and criminal justice officials working with women who have

suffered sexual assault in highly patriarchal societies have adopted practices of confidentiality, closed-door interviews, and other gender-sensitive
approaches designed to avoid exposing victims who tell their stories to
social stigma.[61] In the other strategy, an increasing number of grassroots
organizations, in a variety of postconflict societies, have come forward to
advocate for public disclosure and legal accountability for sexual atrocities.[62] Their actions reflect the finding that organized groups, as opposed to
isolated individuals, may be better able to weather sanctions for violating
existing social norms, and thus better able to effect changes in both the
normative and empirical expectations underlying bad social norms.[63]

Finally, there are cases where social norms prescribing silence are disrupted by unexpected events or "crises" that serve as "catalysts" for norm
erosion.[64] The standard narrative about Holocaust survivors and their willingness to share testimony in their countries of immigration holds that
shortly after the end of World War II, testimony collection efforts ended,
so that it was only after the widely publicized trial of Adolf Eichmann that
the "Era of the Witness" began.[65] With that trial, in which more than a
hundred Holocaust survivors gave public testimony transmitted to global
audiences, it became much harder to sustain the empirical expectation that
others would prefer not to speak or to hear about experiences of the Holocaust. Accordingly, the perceptions of a social norm prescribing silence that
I already noted must have been seriously undermined by this trial. It is perhaps true, as Hannah Arendt famously argued just after these events, that
a criminal trial is an inappropriate venue for writing history or recovering
suppressed memories from victims of genocide. From a normative perspective, however, we may conclude that the trial produced effects extending
far beyond what its architects intended.[66] It is now by no means frowned
upon for survivors of the Holocaust, or other large-scale crimes, to share
their stories in most countries of settlement. Indeed, in many of these
places, bearing witness is now socially prescribed.

The erosion of social norms enjoining silence about ongoing or past
atrocities makes an important, but limited, contribution to mass atrocity
prevention. Reliably constraining large-scale crimes depends on reliable
information about such events; silence is inimical to such efforts, and so
testimony matters.[67] Reaching genuine understanding about the nature,
causes, and responsibility for past atrocities may be the only way of ensuring that old distortions, fabrications, or scapegoating do not reemerge.[68]

It is clear, however, that these initiatives are limited in their effectiveness. They must be supplemented by legal developments and closer examination of existing moral norms. They may also be reinforced by efforts to create new social norms, to which I now turn.

7.3   Creating Social Norms as a Means of Atrocity Prevention

I have argued that silence about past or ongoing mass atrocities generally impedes efforts at mass atrocity prevention. I have also sketched several ways in which social norms prescribing silence about such matters may be eliminated. But not all speech that occurs before, during, or after large-scale crimes serves to reduce intergroup tensions or ease reconciliation. Indeed, some speech, whether in the form of vocal pronouncements, published screeds, or other expressive acts, is explicitly intended to precipitate or prolong mass atrocities. In this section, I consider the significance of incitement to large-scale crimes from the perspective of atrocity prevention. I first briefly review the definition of incitement. I then examine key problems encountered by current legal efforts to define, prohibit, and punish incitement to genocide, mass killing, and other kinds of large-scale crimes. Finally, I defend an alternative preventive response to incitement, one based on the creation of new social norms.

Incitement occurs when an agent uses words (or any other form of expression) to attempt to cause another agent to perform an illicit act. However suitable this may be as a general definition, in law the concept of incitement is subject to significant debate, both with respect to the state of mind (*mens rea*) required for legal charges of incitement and with respect to the requisite causal connection between one agent's expression and another agent's real or potential action.[69] Incitement is generally construed as an inchoate crime—one that does not require that the particular action aimed at by the proscribed expression actually takes place.[70] But the various rulings on incitement issued by the major ad hoc international criminal tribunals, as well as by the International Criminal Court, have not consistently interpreted the crime in this way.[71] The confused state of jurisprudence surrounding incitement to genocide and other forms of mass atrocity has prompted legal scholars to advance alternative theories of incitement, grounded variously in speech act theory, communications research, or a more extensive analysis of different categories of "atrocity speech."[72]

Legal scholar Gregory Gordon provides a particularly clear statement of the obstacles to atrocity prevention arising from current legal prohibitions on incitement to genocide or other large-scale crimes. On the one hand, because of inconsistencies in the way incitement has been interpreted and assessed at the various international criminal tribunals, there is a risk that "would-be defendants will not be put on notice as to what constitutes incitement."[73] This tends to diminish the deterrent effects of these legal prohibitions. On the other hand, unless the definition and limits of the crime of incitement are made clear, "repressive governments will continue to exploit incitement law for purposes of stifling legitimate speech."[74] Different countries afford different constitutional and statutory protections to the speech of their citizens, but the worry for all of them is that parties in power will use laws on incitement or more broadly on hate speech to silence or punish the legitimate speech of political rivals—thus deepening the social marginalization that makes atrocities more likely.[75]

It may be that Gordon and other legal scholars will eventually succeed in streamlining the jurisprudence of incitement and addressing the twin concerns about legality and political exploitation. This may occur by narrowing the range of speech acts that can be charged as incitement, as Richard Ashby Wilson recommends; alternatively, it may occur by adopting a "unified liability theory" for atrocity speech, as Gordon advocates.[76] Still, some of the difficulties raised by legal prohibitions on incitement do not seem to be grounded in the failings of existing legal regimes. They are not, to use the language of jurists, problems of *lex lata*, or law as it exists, but rather problems stemming from the distinguishing features of all legal norms. Because legal norms are subject to standing procedural rules governing their creation and modification, there will always be centralized authorities (whether elected, appointed, or self-proclaimed) empowered to make decisions about the range of their applicability. But however thoroughly delegated this decision-making authority may be, it will always be susceptible to claims of bias against political rivals, thus undermining the legitimacy not only of laws against incitement but of law and legal institutions more broadly. Furthermore, the distinctive legal penalties available for incitement seem ill suited as specific deterrents for this crime, since being jailed does little to prevent an individual's past speech, whether oral or written, from being reproduced or rebroadcast by others.

In light of this, it's worth considering whether a different response to incitement, based not on legal but on social norms, could help constrain such expression while avoiding some of the drawbacks associated with legal prohibitions on speech. Such an approach would place certain kinds of expression outside the bounds of socially acceptable speech, including calls for the elimination or forced removal of whole groups of people from the political community. It would, if successful, work to arrest incitement without requiring the actual arrest of inciters.

To assess the promise of social norms in this domain, we must first consider how they would work: what behaviors they would prohibit and what sanctions might be used to enforce them. We can then consider how such norms might be established within particular populations. Finally, we may look at some lingering fears about social prohibitions on expression.

Existing accounts of the roles social norms perform in shaping political discourse typically focus not on the substance of discussion or debate but rather on the manner in which proposals concerning any given topic may be delivered.[77] Philosophical studies of civility, for example, associate civil or uncivil speech with speech that does or does not conform to established social rules for how others should be addressed in public. These rules range from the use of titles, to tone of voice, to giving the other side a chance to speak. Following such rules, philosopher Cheshire Calhoun argues, is often morally significant because doing so signals respect for conversational partners.[78] Critics of the enforcement of civility in political speech, including Iris Marion Young, also focus on formal requirements for speech and argue that these requirements are used to constrain opportunities for substantive argument, particularly among members of underrepresented groups, and are often tainted by biased judgments about what counts as respectful speech in specific contexts or with specific interlocutors.[79]

Whatever one thinks about these arguments for or against constraints on the manner of political debate, it is clear that social norms prohibiting particular styles of expression are neither necessary nor sufficient as a response to incitement. Although we commonly associate incitement with the demagogue's screed or the fanatic's shout, it is also possible to advance vicious proposals using perfectly polite phrases. Empirical investigation, of the kind advocated by Richard Ashby Wilson, may ultimately reveal whether particular forms of speech or writing are more or less likely to stir up hostile emotions and inspire violent action; the results of such inquiries will bear on our understanding of the contextual conditions for incitement.[80] But what I am interested in investigating are social norms that discourage incitement by prohibiting certain contents of speech rather than by targeting specific modes of expression.

Unlike legal prohibitions on incitement, hate speech, or other forms of expression, social norms against incitement will not be governed by standing procedural rules concerning their emergence or modification; they will also lack institutions specifically charged with codifying, interpreting, or applying them. For this reason, the best way to think about how such norms would operate is to consider how they would affect particular agents' practical deliberations. As we have seen, incitement occurs across a wide range of occasions and venues for expression, ranging from in-person political speeches to printed statements, to television, radio, or Internet streams. It does not typically extend to casual conversations between private persons—though some of the effects of a social norm against incitement might be felt in this context. Instead, incitement to atrocity generally originates with public figures, whether political officeholders, electoral candidates, military officials, or celebrity broadcasters. For this reason, social norms against incitement (as opposed to more generally applicable social norms against, say, hateful expression or demeaning or vulgar language) would need to be applied particularly to these figures.

Who might enforce a social norm against incitement? As already mentioned, social norms do not typically assign responsibility for enforcement to any particular persons. One reason that social norms may help pattern the behavior of unstructured groups (those without substantial capacities for shared agency) is that many different members of those groups can and do act in specific instances to enforce social norms. This wide distribution of sanctioning power supports John Stuart Mill's claim that social sanctions, as compared to legal penalties, leave "fewer means of escape" and "penetrat[e] much more deeply into the details of life."[81] Of course, if the set of agents who can reasonably be accused of incitement to atrocities is limited to public figures, the specific ways in which sanctions can be applied may be affected by this fact, as such figures are often insulated against certain kinds of social sanctions, while being exceptionally exposed to others.

There are two further questions to be answered with respect to social norms against incitement. The first question is what kinds of sanctions can and should be applied against public figures who engage in incitement. The second question is how social norms countering such conduct can be spread across large populations. I will consider each of these questions in turn.

Sanctions against Incitement

The sanctions used to enforce social norms range widely in their publicity, severity, and longevity, from mere "punitive criticism" all the way to deadly violence. Not all of these sanctions are morally permissible; not all are likely to succeed in sustaining particular social norms over time. Here I discuss a few of the most promising options.

Earlier, I cited Linda Radzik's account of social avoidance as a form of social punishment. Radzik has in fact analyzed a broader range of social punishments, emphasizing in each case how they are distinguished from legal punishment by the lack of a centralized decision-making body that could determine proportionality and assign responsibility for enforcement. Among the various types of social punishment she has examined are moral rebukes, gossip, and boycotts.[82] Moral rebukes, Radzik argues, are significant because they are communicative as well as punitive: they do not merely attempt to coercively change an agent's behavior by setting back his or her interests, but also try to convey morally significant reasons for why that change should occur. Boycotts, by contrast, are more akin to social avoidance. By taking steps to withdraw from social interactions with agents deemed to have violated relevant norms and encouraging others to do the same, agents engage in a form of punishment that is open-ended and not directly conducive to moral reason giving. Both of these forms of social punishment, Radzik argues, have advantages and disadvantages. Both are more or less effective in specific circumstances.[83]

Can rebukes and boycotts be effective as sanctions for the kinds of public figures who are in a position to engage in incitement? Here, several considerations are relevant. First, public figures often enjoy certain forms of insulation from criticism, brought about by wealth, prestige, or the privileges of public office. Second, incitement is a form of action whose foreseeable (and intended) harmful effects are likely to follow very quickly, leaving only a small window for imposing preventive sanctions. Third, incitement itself often takes the form of a rebuke, in the sense of an articulation of highly moralized demands accompanied by a threat (more or less explicit) to back up those demands with coercive action if needed.[84] In light of these features, we should consider how either rebukes or social avoidance might work as sanctions justified, at least in part, by their potential to deter specific acts of incitement.

First, consider rebukes for incitement. It is quite common for public figures to call out other public figures for their hateful or, more specifically, inciting, speech. In many cases, of course, those rebukes are offered in private, "between you and me," in which case the analysis will closely follow the one provided by Radzik, where the communicative and punitive aspects of the rebukes are fairly evenly balanced. But the cases of rebukes that actually come to light are generally those where the relevant criticism is uttered publicly, either in person before a crowd or in a broadcast, public letter, or online forum. In these cases, it seems to me, the punitive aspect of the rebuke increases, for here what occurs is not only that a certain agent is criticized, but he or she is seen to be criticized by large numbers of third parties. Even where the addition of such punitive effects is not the intention behind making the rebuke public, as in cases where a former officeholder sees this as the only way to convey a moral message to his or her successor, this heightening of the punitive aspect will occur.

Whether such public shaming is actually effective in deterring incitement will depend on a variety of factors, but one of the most significant of those factors is how factionalized the public is that witnesses the rebuke. In cases of incitement, there will typically already be widespread factionalization on racial, ethnic, or other lines. This is one reason to think that rebukes may not be the most effective means of sanctioning incitement, though they may work to discourage offensive expressions less intimately tied to impending violence.

Turning to boycotts, we should note that in the case of public figures, a far larger proportion of individuals will have virtual ties to those persons than actual face-to-face ties, and so boycotting goods, speeches, or broadcasts may be a more widely available form of sanction than avoidance of physical contact. Where politicians are concerned, avoiding rallies or refusing requests for donations or other kinds of support may be the only way that most people can engage in social avoidance. Although it is sometimes said that elected officials are punished at the polls when voters cast ballots for their rivals, the plurality of reasons for the results of elections, and the many different spins that can be put on those results, make this a less communicative mode of punishment for incitement, even if it is in some ways effective as a means of preventing further wrongs insofar as it removes individuals from positions of authority.

One of Radzik's main concerns in considering social punishment is with determining what forms (or extents) of punishment are proportional to particular violations of norms.[85] Social norms, as we have seen, are not generally created, interpreted, or enforced by centralized bodies, and there is likely to be little "delegation" of authority for imposing sanctions in most cases. Where my analysis departs from Radzik's is in noting that as far as public figures are concerned, often the only effective forms of rebuke or social avoidance require cumulative action by large numbers of persons. This is clearly true of boycotts and may also be true of effective rebukes, at least where factional feeling runs high. In such cases, it is not an appropriate test of proportionality to ask how many different persons participated in applying a sanction, for the effective sanction actually requires the parallel action of many persons. Instead, those concerned with proportionality might be asked to consider the appropriate duration of the boycott, especially once the incitement in question has ended or a public figure has lost his or her status.[86] Should public figures who abuse their positions by engaging in incitement be shunned forever? Should they be blacklisted from all professional or highly remunerative employment, even outside politics or positions of cultural influence? And by what actions or expressions can such figures signal sincere changes of heart that might warrant an end to social sanctions? These are all questions worthy of further study. For now, however, I consider how a social norm against incitement might emerge within particular societies.

Developing Social Norms against Incitement

We saw previously in this chapter that there are many different pathways for the elimination of social norms. What was crucial in each of those cases was that a change in empirical beliefs about the likely conduct of others should proceed, or at least coincide with, a change in normative beliefs about what behaviors are prescribed, permitted, or prohibited. When considering the creation of social norms, the order of operations is reversed: first, new normative beliefs must emerge, followed by new empirical expectations about the conduct of others.[87] With this in mind, we may examine how a social norm against incitement might intentionally be cultivated within modern political societies.

The pathways available for cultivating a social norm against incitement will differ depending on how many of the risk factors for mass atrocity exist within a given society. Where stable democratic institutions and free access to multiple modes of expression are present, campaigns for new social norms may be conducted freely in broadcast media, schools and classrooms, civil society settings, and so forth.[88] Critiques of such initiatives will also receive wide airing. Where populations live in conditions of transitional justice, characterized by inequality, uncertainty, and widespread violations of purported moral and legal norms, the opportunities available for promoting new social norms of any kind will be more limited.[89] Finally, in societies on the very brink of large-scale crimes, where incitement is not a distant prospect but a daily reality, the options for intentionally cultivating a social norm against incitement will be few and the risks to promoters of such a norm substantial.

One method for spreading a new social norm is to graft it onto an existing, widely accepted norm. Political scientist Richard Price defines grafting as a process of strategic exploitation of preexisting norms for the purpose of bringing emergent or previously unregulated modes of behavior under normative control.[90] To say that grafting is strategic means that it does not involve an unconscious process of norm expansion, but rather proceeds via the conscious efforts of interested parties engaged in "active, manipulative persuasion."[91] Grafting seems to work best when the new norm being promoted shares substantial features with the preexisting norm (for example, it has the same modality or applies to the same reference group), and when the preexisting norm is seen as successful in regulating the behaviors it targets.[92]

Existing social norms against bullying are obvious candidates on which to graft a social norm against incitement. Like incitement, bullying is an action defined in part by its public nature; like bullying, incitement seems to be at the same time an expression of strength and of weakness. Furthermore, the modality of social norms against bullying and against incitement is the same. Both are prohibitive, and just as it makes no sense to saying bullying is to be avoided "except under the right conditions," so too a prospective social norm against incitement would presumably apply without exceptions.

There is, however, a key difference between existing social norms against bullying and a prospective social norm against incitement. This concerns the size of the populations in which such social norms would circulate. Social norms against bullying are, in general, small-scale affairs, developed (where they are) in specific offices, schools, arenas, or other places where people regularly gather. This reflects the fact that bullying itself is generally carried on at a small scale against individuals or small groups of people by other individuals or small groups of people. There is, of course, a metaphorical sense in which one nation can bully another nation or one party within a state can bully another party, but these are not the core meanings of bullying, and it is less clear that well-developed social norms exist to constrain bullying in these cases. For that reason, it is not just a difference of scale that makes the possibility of grafting less clear here, but also the less obvious fact of success of a bullying norm at the level of whole populations.

Another pathway for creating new social norms, which does not always involve invocations of preexisting social norms, focuses instead on the persuasive action of norm promoters. Cristina Bicchieri has given substantial attention to the power of "trendsetters" to help create new social norms.[93] Trendsetters, also sometimes referred to as "norm entrepreneurs," are individuals who either visibly infringe existing norms or take unusual steps to establish new norms. They are typically individuals who are less sensitive to risks (particularly, social risks) than others and may also be less likely to perceive risks in specific populations. While these are figured by Bicchieri as differences in basic psychological profiles, there are also differences in social positions that can insulate trendsetters against risks while also making their actions more visible, and hence easier to emulate.[94]

How can trendsetters make a difference in campaigns against incitement? As noted, it is important to be aware of the different opportunities and costs of action in different kinds of societies, but certainly in cases of deeply divided societies, significant risks attach to public criticism of officials who engage in incitement. This is true both where the figures engaging in incitement control the security forces of a state and can use them to attack their critics, and in cases where state institutions are weakened to the point that private ruffians can be used to threaten or attack opponents. One of the most admirable aspects of public rebukes under such circumstances is that they may help disrupt the otherwise ubiquitous appearance that other members of society approve of the hateful messages of incitement that are being targeted at specific groups, thus potentially providing a basis for the development of new empirical, as well as normative, beliefs about the limits of legitimate political speech.

7.4 The Prospects for Social Norms

I have argued that scholars and policymakers should pay more attention to social norms in their search for effective strategies for preventing mass atrocities. My discussion, which has been largely prospective in focus, is likely to attract objections on a variety of points. In this section, I address three of these.

First, it might be objected that the particular social norms I have considered, focusing specifically on speech and silence, are not representative of social norms more broadly, and so they do little to demonstrate the potential of social norms to aid future efforts at atrocity prevention. Expressive acts differ qualitatively from other norm-guided actions that agents perform, insofar as they mainly aim to convey certain ideas, values, or commitments. The norms that most significantly affect whether societies experience mass atrocities, however, are not those that govern what can be said about such crimes, whether retrospectively or prospectively, but rather those that influence individuals' decisions to participate or avoid participation in physical acts of violence.

This objection rightly directs our attention to the fact that the basis for discovering and interpreting particular social norms, especially from the perspective of an outsider, may be more or less difficult depending on whether those norms themselves concern expressive behavior or other kinds of conduct. Testimonial and documentary sources both provide many clues about norms concerning expression or silence, as when a witness to atrocity like Victor Klemperer notes that certain things could not be talked about publicly or when a document issued to military officers explicitly prescribes the use of particular euphemistic words and phrases. In the same way, it is perhaps easier to identify norms needing elimination or describe norms worth developing for preventive purposes when these norms target expression rather than other kinds of action. Nevertheless, I think this objection fails, insofar as social norms governing expression have the same two distinguishing features as other kinds of social norms. They are, in other words, sufficiently representative of social norms bearing on mass atrocity more broadly.

A second objection focuses not on my proposals for identifying or changing social norms, but rather on the one strategy I have rejected: that of modeling prevention on rescue. This objection holds that whereas I have argued that the study of rescue and rescuers provides an inadequate guide to effective prevention, in fact many of the pathways to prevention that I have discussed call for individuals to exhibit virtues very similar to those of rescuers. Accordingly, the objection continues, broad educational campaigns featuring rescuers might be just the sort of thing needed to give individuals who have suffered mass violence the courage to speak out or to inspire soldiers or civilians confronting incitement to make public their criticisms.

I have no problem with the general claim that the virtues manifested by rescuers overlap with those manifested by individuals and groups that attempt at some personal risk to prevent atrocities. But we should be wary of pushing this comparison too far. As Lawrence Blum points out, we may admire, and morally praise, the actions of rescuers even when these do not seem to match traditional conceptions of virtue.[95] A traditional view of courage, for example, is that when carried to excess, it becomes the vice of rashness, but it seems that in cases of rescue (or attempted rescue) from atrocities, this outer limit to courage vanishes; otherwise, how could we praise those who put large numbers of lives at risk in order to save just a few? It is not obvious that the courage exhibited in preventive action has this structure, and this may be why some efforts at gathering testimony from assault victims in patriarchal societies take the form of evading, rather than publicly breaching, social norms (since not only the victim herself but her entire family may be at risk). Similarly, in philosophical discussions of virtue, it is common to draw a distinction between manifestations of virtue in short-term activities and in longer-term plans or projects, but here again, rescue and prevention stand largely on different sides. Accordingly, while persons seeking to prevent genocide and other forms of mass atrocity may learn from rescuers, rescue remains an inadequate model for atrocity prevention.

A final objection targets my proposed social norm against incitement and argues that it is morally unjustifiable or impracticable, or both. Those who believe legal prohibitions on incitement are at least potentially morally justifiable, if implemented in the right way, are likely to think the same about a social norm against incitement. But some liberals and libertarians, particularly those inspired by John Stuart Mill, may believe that even the ugliest forms of expression should be permitted, for epistemic reasons, in democratic societies. Hearing ugly speech or abhorrent proposals, on this account, is important even for those who detest them, because it provides access to the sincere views of some fellow citizens and an outlet for arguments that we must know about if we are to maintain our facility in defeating them.[96] Mill himself might permit social sanctions on forms of expression that reliably lead to interpersonal harms more serious than mere suppression of speech, but given the distinction between incitement and instigation, as well as the general unreliability of claimed causal connections between expression and physical violence, it is hard to see whether, or in what cases, this exception applies.[97] So, the objection goes, we should err on the side of protecting expression and reject social punishment even of vile speech.

One response to this objection, which I do not think is successful, is to say that the kinds of speech that count as incitement are not arguments at all but imperatives, and so the second of Mill's reasons for allowing such expressions does not apply. It is true that many of the specific speech acts that have been prosecuted as incitement do not immediately appear to be arguments, with premises clearly lined up in order to prove a (practical) conclusion. However, what seems to me to be going on here is that those who engage in incitement, like many other political actors, are using enthymemes to advance their agendas. Enthymemes are arguments that, as expressed, contain one or more suppressed premises.[98] An example in this context might be, "All Kulaks are enemies of the revolution," (therefore) "All Kulaks must be eliminated," where the suppressed premise is "enemies of the revolution must be eliminated." My view is that we should not be too quick to deny that acts of incitement express arguments, even if those arguments are outrageous.

Rather than respond to the libertarian objection to prohibitions on incitement as above, I think it is more promising to point to the fact that social punishment of the kind I have recommended is much more likely to be proportional to the harms embodied in or aimed at by incitement than legal punishment, and so more likely to withstand Millian scrutiny. It is true that incitement need not actually lead to the perpetration of mass atrocities in order for it to be socially sanctioned, on my view, but it is a constitutive feature of incitement that the agent performing it intends that such a harm should occur and takes steps to bring it about. It would be disproportionate, in my view, to shoot such a person, or perhaps even to jail him or her for an extended period of time. But it is not disproportionate to ignore that person, to publicly rebuke him or her, to mount a recall election, or to boycott his or her speeches or business. Indeed, even philosophers like Jeff McMahan who strongly condemn boycotts of purportedly offensive speech and tactics like no-platforming make an exception for acts of incitement.[99]

This raises a final point about the relationship between legal and social norms against incitement. It is often argued that legal norms require for their legitimacy support from social norms within the particular populations in which they circulate. This is sometimes taken as a reason for creating or adopting laws against mass atrocity in postconflict societies, as in Sheri Rosenberg and Mark Drumbl's accounts of the expressive functions of international criminal law.[100] But a different lesson is that legal norms that are not closely paralleled by social norms in particular societies are unlikely to be capable of guiding conduct and may thus actually be invalid.[101] If this reasoning is right, then readers who believe in the importance and justifiability of legal norms against incitement should also take up the project of establishing comparable social norms. Both types of norms may work together to arrest incitement and in this way help prevent mass atrocities. Indeed, this strategy encapsulates the overall argument of this book, which is that we must attend equally to moral, legal, and social norms if we are to explain and constrain large-scale crimes.

Conclusion

Meeting the moral and political challenges posed by genocide and mass atrocity requires conceptual clarity and historical acuity. Raphael Lemkin, famous for coining the term *genocide*, well understood these needs. Concerning the need for conceptual clarity, Lemkin wrote, "When people think about [a] new phenomenon, when they speak about it fervently, when they finally reach out for action in connection with this phenomenon, they must have a name for it."[1] Concerning the need for historical acuity, he observed, "One cannot describe a crime by one example; one must rather draw on all available experiences of the past."[2]

In this study, I have named and explained many different roles that norms perform before, during, and after large-scale crimes. I have defined the notion of norm inversion and compared it to alternative processes of norm erosion and norm evasion. I have suggested that soldiers and humanitarian aid workers rely on moral norms against deliberation when facing recurrent moral dilemmas, and described several pathways by which those norms might be revised. At the institutional level, I have argued that political leaders commonly employ legal norms to legitimate persecution or deny atrocities and have spotlighted changes in international law designed to end to impunity for such crimes. Finally, I have shown that social norms, though typically portrayed by philosophers as informal bases of social stability, also help structure episodes of mass violence.

My analysis of the action-guiding power of norms in circumstances of mass atrocity has been informed by authors and scholars in many fields. For my basic account of norm acceptance and norm guidance, I have drawn from philosophers working in meta-ethics, particularly those pursuing naturalistic accounts of norm cognition. For my understanding of the etiology of mass atrocities I have relied on the work of historians, political scientists, and sociologists—even while contesting some of their specific explanatory claims. From the start, I have been inspired by the testimony of survivors of large-scale crimes, who exhibit great courage in reprising their experiences of terror, loss, and abjection, and who provide the clearest picture of life during mass atrocities. Finally, I have learned caution from commentators like Lawrence Langer who contend that out of the "ruins of memory" wrought by large-scale crimes, no special insights into human dignity or human duties can be retrieved.[3]

Given the particular structure of this study—with its separate sections addressing moral, legal, and social norms—readers may be left with lingering questions about the ways in which these three types of norms work together, or work against each other. What happens when institutions nominally governed by egalitarian legal norms are infiltrated by discriminatory social norms? How do the practical commitments and normative attitudes that individuals campaigning for changes in moral norms hold alter when those norms ultimately come to be enshrined in legal prohibitions or prescriptions? And how, in the real world, can disputes about the normative status or prescriptive force of a particular norm or set of norms be resolved?[4]

In response to this last question, we may return to the case of the doctrine of Responsibility to Protect (R2P) discussed in chapter 1 and consider how the analytical framework developed in this study improves our understanding of the status of this much-contested norm.[5]

Conceived as a response to the international community's mixed record of humanitarian intervention during the 1990s, the concept of the Responsibility to Protect was first articulated in writing in the report of the International Commission on Intervention and State Sovereignty in 2001.[6] The specific content of this proto-norm was clarified in the report of the 2005 UN World Summit and in UN Secretary-General Ban Ki-moon's 2009 report, *Implementing the Responsibility to Protect*. Particularly after the invocation of R2P in the Security Council's authorization of air strikes in Libya in 2011, postcolonial, feminist, and pacifist critics raised objections to this new normative approach to sovereignty and the use of force.[7] Today, though state actors seem less enthused about R2P, legal scholars and activists remain immersed in what Sarah Sewall has described as "a period of ferment and experimentation regarding what [this] norm entails in practice."[8]

One major part of this ferment consists in debates about what exactly it means to call R2P a norm, what evidence should count in favor of that judgment, and what practical consequences, if any, follow from such determinations. The analytical framework laid out in this book offers help on each of these fronts. In the first place, I would suggest, debates ostensibly about whether R2P should be called a norm are frequently better understood as debates about whether it has achieved the status of a legal norm. For example, Alex Bellamy and Edward Luck, in their recent book *The Responsibility to Protect: From Promise to Practice*, suggest that one issue "complicat[ing] the question of evaluating whether R2P is a norm" is that "governments and international relations experts mean different things when they use the word 'norm.'"[9] On the one hand, "governments tend to view norms as binding legal principles"; on the other hand, international relations scholars conceive norms as "shared expectations of appropriate behavior for actors with a given identity."[10] What Bellamy and Luck overlook is the fact that these comments do not necessarily implicate two different general conceptions of norms but may equally refer to two different orders of normativity. Advocates of the former view may wish to ask whether R2P has achieved the status of a legal norm. Advocates of the latter view may wish to argue that R2P has already achieved the status of a social norm. Interpreting the alternative positions in this way hardly dissolves the disagreement, but it does make possible a clearer understanding of its stakes.

A similar confusion runs through debates about what sort of evidence would confirm R2P's status as a norm. Even scholars and activists unfamiliar with the analytical framework set forth in this study may be inclined to resist the suggestion, commonly advanced in the literature, that the Responsibility to Protect must become an object of consensus within the international community before it can gain the status of a norm.[11] Setting aside this implausible proposal, the framework I have offered suggests that the kinds of evidence that could confirm R2P's status as a norm vary depending on what particular type of norm we suppose R2P to be. If it is a legal norm, we should expect to see R2P embedded in the practices of states and other institutional actors, and we should equally see the operation of standing procedural rules governing its emergence into those practices. If instead R2P is conceived as a moral norm, then the practical commitments and normative attitudes of individual actors (such as state leaders), linguistically expressed or indicated by actions, may furnish the best evidence of its status as accepted norm.[12]

Finally, what sort of norm we take R2P to be has consequences for its practical effects, and especially the effects of breaching it. As noted in chapter 1, current formulations of this doctrine refrain from portraying forcible protective actions undertaken by the international community as sanctions against leaders who fail to protect their citizens, and any subsequent legal accountability for those leaders is likely to be imposed under the auspices of international criminal law rather than R2P. The standard sanctions deployed by international norm entrepreneurs, naming and shaming, tend to work best when state actors have publicly signed on to relevant treaties, conventions, or other legal instruments, though they can also be employed where leaders have made merely verbal commitments to moral or social norms. Finally, as with the case of Lemkin's earliest antigenocide advocacy, the conscience and moral commitments of individual state leaders may themselves provide an appropriate basis for pressing home the moral responsibilities articulated by R2P.[13]

If debates about the normative status of the Responsibility to Protect illustrate the possibility of overlap and ambiguity among moral, legal, and social norms, the activities of museums and other educational institutions that teach the history of large-scale crimes and claim to promote prevention suggest that distinctions among these several types of norms are already widely recognized. Museums and memorials devoted to mass atrocities, whether the United States Holocaust Memorial Museum in Washington, DC, the Museo Memoria Y Tolerencia in Mexico City, or the Denkmal für die ermordeten Jüden Europas in Berlin, typically incorporate displays that confront their visitors with moral dilemmas. They also tend to elevate particular historical individuals and groups as moral exemplars. In framing education about large-scale crimes in this way, these institutions suggest that mass atrocities are a challenge to our received moral attitudes and commitments. They then go on to emphasize how invidious legal or social norms threaten to confound those commitments. A recent exhibition at the US Holocaust Memorial Museum, "Some Were Neighbors," focused in part on showing how social norms within communities exposed to the Holocaust undermined previously accepted moral norms and in part on demonstrating that other moral norms widely accepted by audiences today (for example, concerning the equality or inherent dignity of persons) were not held by members of relevant populations. Similarly, museum exhibitions on historical and contemporary large-scale crimes commonly highlight restrictive laws, at the domestic and international levels, that prevent effective emigration and asylum claims for those targeted for violence. Such presentations of pernicious legal and social norms take on new urgency when the countries hosting relevant museums are themselves roiled in immigration controversies or ruled by xenophobic ideologues. But the same political circumstances often force directors of such museums to resolve complex ethical challenges.[14]

Here, finally, a general conclusion about the study and teaching of mass atrocities emerges. Individual scholars and educational institutions working on these issues are not immune to moral conflicts and perhaps are not better equipped to deal with them than any other moral agents. However, because of the specific content of their endeavors and given their widely recognized position of norm leadership, a higher ethical standard applies to them. This recalls a point I raised early in this study, where I noted that although few individuals will ever be in a position to prevent mass atrocities, investigation of individual and institutional responses to such crimes may be of considerable value for addressing more routine moral conflicts. Civil disobedience or vocal defiance in the face of unjust laws that do not rise to the level of atrocity remains an important function for museums and educators to perform. Such institutions and individuals also occupy a ready platform for combating pernicious social norms. I do not mean to claim merely that museums and scholars of mass violence enjoy social permission to speak out on these topics. Rather, they are, and are rightly, expected to do so. This will remain true for as long as mass atrocities menace our individual moral commitments and our collective capacities for resistance.

Notes

Introduction

1. See Eric Weitz, *A Century of Genocide: Utopias of Race and Nation* (Princeton, NJ: Princeton University Press, 2003); Christian Gerlach, *Extremely Violent Societies: Mass Violence in the Twentieth-Century World* (Cambridge: Cambridge University Press, 2010); Dan Stone, ed., *The Historiography of Genocide* (New York: Palgrave-Macmillan, 2008); James Waller, *Becoming Evil: How Ordinary People Commit Genocide and Mass Killing* (New York: Oxford University Press, 2002); George Mastroianni, *Of Mind and Murder: Towards a More Comprehensive Psychology of the Holocaust* (New York: Oxford University Press, 2019); Ervin Staub, *The Roots of Evil: The Origins of Genocide and Other Group Violence* (Cambridge: Cambridge University Press, 1992); Harald Welzer, *Täter: Wie aus ganz normalen Mensen Massenmörder werden* (Frankfurt: Fischer Verlag, 2007); Kristen Renwick Monroe, *Ethics in an Age of Terror and Genocide* (Princeton, NJ: Princeton University Press, 2012); Benjamin Valentino, *Final Solutions: Mass Killing and Genocide in the 20th Century* (Ithaca, NY: Cornell University Press, 2005); Scott Straus, *The Order of Genocide* (Ithaca, NY: Cornell University Press, 2006); Mahmood Mamdani, *When Victims Become Killers: Colonialism, Nativism, and the Genocide in Rwanda* (Princeton, NJ: Princeton University Press, 2001); Barbara Harff, "No Lessons Learned from the Holocaust? Assessing Risks of Genocide and Political Mass Murder since 1955," *American Political Science Review* 97, no. 1 (2003): 57–73; Helen Fein, *Genocide: A Sociological Perspective* (London: Sage, 1993); Christopher Powell, *Barbaric Civilization: A Critical Sociology of Genocide* (Montreal: McGill–Queen's University Press, 2011).

2. Alexander Laban Hinton, "The Dark Side of Modernity: Toward an Anthropology of Genocide," in *Annihilating Difference: The Anthropology of Genocide*, ed. Alexander Hinton (Berkeley: University of California Press, 2002); Charles Anderton and Jurgen Brauer, eds., *Economic Aspects of Genocides, Other Mass Atrocities, and Their Prevention* (New York: Oxford University Press, 2016); Thomas Pegelow Kaplan, *The Language of Nazi Genocide: Linguistic Violence and the Struggle of Germans of Jewish Ancestry* (Cambridge: Cambridge University Press, 2009); Marguerite Feitlowitz, *A Lexicon of Terror: Argentina and the Legacies of Torture* (New York: Oxford University Press, 1998).

3. This approach accords with the account of norms recently set out by philosopher Neil Roughley, who writes, "Understanding norms is a two-way process, involving a close interaction between conceptual clarification and empirical research." See Neil Roughley, "Might We Be Essentially Normative Animals?" in *The Normative Animal? On the Anthropological Significance of Social, Moral, and Linguistic Norms*, ed. Neil Roughley and Kurt Bayertz (New York: Oxford University Press, 2019), 3.

4. Nicholas Southwood, "The Moral/Conventional Distinction," *Mind* 120, no. 479 (2011): 761–802; Cristina Bicchieri, *The Grammar of Society* (Cambridge: Cambridge University Press, 2006); Edna Ullman-Margalit, *The Emergence of Norms* (Oxford: Clarendon Press, 1977); Geoffrey Brennan, Robert Goodin, Nicholas Southwood, and Lina Eriksson, *Explaining Norms* (New York: Oxford University Press, 2013).

5. On this point, my account parallels the approach taken by philosopher Claudia Card, who "begins from the premise that atrocities are paradigmatic evils." My project differs from Card's insofar as my focus is not on the concept of evil but on the accepted norms that make atrocities possible and the prospective norms that might help prevent them. Claudia Card, *Confronting Evils: Terrorism, Torture, Genocide* (Cambridge: Cambridge University Press, 2010), 14.

6. Raphael Lemkin, *Axis Rule in Occupied Europe* (Washington, DC: Carnegie Endowment for International Peace, 1944), 79.

7. Specifically, the Convention limits legally recognizable targets of genocide to "national, ethnical, racial or religious group[s]." UN Convention on the Prevention and Punishment of the Crime of Genocide, adopted December 9, 1948; entered into force January 12, 1951. Article II.

8. See, e.g., Deborah Mayersen, *On the Path to Genocide: Armenia and Rwanda Reexamined* (New York: Berghahn Books, 2014), 10.

9. For a good overview of this issue, see Uğur Üngör, "Cultural Genocide," in *The Routledge History of Genocide*, ed. Cathie Carmichael and Richard Maguire (New York: Routledge, 2015), 241–253. For a clear discussion of the place of norms in current anthropological notions of culture, see Christoph Antweiler, "On the Human Addiction to Norms: Social Norms and Cultural Universals of Normativity," in Roughley and Bayertz, *Normative Animal*, 83–100.

10. Lemkin, *Axis Rule*, 87–89.

11. This is the number employed, for example, by the Early Warning Project run by the Simon-Skjodt Center for the Prevention of Genocide at the United States Holocaust Memorial Museum. See http://www.earlywarningproject.com/risk_assessments. Most quantitative approaches stipulate a period of twelve months as the relevant time span for aggregating civilian deaths.

12. Scott Straus, "What Is Being Prevented? Genocide, Mass Atrocity, and Conceptual Ambiguity in the Anti-Atrocity Movement," in *Reconstructing Atrocity Prevention,*

ed. Sheri Rosenberg, Tibi Galis, and Alex Zucker (Cambridge: Cambridge University Press, 2016), 26–27. The qualifier "particularly vulnerable" seeks to capture the fact that scholars of mass atrocity are especially concerned with assaults on noncombatants, or on combatants who have been rendered hors de combat. For critical discussion of the distinction between combatant and noncombatant in international law and politics, see Helen Kinsella, *The Image before the Weapon: A Critical History of the Distinction between Combatant and Civilian* (Ithaca, NY: Cornell University Press, 2011).

13. Some might suspect that by adopting a qualitative definition of *mass atrocity*, I am stacking the deck in favor of my argument concerning the role of norms in explaining and preventing such crimes. But this is not so. Numerous theories of large-scale crimes, including theories based on sadism, inherent evil, and cold strategic calculation, define such crimes qualitatively, while leaving little room for norms in their purported explanations.

14. Mark Osiel, *Obeying Orders: Atrocity, Military Discipline and the Laws of War* (New Brunswick, NJ: Transaction, 1998), 45, cited in David Scheffer, "Genocide and Atrocity Crimes," *Genocide Studies and Prevention* 1, no. 3 (2006): 338. See also Julien Théry, "*Atrocitas/enormitas*: Pour une histoire de la catégorie 'd' énormité' ou 'crime énorme' du Moyen Âge à l'époque moderne," *Clio@Themis: Revue électronique d'histoire du droit* 4 (2011): 5–7.

15. Paul Morrow, "A Theory of Atrocity Propaganda," *Humanity* 9, no. 1 (2018): 45–62.

16. Powell, *Barbaric Civilization*, 33–36, 75–80.

17. Legal scholar David Scheffer advocates *atrocity crimes* as a collective term for offenses now distinguished in law as genocide, crimes against humanity, and war crimes. He claims that this collective term is better suited to "selling to the public the credibility and utility" of international criminal prosecutions, and can enhance the "accuracy and integrity" of those proceedings. In previous work, I have criticized Scheffer's proposal for placing too much weight on the need to speed public consent for military interventions. Here, I follow James Waller, who favors *mass atrocity* over *atrocity crimes* due to the greater "coherence and simplicity" of this term, as well as the fact that it is already "widely embraced." See Scheffer, "Genocide and Atrocity Crimes," 244; Morrow, "Atrocity Propaganda," 55–56; James Waller, *Confronting Evil: Engaging Our Responsibility to Prevent Genocide* (New York: Oxford University Press, 2016), 113–114.

18. The reverse need not be true, of course. Many crimes are large scale but not atrocities.

19. Peter Hayes, *Why? Explaining the Holocaust* (New York: Norton, 2017), xiii.

20. Hayes, *Why? Explaining the Holocaust*, xiv.

21. This sketch necessarily simplifies the distinction between law-governed and non-law-governed explanations. For extended discussion and a variety of viewpoints, see the essays collected in Harold Kincaid, ed., *The Oxford Handbook of Philosophy of Social Science* (New York: Oxford University Press, 2012).

22. Waller, *Becoming Evil*, 265.

23. Evelyn Gertz, Hollie Nyseth Brehm, and Sara Brown, "Gender and Genocide: Assessing Differential Opportunity Structures of Perpetration in Rwanda," in *Perpetrators and Perpetration of Mass Violence*, ed. Timothy Williams and Susanne Buckley-Zistel (London: Routledge, 2018), 135.

24. Mayersen, *On the Path*, 107.

25. Adam Jones, "Gendercide and Genocide," in *Gendercide and Genocide*, ed. Adam Jones (Nashville, TN: Vanderbilt University Press, 2004), 1–38.

26. Sarah Kenyon Lischer, *Dangerous Sanctuaries: Refugee Camps, Civil War, and the Dilemmas of Humanitarian Aid* (Ithaca, NY: Cornell University Press, 2006), 37–38.

27. Cf. Rosenberg et al., *Reconstructing Atrocity Prevention*, 7.

28. Ernesto Verdeja, "Predicting Genocide and Mass Atrocities," *Genocide Studies and Prevention* 9, no. 3 (2016): 13–32.

29. Rosenberg et al., *Reconstructing Atrocity Prevention*, 6.

30. Dwight Raymond, "Military Means of Preventing Mass Atrocities," in *Reconstructing Atrocity Prevention*, ed. Rosenberg et al., 295–318. For the idea of "justified interdiction" to prevent mass atrocities, see David Rodin, "The Myth of National Self-Defense," in *The Morality of Defensive War*, ed. Cécile Fabre and Seth Lazar (New York: Oxford University Press, 2014), 89.

31. Elisa von Joeden-Forgey, "Gender, Sexualized Violence, and the Prevention of Genocide," in *Reconstructing Atrocity Prevention*, ed. Rosenberg et al., 146.

32. Gerlach, *Extremely Violent Societies*, 2010.

33. Primo Levi, *Survival in Auschwitz* (New York: Touchstone, 1996); Lawrence Langer, *Holocaust Testimonies: The Ruins of Memory* (New Haven, CT: Yale University Press, 1993).

34. Jens David Ohlin and Larry May, *Necessity in International Law* (New York: Oxford University Press, 2016), 86.

35. Benjamin Valentino, Paul Huth, and Dylan Balch-Lindsay, "'Draining the Sea': Mass Killing and Guerrilla Warfare," *International Organization* 58, no. 2 (2004): 375–407.

36. Compare Daniel Feierstein, *Genocide as Social Practice: Reorganizing Society under the Nazis and Argentina's Military Juntas* (New Brunswick, NJ: Rutgers University Press, 2014).

37. Holocaust historians will see in this claim tinges of the debate between "intentionalist" and "functionalist" interpretations of the Shoah—the debate about whether the extermination of European Jews proceeded from a conscious plan or from the undirected working of bureaucratic processes. Like most other contemporary scholars of large-scale crimes, I believe this debate presents a false choice. The Holocaust, like other twentieth-century mass atrocities, reflected both intentional action and bureaucratic functioning. For an overview of this debate, see Tom Lawson, *Debates on the Holocaust* (Manchester: University of Manchester Press, 2010), chap. 4.

38. Cristina Bicchieri, *Norms in the Wild: How to Diagnose, Measure, and Change Social Norms* (Oxford: Oxford University Press, 2017).

39. Some readers might worry that this use of primary sources is too selective, providing at best anecdotal evidence for my claims about norms rather than definitive proof. This objection misunderstands the place this study occupies in the scholarly division of labor concerning large-scale crimes. My goal is to provide a conceptually rigorous, analytically capacious account of norms, suitable for use by historians, sociologists, and other scholars undertaking more finely grained studies of specific historical cases of large-scale crimes. The letters, diary entries, and oral testimonies that I analyze are intended to show that this account of norms is not merely a philosophical construct but reflected in the practical deliberations of individuals caught up in various instances of twentieth century mass atrocities.

40. Richard Ashby Wilson, *Writing History in International Criminal Trials* (Cambridge: Cambridge University Press, 2011).

41. Noah Shenker, *Reframing Holocaust Testimony* (Bloomington: Indiana University Press, 2015).

42. This literature is too large to sum up in a single note. Readers eager to know what texts and authors my argument engages may consult the list of works cited at the end of this study.

Chapter 1

1. For the German text of this letter, see Thorsten Suesse and Heinrich Meyer, *Abtransport der "Lebensunwerten"* (Hanover: Verlag Clemens Koechert, 1988), 103–104. The circumstances of composition of this letter, and the text itself, are discussed in Robert Ericksen, *Complicity in the Holocaust: Churches and Universities in Nazi Germany* (Cambridge: Cambridge University Press, 2012), 161–163. My translation.

2. Ericksen, *Complicity in the Holocaust*, 162; Robert Jay Lifton, *The Nazi Doctors: Medical Killing and the Psychology of Genocide* (New York: Basic Books, 2000), 82–88; Henry Friedlander, *The Origins of Nazi Genocide: From Euthanasia to the Final Solution* (Chapel Hill: University of North Carolina Press, 2000), 217.

3. Friedlander, *Origins*.

4. Friedlander, *Origins*, 87–88; Peter Hayes, *Why? Explaining the Holocaust* (New York: Norton, 2017), 118–119.

5. Karl Binding and Alfred Hoche, *Die Freigabe der Vernichtung Lebensuntwerten Lebens: Ihr Mass und ihre Form* (Leipzig: Verlag von Felix Meiner, 1920), excerpted and translated in Steve Hochstadt, ed., *Sources of the Holocaust* (New York: Palgrave Macmillan, 2004), 29–31.

6. These are typically distinguished as statistical norms.

7. I am here making a claim about the existential conditions for norms—the set of facts that must obtain in order for the proposition "there is a norm X in population Y" to be true. This should be distinguished from claims about the epistemic conditions for detecting the existence of norms (though theorists sometimes use this same language of "establishing" when discussing those epistemic conditions). One leading philosopher of social norms, Cristina Bicchieri, objects to references to "attitudes" in theories of norms, arguing that attitudes are difficult to measure and may exert no perceptible influence on action. In my view, her criticisms are better directed at the epistemic connection between norms and attitudes than at the existential connection. See Cristina Bicchieri, *Norms in the Wild* (Oxford: Oxford University Press, 2017), 8–10.

8. In referring to "norm following," "norm conformity," and "norm compliance," I adopt the typology established by Geoffrey Brennan and colleagues to refer to different ways of obeying norms. On this view, following norms implies internalization of those norms: taking on the idea that such prescriptions, permissions, or prohibitions ought to be followed for noninstrumental reasons, while conforming to norms means merely obeying relevant prescriptions or prohibitions without internalizing them. Compliance, finally, serves as a blanket term for actions that follow or conform to particular norms. See Geoffrey Brennan, Robert Goodin, Nicholas Southwood, and Lina Eriksson, *Explaining Norms* (New York: Oxford University Press, 2013), 195–197.

9. Edouard Machery and Ron Mallon, "Evolution of Morality," in *The Moral Psychology Handbook*, ed. John Doris (New York: Oxford University Press, 2012), 3–46; Marco Schmidt and Hannes Rakoczy, "On the Uniqueness of Human Normative Attitudes," in *The Normative Animal? On the Anthropological Significance of Social, Moral, and Linguistic Norms*, ed. Neil Roughley and Kurt Bayertz (New York: Oxford University Press, 2019), 121–135.

10. Cristina Bicchieri, *The Grammar of Society* (Cambridge: Cambridge University Press, 2006); Cristina Bicchieri, Erte Xiao, and Ryan Muldoon, "Trustworthiness Is a Social Norm, but Trusting Is Not," *Politics, Philosophy and Economics* 10, no. 2 (2011): 170–187. See also Ken Binmore, *Natural Justice* (New York: Oxford University Press, 2011).

11. On joint intentions, see Margaret Gilbert, *A Theory of Political Obligation* (New York: Oxford University Press, 2008), 197–204, and Gilbert, *Joint Commitment: How We Make the Social World* (New York: Oxford University Press, 2013); Michael Bratman, *Shared Agency: A Planning Theory of Acting Together* (New York: Oxford University Press, 2014). For children's tendency to infer norms from the actions of others, see Schmidt and Rakoczy, "On the Uniqueness," 127–128.

12. Brennan et al., *Explaining Norms*; Ralph Wedgwood, *The Nature of Normativity* (Oxford: Clarendon Press, 2007); Roughley and Bayertz, *The Normative Animal?*

13. Conventions are also often said to be arbitrary, though this is not a feature that I find particularly valuable for distinguishing them from norms. For the classic philosophical account of conventions, see David Lewis, *Convention: A Philosophical Study* (1969; Malden, MA: Blackwell, 2002). More recent discussions appear in Bicchieri, *The Grammar of Society*, 34–42, and Andrei Marmor, *Social Convention* (Princeton, NJ: Princeton University Press, 2005). I discuss the distinction among conventions, customs, and social norms further in this chapter.

14. On taboos as differing from norms particularly with respect to the normative attitudes underlying compliance with them, see Gerald Gaus, *The Order of Public Reason: A Theory of Morality for a Diverse and Bounded World* (Cambridge: Cambridge University Press, 2011), 205; also see Alan Gibbard, *Wise Choices, Apt Feelings: A Theory of Normative Judgment* (Cambridge, MA: Harvard University Press, 1992), 316.

15. Philosophical accounts of action and agency go back to Aristotle. More recent contributors to this field include Donald Davidson, Elizabeth Anscombe, and Philip Pettit. For a comprehensive overview of topics in this area, see Timothy O'Connor and Constantine Sandis, eds., *A Companion to the Philosophy of Action* (Malden, MA: Blackwell, 2012).

16. John Gibbons, *The Norm of Belief* (New York: Oxford University Press, 2013).

17. Bicchieri, *The Grammar of Society*, 191.

18. Neil Roughley suggests that the "demarcation of … addressees" is one way of understanding the specific character of social norms. It should be clear from my discussion here and in what follows that I don't believe that the fact that a given norm circulates within particular populations is either necessary or sufficient for identifying it as a social norm. Roughley's second suggestion for capturing the specific character of social norms, that is, via the fact that their "*existence grounds in the attitudes or behaviour*" of members of the relevant population, is much closer to what I call the practice-grounded character of social norms. That this feature of social norms is, on my account, shared by legal norms helps clarify the overlap between social and legal norms that Roughley registers. See Neil Roughley, "Might We Be Essentially Normative Animals?" in Roughley and Bayertz, *The Normative Animal?* (emphasis in original), 17.

19. See, for example, Norbert Elias, *The Civilizing Process* (Oxford: Blackwell, 1994); Martha Finnemore and Kathryn Sikkink, "International Norm Dynamics and Political Change," *International Organizations* 52, no. 4 (1998): 887–917; Will Kymlicka, *Multicultural Citizenship: A Liberal Theory of Minority Rights* (New York: Oxford University Press, 1995); Iris Marion Young, *Justice and the Politics of Difference* (Princeton, NJ: Princeton University Press, 1990); Matthew Hornsey, "Social Identity Theory and Self-Categorization Theory: A Historical Review," *Social and Personality Psychology Compass* 2, no. 1 (2008): 204–222.

20. Jason Stanley provides a revisionist account of the relationship between social identities and destructive ideologies in his book *How Propaganda Works* (Princeton, NJ: Princeton University Press, 2015). Jonathan Leader Maynard, who deploys a more traditional definition of ideology, also highlights the relationship between social identities and ideology in "Combating Atrocity-Justifying Ideologies," in *The Responsibility to Prevent: Overcoming the Challenges of Atrocity Prevention*, ed. Serena Sharma and Jennifer Welsh (New York: Oxford University Press, 2015), 189–225. See also Maynard, "Rethinking the Role of Ideology in Mass Atrocities," *Terrorism and Political Violence* 26, no. 5 (2014): 821–841.

21. For the notion of norms as "default" guides to action, see Bicchieri, *Norms in the Wild*, 128.

22. Gaus, *Order of Public Reason*, 54–70.

23. Although these norms rarely come into focus, it may be that we should view their influence too as continuous, serving to rule out even mere consideration of such actions. See Brennan et al., *Explaining Norms*, 251.

24. For a discussion of the "salience," or situational relevance, of norms see Bicchieri, *Grammar of Society*, 46–51.

25. All of these cases are considered in Brennan et al.'s discussion of "norm breaching." Where these authors use the term *norm responsive* to describe such breaches, I prefer the term *norm guided*, as it parallels my definitional claim that norms are capable of guiding the actions of agents. See Brennan et al., *Explaining Norms*, 236–243.

26. Brennan et al., *Explaining Norms*, 29.

27. In making this claim, I endorse the perspective of methodological individualism adopted by philosophers such as Edna Ullman-Margalit, Cristina Bicchieri, and Brennan et al. According to this perspective, claims about the existence of norms ultimately depend on certain facts about individuals (notably facts about the attitudes and commitments of those individuals) rather than on any nonreducible facts about groups. See Bicchieri, *Grammar of Society*, 22; Brennan et al., *Explaining Norms*, 4–5; Edna Ullman-Margalit, *The Emergence of Norms* (Oxford: Clarendon Press, 1977), 16–17. For an extended discussion of the relationship between individualism and holism in philosophical accounts of groups, see Philip Pettit, *The Common Mind: An*

Essay on Psychology, Society, and Politics (New York: Oxford University Press, 1993), chaps. 3, 4.

28. On the significance of social identities for norm emergence, see Finnemore and Sikkink, "International Norm Dynamics," 902–905; also see Brennan et al., *Explaining Norms*, 161–167. On the role of crises, see Richard Price, "Reversing the Gun Sights: Transnational Society Civil Society Targets Land Mines," *International Organization* 52, no. 3 (1998): 613–644. On the role of "trendsetters" or "norm entrepreneurs," see Bicchieri, *Norms in the Wild*, 163–208.

29. For a good discussion of the challenges that confront efforts to directly tie processes of norm emergence to shared social identities, see Brennan et al., *Explaining Norms*, 162–173.

30. On chemical weapons, see Richard Price, *The Chemical Weapons Taboo* (Ithaca, NY: Cornell University Press, 1997). On displaced persons and refugee law, see Phil Orchard, *A Right to Flee* (Cambridge: Cambridge University Press, 2014).

31. While I think there are circumstances in which existing norms objectively fail to address emergent threats to the interests of individuals or groups, the identification of such crises, emergencies, or turning points is often socially contested. This should not come as a surprise, since the interests of group members are rarely affected in the same way, or to the same degree, by failures of existing norms, and since proposed solutions to those failures often have their own disproportionate impacts. For a critique of reflexive discussions of "emergencies" in contemporary humanitarian discourse, see Jennifer Rubenstein, "Emergency Claims and Democratic Politics," *Social Philosophy and Policy* 32, no. 1 (2015): 101–126.

32. Bicchieri, *Norms in the Wild*, chap. 5; Finnemore and Sikkink, "International Norm Dynamics."

33. Lisbeth Zimmerman, *Global Norms with a Local Face: Rule-of-Law Promotion and Norm Translation* (Cambridge: Cambridge University Press, 2017), 207.

34. Gilbert, *Theory of Political Obligation*, 199.

35. For discussion of how judges square their responsibility for resolving such disputes with their general inclination to maintain the predictability of legal norms, see Jeremy Waldron, "The Concept and the Rule of Law," *Georgia Law Review* 43 (2008): 1–61, and "The Rule of Law and the Importance of Procedure," in *NOMOS L: Getting to the Rule of Law*, ed. James Fleming (New York: NYU Press, 2011), 3–33.

36. Cristina Bicchieri offers an account of "moralization," or the transformation of social norms into moral norms, that is very similar to this. See Bicchieri, *Norms in the Wild*, 31, 126–127.

37. I expand on these salient distinctions among legal, moral, and social norms in chapters 2, 4, and 6.

38. Some may deny that norms can undergo changes in modality, and insist that permissive norms may be replaced by prescriptive norms, but cannot be said to become prescriptive themselves. I think that it makes sense to say that a permissive norm can become a prescriptive norm, both from the standpoint of individual agents and from the perspective of populations at large. But as I argue below, I do not think prohibitive norms can turn into prescriptive norms, or vice versa. Thus, I understand if others deny the possibility for any norm to survive a change in modality.

39. For an alternative description of norm inversion in terms of institutionalized rule breaking, according to which initially binding norms are not eliminated but only suspended for a definite period during which contrary norms prevail, see Christoph Antweiler, "On the Human Addiction to Norms: Social Norms and Cultural Universals of Normativity," in Roughley and Bayertz, *The Normative Animal?*, 92–93.

40. In this case, it is doubtful whether even the relevant population should be seen as constant, since Conti himself was deeply involved in the process of narrowing the definition of the *Volk*.

41. Ericksen, *Complicity in the Holocaust*.

42. See, however, my discussion of demoralization in section 2.3.

43. For a recent sketch of such an account, see Christopher Kutz, "How Norms Die: Torture and Assassination in American Policy," *Ethics and International Affairs* 28, no. 4 (2014): 426–430.

44. Olga Kovacs testimony, interview 35369, *Visual History Archive*, USC Shoah Foundation, tape 3, 27:50–28:30. Olga was born on May 23, 1926. Her mother and aunt, she says, were forty-four and thirty-eight, respectively, at the time of their deportation.

45. David Rousset, *L'univers Concentrationnaire* (Paris: Editions du Pavois, 1946); Eric Weitz, *A Century of Genocide: Utopias of Race and Nation* (Princeton, NJ: Princeton University Press, 2003); Christian Gerlach, *Extremely Violent Societies: Mass Violence in the Twentieth-Century World* (Cambridge: Cambridge University Press, 2010).

46. Lee Ann Fujii, "Transforming the Normative Landscape: The Diffusion of a Genocidal Norm in Rwanda," *Journal of Genocide Research* 6, no. 1 (2004): 99–114. The parallel between Fujii's phrasing and the description of norm inversion offered by Dr. Conti in his letter to Dr. Ewald is striking.

47. Fujii, "Transforming the Normative Landscape," 99–100.

48. Fujii, "Transforming the Normative Landscape," 113. In her subsequent book, *Killing Neighbors: Webs of Violence in Rwanda*, Fujii disavows part of the analysis contained in this article. She notes that "while leaders and politicians can frame any conflict in ethnic terms," the reasons for which individuals within local communities

participate in conflict may differ substantially, reflecting distinctively local social and political configurations. This analysis puts Fujii's position closer to that of Christian Gerlach, who has emphasized the role of cross-cutting "coalitions for violence" in perpetrating mass atrocities. See Lee Ann Fujii, *Killing Neighbors: Webs of Violence in Rwanda* (Ithaca, NY: Cornell University Press, 2009), 180; Gerlach, *Extremely Violent Societies*, 274.

49. Fujii, "Transforming the Normative Landscape," 100.

50. Christopher Browning, *Ordinary Men: Reserve Police Battalion 101 and the Final Solution in Poland* (New York: Harper Perennial, 1993).

51. Browning, *Ordinary Men*, 150.

52. Carlos Santiago Nino, *Radical Evil on Trial* (New York: Oxford University Press, 1996), 47.

53. Kenneth Ledford, "Judging German Judges in the Third Reich: Excusing and Confronting the Past," in *The Law in Nazi Germany*, ed. Alan Steinweis and Robert Rachlin (New York: Berghahn Books, 2013), 161–189; David Dyzenhaus, *Judging the Judges, Judging Ourselves* (Oxford: Hart Publishing, 2003).

54. Fujii, "Genocidal Norm," 112.

55. Mark Osiel, *Making Sense of Mass Atrocity* (Cambridge: Cambridge University Press, 2009), 203–217.

56. Osiel, *Making Sense of Mass Atrocity*, 210–213.

57. For foundational statements of the principle of Responsibility to Protect, see "The Responsibility to Protect," *Report of the International Commission on Intervention and State Sovereignty* (Ottawa: International Development Research Center, 2001); also see UN World Summit Outcome, Resolution Adopted by the General Assembly, A/RES/60/1 (2005).

58. Luke Glanville, "On the Meaning of 'Responsibility' in the 'Responsibility to Protect,'" *Griffith Law Review* 20 (2011): 482–504.

59. To be sure, some critics of R2P see such actions as punishments. Venezuela's delegate to the 2005 UN World Summit remarked that R2P would lead to "'States of the [global] South' being 'stigmatized as systematic violators of collective human rights and punished through `humanitarian intervention.'" See UN GAOR, 59th Sess., 89th plenary meeting, 24, UN Doc. A/59/PV.89 (April 8, 2005), cited in Jonah Eaton, "An Emerging Norm? Determining the Meaning and Legal Status of the Responsibility to Protect," *Michigan Journal of International Law* 32 (2010): 788–789.

60. There may still be reputational consequences of such failures. Cf. Glanville, "On the Meaning of 'Responsibility,'" 492–493.

61. Advocates of the Responsibility to Protect have also sometimes been guilty of overlooking the fact that states that express skepticism toward this doctrine due to concerns about sovereignty may also be guided by norms rather than mere calculations of self-interest. See Jennifer Welsh, "Norm Contestation and the Responsibility to Protect," *Global Responsibility to Protect* 5, no. 4 (2013): 365–396.

62. Finnemore and Sikkink, "International Norm Dynamics"; Michael Barnett, *Empire of Humanity* (Ithaca, NY: Cornell University Press, 2011).

63. Philosophers refer to this activity as "mindreading."

64. Bicchieri, *Norms in the Wild*, 64–65.

65. Bicchieri, *Norms in the Wild*.

66. Bicchieri, *Norms in the Wild*.

67. Stanley Milgram, *Obedience to Authority* (New York: Harper Perennial, 2009); Philip Zimbardo, Craig Haney, and Curtis Banks, "Interpersonal Dynamics in a Simulated Prison," *International Journal of Criminology and Penology* 1, no. 1 (1973): 69–97. For an up-to-date critical discussion of criticisms of these experiments and their influence within social psychology, see George Mastroianni, *Of Mind and Murder: Toward a More Comprehensive Psychology of the Holocaust* (Oxford: Oxford University Press, 2018).

68. For the need for evidence concerning norms and norm guidance that is independent of observed behavioral patterns, cf. Bicchieri, *Norms in the Wild*, 57; Antweiler, "On the Human Addiction," 100.

69. Raul Hilberg, *Sources of Holocaust Research: An Analysis* (Chicago: Ivan Dee, 2001); Robert Wolfe, "Nazi Paperwork for the Final Solution," in *Perspectives on the Holocaust: Essays in Honor of Raul Hilberg*, ed. James Pacy and Alan Wertheimer (Boulder, CO: Westview, 1995), 5–6.

70. For detailed discussion of language rules under National Socialism, see Paul Morrow, "Mass Atrocity and Manipulation of Social Norms," *Social Theory and Practice* 40, no. 2 (2014): 255–280. Further analysis of euphemistic or camouflaged language appears in chapter 2 of this study.

71. Yehuda Bauer, *Rethinking the Holocaust* (New Haven: Yale University Press, 2001), 23–24. For a more recent discussion of the advantages and disadvantages of the increasing use of testimony as a source of historical knowledge among Holocaust scholars, see Henry Greenspan, Sara Horowitz, Éva Kovács, Berel Lang, Dori Laub, Kenneth Waltzer, and Annette Wieviorka, "Engaging Survivors: Assessing 'Testimony' and 'Trauma' as Foundational Concepts," *Dapim* 28, no. 3 (2014): 190–226.

72. C. A. J. Coady, *Testimony: A Philosophical Study* (New York: Oxford University Press, 1995); Alvin Goldman, *Knowledge in a Social World* (New York: Oxford

University Press, 1999); Jennifer Lackey, *Learning from Words* (New York: Oxford University Press, 2008).

73. For a clear discussion of the forms of evidence employed at international criminal trials, see Richard Ashby Wilson, *Writing History in International Criminal Trials* (Cambridge: Cambridge University Press, 2011).

74. Coady calls this form of attestation "institutional testimony." See Coady, *Testimony*, 51.

75. I thank participants in two meetings of the "Future of Holocaust Testimonies" conference series at the University of Virginia and Western Galilee College for clarifying my thinking on this issue.

76. See Zoë Waxman, "Transcending History? Methodological Problems in Holocaust Testimony," in *The Holocaust and Historical Methodology*, ed. Dan Stone (New York: Berghahn Books, 2012), 143–157. To be clear, I am using *testimony* here not in its narrow juridical or quasi-juridical sense, but in the broader sense that includes diaries, memoirs, and other types of text and speech as well.

77. Bauer, *Rethinking the Holocaust*, 25.

78. Goldman, *Knowledge*; Coady, *Testimony*.

79. I say more about this issue in my discussion of social norms in chapters 6 and 7.

80. Rebecca Wittmann, *Beyond Justice: The Auschwitz Trial* (Cambridge, MA: Harvard University Press, 2005), 149.

81. Kovacs testimony, tape 3, minutes 16:00–19:00.

82. Benno Cohn testimony, session 15 (April 25, 1961), in *The Trial of Adolf Eichmann: Record of Proceedings in the District Court of Jerusalem* (Jerusalem: Trust for the Publication of the Proceedings of the Eichmann Trial, in cooperation with the Israel State Archives and Yad Vashem, the Holocaust Martyrs' and Heroes' Remembrance Authority, 1992–1995), 1:227.

83. Nicolas Baumard and Dan Sperber, "Evolutionary and Cognitive Anthropology," in *A Companion to Moral Anthropology*, ed. Didier Fassin (Malden, MA: Wiley, 2012), 611–627; Jonathan Haidt, "The Emotional Dog and Its Rational Tail: A Social Intuitionist Approach to Moral Judgment," in *Moral Psychology: Historical and Contemporary Readings*, ed. Thomas Nadelhoffer, Eddy Nahmias, and Shaun Nichols (Malden, MA: Blackwell, 2010), 343–358.

84. Scholars of norms have long acknowledged that their descriptions of norm guidance are in fact reconstructions of deliberative practices and do not provide unmediated access to agents' cognitive processes. What is different about the views I am describing is that they posit processes that are essentially nonrational as the

basic drivers of behavior. See Ullman-Margalit, *The Emergence of Norms*, 1977, 1; Bicchieri, *The Grammar of Society*, 3.

85. Kristen Renwick Monroe, *Ethics in an Age of Terror and Genocide: Identity and Moral Choice* (Princeton, NJ: Princeton University Press 2012).

86. Monroe, *Ethics in an Age of Terror*, 21. One of Monroe's key claims is that individuals who conceive of their identity as more extensive (that is, broadly connected with that of other individuals across space and time) are more likely to perceive threats to the well-being of those others as morally salient, and thus as occasions for moral choice.

87. Monroe, *Ethics in an Age of Terror*, 347. Monroe construes categorization as a cognitive process operating in several distinct stages. First, out of the manifold data of experience, cognitive categorization settles the particular ways in which situations will be framed for actors. Particular frames in turn lead to the activation, or suppression, of particular scripts for behavior. These scripts, finally, count as the proximate causes of observed conduct.

88. Monroe, *Ethics in an Age of Terror*, 23–24.

89. Monroe, *Ethics in an Age of Terror*, 8. Brennan et al. cite Monroe in discussing norms against deliberation. Brennan et al., *Explaining Norms*, 252.

90. At times, Monroe seems to acknowledge this point, for example, in her interview with the Dutch rescuer Tony and his transformation from a fairly conservative, parochial self-conception to a much more liberal and holistic self-image. See Monroe, *Ethics in an Age of Terror*, 66–68, 317–318.

91. An important caveat to this claim is that the extended theoretical discussion Monroe provides at the end of her study draws on many different views in which norms *do* play a central role—for example, her discussion of the theory that humans have an innate moral grammar that makes the cognition of norms both possible and pervasive. See Monroe, *Ethics in an Age of Terror*, chap. 9.

92. This point will be familiar to readers acquainted with constructivist approaches in international relations, though the specific interactions between norms and identity I describe are not fully captured there.

93. For detailed discussion of this distinction, see Paul Morrow, "Identity-Directed Norm Transformations and Moral Progress," *Journal of Value Inquiry* (forthcoming).

94. Friedlander, *Origins*, 1–9. For a discussion of a similar division between scientific professionals and the broader public on this issue in late-nineteenth-century Britain, see Rob Boddice, *The Science of Sympathy: Morality, Evolution, and Victorian Civilization* (Urbana: University of Illinois Press, 2016), esp. chap. 6.

95. Friedlander, *Origins*, 17.

96. Weitz, *Century*, chap. 3. As noted, however, this change in laws does not seem to have succeeded in changing the moral beliefs and attitudes of most Germans toward euthanasia.

97. Telford Taylor, "Opening Statement of the Prosecution, December 9, 1946," in *The Nazi Doctors and the Nuremberg Code*, ed. George J. Annas and Michael A. Grodin (New York: Oxford University Press, 1992), 88; Evelyne Shuster, "Fifty Years Later: The Significance of the Nuremberg Code," *New England Journal of Medicine* 337, no. 20 (1997): 1436–1440.

98. Paul Weindling, "The Origins of Informed Consent: The International Scientific Commission on Medical War Crimes, and the Nuremberg Code," *Bulletin of the History of Medicine* 75, no. 1 (2001): 55, 58.

99. Weindling, "The Origins of Informed Consent," 66–67.

Chapter 2

1. Arthur Conan Doyle, "The Uses of Hatred," *Times*, December 26, 1917, 9.

2. Giovanni Brizzi, "Carthage and Hannibal in Roman and Greek Memory," in *A Companion to the Punic Wars*, ed. B. D. Hoyos (Malden, MA: Wiley-Blackwell, 2011), 483–492.

3. Philip Taylor, *Munitions of the Mind: A History of Propaganda*, 3rd ed. (Manchester: Manchester University Press, 2003), 73–80.

4. Harold Lasswell, *Propaganda Technique in World War I* (Cambridge, MA: MIT Press, 1972), 82. (Originally published in 1927 as *Propaganda Technique in the World War*.)

5. Taylor, *Munitions*; Nicholas O'Shaughnessy, *Politics and Propaganda: Weapons of Mass Seduction* (Ann Arbor: University of Michigan Press, 2005).

6. Christopher Browning, *Ordinary Men: Reserve Police Battalion 101 and the Final Solution in Poland* (New York: Harper Perennial, 1992), xx, cited in James Waller, *Becoming Evil* (New York: Oxford University Press, 2002), 16–17.

7. See, for example, David Enoch, *Taking Morality Seriously: A Defense of Robust Realism* (Oxford: Oxford University Press, 2011); Henry Richardson, *Articulating the Moral Community: Toward a Constructive Ethical Pragmatism* (Oxford: Oxford University Press, 2018), 4–6.

8. See the various essays in James Lenman and Yonatan Shemmer, eds., *Constructivism in Practical Philosophy* (Oxford: Oxford University Press, 2012).

9. J. L. Mackie, *Ethics: Inventing Right and Wrong* (New York: Pelican Books, 1977).

10. Nicholas Southwood, "The Moral/Conventional Distinction," *Mind* 120, no. 479 (2011): 780–781. Southwood's essay is more directly concerned with the ontology

of moral norms than with the role of moral norms in practical reasoning. As his argument makes clear, however, beliefs about the ontology of moral norms may bear directly on the ways in which they guide action. For a similar account of this first salient feature of moral norms, see Ryan Muldoon, "Understanding Norms and Changing Them," *Social Philosophy and Policy* 35, no. 1 (2018): 134–135.

11. Southwood, "Moral/Conventional," 773.

12. The most prominent defender of this view is Lon Fuller. See Fuller, *The Morality of Law* (New Haven, CT: Yale University Press, 1964). More recently, legal philosophers Joseph Raz and Jeremy Waldron have incorporated some of Fuller's claims into their own accounts of the nature and value of the rule of law. See Raz, "The Rule of Law and Its Virtue," in *The Authority of Law,* 2nd ed. (Oxford: Oxford University Press, 2009), 210–232; Waldron, "The Rule of Law and the Importance of Procedure," in *NOMOS L: Getting to the Rule of Law*, ed. James Fleming (New York: NYU Press, 2011), 3–31. For more extended discussion of this feature of legal norms, see chapter 4 below.

13. As philosopher Leslie Green puts it, "There are indeed no 'rules of change' in morality." See Leslie Green, "Escapable Law: Gardner on Law and Morality," *Oxford Legal Studies Research Paper* 15 (2018), 13, https://papers.ssrn.com/sol3/papers.cfm?abstract_id=3261903&download=yes.

14. Philosopher Neil Roughley makes a similar point in analyzing the distinctive domain of moral norms when he suggests that "authority-independence" is a property typically associated with moral judgments. By "authority-independence," he means that "whether or not others are affected negatively by an action or inaction is, with few exceptions, something that does not depend on the proclamations of authority." See Neil Roughley, "Moral Obligations from the Outside In," in *The Normative Animal? On the Anthropological Significance of Social, Moral, and Linguistic Norms*, ed. Neil Roughley and Kurt Bayertz (New York: Oxford University Press, 2019), 224.

15. The philosophical literature on ideology is as robust as that on norms, but the two remain poorly connected. The term *ideology* does not appear anywhere in Geoffrey Brennan, Robert Goodin, Nicholas Southwood, and Lina Eriksson, *Explaining Norms* (New York: Oxford University Press, 2013), or in Cristina Bicchieri's *Norms in the Wild: How to Diagnose, Measure, and Change Social Norms* (Oxford: Oxford University Press, 2017). It is not the place of this study to reconcile these two literatures. However, I do think that ideologies can be sources of individuals' practical commitments and normative attitudes, and in this way serve as a basis for the acceptance of moral norms. For a clear definition of political ideology, which explicitly refers to "normative, semantic, and/or reputedly factual ideas," see Jonathan Leader Maynard, "Combating Atrocity-justifying Ideologies," in *The Responsibility to Prevent: Overcoming the Challenges of Atrocity Prevention*, ed. Serena Sharma and Jennifer Welsh (New York: Oxford University Press, 2015), 191.

16. For a philosophical defense of the possibility of moral testimony, see Linda Zagzebski, *Epistemic Authority: A Theory of Trust, Authority, and Autonomy in Belief* (New York: Oxford University Press, 2012), esp. chap. 8.

17. For the notion of intolerable harm, see Claudia Card, *The Atrocity Paradigm: A Theory of Evil* (New York: Oxford University Press, 2002), 9–13. Card holds that both direct perception and the testimony of victims provide privileged knowledge of "the harm of atrocities."

18. This phrase, routinely encountered in discussions of mass atrocity, originates in a 1784 poem by Robert Burns, "Man Was Made to Mourn." See Mark Celinscak, *Distance from the Belsen Heap: Allied Forces and the Liberation of a Nazi Concentration Camp* (Toronto: University of Toronto Press, 2015), 111.

19. Waller, *Becoming Evil*, 203.

20. Mark Osiel, *Making Sense of Mass Atrocity* (Cambridge: Cambridge University Press, 2009), xi.

21. Paul Bartrop, "Righteousness in the Face of Evil," in *Genocide Perspectives IV: Essays on Holocaust and Genocide*, ed. Colin Tatz (Sydney: UTS ePress 2012), 467.

22. G. M. Gilbert, "The Mentality of the SS Murderous Robots," *Yad Vashem Studies* 5 (1963): 35–41, cited in Waller, *Becoming Evil*, 62.

23. The letter from Leonardo Conti to Gottfried Ewald cited in chapter 1 provides one example of such evidence. Another widely cited example from Holocaust historiography is the speech delivered by SS chief Heinrich Himmler to members of the SS in Posen (Posnau) Poland on October 4, 1943, in which Himmler asserted the existence of a "moral right," as well as "a duty to our people" to exterminate the Jews. For relevant extracts of this long speech, see Steve Hochstadt, ed., *Sources of the Holocaust* (New York: Palgrave Macmillan, 2004), 164.

24. For an alternative criticism of this explanatory thesis, which focuses not on its circularity but on "the profound and enduring *unreliability* of motivations in general and of those expresses by perpetrators in particular," see Arne Johan Vetlesen, "Social Science and the Study of Perpetrators," in *Emotions and Mass Atrocity: Philosophical and Theoretical Explorations*, ed. Thomas Brudholm and Johannes Lang (Cambridge: Cambridge University Press, 2018), 119.

25. See Claudia Koonz, *The Nazi Conscience* (Cambridge, MA: Belknap Press at Harvard University Press, 2005); Eric Weitz, *A Century of Genocide* (Princeton, NJ: Princeton University Press, 2003).

26. These historical accounts lead me to question Derek Matravers's claim—offered in a discussion of fictional, rather than historical, narratives—that "we cannot understand how something could be a moral reason for the denigration of non-white ethnic groups or the mass extermination of Jews." The beliefs and attitudes

that Weitz, Koonz, and other scholars identify as central to genocidal ideologies, such as beliefs about purity, safeguarding one's friends and family, and self-sacrifice in service of a noble cause are recognizably within the universe of moral reasons. These beliefs are simply, horribly misdirected. Saying that we can understand such views from within the moral point of view does not require us to admit that most, or even many, of the individuals who have planned or perpetrated historical large-scale crimes were substantially guided by such moral commitments while doing so. In other words, we can agree that the thesis of moral norm inversion is intelligible without agreeing that it is correct. See Derek Matravers, *Fiction and Narrative* (New York: Oxford University Press, 2014), 144–150.

27. Military historian Christopher Duffy associates morale with each of these different desirable features of fighting units. See Duffy, *The Military Experience in the Age of Reason* (New York: Routledge & Kegan Paul, 1987), 177–188. For a more skeptical view of martial conceptions of morale, see Yuval Noah Harari, *The Ultimate Experience: Battlefield Revelation and the Making of Modern War Culture* (New York: Palgrave, 2008), 117–118.

28. Lasswell, *Propaganda Technique*, 161.

29. John Stuart Mill, *Considerations on Representative Government* (Cambridge: Cambridge Library Collection, 2010), 286.

30. John Wolfenden et al., *The Wolfenden Report: Report of the Committee on Homosexual Offenses and Prostitution* (New York: Stein and Day, 1963), 44.

31. Raphael Lemkin, *Axis Rule in Occupied Europe* (Washington, DC: Carnegie Endowment for International Peace), 89–90.

32. Raphael Lemkin, "The Case of the Spanish in the Peru of the Incas," in *Lemkin on Genocide*, ed. Steven Leonard Jacobs (Lanham, MD: Lexington Books, 2012), 392.

33. Lemkin, "The Case of the Spanish," 390.

34. In this case, as with the others discussed here, dehumanization is likely also to have been a factor. I discuss dehumanization in section 2.4 on evasion of moral norms.

35. For a good, short critique, see Chandran Kukathas's discussion of "Genocide," on *Philosophy Bites*, December 29, 2008. For a more sympathetic discussion of Klemperer's definition, see Larry May, *Genocide: A Normative Account* (Cambridge: Cambridge University Press, 2010).

36. A. Dirk Moses, "Raphael Lemkin, Culture, and the Concept of Genocide," in *The Oxford Handbook of Genocide Studies*, ed. A. Dirk Moses and Donald Bloxham (New York: Oxford University Press, 2010), 28–30.

37. Bernard Williams suggests that we tend to see the interests of larger communities as sources of specifically ethical claims. "Relative to my personal interest,"

Williams writes, "the interests of the town or the nation can represent an ethical demand, but the interests of the town can count as self-interested if the demand comes from some larger identification." Bernard Williams, *Ethics and the Limits of Philosophy* (Cambridge, MA: Harvard University Press, 1986), 15.

38. For Lemkin's personal observations of demoralization in the refugee community in Lithuania following Germany's invasion of Poland, see Raphael Lemkin, *Totally Unofficial: The Autobiography of Raphael Lemkin*, ed. Donna-Lee Frieze (New Haven, CT: Yale University Press, 2013), 60–64. For contemporary uses, see Lynne Briggs and A. D. MacLeod, "Demoralization—A Useful Conceptualisation of Non-Specific Psychological Distress among Refugees Attending Mental Health Services," *International Journal of Social Psychology* 52, no. 6 (2006): 515–524.

39. In the nineteenth century, for instance, American social commentators criticized Northern industrialists for brutalizing the men and women who labored in their factories, and attacked Southern planters for brutalizing the slaves laboring in their fields.

40. Waller, *Becoming Evil*, 210–211.

41. Waller, *Becoming Evil*. On German soldiers during World War II, see Omer Bartov, *Hitler's Army* (New York: Oxford University Press), 1992.

42. Edwin Burrows, *Forgotten Patriots: The Untold Story of American Prisoners during the Revolutionary War* (New York: Basic Books, 2010).

43. Henry Dunant, *A Memory of Solferino* (Washington, DC: American Red Cross, 1939).

44. Waller, *Becoming Evil*, 203.

45. Waller, *Becoming Evil*, 211.

46. Heinrich Himmler infamously expressed concern about the "brutalization" of members of German Order Police through involvement in mass killings on the Eastern Front. His comments indicate that planners of mass violence recognize a difference between techniques of norm evasion, on the one hand, and those of norm erosion, on the other. For the Himmler quote, from January 1942, see Edward Westermann, "Drinking Rituals, Masculinity, and Mass Murder in Nazi Germany," *Central European History* 51, no. 3 (2018): 378.

47. One such connection is the idea that treating other humans like animals reduces those guilty of such treatment to the (moral) status of animals. Historian Mark Celinscak cites the remarks of a Canadian liberator of Bergen-Belsen on this point: "You know, people who treat other people like that can't be human. They *can't* be human." Celinscak, *Distance from the Belsen Heap*, 71.

48. I discuss the significance of such gender-based social norms in chapter 6 of this study.

49. This is borne out by Lemkin's account of the web of legal restrictions confronting refugees.

50. The IWM's Holocaust Exhibit is under renovation at the time of writing, and it is not clear whether this display will be retained. A photograph of the display can be found in Donald Bloxham's *The Final Solution: A Genocide* (Oxford: Oxford University Press, 2009), 26.

51. Marguerite Feitlowitz, *A Lexicon of Terror: Argentina and the Legacies of Torture* (New York: Oxford University Press, 1998).

52. Uğur Üngör and Mehmet Polatel, *Confiscation and Destruction: The Young Turk Seizure of Armenian Property* (London: Continuum, 2011), 6.

53. Feitlowitz, *A Lexicon of Terror*, 50. These terms are, obviously, translations from the original Spanish. The prescribed form of words for discussing uniforms presumably reflects a wish to avoid extending the protections mandated by the Geneva Conventions to members of revolutionary groups.

54. Waller, *Becoming Evil*, 188–189.

55. Feitlowitz, *A Lexicon of Terror*, 50, 52.

56. This point would be weakened in cases where terms that appear euphemistic to outside parties were not or would not be recognized as such by the agents employing them. In the historical cases discussed here, however, there is ample evidence that at least many of the euphemistic terms employed were adopted intentionally through explicit (though secret) "language rules."

57. I provide a more extensive discussion of euphemistic terminology and a more detailed hypothesis of how rules mandating the use of such terms could be manipulatively employed to evade perpetrators' moral inhibitions in my article "Mass Atrocity and Manipulation of Social Norms," *Social Theory and Practice* 40, no. 2 (2014): 255–280.

58. David Welch, *Propaganda: Power and Persuasion* (London: British Library, 2013); Michael Kearney, *The Prohibition of Propaganda for War in International Law* (Oxford: Oxford University Press, 2008).

59. These experiences may be linked by the fact of others' adopting the "objective attitude" toward us. See P. F. Strawson, "Freedom and Resentment," in *Freedom and Resentment and Other Essays* (London: Methuen, 1974), 1–25.

60. David Livingstone Smith, *Less Than Human: Why We Demean, Enslave, and Exterminate Others* (New York: St. Martin's Press, 2011), 26.

61. For Smith's argument concerning the uniqueness of human cruelty, see his *Less Than Human*, chap. 7.

62. Some leading scholars of wartime atrocities have associated these two processes more closely than I wish to do. Historian Janet Bourke, for example, describing narratives commonly used to explain wartime rape, suggests that "processes of dehumanization and brutalization were always portrayed as aberrant: it was the environment of war that led men to act in such ways." It should become clear, in what follows, how the concept of dehumanization I am using differs from the one Bourke employs. Cf. Janet Bourke, "Wartime Rape: The Politics of Making Visible," in *Liberal Democracies at War*, ed. Hilary Footitt and Andrew Knapp (London: Bloomsbury, 2013), 138.

63. Smith, *Less Than Human*, chaps. 2 and 3.

64. Weitz, *Century of Genocide*.

65. Helen Fein, *Accounting for Genocide: National Response and Jewish Victimization During the Holocaust* (New York: Free Press, 1979), 33.

66. The most extensive scholarship in this area concerns the Holocaust. For surveys of experiences within a variety of professions, see Konrad Jarausch, *The Unfree Professions: German Lawyers, Teachers, and Engineers, 1900–1950* (New York: Oxford University Press, 1990); Charles McClelland, *The German Experience of Professionalization* (Cambridge: Cambridge University Press, 1991); Robert Ericksen, *Complicity in the Holocaust: Churches and Universities in Nazi Germany* (Cambridge: Cambridge University Press, 2012). Exemplary studies of particular professions include Alan Steinweis and Robert Rachlin, eds., *The Law in Nazi Germany* (New York: Berghahn, 2013); Henry Friedlander, *The Origins of Nazi Genocide: From Euthanasia to the Final Solution* (Chapel Hill: University of North Carolina Press, 1997); Sabine Hildebrandt, *The Anatomy of Murder: Ethical Transgressions and Anatomical Science during the Third Reich* (New York: Berghahn, 2016); Alan Steinweis, *Studying the Jew: Scholarly Antisemitism in Nazi Germany* (Cambridge, MA: Harvard University Press, 2008).

67. However direct this causal contribution is interpreted to be, it seems that a counterfactual, or "not-without-which," analysis is too strong, since in many cases of atrocities, at least some professionals did refuse to participate, without obviously mitigating the harms imposed.

68. This category clearly includes Dr. Leonardo Conti, discussed in chapter 1.

69. Ericksen, *Complicity in the Holocaust*, 22–23. This conception of complicity diverges from the influential account offered by Christopher Kutz in his book *Complicity*, in which he develops a moral theory of complicity based in the "participatory intentions" of individuals to serve particular roles in larger plans. See Christopher Kutz, *Complicity: Ethics and Law for a Collective Age* (Cambridge: Cambridge University Press, 2000).

70. Michael Davis, "What Can We Learn by Looking for the First Code of Professional Ethics?" *Theoretical Medicine* 24 (2003): 438.

71. Davis, "What Can We Learn," 444.

72. A similar kind of desire for consistency in explanatory models seems to me to stand behind Christopher Browning's suggestion in *Ordinary Men* of repeated inversions in the moral norms accepted by the decidedly nonprofessional members of the Reserve Police Battalion 101.

73. Berel Lang, "The Third Reich and the Breakdown of Professional Ethics," in *The Future of the Holocaust* (Ithaca, NY: Cornell University Press, 1999), 93.

74. Jarausch, *Unfree Professions*.

75. David Dyzenhaus, *Judging the Judges, Judging Ourselves: Truth, Reconciliation, and the Apartheid Legal Order* (Oxford: Hart Publishing, 2003).

Chapter 3

1. Siegfried Sassoon, *Memoirs of an Infantry Officer* (New York: Penguin, 2013), 229.

2. Max Egremont, *Siegfried Sassoon: A Life* (New York: Farrar, Straus and Giroux, 2005), 145.

3. James Waller, *Confronting Evil: Engaging Our Responsibility to Prevent Genocide* (New York: Oxford University Press, 2016), xxx.

4. For the notion of "moral resources," see Jonathan Glover, *Humanity: A Moral History of the Twentieth Century* (London: Jonathan Cape, 1999). See also section 3.4.

5. Sassoon did not initially publish his statement himself, but instead arranged for it to be read out in the House of Commons by Liberal MP Hastings Lees-Smith. See Egremont, *Sassoon*, 163.

6. Alex Bellamy, *Massacres and Morality* (New York: Oxford University Press, 2012), 8–9.

7. Bellamy, *Massacres and Morality*, 14.

8. Geoffrey Brennan, Robert Goodin, Nicholas Southwood, and Lina Eriksson, *Explaining Norms* (New York: Oxford University Press, 2013), 248.

9. Brennan et al., *Explaining Norms*, 251.

10. Note, too, that there is no corresponding legal norm against thinking about killing, as there is in the case of the moral norm against the act of killing.

11. Joseph Raz has argued that all "mandatory norms" have the structure of exclusionary reasons—those that agents have to set aside, rather than assess the strength of, particular practical considerations. To take one of Raz's examples, soldiers who accept a norm of obedience to their superior officers thereby acquire a reason to

exclude considerations of personal well-being, the strategic value of maneuvers, and perhaps even the legality of proposed actions from their decisions. Although I doubt this succeeds as a general analysis of norms—and although I tend to think that norms should be understood as sources of reasons rather than as reasons themselves—I do think some norms exhibit the exclusionary quality Raz identifies, and these are among the norms that I am calling norms against deliberation. See Joseph Raz, *Practical Reason and Norms* (London: Hutchinson, 1975).

12. There may be another way of distinguishing moral norms against deliberation from legal norms, for it is unclear whether there can be binding legal prohibitions on deliberation. Of course, many legal norms, including those most relevant for our thinking about war and peace, require that individual and group actors actually take certain factors into account, with civil or criminal liability attaching if they fail to. But it is less clear whether legal prohibitions on merely deliberating about certain courses of action are tenable. The notion raises worries about criminalizing (or otherwise penalizing) thoughts. As far as I can tell, no similar worries confront the proposal that it may be immoral to deliberate about certain actions—even if, as I have suggested, such thoughts must be allowed at a theoretical or critical level.

13. Not all moral norms directly concerned with deliberation are prohibitive. Some seek to ensure the quality of deliberations by prescribing that they proceed in a particular way, or follow a certain model. Other moral norms are permissive, such as norms of academic freedom that allow researchers to pursue whatever lines of inquiry seem relevant for their research.

14. Note that this is a normative, not a descriptive, question. It seems to be an empirical fact that some individuals or groups are committed to observing particular moral deliberative norms, even to the point of holding them above criticism. What we want is an account of how such a position can be justified and where it is justified. Jerry Gaus takes up a similar question in his discussion of rule following in *The Order of Public Reason*. See Gerald Gaus, *The Order of Public Reason* (Cambridge: Cambridge University Press, 2012).

15. Indeed, in chapter 1, I suggested that such openness to rational reflection is the key factor that distinguishes norms generally, and moral norms specifically, from taboos.

16. Raz, *Practical Reason*.

17. This is not to say that acts and failures to act are morally equivalent, but that their practical effects may be comparable.

18. Dwight Raymond, "Military Means of Preventing Mass Atrocities," in *Reconstructing Atrocity Prevention*, ed. Sheri Rosenberg and Tibi Galis (Cambridge: Cambridge University Press, 2015), 297. For a discussion of the same issue framed specifically

around the doctrine of Responsibility to Protect (R2P), see Sarah Sewall, "Military Options for Preventing Atrocity Crimes," in *The Responsibility to Prevent: Overcoming the Challenges of Atrocity Prevention*, ed. Serena Sharma and Jennifer Welsh (New York: Oxford University Press, 2015), 160–188.

19. Given the focus of this study, it is important to point out that mass atrocities can occur before, during, or after wars; that particular wars (including so-called humanitarian conflicts) may begin precisely because of reported atrocities; and that particular atrocities (such as forced removals) may occur as a consequence of recently concluded wars. Hence my discussion of the deliberations that soldiers take in war, and before entering war, can be instructive about the relationship between war and mass atrocity prevention but cannot be complete.

20. David Luban, "Knowing When Not to Fight," in *The Oxford Handbook of Ethics of War*, ed. Seth Lazar and Helen Frowe (New York: Oxford University Press, 2018), 185–203.

21. Michael Walzer, *Just and Unjust Wars*, 5th ed. (New York: Basic Books, 2015), 127, 344.

22. Seth Lazar, "The Responsibility Dilemma for *Killing in War*: A Review Essay," *Philosophy and Public Affairs* 38, no. 2 (2010): 194. This is not to deny that military and civilian leaders face distinctive epistemic challenges of their own when deliberating about going to war.

23. On the exception for cases of manifest injustice, see Luban, "Knowing When Not to Fight," 195–197.

24. This analysis accords with Neil Roughley's characterization of permissive norms as establishing "prohibitions on others to apply pressure on someone not to do or omit something." See Neil Roughley, "Might We Be Essentially Normative Animals?" in *The Normative Animal? On the Anthropological Significance of Social, Moral, and Linguistic Norms*, ed. Neil Roughley and Kurt Bayertz (New York: Oxford University Press, 2019), 11n6.

25. Walzer, *Just and Unjust Wars*, 44.

26. Jeff McMahan, *Killing in War* (Oxford: Oxford University Press, 2009), 7.

27. McMahan, *Killing in War*.

28. McMahan, *Killing in War*, 92–95.

29. McMahan suggests such norms should be grounded in "principles that govern the distribution of rights of decision-making—in this case the right to make decisions about the resort to war." McMahan, *Killing in War*, 94.

30. Michael Robillard and Bradley Strawser, "The Moral Exploitation of Soldiers," *Public Affairs Quarterly* 30, no. 2 (2016): 186.

31. This assumption is justified if it is true, as Alex Bellamy has argued, that political leaders who make decisions about war are concerned to be perceived as having acted legitimately, whatever their actual interests or incentives for conflict. Cf. Bellamy, *Massacres and Morality*.

32. McMahan, *Killing in War*, 3. Other recent contributions to the ethics of war also contemplate revising existing norms concerning liability to attack. See Cécile Fabre, "Guns, Food, and Liability to Attack," *Ethics* 120 (2009): 36–63; Helen Frowe, *Defensive Killing* (Oxford: Oxford University Press, 2014), 164–187.

33. Elsewhere, McMahan frames his revision of ad bellum deliberative norms in terms of "preventing unjust wars," a goal related to, but not identical with, atrocity prevention. See, for example, Jeff McMahan, "Can Soldiers Be Expected to Know Whether Their War Is Just?" in *Routledge Handbook of Ethics and War*, ed. Fritz Althoff, Nicholas Evans, and Adam Henschke (New York: Routledge, 2013), 21.

34. McMahan, "Can Soldiers Be Expected," 215.

35. It should be clear that episodes of large-scale killing of soldiers who are in fact hors de combat are rightly counted as mass atrocities. The 1940 Katyn massacre, in which roughly 20,000 captured Polish military officers were executed on Joseph Stalin's orders, provides one infamous twentieth-century example. As I will point out, it is also possible for attacks on healthy soldiers in the field to count as atrocities if the means used to kill them is morally impermissible. But we should note that this distinction between morally permissible and impermissible means of killing does not exist in cases of large-scale killing of noncombatants.

36. J. Glenn Gray, *The Warriors: Reflections on Men in Battle* (Lincoln, NE: Bison Books, 1998), 177. For a provocative critique of Gray's account from the perspective of a soldier more directly exposed to front-line combat, see Paul Fussell, *Thank God for the Atom Bomb and Other Essays* (New York: Summit Books, 1988), 13–37.

37. Waller, *Becoming Evil*, 216.

38. For discussion of these legal prohibitions, see chapter 5 of this study.

39. For the philosophical debate over risk taking, see David Luban, "Risk Taking and Force Protection," in *Reading Walzer*, ed. Yitzhak Benbaji and Naomi Sussmann (New York: Routledge, 2014), 277–301. For the morality of killing vulnerable soldiers, see Larry May, "Killing Naked Soldiers: Distinguishing between Combatants and Noncombatants," *Ethics and International Affairs* 19, no. 3 (2005): 39–53. I should note that I am not referring here to soldiers whose vulnerability stems from the fact that they have been rendered hors de combat. In this case, well-established moral and legal norms prohibit their killing.

40. Seth Lazar, *Sparing Civilians* (New York: Oxford University Press, 2016). For a critique of Lazar's account of this principle, see Victor Tadros, "The Moral Distinction

between Combatants and Noncombatants: Vulnerable and Defenceless," *Law and Philosophy* 37, no. 3 (June 2018): 289–312.

41. Lazar, *Sparing Civilians*, 7.

42. *Sparing Civilians*, 2. Like Lazar, I italicize this term in the discussion that follows in order to show that I am referring to his specific conception of this principle.

43. *Sparing Civilians*, 19.

44. *Sparing Civilians*, 74–100.

45. *Sparing Civilians*, 101–122.

46. *Sparing Civilians*, 102–104.

47. *Sparing Civilians*, 105.

48. *Sparing Civilians*, 113–116.

49. Because my application of Lazar's distinction focuses specifically on its value for explaining the distinctive moral wrong done to *targets* of mass atrocities, it avoids some of the paradoxes raised by Victor Tadros concerning the comparative liability of combatants versus noncombatant *perpetrators* of genocide and other large-scale crimes. See Tadros, "Moral Distinction," 295–296.

50. Scott Straus, "What Is Being Prevented? Genocide, Mass Atrocity, and Conceptual Ambiguity in the Anti-Atrocity Movement," in *Reconstructing Atrocity Prevention*, ed. Rosenberg and Galis, 26–27.

51. This kind of large-scale crime does not generally receive as much attention from scholars like Straus who seek to identify key conceptual features of mass atrocities. I agree with Straus that it falls outside the "core conceptualization" of mass atrocity, but it remains worth noting.

52. This conclusion assumes that the combatant/noncombatant distinction can be maintained in practice, without soldiers and commanders resorting to morally dubious proxies such as the sex and age of targeted individuals. For a critique of the existing principle of noncombatant immunity in war that suggests that this distinction cannot be maintained, see Charli Carpenter, *"Innocent Women and Children": Gender, Norms and the Protection of Civilians* (New York: Routledge, 2006).

53. For an example of attempts at empirically measuring the preventive power of legal norms and the criminal sanctions that stand behind them, see Hyeran Jo and Beth Simmons, "Can the International Criminal Court Deter Atrocities?" *International Organization* 70 (2016): 443–475. I engage more closely with empirical approaches to atrocity prevention in chapters 5 and 7.

54. Marc Le Pape, "Epilogue," in *Humanitarian Negotiations Revisited*, ed. Claire Magone, Michael Neuman, and Fabrice Weissman (London: Hurst, 2011), 244–245.

55. Le Pape, "Epilogue," 249.

56. Le Pape, "Epilogue."

57. Notably, MSF traces its very foundation to the rejection of this principle during the Nigerian Civil War (also known as the Biafran War) of the late 1960s. See Joel Pruce, *The Mass Appeal of Human Rights* (Cham, Switzerland: Palgrave, 2018), 85.

58. Hugo Slim, *Humanitarian Ethics: A Guide to the Morality of Aid in War and Disaster* (New York: Oxford University Press, 2015), 19, 66–69.

59. Slim, *Humanitarian Ethics*, 67.

60. Michael Davis "What Can We Learn by Looking for the First Code of Professional Ethics?" *Theoretical Medicine* 24 (2003): 438.

61. Slim, *Humanitarian Ethics*, 70.

62. Slim, *Humanitarian Ethics*, 69.

63. Brennan et al, *Explaining Norms*, 251.

64. Janice Gross Stein, "Humanitarian Organizations: Accountable—Why, to Whom, for What, and How?" in *Humanitarianism in Question: Politics, Power, Ethics* (Ithaca, NY: Cornell University Press, 2008), 128; Larissa Fast, *Aid in Danger: The Perils and Promise of Humanitarianism*, ed. Thomas G. Weiss and Michael Barnett (Philadelphia: University of Pennsylvania Press, 2014), 158–159; Jennifer Rubenstein, *Between Samaritans and States: The Political Ethics of Humanitarian INGOs* (New York: Oxford University Press, 2015).

65. Slim, *Humanitarian Ethics*, 70. One aim of Slim's book, it should be noted, is to distinguish the ideals and methods of humanitarian activism from those of human rights activism. As Slim notes, humanitarian activists who follow traditional norms "often feel bound to stay silent in the face of human rights violations and cooperate closely with evident human rights abusers, both of which count as cardinal sins in human rights orthodoxy." Slim, *Humanitarian Ethics*, 17.

66. For more discussion, see the various contributors to Magone et al., *Humanitarian Negotiations*.

67. Slim, *Humanitarian Ethics*, 55–56.

68. Stein, "Humanitarian Negotiations," 129.

69. Slim, *Humanitarian Ethics*, 56. Slim points to fundamental moral considerations as the basis for the traditional humanitarian principle of impartiality. It reflects, he suggests, a commitment to the universal (and equal) value of human life.

70. I will have more to say about these forms of categorization in my discussion of legal norms and the explanation of mass atrocity in chapter 4.

71. By "direct governance," I mean what political scientist Jennifer Rubenstein calls "conventional governance," for example, "being the sole or almost sole provider of basic goods and services … shaping the rules of coercive institutions, and making large-scale decisions about resources." This contrasts with the forms of global governance I discuss in the next paragraph. See Rubenstein, *Between Samaritans and States,* 8.

72. Bellamy, *Massacres and Morality.*

73. The case humanitarian actors can make for such impartiality is bolstered, as Hugo Slim notes, by the fact that they can always claim it would violate the due process of victims who are themselves suspected of large-scale crimes to deny them aid before they have gone through legal judgment. Slim, *Humanitarian Ethics,* 60.

74. Rubenstein, *Between Samaritans and States.*

75. Rubenstein, *Between Samaritans and States,* 45.

76. Rubenstein, *Between Samaritans and States.* See also Heide Fehrenbach and Davide Rodogno, "'A Horrific Photo of a Drowned Syrian Child': Humanitarian Photography and NGO Media Strategy in Historical Perspective," *International Review of the Red Cross* 97 (2015): 1121–1155.

77. Richard Rorty, "Human Rights, Rationality, Sentimentality," in *Philosophical Papers,* vol. 3: *Truth and Progress* (Cambridge: Cambridge University Press, 1998), 167–185; Lawrence Blum, *Moral Perception and Particularity* (Cambridge: Cambridge University Press, 1994), 65–97.

78. Glover, *Humanity.*

79. Glover, *Humanity,* 23–25. Not all of the attitudinal or emotional responses triggered by such encounters are constructive. Whereas Glover suggests that the disgust often reported by perpetrators at the sight of helpless victims' suffering may count as a final defense against atrocities, Ditte Marie Munch-Jurisic has argued that such disgust often serves instead to distance perpetrators from victims, and so ease violent acts. See Ditte Marie Munch-Jurisic, "Perpetrator Disgust: A Morally Destructive Emotion," in *Emotions and Mass Atrocity: Philosophical and Theoretical Explorations,* ed. Thomas Brudholm and Johannes Lang (Cambridge: Cambridge University Press, 2018), 145–148.

80. Glover, *Humanity,* 26–30.

81. Glover, *Humanity,* 42.

82. Raymond, "Military Means."

83. Glover, *Humanity,* 42.

84. So, for example, Glover describes in some detail the actions of helicopter pilot Hugh Thompson in ending the killing of civilians at My Lai, an episode of

indiscriminate killing that would become the most infamous case of American military atrocity in the Vietnam War. Glover attributes Thompson's actions to his memories of instruction concerning earlier twentieth-century mass atrocities— instruction that he no doubt shared with other members of his generation. But it was the fact that Thompson was positioned on the front lines of war that made it possible for him to respond to this moral education in a way that actually worked to mitigate atrocity. Glover, *Humanity*, 62–63.

85. Glover, *Humanity*, 404.

86. For the distinction between moral and epistemic ignorance, which tracks the distinction I am making, see Gideon Rosen, "Skepticism about Moral Responsibility," *Philosophical Perspectives* 18 (2004): 295–313; Elizabeth Harman, "Does Moral Ignorance Exculpate?" *Ratio* 24, no. 4 (2011): 443–468.

87. Glover, *Humanity*, 42.

88. See Paul Morrow, "A Theory of Atrocity Propaganda," *Humanity* 9, no. 1 (2018): 55.

Chapter 4

1. Gustav Radbruch, *Biographische Schriften*, ed. Günter Spendel (Heidelberg: C. F. Müller Juristischer GmBH, 1988), 168; my translation.

2. Gustav Radbruch, "Gesetzliches Unrecht und übergesetzliches Recht," *Süddeutsche Juristen-Zeitung* 1, no. 5 (1946): 105; my translation. For a full English version of this short text, see Gustav Radbruch, "Statutory Lawlessness and Supra-Statutory Law," trans. Bonnie L. Paulson and Stanley L. Paulson, *Oxford Journal of Legal Studies* 26, no. 1 (2006): 1–11.

3. Radbruch, "Gesetzliches Unrecht," 105.

4. Kristen Rundle, "The Impossibility of an Exterminatory Legality: Law and the Holocaust," *University of Toronto Law Journal* 59, no. 1 (2009): 65–125.

5. Lon Fuller, "Positivism and Fidelity to Law," *Harvard Law Review* 71, no. 4 (1958): 630–672.

6. H. L. A. Hart, "Positivism and the Separation of Law and Morals," *Harvard Law Review* 71, no. 4 (1958): 593–629. See also H. L. A. Hart, *The Concept of Law* (Oxford: Clarendon Press), 1997.

7. Hart, "Positivism," 619–621. For a helpful discussion of the Hart–Fuller debate and its influence on contemporary jurisprudence, see the essays collected in Peter Cane, ed., *The Hart–Fuller Debate in the Twenty-First Century* (Oxford: Hart, 2010).

8. Alon Confino, *A World without Jews* (New York: Columbia University Press, 2014), 51.

9. Confino, *A World without Jews*, 74.

10. Confino, *A World without Jews*, 107.

11. Confino, *A World without Jews*, 170.

12. For a compendium of such exclusionary laws, cited by Confino in his own discussion, see Joseph Walk, ed., *Das Sonderrecht für die Juden im NS-Staat* (Heidelberg: C. F. Müller Juristischer Verlag, 1981).

13. There is a tendency among commentators in some scholarly domains today to distinguish between "norms," on the one hand, and "laws," on the other, suggesting that if something can be described as a norm, it is by definition not a law. I want to make clear that this is not how philosophers use the term *norm*, and it is not how I am using that term in this study. We might interpret this tendency as a case of assuming that the term *norm* applies only to what Brennan et al. call "non-formal norms," that is, social or moral norms. See Geoffrey Brennan, Robert Goodin, Nicholas Southwood, and Lina Eriksson, *Explaining Norms* (New York: Oxford University Press, 2013), chap. 3.

14. I discuss customs and their relationship to social norms in chapter 6 of this study.

15. For an especially illuminating discussion of this point, see Mahmood Mamdani, *When Victims Become Killers: Colonialism, Nativism, and the Genocide in Rwanda* (Princeton, NJ: Princeton University Press, 2001).

16. There are in fact many competing versions of the social fact thesis, most of which take their start from H. L. A. Hart's *The Concept of Law*. I simplify matters for the sake of discussion here. For discussion, see Hart, *The Concept of Law*; Jules Coleman, "Negative and Positive Positivism," *Journal of Legal Studies* 11 (1982): 139; and Joseph Raz, "Legal Positivism and the Sources of Law," in *The Authority of Law*, 2nd ed. (Oxford: Oxford University Press, 2009), 37–52.

17. Raz, "Legal Positivism." Moral principles may still indirectly determine what law there is, on this account, since duly authorized legal actors such as judges and legislators often have recourse to moral principles when reaching their decisions, or drafting their statutes.

18. Radbruch, "Gesetzliches Unrecht." Note again the qualification offered in note 17.

19. Raz, "Legal Positivism," 51.

20. Raz himself acknowledges this point, as I note below.

21. A further advantage of this first feature of legal norms appears in its connection to my general account of practical deliberation. On that account, individual men and women engaged in practical deliberation can and do include in their reflections some attention to what the law in their particular jurisdiction holds with respect to various courses of action. Recognizing the practice-grounded character of legal norms helps align the inquiry researchers make after the fact with the deliberations

undertaken in the moment by individual members of a political society. It does not make those positions equivalent; there is still reason to think that researchers cannot, from their external perspective, directly recreate the reasoning of the individuals they are studying. But insofar as the declarations and interpretations of institutions are publicly available, there seem to be more grounds for confidence here than in, say, ascriptions of guidance by moral norms that proceed without a basis in testimonial or documentary evidence.

22. See chapter 6 for discussion of this point.

23. Although Fuller tends to refer to these as "formal" rules or principles for law-making, I follow Jeremy Waldron in calling them procedural rules. See Jeremy Waldron, "The Rule of Law and the Importance of Procedure," in *NOMOS L: Getting to the Rule of Law*, ed. James Fleming (New York: NYU Press, 2011), 3–31.

24. Lon Fuller, *The Morality of Law* (New Haven, CT: Yale University Press, 1964), 33.

25. Fuller, *The Morality of Law*, 33–38.

26. Joseph Raz, "The Rule of Law and Its Virtue," in *The Authority of Law*, 2nd ed. (Oxford: Oxford University Press, 2009), 223–226.

27. Waldron, "The Rule of Law."

28. See note 24.

29. Barbara Harff, "The Etiology of Genocides," in *Genocide and the Modern Age, Etiology and Case Studies of Mass Death*, ed. I. Wallimann and M. N. Dobkowski (Westport, CT: Greenwood Press, 1987), 41–59.

30. Ernesto Verdeja, "Predicting Genocide and Mass Atrocities," *Genocide Studies and Prevention* 9, no. 3 (2016): 13–32.

31. Verdeja, "Predicting Genocide," 14–15.

32. Barbara Harff, "Countries at Risk of Genocide and Politicide after 2016—and Why," in *Preventing Mass Atrocities: Policies and Practices*, ed. Barbara Harff and Ted Robert Gurr (New York: Routledge, 2018), 27–39; Jennifer Leaning, "Early Warning for Mass Atrocities: Tracking Escalation Parameters at the Population Level," in *Reconstructing Atrocity Prevention*, ed. Sheri Rosenberg, Tibi Galis, and Alex Zucker (Cambridge: Cambridge University Press, 2016), 152–178.

33. David Feierstein, *Genocide as Social Practice: Reorganizing Society under the Nazis and Argentina's Military Juntas* (New Brunswick, NJ: Rutgers University Press, 2014); Scott Straus, *The Order of Genocide* (Ithaca, NY: Cornell University Press, 2006).

34. David Livingstone Smith, *Less Than Human* (New York: St. Martin's Press, 2011); Christopher Powell, *Barbaric Civilization* (Montreal: McGill–Queen's University Press, 2011).

35. Benjamin Valentino, *Final Solutions: Mass Killing and Genocide in the 20th Century* (Ithaca, NY: Cornell University Press, 2005).

36. Powell, *Barbaric Civilization*.

37. Deborah Mayersen, *On the Path to Genocide* (New York: Berghahn Books, 2014), 14–15.

38. Mayersen, *On the Path to Genocide*, 15.

39. Mayersen, *On the Path to Genocide*, 16.

40. Mayersen, *On the Path to Genocide*, 195.

41. In fact, Mayersen does discuss nongenocidal mass atrocities in her account of events preceding specific historical genocides. In the case of the Armenians, for example, she cites mass killings in the late nineteenth century as some of the case-specific precipitating factors.

42. Cf. Joseph Tussman and Jacobus tenBroek, "The Equal Protection of the Laws," *California Law Review* 37, no. 3 (1949): 341–380.

43. Confino, *World without Jews*, 131.

44. Peter Fritzsche, *An Iron Wind* (New York: Basic Books, 2016), 244.

45. Fritzsche, *An Iron Wind*, 245. Fritzsche's discussion of the "lonely individual" created by legal categorization recalls Hannah Arendt's description of loneliness as one end result of totalitarian rule. See Hannah Arendt, *The Origins of Totalitarianism* (New York: Harcourt, 1976), 474–477.

46. Eric Weitz, *A Century of Genocide* (Princeton, NJ: Princeton University Press, 2003), 17.

47. Weitz remarks, "Serb nationalists, and their counterparts among Croats, Slovenes, and, finally, Muslims, sought to 'fix' identities, to establish clearly and cleanly who was a member of what group. Only when that knowledge was firmly established could the state then determine those who deserved the rights and privileges conferred by membership in the nation, and those who had to be driven out and killed." Weitz, *A Century of Genocide*, 201.

48. In part, this was because colonized populations often endured long periods of rule by martial law. See Lyndall Ryan, "Martial Law in the British Empire," in *Violence, Colonialism and Empire in the Modern World*, ed. P. Dwyer and A. Nettelbeck (Cambridge: Cambridge University Press, 2018), 93–109.

49. For the text of this Convention, see https://www.un.org/en/genocideprevention /documents/atrocity-crimes/Doc.32_GC-III-EN.pdf.

50. For the text of this Convention, see https://www.un.org/en/genocideprevention /documents/atrocity-crimes/Doc.32_GC-III-EN.pdf.

51. Raz, "Rule of Law," 225–226.

52. Anthropologist and genocide scholar Alex Hinton highlights this relationship between bare perceptions of difference and institutional avowals of difference when he writes, "If all human beings are born with a propensity to distinguish difference, modern societies are distinguished by the degree to which such differences are reified." Alexander Laban Hinton, "The Dark Side of Modernity: Toward an Anthropology of Genocide," in *Annihilating Difference: The Anthropology of Genocide*, ed. Alexander Laban Hinton (Berkeley: University of California Press, 2002), 12.

53. Mamdani, *When Victims Become Killers*, 190.

54. Mamdani, *When Victims Become Killers*, 129–130. See also Mayersen, *On the Path to Genocide*, 124–132.

55. Alex Bellamy, *Massacres and Morality* (New York: Oxford University Press, 2012), 27–31.

56. Bellamy, *Massacres and Morality*.

57. Geoffrey Best, "Peace Conferences and the Century of Total War: The 1899 Hague Conference and What Came After," *International Affairs* 75, no. 3 (1999): 627.

58. Francisco Javier Guisández Gómez, "The Law of Air Warfare," *International Review of the Red Cross* 323 (1998): 347–364.

59. Christopher Kutz, "How Norms Die: Torture and Assassination in American Policy," *Ethics and International Affairs* 28, no. 4 (2014): 426–430.

60. Cf. Gabriel Finder and Laura Jockusch, eds., *Jewish Honor Courts* (Detroit: Wayne State University Press, 2015).

61. Finder and Jockusch, "Introduction" to *Jewish Honor Courts*.

62. For a helpful discussion of paramilitarism in the context of genocide, see Uğur Üngör, "The Armenian Genocide in the Context of 20th Century Paramilitarism," in *The Armenian Genocide Legacy*, ed. Alexis Demirdjian (New York: Palgrave Macmillan, 2016), 12–14.

63. Stanley Cohen, *States of Denial: Knowing about Atrocities and Suffering* (Malden, MA: Polity Press, 2001), 108.

64. Cohen, *States of Denial*.

65. Victor Klemperer, *I Will Bear Witness, 1942–1945* (New York: Modern Library, 2001), 219–220, 297.

66. Fatma Müge Göçek, *Denial of Violence: Ottoman Past, Turkish Present, and Collective Violence against the Armenians, 1789–2009* (New York: Oxford University Press, 2015), 8.

67. Göçek, *Denial of Violence*.

68. Carlos Santiago Nino, *Radical Evil on Trial* (New Haven, CT: Yale University Press, 1996), 64–65.

69. Robert Jackson, opening statement, "Second Day, Wednesday, 11/21/1945, Part 04," in *Trial of the Major War Criminals before the International Military Tribunal*, vol. 2: *Proceedings: 11/14/1945–11/30/1945*, 98–102 (Nuremberg: IMT, 1947). (Official text in the English language.)

70. Jackson, opening statement. At the close of the tribunal, the US government published an edited collection of documents submitted as evidence at the trial; though containing only a selection of the overall material produced, this collection ran to eight volumes. See US Office of Chief Counsel for the Prosecution of Axis Criminality, *Nazi Conspiracy and Aggression*, 8 vols. (Washington, DC: US Government Printing Office, 1946).

71. Uğur Üngör and Mehmet Polatel, *Confiscation and Destruction: The Young Turk Seizure of Armenian Property* (London: Continuum, 2011).

72. Üngör and Polatel, *Confiscation and Destruction*, 103.

73. Üngör and Polatel, *Confiscation and Destruction*.

74. *Armenians in Ottoman Documents (1915–1920)* (Ankara: Turkish Republic Prime Ministry General Directorate of the State Archives, Directorate of Ottoman Archives, 1982). For clarification of the political and ideological context surrounding this official publication, see Donald Bloxham, *The Great Game of Genocide* (New York: Oxford, 2005), 220.

75. In Turkish, the *Takvim-i Vikâyi*. Üngör and Polatel, *Confiscation and Destruction*, 43n13.

76. Üngör and Polatel, *Confiscation and Destruction*, 45. See also Ümit Kurt, "The Plunder of Wealth through Abandoned Properties Laws in the Armenian Genocide," *Genocide Studies International* 10, no. 1 (2016): 44.

77. Christian Gerlach, *Extremely Violent Societies* (Cambridge: Cambridge University Press, 2010).

78. Gerlach, *Extremely Violent Societies*, 5.

79. Gerlach, *Extremely Violent Societies*, 1.

80. Gerlach, *Extremely Violent Societies*.

81. Gerlach, *Extremely Violent Societies*, 3.

82. Gerlach, *Extremely Violent Societies*, 4.

83. Larry May, *Genocide: A Normative Account* (Cambridge: Cambridge University Press, 2010).

84. Gerlach, *Extremely Violent Societies*, 6.

85. Gerlach, *Extremely Violent Societies*.

86. Gerlach, *Extremely Violent Societies*, 4.

Chapter 5

1. Emily Hobhouse, *The Brunt of the War and Where It Fell* (London: Methuen, 1902).

2. The term "South African War" has for some time been preferred to the name previously given to this conflict: the Anglo-Boer War. See Michael Godby, "Confronting Horror: Emily Hobhouse and the Concentration Camp Photographs of the South African War," *Kronos*, no. 32 (2006): 34. A recent biography of Hobhouse, which provides important details about her life and career, is Elsabé Brits, *Emily Hobhouse: Feminist, Pacifist, Traitor?* (London: Robinson, 2018).

3. Godby, "Confronting Horror." For a discussion of the British use of concentration camps in the South African War, see Dan Stone, *Concentration Camps* (New York: Oxford University Press, 2017), 15–19. Stone reports that the "poor organization" of the camps "led to the deaths of some 45,000 people, about 25,000 Boers and 20,000 Africans" (19).

4. Hobhouse, *Brunt of the War*, xiii.

5. Hobhouse, *Brunt of the War*, xiii.

6. Ruti Teitel, *Humanity's Law* (Oxford: Oxford University Press, 2013), 4.

7. Few Great Powers signed on to the Second Hague convention. The rules it set were designed to expire in five years, anticipating a Third Hague Conference that, in the event, never occurred.

8. This treaty sought specifically to rule out the submarine tactic of sinking merchant vessels carrying civilians when no safe place for offloading those civilians existed. See Nachman Ben-Yehuda, *Atrocity, Deviance, and Submarine Warfare* (Ann Arbor: University of Michigan Press, 2014), 85.

9. Richard Price, *The Chemical Weapons Taboo* (Ithaca, NY: Cornell University Press, 1997), 91.

10. Charles Garraway, "The Law Applies, But Which Law?" in *The American Way of Bombing: Changing Ethical and Legal Norms, from Flying Fortresses to Drones*, ed. Matthew Evangelista and Henry Shue (Ithaca, NY: Cornell University Press, 2014), 91. The failure of these rules in their nonbinding, draft form to constrain surface bombing by both the Axis and the Allies during World War II is notorious. For a philosophically sensitive discussion of real-time debates about the morality of area bombing in that war, see Jonathan Glover, *Humanity: A Moral History of the Twentieth Century* (London: Jonathan Cape, 1999), 83–88.

11. Helen Hintjens, "Reconstructing Political Identities in Rwanda," in *After Genocide: Transitional Justice, Post-Conflict Reconstruction and Reconciliation in Rwanda and Beyond*, ed. Phil Clark and Zachary Kaufman (London: Hurst, 2008), 89–90.

12. International Covenant on Civil and Political Rights, Art. 18(1–4), December 16, 1966, S. Treaty Doc. No. 95-20, 6 I.L.M. 368 (1967), 999 U.N.T.S. 171. Notably, the freedom of religion is held here to be nonderogable.

13. The effectiveness of such legal norms in preventing atrocities should not be taken for granted. Philosophically, laws prohibiting specific forms of hate speech are controversial; empirically, the causal connections between specific instances of hate speech and specific acts of violence against individuals or groups are not well established. For philosophical criticisms, see David Boonin, *Should Race Matter? Unusual Answers to the Usual Questions* (Cambridge: Cambridge University Press, 2012), chaps. 6 and 7. For the empirical connection between hate speech and violence, see Richard Ashby Wilson, *Incitement on Trial: Prosecuting International Speech Crimes* (Cambridge: Cambridge University Press, 2017), 235–236.

14. For the idea of a "regime" of related norms that jointly work to safeguard refugees, see Phil Orchard, *A Right to Flee: Refugees, States, and the Construction of International Cooperation* (Cambridge: Cambridge University Press, 2014), 28–31.

15. For a convenient summary of national-level failures to take in refugees during the Holocaust, see Peter Hayes, *Why? Explaining the Holocaust* (New York: Norton, 2017), 260–273.

16. Orchard, *Right to Flee*.

17. Lon Fuller's notion of a rule of law requirement of "congruence" between declared legal norms and official institutional behavior picks out the particular relationship between the authority of laws and practice that I have in mind. See Colleen Murphy, "Lon Fuller and the Moral Value of the Rule of Law," *Law and Philosophy* 24, no. 3 (2005): 241–245.

18. Christopher Kutz, "How Norms Die: Torture and Assassination in American Policy," *Ethics and International Affairs* 28, no. 4 (2014): 428. Kutz here seems to be referring to norms generally rather than legal norms specifically; his principal cases—torture and assassination—do not lend themselves to further discrimination, since both practices are prohibited by legal *and* moral norms in many contemporary societies.

19. At the time, Lemkin formulated these prohibitions in terms of laws against "barbarism" and "vandalism." See Raphael Lemkin, "Acts Constituting a General (Transnational) Danger Considered as Offences against the Law of Nations," paper for the Fifth Conference for the Unification of Penal Law, Madrid, October 14–20, 1933, http://www.preventgenocide.org/lemkin/madrid1933-english.htm. Also see Raphael Lemkin, *Totally Unofficial* (New Haven, CT: Yale University Press, 2014), 22–23.

20. Raphael Lemkin, *Axis Rule in Occupied Europe* (Washington, DC: Carnegie Endowment for International Peace, 1944), 79–95.

21. UN Convention on the Prevention and Punishment of the Crime of Genocide (adopted December 9, 1948, entered into force January 12, 1951) 78 UNTS 277; Lemkin, *Totally Unofficial*, 176.

22. Lemkin, *Totally Unofficial*, 22–23.

23. Lemkin, *Axis Rule*, 94.

24. Orchard, *Right to Flee*, 105.

25. Orchard, *Right to Flee*, 174–180.

26. Francis Lieber, "General Orders No. 100," in *Military Rules, Regulations and the Code of War: Francis Lieber and the Certification of Conflict*, ed. Richard Shelly Hartigan (New Brunswick, NJ: Transaction, 2011), 48.

27. Hilaire McCoubrey, "From Nuremberg to Rome: Restoring the Defense of Superior Orders," *International and Comparative Law Quarterly* 50 (2001): 387.

28. The distinction between perpetrator and accessory proved particularly important in determining the charges that men and women who engaged in killing actually faced, for in the German law to be a "perpetrator" of murder required both a clear interest in the death of another and a malign will reflected in the act of killing. See Devin Pendas, *The Frankfurt Auschwitz Trial, 1963–1965* (Cambridge: Cambridge University Press, 2006), 56–71; also see Henry Friedlander, "Nazi Crimes and the German Law," in *Nazi Crimes and the Law*, ed. Friedlander and Nathan Stoltzfus (Cambridge: Cambridge University Press, 2008), 27–33.

29. Robert Jackson, "Opening Statement, "Second Day, Wednesday, 11/21/1945, Part 04," in *Trial of the Major War Criminals before the International Military Tribunal*, vol. 2: *Proceedings: 11/14/1945–11/30/1945* (Nuremberg: IMT, 1947), 98. (Official text in the English language.)

30. Dapo Akande and Sangeeta Shah, "Immunities of State Officials, International Crimes, and Foreign Domestic Courts," *European Journal of International Law* 21, no. 4 (2011): 815–852.

31. Akande and Shah, "Immunities of State Officials."

32. Versailles Peace Treaty, June 28, 1919, 225 Parry 188; 2 Bevans 235; 13 AJIL Supp. 151, 385 (1919), Article 227.

33. Jackson Maogoto, "Early Efforts to Establish an International Criminal Court," in *The Legal Regime of the International Criminal Court*, ed. Jose Doria, Hans-Peter Gasser, and M. Cherif Bassiouni (Leiden: Martinus Nijhoff, 2009), 16.

34. Maogoto, "Early Efforts." English economist John Maynard Keynes condemned the proposal to try the Kaiser, deeming it part of a general "concoction of greed and

sentiment, prejudice and deception." John Maynard Keynes, *The Economic Consequences of the Peace* (New York: Harcourt, 1920), 131.

35. Kathryn Sikkink, *The Justice Cascade: How Human Rights Prosecutions Are Changing World Politics* (New York: Norton, 2011); Gill Wigglesworth, "The End of Impunity? Lessons from Sierra Leone," *International Affairs* 84, no. 4 (2008): 809–827.

36. Akande and Shah, "Immunities of State Officials," 840.

37. Mark Osiel, *Obeying Orders: Atrocity, Military Discipline, and Law of War* (New Brunswick, NJ: Transaction, 2001), 51–52.

38. Osiel, *Obeying Orders*, 42; McCoubrey, "From Nuremberg to Rome," 389.

39. Importantly, however, Article 33 of the Rome Statute of the International Criminal Court restores superior orders as a legitimate defense for individuals accused of large-scale crimes in cases where those orders are not manifestly unlawful. The article goes on to stipulate that orders to commit genocide or crimes against humanity are, in fact, manifestly unlawful. For discussion, see McCoubrey, "From Nuremberg to Rome," 392–393.

40. The focus on institutional actors also precludes consideration of certain hypothetical cases, such as the commission of genocide by a lone individual armed with a biological weapon. See David Luban, "A Theory of Crimes against Humanity," *Yale Journal of International Law* 29 (2004): 98n45.

41. Sheri P. Rosenberg, "Audacity of Hope: International Criminal Law, Mass Atrocity Crimes, and Prevention," in *Reconstructing Atrocity Prevention*, ed. Sheri Rosenberg, Tibi Galis, and Alex Zucker (Cambridge: Cambridge University Press, 2016), 153.

42. For discussion of this problem of knowing with certainty when a genocide has actually been prevented, see Kerry Whigham, "Remembering to Prevent: The Preventive Capacity of Public Memory," *Genocide Studies and Prevention* 11, no. 2 (2017): 53–54; see also Scott Straus, *Fundamentals of Genocide and Mass Atrocity Prevention* (Washington, DC: United States Holocaust Memorial Museum, 2016), chap. 6.

43. Whigham, "Remembering to Prevent."

44. Whigham, "Remembering to Prevent," 155; Tom Buitelaar, "The ICC and the Prevention of Atrocities: Criminological Perspectives," *Human Rights Review* 17 (2016): 289.

45. Buitelaar, "The ICC and the Prevention of Atrocities."

46. Rosenberg, "Audacity of Hope," 161.

47. Rosenberg, "Audacity of Hope," 155, 163.

48. For the need to address rival religious ideologies as part of long-term atrocity prevention efforts, see Yehuda Bauer, "Genocide and Mass Atrocities: Can They Be

Prevented?" in *Preventing Mass Atrocities: Policies and Practices*, ed. Barbara Harff and Ted Robert Gurr (New York: Routledge, 2018), 20–22. For the significance of economic programs as long-term prevention measures, see Ted Robert Gurr, "Preventing Genocides and Mass Atrocities: Evidence from Conflict Analysis," in *Preventing Mass Atrocities*, ed. Harff and Gurr, 67.

49. Straus, *The Order of Genocide*.

50. Kenneth Abbott, Robert Keohane, Andrew Moravcsik, Anne-Marie Slaughter, and Duncan Snidal, "The Concept of Legalization," *International Organization* 54, no. 3 (2000): 17–35.

51. Abbott et al., "The Concept of Legalization."

52. Abbott et al., "The Concept of Legalization."

53. The first adopters of this approach to the study of international organizations explicitly refused to "take the position that greater legalization, or any particular form of legalization, is inherently superior." Abbott et al., "The Concept of Legalization," 24.

54. Tuba Inal, *Looting and Rape in Wartime* (Philadelphia: University of Pennsylvania Press, 2013).

55. Inal, *Looting and Rape*, 63–69, 133–134.

56. Inal, *Looting and Rape*, 170–171.

57. Inal, *Looting and Rape*, 173–175.

58. Inal, *Looting and Rape*, 61.

59. Inal, *Looting and Rape*, 98.

60. Inal, *Looting and Rape*, 95.

61. Inal, *Looting and Rape*, 133–135.

62. Inal, *Looting and Rape*, 60.

63. Inal, *Looting and Rape*, 91.

64. Inal, *Looting and Rape*, 179.

65. For discussion of the context of this statement and the significance of German interpretations of military necessity, see Isabel Hull, *A Scrap of Paper: Breaking and Making International Law During the Great War* (Ithaca, NY: Cornell University Press, 2014), 25–33, 41–43.

66. Hull, *A Scrap of Paper*, 13–15. See also William Wohlforth, "Realism," in *The Oxford Handbook of International Relations*, ed. Christian Reus-Smit and Duncan Snidal (New York: Oxford University Press, 2010), 131–149.

67. Lon Fuller, *The Morality of Law* (New Haven, CT: Yale University Press, 1964), 37–38.

68. Fuller, *The Morality of Law*; Jeremy Waldron, "Why Law—Efficacy, Freedom, or Fidelity?" *Law and Philosophy* 13, no. 3 (1994): 259–284.

69. Orchard characterizes a "regime" as "a mechanism through which the appropriate standards of behavior suggested by ... individual norms are linked together to create a response within the complexity of [an] issue area." Cf. Orchard, *Right to Flee*, 6; also see Price, *Chemical Weapons Taboo*, 1997.

70. Sarah Sewall, "Limits of Law: Promoting Humanity in Armed Conflict," in *Law and War*, ed. Austin Sarat, Lawrence Douglas, and Martha Merrill Umphrey (Stanford, CA: Stanford Law Books, 2014), 23.

71. Sarat et al., *Law and War*, 37–38.

72. Hyeran Jo, *Compliant Rebels* (Cambridge: Cambridge, University Press, 2015), 13–15.

73. Ruti Teitel, *Transitional Justice* (New York: Oxford University Press, 2000); Martha Minnow, *Between Vengeance and Forgiveness: Facing History after Genocide and Mass Violence* (Boston: Beacon Press, 1998); Jon Elster, *Closing the Books: Transitional Justice in Historical Perspective* (Cambridge: Cambridge University Press, 2004).

74. Teitel, *Transitional Justice*; Kit Wellman, "Amnesties and International Law," in *War: Essays in Political Philosophy*, ed. Larry May (Cambridge: Cambridge University Press, 2008), 249–265; Margaret Urban Walker, *Moral Repair: Reconstructing Moral Relations after Wrongdoing* (Cambridge: Cambridge University Press, 2006); Colleen Murphy, *A Moral Theory of Political Reconciliation* (Cambridge: Cambridge University Press, 2012).

75. Teitel, *Transitional Justice*; Pablo de Greiff, "Theorizing Transitional Justice," in *NOMOS LI: Transitional Justice*, ed. Melissa S. Williams and Rosemary Nagy (New York: NYU Press, 2012), 31–77; Colleen Murphy, *Conceptual Foundations of Transitional Justice* (Cambridge: Cambridge University Press, 2017).

76. It is doubtful whether this represents a new dichotomy in any case, since an interest in legalization is already evident in discussions of rule-of-law reforms within transitional societies.

77. Mark Drumbl, *Atrocity, Punishment, and International Law* (Cambridge: Cambridge University Press, 2007), 24.

78. Teitel, *Transitional Justice*; Christine Bell, "Of *Jus Post Bellum* and *Lex Pacificatoria*: What's in a Name?" in *Jus Post Bellum: Mapping the Normative Foundations*, ed. Carsten Stahn, Jennifer Easterday, and Jens Iverson (New York: Oxford University Press, 2014), 201.

79. Eric Posner and Adrian Vermeule, "Transitional Justice as Ordinary Justice," *Harvard Law Review* 117, no. 3 (2004): 761–825.

80. Murphy, *Conceptual Foundations*, 24.

81. Murphy, *Conceptual Foundations*, 42.

82. Murphy, *Conceptual Foundations*.

83. Murphy refers to such cases as combining "horizontal" and "vertical" inequalities. Murphy, *Conceptual Foundations*, 47.

84. Teitel, *Transitional Justice*, 44–46, 164–169.

85. Murphy, Conceptual Foundations, 55–56.

86. As I have noted elsewhere in this study, I do not think that such widespread wrongdoing necessarily undermines the moral prohibitions against these actions, since such moral prohibitions are not related to prevailing practices in the same way.

87. Murphy, *Conceptual Foundations*, 67.

88. Murphy, *Conceptual Foundations*, 72–73.

89. David Dyzenhaus, *Judging the Judges, Judging Ourselves: Truth, Reconciliation, and the Apartheid Legal Order* (Oxford: Hart, 2003). See also David Dyzenhaus, *Hard Cases in Wicked Legal Systems* (Oxford: Oxford University Press, 1991).

90. Hakeem Yusuf, *Transitional Justice, Judicial Accountability and the Rule of Law* (Abingdon, UK: Routledge, 2013).

91. Lisa Hilbink, *Judges beyond Politics in Democracy and Dictatorship* (Cambridge: Cambridge University Press, 2011).

92. Stephen Humphreys, *Theatre of the Rule of Law: Transnational Legal Intervention in Theory and Practice* (Cambridge: Cambridge University Press, 2010).

93. Hansjörg Strohemeyer, "Collapse and Reconstruction of a Judicial System: The United Nations Missions in Kosovo and East Timor," *American Journal of International Law* 95, no. 1 (2001): 55.

94. Strohemeyer, "Collapse and Reconstruction."

95. Consider Ruti Teitel's influential description of the status of law in transitional societies: "In transitional jurisprudence, the conception of justice is partial, contextual, and situated between at least two legal and political orders. Legal norms are decidedly multiple, the idea of justice always a compromise." Teitel, *Transitional Justice*, 9.

96. Hobhouse, *Brunt of the War*, 318. Hobhouse became actively involved in post-war rebuilding efforts, establishing schools for wool dying and weaving in multiple locations in the years before World War I. But her general assessment of the power

of laws to constrain large-scale crimes decreased with time. In a new preface written in 1923 for the Dutch edition of *The Brunt of the War,* Hobhouse concluded that the rules of humanitarian law, however "excellent on paper, can easily be, and indeed are eluded in a thousand ways." Emily Hobhouse, "Introduction to the Reprint of 'The Brunt of the War' by Emily Hobhouse," Oxford, Bodleian Library, MS Hobhouse 1, 8–9.

97. Larry May, *After War Ends* (Cambridge: Cambridge University Press, 2011), 194.

98. The contentious character of such determinations is illustrated by Article 231 of the Treaty of Versailles, the so-called war guilt clause. James Morgan Read, *Atrocity Propaganda, 1914–1919* (New Haven, CT: Yale University Press, 1941), viii.

99. Fionnoula Ní Aoláin and Dina Francesca Haynes, "The Compatibility of Justice for Women with *Jus Post Bellum* Analysis," in *Jus Post Bellum,* edited by Carsten Stahn, Jennifer Easterday, and Jens Iverson (New York: Oxford University Press, 2014), 167.

Chapter 6

1. Victor Klemperer, *I Will Bear Witness: A Diary of the Nazi Years 1933–1941,* trans. Michael Chalmers (New York: Modern Library, 1999), 67–68.

2. Saul Friedlander, *Nazi Germany and the Jews: The Years of Extermination* (New York: Harper, 2008), xv.

3. Alon Confino suggests, in a slightly different vein, that such sources provide insight into "the strangeness of the past," specifically into "those elements that can be captured through an analysis of culture, mentalities, and sensibilities." See Alon Confino, *A World without Jews: The Nazi Imagination from Persecution to Genocide* (New Haven, CT: Yale University Press, 2014), 17.

4. Some scholars of mass atrocity employ a notion of norms according to which testimony, even if sincerely given and scrupulously interpreted, cannot supply sufficient evidence for the existence of norms. Such evidence, they claim, emerges only when "actual actions are observed." Without denying the importance of action for identifying norms, I refer to the circularity problem discussed in chapter 1, according to which observations of action are likely to produce self-fulfilling claims about norms. Cf. Christian Gudehus, "Editor's Introduction to 'Social Norms' by Heinrich Popitz," *Genocide Studies and Prevention* 11, no. 2 (2017): 3.

5. For influential philosophical studies of social identity, see Kwame Anthony Appiah, *The Ethics of Identity* (Princeton, NJ: Princeton University Press, 2007); Charles Taylor, *Multiculturalism and "The Politics of Recognition"* (Princeton, NJ: Princeton University Press, 1994); Iris Marion Young, "Five Faces of Oppression," *Philosophical Forum* 19, no. 4 (1988): 270–290.

6. Young, "Five Faces of Oppression"; Marilyn Friedman, "Feminism and Modern Friendship: Dislocating the Community," *Ethics* 99, no. 2 (1989): 275–290; Sally Haslanger, "Gender and Race: (What) Are They? (What) Do We Want Them to Be?" *Noûs* 34, no. 1 (2000): 31–55. For the "intersectional" character of gendered (or sexual) and racial social identities, see Kimberlé Crenshaw, "Demarginalizing the Intersection of Race and Sex," *University of Chicago Legal Forum* (1989): 139–167.

7. See, for example, Katharine Jenkins, "Amelioration and Inclusion: Gender Identity and the Concept of *Woman*," *Ethics* 126, no. 2 (2016): 394–421.

8. To bear a "male" social identity, that is, to be identified as a man in social interactions, does not generally require bearing a "masculine" social identity, though the two are often confused. Put briefly, the social identity of "male" comprehends nonmasculine ways of being a man, just as the social identity of "female" comprehends nonfeminine ways of being a woman. For work addressing this distinction in connection with the Holocaust, see Jason Crouthamel, "Homosexuality and Comradeship: Destabilizing the Hegemonic Masculine Ideal in Nazi Germany," *Central European History* 51, no. 3 (2018): 219–239; Edward Westermann, "Drinking Rituals, Masculinity, and Mass Murder in Nazi Germany," *Central European History* 51, no. 3 (2018): 367–389; and Wendy Lower, *Hitler's Furies: German Women in the Nazi Killing Fields* (New York: Houghton Mifflin, 2007).

9. Cristina Bicchieri, *Norms in the Wild* (New York: Oxford University Press, 2017), 121. Bicchieri goes on to explain how descriptive beliefs about the characteristic traits or behaviors of men and women can shift to become prescriptive rules (135–136).

10. In defining gender and gender-based social norms in this way, my account also bears comparison to the "minimalist approach to gender" adopted by political scientist Charli Carpenter in her study of gendered aspects of the principle of civilian immunity in war. Such an approach, Carpenter explains, "involves demonstrating that a set of inter-subjective beliefs regarding gender relations is socially constructed rather than biologically given; demonstrating that socio-political outcomes are different than would be expected in the absence of those beliefs and the norms constituted by them; and providing a convincing empirical account of the ways in which these beliefs and norms operated to constrain, enable or constitute the outcomes in question." See Charli Carpenter, *"Innocent Women and Children": Gender, Norms and the Protection of Civilians* (New York: Routledge, 2006), 15.

11. H. L. A. Hart, *The Concept of Law* (Oxford: Clarendon Press, 1961); David Lewis, *Convention: A Philosophical Study* (Malden, MA: Blackwell, 2002).

12. Margaret Gilbert, *On Social Facts* (Princeton, NJ: Princeton University Press, 1992); Edna Ullman-Margalit, *The Emergence of Norms* (Oxford: Clarendon Press, 1977).

13. Cristina Bicchier, *The Grammar of Society* (Cambridge: Cambridge University Press, 2006); Bicchieri, *Norms in the Wild*; Nicholas Southwood and Lina Eriksson,

"Norms and Conventions," *Philosophical Explorations* 14, no. 2 (2011): 195–217; Gerald Gaus, *The Order of Public Reason* (Cambridge: Cambridge University Press, 2010); Ken Binmore, *Natural Justice* (New York: Oxford University Press, 2011); Linda Radzik, "Gossip and Social Punishment," *Res Philosophica* 93, no. 1 (2016): 185–204.

14. This philosophical literature on social norms has, in my view, largely superseded the tentative framework developed by Heinrich Popitz in the early 1960s, which has recently been recommended to English-speaking scholars of mass atrocity. See Heinrich Popitz, "Social Norms," *Genocide Studies and Prevention* 11, no. 2 (2017): 5–12. Popitz's discussion of the role of social norms in constructing gender roles across societies is still of value, as I suggest below.

15. On social norms as solutions to collective action problems, see Bicchieri, *Norms in the Wild,* 113–114. On the concept of incompletely theorized agreements, see Cass Sunstein, "Incompletely Theorized Agreements," *Harvard Law Review* 108, no. 7 (1995): 1733–1772.

16. Jerry Gaus refers to human agents generally as "rule following punishers," thus conceptually uniting the disposition to follow a rule with the disposition to punish others for violations. See Gaus, *Order of Public Reason*, 103–112.

17. Geoffrey Brennan, Robert Goodin, Nicholas Southwood, and Lina Eriksson, *Explaining Norms* (New York: Oxford University Press, 2013), 45–46.

18. Although this is not the place to provide a full taxonomy, it should be noted that those punishments differ in both kind and severity. Some standard examples include verbal criticism, gossip, shunning, boycotting, and perhaps expulsion from relevant groups.

19. Paul Morrow, "Mass Atrocity and Manipulation of Social Norms," *Social Theory and Practice* 40, no. 2 (2014): 255–280; Bicchieri, *Norms in the Wild*, 77–78.

20. Marco Schmidt and Hannes Rakoczy, "On the Uniqueness of Human Normative Attitudes," in *The Normative Animal? On the Anthropological Significance of Social, Moral, and Legal Norms*, ed. N. Roughley and K. Bayertz (New York: Oxford University Press, 2019), 121–135.

21. For an analysis of intentional processes of norm translation, which focuses, however, on the spread of legal rather than social norms, see Lisbeth Zimmerman, *Global Norms with a Local Face: Rule-of-Law Promotion and Norm Translation* (Cambridge: Cambridge University Press, 2017). Although many of the institutional mechanisms Zimmerman describes are less relevant in the case of social norms, her general emphasis on interaction and feedback remains helpful.

22. Brennan et al., *Explaining Norms*, 241–243.

23. Bicchieri, *Grammar of Society*, 196–208.

24. Bicchieri, *Grammar of Society*.

25. For philosophical discussions of the ubiquity of testimonial knowledge, see C. A. J. Coady, *Testimony: A Philosophical Study* (New York: Oxford University Press, 1995); Robert Audi, "The Place of Testimony in the Fabric of Knowledge and Justification," *American Philosophical Quarterly* 34, no. 4 (1997): 405–422.

26. Bicchieri defines customs as social practices that are in fact shared across collectives, but that individuals pursue for reasons that do not depend on the conduct of others. She defines conventions as solutions to coordination problems (for example, which side of the road to drive on), which are based on individuals' empirical expectations about the conduct of others, combined with assessments of their own self-interest. The key point is that conventions are, in Bicchieri's words, "self-enforcing," whereas social norms are not. Cf. Bicchieri, *Norms in the Wild*, 16–17, 39.

27. Assuming there is a norm where none in fact exists could of course negatively affect individuals in other ways, for instance, by unnecessarily limiting the careers or educational opportunities they consider or by preventing them from taking liberties they might otherwise take. For a cogent discussion of the rationality of such behavior, see Carel van Schaik and Judith Burkart, "The Evolution of Human Normativity," in Roughley and Bayertz, *Normative Animal*, 147.

28. Bicchieri, *Norms in the Wild*, 39. This is not to say that the negative consequences of breaching conventions are independent of the *actions* of others. A tourist who chooses to drive on the right-hand side of the road in the United Kingdom may face negative consequences in the form of a crash. But that crash will not be intended, by convention-following fellow drivers, as a sanction.

29. It seems possible that conditions of pluralistic ignorance might characterize this case, but the information contained in Klemperer's diary is insufficient to establish this. For analysis of Nazi efforts to discourage public patronage of Jewish-owned businesses, see Robert Gellately, *Backing Hitler: Consent and Coercion in Nazi Germany* (Oxford: Oxford University Press, 2001), 124–125.

30. Emily Hobhouse, *The Brunt of the War and Where It Fell* (London: Methuen, 1902), 313–317.

31. David Roussett, *L'univers Concentrationnaire* (Paris: Éditions du Pavois, 1946), 65–66; my translation.

32. Gaus, *Order of Public Reason*; Gerry Mackie, "Effective Rule of Law Requires Construction of a Social Norm of Legal Obedience," in *Cultural Agency Reloaded: The Legacy of Antanas Mockus*, ed. Carlo Tognato (Cambridge, MA: Harvard University Press, 2017), 313–334.

33. Bicchieri, *Norms in the Wild*; Brennan et al., *Explaining Norms*; John Thrasher, "Evaluating Bad Norms," *Social Philosophy and Policy* 35, no. 1 (2018): 196–216.

34. Some scholars of mass atrocity argue that sexuality, rather than gender, is the more salient concept for capturing the different experiences of men and women, boys and girls during such crimes. Their focus is driven by a concern for the particular forms of sexual and reproductive assault to which women are vulnerable. I am concerned with the ways in which gender structures both perpetration and victimization during atrocities. Accordingly, I focus on gender and gender-based social norms.

35. Karl Mertens, "On the Identification and Analysis of Social Norms and the Heuristic Relevance of Deviant Behavior," in Roughley and Bayertz, *Normative Animal*, 111.

36. Bicchieri, *Grammar of Society*.

37. Elisa von Joeden-Forgey, "Gender, Sexualized Violence, and the Prevention of Genocide," in *Reconstructing Atrocity Prevention*, ed. Sheri Rosenberg, Tibi Galis, and Alex Zucker (Cambridge: Cambridge University Press, 2016), 127.

38. Adam Jones, "Gendercide and Genocide," in *Gendercide and Genocide*, ed. Adam Jones (Nashville, TN: Vanderbilt University Press, 2004), 10.

39. Charli Carpenter, "Beyond 'Gendercide': Incorporating Gender into Comparative Genocide Studies," *International Journal of Human Rights* 6, no. 4 (2002): 85–89.

40. Gabrielle Ferrales, Hollie Nyseth Brehm, and Suzy McElrath, "Gender-Based Violence against Men and Boys in Darfur: The Gender-Genocide Nexus," *Gender and Society* 30, no. 4 (2016): 565–589.

41. Von Joeden-Forgey, "Sexualized Violence." 135.

42. Von Joeden-Forgey, "Sexualized Violence."

43. B. Sabetai and Yvette L. Testimony (HVT-3014), Fortunoff Archive, December 13, 1994, tape 2 (19:00–22:00).

44. This case demonstrates the limits of relying solely on retrospective testimony for evidence of social norms. It should be noted, however, that this line of questioning precisely follows the pattern recommended for field interviews by Bicchieri and other scholars of social norms, insofar as Yvette is asked to describe the beliefs guiding the actions of other members of her community, rather than herself or her family. Cf. Bicchieri, *Norms in the Wild*, 96–99; Karisa Cloward, *When Norms Collide* (New York: Oxford University Press, 2016), 283–284.

45. Marion Kaplan, *Between Dignity and Despair: Jewish Life in Nazi Germany* (New York: Oxford University Press, 1999), 63–64.

46. Kaplan, *Between Dignity and Despair*, 64.

47. This discussion of who took the initiative for planning escape during the 1930s does not contradict the fact that a large proportion of those targets of Nazi genocide who did not escape the process of destruction were women, especially elderly

women. Cf. Kaplan, "Gender: A Critical Tool in Holocaust Research," in *Women and Genocide*, ed. Elissa Bemporad and Joyce Warren (Bloomington: Indiana University Press, 2018), 105.

48. There was, however, a massive exodus of Hutu men and women into neighboring Congo after RDF forces reached the capital of Kigali and made progress toward ending the genocide.

49. For discussion of the dense settlement of Rwanda, see Scott Straus, *The Order of Genocide* (Ithaca, NY: Cornell University Press, 2006), 215–216. For the presence of Hutu roadblocks on the frontier with Burundi, see Charles Kabwete Mulinda, "Crossing a Border to Escape: Examples from the Gishamvu and Kigembe Communities of Rwanda," in *Resisting Genocide: The Multiple Forms of Rescue*, ed. Jacques Semelin, Claire Andrieu, and Sarah Gensburger (New York: Columbia University Press, 2011), 357.

50. Straus, *Order of Genocide*, 163–164. Political scientist Mahmood Mamdani further clarifies the intersection between gender and ethnicity in postcolonial Rwandan society, observing that in cases of intermarriage "social identity is passed on through patrilineal descent.... As the child takes on a unidimensional identity, that of the father, the identity of the mother—whether Hutu or Tutsi—is systematically erased." Mamdani goes on to remark that "today's Tutsi need to be understood as children of mixed marriages who have been constructed as Tutsi through the lens of a patriarchal ideology and the institutional medium of a patriarchal family." Mahmood Mamdani, *When Victims Become Killers* (Princeton, NJ: Princeton University Press, 2001), 53–54.

51. Straus, *Order of Genocide*, 164. Straus later rejects the hypothesis that there was a preexisting "norm of anti-Tutsi killing in Rwandan society." It is not clear whether he sees this as a statistical or a properly normative postulate, for he refers to the hypothesis as holding that the killing of Tutsis was "a routine, even legitimate practice." Either way, this rejection is compatible with recognizing a social norm permitting the killing of women (because of their reproductive potential) and children once violence was underway (175–176).

52. On the notion of "choiceless choices," see Lawrence Langer, *Versions of Survival: The Holocaust and the Human Spirit* (Albany: SUNY Press, 1982); on the idea of the "gray zone," see Primo Levi, *The Drowned and the Saved* (New York: Vintage, 1988).

53. For discussion of Ringelblum's project, and particularly of the differing responses of men and women to ghettoization across Europe, see Nechama Tec, *Resistance: Jews and Christians Who Defied the Nazi Terror* (Oxford: Oxford University Press, 2013), 47–83.

54. Tec, *Resistance*. This historical situation accords with Cristina Bicchieri's observation that "in many cultures, no matter what other roles women may play beyond

the household, women continue to be held strictly accountable for household work and care." Bicchieri, *Norms in the Wild*, 141.

55. Victor Klemperer, *I Will Bear Witness: A Diary of the Nazi Years, 1942–1945*, trans. Martin Chalmers (New York: Modern Library 2001), 7, 43, 151.

56. Peter Hayes, *Why? Explaining the Holocaust* (New York: Norton, 2017), 166. As an indication of the complexities of the roles social norms played here, Hayes notes that once production at the camps turned from outdoor construction to assembly-line processes, women started to be selected for labor at a rate equal to men.

57. Elisa von Joeden-Forgey, "Women and the Herero Genocide," in *Women and Genocide*, ed. Bemporad and Warren, 36–57.

58. Natalia Aleksuin, "Gender and the Daily Lives of Jews in Hiding in Eastern Galicia," *NASHIM: A Journal of Jewish Women's Studies and Gender Issues* 27 (2014): 43.

59. Aleksuin, "Gender and the Daily Lives," 44.

60. Sara Brown, *Gender and the Rwandan Genocide: Women as Rescuers and Perpetrators* (London: Routledge, 2018), 62. Brown attributes this reluctance to kill Ruth and the child she claimed as her own as a product of "Rwandan patriarchal society," which led the Interahamwe to fear Ruth's husband's "violent reprisal." While specific national contexts surely matter in the analysis of social norms, it's worth noting that revenge norms are also commonly used as examples in the more general philosophical literature on social norms—though not always with a specific gendered component. Cristina Bicchieri remarks that "in cases like norms of revenge, the social pressure to conform is real, and this makes such norms particularly robust." Bicchieri, *Grammar of Society*, 180n4.

61. Important studies include Straus, *Order of Genocide*; Waller, *Becoming Evil*; Christopher Browning, *Ordinary Men: Reserve Police Battalion 101 and the Final Solution in Poland* (New York: Harper, 1993); and the essays collected in *Perpetrators and Perpetration of Mass Violence*, ed. Timothy Williams and Susanne Buckley-Zistel (London: Routledge, 2018).

62. Mark Drumbl, *Atrocity, Punishment, and International Law* (Cambridge: Cambridge University Press, 2007), 23–45; Sheri Rosenberg, "Audacity of Hope: International Law, Mass Atrocity Crimes, and Prevention," in *Reconstructing Atrocity Prevention*, ed. Rosenberg et al., 151–174.

63. Rosenberg, "Audacity of Hope," 156.

64. Mamdani, *When Victims Become Killers*; Brown, *Gender and the Rwandan Genocide*. Scott Straus excludes mere looting from his operational definition of perpetration in the Rwandan genocide, restricting this category to individuals "who materially participated in the murder or attempted murder of a noncombatant" (Straus, *Order*

of Genocide, 102–103). More recently, Straus has described looters as "indirect perpetrators." I have no objection to describing looting, especially when opportunistic, as an indirect form of perpetration. However, insofar as genocide and some other forms of large-scale crimes involve the complete displacement of a targeted group or minority population from the social life of a country, then it seems clear that looting, when not merely opportunistic, can be an equally significant tactic for those carrying out this crime. See Scott Straus, "Is a Comparative Theory of Perpetrators Possible?" in *Perpetrators and Perpetration of Mass Violence,* ed. Timothy Williams and Susanne Buckley-Zistel (London: Routledge, 2018), 205.

65. Straus, "Is a Comparative Theory of Perpetrators Possible?" 219.

66. Jean Hatzfeld, *Machete Season: The Killers in Rwanda Speak* (New York: Picador, 2006), 86.

67. Hatzfeld, *Machete Season.*

68. Hatzfeld, *Machete Season,* 73.

69. For the Russian case, see Elissa Bemporad, "Memory, Body, and Power: Women and the Study of Genocide," in *Women and Genocide,* ed. Bemporad and Warren, 5–6. For the Armenian case, see Uğur Üngör and Mehmet Polatel, *Confiscation and Destruction: The Young Turk Seizure of Armenian Property* (New York: Continuum, 2011), 88. Üngör and Polatel write, "Not only did the process [of looting] draw participation from different classes, but it also bridged the gender gap. Women were making themselves useful in the 'national cause.'"

70. Lower, *Hitler's Furies;* see also Lower, "German Women and the Holocaust in the Nazi East," in Bemporad and Warren, *Women and Genocide,* 111–136.

71. Lower, "German Women," 130.

72. Lower, *Hitler's Furies.*

73. This is not to deny that the targets of rape and sexual assault may also be men or that some cases occur in which women rape men. The latter may be relatively underreported due to feelings of shame among victims. For discussion of a case of rape by women on a man during the Rwandan genocide, see Brown, *Gender and the Rwandan Genocide,* 98–99.

74. See, for example, Elisa von Joeden-Forgey, "Genocidal Masculinities," in *New Directions in Genocide Research,* ed. Adam Jones (New York: Routledge, 2012), 90–91.

75. Ferrales et al., for example, conclude that "dominant norms regarding gender influence forms of mass violence, suggesting that gender-based violence establishes, enforces, and reproduces gendered hierarchies within a broader social system." See Ferrales et al, "Gender-Based Violence," 578.

76. For discussion of the "strategic rape theory," see Janet Bourke, "Wartime Rape: The Politics of Making Visible," in *Liberal Democracies at War*, ed. Hilary Footitt and Andrew Knapp (London: Bloomsbury, 2013), 136.

77. Tuba Inal, *Looting and Rape in Wartime* (Philadelphia: University of Pennsylvania Press, 2013), 63, 93.

78. Inal, *Looting and Rape*, 88–91.

79. Elisabeth Jean Wood, "Armed Groups and Sexual Violence: When Is Wartime Rape Rare?" *Politics and Society* 37, no. 1 (2009): 131–162.

80. Inal, *Looting and Rape*, 89–90.

81. Claudia Card, "Rape as a Weapon of War," *Hypatia* 11, no. 4 (1996): 5–18.

82. For Bosnia-Herzegovina, see Alexandra Stiglmayer, ed., *Mass Rape: The War against Women in Bosnia-Herzegovina* (Lincoln, NE: University of Nebraska Press, 1994); Beverly Allen, *Rape Warfare: The Hidden Genocide in Bosnia-Herzegovina and Croatia* (Minneapolis: University of Minnesota Press, 1996). For Guatemala, see Sanford, Victoria, Sofia Dayos Álvarez-Arenas, and Kathleen Dill, "Sexual Violence as a Weapon during the Guatemalan Genocide," in *Women and Genocide*, 207–222. For Sudan, see Samuel Totten, "The Plight and Fate of Females after the Darfur Genocide," in *Women and Genocide*, 268–285.

83. It should be noted that the descriptive term "genocidal rape" is not necessarily coextensive with the international legal definition of rape as one manifestation of the crime of genocide.

84. Elisa von Joeden-Forgey, "Gender and the Future of Genocide Studies and Prevention," *Genocide Studies and Prevention* 7, no. 1 (2012): 89–107.

85. Von Joeden-Forgey, "Gender and the Future," 93.

86. As historian Trude Jacobsen observes, "The same young women who went with their brothers and classmates on patrol were expected to cook upon return to camp, thus adhering to the bourgeois ideals of society prior to the revolution." Trude Jacobsen, "Very Superstitious: Gendered Punishment in Democratic Kampuchea, 1975–1979," in Bemporad and Warren, *Women and Genocide*, 201.

87. In its evaluations of speeches and printed matter preceding and accompanying the genocide, the International Criminal Tribunal for Rwanda interpreted this ubiquitous phrase to mean "go kill the Tutsis and Hutu political opponents of the political regime." See Richard Ashby Wilson, *Incitement on Trial: Prosecuting International Speech Crimes* (Cambridge: Cambridge University Press, 2017), 36. Jean Hatzfeld, discussing interviews conducted with survivors after the genocide ended, also highlights the prevalence of standard occupational terms—for example, "the words *job, cutting*, or *pruning*, taken from the work on banana plantations." Hatzfeld, *Machete Season*, 153.

88. Christian Gerlach, *Extremely Violent Societies: Mass Violence in the Twentieth-Century World* (Cambridge: Cambridge University Press, 2010), 87–88.

89. While I have argued in this chapter that social norms help to structure mass atrocities, it is no part of my argument that it is somehow "better" for the targets of such crimes, or for the societies shaken by them, that social norms play this action-guiding role. This claim seems to be floated by philosopher Josh Thrasher toward the end of an otherwise instructive essay, "Evaluating Bad Norms." Thrasher writes that "often any organization of violence by norms is an important improvement over the alternative." He does not state directly what instances of unorganized violence he has mind as "the alternative" here. But on the basis of the argument set forth in this chapter, it should be clear that twentieth-century mass atrocities do not support his claim and may undercut it, for on the one hand, these crimes are largely structured by norms, while on the other hand, they provide some of the worst imaginable examples of violence. See Thrasher, "Bad Norms," 216.

90. Nechama Tec, *When Light Pierced the Darkness: Christian Rescue of Jews in Nazi-Occupied Poland* (Oxford: Oxford University Press, 1987), 38.

91. Bicchieri, *Norms in the Wild*, 15–16.

Chapter 7

1. The history of Darfur, or the "Kingdom" (*Dar*) of the Fur people, goes back to at least the fourteenth century CE. Turkish and Egyptian colonization of the region began in the 1870s, with British colonial administration following in 1916. Since 1994, the region of Darfur has comprised three states: North Darfur, South Darfur, and West Darfur. For discussion of this region's complex history, see Gerald Prunier, *Darfur: The Ambiguous Genocide* (Ithaca, NY: Cornell University Press, 2005).

2. Prunier, *Darfur*, 128–129.

3. Not everyone interested themselves in this question at first. As UN Secretary General Kofi Annan said in April 2004, "Whatever term it uses to describe the situation [in Darfur], the international community cannot stand idle." Cf. "Darfur Destroyed," *Human Rights Watch* 16, no. 6 (2004): 53. On March 4, 2009, however, the Pre-Trial Chamber of the International Criminal Court issued a warrant for the arrest of then-Sudanese president Omar Al Bashir on charges of war crimes and crimes against humanity. A charge of genocide was latter added to this warrant. See ICC Case Information Sheet, *The Prosecutor v. Omar Hassan Ahmad Al Bashir* (ICC-PIDS-CIS-SUD-02–006/18_Eng), April 2018.

4. Samer Abdelnour and Akbar Saeed, "Technologizing Humanitarian Space: Darfur Advocacy and the Rape-Stove Panacea," *International Political Sociology* 8 (2014): 146.

5. Abdelnour and Saeed, "Technologizing Humanitarian Space.

6. Abdelnour and Saeed, "Technologizing Humanitarian Space."

7. Romy Listo, "Gender Myths in Energy Poverty Literature," *Energy Research and Social Science* 38 (2018): 14.

8. Paul Morrow, "The Thesis of Norm Transformation in the Theory of Mass Atrocity," *Genocide Studies and Prevention* 9, no. 1 (2015): 66–82; Heinrich Popitz, "Social Norms," *Genocide Studies and Prevention* 11, no. 2 (2017): 11–12.

9. For two different ways in which norms can be called "bad," see Geoffrey Brennan, Robert Goodin, Nicholas Southwood, and Lina Eriksson, *Explaining Norms* (New York: Oxford University Press, 2013), 176. For a critical account of "parochial" evaluations of norms as good or bad, see John Thrasher, "Evaluating Bad Norms," *Social Philosophy and Policy* 35, no. 1 (2018): 196–216.

10. Cristina Bicchieri, *Norms in the Wild* (New York: Oxford University Press, 2017); Karisa Cloward, *When Norms Collide* (New York: Oxford University Press, 2016).

11. For discussion of the political dimensions of the designation "Righteous Among Nations," accorded specifically to rescuers during the Holocaust, see Sarah Gensburger, "From the Memory of Rescue to the Institution of the Title of 'Righteous,'" in *Resisting Genocide: The Multiple Forms of Rescue*, ed. Jacques Semelin, Claire Andrieu, and Sarah Gensburger (London: Hurst, 2011), 19–32.

12. Nechama Tec, *When Light Pierced the Darkness: Christian Rescue of Jews in Nazi-Occupied Poland* (New York: Oxford University Press, 1987), 70–84.

13. Tec, *When Light Pierced the Darkness*, 87–98.

14. Ernesto Verdeja, "Moral Bystanders and Mass Violence," in *New Directions in Genocide Research*, ed. Adam Jones (New York: Routledge, 2012), 153–168.

15. Compare this to the definition of "rescue" offered by Jacques Semelin, as "a set of actions, whether covert or not, that aim to legally or physically conceal the identity of wanted persons and/or organize their escape to a place where they will find safety." Where the element of risk, or at least cost, is implicit in Semelin's definition, it is explicit in my own. See Semelin et al., *Resisting Genocide*, 5–6.

16. Tec, *Light Pierced*, 153–154; Kristen Renwick Monroe, *Ethics in an Age of Terror and Genocide* (Princeton, NJ: Princeton University Press, 2012), 221.

17. Bicchieri, *Norms in the Wild*, 170–171; Cloward, *Norms Collide*, 79.

18. For the significance of this distinction, which Bicchieri characterizes as the distinction between "risk sensitivity" and "risk perception," see Bicchieri, *Norms in the Wild*, 172–173.

19. Bicchieri, *Norms in the Wild*, 76–79. Bicchieri goes on to distinguish cases in which there are multiple norms from cases where there are multiple possible

interpretations of the same norm; this latter dynamic also appears in some testimonial accounts of rescue.

20. Sara Brown, *Gender and the Rwandan Genocide: Women as Rescuers and Perpetrators* (London: Routledge, 2018), 73.

21. Istvan Pal Adam, *Budapest Building Managers and the Holocaust in Hungary* (Cham, Switzerland: Palgrave, 2016). In this case, since many of these building managers continued to receive tips from building residents, there is some controversy about whether they should be called rescuers or paid helpers.

22. Samuel Oliner and Pearl Oliner, *The Altruistic Personality: Rescuers of Jews in Nazi Europe* (New York: Free Press, 1988).

23. Oliner and Oliner, *Altruistic Personality*, 188.

24. Oliner and Oliner, *Altruistic Personality*, 209.

25. Oliner and Oliner, *Altruistic Personality*, 189.

26. Oliner and Oliner, *Altruistic Personality*, 221.

27. Oliner and Oliner, *Altruistic Personality*, 258. I understand the final quotation here to be making an epistemic point: social norms are often the means by which individuals come to know of properly moral norms. An alternative perspective on the relationship between social and moral norms, which may be relevant here, holds that many moral norms simply are social norms that have been "moralized," that is, made the object of distinct kinds of practical commitments and normative attitudes. This view is defended in Chad van Schoelandt, "Moral Accountability and Social Norms," *Social Philosophy and Policy* 35, no. 1 (2018): 217–236.

28. Ervin Staub, *Overcoming Evil* (New York: Oxford University Press, 2013); Monroe, *Ethics in an Age*; Semelin et al., *Resisting Genocide*.

29. Lawrence Blum, "Altruism and the Moral Value of Rescue," in *Moral Perception and Particularity* (Cambridge: Cambridge University Press, 1994), 124–143.

30. Blum, "Altruism and the Moral Value," 135.

31. Blum, "Altruism and the Moral Value," 126, 135.

32. Oliner and Oliner, *Altruistic Personality*, 258. Erwin Staub also emphasizes "the possibility of education to reduce hate." See Staub, *Overcoming Evil*, 363–364.

33. For an analysis of the shortcomings of current educational initiatives, along with proposals for tightening the connection between education about genocide and genocide prevention, see Deborah Mayersen, "So the World May Know All: The Importance of Education for Genocide Prevention," in *Last Lectures on the Prevention and Intervention of Genocide*, ed. Samuel Totten (New York: Routledge, 2018), 215–221.

34. Philosopher Tracy Isaacs uses this term to describe perpetrators of some histori-cal large-scale crimes; I believe it applies equally to many rescuer groups. Cf. Tracy Isaacs, *Moral Responsibility in Collective Contexts* (New York: Oxford, 2011), 27–29.

35. Oliner and Oliner, *Altruistic Personality*, 247.

36. Tec, *Light Pierced*, 59.

37. Brown, *Gender and the Rwandan Genocide*, 130.

38. Brown, *Gender and the Rwandan Genocide*, 131.

39. Bicchieri, *Norms in the Wild*, 15.

40. As Fahima Hashim notes, "Darfurian women are known for their significant economic contributions and their participation in market and agricultural econo-mies." By contrast, as Bina Agarwal observes, women in rural India who engage in firewood collection are largely excluded from market and agricultural work. Cf. Fahima Hashim, "Sudanese Civil Society Strategizing to End Sexual Violence against Women in Darfur," in *Darfur and the Crisis of Governance in Sudan*, ed. Salah Hassan and Carina Ray (Ithaca, NY: Cornell University Press, 2009), 236; Bina Agarwal, *Gender and Green Governance: The Political Economy of Women's Presence within and beyond Community Forestry* (New York: Oxford University Press, 2010), esp. chap. 2.

41. Listo, "Gender Myths." For a discussion of the ways in which gender-based social norms have also influenced patterns of sexual violence against men in Darfur, see Gabrielle Ferrales, Hollie Brehm, and Suzy McElrath, "Gender-Based Violence against Men and Boys in Darfur: The Gender-Genocide Nexus," *Gender and Society* 30, no. 4 (2016): 565–589.

42. For the place of "experience-near" ethnographic research in the study of geno-cide, see Alex Hinton, "The Dark Side of Modernity: Toward an Anthropology of Genocide," in *Annihilating Difference: The Anthropology of Genocide*, ed. Alex Hinton (Berkeley: University of California Press, 2002), 33. For a more general philosophical discussion of ethnographic research as one of three distinct "levels" of norm analy-sis, see Thrasher, "Evaluating Bad Norms," 207.

43. Brennan et al., *Explaining Norms*, 176.

44. Bina D'Costa, "*Birangona*: Rape Survivors Bearing Witness in War and Peace in Bangladesh," in *Women and Genocide*, ed. Elissa Bemporad and Joyce Warren (Bloomington: Indiana University Press, 2018), 159–190. For an example of patriar-chal social norms prescribing silence about domestic violence outside the context of mass atrocity, see Karima Manji, "Articulating the Role of Social Norms in Sustain-ing Intimate Partner Violence in Mwanza, Tanzania." (PhD diss., London School of Hygiene and Tropical Medicine, 2018), 94–97.

45. D'Costa, *"Birangona."* See also Elisa von Joeden-Forgey, "Gender and the Future of Genocide Studies and Prevention," in *Genocide Studies and Prevention* 7, no. 1 (2012): 93–94.

46. Annette Wieviorka, *The Era of the Witness* (Ithaca, NY: Cornell University Press, 2006), 72.

47. Lawrence Langer, *Holocaust Testimonies: The Ruins of Memory* (New Haven, CT: Yale University Press, 1993), 61.

48. Brennan et al., *Explaining Norms*, 177.

49. Bicchieri, *Grammar of Society*, 20–22. Some historians dispute claims about a general hesitation among survivors to give testimony during the first decades after the Holocaust. Hasia Diner seeks to dispel the "myth of silence after the Holocaust" among American Jews. Laura Jockusch offers a Europe-centered corrective to claims about survivor silence, highlighting the extent of immediate postwar activism in European displaced persons camps. At the same time, Jockusch acknowledges that many Jews attempting to rebuild their lives after the war encountered hostility or indifference from their interlocutors and were led to "conceal their Jewishness in public, as well as to keep their memories of the recent past private." In light of such controversy, I can only suggest that much more targeted historical inquiry will be required to confirm or disconfirm the hypothesized existence of social norms prescribing silence within specific communities of survivors during this period. Cf. Hasia Diner, *We Remember with Reverence and Love: American Jews and the Myth of Silence after the Holocaust, 1945–1962* (New York: NYU Press, 2009); Laura Jockusch, *Collect and Record: Jewish Holocaust Documentation in Early Postwar Europe* (Oxford: Oxford University Press, 2012), 191.

50. Linda Radzik, "Moral Rebukes and Social Avoidance," *Journal of Value Inquiry* 48 (2014): 648–650.

51. Radzik, "Moral Rebukes." It should be noted that whereas Radzik is concerned with social avoidance as a response to actual violators of moral norms, I am interested in social avoidance merely as a response to real or perceived violations of social norms. I do not think victims of mass atrocities generally fear that they may violate moral norms by speaking about their experience; with social norms, however, such fears are intelligible.

52. Radzik suggests that social avoidance more generally risks misinterpretation because it typically takes the form of a withdrawal from communication; it is for this reason often much more ambiguous than explicit criticism or rebuke. See Radzik, "Moral Rebukes," 650.

53. Alex Bellamy, *Massacres and Morality: Mass Atrocities in an Age of Civilian Immunity* (Oxford: Oxford University Press, 2012), 36. Note that this pathway assumes, as

Bellamy's study argues, that threats of international intervention are at least moderately effective deterrents of mass atrocity.

54. Elazar Barkan, "Historical Dialogue and the Prevention of Atrocity Crimes," in *Reconstructing Atrocity Prevention*, ed. Sheri Rosenberg, Tibi Galis, and Alex Zucker (Cambridge: Cambridge University Press, 2016), 175–195.

55. Barkan, "Historical Dialogue," 192.

56. Kerry Whigham, "Remembering to Prevent: The Preventive Capacity of Public Memory," *Genocide Studies and Prevention* 11, no. 2 (2017): 65.

57. Bicchieri, *Norms in the Wild*. More specifically, Bicchieri refers to shared *second-order* normative and empirical expectations, meaning expectations about what other group members expect. Bicchieri's use of the language of expectations differs from my use of beliefs, attitudes, and commitments, but that difference is driven mainly by her desire to give an operational account of norm transformation—one that can be tested directly in experimental settings.

58. Bicchieri, *Norms in the Wild*, 110. The opposite, as we shall see in the next section, is true of the creation of social norms: for new norms to be created, first new normative expectations must be inculcated and then new empirical expectations formed.

59. Mark Osiel, "The Collective Responsibility of Military Officers," in *Making Sense of Mass Atrocity* (Cambridge: Cambridge University Press, 2011), 203–217.

60. For discussion of the relationship between blackmail and social, or "group," norms, see Richard McAdams, "Group Norms, Gossip and Blackmail," *University of Pennsylvania Law Review* 144 (1996): 2237–2292.

61. D'Costa, *Birangona*, 178. For a general discussion of problems and methods in collecting data about conflict-related sexual violence (CRSV), see Chein Reis, "Ethical, Safety, and Methodological Issues Related to the Collection and Use of Data on Sexual Violence in Conflict," in *Sexual Violence as an International Crime: Interdisciplinary Approaches*, ed. Anne-Marie De Brouwer, Charlotte Ku, Renée G. Römkens, and L. J. Van Den Herik (Cambridge: Intersentia, 2013), 187–210.

62. Milli Lake, "Organizing Hypocrisy: Providing Legal Accountability for Human Rights Violations in Areas of Limited Statehood," *International Studies Quarterly* 58, no. 3 (2014): 515–526.

63. Bicchieri, *Norms in the Wild*, 188–94.

64. For discussion of "catalysts" see Cloward, *Norms Collide*, 86–87. Phil Orchard uses the term *crisis* to refer to such events in his analysis of the evolution of legal protections for refugees. See Phil Orchard, *A Right to Flee* (Cambridge: Cambridge University Press, 2014), 33–34.

65. Wieviorka, *Era of the Witness*.

66. Hannah Arendt, *Eichmann in Jerusalem: A Report on the Banality of Evil* (New York: Penguin, 2006). For two different interpretations of the Eichmann trial and Arendt's analysis of it, see Lawrence Douglas, *The Memory of Judgment: Making Law and History in the Trials of the Holocaust* (New Haven, CT: Yale University Press, 2006), esp. chap. 6; Christian Gerlach, "The Eichmann Interrogations in Holocaust Historiography," *Holocaust and Genocide Studies* 15, no. 3 (2001): 428–452.

67. A few authors take a contrary view and argue that silence may in fact be what is most needed in post-atrocity societies in order to prevent future occurrences. Reporter and social critic David Rieff advances this view in his 2016 book, *In Praise of Forgetting*. However, as other scholars have pointed out, Rieff's account evinces minimal awareness of the state of the art in mass atrocity forecasting or prevention and provides generally weak support for his polemical claims. See David Rieff, *In Praise of Forgetting* (New Haven, CT: Yale University Press, 2016); see also Whigham, "Remembering to Prevent," 53–54.

68. For the importance of front-line journalism as a source of information about large-scale crimes that can inform, or indeed induce, political responses, see Roy Gutman, "Ending the Silence on War Crimes: A Journalist's Perspective," in *Preventing Mass Atrocities: Policies and Practices*, ed. Barbara Harff and Ted Robert Gurr (New York: Routledge, 2018), 73–92.

69. For discussions of the definitional difficulties surrounding incitement to genocide or other large-scale crimes in international law, see Richard Ashby Wilson, *Incitement on Trial* (Cambridge: Cambridge University Press, 2017), esp. chap. 1; Gregory Gordon, *Atrocity Speech Law* (New York: Oxford University Press, 2017), esp. chap. 8; and Susan Benesch, "Vile Crimes or Inalienable Right: Defining Incitement to Genocide," *Virginia Journal of International Law* 48 (2008): 491–498.

70. Wilson *Incitement on Trial*, 72.

71. Wilson *Incitement on Trial*, 32.

72. Legal scholar Gregory Gordon uses the term *atrocity speech* to refer to incitement, instigation, persecution, and other legally proscribed forms of speech related to atrocities. See Gordon, *Atrocity Speech*.

73. Gordon, *Atrocity Speech*, 306.

74. Gordon, *Atrocity Speech*.

75. This worry is not confined to prohibitions on incitement, but extends to any legal regulation of speech. Jeremy Waldron offers a clear account of the basic concern, writing of the "massive power" modern governments enjoy "to suppress dissent, deflect criticism, and resist exposure of … malfeasances." Jeremy Waldron, *The Harm in Hate Speech* (Cambridge, MA: Harvard University Press, 2014), 26.

76. Wilson, *Incitement on Trial*, 66–67; Gordon, *Atrocity Speech*, chap. 11.

77. The studies of social norms prescribing silence about sexual violations considered above may be an exception to this rule, though those norms typically are not specific to political speech.

78. Cheshire Calhoun, "The Virtue of Civility," *Philosophy and Public Affairs* 29, no. (2000): 251–275.

79. Iris Marion Young, *Inclusion and Democracy* (Oxford: Oxford University Press, 2002), 47.

80. Wilson, *Incitement on Trial*, chap. 7.

81. John Stuart Mill, *On Liberty*, in *Collected Works of John Stuart Mill*, vol. 18, ed. J. M. Robson (Toronto: University of Toronto Press, 1977), 220, cited in Linda Radzik, "On Minding Your Own Business: Differentiating Accountability Relations within the Moral Community," *Social Theory and Practice* 37, no. 4 (2011): 577.

82. See Radzik, "Moral Rebukes"; Linda Radzik, "Boycotts and the Social Enforcement of Justice," *Social Philosophy and Policy* 34, no. 1 (2017): 102–122; Linda Radzik, "Gossip and Social Punishment," *Res Philosophica* 93, no. 1 (2016): 185–204.

83. Radzik, "Moral Rebukes."

84. Wilson, *Incitement on Trial*, chap. 7.

85. Wilson, *Incitement on Trial*, 658.

86. Radzik acknowledges the significance of duration as an element in determining the proportionality of social punishments, but does not provide more extended analysis of the appropriate duration of boycotts. See Radzik, "Boycotts," 117, 119.

87. Bicchieri, *Norms in the Wild*, 110–111.

88. Such community-wide campaigns for transformation in social norms receive significant recognition and support from state authorities. For discussion of the normative and practical dimensions of state participation in the design of social norms, see Ryan Muldoon, "Understanding Social Norms and Changing Them," *Social Philosophy and Policy* 35, no. (2018): 146.

89. Colleen Murphy, *Conceptual Foundations of Transitional Justice* (Cambridge: Cambridge University Press, 2017).

90. Richard Price, "Reversing the Gunsight: Transnational Civil Society Targets Land Mines," *International Organization* 52, no. 3 (1998): 613–644.

91. Price, "Reversing the Gunsight," 617.

92. Price, "Reversing the Gunsight."

93. Bicchieri, *Norms in the Wild*, chap. 5.

94. Bicchieri, *Norms in the Wild*, 172–180.

95. Blum, "Moral Exemplars."

96. John Stuart Mill, *On Liberty* (New York: Penguin Classics, 2007), chap. 2.

97. One reason to think that Mill would accept at least social sanctions against such harms is that they are not purely self-regarding, but rather (by definition) intended to harm others. See Radzik, "Minding Your Own Business," 581.

98. This is at least one traditional way of defining an enthymeme. For discussion, see Edward Madden, "The Enthymeme: Crossroads of Logic, Rhetoric, and Metaphysics," *Philosophical Review* 61, no. 3 (1952): 368–376.

99. Jeff McMahan, "I Was No-Platformed. Here's Why It's Counterproductive," *New Statesman*, January 14, 2019, https://www.newstatesman.com/2019/01/i-was-no-platformed-here-s-why-it-s-counterproductive.

100. Rosenberg, *Audacity of Hope*; Mark Drumbl, *Atrocity, Punishment, and International Law* (Cambridge: Cambridge University Press, 2007).

101. Gerald Mackie, "Effective Rule of Law Requires Construction of a Social Norm of Legal Obedience," in *Cultural Agents Reloaded*, edited by Carlo Tognato (Cambridge, MA: Harvard University Press, 2017), 313–334.

Conclusion

1. Raphael Lemkin, "Introduction to Genocide," in *Lemkin on Genocide*, ed. Steven Leonard Jacobs (New York: Lanham, MD: Lexington Books, 2012), 21, 24. For a clear discussion of considerations affecting Lemkin's coinage of the term *genocide*, see Samantha Power, *A Problem from Hell: America and the Age of Genocide* (New York: Basic Books, 2013), 41–45.

2. Donna-Lee Frieze, ed., *Totally Unofficial: The Autobiography of Raphael Lemkin* (New Haven, CT: Yale University Press, 2013), 152.

3. Lawrence Langer, *Holocaust Testimonies: The Ruins of Memory* (New Haven: Yale University Press, 1993).

4. These questions are especially important given the mixture of norms typically in play in practical deliberations. As philosopher Neil Roughley remarks, "Adult judgements of what ought to be done all in all can involve a mixture of moral and conventional—and personal—considerations." See Neil Roughley, "Moral Obligations from the Outside In," in *The Normative Animal? On the Anthropological Significance of Social, Moral, and Linguistic Norms*, ed. Neil Roughley and Kurt Bayertz (New York: Oxford University Press, 2019), 223.

5. I take no position here on the long-term, or near-term, viability of R2P as a norm in global politics.

6. Alex Bellamy and Edward Luck, *The Responsibility to Protect: From Promise to Practice* (Medford, MA: Polity Press, 2018), 18–19.

7. For a helpful survey of those objections, see Noele Crossley, "Is R2P Still Controversial? Continuity and Change in the Debate on 'Humanitarian Intervention,'" *Cambridge Review of International Affairs* 31, no. 5 (2018): 415–436.

8. Sarah Sewall, "Military Options for Preventing Atrocity Crimes," in *The Responsibility to Prevent: Overcoming the Challenges of Atrocity Prevention*, ed. Serena Sharma and Jennifer Welsh (New York: Oxford University Press, 2015), 186.

9. Bellamy and Luck, *Responsibility to Protect*, 18.

10. Bellamy and Luck, *Responsibility to Protect*.

11. For the suggestion that consensus represents a necessary condition for R2P's status as a norm, see, for example, Crossley, "Is R2P Still Controversial?" 416.

12. David Scheffer, "The Fate of R2P in the Age of Retrenchment," in *Globalization and its Impact on the Future of Human Rights and International Criminal Justice*, ed. M. Cherif Bassiouni (Cambridge: Intersentia, 2015), 617.

13. Scheffer, "The Fate of R2P," 627–628.

14. Those challenges are distinct from the aesthetic and symbolic challenges that Holocaust museums routinely face. For discussion, see Jennifer Hansen-Glucklich, *Holocaust Memory Reframed* (New Brunswick, NJ: Rutgers University Press, 2014), 215–218; see also Oren Baruch Stier, *Holocuast Icons: Symbolizing the Shoah in History and Memory* (New Brunswick, NJ: Rutgers University Press, 2015).

Bibliography

Primary Sources: Documents, Testimonies, Diaries, Memoirs, Statutes, Treaties

Binding, Karl, and Alfred Hoche. *Die Freigabe der Vernichtung Lebensuntwerten Lebens: Ihr Maß und ihre Form.* Leipzig: Verlag von Felix Meiner, 1920. Excerpted and translated in *Sources of the Holocaust,* edited by Steve Hochstadt, 29–31. New York: Palgrave Macmillan, 2004.

Cohn, Benno. Testimony of Benno, Session 15 (April 25, 1961). *The Trial of Adolf Eichmann: Record of Proceedings in the District Court of Jerusalem,* vol. 1. Jerusalem: Trust for the Publication of the Proceedings of the Eichmann Trial, in cooperation with the Israel State Archives and Yad Vashem, the Holocaust Martyrs' and Heroes' Remembrance Authority, 1992–1995.

Colby, Elbridge. "Aërial Law and War Targets." *American Journal of International Law* 19, no. 4 (1925): 702–715.

Conti, Leonardo. Letter to Gottfried Ewald. 1940. In *Abtransportder "Lebensunwerten,"* edited by Thorsten Suesse and Heinrich Meyer, 103–104. Hannover: Verlag Clemens Koechert, 1988 and Meyer 1988.

Directorate of Ottoman Archives. *Armenians in Ottoman Documents (1915–1920).* Ankara: Turkish Republic Prime Ministry General Directorate of the State Archives, 1982.

Doyle, Arthur Conan. "The Uses of Hatred." *Times,* December 26, 1917, 9.

Dunant, Henry. *A Memory of Solferino.* Washington, DC: American Red Cross, 1939.

Hatzfeld, Jean. *Machete Season: The Killers in Rwanda Speak.* New York: Picador, 2006.

Hobhouse, Emily. *The Brunt of the War and Where It Fell.* London: Methuen, 1902.

Hobhouse, Emily. "Introduction to the Reprint of 'The Brunt of the War' by Emily Hobhouse." Oxford, Bodleian Library, MS Hobhouse 1 (14 pages), 1923.

Human Rights Watch. "Darfur Destroyed." *Human Rights Watch* 16, no. 6 (2004): 1–75.

ICC. *The Prosecutor v. Omar Hassan Ahmad Al Bashir* Case Information Sheet (ICC-PIDS-CIS-SUD-02–006/18_Eng). April 2018.

ICISS. "The Responsibility to Protect." *Report of the International Commission on Intervention and State Sovereignty.* Ottawa: International Development Research Center, 2001.

Jackson, Robert. Opening Statement, "Second Day, Wednesday, 11/21/1945, Part 04." In *Trial of the Major War Criminals before the International Military Tribunal*, vol. 2. Proceedings: 11/14/1945–11/30/1945. Nuremberg: IMT, 1947. (Official text in the English language.)

Keynes, John Maynard. *The Economic Consequences of the Peace.* New York: Harcourt, 1920.

Klemperer, Victor. *I Will Bear Witness: A Diary of the Nazi Years, 1933–1941.* Translated by Michael Chalmers. New York: Modern Library, 1999.

Klemperer, Victor. *I Will Bear Witness: A Diary of the Nazi Years, 1942–1945.* Translated by Michael Chalmers. New York: Modern Library, 1999.

Kovacs, Olga. Interview 35369. Tape 3, 27:50–28:30. Visual History Archive, USC Shoah Foundation, 1995.

Lemkin, Raphael. "Acts Constituting a General (Transnational) Danger Considered as Offences Against the Law of Nations," conference paper for 5th Conference for the Unification of Penal Law, Madrid, October, 14–20, 1933. http://www.preventgenocide.org/lemkin/madrid1933-english.htm

Lemkin, Raphael. *Axis Rule in Occupied Europe.* Washington, DC: Carnegie Endowment for International Peace, 1944.

Lemkin, Raphael. "The Case of the Spanish in the Peru of the Incas." In *Lemkin on Genocide*, edited by Steven Leonard Jacobs. Lanham, MD: Lexington Books, 2012.

Lemkin, Raphael. "Introduction to the Study of Genocide." In *Lemkin on Genocide*, edited by Steven Leonard Jacobs. Lanham, MD: Lexington Books, 2012.

Lemkin, Raphael. *Totally Unofficial: The Autobiography of Raphael Lemkin.* Edited by Donna-Lee Frieze. New Haven: Yale University Press, 2013.

Lieber, Francis. "General Orders No. 100." In *Military Rules, Regulations and the Code of War: Francis Lieber and the Certification of Conflict*, edited by Richard Shelly Hartigan, 45–71. New Brunswick, NJ: Transaction Publishers, 2011.

Radbruch, Gustav. *Biographische Schriften.* Edited by Günter Spendel. Band 16 in *Gesamtausgabe von Gustav Radbruch.* Heidelberg: C. F. Müller Juristischer Verlag, 1988.

Rousset, David. *L'univers Concentrationnaire*. Paris: Editions du Pavois, 1946.

Sabetai B., and Yvette L. Testimony (HVT-3014), Fortunoff Archive, December 13, 1994.

Sassoon, Siegfried. *Memoirs of an Infantry Officer*. New York: Penguin, 2013.

Taylor, Telford. "Opening Statement of the Prosecution, December 9, 1946." In *The Nazi Doctors and the Nuremberg Code*, edited by George J. Annas and Michael A. Grodin, 67–93. New York: Oxford University Press, 1992.

United Nations. Convention on the Prevention and Punishment of the Crime of Genocide. 78 UNTS 277. 1948.

United Nations. International Covenant on Civil and Political Rights Art. 18(1–4), Dec. 16, 1966, S. Treaty Doc. No. 95–20, 6 I.L.M. 368 (1967), 999 U.N.T.S. 171.

United Nations. U.N. World Summit Outcome, Resolution Adopted by the General Assembly, A/RES/60/1. 2005.

US Office of Chief Counsel for the Prosecution of Axis Criminality. *Nazi Conspiracy and Aggression*, 8 vols. Washington, DC: US Government Printing Office, 1946.

Versailles Peace Treaty. June 28, 1919, 225 Parry 188; 2 Bevans 235; 13 AJIL Supp. 151, 385 (1919).

Wolfenden, John et al. *The Wolfenden Report: Report of the Committee on Homosexual Offenses and Prostitution*. New York: Stein and Day, 1963.

Secondary Sources

Abbott, Kenneth, Robert Keohane, Andrew Moravcsik, Anne-Marie Slaughter, and Duncan Snidal. "The Concept of Legalization." *International Organization* 54, no. 3 (2000): 17–35.

Abdelnour, Samer, and Akbar Saeed. "Technologizing Humanitarian Space: Darfur Advocacy and the Rape-Stove Panacea." *International Political Sociology* 8 (2014): 145–163.

Adam, Istvan Pal. *Budapest Building Managers and the Holocaust in Hungary*. Cham, Switzerland: Palgrave, 2016.

Agarwal, Bina. *Gender and Green Governance: The Political Economy of Women's Presence Within and Beyond Community Forestry*. New York: Oxford University Press, 2010.

Akande, Dapo, and Sangeeta Shah. "Immunities of State Officials, International Crimes, and Foreign Domestic Courts." *European Journal of International Law* 21, no. 4 (2011): 815–852.

Aleksuin, Natalia. "Gender and the Daily Lives of Jews in Hiding in Eastern Galicia," *NASHIM: A Journal of Jewish Women's Studies and Gender Issues* 27 (2014): 38–61.

Allen, Beverly. *Rape Warfare: The Hidden Genocide in Bosnia-Herzegovina and Croatia.* Minneapolis: University of Minnesota Press, 1996.

Anderton, Alexander Charles, and Jurgen Brauer, eds. *Economic Aspects of Genocides, Other Mass Atrocities, and Their Prevention.* New York: Oxford University Press, 2016.

Antweiler, Christoph. "On the Human Addiction to Norms: Social Norms and Cultural Universals of Normativity." In *The Normative Animal? On the Anthropological Significance of Social, Moral, and Linguistic Norms,* edited by Neil Roughley and Kurt Bayertz, 83–100. Oxford: Oxford University Press, 2019.

Aoláin, Fionnoula Ní, and Dina Francesca Haynes, "The Compatibility of Justice for Women with *Jus Post Bellum* Analysis." In *Jus Post Bellum,* edited by Carsten Stahn, Jennifer Easterday, and Jens Iverson, 161–177. New York: Oxford University Press, 2014.

Appiah, Kwame Anthony. *The Ethics of Identity.* Princeton, NJ: Princeton University Press, 2007.

Arendt, Hannah. *The Origins of Totalitarianism.* New York: Harcourt, 1976.

Arendt, Hannah. *Eichmann in Jerusalem: A Report on the Banality of Evil.* New York: Penguin, 2006.

Audi, Robert. "The Place of Testimony in the Fabric of Knowledge and Justification." *American Philosophical Quarterly* 34, no. 4 (1997): 405–422.

Barkan, Elazar. "Historical Dialogue and the Prevention of Atrocity Crimes. " In *Reconstructing Atrocity Prevention,* edited by Sheri Rosenberg, Tibi Galis, and Alex Zucker, 175–195. Cambridge: Cambridge University Press, 2016.

Barnett, Michael. *Empire of Humanity.* Ithaca, NY: Cornell University Press, 2011.

Bartov, Omer. *Hitler's Army.* Oxford: Oxford University Press, 1992.

Bartrop, Paul. "Righteousness in the Face of Evil." In *Genocide Perspectives IV: Essays on Holocaust and Genocide,* edited by Colin Tatz, 465–490. Sydney: UTS ePress, 2012.

Bauer, Yehuda. *Rethinking the Holocaust.* New Haven, CT: Yale University Press, 2001.

Bauer, Yehuda. "Genocide and Mass Atrocities: Can They Be Prevented?" In *Preventing Mass Atrocities: Policies and Practices,* edited by Barbara Harff and Ted Robert Gurr, 11–24. New York: Routledge, 2018. Baumard, Nicolas, and Dan Sperber. "Evolutionary and Cognitive Anthropology." In *A Companion to Moral Anthropology,* edited by Didier Fassin, 611–627. Malden, MA: Wiley, 2012.

Bell, Christine. "Of *Jus Post Bellum* and *Lex Pacificatoria*: What's in a Name?" In *Jus Post Bellum: Mapping the Normative Foundations,* edited by Carsten Stahn, Jennifer Easterday, and Jens Iverson, 181–206. New York: Oxford University Press, 2014.

Bellamy, Alex. *Massacres and Morality*. New York: Oxford University Press, 2012.

Bellamy, Alex, and Edward Luck. *The Responsibility to Protect: From Promise to Practice.* Medford, MA: Polity Press, 2018.

Benesch, Susan. "Vile Crimes or Inalienable Right: Defining Incitement to Genocide." *Virginia Journal of International Law* 48 (2008): 485–528.

Ben-Yehuda, Nachman. *Atrocity, Deviance, and Submarine Warfare*. Ann Arbor: University of Michigan Press, 2014.

Best, Geoffrey "Peace Conferences and the Century of Total War: The 1899 Hague Conference and What Came After." *International Affairs* 75, no. 3 (1999): 627.

Bicchieri, Cristina. *The Grammar of Society*. Cambridge: Cambridge University Press, 2006.

Bicchieri, Cristina. *Norms in the Wild*. Oxford: Oxford University Press, 2017.

Bicchieri, Cristina, Erte Xiao, and Ryan Muldoon. "Trustworthiness Is a Social Norm, But Trusting Is Not." *Politics, Philosophy and Economics* 10, no. 2 (2011): 170–187.

Binmore, Ken. *Natural Justice*. New York: Oxford University Press, 2011.

Bloxham, Donald. *The Great Game of Genocide*. New York: Oxford University Press, 2005.

Bloxham, Donald. *The Final Solution: A Genocide*. Oxford: Oxford University Press, 2009.

Blum, Lawrence. "Moral Exemplars: Reflections on Schindler, the Trocmés, and Others." In *Moral Perception and Particularity*, edited by Lawrence Blum, 65–97. Cambridge: Cambridge University Press, 1994.

Blum, Lawrence. "Altruism and the Moral Value of Rescue." In *Moral Perception and Particularity*, edited by Lawrence Blum, 124–143. Cambridge: Cambridge University Press, 1994.

Boddice, Rob. *The Science of Sympathy: Morality, Evolution, and Victorian Civilization*. Urbana: University of Illinois Press, 2016.

Boonin, David. *Should Race Matter? Unusual Answers to the Usual Questions*. Cambridge: Cambridge University Press, 2012.

Bourke, Janet. "Wartime Rape: The Politics of Making Visible." In *Liberal Democracies at War*, edited by Hilary Footitt and Andrew Knapp, 135–156. London: Bloomsbury, 2013.

Bratman, Michael. *Shared Agency: A Planning Theory of Acting Together*. New York: Oxford University Press, 2014.

Brennan, Geoffrey, Robert Goodin, Nicholas Southwood, and Lina Eriksson. *Explaining Norms*. New York: Oxford University Press, 2013.

Briggs, Lynne, and A. D. Macleod. "Demoralization—A Useful Conceptualisation of Non-Specific Psychological Distress among Refugees Attending Mental Health Services." *International Journal of Social Psychology* 52, no. 6 (2006): 515–524.

Brits, Elsabé. *Emily Hobhouse: Feminist, Pacifist, Traitor?* London: Robinson, 2018.

Brizzi, Giovanni. "Carthage and Hannibal in Roman and Greek Memory." In *A Companion to the Punic Wars*, edited by B. D. Hoyos, 483–492. Malden, MA: Wiley-Blackwell, 2011.

Brown, Sara. *Gender and the Rwandan Genocide: Women as Rescuers and Perpetrators*. London: Routledge, 2018.

Browning, Christopher. *Ordinary Men: Reserve Police Battalion 101 and the Final Solution in Poland*. New York: Harper Perennial, 1992.

Buitelaar, Tom. "The ICC and the Prevention of Atrocities: Criminological Perspectives." *Human Rights Review* 17 (2016): 285–302.

Burrows, Edwin. *Forgotten Patriots: The Untold Story of American Prisoners during the Revolutionary War*. New York: Basic Books, 2010.

Calhoun, Cheshire. "The Virtue of Civility," *Philosophy and Public Affairs* 29, no. 3 (2000): 251–275.

Cane, Peter, ed. *The Hart–Fuller Debate in the Twenty-First Century*. Oxford: Hart, 2010.

Card, Claudia. "Rape as a Weapon of War," *Hypatia* 11, no. 4 (1996): 5–18.

Card, Claudia. *The Atrocity Paradigm: A Theory of Evil*. New York: Oxford University Press, 2002.

Card, Claudia. *Confronting Evils: Terrorism, Torture, Genocide*. Cambridge: Cambridge University Press, 2010.

Carpenter, Charli. "Beyond 'Gendercide': Incorporating Gender into Comparative Genocide Studies." *International Journal of Human Rights* 6, no. 4 (2002): 77–101.

Carpenter, Charli. *"Innocent Women and Children": Gender, Norms and the Protection of Civilians*. New York: Routledge, 2006.

Celinscak, Mark. *Distance from the Belsen Heap: Allied Forces and the Liberation of a Nazi Concentration Camp*. Toronto: University of Toronto Press, 2015.

Cloward, Karisa. *When Norms Collide*. New York: Oxford University Press, 2016.

Coady, C. A. J. *Testimony: A Philosophical Study*. New York: Oxford University Press, 1995.

Cohen, Stanley. *States of Denial: Knowing about Atrocities and Suffering*. Malden, MA: Polity Press, 2001.

Coleman, Jules. "Negative and Positive Positivism." *Journal of Legal Studies* 11, no. 1 (1982): 139–164.

Confino, Alon. *A World without Jews*. New York: Columbia University Press, 2014.

Crenshaw, Kimberlé. "Demarginalizing the Intersection of Race and Sex." *University of Chicago Legal Forum* (1989): 139–167.

Crossley, Noele. "Is R2P Still Controversial? Continuity and Change in the Debate on 'Humanitarian Intervention.'" *Cambridge Review of International Affairs* 31, no. 5 (2018): 415–436.

Crouthamel, Jason. "Homosexuality and Comradeship: Destabilizing the Hegemonic Masculine Ideal in Nazi Germany." *Central European History* 51, no. 3 (2018): 419–439.

D'Costa, Bina. "*Birangona:* Rape Survivors Bearing Witness in War and Peace in Bangladesh." In *Women and Genocide*, edited by Elissa Bemporad and Joyce W. Warren, 159–190. Bloomington: Indiana University Press, 2018.

Davis, Michael. "What Can We Learn By Looking for the First Code of Professional Ethics?" *Theoretical Medicine* 24 (2003): 433–454.

de Greiff, Pablo. "Theorizing Transitional Justice." In *NOMOS LI: Transitional Justice*, edited by Melissa S. Williams and Rosemary Nagy, 31–77. New York: NYU Press, 2012.

Diner, Hasia. *We Remember with Reverence and Love: American Jews and the Myth of Silence After the Holocaust, 1945–1962*. New York: NYU Press, 2009.

Douglas, Lawrence. *The Memory of Judgment: Making Law and History in the Trials of the Holocaust*. New Haven, CT: Yale University Press, 2006.

Drumbl, Mark. *Atrocity, Punishment, and International Law*. Cambridge: Cambridge University Press, 2007.

Duffy, Christopher. *The Military Experience in the Age of Reason*. New York: Routledge & Kegan Paul, 1987.

Dyzenhaus, David. *Hard Cases in Wicked Legal Systems*. Oxford: Oxford University Press, 1991.

Dyzenhaus, David. *Judging the Judges, Judging Ourselves*. Oxford: Hart, 2003.

Eaton, Jonah. "An Emerging Norm? Determining the Meaning and Legal Status of the Responsibility to Protect." *Michigan Journal of International Law* 32 (2010): 788–789.

Egremont, Max. *Siegfried Sassoon: A Life*. New York: Farrar, Straus and Giroux, 2005.

Elias, Norbert. *The Civilizing Process*. Oxford: Blackwell, 1994.

Elster, Jon. *Closing the Books: Transitional Justice in Historical Perspective*. Cambridge: Cambridge University Press, 2004.

Enoch, David. *Taking Morality Seriously: A Defense of Robust Realism*. Oxford: Oxford University Press, 2011.

Ericksen, Robert. *Complicity in the Holocaust: Churches and Universities in Nazi Germany*. Cambridge: Cambridge University Press, 2012.

Fabre, Cécile. "Guns, Food, and Liability to Attack." *Ethics* 120 (2009): 36–63.

Fast, Larissa. *Aid In Danger: The Perils and Promise of Humanitarianism*. Philadelphia University of Pennsylvania Press, 2014.

Fehrenbach, Heide, and Davide Rodogno. "'A Horrific Photo of a Drowned Syrian Child': Humanitarian Photography and NGO Media Strategy in Historical Perspective." *International Review of the Red Cross* 97 (2015): 1121–1155.

Feierstein, David. *Genocide as Social Practice: Reorganizing Society under the Nazis and Argentina's Military Juntas*. New Brunswick, NJ: Rutgers University Press, 2014.

Fein, Helen. *Accounting for Genocide: National Response and Jewish Victimization during the Holocaust*. New York: Free Press, 1979.

Fein, Helen. *Genocide: A Sociological Perspective*. London: Sage, 1993.

Feitlowitz, Marguerite. *A Lexicon of Terror: Argentina and the Legacies of Torture*. New York: Oxford University Press, 1998.

Ferrales, Gabrielle, Hollie Nyseth Brehm, and Suzy McElrath. "Gender-Based Violence against Men and Boys in Darfur: The Gender-Genocide Nexus." *Gender and Society* 30, no. 4 (2016): 567–568.

Finder, Gabriel, and Laura Jockusch, eds. *Jewish Honor Courts*. Detroit: Wayne State University Press, 2015.

Finnemore, Martha, and Kathryn Sikkink. "International Norm Dynamics and Political Change." *International Organizations* 52, no. 4 (1998): 887–917.

Friedlander, Henry. *The Origins of Nazi Genocide: From Euthanasia to the Final Solution*. Chapel Hill: University of North Carolina Press, 2000.

Friedlander, Henry. "Nazi Crimes and the German Law." In *Nazi Crimes and the Law*, edited by Henry Friedlander and Nathan Stoltzfus. Cambridge: Cambridge University Press, 2008.

Friedlander, Saul. *Nazi Germany and the Jews: The Years of Extermination*. New York: Harper, 2008.

Friedman, Marilyn. "Feminism and Modern Friendship: Dislocating the Community." *Ethics* 99, no. 2 (1989): 275–290.

Fritzsche, Peter. *An Iron Wind*. New York: Basic Books, 2016.

Frowe, Helen. *Defensive Killing*. Oxford: Oxford University Press, 2014.

Fujii, Lee Ann. "Transforming the Normative Landscape: The Diffusion of a Genocidal Norm in Rwanda." *Journal of Genocide Research* 6, no. 1 (2004): 99–114.

Fujii, Lee Ann. *Killing Neighbors: Webs of Violence in Rwanda*. Ithaca, NY: Cornell University Press, 2009.

Fuller, Lon. "Positivism and Fidelity to Law." *Harvard Law Review* 71, no. 4 (1958): 630–672.

Fuller, Lon. *The Morality of Law*. New Haven, CT: Yale University Press, 1964.

Fussell, Paul. "Thank God for the Atom Bomb." In *Thank God for the Atom Bomb and Other Essays*, 13–37. New York: Summit Books, 1988.

Garraway, Charles. "The Law Applies, But Which Law?" In *The American Way of Bombing: Changing Ethical and Legal Norms, from Flying Fortresses to Drones*, edited by Matthew Evangelista and Henry Shue, 87–105. Ithaca, NY: Cornell University Press, 2014.

Gaus, Gerald. *The Order of Public Reason: A Theory of Morality for a Diverse and Bounded World*. Cambridge: Cambridge University Press, 2011.

Gellately, Robert. *Backing Hitler: Consent and Coercion in Nazi Germany*. Oxford: Oxford University Press, 2001.

Genocide Prevention Task Force. "Preventing Genocide: A Blueprint for U.S. Policymakers." Washington, DC, 2008.

Gensburger, Sarah. "From the Memory of Rescue to the Institution of the Title of 'Righteous.'" In *Resisting Genocide: The Multiple Forms of Rescue*, edited by Jacques Semelin, Claire Andrieu, and Sarah Gensburger, 19–32. New York: Columbia University Press, 2011.

Gerlach, Christian. "The Eichmann Interrogations in Holocaust Historiography." *Holocaust and Genocide Studies* 15, no. 3 (2001): 428–452.

Gerlach, Christian. *Extremely Violent Societies: Mass Violence in the Twentieth-Century World*. Cambridge: Cambridge University Press, 2010.

Gertz, Evelyn, Hollie Nyseth Brehm, and Sara Brown. "Gender and Genocide: Assessing Differential Opportunity Structures of Perpetration in Rwanda." In *Perpetrators and Perpetration of Mass Violence*, edited by Timothy Williams and Susanne Buckley-Zistel, 133–150. London: Routledge, 2018.

Gibbard, Alan. *Wise Choices, Apt Feelings: A Theory of Normative Judgment*. Cambridge, MA: Harvard University Press, 1992.

Gibbons, John. *The Norm of Belief*. New York: Oxford University Press, 2013.

Gilbert, G. M. "The Mentality of the SS Murderous Robots." *Yad Vashem Studies* 5 (1963): 35–41.

Gilbert, Margaret. *On Social Facts*. Princeton, NJ: Princeton University Press, 1992.

Gilbert, Margaret. *A Theory of Political Obligation*. New York: Oxford University Press, 2008.

Gilbert, Margaret. *Joint Commitment: How We Make the Social World*. New York: Oxford University Press, 2013.

Glanville, Luke. "On the Meaning of 'Responsibility' in the 'Responsibility to Protect.'" *Griffith Law Review* 20 (2011): 482–504.

Glover, Jonathan. *Humanity: A Moral History of the Twentieth Century*. London: Jonathan Cape, 1999.

Göçek, Fatma Müge. *Denial of Violence: Ottoman Past, Turkish Present, and Collective Violence against the Armenians, 1789–2009*. New York: Oxford University Press, 2015.

Godby, Michael. "Confronting Horror: Emily Hobhouse and the Concentration Camp Photographs of the South African War." *Kronos*, no. 32 (2006): 34–48.

Goldman, Alvin. *Knowledge in a Social World*. New York: Oxford University Press, 1999.

Gómez, Francisco Javier Guisández. "The Law of Air Warfare." *International Review of the Red Cross* 323 (1998): 347–364.

Gordon, Gregory. *Atrocity Speech Law*. New York: Oxford University Press, 2017.

Gray, J. Glenn. *The Warriors: Reflections on Men in Battle*. Lincoln, NE: Bison Books, 1998.

Green, Leslie. "Escapable Law: Gardner on Law and Morality." *Oxford Legal Studies Research Paper* 15 (2018).

Greenspan, Henry, ed. "Engaging Survivors: Assessing 'Testimony' and 'Trauma' as Foundational Concepts." *Dapim* 28, no. 3 (2014): 190–226.

Gudehus, Christian. "Editor's Introduction to 'Social Norms' by Heinrich Popitz." *Genocide Studies and Prevention* 11, no. 2 (2017): 3–4.

Gurr, Ted Robert. "Preventing Genocides and Mass Atrocities: Evidence from Conflict Analysis," In *Preventing Mass Atrocities: Policies and Practices*, edited by Barbara Harff and Ted Robert Gurr, 60–69. New York: Routledge, 2018.

Gutman, Roy. "Ending the Silence on War Crimes: A Journalist's Perspective." In *Preventing Mass Atrocities: Policies and Practices*, edited by Barbara Harff and Ted Robert Gurr, 73–92. New York: Routledge, 2018.

Haidt, Jonathan. "The Emotional Dog and Its Rational Tail: A Social Intuitionist Approach to Moral Judgment." In *Moral Psychology: Historical and Contemporary Readings*, edited by Thomas Nadelhoffer, Eddy Nahmias, and Shaun Nichols, 343–358. Malden, MA: Blackwell, 2010.

Hansen-Glucklich, Jennifer. *Holocaust Memory Reframed: Museums and the Challenges of Representation*. New Brunswick, NJ: Rutgers University Press, 2014.

Harari, Yuval Noah. *The Ultimate Experience: Battlefield Revelation and the Making of Modern War Culture*. New York: Palgrave, 2008.

Harff, Barbara. "The Etiology of Genocides." In *Genocide and the Modern Age, Etiology and Case Studies of Mass Death*, edited by I. Wallimann and M. N. Dobkowski, 41–59. Westport, CT: Greenwood Press, 1987.

Harff, Barbara. "No Lessons Learned from the Holocaust? Assessing Risks of Genocide and Political Mass Murder since 1955." *American Political Science Review* 97, no. 1 (2003): 57–73.

Harff, Barbara. "Countries at Risk of Genocide and Politicide after 2016—and Why." In *Preventing Mass Atrocities: Policies and Practices*, edited by Barbara Harff and Ted Robert Gurr, 27–39. New York: Routledge, 2018.

Harman, Elizabeth. "Does Moral Ignorance Exculpate?" *Ratio* 24, no. 4 (2011): 443–468.

Hart, H. L. A. *The Concept of Law*. Oxford: Clarendon Press, 1997.

Hashim, Fashima. "Sudanese Civil Society Strategizing to End Sexual Violence against Women in Darfur." In *Darfur and the Crisis of Governance in Sudan*, edited by Salah Hassan and Carina Ray, 233–243. Ithaca, NY: Cornell University Press, 2009.

Haslanger, Sally. "Gender and Race: (What) Are They? (What) Do We Want Them to Be?" *Noûs* 34, no. 1 (2000): 31–55.

Hayes, Peter. *Why? Explaining the Holocaust*. New York: Norton, 2017.

Hilberg, Raul. *Sources of Holocaust Research: An Analysis*. Chicago: Ivan Dee, 2001.

Hilbink, Lisa. *Judges beyond Politics in Democracy and Dictatorship*. Cambridge: Cambridge University Press, 2011.

Hildebrandt, Sabine. *The Anatomy of Murder: Ethical Transgressions and Anatomical Science during the Third Reich*. New York: Berghahn, 2016.

Hintjens, Helen. "Reconstructing Political Identities in Rwanda." In *After Genocide: Transitional Justice, Post-Conflict Reconstruction and Reconciliation in Rwanda and Beyond*, edited by Phil Clark and Zachary Kaufman, 77–100. London: Hurst, 2008.

Hinton, Alex. "The Dark Side of Modernity: Toward an Anthropology of Genocide." In *Annihilating Difference: The Anthropology of Genocide*, edited by Alex Hinton, 1–40. Berkeley: University of California Press, 2002.

Hochstadt, Steve, ed. *Sources of the Holocaust*. New York: Palgrave MacMillan, 2004.

Hornsey, Matthew. "Social Identity Theory and Self-Categorization Theory: A Historical Review." *Social and Personality Psychology Compass* 2, no. 1 (2008): 204–222.

Hull, Isabel. *A Scrap of Paper: Breaking and Making International Law during the Great War*. Ithaca, NY: Cornell University Press, 2014.

Humphreys, Stephen. *Theatre of the Rule of Law: Transnational Legal Intervention in Theory and Practice*. Cambridge: Cambridge University Press, 2010.

Inal, Tuba. *Looting and Rape in Wartime*. Philadelphia: University of Pennsylvania Press, 2013.

Isaacs, Tracy. *Moral Responsibility in Collective Contexts*. Oxford: Oxford University Press, 2011.

Jacobs, Steven Leonard, ed. *Lemkin on Genocide*. Lanham, MD: Lexington Books, 2012.

Jacobsen, Trude. "Very Superstitious: Gendered Punishment in Democratic Kampuchea, 1975–1979." In *Women and Genocide*, edited by Elissa Bemporad and Joyce W. Warren, 191–206. Bloomington: Indiana University Press, 2018.

Jarausch, Konrad. *The Unfree Professions: German Lawyers, Teachers, and Engineers, 1900–1950*. New York: Oxford University Press, 1990.

Jenkins, Katharine. "Amelioration and Inclusion: Gender Identity and the Concept of *Woman*," *Ethics* 126, no. 2 (2016): 394–421.

Jo, Hyeran. *Compliant Rebels*. Cambridge: Cambridge University Press, 2015.

Jo, Hyeran, and Beth Simmons. "Can the International Criminal Court Deter Atrocities?" *International Organization* 70 (2016): 443–475.

Jockusch, Laura. *Collect and Record: Jewish Holocaust Documentation in Early Postwar Europe*. Oxford: Oxford University Press, 2012.

Jones, Adam. "Gendercide and Genocide." In *Gendercide and Genocide*, edited by Adam Jones, 1–38. Nashville, TN: Vanderbilt University Press, 2004.

Kaplan, Marion. *Between Dignity and Despair: Jewish Life in Nazi Germany*. New York: Oxford University Press, 1999.

Kaplan, Marion. "Gender: A Critical Tool in Holocaust Research." In *Women and Genocide*, edited by Elissa Bemporad and Joyce W. Warren, 97–110. Bloomington: Indiana University Press, 2018.

Kaplan, Thomas Pegelow. *The Language of Nazi Genocide: Linguistic Violence and the Struggle of Germans of Jewish Ancestry*. Cambridge: Cambridge University Press, 2009.

Kearney, Michael. *The Prohibition of Propaganda for War in International Law*. Oxford: Oxford University Press, 2008.

Kincaid, Harold, ed. *The Oxford Handbook of Philosophy of Social Science*. New York: Oxford University Press, 2012.

Kinsella, Helen. *The Image before the Weapon: A Critical History of the Distinction between Combatant and Civilian*. Ithaca, NY: Cornell University Press, 2011.

Koonz, Claudia. *The Nazi Conscience*. Cambridge, MA: Belknap Press of Harvard University Press, 2005.

Kurt, Ümit. "The Plunder of Wealth through Abandoned Properties Laws in the Armenian Genocide." *Genocide Studies International* 10, no. 1 (2016): 37–51.

Kutz, Christopher. *Complicity: Ethics and Law for a Collective Age*. Cambridge: Cambridge University Press, 2000.

Kutz, Christopher. "How Norms Die: Torture and Assassination in American Policy." *Ethics and International Affairs* 28, no. 4 (2014): 426–430.

Kymlicka, Will. *Multicultural Citizenship: A Liberal Theory of Minority Rights*. New York: Oxford University Press, 1995.

Lackey, Jennifer. *Learning from Words*. New York: Oxford University Press, 2008.

Lake, Milli. "Organizing Hypocrisy: Providing Legal Accountability for Human Rights Violations in Areas of Limited Statehood." *International Studies Quarterly* 58, no. 3 (2014): 515–526.

Lang, Berel. "The Third Reich and the Breakdown of Professional Ethics." In *The Future of the Holocaust*, 92–104. Ithaca, NY: Cornell University Press, 1999.

Langer, Lawrence. *Versions of Survival: The Holocaust and the Human Spirit*. Albany: SUNY Press, 1982.

Langer, Lawrence. *Holocaust Testimonies: The Ruins of Memory*. New Haven, CT: Yale University Press, 1993.

Lasswell, Harold. *Propaganda Technique in World War I*. Cambridge, MA: MIT Press, 1972.

Lawson, Tom. *Debates on the Holocaust*. Manchester: University of Manchester Press, 2010.

Lazar, Seth. "The Responsibility Dilemma for *Killing in War*: A Review Essay." *Philosophy and Public Affairs* 38, no. 2 (2010): 180–213.

Lazar, Seth. *Sparing Civilians*. New York: Oxford University Press, 2016.

Le Pape, Marc. "Epilogue." In *Humanitarian Negotiations Revisited*, edited by Claire Magone, Michael Neuman, and Fabrice Weissman. London: Hurst, 2011.

Leaning, Jennifer. "Early Warning for Mass Atrocities: Tracking Escalation Parameters at the Population Level." In *Reconstructing Atrocity Prevention*, edited by Sheri Rosenberg, Tibi Galis, and Alex Zucker, 152–178. Cambridge: Cambridge University Press, 2016.

Ledford, Kenneth. "Judging German Judges in the Third Reich: Excusing and Confronting the Past." In *The Law in Nazi Germany*, edited by Alan Steinweis and Robert Rachlin, 161–189. New York: Berghahn Books, 2013.

Levi, Primo. *The Drowned and the Saved*. New York: Vintage, 1988.

Levi, Primo. *Survival in Auschwitz*. New York: Touchstone, 1996.

Lewis, David. *Convention: A Philosophical Study*. Malden, MA: Blackwell, 2002.

Lifton, Robert Jay. *The Nazi Doctors: Medical Killing and the Psychology of Genocide*. New York: Basic Books, 2000.

Lischer, Sarah Kenyon. *Dangerous Sanctuaries: Refugee Camps, Civil War, and the Dilemmas of Humanitarian Aid*. Ithaca, NY: Cornell University Press, 2006.

Listo, Romy. "Gender Myths in Energy Poverty Literature." *Energy Research and Social Science* 38 (2018): 9–18.

Lower, Wendy. *Hitler's Furies: German Women in the Nazi Killing Fields*. New York: Houghton, 2007.

Lower, Wendy. "German Women and the Holocaust in the Nazi East." In *Women and Genocide*, edited by Elissa Bemporad and Joyce W. Warren, 111–136. Bloomington: Indiana University Press, 2018.

Luban, David. "A Theory of Crimes against Humanity." *Yale Journal of International Law* 29 (2004): 85–167.

Luban, David. "Risk Taking and Force Protection." In *Reading Walzer*, edited by Yitzhak Benbaji and Naomi Sussmann, 277–301. New York: Routledge, 2014.

Luban, David. "Knowing When Not to Fight." In *The Oxford Handbook of Ethics of War*, edited by Seth Lazar and Helen Frowe, 185–203. New York: Oxford University Press, 2018.

Machery, Edouard, and Ron Mallon. "Evolution of Morality." In *The Moral Psychology Handbook*, edited by John Doris, 3–46. New York: Oxford University Press, 2012.

Mackie, Gerry. "Effective Rule of Law Requires Construction of a Social Norm of Legal Obedience," In *Cultural Agents Reloaded: The Legacy of Antanas Mockus*, edited by Carlo Tognato, 313–334. Cambridge, MA: Harvard University Press, 2017.

Mackie, J. L. *Ethics: Inventing Right and Wrong*. New York: Pelican Books, 1977.

Madden, Edward. "The Enthymeme: Crossroads of Logic, Rhetoric, and Metaphysics." *Philosophical Review* 61, no. 3 (1952): 368–376.

Magone, Caire, Michael Neuman, and Fabrice Wiessman, eds. *Humanitarian Negotiations Revealed: The MSF Experience*. London: Hurst, 2011.

Mamdani, Mahmood. *When Victims Become Killers: Colonialism, Nativism, and the Genocide in Rwanda*. Princeton, NJ: Princeton University Press, 2001.

Manji, Karima. "Articulating the Role of Social Norms in Sustaining Intimate Partner Violence in Mwanza, Tanzania." PhD diss., London School of Hygiene and Tropical Medicine, 2018.

Maogoto, Jackson. "Early Efforts to Establish an International Criminal Court." In *The Legal Regime of the International Criminal Court*, edited by Jose Doria, Hans-Peter Gasser, and M. Cherif Bassiouni. Leiden: Martinus Nijhoff, 2009.

Marmor, Andrei. *Social Convention*. Princeton, NJ: Princeton University Press, 2005.

Mastroianni, George. *Of Mind and Murder: Towards a More Comprehensive Psychology of the Holocaust*. New York: Oxford University Press, 2019.

Matravers, Derek. *Fiction and Narrative*. New York: Oxford University Press, 2014.

May, Larry. "Killing Naked Soldiers: Distinguishing between Combatants and Noncombatants." *Ethics and International Affairs* 19, no. 3 (2005): 39–53.

May, Larry. *Genocide: A Normative Account*. Cambridge: Cambridge University Press, 2010.

May, Larry. *After War Ends*. Cambridge: Cambridge University Press, 2011.

Mayersen, Deborah. *On the Path to Genocide: Armenia and Rwanda Reexamined*. New York: Berghahn Books, 2014.

Mayersen, Deborah. "So the World May Know All: The Importance of Education for Genocide Prevention." In *Last Lectures on the Prevention and Intervention of Genocide*, edited by Samuel Totten, 215–221. New York: Routledge, 2018.

Maynard, Jonathan Leader. "Rethinking the Role of Ideology in Mass Atrocities." *Terrorism and Political Violence* 26, no. 5 (2014): 821–841.

Maynard, Jonathan Leader. "Combating Atrocity-Justifying Ideologies." In *The Responsibility to Prevent: Overcoming the Challenges of Atrocity Prevention*, edited by Serena Sharma and Jennifer Welsh, 189–225. New York: Oxford University Press, 2015.

McAdams, Richard. "Group Norms, Gossip and Blackmail." *University of Pennsylvania Law Review* 144 (1996): 2237–2292.

McClelland, Charles. *The German Experience of Professionalization*. Cambridge: Cambridge University Press, 1991.

McCoubrey, Hilaire. "From Nuremberg to Rome: Restoring the Defense of Superior Orders." *International and Comparative Law Quarterly* 50, no. 2 (2001): 386–394.

McMahan, Jeff. *Killing in War*. Oxford: Oxford University Press, 2009.

McMahan, Jeff. "Can Soldiers Be Expected to Know Whether Their War Is Just?" In *Routledge Handbook of Ethics and War*, edited by Fritz Althoff, Nicholas Evans, and Adam Henschke, 13–22. New York: Routledge, 2013.

McMahan, Jeff. "I Was No-Platformed. Here's Why It's Counterproductive." *New Statesman,* January 14, 2019. https://www.newstatesman.com/2019/01/i-was-no-platformed-here-s-why-it-s-counterproductive.

Mertens, Karl. "On the Identification and Analysis of Social Norms and the Heuristic Relevance of Deviant Behavior." In *The Normative Animal? On the Anthropological Significance of Social, Moral, and Legal Norms*, edited by Neil Roughley and Kurt Bayertz, 101–120. Oxford: Oxford University Press, 2019.

Milgram, Stanley. *Obedience to Authority*. New York: Harper Perennial, 2009.

Mill, John Stuart. *On Liberty*. New York: Penguin Classics, 2007.

Mill, John Stuart. *Considerations on Representative Government*. Cambridge: Cambridge Library Collection, 2010.

Minnow, Martha. *Between Vengeance and Forgiveness: Facing History After Genocide and Mass Violence*. Boston: Beacon Press, 1998.

Monroe, Kristen Renwick. *Ethics in an Age of Terror and Genocide: Identity and Moral Choice*. Princeton, NJ: Princeton University Press, 2012.

Morrow, Paul. "Mass Atrocity and Manipulation of Social Norms." *Social Theory and Practice* 40, no. 2 (2014): 255–280.

Morrow, Paul. "The Thesis of Norm Transformation in the Theory of Mass Atrocity." *Genocide Studies and Prevention* 9, no. 1 (2015): 66–82.

Morrow, Paul. "A Theory of Atrocity Propaganda." *Humanity* 9, no. 1 (2018): 45–62.

Morrow, Paul. "Identity-Directed Norm Transformations and Moral Progress." *Journal of Value Inquiry* (forthcoming).

Moses, A. Dirk. "Raphael Lemkin, Culture, and the Concept of Genocide." In *The Oxford Handbook of Genocide Studies*, edited by A. Dirk Moses and Donald Bloxham, 19–41. New York: Oxford University Press, 2010.

Muldoon, Ryan. "Understanding Norms and Changing Them." *Social Philosophy and Policy* 35, no. 1 (2018): 128–148.

Mulinda, Charles Kabwete. "Crossing a Border to Escape: Examples from the Gishamvu and Kigembe Communities of Rwanda." In *Resisting Genocide: The Multiple Forms of Rescue*, edited by Jacques Semelin, Claire Andrieu, and Sarah Gensburger, 345–361. London: Hurst, 2011.

Munch-Jurisic, Ditte Marie. "Perpetrator Disgust: A Morally Destructive Emotion." In *Emotions and Mass Atrocity: Philosophical and Theoretical Explorations*, edited by Thomas Brudholm and Johannes Lang, 142–161. Cambridge: Cambridge University Press, 2018.

Murphy, Colleen. "Lon Fuller and the Moral Value of the Rule of Law." *Law and Philosophy* 24, no. 3 (2005): 239–262.

Murphy, Colleen. *A Moral Theory of Political Reconciliation*. Cambridge: Cambridge University Press, 2012.

Murphy, Colleen. *Conceptual Foundations of Transitional Justice*. Cambridge: Cambridge University Press, 2017.

Nino, Carlos Santiago. *Radical Evil on Trial*. New York: Oxford University Press, 1996.

Ohlin, Jens David, and Larry May. *Necessity in International Law*. New York: Oxford University Press, 2016.

Oliner, Samuel, and Pearl Oliner. *The Altruistic Personality: Rescuers of Jews in Nazi Europe*. New York: Free Press, 1988.

Osiel, Mark. *Obeying Orders: Atrocity, Military Discipline and the Laws of War*. New Brunswick, NJ: Transactions, 1998.

Osiel, Mark. *Making Sense of Mass Atrocity*. Cambridge: Cambridge University Press, 2009.

Pettit, Philip. *The Common Mind: An Essay on Psychology, Society, and Politics*. New York: Oxford University Press, 1993.

Popitz, Heinrich. "Social Norms." *Genocide Studies and Prevention* 11:2 (2017): 5–12.

Powell, Christopher. *Barbaric Civilization: A Critical Sociology of Genocide*. Montreal: McGill–Queen's University Press, 2011.

Power, Samantha. *A Problem from Hell: America and the Age of Genocide*. New York: Basic Books, 2013.

Price, Richard. *The Chemical Weapons Taboo*. Ithaca, NY: Cornell University Press, 1997.

Price, Richard. "Reversing the Gun Sights: Transnational Society Civil Society Targets Land Mines." *International Organization* 52, no. 3 (1998): 613–644.

Pruce, Joel. *The Mass Appeal of Human Rights*. Cham, Switzerland: Palgrave, 2018.

O'Connor, Timothy, and Constantine Sandis, eds. *A Companion to the Philosophy of Action*. Malden, MA: Blackwell, 2012.

O'Shaughnessy, Nicholas. *Politics and Propaganda: Weapons of Mass Seduction*. Ann Arbor: University of Michigan Press, 2005.

Orchard, Phil. *A Right to Flee*. Cambridge: Cambridge University Press, 2014.

Pendas, Devin. *The Frankfurt Auschwitz Trial, 1963–1965*. Cambridge: Cambridge University Press, 2006.

Posner, Eric, and Adrian Vermeule. "Transitional Justice as Ordinary Justice." *Harvard Law Review* 117, no. 3 (2004): 761–825.

Prunier, Gerald. *Darfur: The Ambiguous Genocide*. Ithaca, NY: Cornell University Press, 2005.

Radbruch, Gustav. "Gesetzliches Unrecht und übergesetzliches Recht." *Süddeutsche Juristen- Zeitung* 1, no. 5 (1946): 105–108.

Radbruch, Gustav. "Statutory Lawlessness and Supra-Statutory Law." Translated by Bonnie L. Paulson and Stanley L. Paulson. *Oxford Journal of Legal Studies* 26, no. 1 (2006): 1–11.

Radzik, Linda. "On Minding Your Own Business: Differentiating Accountability Relations within the Moral Community." *Social Theory and Practice* 37, no. 4 (2011): 574–598.

Radzik, Linda. "Moral Rebukes and Social Avoidance." *Journal of Value Inquiry* 48 (2014): 648–650.

Radzik, Linda. "Gossip and Social Punishment." *Res Philosophica* 93, no. 1 (2016): 185–204.

Radzik, Linda. "Boycotts and the Social Enforcement of Justice." *Social Philosophy and Policy* 34, no. 1 (2017): 102–122.

Raymond, Dwight. "Military Means of Preventing Mass Atrocities." In *Reconstructing Atrocity Prevention*, edited by Sheri Rosenberg, Tibi Galis, and Alex Zucker, 295–318. Cambridge: Cambridge University Press, 2016.

Raz, Joseph. *Practical Reason and Norms*. London: Hutchinson, 1975.

Raz, Joseph. "The Rule of Law and Its Virtue." In *The Authority of Law*, 2nd ed., 210–232. Oxford: Oxford University Press, 2009.

Raz, Joseph. "Legal Positivism and the Sources of Law." In *The Authority of Law*, 2nd ed., 37–52. Oxford: Oxford University Press, 2009.

Read, James Morgan. *Atrocity Propaganda, 1914–1919*. New Haven, CT: Yale University Press, 1941.

Reis, Chein. "Ethical, Safety, and Methodological Issues Related to the Collection and Use of Data on Sexual Violence in Conflict." In *Sexual Violence as an International Crime: Interdisciplinary Approaches*, edited by Anne-Marie De Brouwer, Charlotte Ku, Renée G. Römkens, and L. J. Van Den Herik, 187–210. Cambridge: Intersentia, 2013.

Richardson, Henry. *Articulating the Moral Community: Toward a Constructive Ethical Pragmatism*. Oxford: Oxford University Press, 2018.

Rieff, David. *In Praise of Forgetting*. New Haven, CT: Yale University Press, 2016.

Robillard, Michael and Bradley Strawser. "The Moral Exploitation of Soldiers." *Public Affairs Quarterly* 30, no. 2 (2016): 171–195.

Rorty, Richard. "Human Rights, Rationality, Sentimentality." In *Philosophical Papers*, vol. 3: *Truth and Progress*, 167–185. Cambridge: Cambridge University Press, 1998.

Rosen, Gideon. "Skepticism about Moral Responsibility." *Philosophical Perspectives* 18 (2004): 295–313.

Rosenberg, Sheri P. "Audacity of Hope: International Criminal Law, Mass Atrocity Crimes, and Prevention." In *Reconstructing Atrocity Prevention*, edited by Sheri Rosenberg, Tibi Galis, and Alex Zucker. Cambridge: Cambridge University Press, 2016.

Rosenberg, Sheri, Tibi Galis, and Alex Zucker, eds. *Reconstructing Atrocity Prevention*. Cambridge: Cambridge University Press, 2016.

Roughley, Neil. "Might We Be Essentially Normative Animals?" In *The Normative Animal: On the Anthropological Significance of Social, Moral, and Linguistic Norms*, edited by Neil Roughley and Kurt Bayertz, 3–37. New York: Oxford University Press, 2019.

Roughley, Neil. "Moral Obligations from the Outside In." In *The Normative Animal: On the Anthropological Significance of Social, Moral, and Linguistic Norms*, edited by Neil Roughley and Kurt Bayertz, 214–242. New York: Oxford University Press, 2019.

Roughley, Neil, and Kurt Bayertz, eds. *The Normative Animal? On the Anthropological Significance of Social, Moral, and Linguistic Norms*. New York: Oxford University Press, 2019.

Rubenstein, Jennifer. "Emergency Claims and Democratic Politics." *Social Philosophy and Policy* 32:1 (2015), 101–126.

Rundle, Kristen. "The Impossibility of an Exterminatory Legality: Law and the Holocaust." *University of Toronto Law Journal* 5, no. 1 (2009), 65–125.

Ryan, Lyndall. "Martial Law in the British Empire." In *Violence, Colonialism and Empire in the Modern World*, edited by P. Dwyer and A. Nettelbeck, 93–109. Cambridge: Cambridge University Press, 2018.

Sanford, Victoria, Sofia Dayos Álvarez-Arenas, and Kathleen Dill. "Sexual Violence as a Weapon during the Guatemalan Genocide," In *Women and Genocide*, edited by Elissa Bemporad and Joyce W. Warren, 207–222. Bloomington: Indiana University Press, 2018.

Scheffer, David. "Genocide and Atrocity Crimes," *Genocide Studies and Prevention* 1, no. 3 (2006): 229–250.

Scheffer, David. "The Fate of R2P in the Age of Retrenchment." In *Globalization and Its Impact on the Future of Human Rights and International Criminal Justice*, edited by M. Cherif Bassiouni, 617–628. Cambridge: Intersentia, 2015.

Schmidt, Marco, and Hannes Rakoczy. "On the Uniqueness of Human Normative Attitudes." In *The Normative Animal? On the Anthropological Significance of Social, Moral, and Linguistic Norms*, edited by Neil Roughley and Kurt Bayertz, 121–135. New York: Oxford University Press, 2019.

Semelin, Jacques, Claire Andrieu, and Sarah Gensburger, eds. *Resisting Genocide: The Multiple Forms of Rescue.* New York: Columbia University Press, 2011.

Sewall, Sarah. "Limits of Law: Promoting Humanity in Armed Conflict." In *Law and War*, edited by Austin Sarat, Lawrence Douglas, and Martha Merrill Umphrey, 23–47. Stanford, CA: Stanford Law Books, 2014.

Sewall, Sarah. "Military Options for Preventing Atrocity Crimes." In *The Responsibility to Prevent: Overcoming the Challenges of Atrocity Prevention*, edited by Serena Sharma and Jennifer Welsh, 160–188. New York: Oxford University Press, 2015.

Shenker, Noah. *Reframing Holocaust Testimony.* Bloomington: Indiana University Press, 2015.

Shuster, Evelyne. "Fifty Years Later: The Significance of the Nuremberg Code." *New England Journal of Medicine* 337, no. 20 (1997): 1436–1440.

Sikkink, Kathryn. *The Justice Cascade: How Human Rights Prosecutions Are Changing World Politics.* New York: Norton, 2011.

Slim, Hugo. *Humanitarian Ethics: A Guide to the Morality of Aid in War and Disaster.* New York: Oxford University Press, 2015.

Smith, David Livingstone. *Less Than Human: Why We Demean, Enslave, and Exterminate Others.* New York: St. Martin's Press, 2011.

Southwood, Nicholas. "The Moral/Conventional Distinction." *Mind* 120, no. 479 (2011): 761–802.

Southwood, Nicholas, and Lina Eriksson. "Norms and Conventions." *Philosophical Explorations* 14, no. 2 (2011): 195–217.

Stanley, Jason. *How Propaganda Works.* Princeton, NJ: Princeton University Press, 2015.

Staub, Ervin. *The Roots of Evil: The Origins of Genocide and Other Group Violence.* Cambridge: Cambridge University Press, 1992.

Staub, Ervin. *Overcoming Evil.* New York: Oxford University Press, 2013.

Stein, Janice Gross. "Humanitarian Organizations: Accountable—Why, to Whom, for What, and How?" In *Humanitarianism in Question: Politics, Power, Ethics*, edited by Thomas G. Weiss and Michael Barnett, 124–142. Ithaca, NY: Cornell University Press, 2008.

Steinweis, Alan. *Studying the Jew: Scholarly Antisemitism in Nazi Germany.* Cambridge, MA: Harvard University Press, 2008.

Steinweis, Alan, and Robert Rachlin, eds. *The Law in Nazi Germany.* New York: Berghahn, 2013.

Stier, Oren Baruch. *Holocaust Icons: Symbolizing the Shoah in History and Memory.* New Brunswick, NJ: Rutgers University Press, 2015.

Stiglmayer, Alexandra, ed. *Mass Rape: The War Against Women in Bosnia-Herzegovina.* Lincoln: University of Nebraska Press, 1994.

Stone, Dan, ed. *The Historiography of Genocide.* New York: Palgrave-Macmillan, 2008.

Stone, Dan. *Concentration Camps.* New York: Oxford University Press, 2017.

Straus, Scott. *The Order of Genocide.* Ithaca, NY: Cornell University Press, 2006.

Straus, Scott. *Fundamentals of Genocide and Mass Atrocity Prevention.* Washington, D.C: United States Holocaust Memorial Museum, 2016.

Straus, Scott. "What Is Being Prevented? Genocide, Mass Atrocity, and Conceptual Ambiguity in the Anti-Atrocity Movement." In *Reconstructing Atrocity Prevention*, edited by Sheri Rosenberg, Tibi Galis, and Alex Zucker, 17–30. Cambridge: Cambridge University Press, 2016.

Straus, Scott. "Is a Comparative Theory of Perpetrators Possible?" In *Perpetrators and Perpetration of Mass Violence*, edited by Timothy Williams and Susanne Buckley-Zistel, 204–209. London: Routledge, 2018.

Strawson, P. F. "Freedom and Resentment." In *Freedom and Resentment and Other Essays*, edited by P. F. Strawson, 1–25. London: Methuen, 1974.

Strohemeyer, Hansjörg. "Collapse and Reconstruction of a Judicial System: The United Nations Missions in Kosovo and East Timor." *American Journal of International Law* 95, no. 1 (2001): 46–63.

Suesse, Thorsten, and Heinrich Meyer. *Abtransportder "Lebensunwerten."* Hannover: Verlag Clemens Koechert, 1988.

Sunstein, Cass. "Incompletely Theorized Agreements." *Harvard Law Review* 108, no. 7 (1995): 1733–1772.

Tadros, Victor. "The Moral Distinction between Combatants and Noncombatants: Vulnerable and Defenceless," *Law and Philosophy* 37, no. 3 (2018): 289–312.

Taylor, Charles. *Multiculturalism and "The Politics of Recognition."* Princeton, NJ: Princeton University Press, 1994.

Taylor, Philip. *Munitions of the Mind: A History of Propaganda*, 3rd ed. Manchester: Manchester University Press, 2003.

Tec, Nechama. *When Light Pierced the Darkness: Christian Rescue of Jews in Nazi-Occupied Poland.* Oxford: Oxford University Press, 1987.

Tec, Nechama. *Resistance: Jews and Christians Who Defied the Nazi Terror.* Oxford: Oxford University Press, 2013.

Teitel, Ruti. *Transitional Justice.* Oxford: Oxford University Press, 2000.

Teitel, Ruti. *Humanity's Law.* Oxford: Oxford University Press, 2013.

Théry, Julien. "*Atrocitas/enormitas:* Pour une histoire de la catégorie d' 'énormité' ou 'crime énorme' du Moyen Âge à l'époque moderne." *Clio@Themis: Revue électronique d'histoire du droit* 4 (2011): 1–45.

Thrasher, John. "Evaluating Bad Norms." *Social Philosophy and Policy* 35, no. 1 (2018): 196–216.

Totten, Samuel. "The Plight and Fate of Females after the Darfur Genocide." In *Women and Genocide*, edited by Elissa Bemporad and Joyce W. Warren, 268–285. Bloomington: Indiana University Press, 2018.

Tussman, Joseph, and Jacobus tenBroek. "The Equal Protection of the Laws." *California Law Review* 37, no. 3 (1949): 341–380.

Ullman-Margalit, Edna. *The Emergence of Norms.* Oxford: Clarendon Press, 1977.

Üngör, Uğur. "Cultural Genocide." In *The Routledge History of Genocide*, edited by Cathie Carmichael and Richard Maguire, 241–253. New York: Routledge, 2015.

Üngör, Uğur. "The Armenian Genocide in the Context of 20th Century Paramilitarism." In *The Armenian Genocide Legacy*, edited by Alexis Demirdjian, 11–25. New York: Palgrave Macmillan, 2016.

Üngör, Uğur, and Mehmet Polatel. *Confiscation and Destruction: The Young Turk Seizure of Armenian Property.* London: Continuum, 2011.

Valentino, Benjamin. *Final Solutions: Mass Killing and Genocide in the 20th Century.* Ithaca, NY: Cornell University Press, 2005.

Valentino, Benjamin, Paul Huth, and Dylan Balch-Lindsay. "'Draining the Sea': Mass Killing and Guerilla Warfare." *International Organization* 58, no. 2 (2004): 375–407.

van Schaik, Carel, and Judith Burkart, "The Evolution of Human Normativity." In *The Normative Animal? On the Anthropological Significance of Social, Moral, and Legal Norms,* edited by N. Roughley and K. Bayertz, 139–153. New York: Oxford University Press, 2019.

van Schoelandt, Chad. "Moral Accountability and Social Norms." *Social Philosophy and Policy* 35, no. 1 (2018): 217–236.

Verdeja, Ernesto. "Moral Bystanders and Mass Violence." In *New Directions in Genocide Research,* edited by Adam Jones, 153–168. New York: Routledge, 2012.

Verdeja, Ernesto. "Predicting Genocide and Mass Atrocities." *Genocide Studies and Prevention* 9, no. 3 (2016): 13–32.

Vetlesen, Arne Johan. "Social Science and the Study of Perpetrators." In *Emotions and Mass Atrocity: Philosophical and Theoretical Explorations,* edited by Thomas Brudholm and Johannes Lang, 104–120. Cambridge: Cambridge University Press, 2018.

von Joeden-Forgey, Elisa. "Genocidal Masculinities." In *New Directions in Genocide Research,* edited by Adam Jones, 76–95. New York: Routledge, 2012.

von Joeden-Forgey, Elisa. "Gender and the Future of Genocide Studies and Prevention." *Genocide Studies and Prevention* 7, no. 1 (2012): 89–107.

von Joeden-Forgey, Elisa. "Gender, Sexualized Violence, and the Prevention of Genocide." In *Reconstructing Atrocity Prevention,* edited by Sheri Rosenberg, Tibi Galis, and Alex Zucker, 125–148. Cambridge: Cambridge University Press, 2016.

von Joeden-Forgey, Elisa. "Women and the Herero Genocide." In *Women and Genocide,* edited by Elissa Bemporad and Joyce W. Warren, 36–57. Bloomington: Indiana University Press, 2018.

Waldron, Jeremy. "Why Law—Efficacy, Freedom, or Fidelity?" *Law and Philosophy* 13, no. 3 (1994), 259–284.

Waldron, Jeremy. "The Concept and the Rule of Law." *Georgia Law Review* 43 (2008): 1–61.

Waldron, Jeremy. "The Rule of Law and the Importance of Procedure." In *NOMOS L: Getting to the Rule of Law,* edited by James Fleming, 3–33. New York: NYU Press, 2011.

Waldron, Jeremy. *The Harm in Hate Speech.* Cambridge, MA: Harvard University Press, 2014.

Walk, Joseph, ed. *Das Sonderrecht für die Juden im NS-Staat.* Heidelberg: C. F. Müller Juristischer Verlag, 1981.

Walker, Margaret Urban. *Moral Repair: Reconstructing Moral Relations after Wrongdoing*. Cambridge: Cambridge University Press, 2006.

Waller, James. *Becoming Evil: How Ordinary People Commit Genocide and Mass Killing*. New York: Oxford University Press, 2002.

Waller, James. *Confronting Evil: Engaging Our Responsibility to Prevent Genocide*. New York: Oxford University Press, 2016.

Walzer, Michael. *Just and Unjust Wars*, 5th ed. New York: Basic Books, 2015.

Waxman, Zoë. "Transcending History? Methodological Problems in Holocaust Testimony." In *The Holocaust and Historical Methodology*, edited by Dan Stone, 143–157. New York: Berghahn Books, 2012.

Weindling, Paul. "The Origins of Informed Consent: The International Scientific Commission on Medical War Crimes, and the Nuremberg Code." *Bulletin of the History of Medicine* 75, no. 1 (2001): 37–71.

Weitz, Eric. *A Century of Genocide: Utopias of Race and Nation*. Princeton, NJ: Princeton University Press, 2003.

Welch, David. *Propaganda: Power and Persuasion*. London: British Library, 2013.

Wellman, Kit. "Amnesties and International Law." In *War: Essays in Political Philosophy*, edited by Larry May, 249–265 Cambridge: Cambridge University Press, 2008.

Welsh, Jennifer. "Norm Contestation and the Responsibility to Protect." *Global Responsibility to Protect* 5, no. 4 (2013): 365–396.

Welzer, Harald. *Täter: Wie aus ganz normalen Mensen Massenmörder werden*. Frankfurt: Fischer Verlag, 2007.

Westermann, Edward. "Drinking Rituals, Masculinity, and Mass Murder in Nazi Germany." *Central European History* 51, no. 3 (2018): 367–389.

Whigham, Kerry. "Remembering to Prevent: The Preventive Capacity of Public Memory." *Genocide Studies and Prevention* 11:2 (2017): 53–71.

Wieviorka, Annette. *The Era of the Witness*. Ithaca, NY: Cornell University Press, 2006.

Wigglesworth, Gill. "The End of Impunity? Lessons from Sierra Leone." *International Affairs* 84, no. 4 (2008): 809–827.

Williams, Bernard. *Ethics and the Limits of Philosophy*. Cambridge, MA: Harvard University Press, 1986.

Williams, Timothy, and Susanne Buckley-Zistel, eds. *Perpetrators and Perpetration of Mass Violence*. London: Routledge, 2018.

Wilson, Richard Ashby. *Writing History in International Criminal Trials*. Cambridge: Cambridge University Press, 2011.

Wilson, Richard Ashby. *Incitement on Trial: Prosecuting International Speech Crimes*. New York: Cambridge University Press, 2017.

Wohlforth, William. "Realism." In *The Oxford Handbook of International Relations*, edited by Christian Reus-Smit and Duncan Snidal, 131–149. New York: Oxford University Press, 2010.

Wolfe, Robert. "Nazi Paperwork for the Final Solution." In *Perspectives on the Holocaust: Essays in Honor of Raul Hilberg*, edited by James Pacy and Alan Wertheimer, 5–38. Boulder, CO: Westview, 1995.

Wood, Elisabeth Jean. "Armed Groups and Sexual Violence: When Is Wartime Rape Rare?" *Politics and Society* 37, no. 1 (2009): 131–162.

Young, Iris Marion. "Five Faces of Oppression." *Philosophical Forum* 19, no. 4 (1988): 270–290.

Young, Iris Marion. *Inclusion and Democracy*. Oxford: Oxford University Press, 2002.

Yusuf, Hakeem. *Transitional Justice, Judicial Accountability and the Rule of Law*. Abingdon, UK: Routledge, 2013.

Zagzebski, Linda. *Epistemic Authority: A Theory of Trust, Authority, and Autonomy in Belief*. New York: Oxford University Press, 2012.

Zimbardo, Phillip, Craig Haney, and Curtis Banks. "Interpersonal Dynamics in a Simulated Prison." *International Journal of Criminology and Penology* 1, no. 1 (1973): 69–97.

Zimmerman, Lisbeth. *Global Norms with a Local Face: Rule-of-Law Promotion and Norm Translation*. Cambridge: Cambridge University Press, 2017.

Index